Building Classic Small Craft

Volume 1

Building Classic Small Craft

Volume 1

John Gardner

INTERNATIONAL MARINE
Camden, Maine

Published by International Marine

Eight hardcover printings. First paperback printing, with revisions to appendix, 1991

10 9 8 7 6 5 4 3

Library of Congress Catalog Card Number 76-8778
International Standard Book Number 0-87742-299-0

Questions regarding the content of this book should be addressed to:

International Marine
P.O. Box 220
Camden, ME 04843

Typeset by A & B Typesetters, Inc., Concord, NH
Printed by Malloy Lithographing, Inc., Ann Arbor, MI

To all the boatbuilders gone before whom I have learned from, and to those yet to come who may read this book, finding herein something of what I learned that they can use.

Contents

Preface

This is a book of small craft for amateur builders. It is comprised of a selection of material published in the *Maine Coast Fisherman* and later the *National Fisherman* over the last twenty-six years. Actually the material goes back farther than that, although it did not start getting into print until the spring of 1951.

In 1942 I was hard at it planking 38-foot Coast Guard picket boats on the second shift at James E. Graves's lower yard down at Barnegat off Front Street in Marblehead, Massachusetts. We were at war. German submarines were reported close offshore, so close, that, believe it or not, guns collected about town were brought into the yard, and the boatshop crew were assigned defense stations behind the rocks and ledges which skirted the waterfront. Upstairs in the joiner shop the foreman put someone at the lathe turning out billy clubs for the blackout wardens, although I never heard that these implements of persuasion were ever needed or used.

Young and old were caught up in the war effort, which brought together an assemblage of boatbuilding talent and experience that will not be seen again. Not only in Marblehead but all up and down the coast the oldtimers came out of retirement for one last hurrah, and for a brief interval the clock stood still while an era of wooden boat construction, which had all but passed away, was revived and renewed. Some of us who were younger sensed that we were involved in something special and absorbed as much of it as we could, but how special this was we did not realize then, and only came in time to know.

At his bench at the head of the stairs, Charlie Lawton, soon to be ninety, still did a day's work, and in odd moments snatched from the job turned out the prized planes for which he was famous, artfully shaped from selected chunks of ironwood, rosewood, lignum vitae, or native beech. As a young man in the late 1880's, Charlie had come down to Boston from Saint John, N.B., to work for the Partelows in their canoe factory at Riverside on the Charles River, building St. Lawrence River skiffs and fancy Whitehalls. Later at the Boston Naval Shipyard he made a name for himself, and as the years passed his reputation as a boatbuilder grew. When I got to know him his skill had become a legend, and he stood at the pinnacle of his trade. Dignified, self-assured, and crusty when crossed, Charlie did not hesitate to express his opinions in positive and forthright language, as he did on one well-remembered occasion when he gave L. Francis Herreshoff a dressing down over some differences involving the planking of a fancy yacht tender of Herreshoff's design. Herreshoff, who occasionally dropped in at the shop, cut an odd figure about town in those days with his beard and his dogs.

In 1941, H.I. Chapelle's *Boatbuilding* was published, and I wasted no time in getting a copy, which I read like a Bible, for although I had not yet come to know Chap in person, his ground-breaking studies of classic American small craft published in *Yachting* magazine during the 1930's had made me a devoted disciple. Sometime later on I brought my copy of *Boatbuilding* into the shop to show to the head joiner, Dan Grant, who had just returned to Graves from an interval as woodworking boss at the Robinson shipyard in Ispwich, Massachusetts, where Chapelle was the naval architect. Dan proceeded to take me down a peg. "The book is old fashioned and out of date," he told me, "and I ought to know," he continued, "for he got most of it from me." That may have been stretching it somewhat, but probably Chapelle did get quite a lot from Dan, as Dan had a lot to give. A Nova Scotia Scotchman who had come to the States as a young man to work at the carpenter's trade, Dan was a superb natural mechanic. As a joiner, patternmaker, and sparmaker, he was unexcelled. He had ruined his eyesight, he claimed, although it was not evident from his work, making violins at night, and very good ones, which he sold to defray the cost of medical treatment for a son crippled by infantile paralysis. In his old age when I knew him, his spare time was devoted to perfecting an elaborate machine that he had devised for turning out wooden lobster plugs by the bushel. The machine was kept out of sight in his attic because it would have been too costly to patent it.

Then there was Jess Hammond, an old-fashioned mechanic, who could do anything, it seemed, or almost anything. Jess, the last in a long line of independent Yankee artisans, had never worked for another man's wage a day in his life until he joined the Graves crew at the beginning of the War when he was nearing seventy. In his Danversport shop over the previous fifty years, Jess had turned out many fine boats, particularly power launches and dories, including some of the first power dories built around the turn of the century. In fact it was one of Jess Hammond's dories that was the subject of my first published article in the *Maine Coast Fisherman* in May, 1951, of which more later on.

There were others: Trim Robarts, rigger and splicer par excellence, whose domain was the spar loft, and his brother Jack, one-time yard boss for Sterns & McKay on Front Street, and a deep-water sailor in his youth. "Pot-lead" Conners who could plank circles around the best of them, and Ben Tutt, native of Marblehead, old Beachcomber sailor, and one-time hand at the ill-fated Burgess Plant where for a brief time wooden seaplanes designed by Starling Burgess were built during World War I.

About town there were still others. For a journeyman boatbuilder looking to learn, there was much to see and absorb. Captain Charleton Smith, then in his mid-eighties, sailor, author, and friend of W. P. Stephens, was still to be found at work in his shop, locally known as the Home of the Brutal Beast, after the little sailboat got up by Starling Burgess for youngsters to learn to sail in. And up at Fort Sewell in his shop in an ancient building once a fish house, Bill Brown built Yankee Sailing Dories designed by his brother, Sam, held in highest esteem by his fellow Marblehead townsmen as a naval architect.

Hauled out on the beach at Barnegat, where the lobstermen put in, lay an elegant double-ender, somewhat the worse for wear, it is true, and shabby of paint, but otherwise as trim and shapely as the day she was launched. She caught my eye from the first, and upon inquiry I learned that she had been Bill Chamberlain's own gunning dory built for winter duck hunting in the rough seas among the islands of the outer harbor. Nineteen feet, five inches over all, her rounded sides and graceful sheer made her, I thought, about the handsomest boat I had ever seen. Lightly built of cedar, she was hardly suited for the rough work of hauling lobster pots, the use to which Charlie Briggs had converted her.

As soon as work slacked enough in the shop for me to be spared for a Saturday, I took off the lines of the dory and carefully recorded the details of her construction in anticipation of the day when I should want to build another. It was a good thing I did. Too lightly constructed for lobstering and weakened by age, she went to pieces over the next few years and was broken up.

I did not build another right away, in fact it was over twenty years before I got around to building one myself. But in the meantime, in the February, 1960, issue of *Outdoor Maine,* a rival of the *Maine Coast Fisherman* that has long since folded, I had a story about the gunning dory, and her lines were published for the first time. Jim Rockefeller of Camden saw them and had Veli Holstrum of Vinalhaven build one for him for winter duck hunting in Penobscot Bay. He was more than pleased with the boat as was extensively reported at the time in several issues of the *National Fisherman.* Then Lew Dietz, one of Jim Rockefeller's duck-hunting companions, wrote a story about the boat for *Field & Stream.* So many inquiries about the boat ensued with requests for building plans that I got busy and put together four large sheets of building details and instructions for amateur builders, the same that you will find reproduced in this book. Since then, over 160 sets of these plans have been sold all over the United States and Canada, and some abroad. Just how many boats have been built from them I do not know, but there are gunning dories afloat today from the Gulf of Maine to Puget Sound, and from the Chesapeake to Alaska, and I have never had a bad report from the owners of any of them.

Also dating from these early years are the lines and details, reproduced herein, which were developed from the 19-foot surf dory, also built by Chamberlain. The boat I took them off was a life-saving dory that the Metropolitan District Commission used to keep on a cart at the entrance to King's Beach in Lynn, Massachusetts, during the summer season. Ten or twelve years later, in the mid-1950's, Dick Dion and I built one in Salem, Massachusetts, for the Texas Company to use in landing operations in the heavy surf off the west coast of Nicaragua. The boat worked out so well for this that more were built later. At one time in Swampscott, George Chaisson also built surf dories of much the same model that were widely used along the coast as far south as Florida.

Plans for the Chamberlain dory skiff were likewise obtained back in the War years when I was working at Graves. I gained them from a former employee of Chamberlain who apprenticed at his Orne Street shop near the end of Chamberlain's career when he was going blind. Embittered by the loss of his sight, Chamberlain had begun to destroy his patterns and molds before giving up his shop. If the patterns of this fine skiff had not been copied at the time, they would probably have been lost forever. As it was they had been stashed away and forgotten until recalled to mind by my take-off of the gunning dory lines. In turn I filed them away and did not publish them until June, 1951. Since then, this skiff has been widely built on both coasts and for use on numerous inland lakes and rivers. Intended originally for rowing, various modifications of it have been successfully rigged for sail, particularly the widened version now in limited production at Mystic Seaport.

Over the past quarter of a century I have published my share of dories, but the first one to see print was special. This was one of Jess Hammond's, a 15-foot 10-inch LOA knuckle-sided Danversport dory, which I described in the May, 1951, issue of the *Maine Coast Fisherman.* Shortly after this appeared, I got a call from the Peabody Museum in Salem. Would I drop by on Saturday afternoon, there was someone interested in dories who would like to meet me? Drop by I did, and, gathered in Charles Copeland's office, I found a small group intently conversing with a tall man with thick, mussed hair and a wrinkled blue sport shirt. I was introduced to Howard Chapelle. For a long time I had admired the man and his work from afar, but unexpectedly to meet him, to be in the same room with him, and to talk with him was almost too much. The talk flowed on and was continued down the street at the Hawthorne Hotel where we went for dinner.

This was the beginning of a cordial relationship that lasted until Chapelle's recent death. His enthusiasm for boats and his encyclopedic knowledge of them, past and present, was equalled only by the generosity with which he spread this knowledge around, providing encouragement and inspiration for so many like myself who will always stand in his debt. For the wide-spread renewal in the use of traditional native watercraft that looms so large on the American boating scene today, Chap, more than anyone else, was directly responsible.

The small craft renewal that we are experiencing, the revival of traditional wooden boats, Whitehalls, peapods, St. Lawrence River skiffs, Rangeley Lake boats, wherries, Adirondack guideboats, sneakboxes, wooden sailing canoes, and all the rest, is something which to a large extent has taken place since the earliest of the articles reproduced herein were written. Whitehalls are no rarety these days; they are both amateur and commercially built. Indeed, Whitehalls are now numerous and popular for recreational boating on both the East and West coasts, but for several decades, until the 1960's, hardly any were to be found in use anywhere. In Marblehead in the 1940's, when I was eagerly absorbing all that old Charlie Lawton could tell me about the Whitehalls he had built in Boston before the turn of the century, my searches turned up only one lone surviving example of the type. Based on this boat, on what Charlie taught me and what I learned from Capt. Charleton Smith, I designed a 17-foot rowing Whitehall published in the *Maine Coast Fisherman* in 1953 in several issues and reprinted here. Except for the two Whitehalls in Chapelle's *American Small Sailing Craft,* 1951, these were the first detailed plans for a rowing Whitehall for amateur construction to be published, and in important respects the details were more complete than those furnished by Chapelle. A number of these Whitehalls have been built, one of the most recent is a clinker version launched last year by Bob Coe of Waldren Island, Washington, a boat that the owner cannot praise too highly.

Originally and primarily, Whitehalls were pulling workboats. Frequently a small sail laced to a short mast was carried in the boat to be raised when the wind favored for running or reaching; but into the wind, a straight pull with oars was much faster than tacking. Practically none of the old working Whitehalls had centerboards, although Chapelle does show one in a boat with an uncharacteristic flat, plank keel. There is now, however, a growing demand in recreational boating for Whitehalls capable of sailing on all points. The 14-foot sailing Whitehall detailed herein was designed to fill this need. By changing the position of the molds, as used to be the practice, it is possible to build this boat in four lengths from 14 feet to 17 feet 3 inches. Installing a centerboard in a boat like this with its strip, or "scantling," keel instead of a flat, plank keel, presents some problems. One way of dealing with this is by the method detailed here. It is simple, does not weaken the hull, and requires only minimal changes to the basic structure of the boat.

Thirty years ago the working peapods of Maine lobstermen had been replaced in the fishing industry, to a great extent, by larger, motorized craft, and these fine sea boats seemed well on the way to extinction. Built by the fishermen themselves and in small boatshops along the coast, the lines and construction of these fishing pods had never been recorded and were unavailable to amateur builders. The first to put peapods in print, with the exception of a single isolated article in *Yachting* magazine in the 1930's, was Chapelle in *American Small Sailing Craft* in 1951. Two years later I followed in the *Maine Coast Fisherman* with more pods and building information, much of which is reproduced here. The following year I published the details for a 15-foot clinker-planked Matinicus Island peapod, selected for production twenty years later by the Apprenticeshop of the Bath Marine Museum at Bath, Maine, and successfully built and sold by them. Then just last year I worked out the details for another clinker pod and directions for planking it, which were published in the *National Fisherman* and are included here. My contention is that, for many small boats, pods included, it is simplier, easier, quicker, and less expensive to plank clinker rather than carvel, once the method is correctly understood and followed. Unfortunately, up to now clinker planking technique had remained largely a mystery to amateur builders, in part because little about it had been published, but in greater part because what had been written about it had not been explicit enough about basic clinker procedures. The detailed step-by-step explanation of essential clinker techniques included in this book in the sections on the Herreshoff pram, the Rangeley Lakes boat, and peapods, as already indicated, do together comprise, I believe, a fuller account of the clinker planking process, including lining, spiling, beveling, fitting, and fastening than is to be found elsewhere. It is complete enough for the inexperienced amateur to follow successfully. You will also find extensive explanations of clinker planking in the Appendix.

The details and directions for building a Rangeley Lakes boat are the only ones yet published, so far as I am aware, for this able craft developed for large, rough lakes. The section on the St. Lawrence River skiff is reproduced from articles written when this exceptional craft had all but dropped from sight, use, and memory, and helped, we like to think, in bringing about its current revival.

There are two small prams, one a 10-foot varnished cedar beauty after one by L. Francis Herreshoff, the other a 9-foot-plus plywood utility pram designed by me that has been widely built, proving sea-kindly, easy to row, and simple and inexpensive to build. For additional variety there is a 16-foot Sea Bright skiff rigged to sail, a New England wherry, a Barnegat Bay sneakbox of modified construction simplified and adapted for home building, and others as well.

Some boats had to be left out. Long-time readers of the *National Fisherman* may miss a favorite craft. It is not likely that the selection included will satisfy everyone in all respects. We regret this, but clearly not every one of the several hundred boating articles that I have contributed over the past twenty-six years to the *National Fisherman,* and earlier to the *Maine Coast Fisherman,* could be crowded between the covers of a single book. Yet we do believe that the selection is extensive enough and varied enough for nearly everyone looking for a small boat to build to find something worth his consideration, or at least to enlarge his knowledge and appreciation of our native small craft.

John Gardner
Mystic, Connecticut
1977

Building Classic Small Craft

Volume 1

Introduction:
Selecting and Building Classic Small Craft

If you were to discover that someone was attempting to teach the fine points of horsemanship with water buffaloes or camels for mounts, you might be amused or indignant, depending upon your feeling for horses and the extent of your regard for the equestrian art. A not entirely dissimilar situation now obtains in this country with respect to rowing. Thousands of youngsters each summer in a multitude of camps and recreational programs are being introduced to rowing in boats which were never designed or intended for this, and which, in fact, row abominably, even to the extent of being unsafe in rough water.

The net result is that, in all too many cases, the novice is conditioned against rowing for life. After tugging and sweating at leaden oars in order to move the clumsy and unresponsive hulk provided him in lieu of a proper rowboat, he soon decides that this is not for him, and he can hardly wait to throw away his oars and get in front of an outboard motor instead. To deduce from this any contrived and Machiavellian plot on the part of the outboard motor industry would be too absurd and verging on paranoia, yet outboard motors are the beneficiaries of poor rowboats.

Lacking suitable boats for rowing, people have forgotten how to row. They have forgotten that rowing, aside from any utilitarian application, is, or can be, a pleasurable and beneficial form of recreation. Recreational rowing is a delightful, wholesome, relatively inexpensive outdoor sport that young and old, and all ages in between, can enjoy.

Recreational rowing is no competition to the use of the outboard motor for basic transportation. There are a thousand and one applications of the outboard to basic waterborne transportation in small boats; the outboard motor is supremely suitable for its proper use. No one, I think could reasonably argue its abandonment and the consequent return to oars, where it is simply a matter of getting something or someone over an expanse of water quickly and easily. Here, propulsion is merely a means to an end that is most effectively and economically accomplished by a machine.

Something more than mere transportation is involved in recreational rowing. Here, rowing becomes to some extent an end in itself. Ideally, the oarsman and his boat act together in a harmony of motion and balance not unlike a similar unity of response and action achieved by the equestrian and his mount. Indeed, not infrequently the old-time oarsman thought and spoke of his boat as a live thing.

Obviously, one must have the right sort of boat to feel this way, and unfortunately such are not easily obtainable at this time. The numerous mass-produced boats of aluminum or plastic now commonly available in the market are outboard boats and basically unsuited for rowing. Skilled handwork is so costly today that superior pulling types of traditional form and construction produced singly or on a limited scale would be far too expensive to compete with factory-produced craft now manufactured in great numbers for large-scale distribution.

This is not to say that good rowing boats, as well as outboard boats, could not be so produced, but this has not been done to any great extent. So far, there has been such a demand for outboard types that manufacturers have concentrated on these, thinking that such could also be made to do for rowing—at least, so it would seem. But these wide, shallow, broad-stern outboard hulls cannot be made to serve as rowboats with any degree of success, in spite of the rationalizations put forward in support of their versatility by those supplying them.

SAFETY AND STABILITY

First and foremost of the specious arguments for these ultra-wide, flat, outboard hulls is the claim for "safety." Thus a spokesman for the Boating Industry Association in a letter to Bulkeley Smith of Hamden, Connecticut, a lifelong rowing enthusiast, a Scout leader since 1919, and a prime mover in the cause of better rowboats for beginners, concluded as follows: "The old wooden rowboats that slipped through the water so easily, just do not handle satisfactorily with the outboard motors people wish to use on boats of this size. They were also tippy (*sic*). The emphasis today on the part of all safety authorities stresses stability."

First off, it should be noted that the writer does not seem to realize that two distinctly different types of small craft might well be produced, one for outboards and the other for oars, and that there would probably be sufficient demand for the latter to make its production in quantity profitable. The Boy Scouts alone have around 5,000 rowboats in commission. Then there is the Red Cross, as well as hundreds of privately run summer camps using rowboats. The potential market for a superior, mass-produced, general-utility rowing hull, whether in wood, metal, or plastic, easily reaches into the thousands.

But this is not the crux. The key is "stability." Apparently the BIA spokesman does not know very much about boats, at least about rowboats. He makes the fatal mistake of confusing stability, that is ultimate stability, with initial stability. There is a world of difference. I have used the word "fatal" in the previous sentence advisedly, for an ultra-wide, flat, light, shoal-draft outboard boat of great initial stability used as a rowboat, should it get caught in really rough water, might easily capsize or otherwise founder with the chance of drowning the unfortunate oarsman. Meanwhile, one of those "old wooden rowboats" characterized as "tippy," with a good man at the oars, would have a far better chance of coming through safely.

A large, rectangular box floating on the surface of a mill pond would have about maximum "initial stability," but that does not make such a safe boat. If the box is wide enough and the pond sufficiently calm, an occupant can stand up and walk around almost as if he were standing on terra firma. But start tipping the box to one side, and soon a point is reached where all of the initial stability is lost, and over she goes in a twinkling. Take the box into rough water. Heavy seas slam at its wide, flat bottom and square chine knuckles. If the box does not straightaway capsize or fill, it will nevertheless take a terrible pounding, so violent, in fact, as to make it nearly unmanageable. Some of the aluminum outboard hulls now passed off as rowboats are hardly different in shape from rectangular boxes, even though one end may be pointed.

The rounded hull of good design is treated much more kindly by the sea. For this reason naval architects often characterize such hulls as "sea kindly." There is nothing flat or square for surging seas to grab or slam against. Like the seasoned boxer, they "roll with the punches." The initial stability of such a hull may not be great because of the relatively sharp, easy lines of its underbody, so that it will start to roll quite easily. Yet, if competently designed with ample side flare, freeboard, and beam, as well as adequate overall length, it will rapidly pick up stability as it rolls down. Thus, it will go only so far and no farther, to pause briefly before starting to roll back. The ultimate stability of such a boat will, under almost all conditions, prove more than ample.

Safety in a small rowboat must not be judged by absence of motion, but rather by its control. Only a boat which responds freely, lightly, quickly, and easily to the motion of water can be considered safe. The sea is much too powerful to fight. Safety lies in being able to evade the sea. Like a sea duck riding the crests and dipping easily into the troughs, the superior small rowboat can take an amazing amount of weather.

A BOAT FOR ITS INTENDED USE

I must state categorically that there is just no such thing as the superior, all-purpose rowboat, just as there is no such animal as the superior, all-purpose dog. Border collies were bred for herding sheep, dachshunds for digging out badgers, malamutes for hauling sleds, Dobermans for police work, and Dalmatians for running after coaches.

Peapods are fine for setting lobster pots around rocky shores and ledges, guideboats for portaging through the Adirondack brush, salmon wherries for launching stern first into the surf, Whitehalls for fast taxi service across the bay before motors came into use—but swap these functions around at your peril! Whether a rowboat is any good or not depends to some extent on what it is used for and who uses it.

In former times, when men rowed boats in the course of their daily occupations, depended upon them for their livelihood and often for their lives, an intimate relationship existed between a man and his boat. Choosing a boat was a serious business, somewhat on the order of selecting a wife. There was a wide field to choose from, and many factors to take into account. Trim, smart lines were a consideration, to be sure, but not the whole story, by a long shot.

It is no accident that such superlative watermen as Adirondack guides and Maine coast fishermen frequently built their own boats in bygone days. So much depended upon having a boat uniquely suited to their own individual needs and preferences that they did not trust the job to anyone else. To the city sport entering the North Woods for the first time, all guideboats must have looked pretty much alike. Not so to the guides. Likewise to the average summer visitor, all downeast peapods would have appeared double-ended, but precious little else besides. The uninformed eye simply cannot pick out all the little differences that add up to the Big Difference. To the fisherman, each boat had individuality, and each was as different in its own way as the man who owned it.

Even professional builders, formerly, did not always build all boats of the same model just the same. It is known that Bill Chamberlain in Marblehead never made any two of his famous dories exactly alike, but was always making slight changes and experimenting.

What it all comes down to is that if a man wants a really superior rowboat suited to his own needs and preferences, provided he knows what these are, he had best build it himself to his own personal specifications; and if he is not capable of this, he should have it custom built for him by a competent professional builder. This is to obtain the best. If he will be satisfied with something less, there are good stock rowboats to be had, from which he can probably choose one that will be adequate, provided he follows some fairly simple rules or guides.

Length is an absolute. Other factors being more or less equal, the longer boat (within limits) will always row faster and easier than the shorter one. But there is a perverse tendency today generally to make rowboats too short. The outboard motor can be blamed for this. Planing hulls for outboard power do not need length, and, as stated previously, most boats suitable for outboards are entirely unsuited for rowing.

In addition, traditional pulling types are

often ruined by scaling down their length. The automobile is partly responsible for this. People who know next to nothing about boats, but who want to haul one on top of a car, think they can take one of the better old types 16 to 18 feet in length, and scale it down to 10 feet or 12 feet, and still retain the superior qualities of the original. They could not be more mistaken. Disaster is almost always the invariable result. Some scaled-down "dories" are dangerous. They are anything but dories, and should not be labeled such under penalty of law.

The standard 16-foot guideboat is far superior to the 12-footer in all respects, except that the latter is lighter and easier to carry through the woods. Some well-designed yacht tenders of 12 feet and even 10 feet in length row fairly well, but the best of them cannot compare in speed or rowing ease with equally well-designed pulling craft 4 or 5 feet longer.

As for the greater safety of the longer boat, a boatbuilder and guide at Rangeley, Maine, once explained to me that rowboats under 17 feet in length were unsafe for treacherous lakes like those in the Rangeley chain, whose shallow water can grow dangerously rough in minutes when sudden winds whip down from the surrounding mountains.

Small pulling boats, mostly under 18 or 19 feet in length, such as are generally rowed by one man, are purely displacement hulls, never attaining planing speeds under oars. They cut through the water rather than skim over it. To knife along with as little fuss as possible at rowing speeds, the hull requires a sharp, thin entrance and an equally sharp exit, with long, easy flowing lines between. If the boat has a transom stern, this must sit high above the water for best results. To the extent that the transom is immersed, it will drag, cutting down rowing speed. This is a principal reason, of course, why boats with wide, low sterns to support outboard motors row poorly, or sometimes will hardly row at all.

While both the wherry and the Whitehall have transom sterns, they are both double-enders on the water. Likewise, the Banks dory, with its narrow "tombstone" stern, comes close to being a double-ender at the waterline.

A deep, sharp forefoot at the bottom of a perpendicular stem, such as is characteristic of the Whitehall, is excellent for holding the boat on a straight course, but a boat with such a forefoot turns slowly, tows badly, and is dangerous in surf. A more raking stem, and a rounder, more cut-away forefoot is required for quick maneuvering in broken water.

To gain displacement depth for stability in open water and rough seas, the bottom of the Banks dory is heavily "rockered" or cambered fore and aft. But in the shore fishery it is desirable for the dories used to ground out as high up on the beach as possible and out of the surf, so their depth of displacement is reduced to a minimum by building them perfectly flat on the bottom.

These are but a few of the many possible variations in underwater shape to be considered in choosing a rowboat, depending, as already mentioned, on what the boat is to be used for and who is to use it.

The portion of the hull above water must be taken into account. Windage, that is, the force of the wind against the topsides, can cut rowing speed markedly and make the boat difficult to manage, yet adequate freeboard is required to keep the boat from swamping. In racing shells confined to comparatively smooth and sheltered waters, freeboard can be minimal. Banks dories, on the other hand, operating in rough water and carrying tremendous loads of fish, are built high-sided. In a light condition they stick so far out of water that they are extremely difficult to handle in a wind. Contrary to the popular notion, the Banks dory for this, as well as for other reasons, is not a particularly easy boat to row. Quite the contrary. Yet it is well-suited on the whole to the purpose for which it was developed.

Wood and reinforced thermoplastic resin are the materials mainly considered in the boats discussed in this book. Construction combining both has come to be known as composite construction. When properly engineered, composite construction retains most, if not all, of the superior characteristics of wood with additional advantages derived from the plastic.

I have never seen an aluminum rowboat that I wanted any part of. This is merely my personal feeling, and it is true that aluminum does serve quite well for some inexpensive, light, cartop boats. Furthermore, I have seen few or no molded fiberglass rowboats that I considered equal to their wooden prototypes; most of them I judge to be quite inferior. Too often, changes in shape are made to make it easier to mold the boat, and while these changes may appear to be slight, the result can be serious.

Fiberglass is a much heavier material than cedar or pine. A hull thickness required to obtain a stiffness equivalent to wood means extra weight which, if added in the wrong places, can spoil the balance of the hull. One example of this is the fiberglass replica of a 10-foot yacht tender formerly planked with cedar by a famous Marblehead boatbuilder. The fiberglass replica is quite heavy, not a serious defect, if a defect at all, so far as rowing is concerned, but bad in a tender which must be lifted in and out of the water. This tender rows quite well for its 10 feet, yet it is definitely less steady than its wooden prototype. Apparently this is because of the additional weight of fiberglass concentrated in the topsides.

In some cases, to keep down weight, fiberglass hulls are made thin and flimsy, and the finish and general appearance of molded fiberglass small craft is still generally much inferior to first-class wood construction. Some of the small molded fiberglass prams and dinghies make adequate yacht tenders, but are not in a class with the rowing craft we are considering.

A boat that is framed with wood, although it may have a fiberglass skin, is not a fiberglass boat, strictly speaking. It is a composite boat. Furthermore, if weight is a consideration, it is far better to cover such a boat with polypropylene, which is only one-third the weight of glass, and tougher and more resilient, besides. As for molded fiberglass guideboats, at least two attempts to build them on a commercial scale have failed, because of the inferiority of the molded boats.

Except for extreme types, notably racing shells, moderate hull weight, if properly distributed, is an asset rather than a detriment in the rowing hull. This is particularly true in rough water where the inertia from moderate weight keeps the boat moving smoothly ahead between strokes of the oars. Only when boats have to be lifted frequently in and out of the water, or portaged, is moderate weight a liability.

The trouble is that today boats that are mediocre or worse are frequently passed off as excellent in all good faith, and accepted as such, because no one involved has ever seen a really superior rowboat or rowed one, or has any idea what such a boat is like. It is one thing to look at a picture or a model, or to read an account in a book. It is quite another thing to sit in an actual boat and to pull the oars. In this book are a number of designs and building instructions for boats that make superior rowing, and sometimes sailing, craft. They are intended for amateur construction, so if you want to feel what it is like to row a truly excellent boat, the realization of your wish is in your own hands.

AMATEUR CONSTRUCTION

Since our approach here is from the standpoint of the amateur builder rather than the professional, a few introductory words on building small craft are in order. The boats discussed in this book are not especially simple or easy to build, but, to the contrary, require careful and precise workmanship and some familiarity with tools and materials, none of which is beyond the reach of reasonable diligence on the part of the serious amateur.

The amateur has one immense advantage over the professional. His time is worth nothing, so he can be lavish in its expenditure. A simple model will suffice to explain why: Let us say it takes 200 man-hours to custom-build a varnished cedar pram in the old way; yet the factory can turn out molded fiberglass prams in lots of 100 or more at an average expenditure of only 20 man-hours or less per pram. At five dollars per hour for labor, plus whatever else the materials, advertising, marketing, and the rest come to, the fiberglass pram might be sold at a good profit for $500, while labor alone for the cedar pram has cost twice that much, or $1000. This is only a model, of course, yet if the figures are not precise, they are still close enough so that the picture given is in general a true one.

In all fairness to fiberglass, if you are going to buy a pram, the fiberglass one will probably serve adequately. While neither as handsome as a varnished cedar pram, nor as lightweight to lift in and out of the water, the glass job will row and tow almost as well (provided the model is the same), will stand more abuse and pounding on the beach, and has no seams to dry out and open up. Yet if you have the time and inclination to build your own pram, and especially the inclination, the advantages are all with the cedar one.

It would be next to impossible to produce a one-shot fiberglass pram in the home workshop; that is, one comparable in quality and finish to the factory-made product. However, as has been proved many times, the painstaking amateur can produce a superior wooden boat if he is willing to give it the required effort and if cost is any consideration. Materials for a cedar pram will stand him less than those required for glass.

The deciding consideration may very well be one of aesthetics. For some of us, the well-made wooden boat of superior traditional design is a thing of beauty, quite aside from its functional utility. Why it is would be difficult to explain, nor is it necessary to do so. It just is, and it is enough to recognize the fact and to acknowledge it.

The creation of beauty is more satisfying and joyous than mere possession. For the person who loves boats, and who has time on his hands, what better way to spend some of it than to build himself a boat that will please him every time he looks at it or uses it. It will take some pains, both in the figurative and the literal sense, for the creative process at levels of excellence is never easy, and often its demands are rigorous and its discipline is severe.

As others have often found in the building of boats, one is likely to come close to tears more than once before everything is shipshape and the job is finally and creditably done. But then that is life, and some travail would seem a nearly inevitable part of the accomplishment of any challenging and worthwhile aim.

In order to build successfully a boat like a cedar pram, and the others in this book, a number of requirements must be met. One prerequisite is a suitable place to work, with good light, bench room, and sufficient heat in winter for gluing. It is almost as essential to have a place where things can be left lying about without their being disturbed when the builder is absent—tools on the bench or lying under the boat waiting to be picked up when work is resumed.

Tools required: a large outlay for power tools is not necessary for most of the boats discussed here. Ordinary hand tools, provided they are of good quality, and the edged ones sharp, are all that are needed. But sharp they must be. Acceptable work cannot be done otherwise. One should have a grinder and oil stones and know how to get a keen edge.

Care and patience: Measurements must be exact. Fits close. To tolerate less is fatal. Just as the surgeon demands complete asepsis in the operating room, so the competent boatbuilder strives for precise and errorless measurement and layout in the shop.

Also, as the amateur builder is not driven by time, he need not be reluctant to discard pieces which he "spoils," or that otherwise are found to be defective in any way. Planks that do not fit should be put to the saw without hesitation, and new and corrected ones made.

Special knowledge of the type of craft abuilding, trade knowhow which is the fruit of practice, these we shall attempt to explain here, at least to an extent sufficient to guide the inexperienced builder over some of the hurdles and around some of the pitfalls.

SCANTLINGS IN SMALL CRAFT

The amateur boatbuilder frequently finds himself involved in problems of design that he is not prepared to handle. For instance, he may come across a set of lines that seem to be just what he has been looking for, but there is no construction plan or any scantling dimensions to speak of. If he is going to build the boat, he will have to work out construction details, and what he needs is not always to be found in books. There are no tables of standards for figuring the sizes and spacing of timbers for small wooden boats, the thickness of planking, size of gunwales and risers, width of thwarts, width of stem aprons, or a number of other values he will have to determine with some precision.

While it is obvious that the lighter the construction, the more critical the scantling dimensions, just how critical these may be is not easy to calculate. Sometimes it takes only a sixteenth of an inch plus or minus to make all the difference. There are a great many variables. The various species of wood show marked differences in strength, weight, and flexibility, not to mention durability, and even appreciable differences are sometimes found in various lots of boat timber from the same species. Another factor that must be taken into account is the complex structural interrelationships among the members that make up the hull fabric.

It hardly needs saying that the structural design of traditional wooden small craft has not been put on a scientific basis, and while it could be, no doubt, it is not likely to be. In the past, those who practiced boatbuilding as a trade in the small shops relied on imitation of previously built boats and on their boatbuilder's judgment, the latter largely a matter of accumulated experience and observation retained in part at the subconscious level. In most cases, also, the builder was more or less a specialist whose efforts were confined to a relatively few local types with which he was thoroughly familiar. When he ventured outside his specialty, it was generally with caution and reluctance. Sometimes the result was less than happy. I recall one instance when what was supposed to be a small round-bottom sailboat came out looking strangely like a dory when it was built by a dory builder.

We know very little about small craft in early America and how they were built. It does appear, however, that the earlier boats were rather standardized and quite heavily constructed. Timber sawn from root crooks and limb crooks seems to have been used exclusively, and screws and small sizes of machine-made copper and iron nails did not become available to boatbuilders until well along into the nineteenth century.

The nineteenth century was an era of continuous and rapid technological development and growth, which accelerated as the century advanced, and this was true in the area of small craft as elsewhere. Local diversification in boats took place on a broad scale, with progressive and marked refinements in structure, especially as older working types were taken over for recreational use. In almost all cases improvement took the same course: reduction in weight was sought without reduction in strength or durability. Generally the changes that were made came gradually.

Two of the most striking examples are the Adirondack guideboat and the yachts designed and constructed by the Herreshoff Manufacturing Company at Bristol, Rhode Island. In the 1840s or thereabouts the boats used by the trappers and market hunters in the Adirondack wilderness were heavily and crudely made. In the course of the next 40 or 50 years, by a process of gradual evolution, the hunter's and the guide's boat was transformed into a guideboat, a marvel of lightness with strength. The guideboat could never have happened except for the very small machine-made brass screws and tiny copper tacks which it required in great numbers. And its scantling sizes attained ultimate reduction by the removal of literally one shaving at a time.

In much the same way, the Herreshoff Manufacturing Company lightened yacht construction and revolutionized yacht design, although scientific calculations were used as well. Scantling sizes were gradually and daringly reduced until the ultimate combination of light weight with adequate strength was reached. Few since have even approached Herreshoff's mastery of lightweight yacht construction. That scantling reductions were not excessive is attested by the fact that a number of Herreshoff yachts built in the first decade of the present century are still sailing today.

In some cases the process of refinement was carried too far. This appears to have been the case for some of the later Great South Bay catboats to come from the Gilbert Smith shop in Patchogue, Long Island. While unexcelled for speed and appearance, some of his later catboats did not hold up too well in hard use over the years.

In the construction of light yacht tenders, reduction of weight was sometimes carried to an extreme to save what could hardly have been more than ounces, certainly not more than two or three pounds. Bent oak ribs were made so small in section that they broke quite easily. Here $\frac{1}{16}$ inch, which doesn't amount to much in some places, might well have been critical.

How to know whether to leave on that final shaving or take it off? About the only way is to examine other boats of a similar nature whose history is known, before deciding. Essentially that is the way most yachts have been, and are still, designed. In one way or another, architects accumulate files of lines and structural data, which they draw upon when commissioned to design new boats.

It should be understood, of course, that there isn't any such thing, really, as a new boat. New boats are all combinations of old boats worked over. An occasional feature may be new, but that is all. Likewise, the old-time boatbuilder accumulated a shop full of patterns, molds, and templates, and then whenever he was in doubt, he would go out on the waterfront with his rule to measure actual boats. The amateur builder can also go out on the waterfront with his rule, and should do so by all means. In addition, he should have a notebook and camera with him.

A lot can be learned in boatyards, especially storage yards of the less exclusive sort where usually can be found numbers of old boats in various stages of decrepitude. In addition, there are also today a number of marine museums with extensive small craft collections, where they are beginning to make provision to assist amateur builders and antique boat buffs. One of these is Mystic Seaport, whose collection of small craft now totals over 200 and is still growing, the largest such collection in North America. While it is generally not expedient for a museum to permit all visitors to do their own measuring of boats in the exhibit collections, this is easily gotten around by having the museum staff do the measuring, beforehand, if possible, in anticipation of the public's needs. Already at Mystic Seaport, plans for a sizable selection of its small craft have been prepared by the museum staff, with prints furnished to the public for the cost of reproduction. In addition to various conventional exhibits of small craft at Mystic, a considerable number are now to be found in a separate building where they may be seen and studied upon request by persons with a particular interest in small craft.

Having made these several remarks about the choosing and construction of classic small craft, let us now go on to consider in turn a number of specific boats of good design. We will discuss a bit of their history and development, their form, and the details of their construction, together with something of their equipment and use.

1 The Common Punt

The simplest and easiest to build of all small workboats is what I learned to call a punt as a boy growing up in Maine on the St. Croix River. Names vary, however, both in time and place, so that some of our readers may be accustomed to designate this type of craft by another name, such as scow.

A punt has square ends and straight sides, giving it a rectangular shape in plan view. Its sides are vertical, and its bottom is quite flat athwartships, although fore and aft the bottom will show rocker, the amount varying from boat to boat. It has no sheer curve, being perfectly straight on top. In short, the shape is that of a rectangular box, except for the longitudinal curve of the bottom, which lifts the ends, cutting down resistance and making it easier to push the punt through the water. Some punts with well-proportioned sled-form bottoms offer surprisingly little resistance when moving, and, if lightly built, can be brought up to planing speeds by a high-speed outboard motor of sufficient power. (In fact, the extremely popular Boston Whaler is virtually a punt in form, although with secondary modifications which improve its appearance as well as its performance with an outboard motor.)

If my memory serves me, Punt is an ancient Egyptian name for a part of northern Africa; perhaps the name could be connected with the dugouts used on the River Nile and other African rivers and lakes from time immemorial. Indeed, the punt may be thought of as a replacement for the log dugout, more easily constructed of boards after sawn lumber became available.

However, what I am accustomed to call a punt, others call a scow, reserving the term punt for a slightly more sophisticated vessel. Thus, W. P. Stephens in his classic *Canoe and Boat Building*, published in the 1880s, designates the simplest and crudest form as a scow with a sketch of what is nothing more than a low, flat, rectangular box, somewhat wide and short in its proportions, and cross-planked on the bottom. This rises at the ends, not in a curve, but merely in a flat, straight incline, beveled back from either end about a quarter of the length of the boat.

Stephens's punt is a more shapely little vessel. The low side is still made of a single, wide board set on edge, but both sides are bent in plan view to give a slight but pleasing curve, and in profile they show a bit of sheer as well. The bottom is given considerable rocker fore and aft, and it is planked lengthwise. The ends are identical and square.

More frequently today the term scow is used for large vessels, while I can recall no instances in which punt is employed to designate anything larger than a rowboat. Some of the large sailing scows of the past were intricately

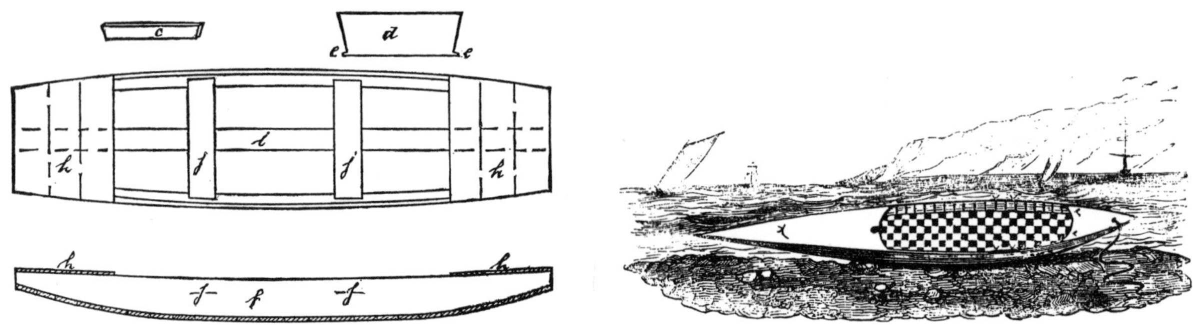

Stephens's punt (left) and Folkard's gunning punt (right).

developed and powerfully rigged craft. Howard I. Chapelle, in his *American Small Sailing Craft*, lists and describes a variety of sailing scows, including the New Jersey garveys.

In America, the term punt is most commonly applied to a small scow to be rowed, paddled, or poled; in England, it seems to cover round-bottomed boats as well. The English writer, H. C. Folkard, who was no less an authority in his country than was his contemporary, W. P. Stephens, in America, published in the sixth edition (1906) of *The Sailing Boat*, published in London in 1906, an engraving of a curious little double-ended, round-bottomed boat, which he calls a "gunning-punt," built "after the author's invention, suitable both for sailing and paddling in pursuit of wild-fowl." But only in sheltered waters. This English gunning punt has little freeboard or stability. Thus Folkard concludes: "The young wild-fowler is cautioned not to venture into rough water with the sailing-punt, for a sportsman's life is supposed to be of more value than that of a duck."

Another English authority, T. C. Lethbridge, in his *Boats and Boatmen*, suggests that the word punt is derived from the Latin *ponto*, in turn related to *pons*, a bridge. Webster substantiates this etymology, "ponto, punt, pontoon," defining punt as a "long, narrow, flat-bottom boat with square ends, usually propelled by a pole,—chiefly used in England." This last observation is probably not quite true, but the identification of punt with pontoon is highly significant. Flat, square-ended, wide boats of rough construction have been in use in Europe by the military since ancient times as pontoons to support bridges.

THE CHARLESTON BATEAU

Here, then, are the plans for what I would call a punt but which is called by its users a "Charleston bateau." It was brought to my attention for the first time by Richard H. Randall, chairman of the Maritime Committee of the Maryland Historical Society in Baltimore, whose friend, Hugh Benet, who grew up in Charleston, South Carolina, had one as a boy. His brother had one also. They bought them for 50 cents apiece secondhand from raft men who, after having delivered their logs, had no further use for the boats. As Mr. Randall explained:

> At the turn of the century much logging was being carried on in that part of South Carolina. Rafts of timber and logs, roughly cut planks piled on log rafts, were floated down the rivers bound together as most log rafts were bound on the Delaware, Susquehanna, and other American rivers—a few angle irons driven into the outside logs, a few cross timbers through-bolted, again to the outside logs. These rafts were steered by a long oar, or sweep mounted on a raised Y-post securely braced. Usually two other sweeps were pinned on the port and starboard just ahead of midships.
>
> Now, these raft men built at least one bateau per raft—frequently more. They were always the same, the hull was double-ended, with a punt-raised floor under the bow, so the bottom boards had to be shaped accordingly. The sides were nailed to the bottom boards, and cross cleats were likewise nailed to the bottom and sides, with seldom more than six cross cleats per boat. No thwarts or seats.
>
> Occasionally a triangular piece at bow and stern helped to hold the sides in position. They were built of the cheapest pine and propelled by a paddle or two—

usually homemade by the purchaser, when the bateaux were sold at the end of the trip for no more than 50 cents apiece. Obviously these bateaux swamped easily.

Of course the rafters needed at least one to get ashore if the raft grounded, to help get tackle rigged to pull her out into the stream again, also to repair the raft if the logs slipped or got loose. Rafters used the paddle too.

The shores of the Ashley and Cooper Rivers at Charleston were muddy and swampy—still are at the southern entrance of the Inland Waterway. This swamp shore was called plough mud [pronounced pluff] and the boys had to dig into the mud with their paddles and slide the bateaux along to gain solid ground. Remember how terrible that mud smelled? And the Intercoastal still does!

With no caulking the seams would dry out overnight and these boats were not taken from the water, so the kids sank them every time they came home, and emptied them the next time they were used.

Charleston was settled by many French Huguenots, so perhaps that is how the name bateau became connected with this type of craft.

Following Hugh Benet's sketch closely, which he drew from memory, I made the drawings which accompany this description.

The lengthwise planking of the bottom is not what I am familiar with for small scows or punts like this. I believe that cross-planked construction is more usual, yet fore-and-aft bottom planking is probably better—certainly it would offer less resistance in sliding over mud, if there was much of this to be done. Also there would be fewer seams to open and leak. As we have already seen, W. P. Stephens designed his rather nicely modeled punt with the bottom planks running lengthwise.

There might be some difficulty in bending these bottom planks if the bottom curve or "rocker" were rounded too abruptly. The bottom curve I have shown in Profile 1 on the drawing closely reproduces the curve on Benet's sketch, and in my judgment might require steaming the planks. In Profile 2, I have eased this curve enough so that I think that softwood boards (pine, cedar, cypress), if not too dry, could be sprung in place without steaming. In a second sketch, I show the proper way of going about this: Nail one end securely, and then use the length of the board as a lever to spring the board down in place gradually, nailing securely as you proceed, both through the cross cleats of

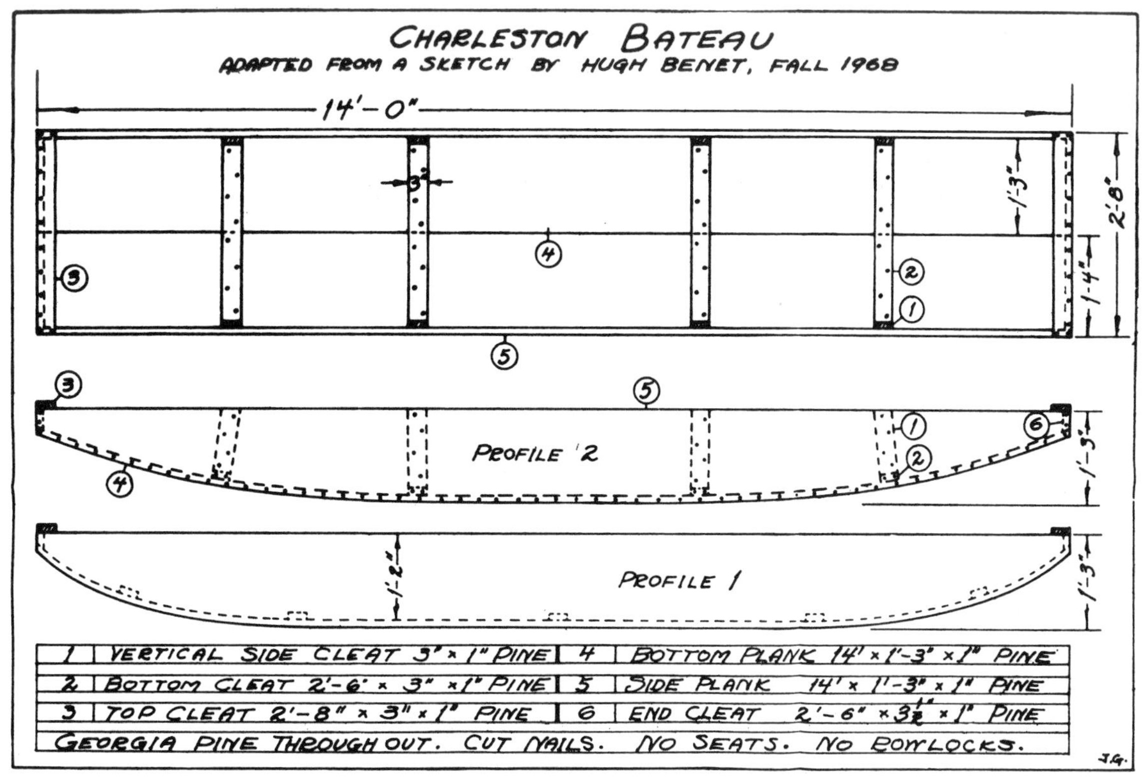

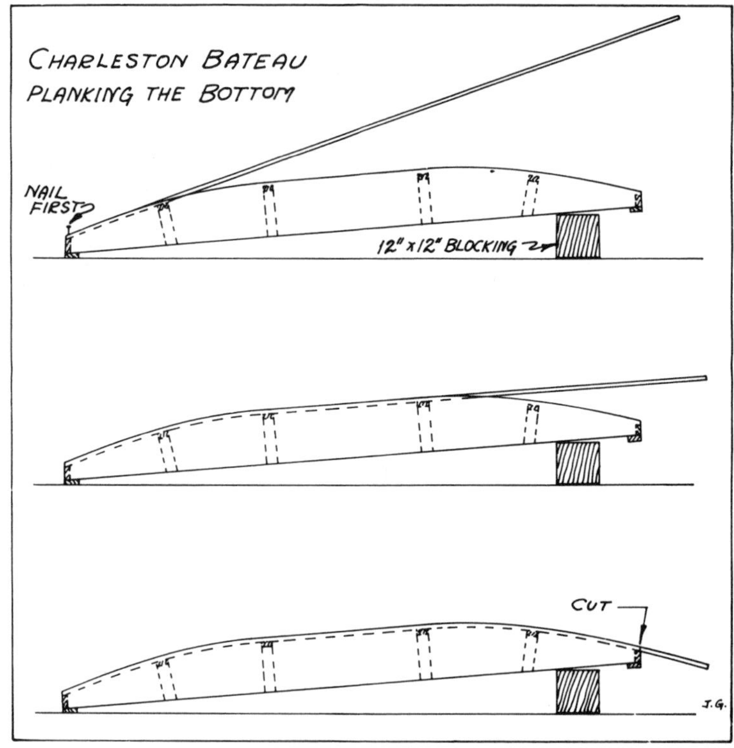

the bottom and through the side edges. Boards several feet longer than the bottom should be used in order to gain leverage and to get the other end down into place. When the planks are securely nailed, the excess is sawed off.

Boards as wide as were used originally, as shown in the drawings, are not necessary. The bottom can just as well be made of four boards instead of two, and the sides of two boards each instead of one wide one. The narrower boards will bend into place more easily.

Benet in his sketch did not show any cleats on the sides. Possibly these are not absolutely necessary and were not used for the cheapest construction, but I have put them in. They support the bottom cross cleats during construction when a lot of pressure is put on the cross cleats in springing the bottom boards into place. Also, side cleats brace the sides and help to keep the wide side planks from warping or splitting. If two planks were used for the side instead of one wide one, side cleats would, of course, be required.

This is a very easy and inexpensive boat to build, and either as it is, or with minor modifications, could prove a most useful craft under many different conditions and circumstances. It is capable of carrying heavy loads, is extremely stable in calm water, and will row or paddle more easily than might appear. It will take a lot of abuse and should not require much care or upkeep.

As a utility craft or small workboat on the waterfront—a river, lake, or ocean—this punt has real possibilities. It could be used with an outboard motor and would even sail with a few slight modifications. Its fore-and-aft bottom planking makes installation of a centerboard very easy.

This is a basic hull with which a great deal can be done for very little.

A UTILITY PUNT

Every boatyard needs one of these rugged punts. Likewise, summer camps and shore resorts, alongside fresh or salt water. This sturdy little vessel would more than earn its keep any place along the waterfront where work has to be done on or from the water. This punt would certainly give a good account of itself for a variety of jobs. For one thing, as it is roomy, fairly high-sided, and impossible to tip over, it would make a grand play boat for children in sheltered waters. Its flat bottom and sled bow are well adapted for beaching, although it would have to be built rather light to be pushed off the beach by children.

For a chunky, blunt-ended craft, this punt rows and handles remarkably well, and it is as steady as a small raft for carpenter work and painting. Its carrying capacity, for a boat not 12 feet long, is enormous. The original punt, from which the present design was faithfully copied, had as many as nine men aboard on occasion. Over its long career, it carried innumerable and varied heavy loads, such as hard pine blocking, lumber, sand, stone, and cement. Its main job was tending the two marine railways at F. J. Dion's yard in Salem, Massachusetts. The punt met its end recently when it got caught and crushed beyond repair in the larger railway. Fred Dion, who some thirty years before had designed and built the original, built a second punt copied from it. The lines, dimensions, and details are given herewith.

The idea for the first punt came from larger working punts developed on the Cape Cod cranberry bogs. These were sometimes dragged like sleds on the surface of the bogs by horses and were large enough to float a horse to parts of the bogs accessible only by water. Mr. Dion, in adapting the design, kept the general shape and proportions of the bog punt, but reduced the size to the requirements for a yard boat.

This punt, when properly handled, is surprisingly able in rough water. I witnessed its performance in the big hurricane of 1954, when the punt was used to put out extra dock lines. At the time it was blowing so hard that two men facing each other were required to hold one pair of oars in the water. At times the punt would drop nearly out of sight in the trough, and for long spells the boat seemed not to make an inch of headway. But finally the lines were set and secured, and the punt returned safely and completely dry to the float. This was a stiff test for any 12-foot boat, and some good yacht tenders could not have made it.

The construction shown in the accompanying drawings is extra heavy. This boat was built to take abuse of the heaviest and hardest sort and to last for many years. Since the boat was designed to remain in the water the whole

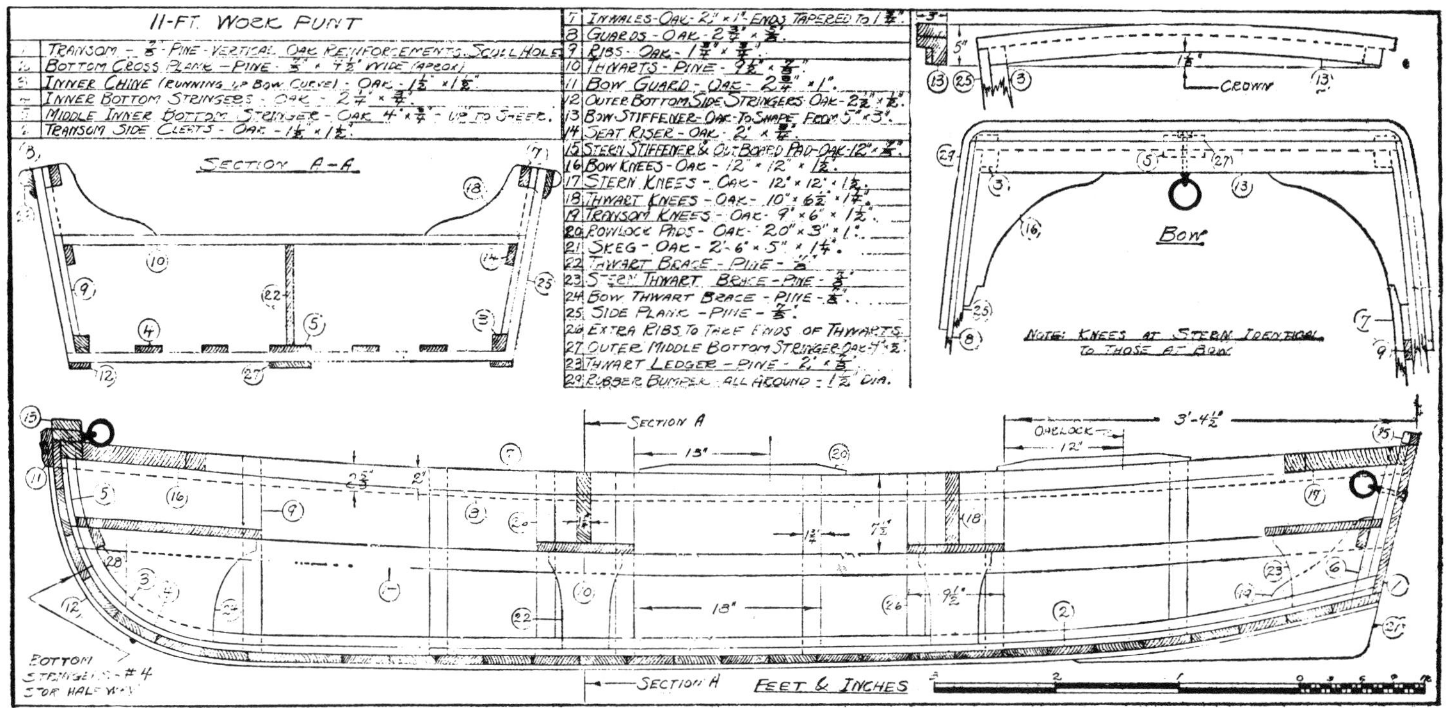

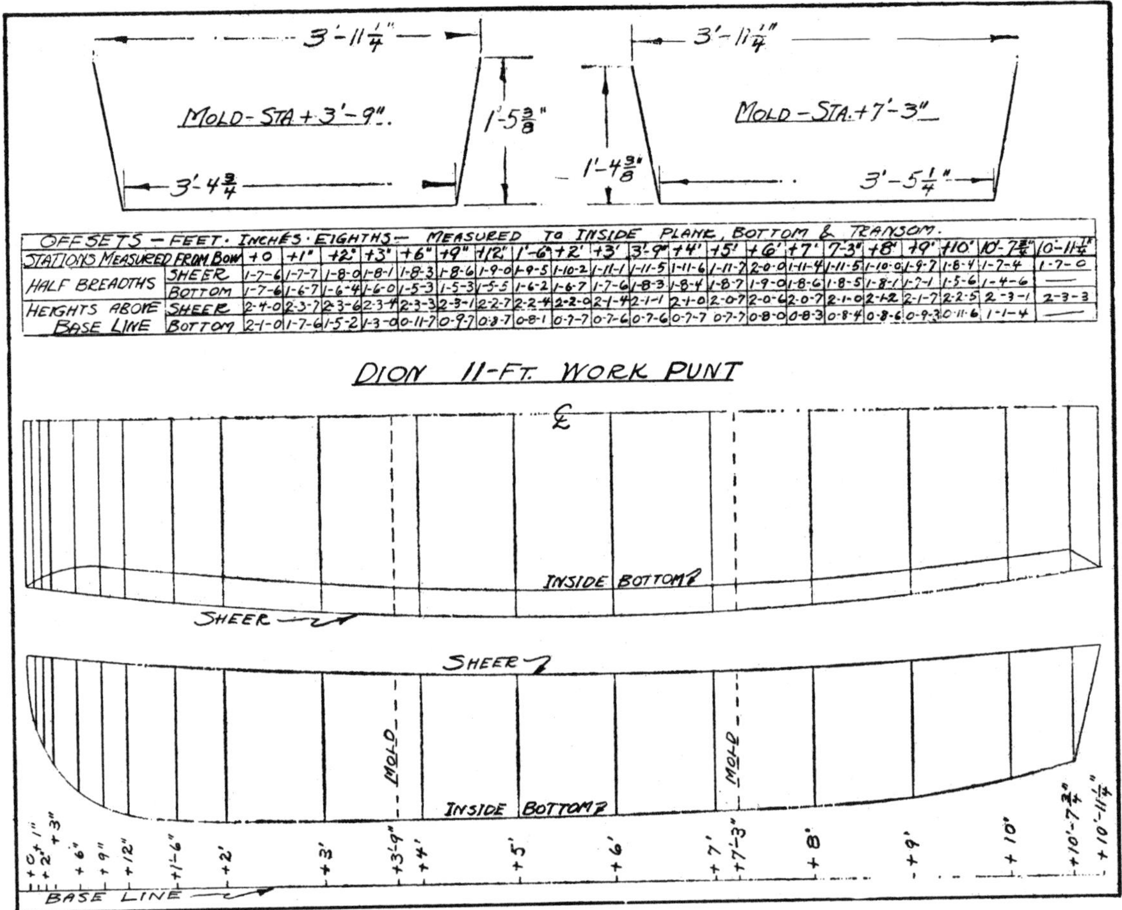

OFFSETS — FEET · INCHES · EIGHTHS — MEASURED TO INSIDE PLANK, BOTTOM & TRANSOM.

STATIONS MEASURED FROM BOW		+0	+1"	+2"	+3"	+6"	+9"	+12"	1'-6"	+2'	+3'
HALF BREADTHS	SHEER	1-7-6	1-7-7	1-8-0	1-8-1	1-8-3	1-8-6	1-9-0	1-9-5	1-10-2	1-11-1
	BOTTOM	1-7-6	1-6-7	1-6-4	1-6-0	1-5-3	1-5-3	1-5-5	1-6-2	1-6-7	1-7-6
HEIGHTS ABOVE BASE LINE	SHEER	2-4-0	2-3-7	2-3-6	2-3-4	2-3-3	2-3-1	2-2-7	2-2-4	2-2-0	2-1-4
	BOTTOM	2-1-0	1-7-6	1-5-2	1-3-0	0-11-7	0-9-7	0-8-7	0-8-1	0-7-7	0-7-6

STATIONS MEASURED FROM BOW		3'-9"	+4'	+5'	+6'	+7'	7-3"	+8'	+9'	+10'	10'-7¾"	10'-11¼"
HALF BREADTHS	SHEER	1-11-5	1-11-6	1-11-7	2-0-0	1-11-4	1-11-5	1-10-0	1-9-7	1-8-4	1-7-4	1-7-0
	BOTTOM	1-8-3	1-8-4	1-8-7	1-9-0	1-8-6	1-8-5	1-8-1	1-7-1	1-5-6	1-4-6	—
HEIGHTS ABOVE BASE LINE	SHEER	2-1-1	2-1-0	2-0-7	2-0-6	2-0-7	2-1-0	2-1-2	2-1-7	2-2-5	2-3-1	2-3-3
	BOTTOM	0-7-6	0-7-7	0-7-7	0-8-0	0-8-3	0-8-4	0-8-6	0-9-3	0-11-6	1-1-4	—

season, from early spring to late fall, extra weight does not matter, as it would in a boat that has to be pulled in and out of the water frequently. For rowing, especially in rough water, considerable weight is an advantage, as it keeps the boat moving steadily between strokes once headway has been gained. Also, weight suppresses undue bobbing, jumping, and heeling, an important feature when a boat is to be used for carpenter work and painting, and as a tender around marine railways.

It would be easy, however, to make a much lighter boat to the same lines and general details. Such a boat would be amply strong for general use if the sides were made of marine fir plywood ½ inch thick, or even ⅜ inch thick if a very light boat were desired. The ribs could be cut to 1¼ inches, the chines to 1¼ inches, the inwales and risers to 1½ inches, and the guards to 1¾ inches. Two of the inner bottom stringers could be eliminated, the size of the knees could be reduced by one third, and the thickness of the skeg could be reduced to ⅞ inch. The heavy oak bow stiffener could be eliminated, the stern outboard pad narrowed to 9 inches, and the oarlock pads shortened by one third. All in all, it would not be hard to reduce the total weight by 25 per cent and more without weakening the boat for ordinary use.

While marine fir plywood would make an excellent alternative material for the sides, plywood is not recommended for the bottom.

The white pine bottom cross plank should not be reduced in thickness to under a minimum of ¾ inch.

The boat shown here was fastened throughout with screws, except for the inwales, which were rivet-fastened through the topsides and timberheads with 20d copper wire nails headed over burrs. Screws used were mostly No. 12s and No. 14s, from 1½ inches to 2 inches long. To fasten the ends of the cross plank into the sides, No. 10s 2¼ inches long were used. The cross planks were also fastened into each stringer with two screws. Altogether, the fastening was extra generous. Galvanized nails could be used instead of screws if desired. Such would be cheaper, possibly quicker to drive, and sufficiently strong and lasting for all ordinary purposes.

Construction is quite simple. First, the two sides are made up in the flat. Comprised in this assembly are the side planks, inner chines, and ribs. The sides are then bent bottom up around the two molds, which are indicated in the lines plan. The fore and aft ends are hauled in with door clamps to the proper widths and secured with temporary stay-laths. After this assembly has been checked, horned, and plumbed for symmetry and conformity to the lines dimensions, and securely stayed with ample braces, the transom and bottom cross planking are put on.

The structure is next turned right side up. The inner bottom stringers, risers, bow stiffener, knees, inwales, etc., are installed. When all interior members are in and fastened, the boat is turned bottom up again to receive the outer bottom stringers and skeg. Before the stringers and skeg are fastened on, the bottom seams are caulked with a thread of cotton, payed with primer, and puttied. It is important to do a thorough caulking job on the ends of the cross plank where they meet the sides.

For yacht work, the continuous rubber bumper around the sheer and ends is a must. Also, it should be noted that the sheer guard is well beveled on its lower edge so as not to catch on things when the boat settles in a swell. Heavy ring bolts are shown in each end, ample enough to be used as lifting rings; both are fitted with painters. The location of the rowlocks is indicated. These are galvanized iron of the Davis pattern that slip out of an upright position when not in use and hang down inside the boat. This also is a "must" for yacht work, as the ordinary rowlock can give a nasty dig on occasion in the overhanging counter of a yacht. Most of the rowing will be done from the forward center thwart, but the rowlocks are located so that a man can row pushing by facing forward from the after cross thwart. Thus two men can work at the same pair of oars in an emergency—one pushing and one pulling.

The thwarts and end seats are well braced and posted because men frequently have to jump from a height into the boat when working around railways. Also, heavy blocking is sometimes dropped into the boat. Such hard usage is one reason for the close stringers. In the old punt, thirty years of hard work had worn hollows in the pine cross planking exposed between the bottom stringers.

Finally, we should not forget the scull hole in the transom, although the art of sculling, as well as ordinary rowing, is fast being forgotten in this day of the ubiquitous outboard motor. An oak reinforcement suitable for mounting an outboard motor is indicated for the transom, but to my knowledge the old punt was never submitted to the indignity of an outboard. A motor would probably work all right, although the up-turn of the bottom aft is not suitable for efficient outboard performance. For best results with an outboard, the run of the bottom aft should be straight and flat. But this would drag water when the boat is rowed. "You pays your money and you takes your choice."

2 L. Francis Herreshoff's Pram

Along the waterfront these days prams are everywhere in evidence. Made of plywood and plastic, these snub-nosed craft now are probably our most popular and common type of small tender. Some are quite diminutive and boxy and can hardly be classed as sea boats, yet they serve quite adequately on calm days to negotiate the several hundred yards or less between the mooring and the float, which is about all that many require of a tender.

The advantages of such prams are several. They are light, compact, easy to handle and take aboard, and stow to advantage on deck, taking up a minimum of room. Some of the plastic ones are transparent, permitting them to be placed bottom-up over skylights or hatches without cutting off the light below.

Their form is such that they are relatively simple and easy to construct, and they are adapted, as well, for mass production. The lower building costs resulting sometimes carry over to the final selling price, although some of the more fancy plastic prams are priced about as high as the traffic will bear, and then some.

Yes, for fair weather use in sheltered harbors, most of these modern, mass-produced prams serve nicely enough, but if one is looking for something more in a tender—that is to say for a boat that will tow, that will pull easily over a distance, that will stand some rough water—then the ordinary run-of-the-mill pram, as commonly seen today, just won't do.

But there are prams and there are prams. In Scandinavian waters, where prams originated long ago, they proved themselves fine sea boats, as some still are, and if properly designed, they tow beautifully. We have this from no less an authority than the late L. Francis Herreshoff, one of the greatest American yacht designers, sailor and yachtsman of wide experience, and in addition, one who knew small craft and the details of their construction as have few others. In addition to his other numerous accomplishments, Herreshoff was a proficient boatbuilder.

Back in the 1940s, Herreshoff wrote for *Rudder* magazine a long series of articles afterwards published in book form as *The Common Sense Of Yacht Design*, which has been reprinted by Caravan-Maritime Books, Jamaica, New York. The series was immensely popular. We waited with mounting anticipation for each new installment. We cherished the back issues—in fact, I have mine still, and they fill a rather large box. I well remember the appearance of the section on small craft, now Chapter XIX in the Caravan reprint, and how avidly I read it. Figure 362 of this section, reproduced here, is an undimensioned lines sketch showing the proportions of the pram that Herreshoff designed for the deck of the M boat he designed,

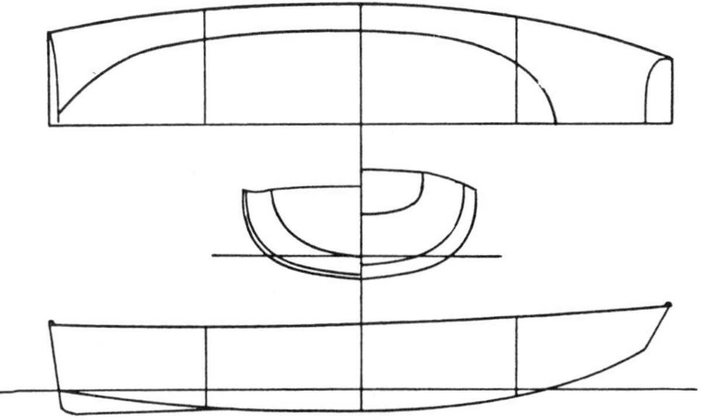

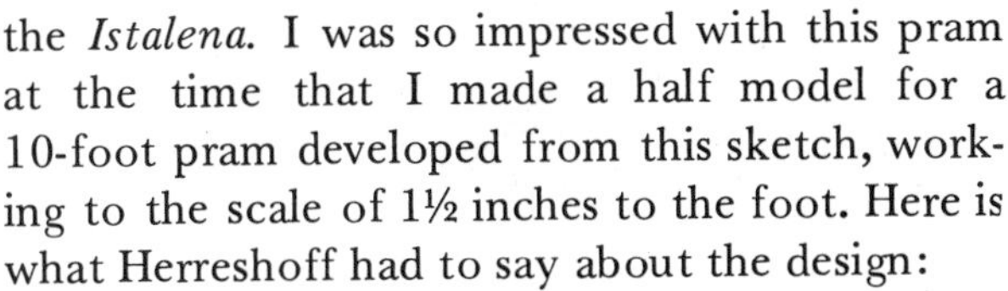

Racing tender designed by L. Francis Herreshoff for the deck of the M boat Istalena *(from* The Common Sense of Yacht Design, *Caravan Maritime Books)*

Folkard's praam.

the *Istalena.* I was so impressed with this pram at the time that I made a half model for a 10-foot pram developed from this sketch, working to the scale of 1½ inches to the foot. Here is what Herreshoff had to say about the design:

> After World War I yachts became smaller and smaller, so that a good dinghy (particularly for the deck of a racing yacht) became quite a problem, for when the usual models of dinghies are made too small they are not safe or comfortable. In England about this time the smaller yachts were using what is called a pram dinghy, that is, one with a transom both forward and aft. While somewhat similar models called square toes had been used in this country, as a general rule they were so poorly modeled that they were not a success.
>
> In 1921 when I was racing at Cowes in England, I had an opportunity to try one out in rough water on a day when the tide was setting up against a stiff breeze. I rowed one from Cowes Roads nearly to Southampton waters and back, and was so much impressed with the performance of that pram that ever since I have considered it the best model for a small tender.... These little prams tow as well as, if not better than, any other dinghy and on account of their low freeboard stow well on deck.

It is clear that the pram was known and used in England a considerable time before the period cited by Herreshoff. It was used as a rowing boat and as a sailboat in the larger sizes. In the sixth edition (1906) of *The Sailing Boat* by H. C. Folkard, London, there is printed a steel engraving, reproduced here, of a "large Sailing-Praam, adopted and rigged in British waters with two masts and lug-sails..." It is shown running before the wind with the foresail or jib "hauled aweather," which, according to Folkard, was the usual method for steadying a boat in a seaway. What Folkard has in general to say about the pram is worth quoting here:

> The Praam (Praham) is also a boat of Norwegian contrivance, and of peculiar form. The Praams, like the yawls, are built of "Norway deal," but without nails, the planks being fastened to the keelson and timbers with hard wooden pegs; notwithstanding which they are very tight and secure, as well as strong and durable.
>
> The shape of the Praam is similar to a wooden boat scoop without a handle, having a broad, round shaped bottom; the greatest width of beam is at the stern, the head and bows gradually rising forward, and sometimes finishing with a carved figurehead. Small-sized Praams are used generally as rowing boats; it is only the larger size that are sailed.

Two characteristics of the Norway praam noted by Folkard call for comment. First is the manner of fastening with "hard wooden pegs." Treenail fastening was a common method for traditional Norse fishing small craft. Detailed drawings for shaping and wedging such treenails may be seen in the plans of a heavy, flat-bottomed boat of pram shape reproduced here from *Nordens Batar*, by Arne Emil Christensen, Jr. Treenail fastening, however, requires thick wood to be effective, and this, in turn, means relatively heavy scantlings. For a light tender, such as we are considering, construction of this sort is entirely unsuitable. Recommended for our purposes is white cedar planking, ¼-inch thick, fastened with small copper rivets. Instead

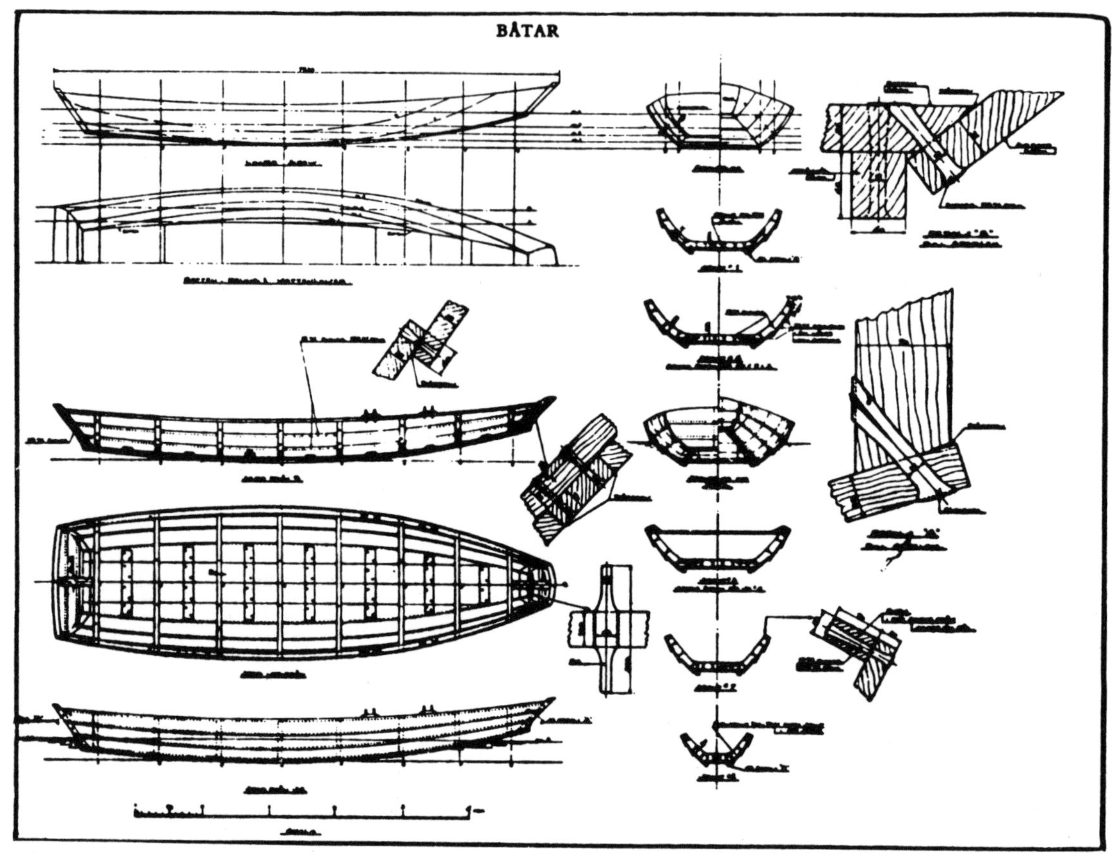

A heavy Scandinavian work pram shown in Nordens Bater. *Although of flat-bottomed construction, she is similar in shape to the 10-foot pram based on Herreshoff's lines.*

of heavy, hewn, natural-crook timbers such as were traditional with the Norwegian boats, our pram will be framed with slight, steam-bent ribs of white oak, closely spaced.

Second, according to Folkard's description, the praam's greatest breadth of beam came at the stern with the hull tapering forward to a small transom at the bow. The result was a somewhat pointed appearance combined with a marked amount of rocker. In the Herreshoff pram, although the stern is fairly wide, the greatest beam comes nearly amidships. The bow transom is not particularly small, nor is the profile curve of the bottom in any way excessive. In short, Herreshoff retained the characteristic pram shape, but without going to extremes in any particular. The result is an especially easy shape to plank without twists or hard bends of any sort. With proper lining, the strakes should run nearly straight, and none will require steaming.

From the half model of Herreshoff's pram that I made so many years ago, I have taken off the lines, which are reproduced here, along with the offsets. From these, an excellent tender can be made, I feel sure. It is a relatively easy one to build, a consideration not to be minimized by the inexperienced amateur. The pram is to be planked lapstrake or clinker, which is the way the Norwegians first built their praams, and the proper way of doing it still. Not only is clinker construction the easiest and strongest method for building this pram, and the lightest even, but also it makes a more stable boat, for the laps grab the water, helping to keep the boat from rolling, which this type of hull has a tendency to do.

The building process for this pram may be divided into four stages: (1) setting up, which includes laying down the full-size lines, and making the molds and setting these up with the two transoms and the keel strip in place, ready to receive the planking; (2) planking, which comprises lining off the plank shapes on the molds, spiling the shape of each plank in turn and getting it out of planking stock, and finally hanging it, that is bending and fastening the plank on the boat; (3) timbering with white oak frames, steamed and bent in, and riveted through the laps after the planking is in place; and (4) finishing, the addition of thwarts, rowlocks, gunwales, knees, and miscellaneous hardware.

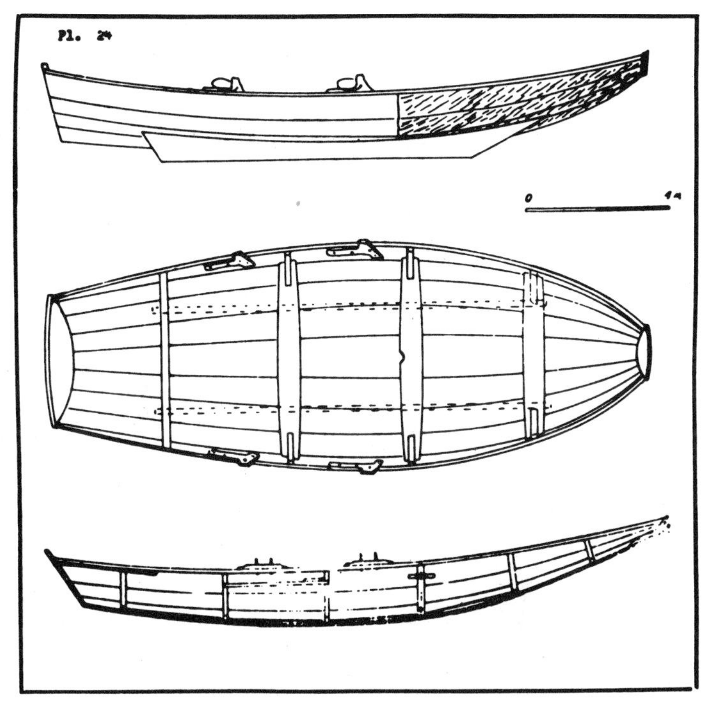

Two Norwegian prams from Norske Bater *by Arne Emil Christensen, Jr. The pram at the top is not unlike the Herreshoff pram, although the latter's lines are much less extreme. Note the twin skegs that serve as both runners and keels.*

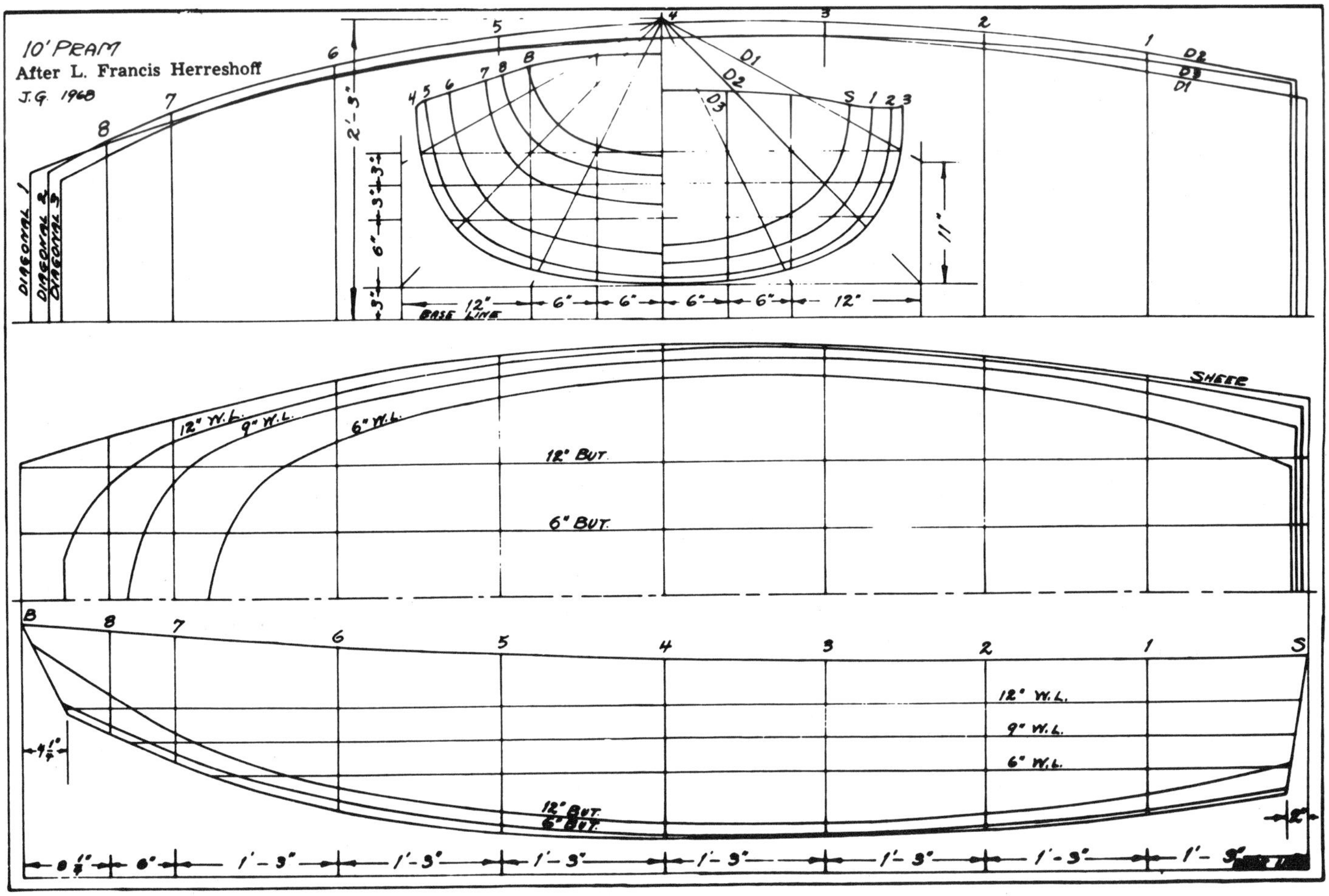

10' PRAM
After L. Francis Herreshoff
J.G. 1968

SETTING UP

The "ladder-frame" method I am proposing here for setting up is a bit unusual, and very likely the professional builder might do it differently to save time. But occasionally, as the old saying goes, "the longest way 'round is the shortest way home." The extra labor expended in making this ladder-frame setup will not be lost, let me assure you. Not only will it insure a fair shape, as well as an easy means of positioning the molds and holding them rigid, but also it will permit fastening the garboards without interference from posts or other kind of underpinning as might be in the way if the boat were set up on posts or a plank-on-edge, two of the more usual ways of doing this.

For the "ladder", two 12-foot 2 by 4s are required. These must be perfectly straight, otherwise the setup will not be fair. These are laid out side to side on edge on the bench or the floor, and the mold spacing from the lines plan is measured off on them and squared across both and marked. The two sides of the "ladder" are then separated so that they run parallel and are exactly 2 feet apart from outside to outside.

Cross cleats, previously prepared, are securely nailed on at the mold stations conforming exactly to the squared lines as

OFFSETS 10' HERRESHOFF PRAM

STATIONS		STERN	1	2	3	4	5	6	7	8	BOW
HEIGHTS	BOTTOM	0-6-4	0-4-7	0-3-5	0-3-1	0-3-1	0-3-5	0-5-6	0-10-1	1-0-7	1-2-5
	6" BUT.	0-7-1	0-5-4	0-4-0	0-3-5	0-3-4	0-4-2	0-6-5	0-10-7	1-1-5	1-3-6
	12" BUT.	0-9-3	0-6-6	0-5-1	0-4-3	0-4-4	0-5-5	0-8-0	1-0-7	1-4-3	1-9-3
	SHEER	1-7-1	1-6-7	1-6-6	1-7-0	1-7-2	1-7-6	1-8-4	1-9-5	1-10-0	1-10-6
HALF-BREADTHS	6" W.L.	0-11-2	1-3-7	1-6-3	1-7-6	1-7-6	1-6-1	1-2-3	—	—	—
	9" W.L.	1-3-1	1-6-1	1-8-2	1-9-3	1-9-3	1-8-1	1-5-1	0-10-5	—	—
	12" W.L.	1-4-6	1-7-1	1-9-0	1-10-1	1-10-2	1-9-1	1-6-4	1-2-3	0-10-3	0-3-3
	SHEER	1-5-4	1-7-4	1-9-3	1-10-3	1-10-6	1-9-7	1-7-5	1-4-2	1-2-6	1-0-3
DIAGONALS	D 1	1-7-6	1-10-6	2-0-0	2-1-1	2-1-2	2-0-1	1-9-5	1-6-0	1-4-0	1-1-3
	D 2	1-9-3	1-11-7	2-1-5	2-2-6	2-2-6	2-1-4	1-11-0	1-6-6	1-4-1	1-1-4
	D 3	1-9-0	1-11-1	2-0-5	2-1-3	2-1-3	2-0-3	1-10-1	1-5-6	1-2-7	1-0-7

BOTTOM HEIGHTS AT CENTER LINE OF HULL. MEASUREMENTS TAKEN TO INSIDE OF PLANKING.

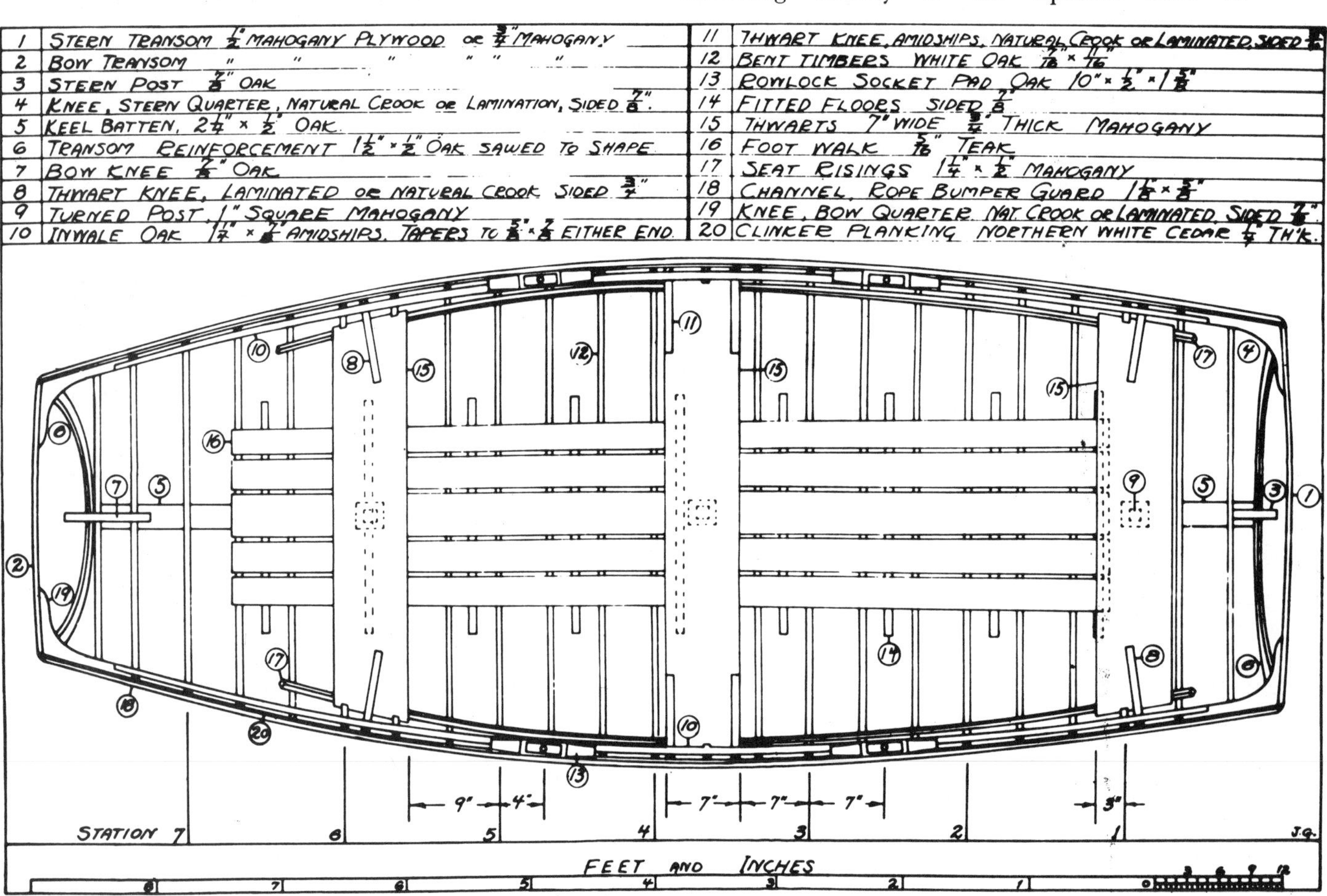

previously marked. These cross cleats of 4-inch wide strips of one-inch spruce or pine boards must all be exactly 2 inches long with accurately squared ends. Not only will the sides of the ladder-frame when assembled be exactly parallel, but also the seven cross cleats at right angles to the sides will all be evenly spaced 15 inches apart and parallel with each other.

When the molds are located on this ladder-frame at their respective stations, their accurate positioning is virtually automatic. At the same time they are rigidly secured in place. The two beveled end cleats that hold the bow and stern transoms need not be fitted until the backbone assembly is put on the molds and fastened down.

The molds, to be located vertically, that is at their correct relative heights, are made with extensions which raise them the proper distance above the ladder-frame. The various lengths to make these extensions as required by different molds are determined from a line added to the profile view of the lines drawing. It corresponds to the ladder-frame and is laid out parallel to, and 25 inches above, the baseline from which the offsets are measured. The molds are all extended to this line.

The keel batten, which provides backing for the garboards and to which they are riveted along their lower edges, is a strip of ½-inch by 2¼-inch oak. The molds must be notched to receive it, and, because it takes considerable bend, especially forward, some practicable means must be devised for holding it in position during the first stages of construction. This is accomplished by another batten, a temporary set-up batten, also oak and of the same dimensions except that it is shorter, extending from mold No. 1 to mold No. 7. This set-up batten is located inside, or rather, under, the keel batten, which rests on it and to which it is temporarily fastened by a number of one-inch No. 10 screws

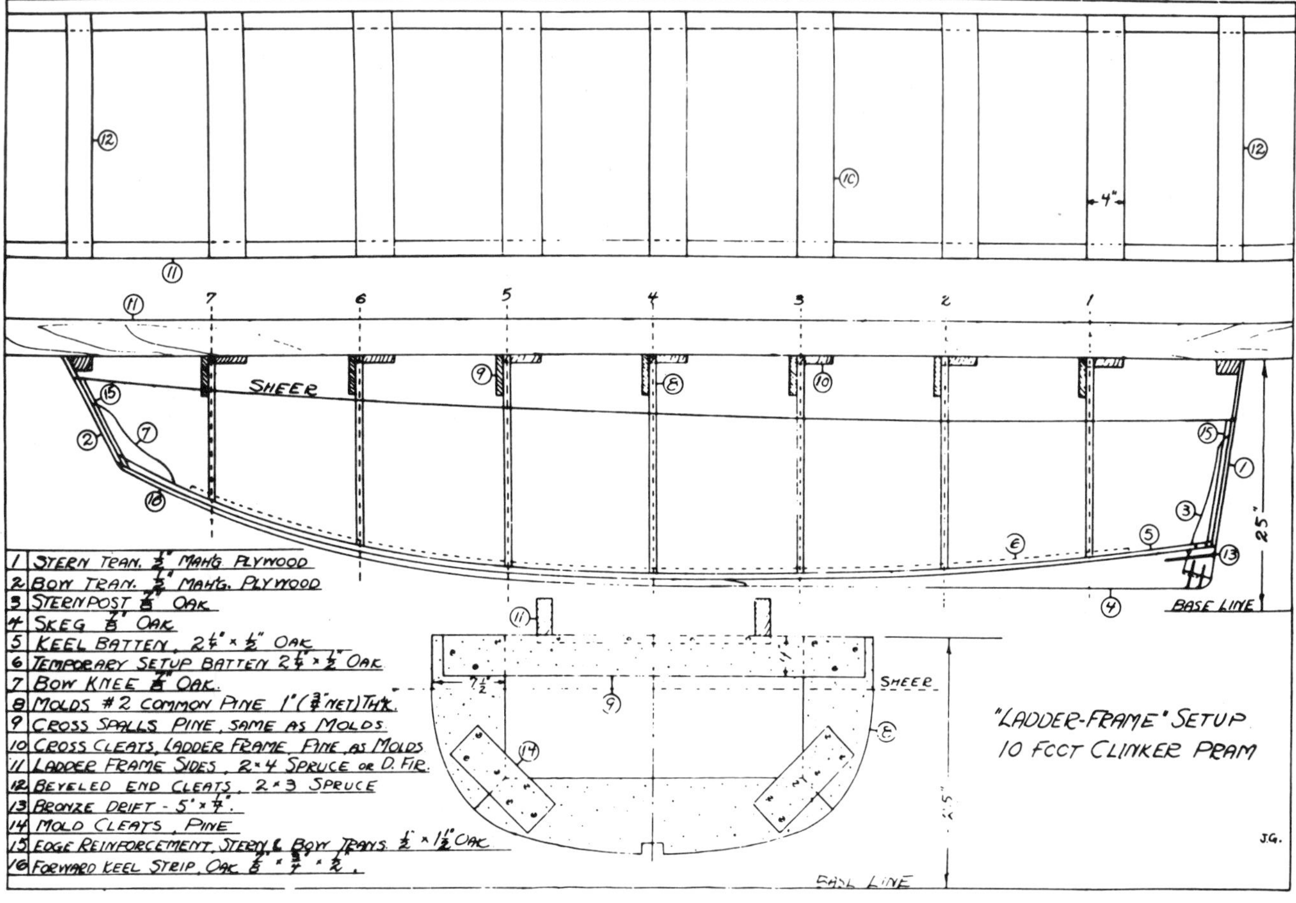

put in from the inside of the boat and thus easy to get at when the molds are removed after planking.

Besides acting as a form to bend the keel batten on and to help hold the backbone in position for planking, the temporary set-up batten has another function: It serves to brace the molds and to hold them perpendicular to the ladder-frame and parallel to each other. The set-up batten is screwed securely into each mold, the keel batten notches in the molds having been cut an additional ½ inch deeper to receive it. With the tops of the molds secured to the ladder-frame cleats and the bottoms attached to the set-up batten, the result is quite rigid, as it will be absolutely immovable when the backbone assembly is fastened on with the bow and stern transoms screwed to the beveled end blocks nailed to the ladder frame.

One thing to mention about the molds, lest it be overlooked: They are not located in the usual way either at one side or the other of the section lines, but directly over them, so that temporary fastenings into them through the plank may later be drawn and the same plank holes used to fasten through to the timbers, every third one of which will fall directly on a section line. Consequently, the end molds will have to be beveled slightly on one side or the other, but for only half the thickness of the mold.

Old-time builders of lapstrake boats fre-

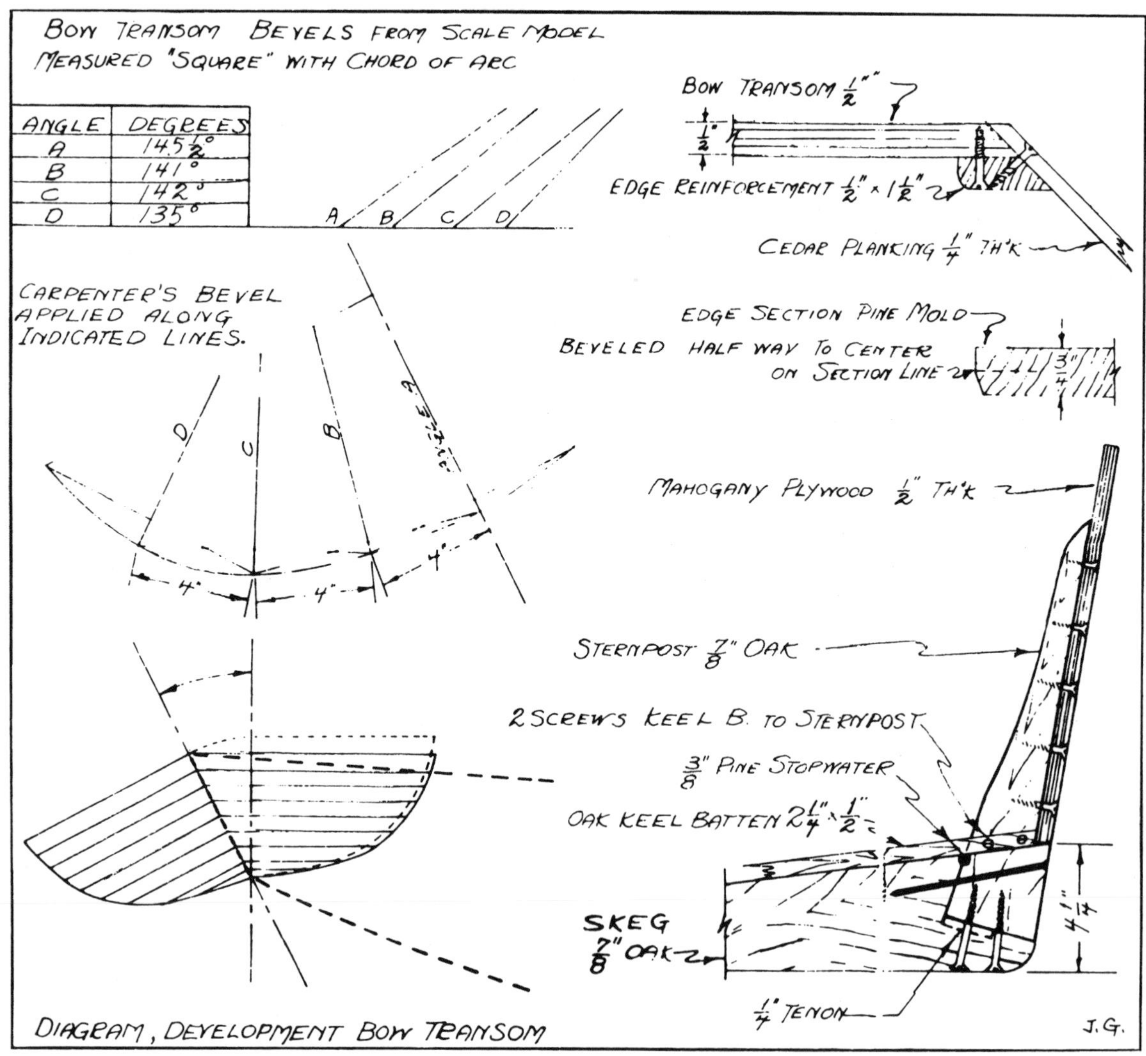

quently used only one mold, called the "shadow," which was set up amidships. Depending on this alone, they were able to control the shape of the boat as they planked, keeping it symmetrical and fair. But this method required a high order of skill attainable only through long practice, and, I dare say, even so, boats did not always shape out exactly as planned.

In this boat, two of the intermediate after molds, where the shape does not change quickly, could be left out, but for a beginner I would certainly recommend staying with all seven molds, although the 15-inch spacing between stations may seem pretty close.* There is a reason for spacing these molds exactly 15 inches apart on centers. The steamed white oak timbers, bent in place and riveted through the laps after planking is complete, are located 5 inches apart on centers. Thus, two timbers come between each two molds, and when the molds are removed timbers take their places, giving a uniform 5-inch timber spacing throughout the boat.

The timber "bays," that is, the spaces between the timbers, are divided to allow two riveted lap fastenings between every two riveted timber fastenings, so that the rivet heads on the outside of the laps are all spaced equally the length of the boat. The intermediate lap fastenings are put in and headed up tightly over roves or burrs as the planking goes on. This, of course, takes place before the molds are removed and the timbers bent in. Obviously, it is essential to space these intermediate lap fastenings correctly, leaving spaces for rivets which will fasten into the timbers later.

In this boat as laid out, it is easy to determine the location of the timbers by measurement from the molds, and thus to lay out the precise rivet spacing between timber locations as the planking proceeds. With the ladder-frame set-up, the molds are bound to be positioned right. With a little care the fastenings can be spaced perfectly. This is more important than might seem in a varnished boat where all the rivet heads will show, and any departures from a regular, uniform pattern will stand out like the proverbial "sore thumb."

Once the molds are in place, the bow and stern transoms are both got out with enough additional wood at their upper ends to allow them to be fastened to the end blocks on the ladder-frame. After the boat is planked and the molds have been removed, this excess is cut off and the ends are given their designed shape.

To save weight without loss of strength, ½-inch mahogany plywood of the best marine quality is suggested for the transoms. Solid mahogany could be used, but it should not be less than ⅝-inch thick. Perhaps ¾-inch thick would be better if weight were not too compelling a consideration. If plywood is used, it will be necessary to add a reinforcement around the inner edge to provide secure fastening for the screws which hold the ends of the planking. Such reinforcing pieces got out to the required curves can be either oak or mahogany and need not be more than ½-inch thick and 1½-inch wide. They should be nicely cut, well smoothed, and neatly beveled or rounded on the inside so as to look well when varnished. These pieces should be glued to the inner face of the transom with epoxy adhesive, in addition to being well fastened with ⅞-inch No. 8 bronze wood screws spaced not more than 2 inches apart, with the heads set just below the surface of the wood.

The side and bottom edges of the plywood transom will be covered with planking after beveling. The top edges of the plywood transoms need not be left exposed. There are various neat ways of protecting and hiding the end wood. One is by covering it with fiberglass tape set in epoxy, with the excess width trimmed off flush with the surface after the resin has hardened. Another is by the addition

*While it is nice to have plenty of molds to insure a fair and accurate shape, the spacing recommended would be pretty close when it came to riveting the laps of the bottom planks. Amidship, especially, it would be hard to reach in between molds set as close as this to get at the rivets conveniently in order to do the careful, painstaking job in heading them up which is so important and critical, as will be explained.

So on second thought I think it will be desirable (certainly for fat men) to make do with molds on the even numbered stations only, omitting molds on stations 1, 3, 5 and 7. Some might want to keep the mold at station 7 because of the greater bend in the plank close to the bow and the danger of getting a flat spot there.

of a thin strip or half oval of mahogany put on with epoxy adhesive and very fine brads.

The sternpost construction is typical of the best traditional design. It imparts strength and bracing action to the whole after end of the boat without adding extra weight. Note that it is shouldered to support the transom, and that it extends up the inside of the transom to brace it. The sternpost should be glued to the transom with epoxy adhesive, and fastened through from the outside with 1-inch and 1¼-inch No. 10 bronze screws 2 inches apart, with the heads carefully set just barely below the surface and with the slots lined the same way, which will look all right varnished. They should not be bunged, as the ½-inch plywood is not thick enough to take a bung and still retain its strength around the fastening.

The sternpost is of ⅞-inch thick oak like the skeg and the outer forward keel strip. It mortises snugly through the after end of the keel batten and comes down through the bottom of the boat to "marry," as the English boatbuilders say, with the skeg. Note how it is securely pinned with copper rod, and particularly how a small tenon on the inner side of the lower end fits into a mortise in the skeg and thus holds the two in perfect alignment, even though the tenon is only ¼-inch thick and ¼-inch deep. Note also how the end of the sternpost is fitted to the skeg with a raking joint in order to cover and to protect its end wood. By this arrangement the skeg is so solidly braced that it can sustain heavy shocks and even pounding on the beach without straining or moving or getting knocked sidewise, as would easily and most certainly happen if it were merely fastened on the bottom with a few screws through the keel batten. In such a case in a boat as lightly constructed as this one, even slight strain on the skeg might produce leverage enough to spring it sidewise, producing a split or a leak.

Where the sternpost mortises through the keel batten, outside strips of the batten 11/16-inch wide remain on each side. These should be fastened sidewise into the sternpost on each side with two 1¼-inch No. 8 bronze screws. The after ends of the garboard planks will be held in place by rivets driven through these cheek pieces.

Before planking starts, a ⅜-inch hole should be bored centering on the joint between the end of the skeg and the sternpost and just below the keel batten. Through this a tight pine stopwater is driven, and its ends trimmed off flush with the surface of the sternpost. The ¼-inch planking when it is on will not cover all the stopwater, but that does not matter. Better to have a stopwater too large than too small. The planking should fit tightly against it, but not so tightly that a thin thread of cotton cannot be driven in against this stopwater on either side. A bit of caulking may also be needed where the transom sits in its notch in the sternpost. No other caulking should be required in this boat.

After the mold assembly is completed on the ladder-frame, and the backbone assembly has been bent on and secured in place, the set-up is ready for planking, provided the molds don't require some final slight fairing. Of course this will be checked for and done if needed.

But before planking can start, the set-up assembly must be turned over and securely positioned in some manner at a convenient height for working, for in order for one man to rivet the laps of clinker planking as the several strakes go on up the sides starting from the garboards, the boat must sit right side up. This is so the planker can push against the rivet head on the outside with a weight in his left hand, perhaps assisted by his knee, while he heads up the rivet on the inside of the lap with his riveting hammer in his right hand. If riveting is attempted with the boat bottom up, two persons will be required for this operation, and even so they may not be able to coordinate their efforts to do it properly.

How to hold or suspend the set-up securely and at the correct position for planking to proceed? Possibly the extended ends of the ladder-frame can be supported by a couple of high horses. Or an arrangement of posts at either end may be substituted. Cleats nailed to a convenient wall could serve nicely to take one end of the ladder-frame, while a horse or posts hold up the other end.

Much will depend on the place serving for a

shop, and something needs be left to the builder's ingenuity. A few stay-laths, either pieces of strapping or long edgings, run from the set-up to convenient spots on the wall and/or ceiling and temporarily nailed, will steady the set-up wonderfully, and, after the garboards are on, a couple of light posts as props underneath will make things as solid as the Rock of Gibraltar. Several outside legs clamped to the outside of the wider molds and running to the floor will provide the finest kind of support without getting in the way of the planking enough to bother the builder excessively.

PLANKING AND TIMBERING

Though this 10-foot pram would admit construction by several methods using a variety of materials in different scantling sizes, the intention here is to build a fancy varnished tender, ultra light in weight, yet adequately strong and lasting if properly handled and cared for. For a quality tender of this sort nothing can equal clinker planking of northern white cedar.

J. H. Rushton of Canton, New York, one of this country's leading builders of small craft in the latter part of the nineteenth century, specialized in light lapstrake cedar boats. One of these, the "Nessmuk featherweight canoe," 10½ feet long and 27 inches in beam, was advertised in the Rushton catalog as weighing between 20 and 22 pounds. Rushton explained why he preferred northern white cedar:

> Do not confound our White Cedar, which grows only in the most Northern States and Canada, with the White Cedar of New Jersey and Virginia. The former is the lightest known wood of this or any country that is suitable for planks for small craft. One cubic foot, air seasoned (not kiln-dried) weighs but eighteen pounds, while the White Cedar of New Jersey and Virginia weighs 28 pounds.
>
> The Northern Cedar is soft, tough and durable. You can give it a vast amount of hard useage with but little injury, and time makes little impression on it, as I have known the Cedar planking in a boat to be sound and perfect after twenty years' constant use every summer, and having only such shelter winters as may be found in a woods camp.

In building clinker or lapstrake, thinner planking can be used than is required for carvel, because the doubling at the laps in the former makes up in strength and stiffness for the slighter thickness. Besides, carvel planking generally must be thicker to hold caulking, which clinker does not require. Rushton built "Pleasure Row Boats" as long as 16 feet with a beam of 42 inches, planked lapstrake of northern cedar ¼-inch thick. For our 10-foot pram, a ¼-inch plank thickness will be quite adequate. We might use 5⁄16-inch planking but little would be gained by it except a somewhat heavier boat. As old Charles Lawton used to say in this connection (Charlie was for many years the leading small-boat builder in Marblehead), "Three-eighths planking will smash just as quick on the rocks," meaning that for normal use ¼-inch planking was adequate for the small clinker tender, and that under conditions of extreme abuse, extra plank thickness availed little or nothing.

Of course, it should be understood that thin planking must be adequately reinforced and supported by suitable timbers or ribs. If these are made of choice white oak, they may be fairly small in cross section, but at the same time they should be rather closely spaced, as we shall see when we get to timbering.

The main event in building this pram is the planking. Setting up, and in general getting ready to plank, requires careful, accurate, methodical work, it is true, but is, in a sense, routine. Finishing the boat after planking is complete is not to be done haphazardly, but is anticlimactic and something of a letdown. It is the planking that separates the boatbuilders from the shoemakers, as they used to say in Marblehead. In planking, variables come into play requiring exercise of judgment. Aesthetics are involved to a critical extent. In fact planking is something of an art, perhaps one reason none of the boatbuilding books I have seen treat its mysteries adequately.

Fortunately, our pram has an easy shape to plank. Strakes can be lined out nearly straight, for the greater part, and go on without twist or sny. One advantage obtained from the pram's transomed bow is the elimination of twist in the

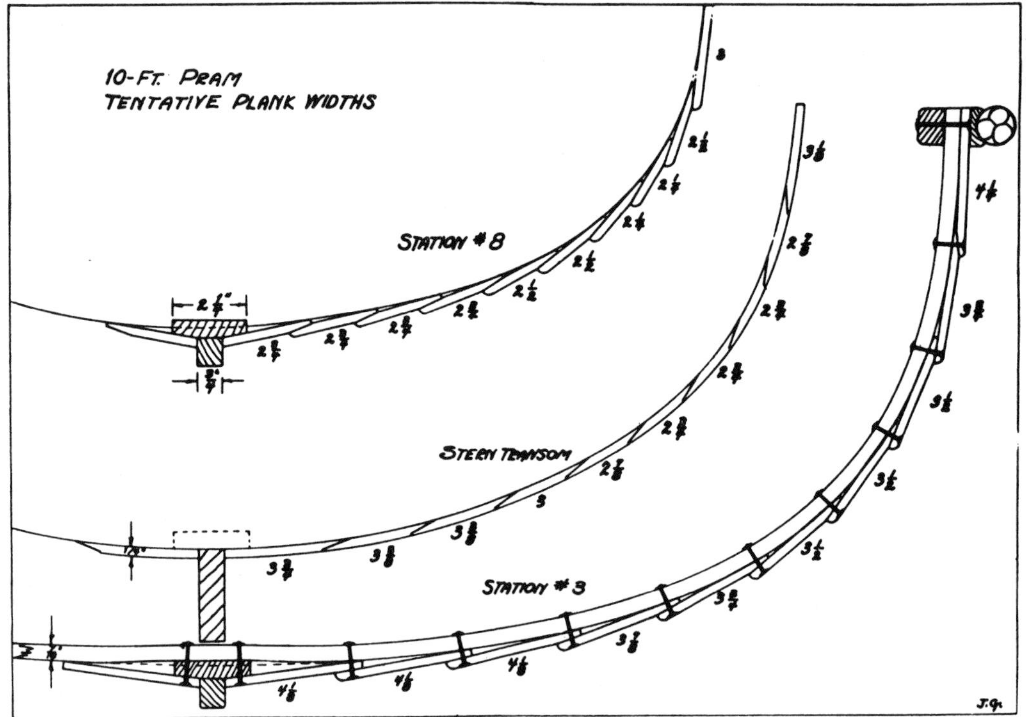

fore ends of the lower plank, especially the garboard. In a comparatively short, wide boat with a sharp bow and nearly upright stem like the well-known Lawley tender, for instance, the hood ends of the lower plank, which land in the stem rabbet, require steaming and can prove vexatious to fit and hang even for experienced boatbuilders. With the pram, all this is avoided. The thin, narrow planks bend easily into place with a minimum of clamping and no forcing, if accurately spiled. No hollowing or rounding is required as with carvel planking.

To begin planking, the hull surface must be lined, that is divided up to best advantage with the widths and sweeps of the several planks marked off on the edges of the molds. Special devices employed in this operation, namely the lining batten and the diminishing batten, are described in the Appendix and need not be taken up here.

In lining plank, one of the first steps is to decide on the number of planks. For this pram I should think 10 strakes about right in order to give rather narrow widths, for narrow plank for a clinker boat of this sort are an advantage over wide planks, if not a necessity. Narrow planks are not likely to split or rent. They do not move as much in swelling and shrinking as wider widths. They fit the curve of the sides better where the turn is sharp, and they are easier to get out of ordinary planking stock, where it is often desirable to dodge knots or other defects. Narrower planks mean more laps, however, and more riveting as well. An extra strake or two lengthens the building time somewhat, but this should not bother the amateur.

Plank shapes need to run in smooth, easy, continuous sweeps or curves, diminishing evenly in breadth from the wider mid-portion of the hull to its narrower ends. Not only is this necessary for appearance, so that the boat will "look right," but it would be difficult, if not impossible, to attain a watertight hull if the planks were of erratic shapes and made abrupt changes in contour.

Numerous considerations, sometimes conflicting ones, enter into the determination of plank widths. Compromise is often necessary. For one thing, hood ends must not be made so narrow as to preclude room for adequate fastening. As a general rule, plank should be fairly straight when laid out in the flat, both to avoid weak cross-grain and for economical utilization of planking stock. The apportionment of width in the strake has much to do with the amount of crook developed in its shape. Furthermore, in clinker plank, widths have a direct relationship to lap bevels and should correspond to the curvature of the frame, so that the sharper the rib bend, the narrower the plank will need to be.

The accompanying drawing shows tentative plank widths for three stations for the pram, for No. 3 in the mid-portion of the hull, No. 8 just abaft the bow transom, and for the stern transom. It should be noted that the planks are wider on the bottom and in the topsides next to the sheer, and narrower at the turn of the bilge and just above, where the most curve is found. The reason for such variation in plank width should be obvious.

As stated, these are "tentative" widths, which will need to be checked on the hull with the lining batten. Undoubtedly some adjustment in these preliminary widths will be required, although probably not much. There is no precise way of exactly determining plank widths in advance of building, except that it is possible to lay out close approximations on an accurate scale model.

In a lightly built clinker boat like this pram, it is desirable for strength to leave as much wood as possible in fitting the laps. The lap bevels can be controlled to some extent through plank widths. From the planking diagram for station No. 3 on the drawing, it will be found that the laps fit with little or no beveling. However, at station No. 8 the laps are beveled considerably more. This is because this station is close to the bow transom where the beveling must be increased to permit the hood ends of the plank to lie flat and smooth on the edge of the transom without any of the lap protruding.

This, of course, is what is also seen at the stern transom. Sometimes each of the meeting lap surfaces at the ends of adjoining plank are shaved to a sharp, or "feather," edge, so that they lie flush and continuous when brought together. The feather edge is more prone to break, so according to the best practice, as shown in the accompanying drawing, the edge of the outer lap is left a little blunt or "strong," so as to let in flush to a slight rabbet cut in the underpiece. This makes a neater and more secure job.

It must be admitted that the changing lap bevels required for this pram are fairly tricky and call for special attention. Yet they are nothing that cannot be handled, given care and a little study. For the novice who finds these bevels difficult or puzzling at the start, it might help to lay them out precisely and full-size on the drawing board, for several stations at different parts of the boat.

Incidentally, clinker plank may be finish-sanded on the bench before hanging. A small power belt sander, if available, serves famously for this, although the old fashioned sandpaper block run by potato power does just as good a job.

The planking may be got out of cedar boards even slightly thinner than one inch in the rough. A plank shape is laid out on such a board and cut out, and the edges are planed to the line. Then the piece is split in two lengthwise, giving two planks of identical shape, one for either side of the boat.

Copper rivets are indicated for fastening the planking laps of this boat, both through the timbers and between them, instead of clinched fastenings. Although rivets may mean a little more work, I believe they pull up tighter and are not so apt to work loose when properly put in. (For further information on this, including instructions on riveting, see the Appendix.) For the laps of this pram, a nail ¾-inch long is big enough. For riveting through laps and timbers together, a 1¼-inch nail is needed. For riveting the inwales and thwarts, a 2-inch nail is required.

Timbers in this pram run continuously from gunwale to gunwale and are spaced exactly on 5-inch centers. As previously indicated, the body sections in the lines have been laid out with this in mind, being drawn 15 inches apart, so that when timbers are located on the section lines, the spaces, or "bays," between will each divide evenly for two sets of timbers. Thus, it is easy and convenient to lay out on the inside of the planking, measuring from the molds, and using a thin, flexible batten for marking, the exact position to be occupied by each continuous timber or rib. The timbers are to be white oak. For instructions on steaming, placing, and riveting them, see the Appendix.

FINISHING OUT

After the boat is timbered, the finish work can begin. The fitted floors are scribed, cut to shape, and fastened in. Incidentally, these, while spaced approximately on 10-inch centers, should be shifted slightly one way or the other to miss fastenings already put in. The fitted floors add a little extra weight and some extra work, but are worth it in added strength. They must be well fitted, not less than ½-inch thick (molded thickness) where they notch over the keel batten. Don't forget the limbers to permit water to drain along the laps. The floors hold not only the inside walkway, but also the rubbing strips on the outside.

The walkway strips come next and should not be varnished, for more secure footing, and are best made of teak. Port Orford (Alaskan) cedar, or even ordinary white cedar could be used, however. The strips are fastened into the fitted floors with 1-inch No. 6 or No. 8 bronze wood screws. A round hole may be cut through these strips under the middle thwart for sponging out the boat. Strips, or "stretchers," are easily screwed on the walkway strips, to brace the feet when rowing.

Next, the seat risers can be installed, as well as the thwarts and thwart knees. The turned posts under the thwarts permit the thwarts to be made only ¾-inch thick, and thus save a great deal more than their own weight. The ¼-inch chamfer on the edges of the thwarts is for appearance, making the thwart look even thinner than it is. The thwarts, with their knees and center posts, or supports, are very important strengthening members. The bracing knees as shown are absolutely essential for strength.

The four quarter knees are installed next. These and the eight thwart knees may be made either of natural crooks or of laminations. In the past, the finest light tenders often had their knees made from apple limb crooks. These are still good, but not easy to obtain.

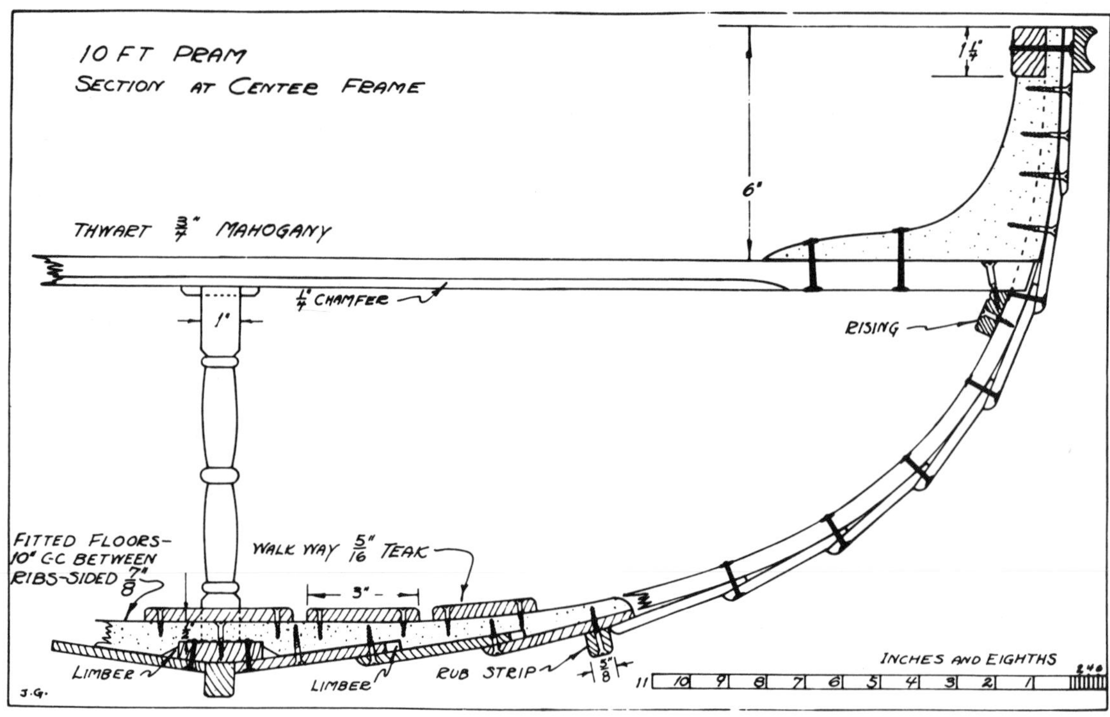

Laminated knees when properly made and finished look good and are very strong. A form should be made for bending and gluing thin strips (about 1/16-inch thick) to produce a blank of the right size from which to cut out the finished knees. The form is made in two parts, an inside and an outside part, which are drawn together, with the strip assembly between. Large C-clamps are most commonly used for clamping. All parts of the gluing form must be well waxed to prevent the glue from sticking to them. Strips are got out on the circular saw from stock 2-inches thick, let us say, so as to produce a blank that when glued will give two knees of 7/8-inch thickness, finished. Wood for laminated knees may be mahogany, ash, or Sitka spruce. Strips should not be too smooth for good results with epoxy glue—just as they come off the ordinary circular saw (*not* a planer-tooth saw) is fine.

Any good epoxy glue can be used but it should be rather heavy. The form should be arranged so the glue does not run out easily before it hardens. A proprietary epoxy glue may be used or any rather heavy epoxy resin mixed 50/50 with Versamid 140 as the hardener.

After the knees are in place, the oak inwale is fastened with rivets through the sheer plank and timberheads and through the ends of the quarter knees, bow and stern. Then the following items must be installed: rowlock sockets and pads; the outside channel strips to hold the cotton rope bumper; bronze eye bolt and ring for towing put in through the bottom of the bow transom into the bow knee, and lifting rings in the bottom, inside, if desired.

The final finishing includes sponging outside with hot water to take out dents, as well as inside around rivet heads, the final sanding, a coat of sealer, and three coats of varnish. Then the cotton rope bumper and painter is installed.

While ½-inch thick mahogany plywood with the edge reinforcement, as shown in the drawings, will make a strong, light transom without seams, the top edge will have to be protected in some way, possibly with a strip of solid mahogany securely fastened on with epoxy glue and 2-inch No. 6 or No. 8 bronze screws. Those who don't like the idea of plywood here can substitute solid mahogany ¾-inch thick, but it will add a little to the weight of the boat.

Screws needed for the thwart knees, risers, fitted floors, and rub strips are No. 8 bronze 1-inch and 1¼-inches long. For the ends of the planking and the transom reinforcements, 7/8-inch No. 6 bronze screws will do, although those for the transom edge reinforcements might better be size No. 8. For the outside channel strips for the rope bumper, 7/8-inch No. 6 or No. 8 screws are needed to go through the sheer plank into the timber heads. For the sternpost, bow knee, outer keel strip, and skeg, assorted bronze screws of sufficient size and number will be required to give solid fastening. Plenty of fastenings are needed. Do not skimp.

Glue should be used throughout, especially for reinforcing knees and for securing the reinforcing strips around the edges of the transoms.

For flotation, six Styrofoam blocks may be affixed to the under sides of the thwarts. These may be made up the width of the thwarts to go on either side of the center posts, and covered with a thermoplastic coating of some sort for cleanliness and appearance. If fastened to a thin plywood backing, these flotation units may be secured with round-head screws so as to be removed easily if desired.

3 A Plywood Pram

This pram is all boat, and quite a vessel for less than 9½ feet of length. I took a lot of pains with my design, not only in the preliminary stage of gathering and comparing dimensions and other data, but in laying out trial lines and in making a working half model to see how the proportions looked in wood. After a year of use, it has more than met my expectations in all but one respect: the weight is slightly more than I had hoped. But weighing just under 100 pounds, the boat is not that heavy. Two persons can easily carry it. It could have been built lighter, but I chose to make it more than amply strong and rugged, and whenever it was a question of gaining extra strength by adding a little more weight or a slightly larger scantling, I decided for the extra strength.

The pram is very stiff and surprisingly seaworthy. It takes four adults easily, its bottom rocker and fairly deep vee give it a good grab beneath the surface, and its 55 inches of beam assure ample stability. Yet in spite of its exceptional width the boat is not tubby. It rows easily for a short boat and handles well. The considerable bottom rocker and vee plus the long slant of the bow transom largely account for superior performance here, I am inclined to think.

This pram builds easily according to the method devised for it, and it builds inexpensively, too. With the compartments under each of its three seats filled with Styrofoam, it is unsinkable, and no matter how long it lies hauled out in the hot sun it will not leak a drop.

The basic material is exterior fir plywood in ¼-inch and ⅜-inch thicknesses. The boat is glued throughout with epoxy resin, and its seams are reinforced with 3-inch fiberglass tape set in epoxy. The lengthwise reinforcing pieces, namely the inner keel strip or keelson, the chine strips, the risers, and the gunwales, are spruce, as are the beams and framing for the plywood seats. Spruce is used for the strips that frame the edges of the bow and stern transoms and those around the three interior plywood bulkheads, which serve both as building molds and fronts for the underseat compartments and as athwartship reinforcement for the boat. The skeg is likewise spruce, along with the four, long, outside bottom strips and the short, interior cross floors and stiffeners for the bottom. In short, all the wood in the boat other than the fir plywood is spruce got out of rough ⅞-inch Nova Scotia spruce ledger boards bought from a local lumber yard.

Spruce ledger boards used for building stagings are tough, light, and strong. They are moderately priced, going for a fraction of what Sitka spruce would cost. Yet by picking out good boards and getting a couple of extra ones, and in using care in splitting them on the circular saw, it is possible to dodge the knots, getting

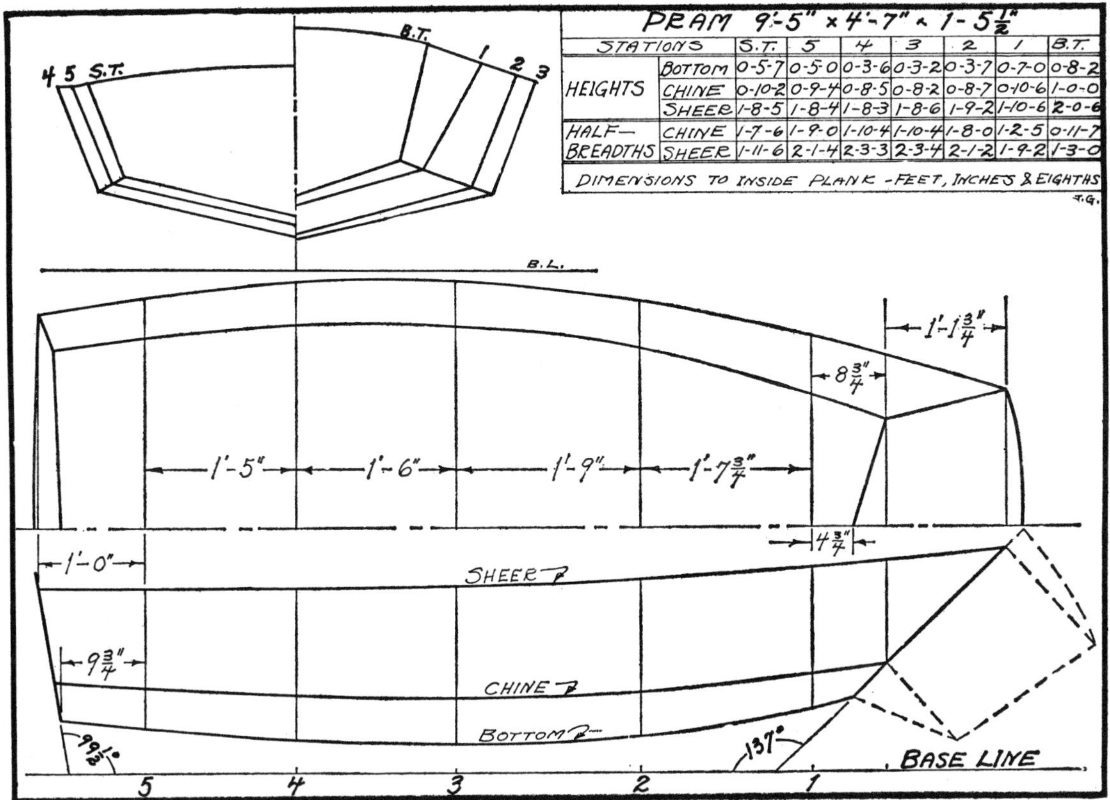

PRAM 9'-5" × 4'-7" × 1-5½"

STATIONS		S.T.	5	4	3	2	1	B.T.
HEIGHTS	BOTTOM	0-5-7	0-5-0	0-3-6	0-3-2	0-3-7	0-7-0	0-8-2
	CHINE	0-10-2	0-9-4	0-8-5	0-8-2	0-8-7	0-10-6	1-0-0
	SHEER	1-8-5	1-8-4	1-8-3	1-8-6	1-9-2	1-10-6	2-0-6
HALF—BREADTHS	CHINE	1-7-6	1-9-0	1-10-4	1-10-4	1-8-0	1-2-5	0-11-7
	SHEER	1-11-6	2-1-4	2-3-3	2-3-4	2-1-2	1-9-2	1-3-0

DIMENSIONS TO INSIDE PLANK - FEET, INCHES & EIGHTHS

clear wood throughout for the necessary strips. Although the boards I selected had been piled in the open, they were dry and thoroughly seasoned. Air-cured Eastern spruce like this is tough, glues well, and holds fastenings well. Wet, unseasoned stock should not be considered.

This boat is glued together with epoxy resin wherever wood meets wood. For the greater part, two-penny galvanized wire lath nails can be used to tack the joints in place and also to add mechanical reinforcement. Small screws might be used, but these will cost more and take longer to put in. Screws are employed only where special reinforcement is required, as for holding on the bottom strips and for fastening through the inner cross floors into the first of the outside bottom longitudinals. Screws are also used to tie the keelson and chines to the bulkheads and to reinforce the ends of the four laminated knees bracing the center thwart.

All outside plywood joints butting on the keelson, chines, and ends are bound with two layers of 3-inch fiberglass tape set in epoxy resin. This covering protects the plywood edges, ensures that the seams are perfectly and permanently tight, and binds the seams together with much additional reinforcement. Strips of fiberglass tape and epoxy are also used inside and out to bind and reinforce the corners where the ends of the sheer meet the stern and bow transoms. These tape strips are lighter and less bulky than the conventional wooden knees commonly used for reinforcement here.

One of the distinctive things about this pram is the easy method devised for setting it up for building. Two straight 10-foot 2 by 4s are laid level and parallel on horses and cleated together securely so that their inner edges are exactly 22 inches apart. The several stations shown in the plan are marked on them and squared across from side to side.

The end transoms are got out of ⅜-inch exterior fir plywood according to the dimensions furnished, and their edges are framed with glued spruce strips. Beveling may be postponed until after the boat is set up for planking. The three interior ¼-inch plywood bulkheads are cut out and prepared with spruce strips glued

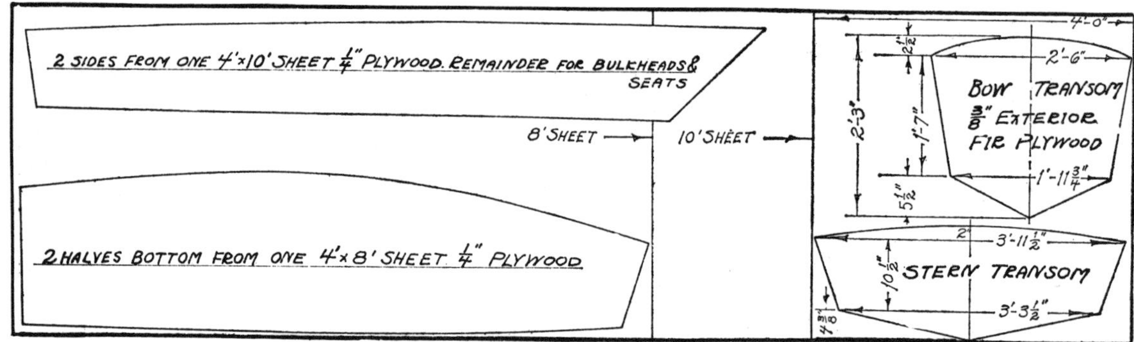

around their edges. Also made up are the two temporary molds that remain at stations 2 and 4 until the bottom and sides are on.

There are seven sub-assemblies in all; on each of them a pair of legs made from strapping or other strips of board is fastened parallel and equidistant to the centerline of the boat as marked on these molds and bulkheads, exactly 22 inches apart from outside to outside. These legs or posts are intended to fit between the horizontal 2 by 4s. Each pair is marked, according to the plan, so that the bulkheads, transoms, and molds will be located at the correct distance from the given baseline. When these marks are positioned to correspond with the top edge of the 2 by 4s, the sub-assemblies will be set at the correct height, and the legs can be clamped to the horizontal form or temporarily nailed. After the keel strip, the chines, and the risers are notched in and fastened, final adjustment may be made by moving the legs slightly up or down, if necessary, to remove any minor unfairness that might show up at this stage. Then the final fairing and beveling for the plywood bottom and sides is completed.

When the forms show fair throughout, with the keel strip, chines, and risers serving as longitudinal ribbands, the adjusted set-up is securely nailed and braced. All bevels should be checked and touched here and there with the plane if needed. Quite a bit of exacting beveling is required around the edges of the bow transom.

The bottom, in two pieces, is put on first. This is ¼-inch exterior fir, and a 4-foot by 8-foot sheet will suffice for the two panels. These must be carefully fitted down their inner edges, which take a slight curve due to the rocker of the bottom. It doesn't matter if the outside edges of the two bottom halves project slightly beyond the chines; the excess is easily planed off after the bottom panels are glued and fastened in place. They will have to be faired to the correct bevels whether they project beyond the chines or not.

The side panels are put on next. They may be slightly larger for planing to exact shape after they are fastened and glued in place. One-piece sides require a 10-foot sheet of plywood, but they can be spliced up from shorter stock with an ordinary glued, tapered scarph, as I did on my own pram. Not much is saved, however, since the 10-foot sheet will yield besides the sides, enough extra plywood for the bulkheads and seats.

When the bottom and sides are on, the four lengthwise bottom strips may be glued and screwed on outside. These four strips running the whole length of the bottom are a distinctive and important special feature of this pram. They are needed to stiffen and to protect the wide, light bottom of ¼-inch plywood, and they help greatly in preventing the boat from slipping sideways in the water.

This is a good time to put on the bindings of fiberglass tape; installing the skeg should be left until later. The outside gunwales are not put on until the boat is turned over.

When the boat is turned over, most of the bracing and false work can be discarded, as can be the two temporary molds at stations 2 and 4. Then put in the low cross floors on either side of the bulkhead at station 3. These slight cross

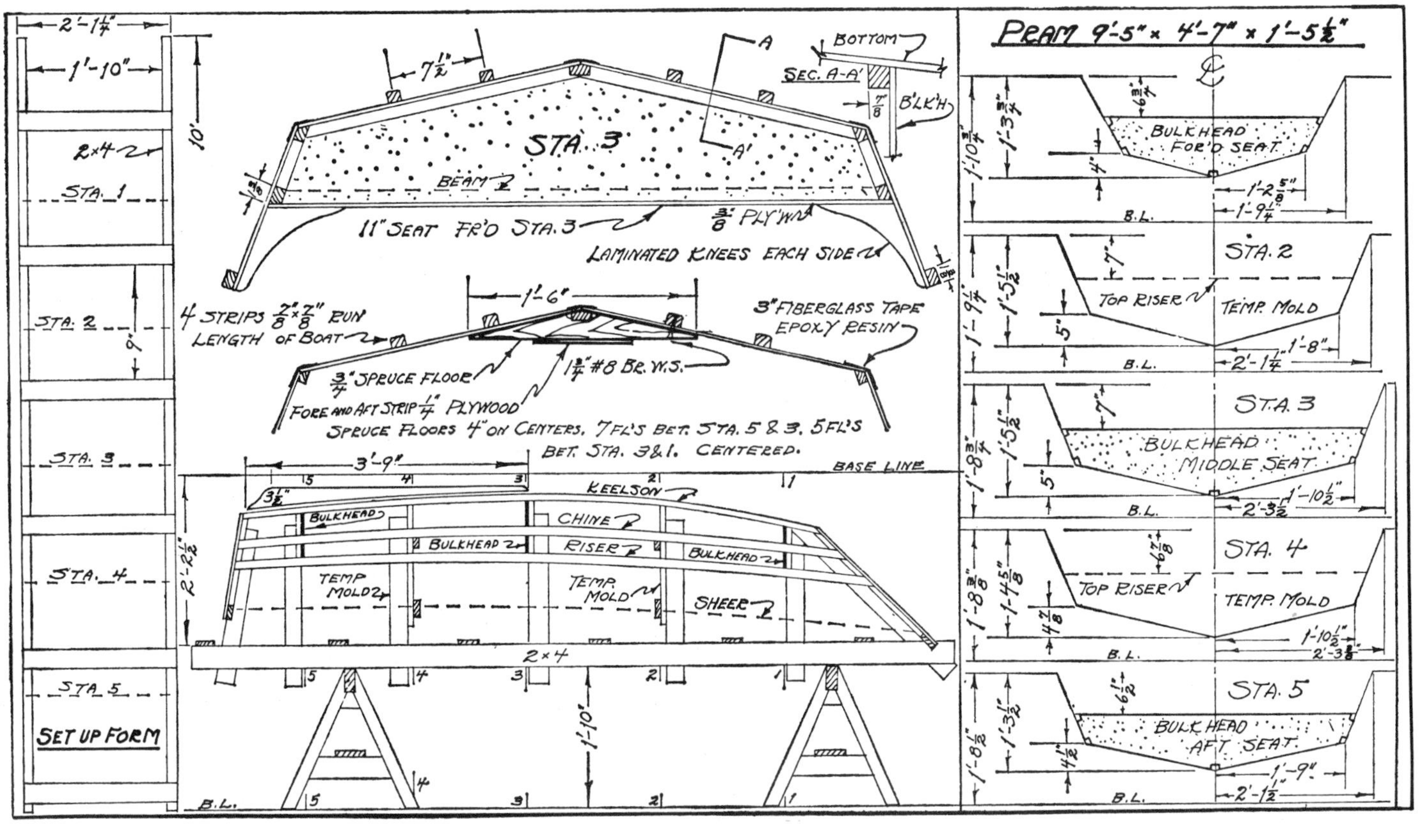
PRAM 9'-5" x 4'-7" x 1'-5½"
SET UP FORM
STA. 1
STA. 2
STA. 3
STA. 4
STA. 5
2×4
10'
2'-1¼"
1'-10"
STA. 3
BEAM
11" SEAT FR'D STA. 3
⅜" PLY'WD
LAMINATED KNEES EACH SIDE
SEC. A-A'
BOTTOM
B'LK'H
4 STRIPS ⅞"×⅞" RUN LENGTH OF BOAT
3" FIBERGLASS TAPE EPOXY RESIN
¾" SPRUCE FLOOR
1¾" #8 BR. W.S.
FORE AND AFT STRIP ¼" PLYWOOD
SPRUCE FLOORS 4" ON CENTERS. 7 FL'S BET. STA. 5 & 3. 5 FL'S BET. STA. 3 & 1. CENTERED.
BASE LINE
KEELSON
BULKHEAD
CHINE
RISER
TEMP. MOLD
SHEER
B.L.
BULKHEAD FOR'D SEAT
TOP RISER
TEMP. MOLD
BULKHEAD MIDDLE SEAT
BULKHEAD AFT SEAT

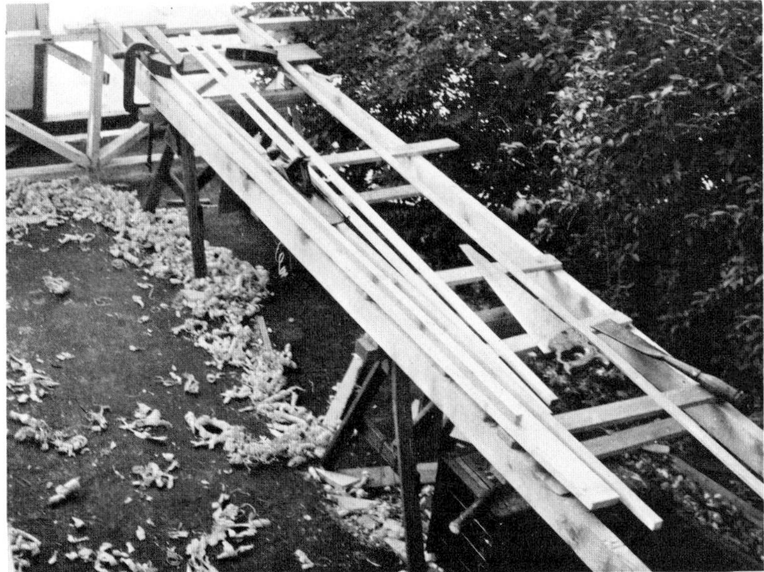

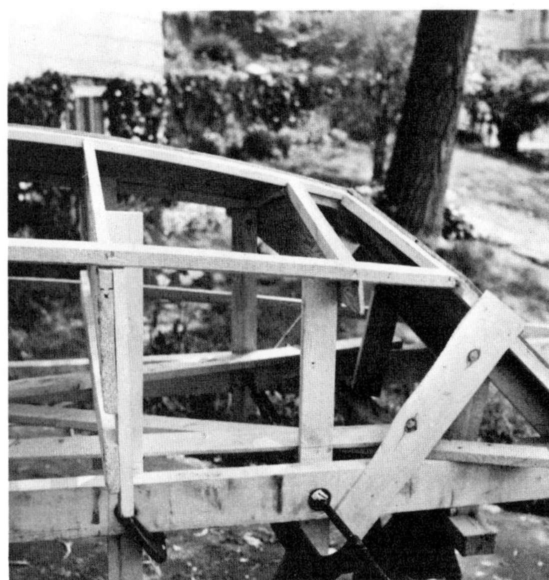

(Left) The building jig completed and set up on horses. (Right) The chine and keelson in place. Note the temporary legs extending down from the frame and fastened to the 2 x 4 building jig.

Side plank going on. Note the splice in the plywood near the bow.

The boat has been turned over after the seams were taped. The risers are being installed.

The seats are almost completed. Note the Styrofoam in the compartment under the middle seat, which has yet to be fastened in place.

The completed pram.

floors add little weight, but strengthen and stiffen the thin plywood bottom wonderfully. They screw fasten into the keelson, through the bottom, into the first pair of outside longitudinal rub strips. Like all parts of the boat, the cross floors are glued with epoxy. Limbers next to the keel strips must not be forgotten. On top of the cross floors two strips of ¼-inch plywood are nailed; they should be narrow, but wide enough to step on. Most of the stepping inside the boat can be done on these two strips.

The ¼-inch plywood bulkheads extending as high as the riser at stations 3 and 5 serve as foundations for the end seats and make compartments for Styrofoam flotation. Sufficient light spruce beams and cleats are put in to stiffen the thin plywood seats for sitting. Cleats are glued to the ends and the seats are screwed and glued to them and the risers, so the seats firmly brace the ends of the boat.

The middle seat, 11 inches in width, is strengthened with reinforcing strips underneath and tied to the sides of the boat at each of its four corners with knees laminated from thin spruce strips glued with epoxy. These four knees fasten securely with glue and screws to the sides and the gunwales, and to the thwart beams and the bulkhead underneath. The resulting structure forms a light but very strong and rigid truss at the center of the boat. In addition to the bulkheads and transoms at the ends, this framing makes a tremendously strong hull that would not smash or let go if dropped from a considerable height into the water. The space under the 11-inch middle seat is also packed with Styrofoam, having a capacity of at least three cubic feet.

Rowing is done from the middle seat facing the stern and pulling the oars in the usual way, or one may face the bow and push the oars from the stern sheets facing forward. The short cross floors, set 4 inches on centers in the bottom and tied together with their plywood strips, give good bracing for the oarsman's feet in all positions of rowing.

Rowlocks are located about 12 inches from either edge of the center seat on small pads glued to the inside of the plywood topsides and screwed through into the outside gunwale.

A novel feature to save weight is a number of ⅞-inch holes, in lieu of cleats and rings, which pierce the topsides just below the gunwales and through the stern and bow transoms close to the corners and just below the inside reinforcement of flat spruce the width of the outside gunwales. A special feature of these holes is to provide for lashing the boat to its cartop carriers. To strengthen the wood around these lashing holes and keep lines from wearing the plywood surface inside and outside, the edges of the holes are covered for a few inches on either side with epoxy and fiberglass.

Before any paint goes on the plywood and the spruce, the boat should be thoroughly soaked inside and out with a good wood preservative; it should also receive a coat of thinned and heated linseed oil if there is time for it to dry thoroughly. Oils will not harm the epoxy glue once it has set. It is of great importance to seal the wood, not only to forestall rot, but also to keep the boat from adding weight by taking up water, which will occur even though the edges of the plywood are all bound and sealed with epoxy and fiberglass. The preliminary oil treatment cannot be used if epoxy paint is to be put on later. When it comes down to hard choices like that, I'd rather forego the epoxy paint for a good preliminary treatment of oil-based wood preservative, followed by good, standard, oil paint.

4 A Sailing Flattie

As a sop to the traditionalists, let me point out at the beginning that the sailing flattie is an antique boat; that is, it is a modernized adaptation of an antique boat or type, and if there should be muttering in the background of less complimentary term, may I add that the old order changeth, and not always for the worse.

What is an antique boat? According to ground rules laid down several years ago by the Thousand Islands Antique Boat Show, it must have been built before 1930. Well, this flattie goes back to the 1890s and before. The lines and principal dimensions follow closely those of a racing flattie published by Charles G. Davis in *Rudder* in November, 1895, although the construction, rig, and sail plan are quite different. Davis mentions that his starting point in making up the design was a class of racing flatties on New York Bay at that time with a limit on the waterline length of 14 feet, which he thought was a good size.

Rudder magazine at the time had just completed its first five years of successful publication under its able editor and founder, Thomas Fleming Day, who inaugurated a pioneering department for amateur builders, titled "Designing" and presided over by Charles G. Davis. Davis, who was 25 years old at the time, had done considerable sailing in flatties. He had cruised in one with his brother, and had raced in them under conditions where crews of three or four men were required to keep them on their feet. In introducing flatties to *Rudder*'s following of amateur builders in 1895, Davis made the following assertion: "For fifty dollars any man or boy can build a good, serviceable, flat-bottomed sloop, capable of carrying three or four men, and able if built to a proper shape to stand as heavy weather as anyone would care to be out in."

Davis's 14-foot flattie has a gaff and bowsprit. "Her rig," he explained, "is large, 238 square feet, 'but you can't fly unless you have wings,' and they are about as large wings as you can handle on such a boat, and then you want three or four fellows to hang out to windward for you." Should this sort of sailing appeal to you, I suggest you go back to Davis's original design. But for the less strenuous and chancy sailing, I have brought the rig entirely inboard with a sail area just under 100 square feet, which should be ample, although not excessive for a hard-chined boat with a waterline length of 14 feet and a beam of 5 feet.

The rig shown, however, is only one of a number of possibilities for this boat and is offered somewhat tentatively for consideration and experimentation. On a boat of this size it is not easy to tell how a rig will balance until it has been tried out. There are a lot of variables involved and no precise formulas for engineering this ahead of time. Some guesswork is involved,

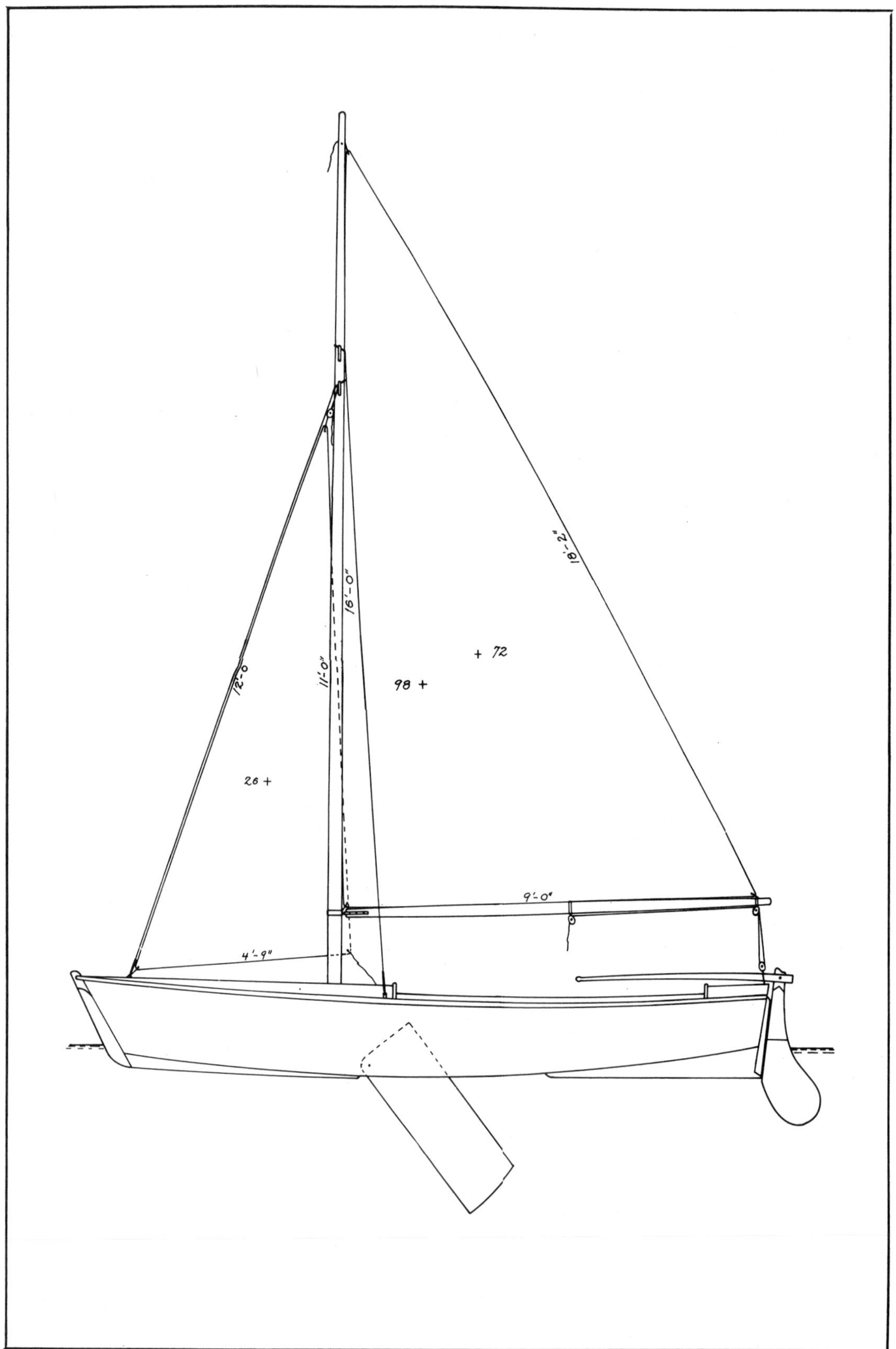
18'-2"
16'-0"
11'-0"
12'-0
+ 72
98 +
26 +
9'-0"
4'-9"

and even educated guesswork is still guesswork. Consequently, I do not presume to guarantee that the rig as shown will prove entirely satisfactory without adjustment. Only trial on the water can give the final word.

The hull construction, on the other hand, is a different matter. This we can fully guarantee ahead of time, and, if directions are faithfully followed, a sturdy craft will result that is serviceable and tight. The weatherly qualities of a hull of this sort and its ability to carry sail hardly need extended comment. Flatties were a well known and proven type long before Davis's time. It is sufficient to say that when it gets too rough for a boat of this kind with a capable sailor at the helm, it is time to come in anyway. Naturally they are neither intended, nor offered, for crossing the Atlantic.

In choosing this particular boat, we were governed by a number of considerations. A lot of interest has been shown of late in small, easily built sailboats. To meet this demand, we at first cast about for a boat that could be both sailed and rowed, but these are distinctly different functions that do not combine with optimum effectiveness as a rule, although there are exceptions, like the St. Lawrence River skiff. But as particular interest seemed to be manifested in sail, we decided for this once to confine our efforts to sail.

General requirements decided upon went somewhat as follows:

1. Safe and seaworthy within reasonable limits for size and type.

2. Good performance under sail—while not the fastest boat on the bay, not the slowest either.

3. Sturdy, rugged, and able to take it, yet

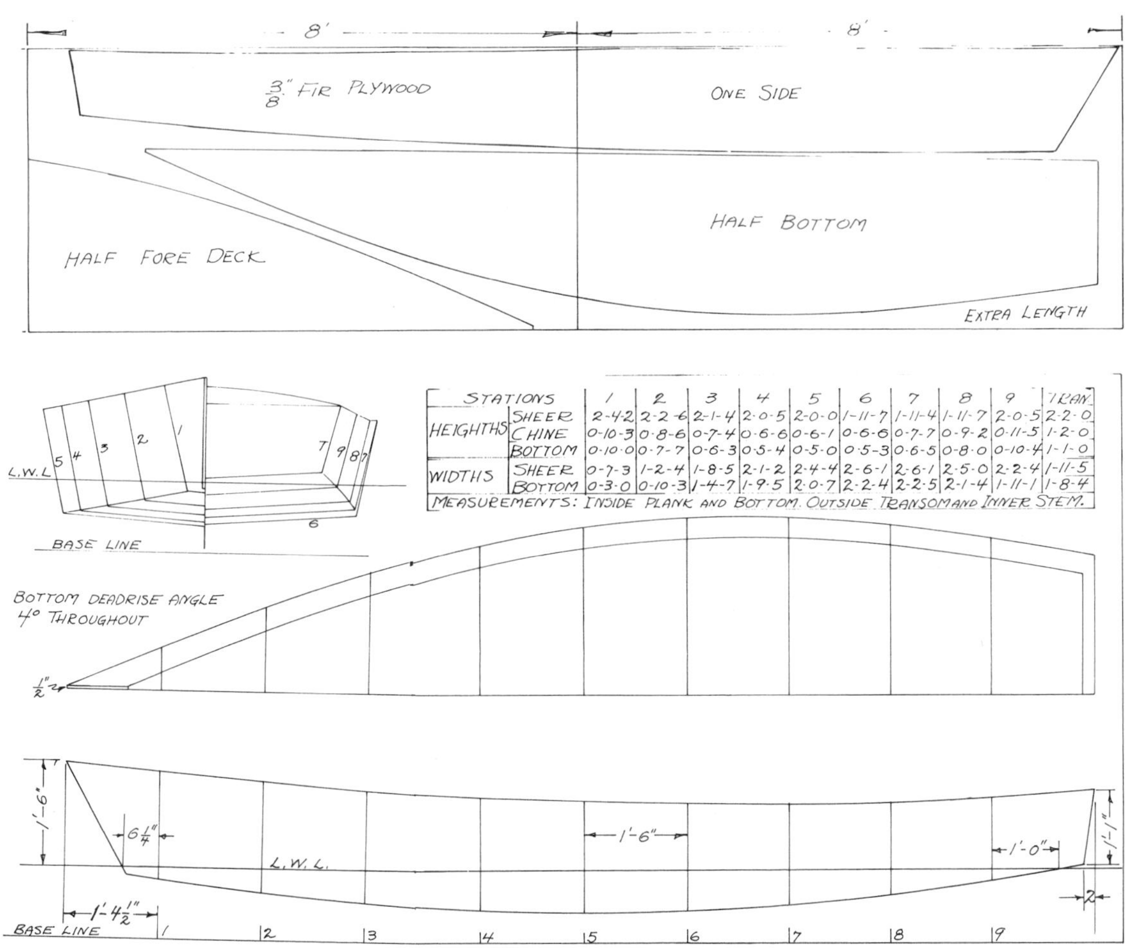

STATIONS		1	2	3	4	5	6	7	8	9	TRAN.
HEIGHTHS	SHEER	2-4-2	2-2-6	2-1-4	2-0-5	2-0-0	1-11-7	1-11-4	1-11-7	2-0-5	2-2-0
	CHINE	0-10-3	0-8-6	0-7-4	0-6-6	0-6-1	0-6-6	0-7-7	0-9-2	0-11-5	1-2-0
	BOTTOM	0-10-0	0-7-7	0-6-3	0-5-4	0-5-0	0-5-3	0-6-5	0-8-0	0-10-4	1-1-0
WIDTHS	SHEER	0-7-3	1-2-4	1-8-5	2-1-2	2-4-4	2-6-1	2-6-1	2-5-0	2-2-4	1-11-5
	BOTTOM	0-3-0	0-10-3	1-4-7	1-9-5	2-0-7	2-2-4	2-2-5	2-1-4	1-11-1	1-8-4

MEASUREMENTS: INSIDE PLANK AND BOTTOM. OUTSIDE TRANSOM AND INNER STEM.

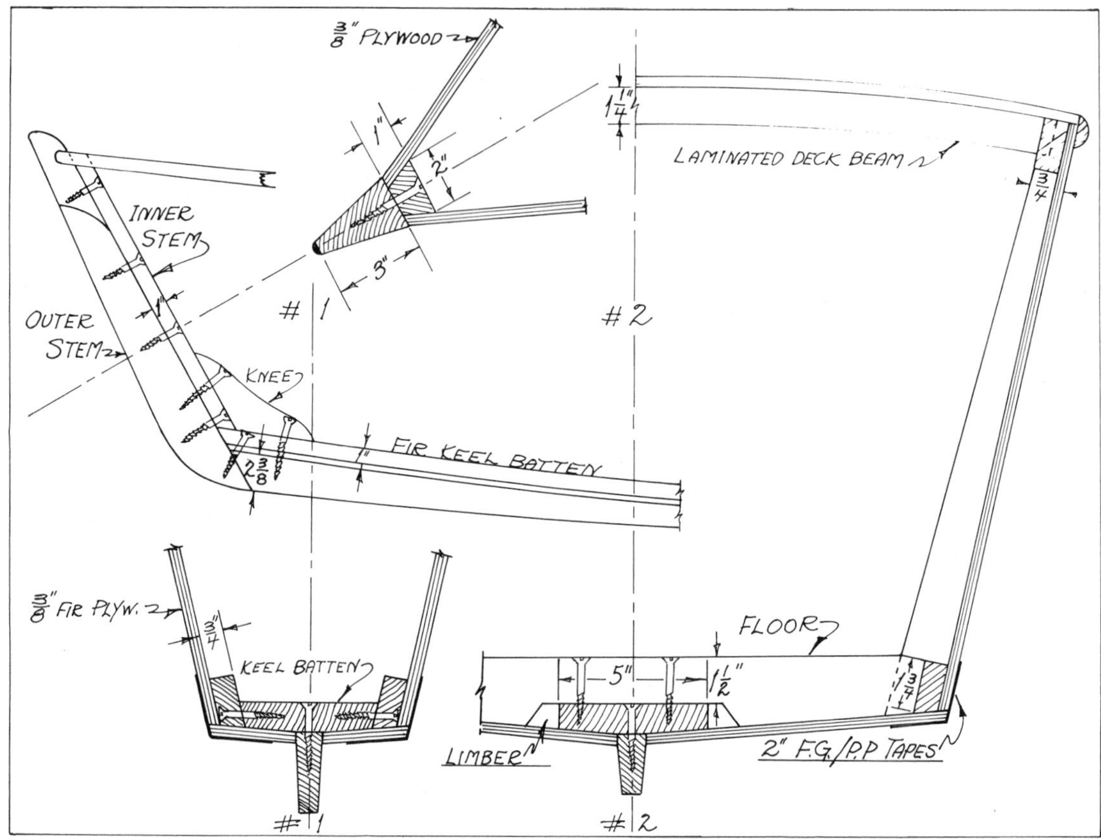

not too heavily built.

4. Pleasing appearance—must not look like a box or a tub.

5. Easy and inexpensive to build. This means, among other things, that materials should be standard and readily obtainable, and that no costly or unusual tools or building equipment should be required.

MATERIALS

Davis, in introducing his design, emphasized the necessity for light construction, that is, for not loading up the hull with unnecessary wood. For the two sides he recommended getting a white pine plank 18 inches wide, 1¼ inches thick, and 16 feet long. This was to be ripped into two boards to be dressed down to a finished thickness of ½ inch. The bottom, with the exception of an oak center plank ⅝ inch thick, was to be of ½-inch pine like the sides. Today, select white pine of these dimensions would be prohibitively expensive, if it could be found. Fortunately there is an excellent substitute at hand, namely ⅜-inch fir plywood. It is a standard material, obtainable everywhere, and not expensive as compared with other materials today.

Fir plywood has several definite advantages over pine. It will not rent or split in wide widths, as sides made of single widths of pine boards are apt to do, and it ensures that there will not be any bottom seams to caulk or to open when the boat dries out. Plywood ⅜ inch thick is also somewhat lighter than pine ½ inch thick.

The two sides, the bottom and the foredeck can be got out of four standard 4-foot by 8-foot sheets, provided the half lengths are joined with glued splices or scarfs. Such splices are easily made. All that is required in the way of tools is a sharp, low-angle block plane. Glued splices in plywood are not difficult, except that they must be carefully done. (See the Appendix for specific instructions.) Success in building this boat will depend more upon painstaking attention to construction details than upon special woodworking skill.

Two additional 4-foot by 8-foot sheets of ⅜-inch plywood should more than suffice for gluing up the centerboard, rudder, and for the short afterdeck and the waterways, so the plywood inventory adds up to six 4-foot by 8-foot sheets in all. If need be, everything else can be got out of ordinary Douglas fir construction lumber, selected to obtain material as free from knots as possible. Standard sizes 2 inches and 4 inches thick can be stripped on the circular saw and glued without further smoothing just as they leave the saw. Chines and inwales can be built up by gluing together several thinner strips. Properly done, the result is stronger and stiffer than a single sawn strip.

For these reasons, it is desirable, if not almost essential, to have the use of a power circular saw in building this flattie. The boat could be built entirely with hand tools, but it would be harder to do and would take longer.

The inside keel batten, or keelson, as some might term it, is shown as 5 feet wide and 1 inch thick. This runs the length of the bottom and takes a considerable amount of curve. It would bend easier if glued together in place from two ½-inch layers, and the result would be both stiffer and stronger.

Deck beams should be laminated by gluing thin strips of spruce. For these, spruce staging boards or planks can often be found free or nearly free of knots. These come unplaned, but no planer is required to work them up for the boat, as a sharp saw blade will size them and smooth them enough for gluing.

If oak is available it can be used to advantage for the outer stem piece, for the fore and aft skegs, the outside rudder post and even for the keel batten. But oak is not required, and good quality Douglas fir will do nicely.

Material for the spars, as well as how to make them is covered later.

About fastenings: This boat is literally held together by glue, specifically epoxy glue. The metal fastenings are secondary, and in a number of places serve only to hold wooden members in position until the glue has hardened. With the glue now available, we can do things with wood today undreamed of when Charles G. Davis worked up his original design. For those uninformed about epoxy glue, and who want a detailed explanation plus a list of supply sources, I recommend the reprint of *National Fisherman* articles on this subject, *The Use Of Plastics In Boatbuilding*, which is available from International Marine Publishing Company, 21 Elm Street, Camden, Maine; the price is $3.00.

In building this flattie, it is recommended that all plywood edges which otherwise might be exposed be covered with epoxy-bonded polypropylene or fiberglass tape, and that the centerboard and the rudder blade, both of plywood, should be sheathed with epoxy-bonded Versatex PP fabric or fiberglass. Complete directions for a covering job of this sort can be found on the last page of *The Use of Plastics in Boatbuilding.*

BUILDING PROCEDURE

It is imperative to follow the correct building procedure or order of operations. This is as follows:

The boat is started upside down using the ladder-frame method of setting up. The 9-foot 6-inch plywood pram, whose construction is explained in Chapter 3, is built by this method. The ladder frame, made of two straight two-by-fours with spacers nailed across, serves as a base to locate and secure the building molds in position and at the correct height. Three molds plus the transom are sufficient for this boat. The molds are notched to take the keel batten, the chines, and the inwale strips or clamps.

It is not necessary to rabbet the stem, an operation that more often than not gives the novice trouble. The two-piece stem as shown in the drawing is just as strong, just as tight, and much easier to do than a one-piece stem. In this boat the inner stem piece is given the same bevel throughout and is attached to the keel batten by the stem knee with screws, but without any glue at first.

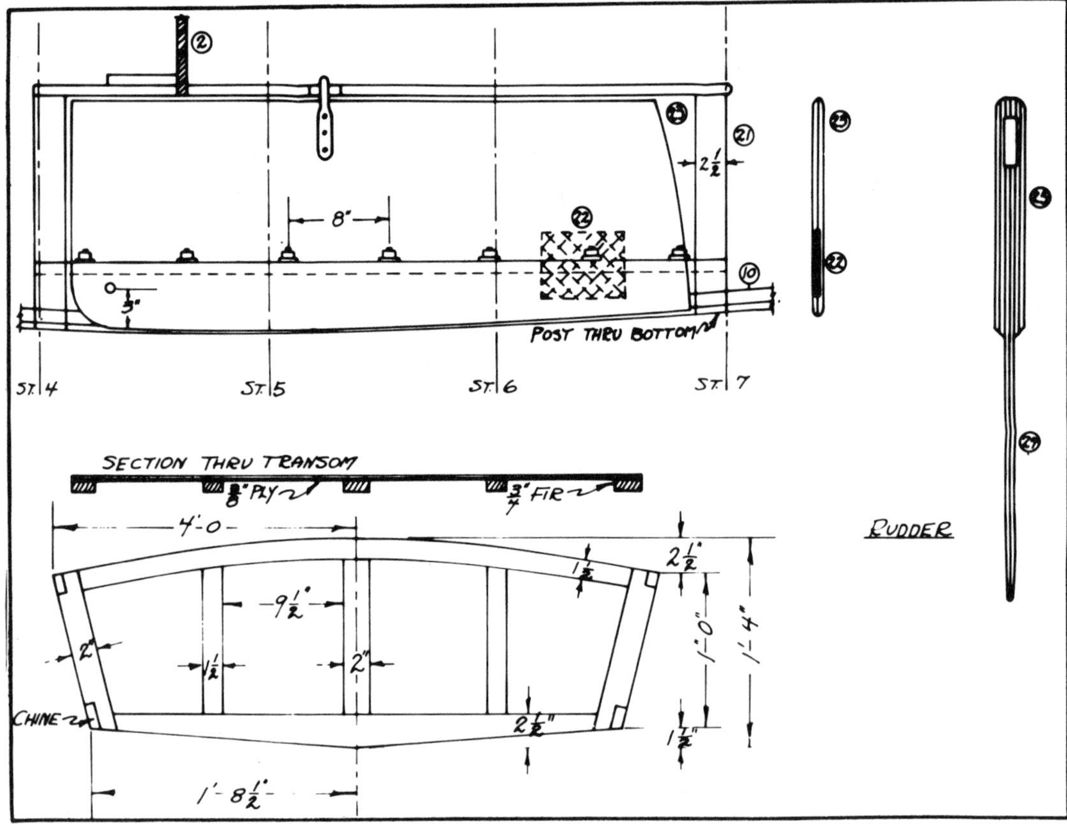

The plywood sides are then fastened to the inner stem both with glue and screws. The sides do not have to fit exactly, that is, they can project slightly, for after fastening, their outer ends will be faired with a sharp block plane to receive the outer stem piece, which can be prepared ahead of time at the bench. The outer stem is put on with glue and fastened with screws through the inner stem piece from the inside. To get screws through the bottom end, the stem knee must be temporarily removed, to be put back permanently afterwards with a liberal application of glue and the original screws. Before the hull is removed from the molds and ladder frame and turned right-side up, the fore and after skegs and outside stern post should be fitted and fastened. These can be only partly fastened from the bottom or outside of the boat. Fastening is completed as soon as the boat is removed from the molds and the ladder frame and turned right-side up to finish.

The frames, floors, and deck beams are fitted and glued in place with some nails and screws to reinforce the glue and to hold the various members in place until the glue has hardened. Pieces of board glued to the plywood sides of the boat and under the inwale stringer or clamp hold the chainplates, which are put on from the inside before the boat is decked; they extend through the deck. The mast step is nailed and glued to the inside keel batten or keelson. The ⅜-inch fir plywood deck is installed, and the fore-and-aft mast partners are fitted between the deck beams and glued to the underside of the deck.

The centerboard case (or trunk) and the centerboard are made up as a completed assembly apart from the boat, with bed logs carefully shaped to fit the curve of the keel batten where they are to go. Before the case is assembled, each bed log is set in place on top of the keel batten to test the fit and, if need be, planed until there is a touching fit throughout. When the centerboard case is assembled, the end posts are left long enough so that they will project through the bottom of the boat an inch or so when the case is bolted on. Later they are sawn off flush with the bottom. The sides of the case should be glued to the posts and through-riveted, if rivets are available, otherwise well screwed. The ends of the bed logs should be glued to the posts and through-bolted with two ⁵⁄₁₆-inch bolts in each end.

The centerboard slot is not cut through the bottom until the case is made. The slot should be mortised carefully so the two end posts push through with a snug fit. It is best to locate and bore the bolt holes through the bed logs at the bench when the case is out of the boat. Then when the case is back in the boat and hauled down tight with a couple of door clamps through the slot, or some other clamping arrangement, the bolt holes are completed through the keel batten and bottom.

The bolts, which should fit their holes snugly, but not too tightly, are driven up from the bottom, but before this is done the logs are bedded in a generous application of thick glue. Three-eighths-inch galvanized carriage bolts are used. The bottom plywood is countersunk just enough so that the bolt heads will be just below flush when the bolts have been set up tightly. These countersunk holes should not be deep enough to penetrate the keel batten. It will be noted that as the sided thickness of the bed logs is 2¼ inches, they will project ⁵⁄₁₆ inches over the edge of the keel batten, which is 1¹⁵⁄₁₆ inches wide on either side of the 1⅛-inch centerboard slot. The bolts should be gradually tightened in turn until there is a firm, even strain on them all and their heads are pulled in just under flush, so they can be smoothed over with a plastic surfacer and painted.

MAKING THE SPARS

If fairly knot-free spruce ledger boards can be found at the local lumberyard to make the mast and boom, this is the material to use;

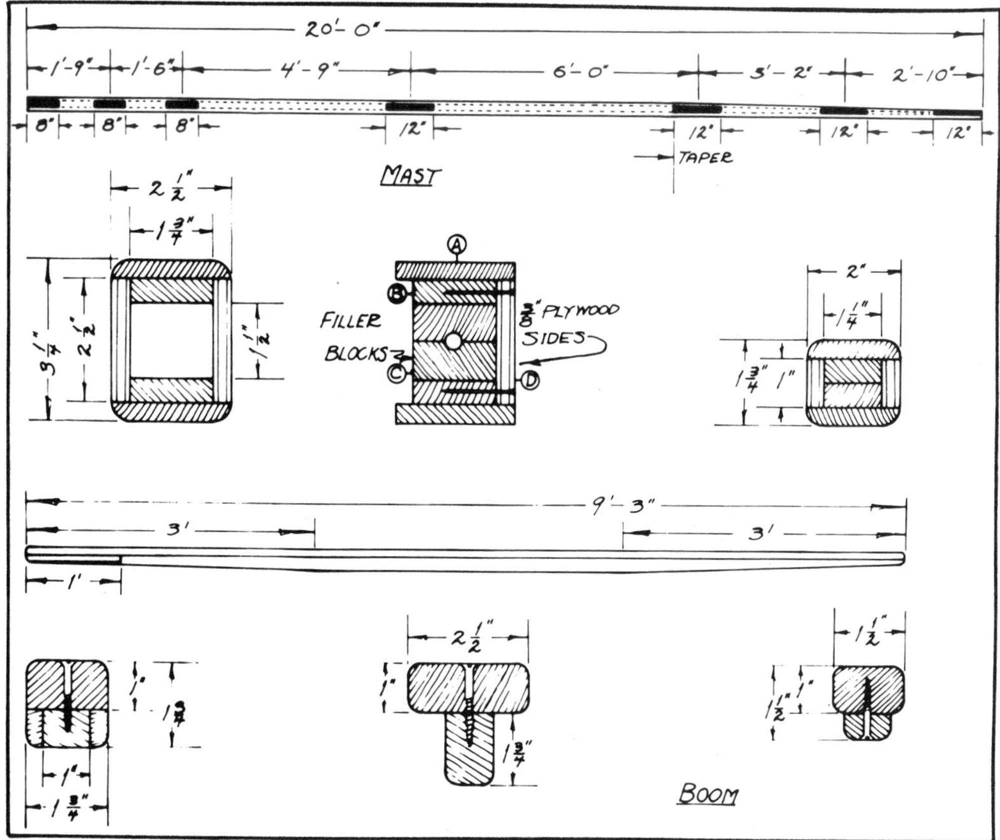

otherwise it should be clear Douglas fir stripped to size from a seasoned floor joist, four-by-four, or other similar piece of timber. Good quality fir is excellent for spars, except that it is heavier than spruce.

It is not likely that a stick will be found that is long enough to get out the strips for the mast in one length, nor is it easy to handle timber of this length on the saw. It is perfectly admissible to splice the strips which form the mast, provided the scarphed joints are well separated.

The construction of the boom is so simple that it is perfectly obvious from the drawing. The procedure for assembling the mast is not involved, but needs to be briefly outlined. A pair of the A strips and a pair of the B strips (see drawing) are first got out on the circular saw. They will probably have to be spliced to get sufficient length; after the glue has set they are sized on the circular saw and dressed with a bench plane if necessary. The taper on their upper ends is put on at the bench with a hand plane. Then strip B is located on strip A, and the two are glued together. Small brads through B into A hold the two in position and together while the glue is setting. In the meantime, the seven solid-core blocks are made up from ¾-inch dry soft wood and glued together, but with a hole through the middle of each so there will be a passage for air to circulate inside the hollow mast after it is glued up. As soon as the center blocks are in and glued in place, the plywood sides can be fitted into place and glued. The brads shown in the drawing contribute some strength, but are mainly used to pull the D strips into place and hold them until the glue hardens.

If at all possible, a gluing jig should be set up on the floor or other suitable place to keep the mast straight while it is being assembled. A chalk line is snapped to give a straight line on which a series of blocks are set and temporarily nailed in place. These are used to clamp to or to brace against. The after side of the mast, which is perfectly straight the entire way, can be lined up and held against the row of blocks until the glue hardens. Otherwise the mast is likely to have kinks in it. Finally, the mast is lightly smoothed on all four sides, the corners rounded, the whole sanded, and then the various required fittings are installed.

Rigging details are straightforward and need not be elaborated on here. These can be closely similar to those for the 15-foot trailer sloop *Titmouse*, which can be found fully detailed starting on page 152 in S. S. Rabl's *Boat Building In Your Own Backyard*, Cornell Maritime Press, Cambridge, Maryland.

NUMBERED REFERENCES

1. Mast step. 1″ fir nailed and glued to the keel batten.
2. Coaming piece. Covers after end of the fore decking and braces the centerboard trunk. Notched over the trunk capping and screwed to cleat behind. Nailed and glued to deck beam.
3. Cleat. ¾″ fir or pine.
4. Side decking. ⅜″ fir plywood.
5. Side deck gusset. ⅜″ fir plywood glued and nailed to frame and deck beam.
6. Side deck carling. 2″ x ¾″ fir or pine.
7. Coaming. 3½″ x ⅝″ fir or pine.
8. Side frames. ¾″ fir, tapers from ¾″ molded width at top to 1½″ molded width at bottom end.
9. Floors. ¾″ fir sided thickness. Maximum molded depth 2½″, notched to fit over 1″ thick fir keel batten with limbers either side. Molded depth at outboard ends 1½″.
10. Keel batten. 1″ x 5″ fir.
11. Deck beams. Laminated from glued strips of spruce or fir. Sided thickness ¾″. Molded depth 1¼″.
12. Fore skeg. 1″ fir or oak, tapered to ¾″ at bottom edge. See drawing detail.
13. After skeg. 1″ fir or oak tapered to ¾″ at the bottom edge. Glued to bottom, spiked through keel batten from inside. Screwed from outside into keel batten where width permits. After end braced and secured by outside sternpost. Bore for spikes.
14. Sternpost. 1¾″ fir or oak. Molded 2¼″ at lower end, 1″ upper end. Glued and screwed to transom. Spiked and glued to skeg. Bore for spikes.

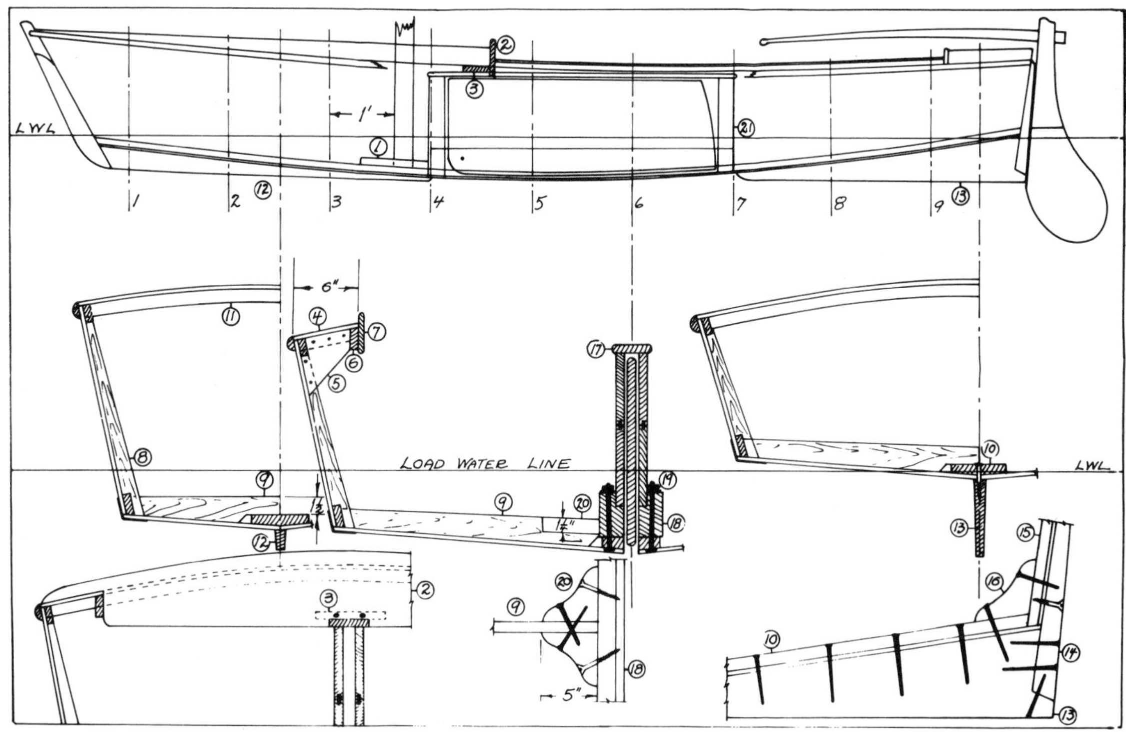

15. Transom framing. ¾" fir to brace ⅜" fir plywood.

16. Stern knee. Fir or oak sided 1½".

17. Cap, centerboard case. ¾" fir or pine.

18. Bed logs, centerboard case. Fir or pine, 2¼" sided thickness. Maximum molded depth, 4".

19. Bed log bolts. ⅜" galvanized carriage bolts set on 8" centers.

20. Knees. Fir or oak sided thickness 1¼". Secure ends of floors to bed logs. Glued, nailed and/or screwed in place.

21. End posts, centerboard case. 1¼" x 2½" fir.

22. Lead weight in centerboard.

23. Centerboard. ¾" thick glued up from two thicknesses of ⅜" fir plywood. Recess for sheet lead cut before the two halves are put together. For best results, sheath with polypropylene fabric, Dynel, or fiberglass.

24. Rudder. Made the same as centerboard.

25. Rudder cheek pieces. Glued and through-fastened with copper rivets.

5 A Chamberlain Skiff

This 14-foot skiff is offered as one possibility to be considered in the selection of a general-purpose rowboat, one which will row easily and be a good sea boat, as well, within the limits of its size. It is a proven model, being a slightly altered and enlarged version of the 13-foot 6-inch dory skiff designed and formerly built in the early decades of this century by William Chamberlain of Marblehead.

From the load line as drawn in the lines plan, the depth of draft, including the thickness of the bottom, is 6¾ inches, and displacement at this depth is approximately 9 cubic feet, or something like 560 pounds. After allowing 150 pounds for the weight of the ⅜-inch marine fir plywood hull, the remaining displacement would be about equivalent to the combined weight of three medium-size persons. With this loading, the bottom of the transom would barely touch the water. There would be no stern drag. The entrance is fairly sharp—the additional 6 inches at the bow helped this—and with its somewhat narrow bottom and relatively steep deadrise in the sides, this hull is bound to row easily.

Because of the characteristics just noted, this boat's initial stability will prove somewhat tender, so that a landlubber stepping into her carelessly when she is light might get a start. Yet this is a stable hull where stability counts, and because of her ample side flare, beam, and length, a fair size boy could sit on her rail without putting it under.

In spite of its flat bottom, which of course is relatively quite narrow, this dory skiff has virtually a round hull, and for all practical purposes behaves as a round-bottomed boat. Indeed, this skiff closely resembles the old-time New England wherry, which was a fine sea boat. It is worth mentioning that this skiff fitted with a centerboard and a proper rig would sail smartly, but she is unsuited for an outboard.

For the utility rowing skiff, two building options in wood are open. One is classic dory construction planked with clinker strakes of sawn boards. The other is to use plywood for planking. The plywood strakes may be butted on internal seam battens to which the strakes are both glued and screwed. When such a seam is covered on the outside with a tape of either glass or synthetic fiber and cemented with epoxy thermoplastic, the result is both extremely strong and permanently watertight.

For this particular boat an alternate method for plywood is shown which omits the internal wooden seam batten, yet gives a construction that is adequately strong and watertight as well. This is a substantial simplification of building procedure. Sometimes inexperienced builders have difficulty with seam battens. They frequently find notching the battens into the frames as well as beveling the battens between frames to be a taxing and tedious operation. Besides, seam battens add nothing to the finished appearance of the boat, and frequently

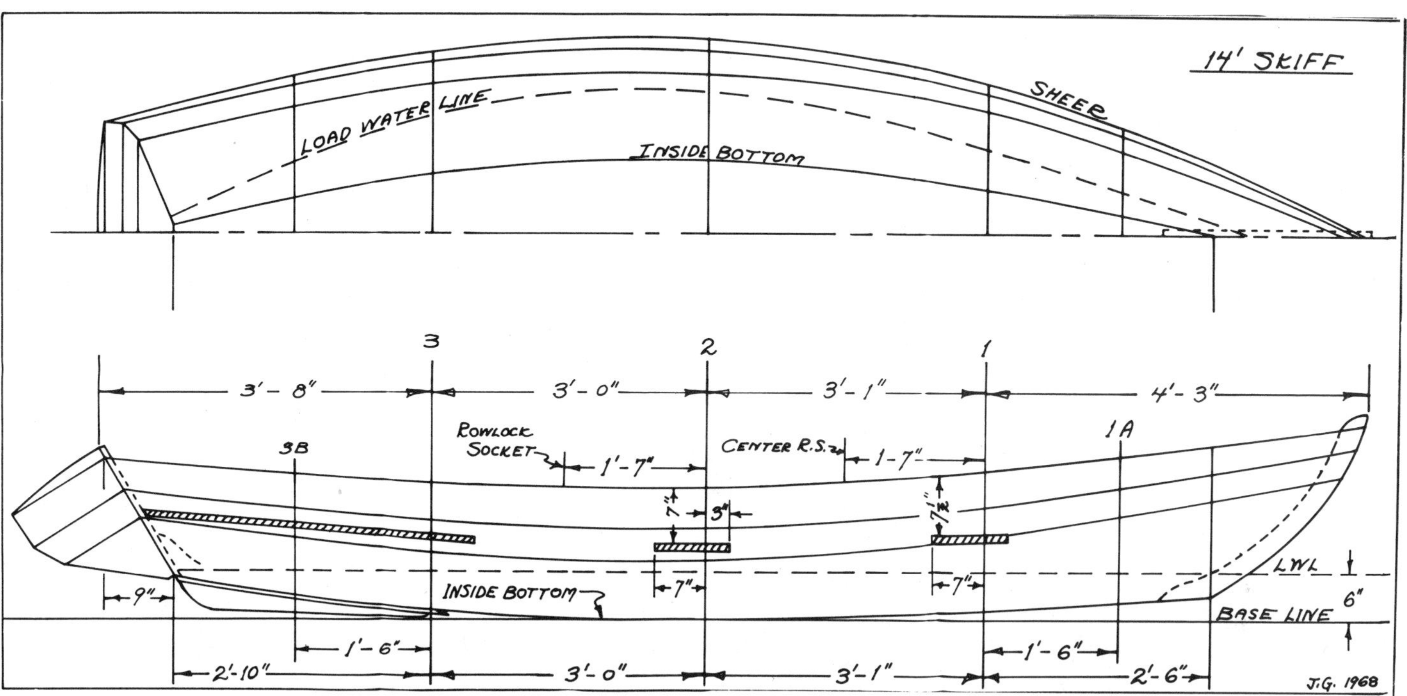

appear crude and clumsy. Leaving them out of this boat, as can be done without structural impairment, is a real gain, I believe. However, should anyone still prefer to retain the seam battens, there is nothing to prevent him from doing so.

Length of planking is no problem; glued splices will provide planking of any length. A properly made, epoxy-glued splice is practically as strong as natural unbroken lumber. This is the case for either sawn boards or plywood. (For splicing techniques, see the Appendix.)

As you can see, the strength of the planking seams is dependent on binding and reinforcing the seams with tapes set in thermoplastic resin. Because the plywood does not swell and shrink to any extent, comparatively inflexible tapes of glass fiber will serve adequately. Fiberglass tapes are much easier to obtain and to apply than a binding of synthetic fibers, particularly polypropylene. If there were much movement of the underlying wood as occasioned by swelling and shrinking with changes in the moisture content, then a flexible synthetic like polypropylene would be required.

A 3-inch-wide glass tape will do nicely. For

OFFSETS – 14 FT. SKIFF

	Stations	Stem	1A	1	2	3	3B.	Tran.
Heights	Sheer	2-1-0	1-8-7	1-7-0	1-4-6	1-5-4	1-6-4	1-8-4
	1st Knuckle	1-10-0	1-4-6	1-2-3	0-11-5	1-0-4	1-2-1	1-4-2
	2nd Knuckle	1-6-4	1-1-2	0-10-4	0-7-4	0-8-4	0-10-4	1-1-0
	Inside Bottom	0-3-0	0-2-2	C-1-1	0-0-0	0-1-1	0-3-0	0-5-4
Half-Breadths	Sheer	0-0-0	1-1-4	1-7-1	2-0-6	1-11-2	1-8-0	1-2-0
	1st Knuckle	0-0-0	1-0-5	1-5-7	1-11-2	1-9-6	1-6-6	1-1-7
	2nd Knuckle	0-0-0	0-10-4	1-3-6	1-8-2	1-7-0	1-4-0	0-11-6
	Inside Bottom	0-0-0	0-2-4	0-5-4	0-9-3	0-7-4	0-4-4	0-1-0

LINES TO INSIDE PLANK, INSIDE BOTTOM, OUTSIDE TRANSOM AND STEM.

T 2,3 3B 1A 1 2

LWL 6" BASE LINE

FEET AND INCHES 3 2 1 0

J.G. 1968

covering the chine, that is, where the bottom edge of the garboard is nailed to the bottom, a 4-inch-wide glass tape would be better. When seam battens are omitted, two layers of tape over the seams between the large frames on the inside of the boat will be required. The short

A 13½-foot Chamberlain skiff, similar to the one described here but slightly smaller. She was built of plywood and fiberglass.

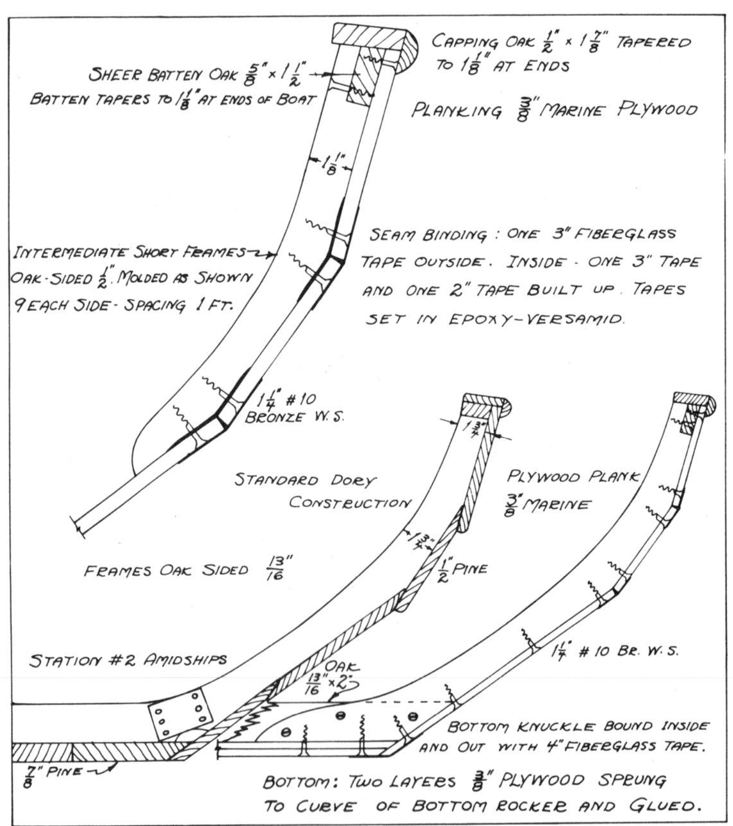

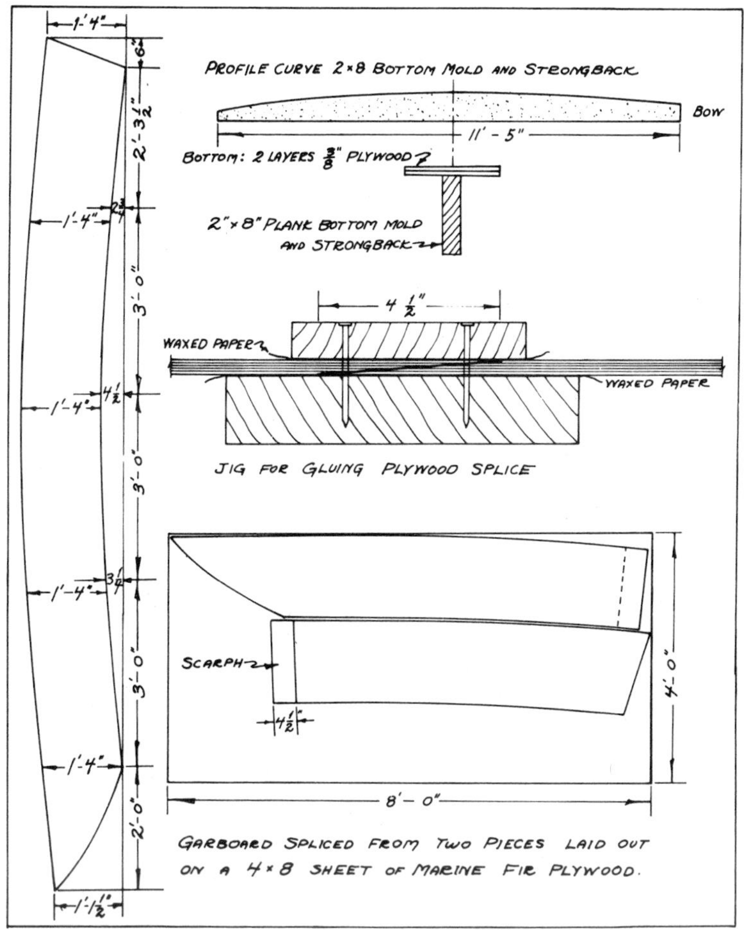

intermediate frames, extending down from the gunwales on the inside between the frames, go in after the interior tapes have been laid in place and saturated with epoxy adhesive. It is best to have these short intermediates fitted and bored for screws beforehand so that they can be put in and drawn tight with screws while the tapes over the seams are still wet.

There will be nine of these intermediate short frames on a side. They are to be spaced approximately on one-foot centers. Two will come aft of frame 3, two between frame 3 and frame 2, two between frame 2 and frame 1, and three forward of frame 1.

A siding of ½ inch will be ample for these intermediates, and they should not be made heavier because it is desirable to keep down weight. If they can be cut from oak with curved grain approximately the same as the curve of these members, they will be that much stronger, although actually these intermediates are fairly straight.

The three sets of main frames, which are located at stations 1, 2, and 3, are to be made of the best dry oak, of course, and are sided 13/16 inch. For these, boards with curved grain would be highly desirable. It is of greatest importance to lay out the shape of the frames on the boards before cutting, taking care to get as little cross grain as possible; that is, the pattern should be placed so that the grain of the boards runs lengthwise on it and not crosswise, or at least with as little crosswise grain as possible. It will pay to go to some trouble in this respect not only in laying out the frames, but also in obtaining crooked boards to begin with. Boards for this purpose should not be straight-edged, but rather live-edged or flitch sawn, that is, sawn

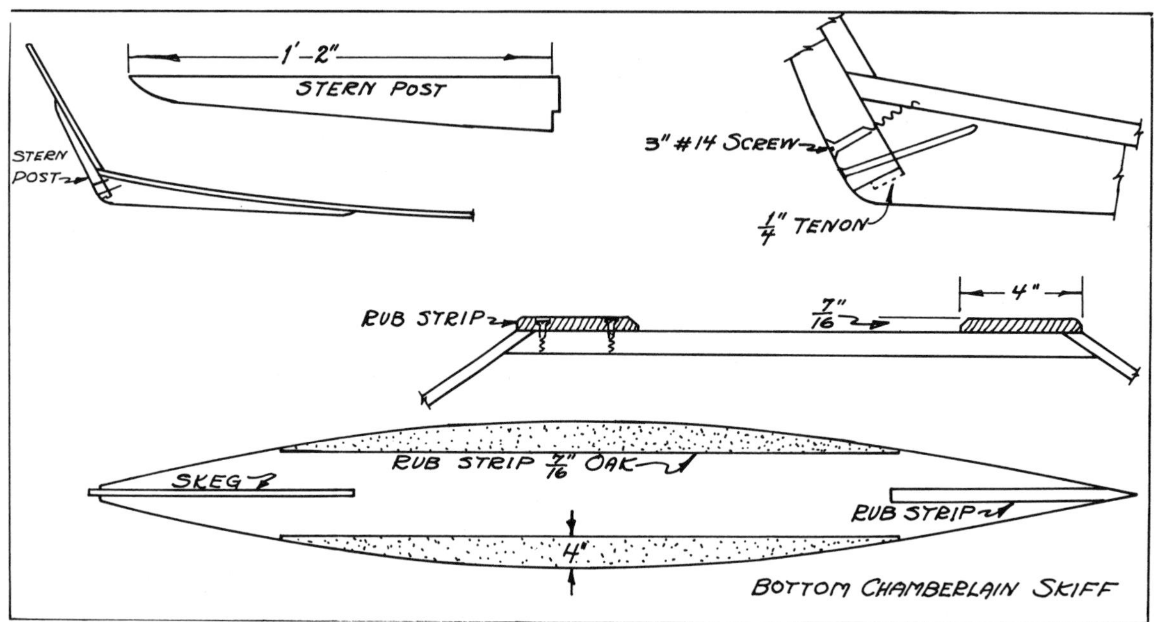

with the bark remaining on the edges.

The main frames can be made up like standard dory frames with metal clips through-riveted at the bottom knuckle to hold the side futtock to the bottom cross piece. For the plywood boat, a somewhat different arrangement is shown which might prove easier; if this is used, the limber for letting the water drain would not come in the bottom knuckle as is usual, but rather would be cut midway in the piece across the bottom.

The bottom could be made in the usual way of pine boards ⅞ inch thick and run lengthwise. Two or more boards would be required, and the seam or seams between would have to be caulked, and would open when the boat dried out. Besides, the rocker of the bottom is considerable aft, perhaps requiring more of a bend than the pine would take without steaming.

Rather than suggest pine boards for the bottom, I am going to suggest plywood, a double thickness, glued together of the same ⅜-inch plywood used for planking the sides. Both layers, top and bottom, will have to be spliced, and the splices in the two layers positioned so as not to come together. Plywood ⅜ inch thick will bend easily, and when two layers are bent over a form and glued, they will hold their curve after the glue has set. Here, the gluing form will be the same strongback shaped from a 2-inch by 8-inch plank that will support the boat in an upside-down position while it is being planked. With care, both the bottom and the side plank for this boat can probably be got out of three 4-foot by 8-foot sheets. Of course, numerous splices will be required, which will take time. This would be expensive for the boatshop, but for the home builder who does not figure his time, splicing can mean real economy.

A few words about fastenings: Bronze screws are strong, lasting, pull up tightly, and generally are a pleasure to use, but they are very expensive. Nails can be substituted. Some of the modern annular nails (Anchorfast is one trade name) of bronze or monel have great holding power in dry oak. Galvanized nails also can be used, except that suitable galvanized nails are getting difficult to obtain.

If a plywood bottom is used, the garboards should be glued to the bottom as well as nailed. If this bottom knuckle is covered inside and out with a reinforcement of epoxy-bonded fiberglass tape, the garboard can be nailed to the bottom with eight-penny galvanized wire nails spaced 2½ inches to 3 inches apart. This will make a very strong job. It hardly needs saying that the nails are put in before the tapes are glued on.

If the sides are planked with plywood, there

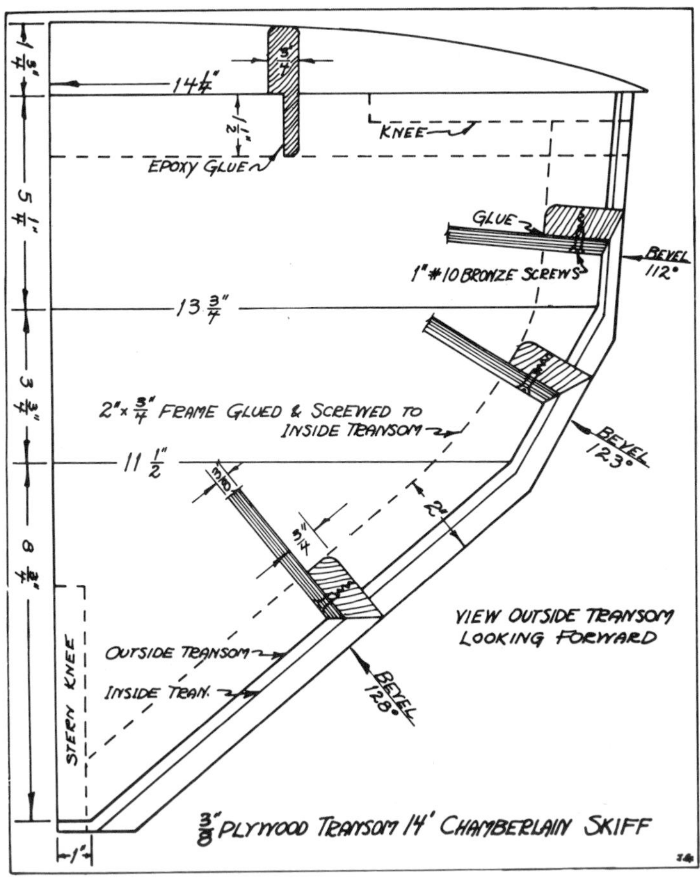

is good reason for making the transom of plywood also, as is shown here. Three-eighths-thick plywood is specified and is adequate, but some might want to use ½-inch plywood instead.

The lines show the outside of the transom, so that when the transom is laid out, extra wood must be left for beveling. This also applies, of course, to the reinforcing strip or frame which extends around the inside of the transom to receive the fastenings for the ends of the planking, and allowance must be made for beveling here as well. This inner strip should be a hard wood like oak or mahogany.

In a transom set on as much of a rake as is found in the Chamberlain skiff, getting the transom bevels can be a fairly tricky operation for one not accustomed to it. Those given in the sketch should be fairly exact as they were taken from an accurately made half model. Notice that they are taken "square" with the edge of the transom, and should be so applied when beveling. Transom bevels should not be taken in the direction that the planking runs on the sides of the boat. Let the stock of the carpenter's bevel be placed flat against the outer surface of the transom and at an angle of 90 degrees with that portion of the transom edge where the bevel is being taken. This is the procedure used when bevels are taken and when applied, and only by this method can one be sure of the results.

This transom is not intended for an outboard motor; if it were, heavier internal bracing would have been shown. However, additional bracing, not indicated in the sketch, will be obtained from the stern bench, which extends aft to fit tightly against the transom. The bench rests upon, and is fastened to, a cleat extending across the inner face of the transom, and is glued and screwed to it like the strips around the edges of the transom. This arrangement adds greatly to the structural rigidity of the stern.

6 A Modified Quincy Skiff

This modified Quincy skiff should row well, but build easily and cheaply. This is not a racing shell, obviously, nor is it intended for the open sea. This simple skiff should do well on lakes, large rivers, and sheltered waters along the coast. For someone interested in rowing for exercise, but only to the extent of committing a modest investment for this purpose, the Quincy skiff has much to offer.

Because of the length of the Quincy skiff, two can row together without crowding, as is not the case with most shorter boats, yet one person can handle the 18-foot version of this skiff by himself, without difficulty. The original Quincy was a rowing workboat capable of carrying heavy loads, but so lined as to move easily through the water either in a light or loaded condition. Her fine entrance and long, slim underbody offer a minimum of resistance. At the same time, her great amount of side flare picks up displacement fast, so even with heavy loads she does not become logy or drag water. It has been said that the old lumbermen's Quincys could take a thousand pounds of rafting chain in their stern sheets without settling unduly.

I judge that the Quincy skiff would show best with a moderate load, but that she might prove somewhat quick or "tiddly" in a light condition with only one occupant—not to an extent to give trouble, but requiring some attention to trim, nonetheless. While I have never been in a Quincy, I base my surmise on the performance of the Quincy's eastern cousin, the bateau of the Maine lumberman, a craft with which I am quite familiar. These two boats have a great deal in common, but especially notable is their extreme, and nearly identical, amount of side flare, considerably more than is found in any other member of the dory family either in America or abroad.

There can be no doubt that the Quincy is a derivation of the bateau devised for western rivers and large lakes by New England watermen when lumbering moved westward during the nineteenth century. The form is definitely a modified bateau, except that the high, sharp, raking ends needed for shooting the roaring pitches of rapid eastern rivers, the Penobscot in particular, have been changed.

In construction the Quincy and the lumberman's bateau are basically identical, with sides and bottoms planked fore-and-aft with white pine boards on oak frames, preferably cut from natural root or limb crooks. But in appearance the basic similarity of these two boats is considerably disguised by the Quincy's plumb, rabbeted stem and cut-off, transom stern, features more normal in a general-purpose workboat not required to run the violent, rocky rapids of the eastern rivers.

Our knowledge of the classic Quincy skiff is derived from a plan by Allen D. Woods, N.A.,

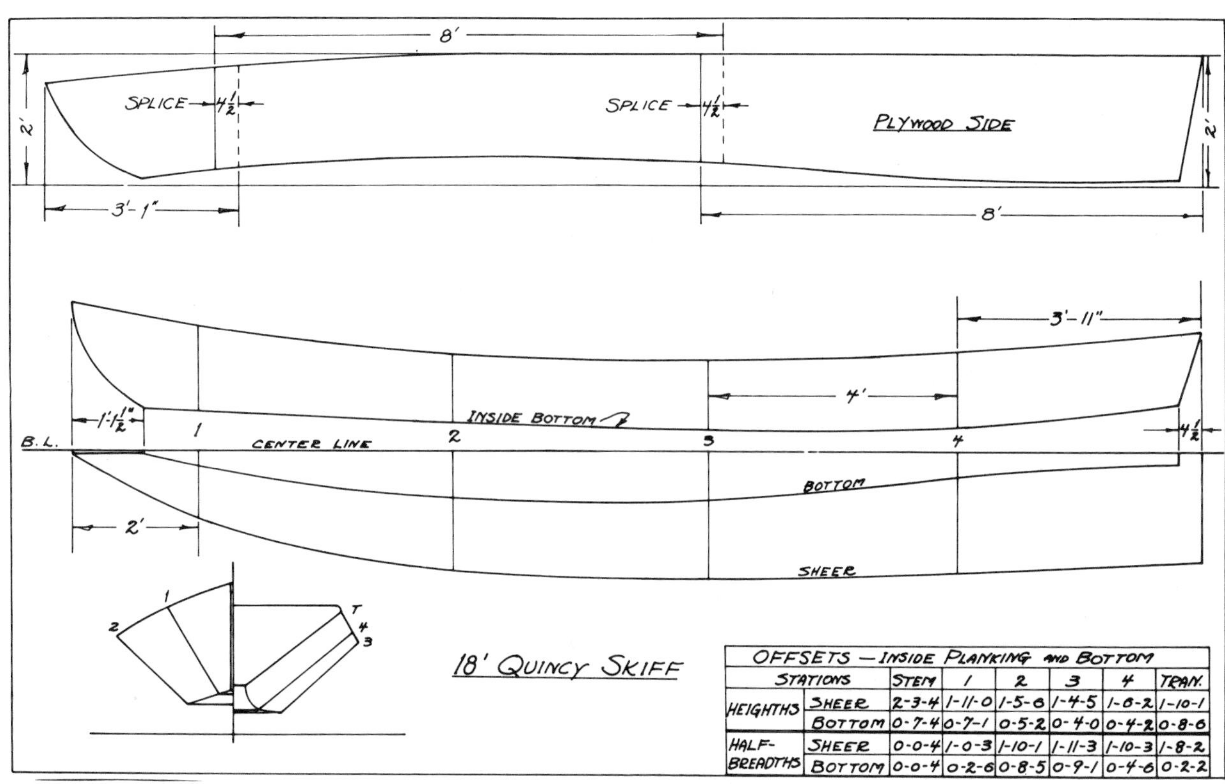

OFFSETS — INSIDE PLANKING AND BOTTOM							
STATIONS		STEM	1	2	3	4	TRAN.
HEIGHTHS	SHEER	2-3-4	1-11-0	1-5-6	1-4-5	1-6-2	1-10-1
	BOTTOM	0-7-4	0-7-1	0-5-2	0-4-0	0-4-2	0-8-6
HALF-BREADTHS	SHEER	0-0-4	1-0-3	1-10-1	1-11-3	1-10-3	1-8-2
	BOTTOM	0-0-4	0-2-6	0-8-5	0-9-1	0-4-6	0-2-2

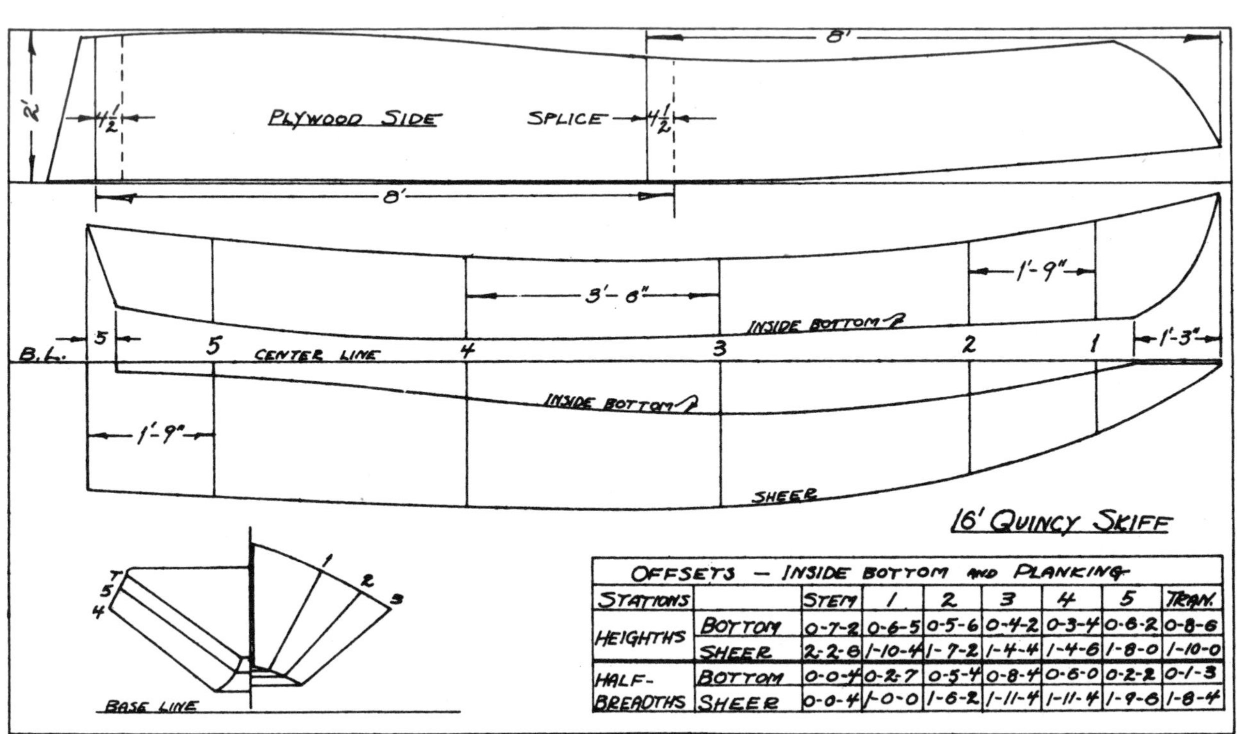

OFFSETS — INSIDE BOTTOM AND PLANKING								
STATIONS		STEM	1	2	3	4	5	TRAN.
HEIGHTHS	BOTTOM	0-7-2	0-6-5	0-5-6	0-4-2	0-3-4	0-6-2	0-8-6
	SHEER	2-2-6	1-10-4	1-7-2	1-4-4	1-4-6	1-8-0	1-10-0
HALF-BREADTHS	BOTTOM	0-0-4	0-2-7	0-5-4	0-8-4	0-6-0	0-2-2	0-1-3
	SHEER	0-0-4	1-0-0	1-6-2	1-11-4	1-11-4	1-9-6	1-8-4

who drew it from measurements made at Winona, Minnesota, in the summer of 1902 from a boat used in rafting operations on the upper reaches of the Mississippi River. I believe that the original plan or a copy of it is preserved at the Smithsonian Institution in Washington, D. C., from whence I obtained a blueprint copy a number of years ago. None of the original boats have survived to my knowledge.

The boat selected as typical by Woods was 18 feet long, and considering the boat's slim lines and comparatively shallow depth and light construction, this is not as big a boat as might appear, nor too large, I think, for one person to manage alone. Personally, I would favor the original 18-foot length. Nevertheless, I have also worked out a shortened version 16 feet long. Beam, depth, and other principal dimensions have not been changed. The shorter boat is not likely to row quite as well as the larger and possibly will prove slightly more tender, yet not enough to matter. It will prove a good boat and some may prefer it.

The original construction has much to commend it, but I shall not attempt to detail it here. I suggest that anyone interested take steps to obtain a print of Woods's drawing. If suitable materials were available, the experienced boatbuilder might want to follow the original plan. There is no doubt that the plumb, rabbeted stem adds considerably to the appearance. Ideally, this stem would require an oak or hackmatack knee and might tax the capability of the novice.

What I have attempted here is to simplify the building requirements, while retaining the lines and integrity of the original soundness of construction, so that the boat can be easily and inexpensively built with a minimum of specialized skill from stock materials readily obtainable from any ordinary local retail lumberyard or building supply firm.

MATERIALS

With one exception, the fastenings called for are galvanized common nails. No special tools or equipment are required. In fact this boat can be built entirely with a few common hand tools, although a power circular saw can be used to advantage and would speed up the job.

All lumber specified is standard dimensioned stock of species widely used for building construction and repair. Anyone able to do ordinary house carpentry should be able to put together this modified Quincy skiff without too much sweat. For those unfamiliar with the standard lumber sizes, "one-inch" boards, so called, come from the surface planer approximately ¾ inch thick. It is frequently possible, however, to obtain unplaned spruce ledger boards, which are actually 1 inch thick, or close to it. These can be bought in 8-inch and 10-inch widths, and usually can be selected so as to be free from large knots or other serious defects. In most cases if the buyer asks to pick out his own boards, he will be permitted to do so, especially where terms are cash and carry. Spruce is both stiff and strong, and such spruce boards are not only excellent for bracing the ladder frame and for making the molds, but are the finest kind for the rowing thwarts. This spruce can also be used for the inwale strips, the gunwales, and the capping strips.

When made a part of the structure of the boat, rough spruce will require a light brushing with a sharp hand plane (jack or smoother), otherwise these boards can be used as they come. Spruce is not recommended for planking the bottom, as it does not last too well in places where the water gets at it. For thwarts and gunwales and the like, if kept well painted, there is less danger of rot, so that spruce would be quite acceptable there.

In different parts of the country, the softwood species available from lumberyards will vary considerably. For planking the bottom, either pine or Douglas fir boards, or both, will generally be available. Northern white pine is excellent for bottom planking and need not be clear (select grade) as it is tougher and stronger with some sound knots of moderate size. Besides, the clear or select stock carried for interior finish is far too expensive. The short pieces required for cross planking can be cut from No. 2 common grade so as to avoid any bad knots or other serious defects. Southern pine, either longleaf or loblolly, is good, but relatively heavy, so that its use for bottom planking will mean a somewhat heavier boat. The pines used for interior finish, in particular ponderosa pine and sugar pine, are not suitable, as these species rot easily when exposed to the weather.

Other softwood species that can be used for bottom planking include white cedar, western red cedar, and Alaskan cedar. The first two, while rot resistant and lasting, are quite soft. Alaskan or Port Orford cedar is superior in all respects, but generally expensive and not readily obtainable except in the Pacific Northwest. Cypress, another superior species, might be obtainable in a few southern localities but unobtainable elsewhere.

Oak might be used to advantage for the gunwale cap and for the stem, especially if a curved piece could be found to make laminating unnecessary. Oak could even be used for the chines but might be rather heavy in the size indicated.

CONSTRUCTION

No full-size lay down of lines is required. The drawings give exact dimensions for the molds, although these could be taken from the lines printed herewith. The molds are placed upside-down on a ladder form made of two 2 x 4's cross-braced at the mold stations with 1-inch boards well-nailed with 10d nails and set on two horses at a convenient height for working. The molds are securely braced and fastened to the ladder frame.

Next, attention is given to the chine logs. For these, standard Douglas fir 2-inch joists are recommended; in actual thickness they are slightly more than 1½ inches. To make the full-length log for either side, an 8-foot section of 2-inch by 8-inch joist and a 12-foot section of 2-inch by 6-inch joist are glue-spliced together as shown in the drawing. After the glue has cured, this assembly is cut to the contour required by the molds and beveled to conform to the slope of the sides.

The beveling operation probably can best be done, or at least finished, with the chine logs securely in place on the molds. The fore-and-aft curve or rocker of the bottom is so gradual there will be no difficulty in springing the logs down into place. The two side logs fit together at both ends of the boat and are glued together in the same manner in which they are spliced. The glue joints should be reinforced by nailing with 3-inch and 4-inch galvanized wire nails, or staging nails as explained in the Appendix, but not so as to come in the way of the beveling.

After the chine logs are in place and beveled, the stem and the stern transoms are fastened in place. After they have been secured and well braced, their bevels are checked with a batten laid across the molds, and if necessary, they are faired with a sharp plane.

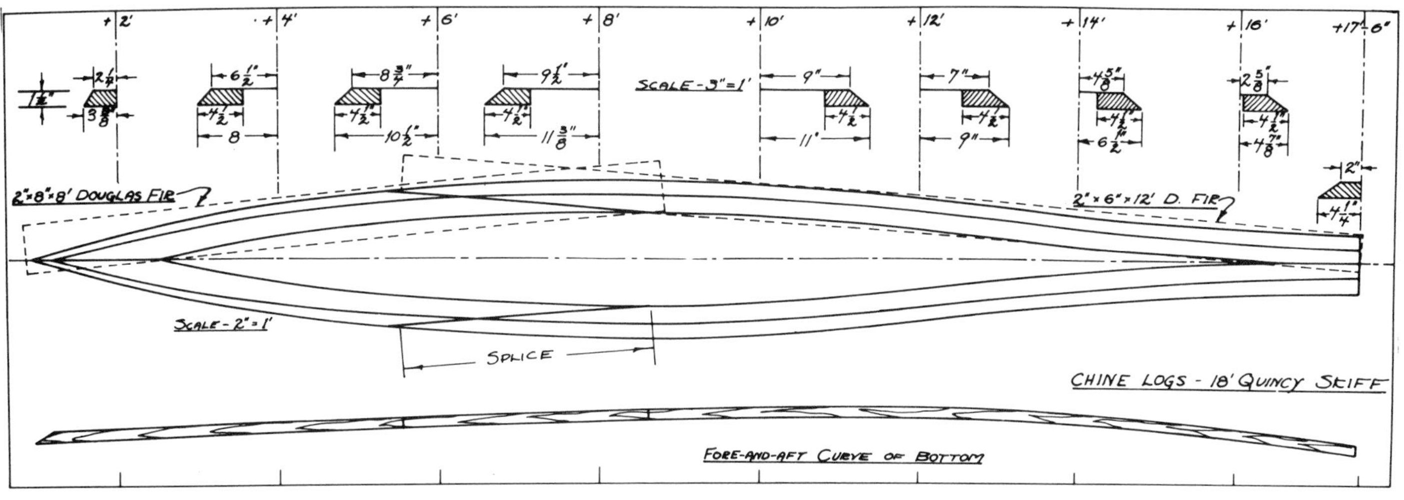

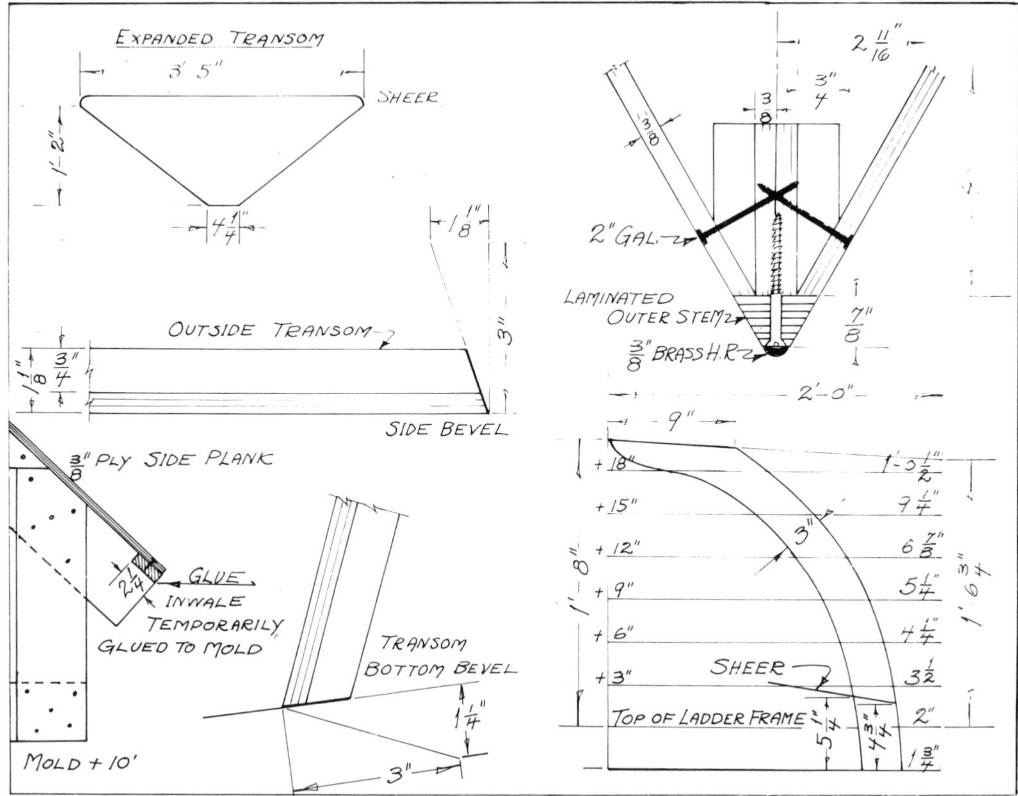

The stem, that is to say the inner stem, is a glued-up lamination assembled from four layers, two of ⅜-inch fir plywood on the inside, covered on the outside, either side, with a layer of pine, fir, or other softwood, ¾ inch thick. Gluing pressure is applied with C-clamps, as well as with 2½-inch staging nails, later removed. When the glued-up stem is later sawn to the shape as shown in the drawing, but before it is attached to the bottom, it can be used as a form for gluing the laminated outer stem, made of ⅛-inch thick strips, bent to shape on the form and clamped to it.

The stern transom is also a glued-up lamination, consisting of one layer of ⅜-inch plywood on the inside and boards ¾ inch thick outside, put on horizontally. The outer boards are glued to the plywood underneath and are edge-glued to each other as well. This forms a transom which is both strong and tight, yet easily made. The plywood reinforcement is covered on the inside of the boat, and the short grain at the bottom of the outer layer is reinforced against splitting.

The last operation before the sides go on is to install the inwale strips, to which the upper edges of the plywood sides will fasten with glue and short nails. The inwales are strips of fir, pine, or spruce, 2¼ inches by ¾ inch in section and running the length of the boat.

To get one continuous length from bow to stern, these strips will probably have to be glue spliced. In making such a splice, the tapered scarph should be 12 times the thickness of the strip, or 9 inches. The forward end of the inwale strip is beveled to fit against the side of the stem to which it is glued and nailed. The after end of the inwale strip, which is let into a blind recess in the side of the stern transom, is also glued and nailed in place.

Where the inwale strip lies in the notches cut for it in the ends of the molds, it is held by a spot of glue. Glue is applied at the underside where it meets the mold; be careful not to get any on the lower edge. A staging nail holds the strip down in place until the glue has set, after which the nail is drawn to permit the plywood side to go on. After the boat is planked and has been turned right side up, a fine saw run between the inwale strip and the mold will separate the latter so that it may be removed from the boat. The inwales installed in this manner stiffen the plywood sides and hold them in shape until the thwarts are put in and the gunwales and capping strips are added.

The sides are panels of ⅜-inch exterior fir plywood, good both sides. In no place are the plywood sides wider than 2 feet and for most of their length they are appreciably less, so that the standard 4-foot-wide plywood panels used for planking can be cut in two lengthwise. These pieces will have to be spliced in two places to make a continuous length sufficient to cover the side.

The side panels are fastened both with glue and nails to the chine logs, the transom, the stem, and the inwale strips. The only frames required are those which support the rowing thwarts, and these are installed after the boat is

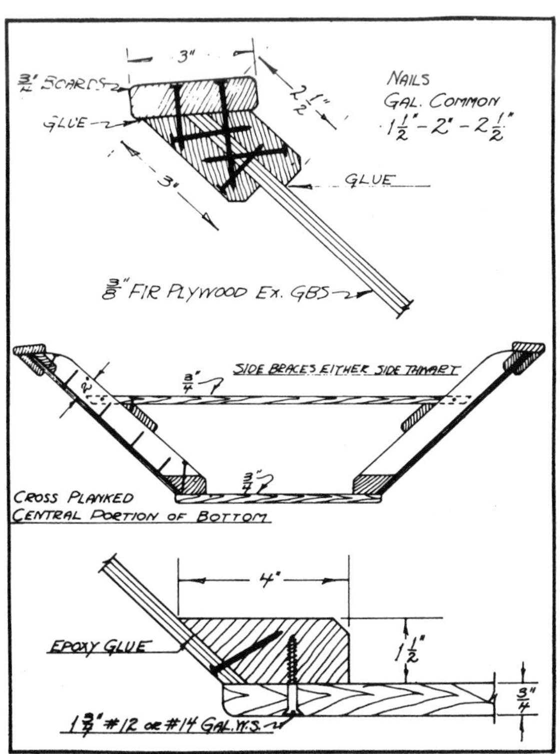

planked and has been turned right side up. But before this is done, the outside is finished; that is, the bottom is planked and the outer stem and stem band, the skeg, the sternpost, and the outside keel strip are put on.

At either end the bottom is too narrow for cross planking. Short lengths of board with the grain running fore and aft are used here. For the 18-foot boat, the bow section will require a 2-foot by 11-inch board; the stern section needs a 4-foot by 11-inch board. In the central portion of the bottom, cross planking serves to tie the chine logs together. The combined result is an extremely strong bottom, which is by far the strongest part of the entire structure. Further, a considerable part of the total weight of this boat is in the bottom, which makes for stability.

The ends of the cross planking as well as the edges of the end planks are not beveled but are left square to cover and to protect the edges of the plywood side planking. Cross planking should be under 5″ wide to prevent cupping, and to minimize opening at the seams through shrinkage. If the chine logs are liberally coated either with white lead or a good flexible bedding compound before the bottom planking is put on, no caulking of the garboard seam will be required. Screws need only be used for fastening the bottom; they should be 1¾-inch No. 12 galvanized flat-head wood screws.

Additional reinforcement for the bottom is secured from an outside keel strip 4 inches wide which runs the length of the bottom. The after end is slotted to fit around the skeg—this helps to keep the skeg from twisting.

The skeg must be well fastened from the inside of the boat with a ⅜-inch drift pin driven through the lower end of the stern knee and the bed logs. In addition the skeg is pinned through the lower end of the sternpost, which is bolted through the transom and the stern knee, as well as being screwed to the transom.

Once the outside of the boat is completed, it can be turned over. Before the molds are removed, two temporary cross spalls bracing the inwales apart are fitted. These remain in place until the thwarts are in and the gunwales and the cappings are in place (see detailed drawing).

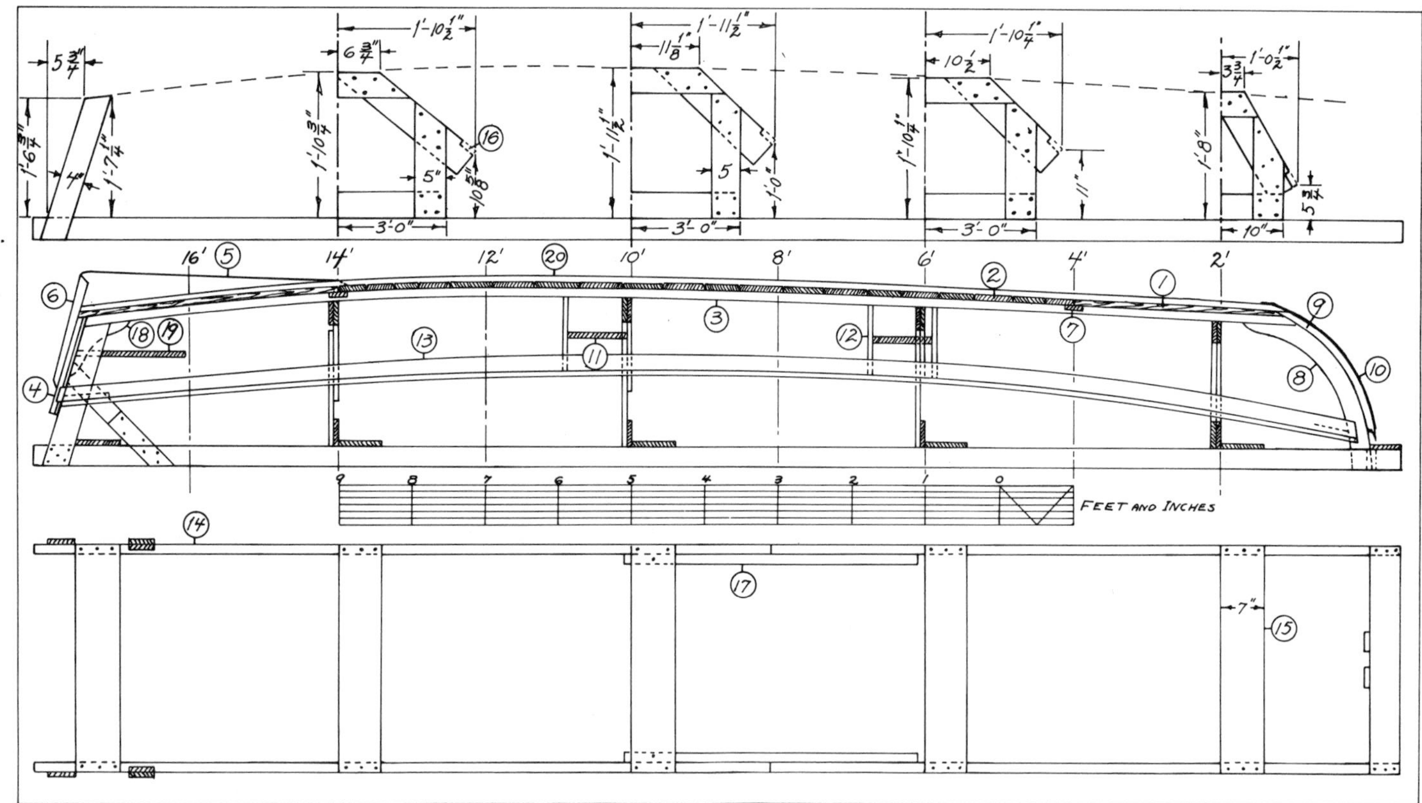

Before the capping strip goes on, the surface underneath should be thoroughly sealed with thick paint. The usual breasthook and stern quarter knees are also installed.

Rowlocks are centered 12 inches aft of the after edge of the rowing thwarts. If the cap is to be bored for thole pins, it should be given a little additional width in the center portion of the boat.

With the boat sitting upright before painting, and provided the bottom has been caulked tight, it would be a good idea to pour in a gallon of linseed oil thinned with a pint of turps, allowing the bottom to soak up as much as it will take. While the bottom is soaking, frequently brush the oil on the upper surface of the bed logs and on the plywood sides.

A few words about caulking the bottom: The cross planking is wedged tightly on the inside, but is beveled so as to stand open on the outside about 1/16 inch to 1/8 inch. A double strand of soft caulking cotton is rolled into these seams and set down with a caulking iron and mallet, but not hard enough to force it through the inside. The seams are thoroughly saturated with paint. After this is dry, the space remaining in the seam is filled with a flexible seam compound.

NUMBERED REFERENCES ON DRAWING

1. Fore end bottom. Runs fore and aft. Two widths of fir, pine or other glued together to give a maximum width of 13".

2. Cross planking, midsection bottom. Maximum width 5". Ends left square, not beveled to match the sides of the boat.

3. Bed logs from 2" fir joists. Neat thickness 1½". Molded width of bed logs changed from 4" to 4½".

4. Transom, glue laminated. 3/8" fir ply inside. "One-inch" (¾") fir or pine boards outside running horizontally.

5. Skeg, fir, hard pine, oak. Neat thick-

ness where it lands on the bottom, one inch tapering to about ¾″ at the edge. Set down into slot in keel strip, No. 20.

6. Stern post. Materials and thickness to match skeg.

7. Strips running athwartships and let into bed logs to catch ends of the fore-and-aft bottom planks.

8. Stem. Glued lamination. Two thicknesses of ⅜″ fir ply inside covered either side by one thickness "one-inch" fir or pine board.

9. Laminated outer stem covers ends of plywood side planking.

10. ½″ brass half-round or half-oval.

11. Rowing thwarts. Thicker than a neat ¾″ if possible, for stiffness.

12. Vertical frames or ribs either side of the rowing thwarts and supporting them. See detail in drawing.

13. Inwales. 2¼″ strip of "one-inch" board glue-spliced to give continuous length from bow to stern.

14. Sides of ladder frame 2 x 4's butt-spliced to give continuous length.

15. Cross braces for ladder frame well nailed.

16. Cutouts in molds for inwale strips.

17. Reinforcement for side splice in ladder frame. Fastened with 3″ nails.

18. Stern knee. Laminated like stem. Through fastened into skeg and stern post.

19. Stern sheets. Same wood as rowing thwarts. Fitted and screwed to cleats which are glued and screwed to plywood sides and transom. Braces stern. (Not shown on drawing.)

20. Outer keel strip. Slotted to take skeg. Screwed to bottom. Keeps cross planking amidships from working. Put on after bottom is caulked and puttied.

7 A Lowell Dory Skiff

Here we have a tried and tested dory skiff of large size. This substantial rowboat will give good service for fishing and general recreational use on all but the most exposed waters. This is a sturdy craft, built for rough treatment, and stout enough for a workboat. Its flat bottom and shallow draft make it easy to beach. Considering its weight and size, this skiff rows easily and handles well. But it should be well understood at the beginning that this skiff is not a model for the violent, open sea, and that in this respect it is not in a class with such rough-water types as the larger Banks and Swampscott dories, the peapod, or the Rangeley Lakes boat.

The flat, comparatively wide bottom of this skiff affords great initial stability, making it a steady, comfortable boat to fish from, and one that dogs and children cannot tip easily. The flat bottom draws little water even under a load, giving a craft well suited to extremely shallow water. While the boat would row easier with a narrower bottom, it would lose in steadiness.

A small outboard motor can be used to push this dory skiff along at moderate speeds, but considerable alteration of its lines would be required to make this boat suitable for large motors and high speeds. Features that make this skiff row easily and handle well under oars would need changing. The rocker would have to be taken out of the bottom, aft, to make a straight, flat run from amidships to the transom. The transom would need widening and should be set more upright—by at least 15 degrees—to give a better angle for the motor. These are not difficult changes to make, and might well be considered if one were interested primarily in an outboard boat capable of a smart turn of speed. The resulting craft would be what is now frequently called a "semi-dory" (See Chapter 8). Boats of this type are now popular and widely used with large outboard motors. If one is mainly interested in rowing, however, the skiff is best left as she is.

The lines and the construction details in the accompanying drawing were taken from a boat owned by Mr. H. C. Riggs in Essex, Massachusetts. This boat was built for Mr. Riggs by Hiram Lowell & Sons, Amesbury, Massachusetts. The model was the old New York Yacht Club tender, so called, lengthened by two feet. Originally, this tender was designed and built by Toppan of Medford, Massachusetts, at one time a famous dory building concern, whose advertisements, incidentally, may be seen in the back files of *Rudder* of 50 years ago.

This boat could be built first-class, rather than with materials used in standard dory construction. You could use cedar planking, genuine white oak frames, and copper and bronze fastenings throughout, except for the lower edge of the garboard, which should be fastened to the bottom with 8d Anchorfast

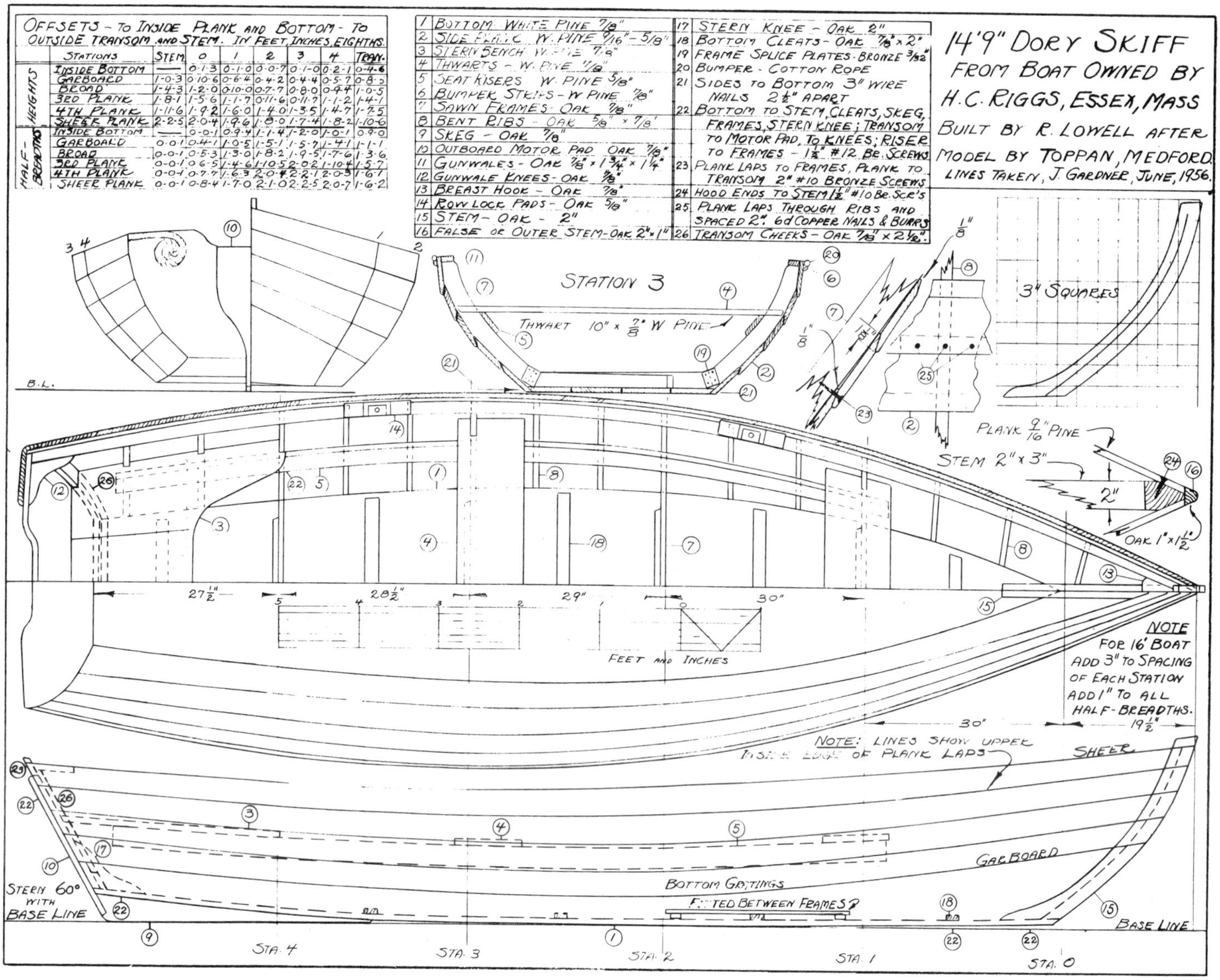

OFFSETS - TO INSIDE PLANK AND BOTTOM - TO OUTSIDE TRANSOM AND STEM. IN FEET, INCHES, EIGHTHS.

	STATIONS	STEM	0	1	2	3	4	TRAN.
HEIGHTS	INSIDE BOTTOM	—	0-1-3	0-1-0	0-0-7	0-1-0	0-2-1	0-4-6
	GARBOARD	1-0-3	0-10-6	0-6-4	0-4-2	0-4-4	0-5-7	0-8-5
	BROAD	1-4-3	1-2-0	0-10-0	0-7-7	0-8-0	0-9-4	1-0-5
	3RD PLANK	1-8-1	1-5-6	1-1-7	0-11-6	0-11-7	1-1-2	1-4-1
	4TH PLANK	1-11-6	1-9-2	1-6-0	1-4-0	1-3-5	1-4-7	1-7-5
	SHEER PLANK	2-2-5	2-0-4	1-9-6	1-8-0	1-7-4	1-8-2	1-10-6
HALF-BREADTHS	INSIDE BOTTOM	—	0-0-1	0-9-4	1-1-4	1-2-0	1-0-1	0-9-0
	GARBOARD	0-0-1	0-4-1	1-0-5	1-5-1	1-5-7	1-4-1	1-1-1
	BROAD	0-0-1	0-5-3	1-3-0	1-8-2	1-9-5	1-7-6	1-3-6
	3RD PLANK	0-0-1	0-6-5	1-4-6	1-10-5	2-0-2	1-10-4	1-5-7
	4TH PLANK	0-0-1	0-7-7	1-6-3	2-0-4	2-2-1	2-0-3	1-6-1
	SHEER PLANK	0-0-1	0-8-4	1-7-0	2-1-0	2-2-5	2-0-7	1-6-2

1	BOTTOM WHITE PINE 7/8"	17	STERN KNEE - OAK 2"
2	SIDE PLANK W. PINE 9/16"-5/8"	18	BOTTOM CLEATS - OAK 7/8" x 2"
3	STERN BENCH W. PINE 7/8"	19	FRAME SPLICE PLATES - BRONZE 3/32"
4	THWARTS - W. PINE 7/8"	20	BUMPER - COTTON ROPE
5	SEAT RISERS W. PINE 5/8"	21	SIDES TO BOTTOM 3" WIRE NAILS 2½" APART
6	BUMPER STRIPS - W PINE 7/8"		
7	SAWN FRAMES - OAK 7/8"	22	BOTTOM TO STEM, CLEATS, SKEG, FRAMES, STERN KNEE; TRANSOM TO MOTOR PAD, TO KNEES; RISER TO FRAMES - 1½" #12 Be. SCREWS
8	BENT RIBS - OAK 5/8" x 7/8"		
9	SKEG - OAK 7/8"		
10	OUTBOARD MOTOR PAD OAK 7/8"		
11	GUNWALES - OAK 7/8" x 1¾" x 1¼"	23	PLANK LAPS TO FRAMES, PLANK TO TRANSOM 2" #10 BRONZE SCREWS
12	GUNWALE KNEES - OAK 7/8"		
13	BREAST HOOK - OAK 7/8"	24	HOOD ENDS TO STEM 1½" #10 Be. SCR'S
14	ROW LOCK PADS - OAK 5/8"	25	PLANK LAPS THROUGH RIBS AND SPACED 2". 6d COPPER NAILS & BURRS
15	STEM - OAK - 2"		
16	FALSE OR OUTER STEM - OAK 2" x 1"	26	TRANSOM CHEEKS - OAK 7/8" x 2½"

14'9" DORY SKIFF
FROM BOAT OWNED BY
H.C. RIGGS, ESSEX, MASS
BUILT BY R. LOWELL AFTER
MODEL BY TOPPAN, MEDFORD.
LINES TAKEN, J. GARDNER, JUNE, 1956.

STATION 3

THWART 10" x 7/8" W PINE

3" SQUARES

PLANK 9/16" PINE

STEM 2" x 3"

OAK 1" x 1½"

27½" 28½" 29" 30"

FEET AND INCHES

NOTE
FOR 16' BOAT ADD 3" TO SPACING OF EACH STATION ADD 1" TO ALL HALF-BREADTHS.

NOTE: LINES SHOW UPPER INSIDE EDGE OF PLANK LAPS

SHEER

GARBOARD

BOTTOM GRATINGS FITTED BETWEEN FRAMES?

STERN 60° WITH BASE LINE

BASE LINE

STA. 4 STA. 3 STA. 2 STA. 1 STA. 0

The Lowell dory skiff owned by H.C. Riggs of Essex, Mass.

(Above and below, right) Two views of the construction of H.C. Riggs's Lowell dory skiff.

monel nails. It goes without saying that such materials make a boat of superior lasting qualities. Nevertheless, a good, serviceable boat can be constructed at considerably less expense with native pine planking and galvanized iron fastenings.

This need not be an expensive boat to build, nor should it be a difficult model for the amateur builder. There are no hard bends, and no steaming is required. Even fitting the laps is not hard, if the beginner will take time to study the operation. While some might find it easier to fasten the laps with copper nails riveted over burrs, the knack of properly clinching chisel point nails is not difficult to acquire with a little preliminary practice. When correctly turned and tightened, the chisel point nail is a good method of fastening. Planks spliced with epoxy glue can be got out economically from the shorter lengths of boards, which are cheaper and easier to obtain. If the amateur is interested in economy, and has plenty of time, he can build himself a good, serviceable boat of this sort, with a very moderate outlay of cash.

8 A Semi-dory

This 14-foot semi-dory is a good boat for the beginning amateur boatbuilder. It is a tried and tested model, not too difficult to build, and a safe boat for children—one they can learn in and have a lot of fun with. It is also one that will take Dad fishing and that Mother can sail afternoons, if she has a mind to. While this semi-dory has proved to be an excellent family boat, it was not offered as such in the first place. The lines for this particular boat were drawn for a series on tabloid lobsterboats printed in the *Maine Coast Fisherman* in the spring of 1954. Considered in the series were a number of small fishing workboats suitable for outboard motors.

The semi-dory, sometimes called a half-dory, gets its name from its resemblance to the forward half of a large Swampscott dory, as if the after half of the dory had been cut away and removed. Of course, this is not the case. Rather, standard Swampscott dory lines are widened aft to give a stern section wide enough and powerful enough to support an outboard motor without settling or "squatting." In the semi-dory, the after part of the bottom is also changed somewhat by widening it and by taking out the rocker to produce a nearly straight run aft. Twenty or twenty-five years ago, semi-dories were a popular and much-used small craft type in New England, both for work and for sport.

Richard W. Hodgdon built the boat from the 1954 plans, and, as an outboard boat it more than came up to expectations. Surprisingly, it rowed quite well, also; his young son, even, had no difficulty rowing it. This is exceptional for an outboard boat. Most are terrible under oars, as hardly needs saying. Enough of the Swampscott dory characteristics remain in the design so that this semi-dory would sail fairly well, also. A sail plan was worked out by Hodgdon's long-time friend E. D. McIntosh of Dover, New Hampshire, a well-known builder, designer, and sailing skipper. The result is not a racing machine, certainly, but a good sailing knockabout. Lifting out the mast and unshipping the rudder turns the boat back into an outboard boat as before. It performs well with motors ranging from 6 to 20 hp. The centerboard, when pulled up into its box, should not interfere with rowing.

As first designed in 1954, this semi-dory was intended for straight, old-time dory construction with sawn lumber. Since then, other methods of small craft construction have been worked out utilizing plywood, thermoplastic adhesives, and synthetic and glass reinforcements. I have therefore redesigned the boat for more modern wooden construction, and in the process I have made some changes to the sailing rig put in by Hodgdon.

Hodgdon's rig had a combined sail area of 115 square feet. This seems to me to be excessive, especially if the boat is to be sailed outside sheltered waters, where strong winds might

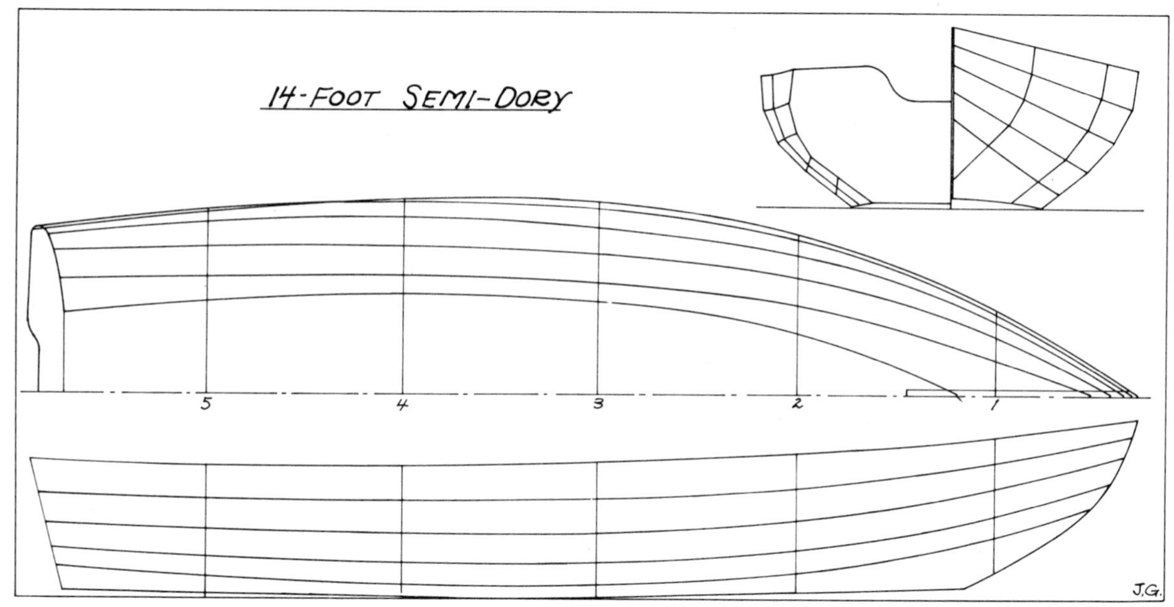
14-FOOT SEMI-DORY
5
4
3
2
1
J.G.

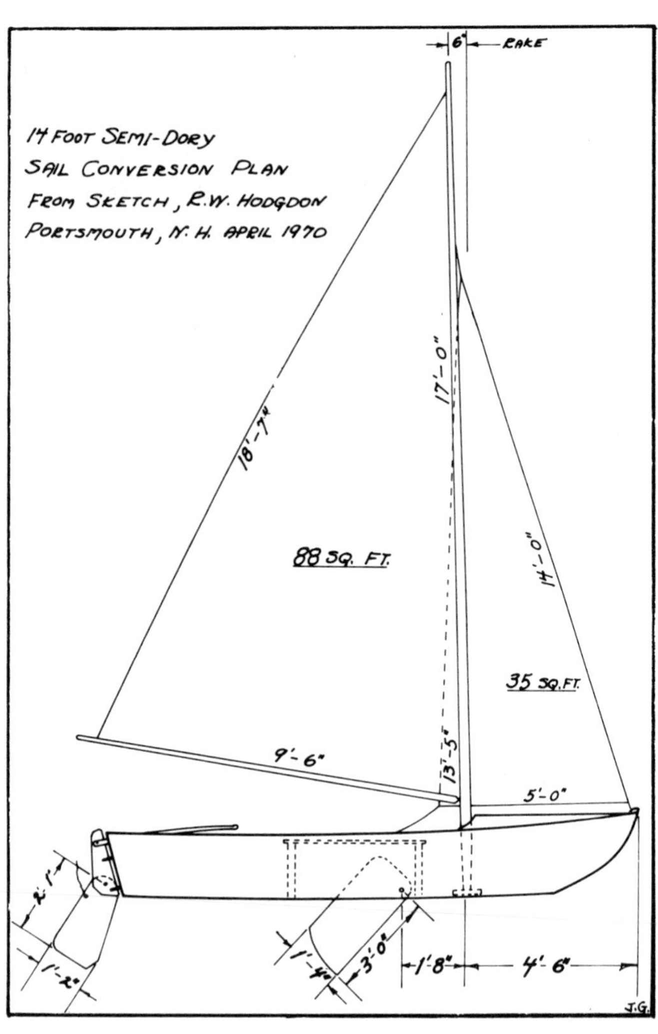
14 FOOT SEMI-DORY
SAIL CONVERSION PLAN
FROM SKETCH, R.W. HODGDON
PORTSMOUTH, N.H. APRIL 1970
6"
RAKE
18'-7"
17'-0"
88 SQ. FT.
14'-0"
35 SQ.FT.
9'-6"
13'-5"
5'-0"
2'-1"
1'-2"
1'-4"
3'-0"
1'-8"
4'-6"
J.G.

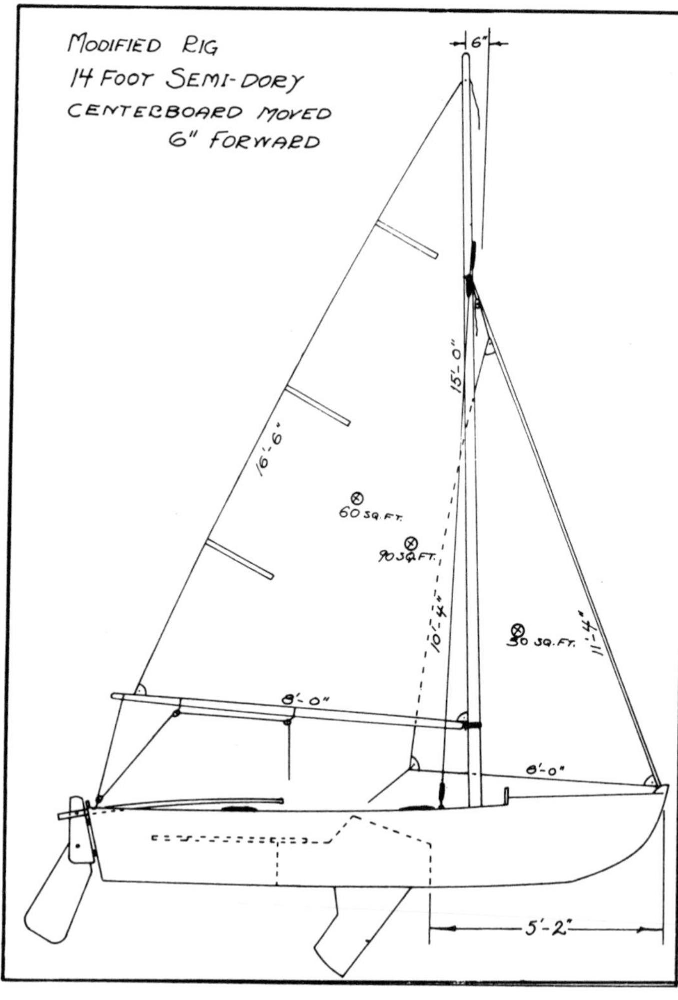
MODIFIED RIG
14 FOOT SEMI-DORY
CENTERBOARD MOVED
6" FORWARD
6"
15'-0"
16'-6"
60 SQ.FT.
90 SQ.FT.
10'-4"
30 SQ.FT.
11'-4"
8'-0"
6'-0"
5'-2"

be encountered. I have consequently reduced the sail area—the combined sail area for the alternate rig shown here has been reduced to 90 square feet, the mast has been shortened from 19 feet 2 inches above the deck to 17 feet 8 inches, and the boom has been raised high enough to clear the heads of those seated in the boat.

Hodgdon's drop rudder, convenient if the boat is beached frequently, has been retained. The details show one way of building it: not the only way, certainly, and not necessarily the best way, but it is one that will work.

14-FOOT SEMI-DORY												
	HEIGHTS ABOVE BASE						HALF-BREADTHS					
	BOT.	GAR.	2	3	4	SHEER	BOT.	GAR.	2	3	4	SHEER
STEM	—	1-1-4	1-5-4	1-9-1	2-0-1	2-2-6	0-1-0	0-1-0	0-1-0	0-1-0	0-1-0	0-1-0
STATION 1	0-1-6	0-9-1	1-0-2	1-4-2	1-8-0	1-11-7	0-1-0	0-5-3	0-8-5	0-11-0	1-0-2	1-0-5
STA. 2	0-0-7	0-3-6	0-7-1	0-11-3	1-4-1	1-9-3	0-9-1	1-1-1	1-5-1	1-8-5	1-10-7	1-11-5
STA. 3	0-0-1	0-2-1	0-5-3	0-9-5	1-2-4	1-8-2	1-1-5	1-4-3	1-8-6	2-0-5	2-3-3	2-4-4
STA. 4	0-0-1	0-2-1	0-5-2	0-9-5	1-2-3	1-7-4	1-2-6	1-5-4	1-9-6	2-2-1	2-4-2	2-4-5
STA. 5	0-0-2	0-3-1	0-6-2	0-10-1	1-2-5	1-7-5	1-1-5	1-5-2	1-9-5	2-1-2	2-3-1	2-2-5
TRANSOM	0-0-6	0-4-6	0-7-3	0-11-0	1-3-4	1-8-2	1-0-0	1-5-0	1-9-1	1-11-3	2-0-4	2-0-0
OFFSETS IN FEET, INCHES, & EIGHTHS TO INSIDE PLANK, BOTTOM AND OUTER STEM PROFILE. STATIONS SPACED 30". TRANSOM AT SHEER 26 3/4" AFT STA. 5. RAKED 5".												

The centerboard details, worked out some time ago for a slightly larger round-sided sailing dory, are typical, and are suitable for this semi-dory without any reduction in size.

The drawing showing how to set the boat up as well as how to proceed with the planking,

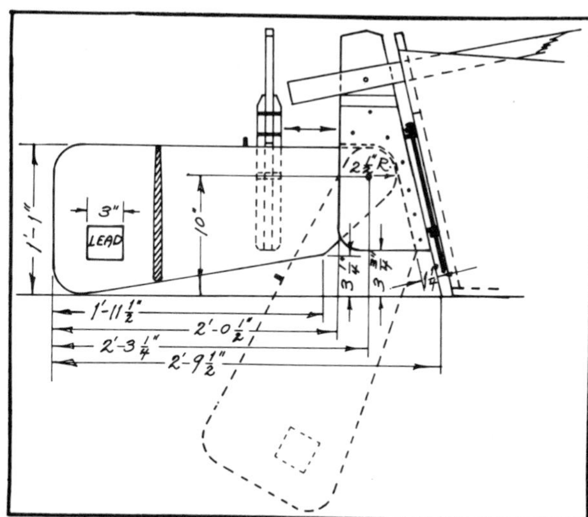

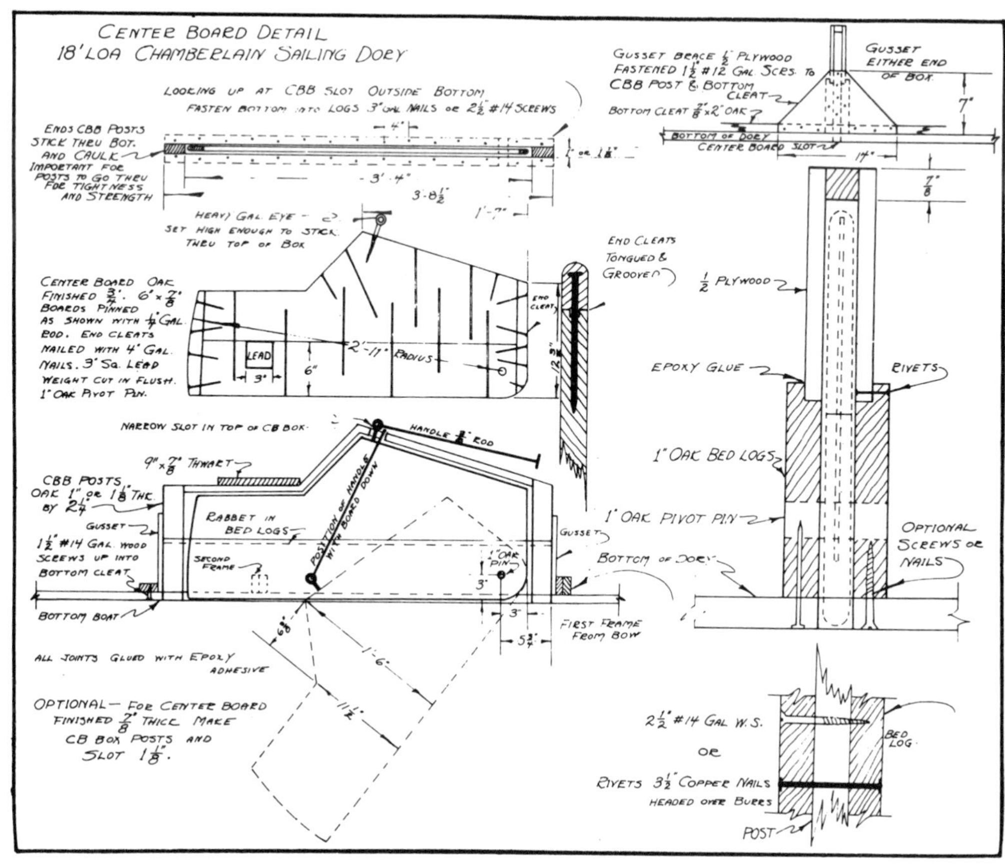

Richard Hodgdon's 14-foot semi-dory rigged for sail, oars, and even motor.

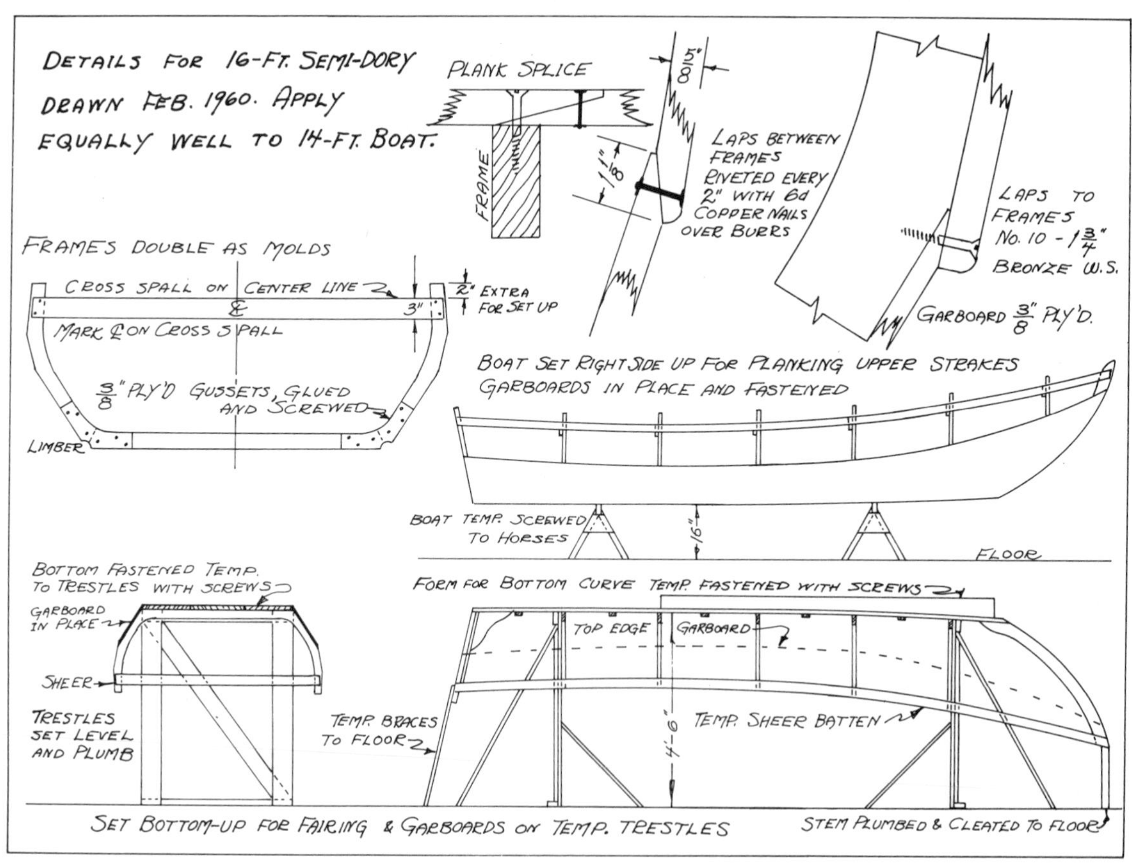

the manner of fastening the laps and so forth, was done for a 16-foot semi-dory, an enlargement of this 14-foot boat, so it applies equally well here. It will be noted that the 16-footer is a four-plank boat, while the 14-footer is a five-plank boat. In both cases the garboard and the next plank above are treated as a single plank, being made of plywood. This could not be done with natural lumber, as the width required would be too great, but is easily done with plywood, saving both labor and material. If one wanted to, however, this dory could be planked in the traditional manner with two bottom strakes of natural lumber replacing the one wide plywood strake as shown.

As can be seen, the various parts of the dory hull have been numbered. The numbers refer to the building descriptions, which follow:

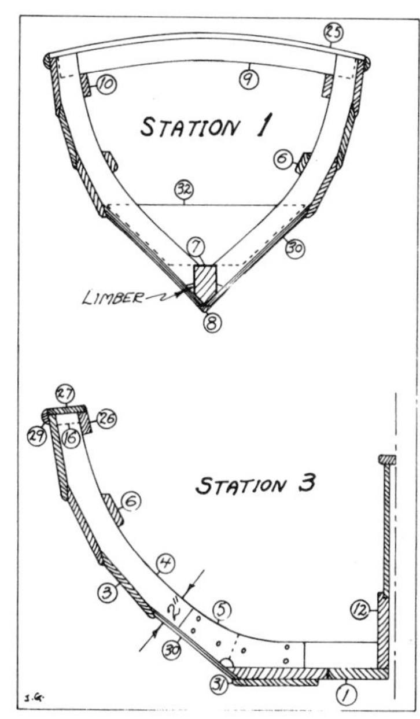

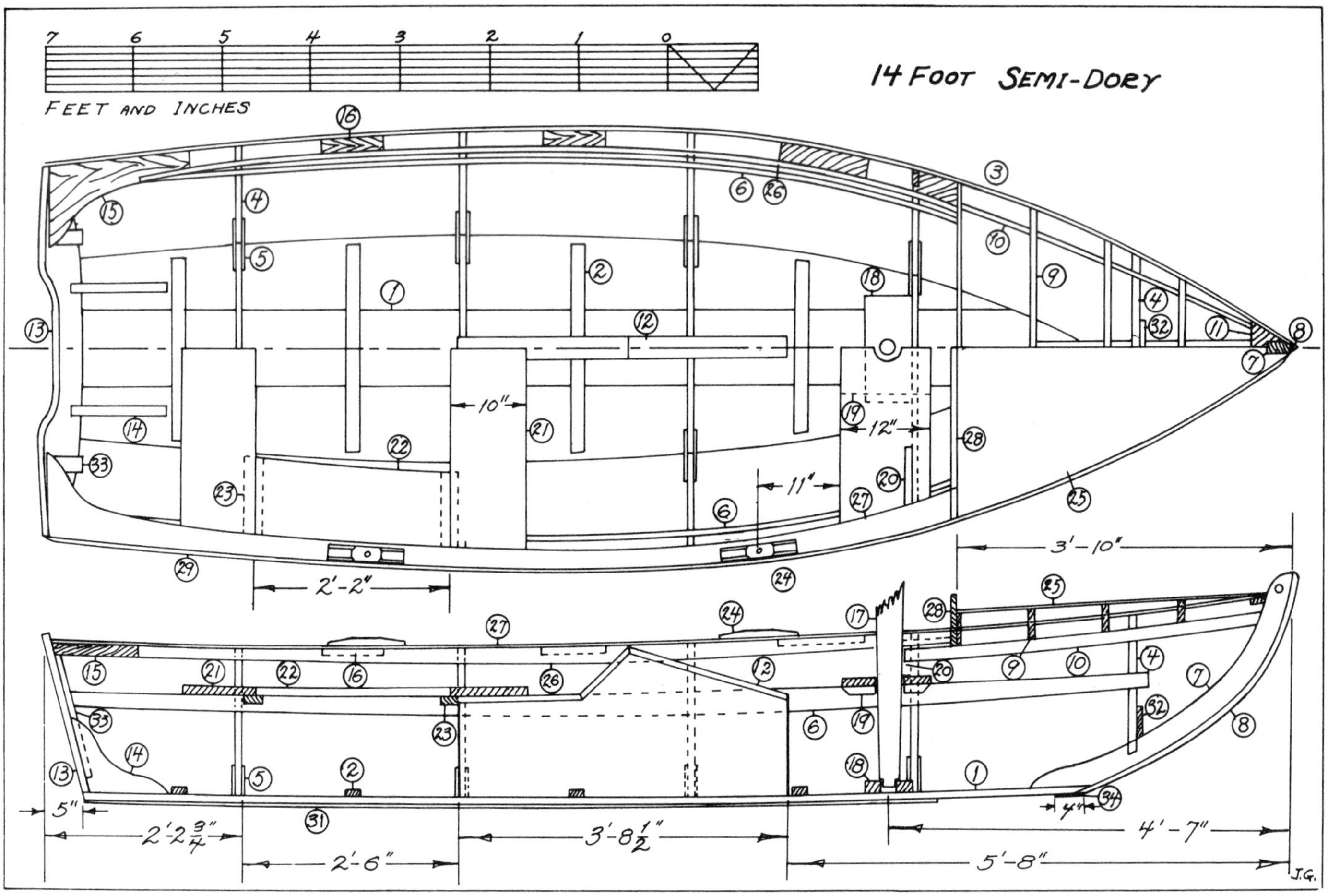

1. Bottom. Northern white pine, Philippine mahogany, cypress, cedar. Pine preferred. Thickness ⅞". Make out of three or four boards. Fasten to bottom cleats with No. 12 or No. 14 wood screws, 1½" long; likewise to frames, stem, transom, and stern knees.

2. Bottom cleats. Oak, ⅞" thick, 2" wide. Install midway between frames to stiffen bottom.

3. Side plank. First two strakes from the bottom (garboard and broad) made as a single plank of ⅜" marine plywood. Glued to bottom, stem, and transom with epoxy, polysulphide caulk, or equivalent. Nailed to bottom with 8d or 10d monel Anchorfast nails, bronze Anchorfast, or galvanized wire nails, spaced approximately 2" apart. Fastened to stem with 1¼" No. 10 or No. 12 screws; to transom with 1½" No. 10 or No. 12 screws. Can also be made as two planks, lapped and fastened like the upper plank. The upper plank to be made of northern white pine, Philippine mahogany, cypress, or cedar 9/16" thick and lapped 1⅛". Fasten through laps into frames with No. 10, 1½" or 1¾" screws. On the upper transom use longer screws in the end grain. Fasten laps between frames with copper nails riveted over burrs spaced approximately 2½".

4. Frames. Oak, ⅞" thick, molded approximately 2". Side futtocks joined to bottom cross frame with plywood gussets both sides.

5. Frame gussets. ⅜" marine plywood fastened to oak frames with glue and 1" No. 10 screws.

6. Risers. Same material as side plank, 3" wide amidships tapering at the ends to 2". Fasten to frames with No. 10, 1½" screws.

7. Stem. Oak 2" thick, molded 3". Grain to follow the curvature of the stem as much as possible.

8. Outer stem. Oak. Steam-bent strip applied after planking is complete. Fastened with No. 10, 1¾" screws, and faired to conform to the shape of the boat.

9. Deck beams. Oak or mahogany ⅝" thick, molded 2", and laid out to a curve rising 3" at the forward end of the deck.

10. Deck beam clamp. Same material as the thwart risers. Fastened the same. Molded 2". Fastened to the two forward frames and the stem to support the ends of the deck beams.

11. Breast hook. Oak, ⅞" thick. Grain runs athwartships. Fastened to stem with long screw or drift. Takes fastenings from the sheer strakes and the fore end of the deck.

12. Centerboard and centerboard box. Fully detailed in accompanying drawing.

13. Transom. Philippine mahogany 1" thick. Two or three pieces running athwartships glued and dowelled with ⅜" white oak dowels. Reinforced with stern knees and transom cleats.

14. Stern knees. Oak, 1¼" thick, 10" length of either limb. Molded and located as shown. Fastened through the stern with No. 12 or No. 14, 2" to 2½" screws bunged and plugged. Bottom fastenings may be longer than 1½".

15. Stern quarter knees. Oak, 1¼" to 1½" thick. 10" bearing on transom. Molded as shown. Fastening through transom same as stern knees. Sheer plank and inwale both screw into stern quarter knees with No. 10, 1½" screws.

16. Filler blocks. ⅞" oak, mahogany, pine, located as shown. Fastenings from sheer plank, inwales, and capping.

17. Mast. Spruce. 19'6" from step to head. 3½" diameter at deck, tapering to 2" diameter at head.

18. Mast step. Oak, 1¼" to 1½" thick. To overlap at least two bottom planks.

19. Mast hole cleat. ⅞" thick oak, 12" square. Underside of the center of the forward thwart, with grain running fore and aft, for reinforcement. Fastened with No. 12, 1½" screws bunged and plugged.

20. Thwart knees. Either side of the forward thwart to brace the mast. ⅞" thick. Preferably natural crooks of hackmatack, apple, oak, or other suitable hardwood. Can be glued laminations. Fasten to thwart, side planking, inwale, and capping.

21. Thwarts. Pine, Philippine mahogany, cypress, spruce. ⅞" thick. Notched around frames. Screwed to risers with No. 12, 1¾" to 2" screws bunged and plugged.

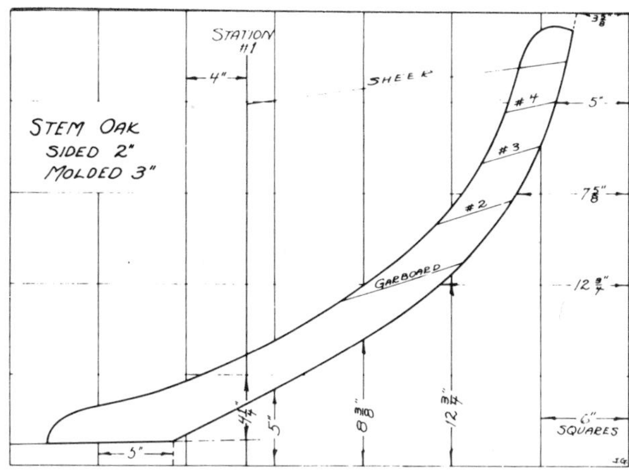

22. Side benches. Same material as thwarts. Between second and third thwarts either side. Fastened to thwarts by cleats on underside with 1½" No. 12 screws bunged and plugged. Fastened to risers, as well.

23. Side bench cleats. ⅞" oak, 3" wide.

24. Rowlock cleats. Oak strips, 11" x 2" x ⅞" beveled as shown and screwed into capping and filler blocks.

25. Fore deck. ⅜" plywood. Screwed to deck beams, sheer strake, and breast hook with 1¼" No. 8 wood screws. Filler blocks along the outside between the deck beams and fastened to the sheer strakes can be installed for added fastening and reinforcement. Can be covered with thin canvas laid in paint, with fiberglass or polypropylene, or can be merely painted. Outside edges may be covered with fiberglass or polypropylene tape under half oval trim.

26. Inwale. Oak or Philippine mahogany ⅞" thick, 2" wide amidships tapering to 1½" at ends. Fastened to stern quarter knees, frames, and filler blocks with No. 12, 1¾" to 2" screws.

27. Side capping. Pine or Philippine mahogany ½" thick. Forward end thinned slightly to fair into ⅜" thick fore deck. Put on in two pieces. Butt splice under after oarlock cleat. Fastened to stern quarter knees, inwales, filler blocks, and sheer strakes with No. 10, 1¼" to 1½" screws. Heads slightly countersunk and puttied.

28. Deck coaming. Philippine mahogany ⅝" thick. Finishes after end of deck, covering the after deck beam and projecting 2" above the deck. Rounded ends cover the joints between the deck and side capping and extend to the outside of the boat. Can be finished bright; if so, the inwales, side capping, and half oval trim can be made of Philippine mahogany to correspond and can be finished bright also. All fastenings through these members to be bunged and plugged.

29. Half oval trim. Philippine mahogany or oak 1" wide. Fore end approaching the stem tapered to ¾". Fastened with No. 8, 1" screws, bunged ⅜", and plugged.

30. Plywood garboard. (See No. 3.)

31. Bottom strip. Oak or Philippine mahogany ½" thick. To protect the lower edge of the garboard and to take wear on the bottom. Inside edge of bottom strip must be straight and parallel with the centerline of the boat, otherwise it will create drag and slow the boat. Thus these strips will be 8" wide at the center of the boat, dying out to a point about 6" forward of the second frame, slightly forward of the mast location. Fastened with No. 10, 1" screws bunged and plugged. Before the bottom strips are put on, and before any paint is put on the bottom, the lower edge of the garboard is to be reinforced with fiberglass or polypropylene tape 3" wide, equally lapped on bottom and up side. Tape to be bonded with epoxy-Versamid mix. A double thickness of tape to be applied at the base of the stem.

32. Frame cleat. ⅜" or ½" plywood glued and screwed to the two sides of the forward, or No. 1, frame.

33. Transom cleats. Oak strips ⅞" thick by 2" wide extending from the underside of the stern quarter knees to the bottom to reinforce the transom. Fastened with No. 12, 1½" screws bunged and plugged.

34. Bottom plate. Triangular piece of flat brass or bronze to cover lower end of false stem and fore end of bottom. Fasten with No. 8, 1" screws, countersunk.

9 A Car-top Semi-dory

There is definitely a demand for a car-top boat. The requirements, when boiled down, are more or less uniform and quite specific:

1. It must be as light as possible for easy handling.

2. It should be large enough to carry at least three persons in moderately rough water with safety.

3. It must be tight, and must stay tight, even when exposed to drying winds and the direct rays of the hot summer sun when it is on top of a car.

4. It should be a model that rows at least moderately well, that will drive easily with a small outboard motor, and that can be adapted for sailing if the owner so wishes.

5. It must be capable of being built inexpensively and easily, that is to say its construction must come well within both the capability and the pocketbook of the average home builder.

This is asking quite a lot, yet not the impossible, by any means. A generation ago the fulfillment of all five requirements would have been impossible. A skilled professional boatbuilder taking pains and not sparing expense could probably have achieved the first four requirements, if he covered the hull with canvas. Few home builders could have made the grade. In attempting to make a permanently tight hull, the amateur would have likely built the boat too heavy. In seeking to keep the weight down, he might have built it either too light or too flimsy.

Since the advent of thermosetting adhesives and reinforcements of glass and synthetic fibers in the last 15 to 20 years, it has become possible for amateur builders to build the kind of boat we are considering.

In the June, 1961, issue of *Outdoor Maine*, I offered the lines, construction details, and building directions for a car-top boat for the sportsman and amateur builder. In shape, the boat—12 feet LOA, 4 feet 2 inches beam, 1 foot 4 inches depth amidships—was that of a knuckle-sided semi-dory with four planks to a side. The planks, of 5mm Utile mahogany plywood (approximately 3/16 inches thick), were screwed and glued to Sitka spruce seam battens, with the joints covered on the outside with a narrow fiberglass tape bonded with epoxy resin. An entire covering of the outer surface of the hull with fiberglass was not advocated, as this would have added too much weight. The narrow tape was sufficient to waterproof and reinforce the planking seams, and was not too unsightly on the finished boat, if care was taken in putting on the tapes and in feathering out their edges by careful sanding before the final coats of paint were applied.

Such seam-batten construction, although it has proved quite successful, up to a certain point, is now obsolete. It is obsolete because the

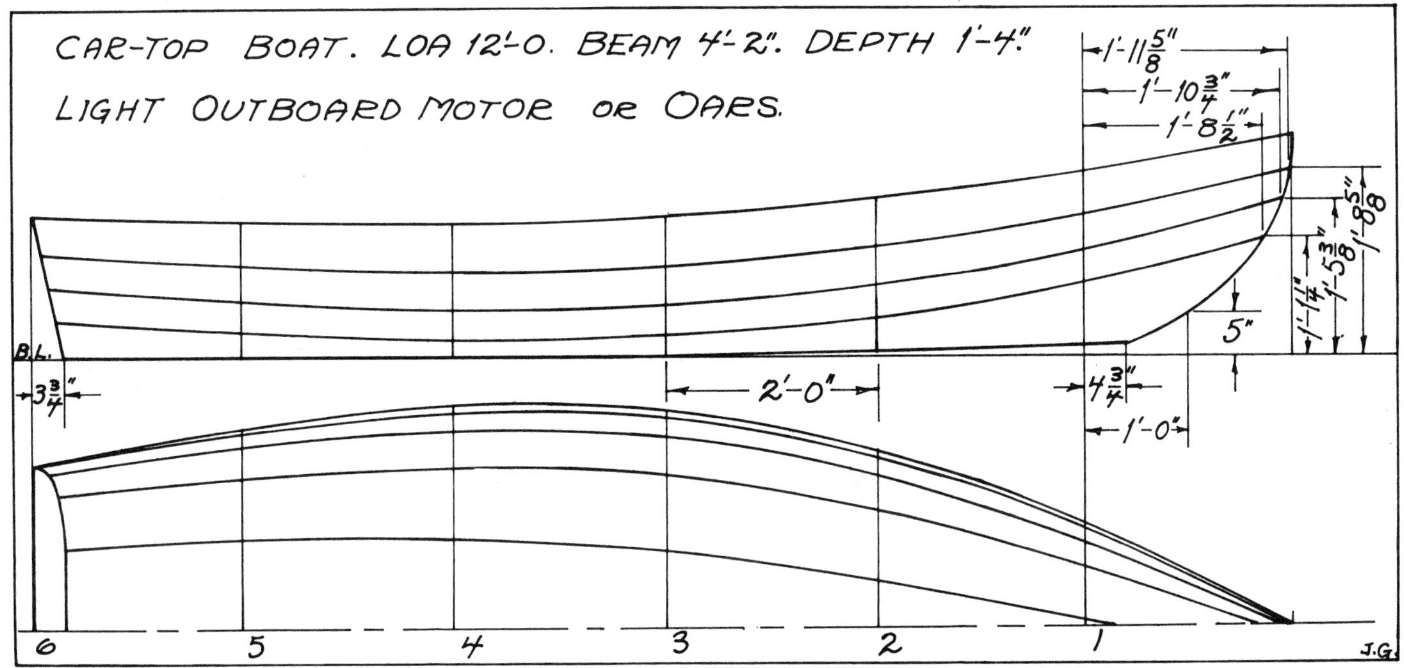

(Above and below) The plans for the car-top semi-dory as originally designed for four strakes per side. The five-strakes-per-side version appears on pages 74 and 75.

battens can be eliminated, giving way to a less expensive and much easier construction—one that permits a number of improvements in design.

Instead of wooden seam battens, an arrangement of Vectra polypropylene tapes bonded with epoxy can be used to join the edges of the strakes of plywood planking. The introduction of Vectra polypropylene has provided the amateur builder a fabric with flexibility, toughness, strength, and light weight—equivalent fiberglass reinforcement is approximately two and one-half times as heavy. (Note: if Vectra is unobtainable, then fiberglass tape may be substituted.)

The advantages gained by eliminating seam battens are worth considering. Seam battens must be fitted and beveled accurately, which sometimes calls for greater skill than the amateur can muster. If the edges of the plywood planks are screwed as well as glued to the battens, as is recommended, several gross of small brass or bronze screws are required, which add to the expense, take time to put in, and add weight. In addition, there are several objections to having seam battens on the inside of the boat.

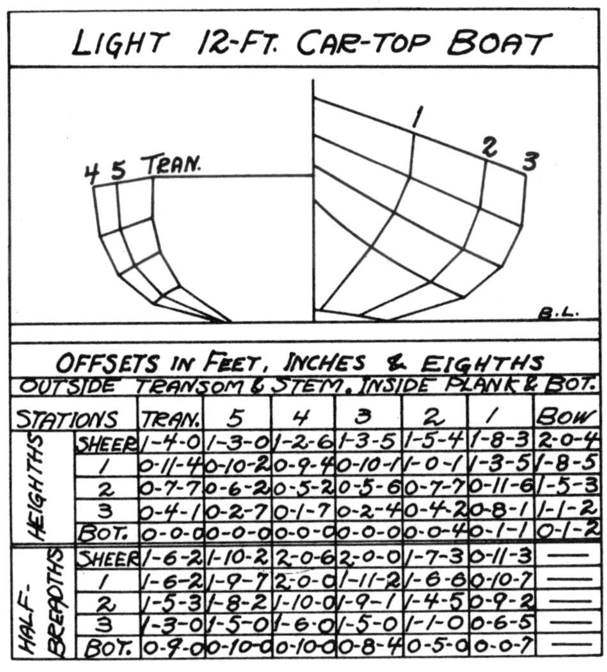

OFFSETS IN FEET, INCHES & EIGHTHS
OUTSIDE TRANSOM & STEM. INSIDE PLANK & BOT.

STATIONS		TRAN.	5	4	3	2	1	BOW
HEIGHTS	SHEER	1-4-0	1-3-0	1-2-6	1-3-5	1-5-4	1-8-3	2-0-4
	1	0-11-4	0-10-2	0-9-4	0-10-1	1-0-1	1-3-5	1-8-5
	2	0-7-7	0-6-2	0-5-2	0-5-6	0-7-7	0-11-6	1-5-3
	3	0-4-1	0-2-7	0-1-7	0-2-4	0-4-2	0-8-1	1-1-2
	BOT.	0-0-0	0-0-0	0-0-0	0-0-0	0-0-4	0-1-1	0-1-2
HALF-BREADTHS	SHEER	1-6-2	1-10-2	2-0-6	2-0-0	1-7-3	0-11-3	—
	1	1-6-2	1-9-7	2-0-0	1-11-2	1-6-6	0-10-7	—
	2	1-5-3	1-8-2	1-10-0	1-9-1	1-4-5	0-9-2	—
	3	1-3-0	1-5-0	1-6-0	1-5-0	1-1-0	0-6-5	—
	BOT.	0-9-0	0-10-0	0-10-0	0-8-4	0-5-0	0-0-7	—

They look clumsy and add weight, they can catch water and dirt, and they prevent the use of bent frames, either steam bent or put in as laminations of thin, glued strips.

There is a further consideration, as well. The elimination of seam battens makes it easier to put more and narrower planks on a side. This

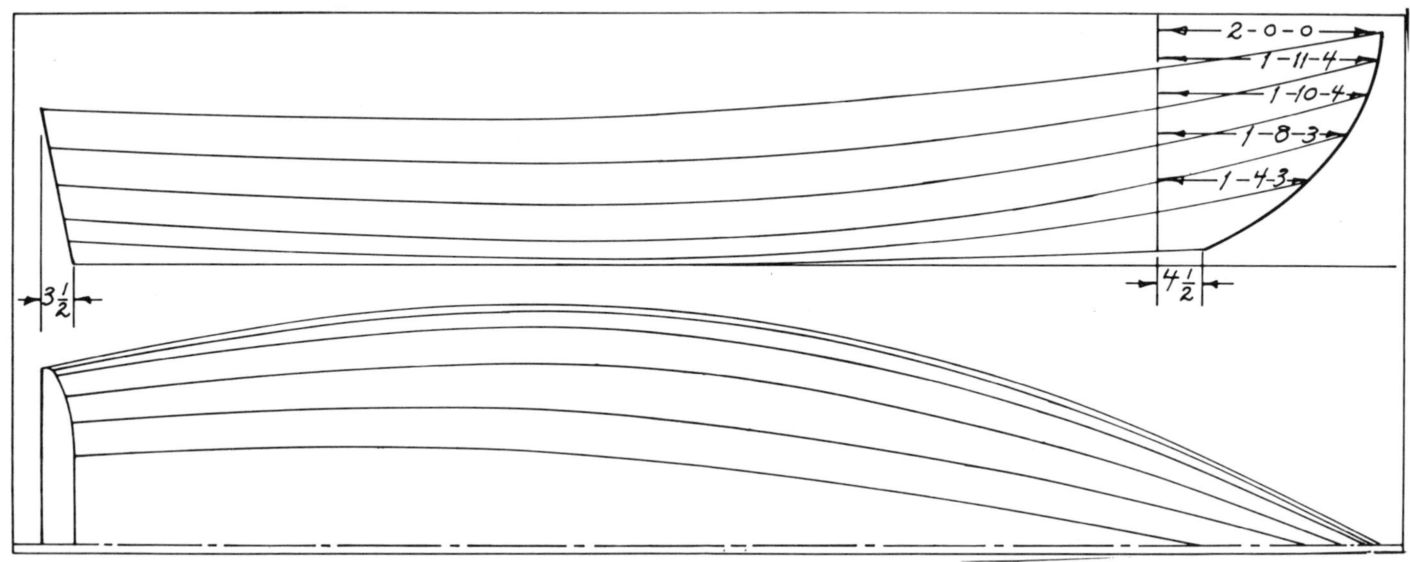

(Above and opposite page) The plans for the car-top semi-dory as newly designed for five strakes per side.

is no small factor. The original boat designed for *Outdoor Maine* had but four planks to a side. It would have been a better boat with five, but the number was kept at four in order to eliminate the additional labor and expense, not to mention weight, of an extra seam batten.

The original 12-foot car-top boat has now been redrawn for five strakes of plank instead of four as first laid out, and the revised lines and offsets are given herewith. The result is a more rounded hull with slightly increased displacement or capacity, which will be easier to plank because of its narrower strakes. The strakes can be cut out of standard 4-foot by 8-foot panels of ¼-inch marine grade fir plywood with very little waste, if the 12-foot strakes are spliced together from two or more shorter pieces. (See the Appendix for details on splicing.)

CONSTRUCTION

Following is a description of the method to be used in building this boat with Vectra reinforced seams instead of seam battens. It should be understood that this method of building is equally suited to a wide range of small craft, from kayaks to powerboats and sailboats up to 20 feet long, and even larger. Without altering the design to any significant extent, many round hulls can be treated as if they were multi-chine or knuckle-sided and so built by this method easier than if standard carvel planking were used. To the inventive and resourceful amateur builder, this method of building offers a chance to experiment with novel and imaginative variations of traditional design. It should not be overlooked by the professional designer either; some of them, I must say, tend to be far too conservative in their approach to small craft.

To begin with, the lines, as always, must be laid down full size and faired. From these adjusted lines molds are made in the usual way with pine boards, so that they can be nailed into, and are set up carefully and checked and adjusted for fairness. They should not be too far apart, not more than 2 feet in any case, for there will be nothing between them to support the edges of the plywood strakes. If the molds were too far apart, the adjoining edges of the planks might not hold together tightly where there are hard bends or twists.

After each strake is shaped and fitted, but before it is nailed in place, a very shallow cut into the outer face is made along each edge. This is best done with a small, high-speed power hand router using a special gauge made for this purpose. The cut should be about one inch wide and not more than ⅓₂″ deep. The purpose of this cut is to allow the Vectra tape,

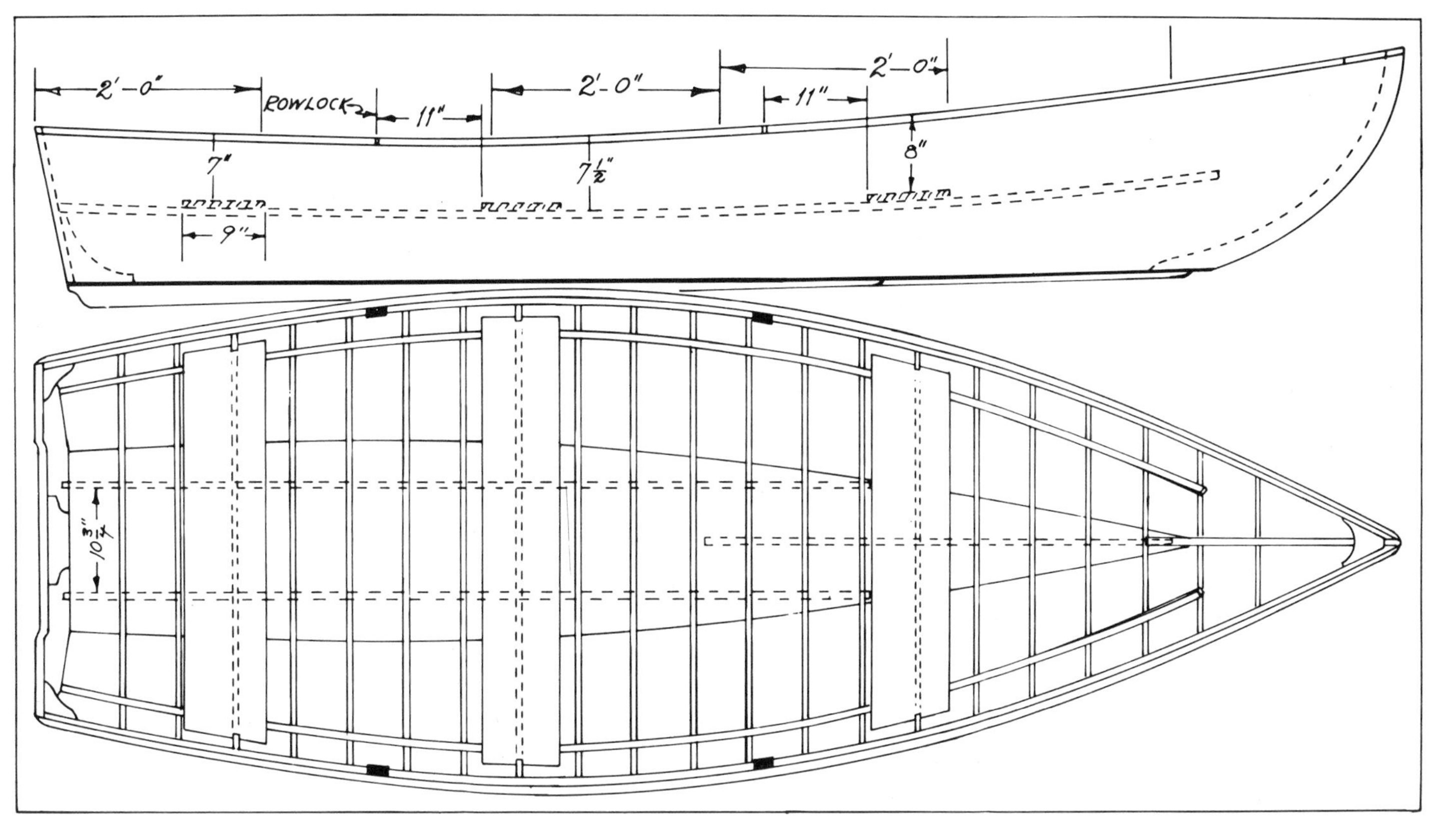

which will eventually bind the seam, to lie flush with the surface of the plywood. Thus, when the final outer covering of polypropylene fabric is applied, the seams will not stand out from the rest of the hull as they otherwise would.

In planking, when the plywood strakes are fitted one to the other, the edges should be beveled to fit tightly on the inside, yet stand open on the outside, say about ⅛-inch for ¼-inch plywood planking. The strakes as they are fitted are nailed to the molds. As these nails are only temporary and must be drawn later when the hull shell is removed from the molds, some provision must be made for getting at the heads, although the nails must be set down with enough force to hold the strakes firmly against the molds. This can be done by putting washers of leather or thick cardboard under the heads, or by using a double-headed staging nail. The six-penny size should be large enough for ¼-inch plywood.

OFFSETS IN FEET, INCHES & EIGHTHS TO OUTSIDE OF TRANSOM AND STEM, INSIDE PLANK & BOT.

STATIONS		TRAN	5	4	3	2	1	BOW
HEIGHTS	SHEER	1-4-1	1-3-4	1-3-2	1-3-6	1-5-7	1-9-0	2-0-3
	1	1-0-2	0-11-2	0-10-5	0-10-7	1-0-7	1-4-3	1-9-4
	2	0-8-2	0-7-0	0-6-2	0-6-4	0-8-6	1-0-5	1-5-7
	3	0-4-5	0-3-4	0-2-3	0-2-6	0-4-6	0-8-5	1-1-5
	4	0-2-3	0-1-4	0-0-6	0-0-4	0-2-4	0-5-4	0-8-6
	BOT.	0-0-0	0-0-0	0-0-0	0-0-0	0-0-5	0-1-3	0-1-4
HALF-BREADTHS	SHEER	1-6-3	1-10-6	2-0-7	2-0-0	1-7-4	0-11-4	—
	1	1-6-2	1-10-1	2-0-3	1-11-4	1-6-6	0-10-6	—
	2	1-5-5	1-8-5	1-10-6	1-9-4	1-5-2	0-9-4	—
	3	1-3-4	1-5-5	1-6-7	1-5-6	1-1-4	0-7-2	—
	4	1-0-6	1-1-6	1-2-3	1-0-6	0-9-2	0-4-2	—
	BOT.	0-9-0	0-10-1	0-10-0	0-8-2	0-5-3	0-0-7	—

4 5 T.
1
2 3

After all the strakes are fitted and nailed in place on the molds, as well as permanently screwed to the transom and inner portion of the stem, the V-ed openings along the meeting edges of the strakes or planks are filled with a stiff epoxy-Thiokol caulk, which when it cures will be both strongly adhesive and somewhat resilient. It will not push through to the inside if the strakes fit tightly on their inner surface, but if they do not fit in some places, no matter, for temporary strips of masking tape applied on the inside will keep the caulk from oozing through.

After this caulk has cured and the excess has been cut or sanded away, 2-inch Vectra tapes are laid in the shallow depressions previously cut for them and are stapled or tacked where necessary to hold them in place. The tapes are then saturated with epoxy resin. When this has hardened (and it is best to let it cure at least a couple of days for full strength), all the nails through the planks into the molds are drawn. The shell can then be lifted clear of the molds and turned right side up.

Now the inside of the seams is reinforced. First a narrow tape of Vectra set in epoxy resin is applied straddling the inside of each seam. For width, 1½ inches is ample for this first tape. Over it, another and wider tape is glued. This one should be 2½ inches to 3 inches wide, extending equally on either side of the seam. After this double-tape reinforcement is in place and cured, the hull is ready for framing or timbering.

The builder can buy his polypropylene tape already cut, or he can cut it himself. For the one-shot builder who would not have need for polypropylene tapes except for this particular job, it might be simpler and no more expensive to buy his tapes all cut rather than cut his own from cloth. Polypropylene tapes in various widths can be bought from many marine suppliers. For the outside of this boat one 50-yard roll of the 2-inch tape would suffice. For the inside, a 50-yard roll each of the 2-inch and the 3-inch tapes will do.

If the builder wishes to cut his own, he can heat-cut his tapes from standard 4.3-ounce Vectra or Versatex polypropylene boat fabric. This can be done with an ordinary soldering iron with a sharp tip, but it is best and easiest done with the type of soldering gun commonly used today by sailmakers to cut the modern synthetic sailcloths.

Another possibility for the amateur builder is to stretch out 12-foot lengths of polypropylene fabric on a clean floor or on two sheets of plywood laid end to end. This could be the plywood he plans to use for planking, but before it is cut. A few ¼-inch staples here and there, later to be removed with ice pick and pliers, will hold the cloth in place and keep it taut. After the cloth is stretched out and the widths of tape marked on it with a soft pencil and straight edge, or even a chalk line, a thin application of flexible epoxy/Thiokol mix is sparingly applied in a narrow strip along each dividing line. When this has set, the tapes are cut apart with shears along the previously marked dividing lines. The thin edging of the cured epoxy/Thiokol prevents raveling, yet is flexible enough not to interfere with the application of the tape to the seams.

It should be mentioned here that polypropylene fabric creases easily, and such creases are hard to get out except with a warm iron, hence lengths of cloth should not be folded, but should always be rolled for shipment or storage.

It should be obvious, even without specific mention, that a stapling gun is almost an essential for working with synthetic and glass fabrics used for reinforcing thermosetting resins. In many cases it is possible to put on the covering fabric dry, stretching it in place and tacking it with staples to prevent blisters, and then saturating it with a low viscosity resin formulation thin enough to penetrate through the fabric to the bonding surface beneath. In most cases of this sort, the resin is best applied sparingly—just enough to achieve a bond, but not enough to run or sag. After the resin has hardened, subsequent applications can be made, as desired, to build up the surface. For this, the advantage of a formulation that does not run off, even on a vertical surface, can hardly be overestimated.

FRAMING

For framing the hull, there are three options:

1. Sawn frames of several sorts can be scribed in and fitted.
2. Steamed timbers continuous from gunwale to gunwale can be bent in. These will touch the center of each strake of plank and may be fastened through from the outside with either rivets or small bronze screws. The spacing and cross section of such steam-bent ribs, preferably select white oak from butt logs, will depend on the size and type of the hull. They need not be large to add greatly to the strength of the hull.
3. Instead of steam-bent ribs, glued laminated ribs make an excellent substitute. Perhaps substitute is not just the right word, for such laminated ribs if properly installed will be just as good or better than steamed ones. These are also put in continuous from rail to rail. Strips of spruce, or possibly ash, thin enough to bend easily to the shape of the hull, are used. Epoxy adhesive is applied to the number required to make up the desired thickness. These are bent in, forced down into place so as to fit snugly against the sides of the boat like steamed timbers, and the layered strips are lined up with several small wooden-jawed clamps until the lamination can be secured in place. The fastenings can be either rivets or screws, put in from the outside directly before the adhesive hardens, exactly as in the case of steamed frames. These fastenings will hold the laminations in place until the glue hardens.

In the drawing I have shown the frames as located on 6-inch centers. This spacing need not be followed exactly. Somewhat smaller frames could be put in closer together, and larger ones farther apart. I would not recommend frames smaller than ⅝-inch square in cross-section, and would judge that a width of ¾ inch might be better with a thickness or molding of 9/16 inch.

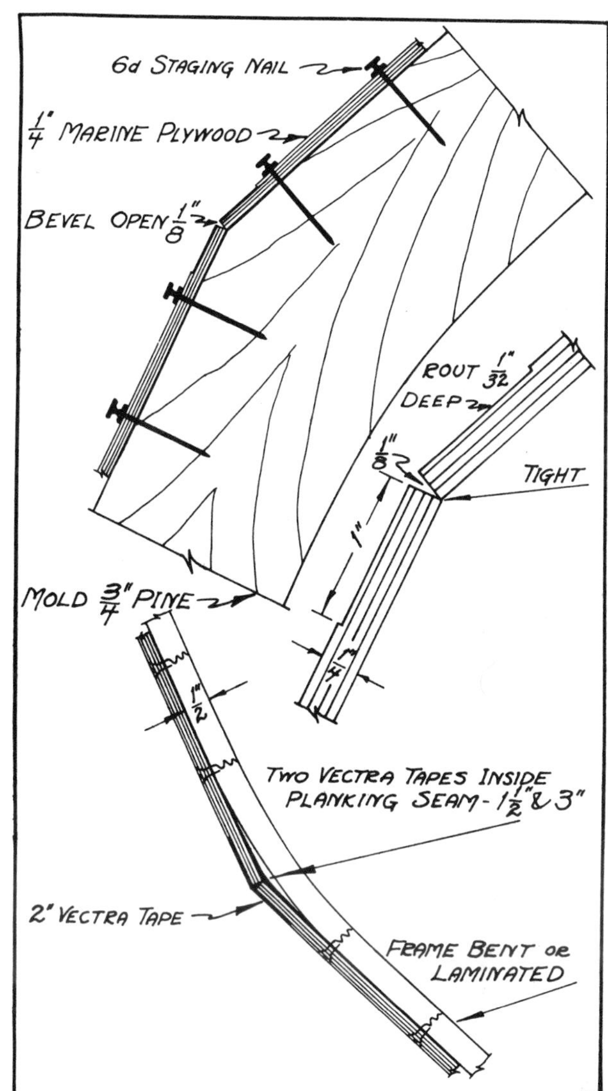

FINISHING OFF

After the ribs are fitted and in, the whole interior can be finished: risers, thwarts, breast hook, stern quarter knees, and inwales. When this work is complete, the boat is turned over.

The heads of rib fastenings and nail holes are faced with a stiff mix of epoxy resin and phenolic microballoons, or something equivalent. The Vectra strips covering the plank seams are also faced carefully. When this is hard, the whole outer surface of the hull is carefully sanded smooth and even in preparation for the outer covering of Vectra fabric.

The Vectra is put on dry, pulled tight, and

stapled where necessary to prevent wrinkling. After the first coat of resin has hardened, staples that show can be removed quite easily with an ice pick and pliers, but staples that come where the gunwales and outer stem are to be added may be left in, provided they are bronze or Monel.

The resin formulation for bonding the outside covering of Vectra should be quite thin and applied sparingly, yet there should be enough to penetrate the polypropylene fabric and to saturate it thoroughly. Any excess beyond this will tend to run and sag before it hardens, necessitating sanding and scraping in order to obtain a smooth surface before the second and final coat of resin is applied. Some may want to add an extra thickness of Dynel fabric on the bottom before the skegs go on, because of the superior abrasion resistance of Dynel. Instead of covering the outside with polypropylene fabric, Dynel fabric may be substituted with excellent results. Also, fiberglass tapes may be used instead of polypropylene tapes without adding enough weight to matter.

Last of all, the gunwale strips, outer stem and skeg or skegs are fastened on. The outer stem is made the same as in the Rangeley boat and is fastened on through the inside stem with several long screws. It merely finishes off the bow—the boat is quite tight without it. Finally, enough foam flotation should be installed under the seats to support four persons easily.

A 12-foot boat built in this manner with ¼-inch fir plywood, marine quality, should weigh under 100 pounds, and even appreciably less, if care is taken not to make the scantlings larger than they need to be. Of course, the addition of a centerboard, should one plan to sail the boat, will add weight. The 12-foot boat as originally designed had a stern buoyant enough to support an outboard motor up to 7 hp or thereabouts.

10 The Dory

The common, straight-sided fisherman's dory, also known as the Grand Banks dory, is an old favorite with amateur builders. If you think you might ever want to build yourself a dory, here are a couple to consider.

Banks dories used to be designed by the bottom length; the two dories detailed here are dories with 12- and 15-foot bottoms, respectively. The 12-footer is about as small as is generally useful and safe, yet it is not too large to be handled easily by a single oarsman. The 15-footer can be rowed by one man, but it takes two good oarsmen to handle it in rough water. There are dories 16 feet on the bottom, and larger, but one with a 15-foot bottom is about as large as most people want, though if you must, it would be quite easy to make this 15-footer (19 feet 5 inches LOA) a few feet longer.

The lines and specifications for the 12-footer were worked out carefully by myself from study and comparison of numerous dories for an article on the dory published in *Yachting* in March, 1954. The plans for the 15-footer are those of a dory designed and built during World War II for the U. S. Coast Guard by Hiram Lowell & Sons, the famous Amesbury, Massachusetts, dory builders. For all-around general use it is probably the best Banks dory model ever worked out. It is less heavy and clumsy than some of the old fishing models, which were generally made very deep to carry enormous loads of fish. Such deep models in a light condition are cranky and hard to handle. In making this dory shallower, it was possible to give the sides greater flare, all in all resulting in a boat much better suited for general use.

It goes without saying that the lines for either of these dories must be laid down full size. The lines are given to the inside of the plank, as is proper for lapstrake boats. The frames serve as molds.

Anyone who is building a dory for the first time, especially an amateur, should make a half model. The right scale is 1½ inches to the foot. On the half-model, the run, width, and laid-out shape of the plank can be found and taken off quite accurately if the model is carefully made. To get the run of the plank, one of the jobs that often gives the amateur trouble, use a thin strip of wood wide enough so that it cannot bend edgewise. Hold the strip or lining batten in position with thumbtacks. The straight sides of this dory make lining out the plank easy.

The first building operation is making the bottom assembly. The three or four pine boards that comprise the bottom are cut roughly to length, given straight edges with a slight caulking seam on the outside, and clamped together tightly; then the bottom

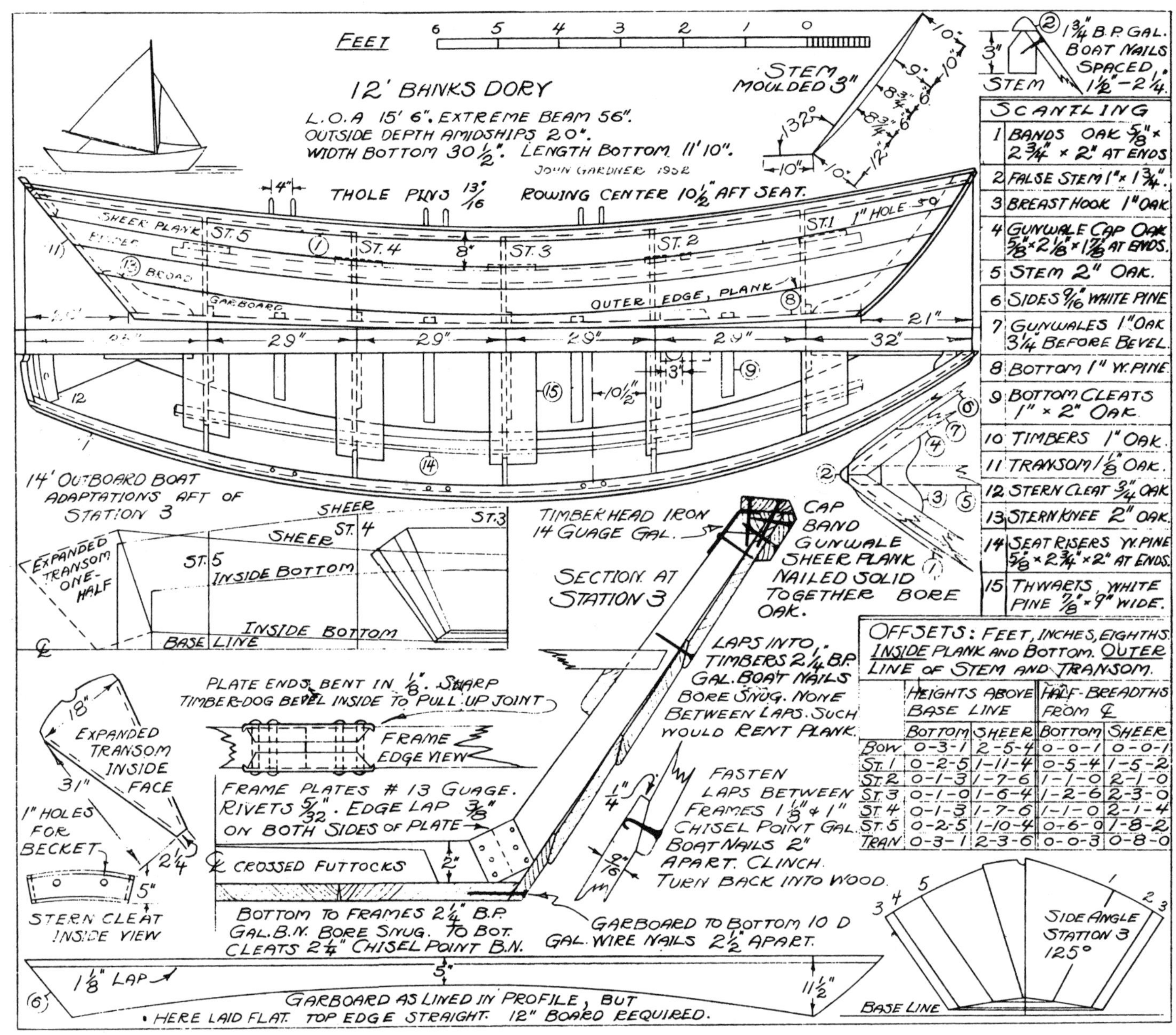

	HEIGHTS ABOVE BASE LINE		HALF-BREADTHS FROM ℄	
	BOTTOM	SHEER	BOTTOM	SHEER
BOW	0-3-1	2-5-4	0-0-1	0-0-1
ST. 1	0-2-5	1-11-4	0-5-4	1-5-2
ST. 2	0-1-3	1-7-6	1-1-0	2-1-0
ST. 3	0-1-0	1-6-4	1-2-6	2-3-0
ST. 4	0-1-3	1-7-6	1-1-0	2-1-4
ST. 5	0-2-5	1-10-4	0-6-0	1-8-2
TRAN	0-3-1	2-3-6	0-0-3	0-8-0

cleats are put on. The frame stations are marked, and the stem and transom are fastened on.

The next step is to set up for planking. This can be done either upside down or right-side up. The latter way makes it easier to clinch the lap fastenings as the planking proceeds. The bottom-up method is better for fairing and beveling the frames, bottom, stem, and transom surfaces to receive the garboards. This is difficult for beginners, and for that reason, the bottom-up method is possibly the best for the inexperienced.

When a dory is planked upside down, the bottom assembly is shored down and secured over a strongback, which is a wide, two-inch plank set on edge at a convenient height from the floor for working, rounded on its top edge to the curve of the rocker of the bottom, and notched out to take the frames and the bottom cleats. The strongback is set up over a centerline on the floor; this gives the location for the temporary cleating of the stem and transom of the floor while planking is in progress. The frame stations are squared out from the centerline, so that the frames can also be temporarily cleated to the floor, for which they are often left long to be sawed off when planking is finished.

After the bottom assembly with the frames attached has been set up as accurately as possible and secured, it is necessary to fair the framework for planking. This is a job that can't be hurried or slighted. It calls for patience and exactitude, and the final quality of the boat depends upon it. It is better to work over the whole boat several times, taking thin shavings sparingly here and there until the whole thing suddenly comes right all at once, than it is to attempt to do a finished fairing job a small piece at a time.

What is required for fairing is a thin, wide batten, say three or four inches wide, one-quarter or three-eighths of an inch thick, and long enough to reach across three or four frame stations. By bending this around the frames, bottom edge, and stem and transom bevels, it is easy to detect any lumps, unfairness, or wrong bevels.

The garboards must fit perfectly, that is, wood to wood along the entire length of the bottom and up on the fayed edges of the stem and transom. Otherwise, the boat will leak. The secret of a tight boat is to bevel the bottom and other parts so that the inside is a little strong, and the outside a little slack. Never the other way. Thus, when the fastenings are in and pulled up tight, the upper, inside edge of the bottom will press very tightly against the inside of the plank, or even dig into the soft pine or cedar a little. If the outside stands open slightly, no matter. A thin thread of cotton can be tucked in carefully, but never hard enough to force the plank.

The garboard is fastened to the bottom with 10d galvanized wire nails. It is best to drill a fine lead hole for the nail to follow, but not large enough to cut down the holding power of the nail. Try drilling in a scrap block of pine to get the right fit. To get the right angle for the drill, so as not to split out through the bottom, sight for the lead holes parallel to a piece of board laid flat across the bottom. Such directions may seem elementary, but fastening the garboards is critical, and the inexperienced builder had best take all the precautions necessary on this one to avoid mistakes. A little extra bottom thickness helps in construction; it also helps later when the boat is dragged over rocks and beached. For myself, I'd rather have the bottom of 1-inch-thick pine than the ⅞-inch dimension shown on the Lowell plan.

The laps are not hard to do on a straight-sided dory. If a person is not used to chisel-point nails, it is well to practice clinching a few before going on the laps. Please remember that they must be driven with their wide chisel edges cutting across the grain and shearing it, otherwise they will act as wedges, surely splitting the laps. In clinching, the thin points must be turned by the hold-on so that they return and re-enter the wood, drawing up tight with the finishing raps of the hammer. In place of chisel point nails, rivets may be used to fasten the laps. For rivets use 6d copper cut or wire nails headed up over burrs. Today, chisel point dory nails are all but impossible to obtain, so copper rivets will probably be used.

The planks should be fastened to the frames or ribs with a single fastening only, through the lap, as specially indicated on the detail for the 12-foot dory. Other fastenings into the frames through the middle of the planks, and especially in the middle of the garboards, will surely split the planks in time. The wider the dory planks, the more chance they need to come and go.

Standard dory fastenings are galvanized nails. But screws may be substituted throughout. Perhaps screws are easier for the amateur. I, myself, would not change the 10d galvanized wire nail fastening for the garboards in the bottom. Some are trying Monel Anchorfast nails for this. But ordinary galvanized wire nails hold well, and last as long as the wood.

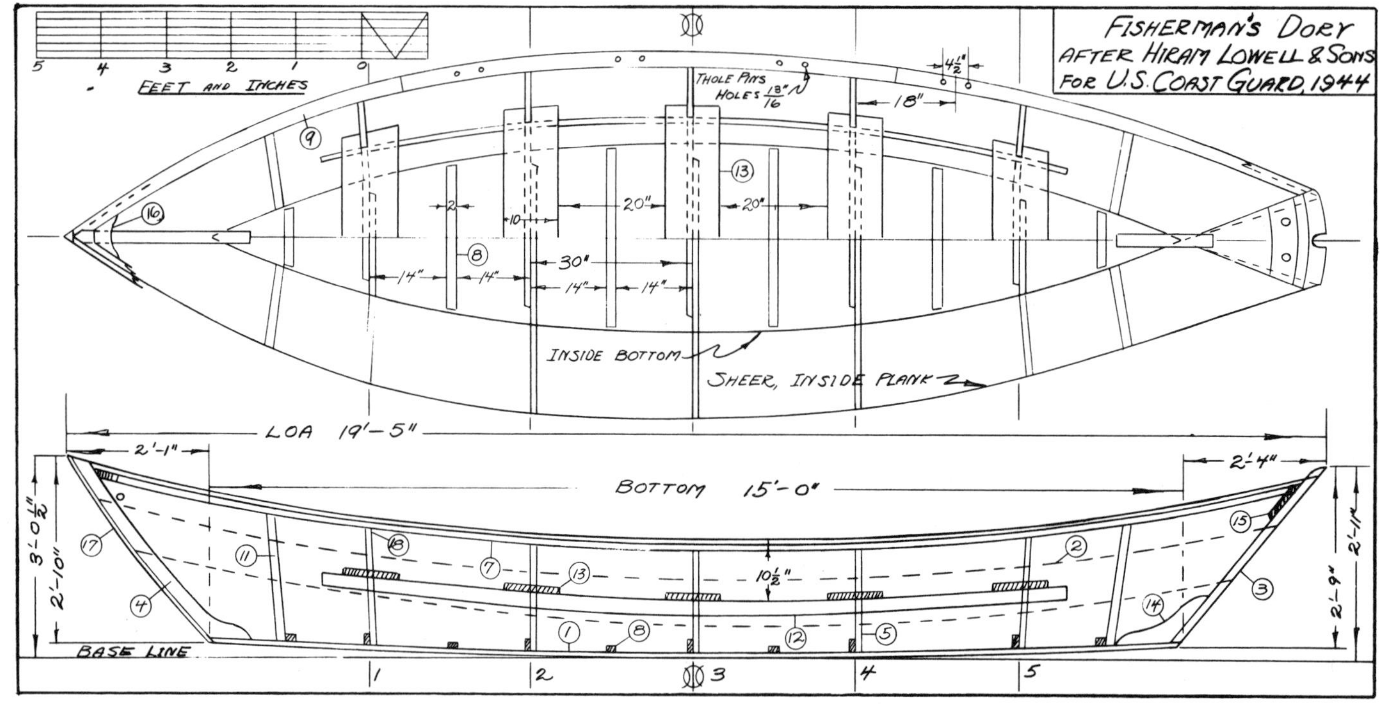

White pine is the standard planking wood for dories. In New England, where the dory originated, good, country white pine is still fairly easy to come by, but not always in wide widths. A few knots, even loose ones, do no harm. In fact, they mean tougher lumber. Loose knots can be bored out and replaced by a tapered pine plug. The old dory builder often puts loose knots back, nailing them in with a small clinch nail going through one edge, bored for, of course. (See the next chapter, on the Swampscott dory, for more on dory lumber.)

The 15-foot dory is shown with three strakes. The boat might just as well be planked with five. The garboard need not be more than three inches wide at its narrowest part amidships. (See the typical dory garboard shape in the detail drawing for the 12-foot dory.) In fact, the garboards could be made of two pieces, spliced at the midpoint. The sheer strake can be spliced also, as was always done in the case of Swampscott dories whose shape gave a very crooked sheer strake.

If, as has been suggested, the planking is worked out first on a half-model, it may be planned to utilize available widths and lengths of boards, and real economy can be achieved in this day of scarce and expensive lumber. Actually, every strake in the boat could be spliced up out of two pieces, provided the splices were, with the exception of the garboards, kept at least within one-third of the length of the boat from the ends. Closer to the ends would be better, for the greatest strain is at the center of the boat. Also, splices would need to be alternated from one end to the other of the boat—one strake spliced near the bow, the next near the stern, and so on.

The straight sides of a Banks dory are easily covered with plywood in a single sheet. But with a little planning to utilize available and inexpensive lumber, standard planking is no doubt cheaper and better for the amateur.

After the dory is planked, the rest is easy, hardly requiring any special directions or comment. Finishing is adequately covered in the detail drawings.

Banks dories often carried a short, detach-

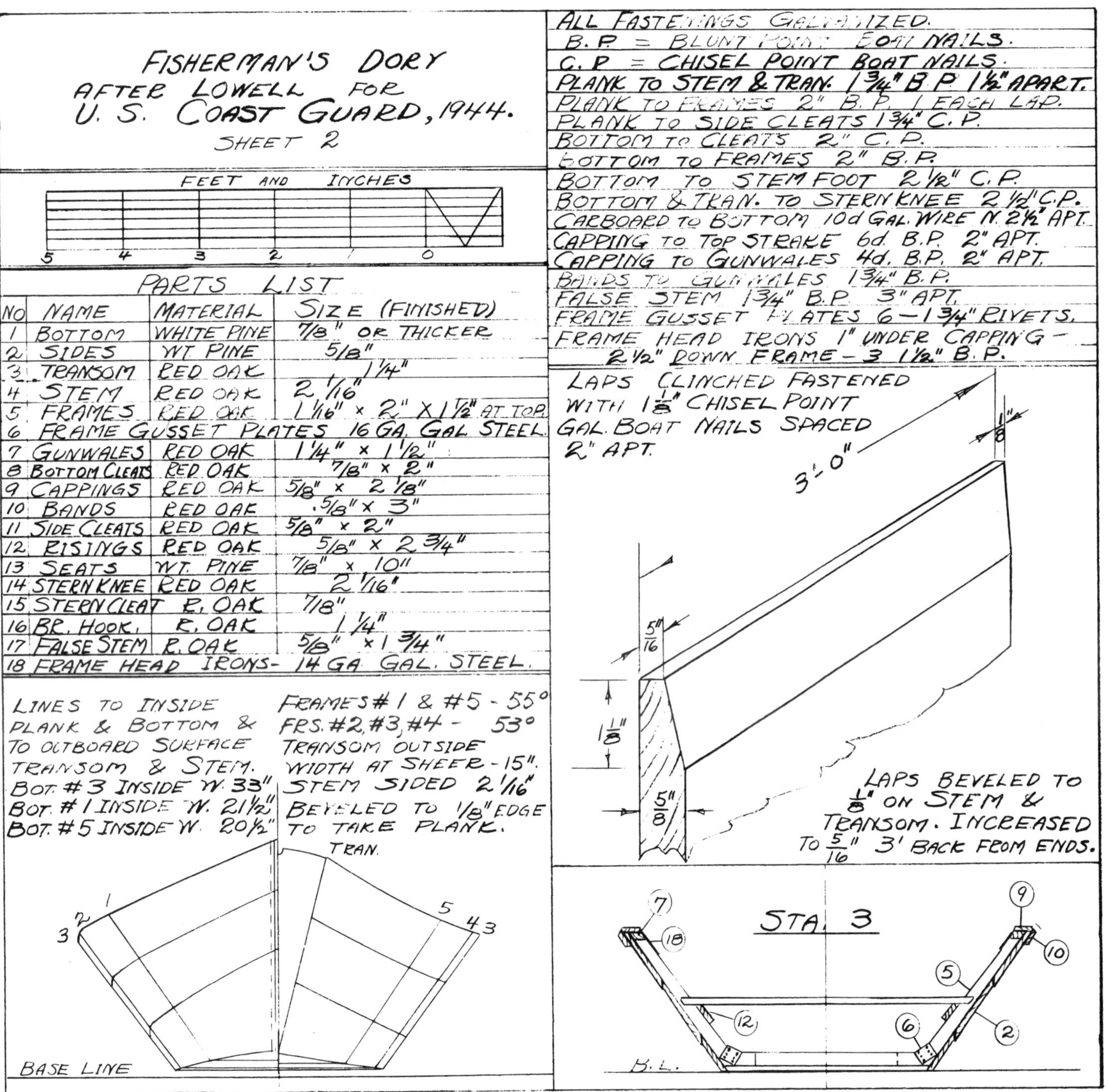

able mast and a small loose-footed sail, and were steered with an oar. It is easy with their flat bottom to install a centerboard. A modified Banks dory with centerboard and sailing rig can be found on page 91 of Howard Chapelle's *American Small Sailing Craft*, W. W. Norton, New York, 1951. Chapelle features a Cape Ann sailing dory from Annisquam, Mass., just outside of Gloucester.

11 A Modified Swampscott Dory

Here is a Swampscott dory that is not too large for one man, or even a strong boy, to handle, yet large enough to retain all of the excellent qualities for which the type is noted. Certain minor modifications have been made to adapt it for amateur construction and to permit the use of materials currently to be had at most retail lumber dealers. Its overall length is not so great as to require building space in excess of what is available in most home workshops.

This dory is much like a 17-foot model built in the Small Craft Boatshop at Mystic Seaport. By only slightly lifting the angle of the tombstone stern and at the same time raising the stem profile by a like amount, I have shortened the overall length of this boat by a foot without affecting its seakeeping qualities to the slightest degree. The waterline length remains almost the same.

Built as drawn, the modified model as measured on top from the extreme overhang of the transom to the fore edge of the false stem, will not exceed 16 feet by more than 3 inches. But if the spacing of the three frames is decreased from 34 inches to 32 inches, it is possible to bring the overall length a few inches under 16 feet.

First, let me say that I don't believe that shortening the boat in this way would affect its performance to any significant extent. Actually, I doubt if any difference could be noticed under ordinary conditions of use. Perhaps the shortened model would be a few seconds slower in a race. I doubt if the boat's weatherly qualities would suffer at all.

However, this difference in length could be important in a situation where 16 feet of overall length has been set by statute or administrative edict as the cut-off point between regulation of various sorts. Some of the regulations applying to small craft are arbitrary, ill-advised, and in general nuisances well worth bypassing if possible.

Decreasing the frame spacing by only 2 inches will not require any significant alteration in the lines. They will still fair easily. The only adjustment called for will come in lining out the bottom, and this will hardly be noticeable, requiring only slight shifts in the batten to get a fair curve. The stem, stern transom, and frames will all remain exactly the same as presently drawn.

Shortening the dory will not affect her appearance in the slightest. This dory, by the way, is a really handsome model, as I was able to observe when I had completed the working half model on the scale of 1½ inches to the foot, made to prove the lines and to lay out the spacing and shapes of the planks.

The true Swampscott dory, of which this boat is a good example, is essentially a round-

Rowing craft in the harbor at Marblehead, Massachusetts, were photographed by Fred Preu shortly after 1900. The Swampscott dory in the middle foreground is similar to the one under consideration. (Photo courtesy of the San Francisco Maritime Museum)

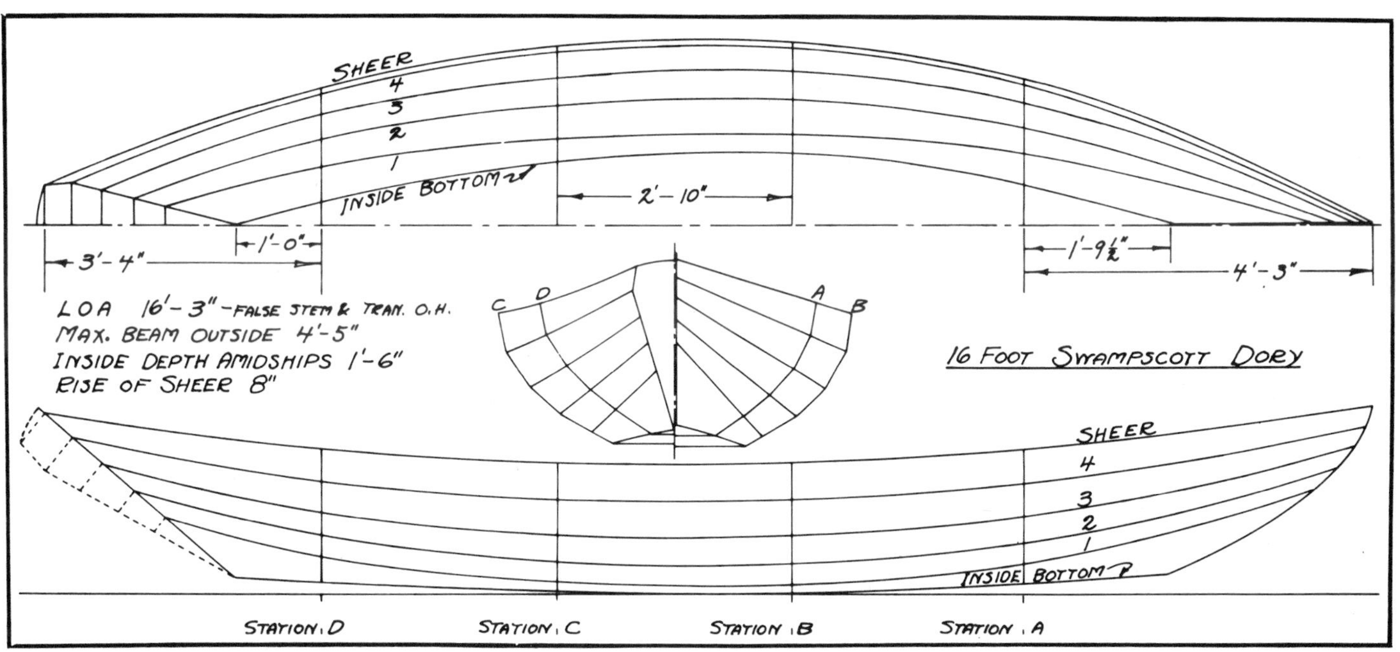

bottom boat, yet with enough flat in its relatively narrow board bottom to sit upright on the beach when it grounds out. For a boat that is to be beached frequently, this is an especially desirable feature, particularly as it permits a double bottom, the outer layer of which is easily renewed when it wears thin from dragging over rocks.

These Swampscott boats are the aristocrats of the dory clan, and are not to be confused with their clumsier, more crudely built cousins, the heavy, slab-sided working dories of the Grand Banks fishermen. True, in some features of their construction Swampscott and Grand Banks dories are similar, but in performance there is a vast difference. Swampscott dories row and handle so much easier than the Banks model. Whether they are faster under oars remains open to argument, but certainly they are every bit as good sea boats. Their marked

16 FOOT SWAMPSCOTT DORY							
		STEM	STA. A	STA. B	STA. C	STA. D	STERN
HEIGHTS	BOTTOM	0-2-7	0-1-3	0-0-0	0-0-3	0-1-5	0-2-2
	1	1-2-5	0-4-1	0-1-2	0-1-6	0-5-2	0-10-7
	2	1-5-6	0-7-1	0-4-1	0-4-4	0-8-2	1-2-4
	3	1-8-7	0-11-0	0-8-0	0-8-2	0-11-4	1-6-2
	4	1-11-6	1-3-5	1-1-2	1-1-2	1-3-7	1-10-0
	SHEER	2-2-4	1-8-4	1-6-4	1-6-4	1-8-3	2-1-4
WIDTHS	BOTTOM	0-0-1	0-5-6	0-10-1	0-8-7	0-3-3	0-0-2
	1	0-0-1	0-10-1	1-0-6	1-0-2	0-8-3	0-2-4
	2	0-0-1	1-1-6	1-5-6	1-4-7	1-0-0	0-3-5
	3	0-0-1	1-5-2	1-9-6	1-8-6	1-3-5	0-4-7
	4	0-0-1	1-7-7	2-1-0	2-0-4	1-6-6	0-6-0
	SHEER	0-0-1	1-8-5	2-1-6	2-1-4	1-7-4	0-5-4
OFFSETS MEASURED IN FEET, INCHES & EIGHTHS TO INSIDE OF PLANKING & BOTTOM & TO OUTSIDE OF STEM & TRANSOM.							

superiority over the Banks model for recreational use lies in their greater ease of handling. In normal conditions a youngster could manage the boat under consideration easily, but he definitely could not handle a Banks dory of the same size.

Yet, this is not a small boat by any means. With an inside depth amidships of 18 inches and a maximum inside beam of 52 inches, this boat could easily take six men or an equivalent load without undue reduction of freeboard. Because of its ample beam and depth, this boat would do well if rigged to sail, for which it can be adapted quite easily. Its flat board bottom makes the addition of a centerboard trunk easy.

MATERIALS

New England dories came into being when native lumber was plentiful and cheap, when beautiful clear boards of northern white pine 14 inches, 15 inches, and even 18 inches wide were to be had for a few cents a board foot. Dories were designed to be built with a few wide strakes, generally four to a side, in order to be planked up quickly and thus save labor and cut building costs. In all probability, neither the Banks dory nor the round-sided Swampscott dory would ever have taken form except for an abundance of wide pine boards.

Now that the supply of wide pine dory boards has almost run out, we have to find other means of keeping these fine old heritage boat types alive. It is possible to build dories from plywood, but plywood has a number of disadvantages and has recently jumped sky-high in price. Besides, some people just don't like plywood in boats.

For this dory we have worked out an alternate method whereby pine can still be used for planking in the old way. This was done by relining the hull for five strakes of plank instead of four, and by specifying composite strakes made up of two or three short lengths joined by glued splices. This permits the use of ordinary No. 2 common white pine boards.

No. 2 common pine is still fairly reasonable in price, as present-day prices go, and generally available. Except for the garboards, which will take 10 inch widths, the boards required will only be 8 inches or less. When planks are pieced up from two or three short lengths, it is often possible to cut out and get rid of bad knots and other defects which otherwise would make the board unusable for a single-length strake. Sound, tight, round knots of small or medium size, when not too numerous and bunched too closely together, are quite acceptable. In fact, a few sound knots scattered through a plank strengthen rather than weaken it, making it less liable to split or "rent," as the boatbuilders say. In the old dories the wide ends of the garboards frequently split as the boat aged, especially if the boat was planked with clear, knot-free lumber. This was one of the weakest points of traditional dory construction, which now with narrower planks and knotty lumber, can be avoided all but completely. The size, number, placement, and type of knots that are allowable is a matter of judgment for which there is no hard and fast general rule. Common sense must govern.

Small, loose knots should be bored out and plugged. Holes reamed to take plugs should be slightly larger on the outside, and pine plugs must be carefully planed to the right taper to fit. These are driven tightly, but not so tightly as to split the plank. Glue should be applied to bond them securely, although in the past, before we had waterproof glue, plugs put in without glue held perfectly well.

The boards for the bottom, also pine, can have numerous sound knots, more than the side plank and larger, because the bottom boards are thicker, and because they don't have to withstand bending strains. In fact a pine bottom will be tougher and wear better with plenty of knots, but these should be kept away from the edges as much as possible so as not to interfere with the garboard fastenings. In both sides and bottom, "spike" knots, so called, which cut across a board and weaken it unduly, should be avoided.

The idea that one has to have clear lumber, and that a sound, serviceable boat, at least a dory, cannot be built without it, is a holdover from former times and is just not so. Of course as already noted, common sense must be used, but what is involved is not so critical that there is likely to be any trouble, if one observes the cautions and follows the directions given.

Splices, if properly made, are just as strong as the uncut board, and when planed smooth and painted cannot be detected. Their locations should be staggered, that is, the splices in any one strake should be separated by a couple of feet or so from those in the strakes directly above or below it.

In this boat the garboards might well be made up of three pieces of equal length, the plank above of two pieces spliced in the middle, the third plank of three lengths and so on. Of course, if full length boards for the straighter strakes should be available, so much the easier and better.

Curved strakes are better spliced up from several shorter lengths. They are frequently stronger than unspliced strakes because in the spliced strake, short, cross grain can be avoided. All of the strakes in the Adirondack guideboats were spliced from two and three shorter pieces for this reason; these strakes were plenty strong even though the builders did not have modern waterproof glue. In this dory the only strake besides the garboard that has any curve to speak of is the sheer, and the sheer planks in Swampscott dories were always spliced anyway, the splice coming about one-third of the way from the stern. In this boat two of the five strakes are nearly dead straight.

The planking layout or diagram given on page 88 for this dory was carefully spiled from an accurately made half model, and so the planking shapes and widths shown should be pretty close, close enough to use as a reliable guide in the selection and splicing of plank. By allowing a little extra width, the plank can be laid out and spliced up ahead of time. Of course the exact shape will have to be spiled directly from the planking set-up of the bottom frame assembly. So far as I know, this is the first time a dimensioned planking diagram has ever been worked out for a how-to design for building a dory. It will make the planking job simpler and easier, and should save a lot of time and lumber.

Plank splices could be fitted and glued on the boat as the planking operation proceeds, but I don't recommend this. It will be far better and easier to lay out the splices and glue them ahead of time. They can then be planed smooth and the full length plank spiled and laid out in one operation. There is much less chance of error.

To a great extent the strength of this hull will depend on its clinker construction, and good lap fastenings are of particular importance. Copper rivets should be used. I strongly recommend the heavier European dished roves and the square-section copper boat nails now available in this country from several suppliers. They are well worth the high price. The dished roves have greater holding power and grip the wood with greater compressive force when the rivet is made up, and are in every way far superior to ordinary flat roves or burrs.

I have shown the hood ends of the plank fastened into the stem with 2-inch galvanized boat nails; 1½-inch or 1¾-inch No. 12 screws could just as well be used.

First choice for the stem stock, sided 2

inches and molded 2½ inches, is dry white oak. Red oak is almost as good. If a plank can be found with a run of grain which favors the curve of the stem, so much the better. If not, straight grain will do, but the stem should be laid out so that the cross grain is equally distributed and does not come all in one end.

If oak is not to be had, any lasting hardwood can be substituted, preferably with a grain that favors the stem curve. Locust, although heavy, would be excellent; should locust be used, the stem could be molded slightly smaller, say 2¼ inches instead of 2½ inches. Apple wood also would be fine. In fact, there is nothing better for dory frames than sound apple limbs of the right bend or curvature.

In case suitable hardwood is not available, good quality Douglas fir or even longleaf yellow pine may be substituted for the stem. When these softer woods are used, it would be wise to increase the molded dimension somewhat to compensate, say to ¾ inches or even as much as 3 inches. The extra weight would be negligible. Also if softer wood is used for the stem, the fastenings through the hood ends of the planking should be larger.

Another possibility is a glued-up stem using epoxy adhesive. This can be made of smaller pieces fitted together, if a single large plank of sufficient size cannot be found (see the Appendix for more on laminating).

The transom can be Douglas fir or yellow pine just as well as oak. If oak is used, it could be planed to 1¹⁄₁₆ inches thick to save weight. It is better to use red oak than white, because

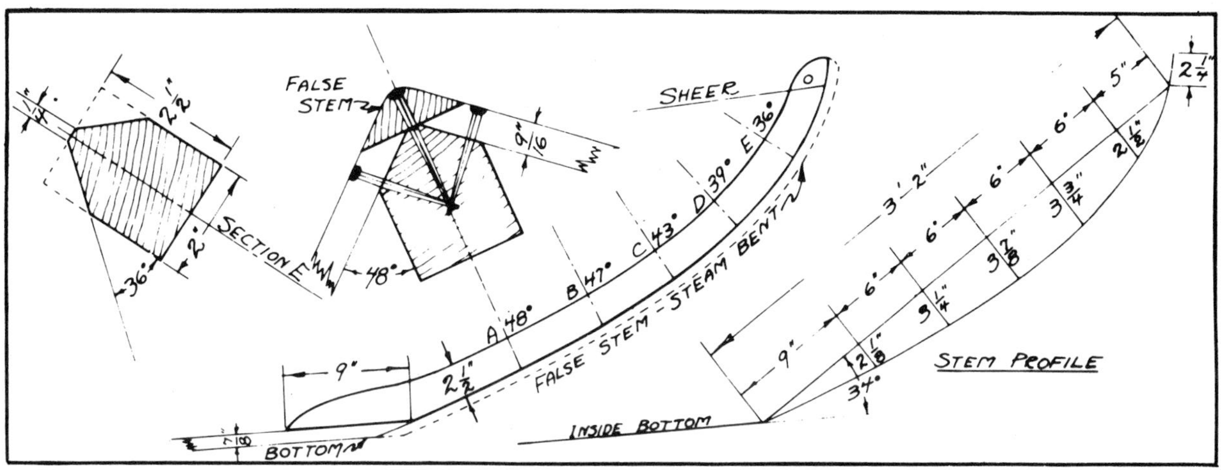

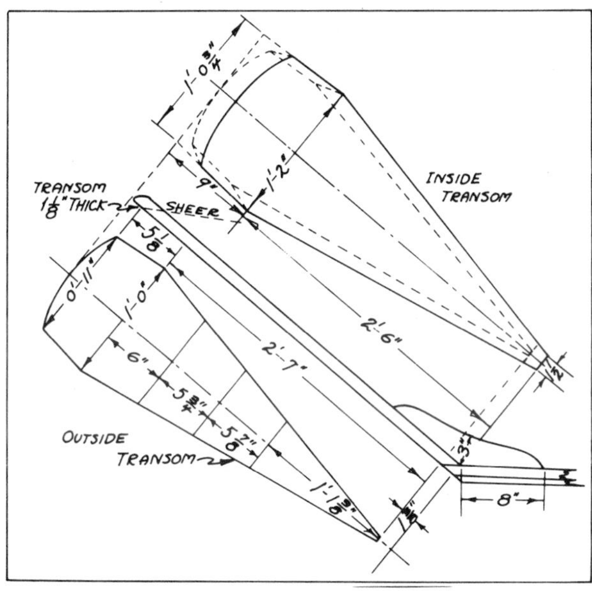

white oak is heavier and is more apt to pull out of shape in wide widths. A maximum width of 14 inches is required, which in most cases would mean making up the transom from two pieces. A heavy cleat across the inside face just below the sheer serves to tie the stern together, if the transom is made of two pieces, and to prevent splitting if it's got out of a single width of plank. The dimensions and bevels for the transom given in the drawing were derived from the lines layout and checked against the working half-model, which was accurately made to scale. They should be close. However, it would be prudent in beveling not to cut to the line at first, but to leave a little wood for final fairing after the set-up has been made, preliminary to planking. This goes for the stem as well.

CONSTRUCTION

The boat should be planked bottom up. The bottom is laid out first, cut to shape, and cleated together. Its edges may be beveled to receive the garboard planks, but for someone building a dory for the first time, it is probably best to leave this beveling operation until the completed frame and bottom assembly is secured bottom-up and in place on the strongback. When the bottom has been cut out and cleated, the stem, the frames, and the stern transom and knee, which have been made up separately, are put in position on the bottom and fastened. All of these members will have to be beveled.

Bevels can be taken ahead of set-up from the full-size laydown of the lines, which according to good boatbuilding practice should be made and faired before any woodwork is started. However, for the beginner who may not trust completely the bevels he takes from his laydown, it would be best, perhaps, not to cut the bevels down all the way to their lines until the boat has been set up and he can check these bevels with a batten. Wood is easily taken off when necessary, but it is much

A 17-foot swampscott dory in frame on a strongback at the Mystic Small Craft Boatshop. The boat is just about ready for planking. (Photo by Mary Anne Stets)

more difficult to pad out bevels that were cut too deep. Besides, in almost all cases it will be necessary to fair the bottom-and-frame assembly more or less extensively after it is set up and before planking starts.

The set-up is made over a strongback, which is a wide 2-inch plank secured on edge at working height, with its upper edge cut to the curve of the inner bottom and notched to receive the frames and bottom cleats. The ends of the strongback are likewise cut to receive the stern knee and the bottom end of the stem. The strongback supports the preliminary assembly of bottom, frames (which serve as molds), stem, and stern transom during the planking operation. After planking is completed, the planked-up shell is lifted off the strongback, turned right-side-up, and the laps are riveted in one operation. Of course, all the nails were previously in place, having been driven as the planks went on.

If the planks are carefully fitted and properly beveled, the riveting operation can be put off until the boat is turned over, when it is done all at once. Of course, the boat could be built right-side-up, and the laps riveted plank by plank, but it would be ever so much harder to bevel the bottom correctly to receive the garboards and to fit the changing lap bevels. The planking operation is far easier and surer when done bottom up over a strongback.

The accompanying drawings will bear some study. Comments and explanations for the numbered references follow:

1. Sheer plank, ½″ thick white pine. For a boat intended for extra hard use, a plank thickness of 9/16″ is recommended. The weight of the boat would not be greatly increased

thereby. This plank has some curve and could be just as well spliced from three pieces. The inwale and cap add extra reinforcement.

2. Frames sided ⅞″, molded 2″ to 3″. Approximately 2¼″ through the knuckles, tapering to 1½″ at the top. Oak should be used, although substitutes such as Douglas fir can be used with proportional increase in dimensions to give equivalent strength. As shown here, two halves are reinforced with a strip of ⅞″ oak across the bottom. Should be cut from natural-crook lumber to avoid cross grain.

There are a number of ways of making dory frames. They can be made in three sections cut out of ordinary oak boards spliced where bottom and sides come together with galvanized iron gusset plates on either side, through riveted. Instead of iron gusset plates, longer plywood gussets on either side, glued and screwed or riveted are acceptable. It is even possible to laminate continuous one-piece frames from thin strips glued on a form.

3. Reinforcing strip connecting to frame halves. Oak, ⅞″ x 2⅛″.

4. Also Nos. 16 and 17. Bottom 15/16″ pine. To be not less than ⅞″ nor more than 1″. Can be two or three boards wide.

5. Outer or false bottom. ½″ thick. Pine, spruce, oak, elm, etc. Put on with screws to be removable and renewable. Function, to take wear from dragging over beaches and rocks.

6. Seat riser, ⅝″ pine, 3½″ wide tapering to 2½″ at ends. Same as No. 21.

7. Thwarts. Pine or spruce ⅞″ to 1″ thick, 8″ wide. Removable, notched to fit frames but not fastened to risers.

8. Inwale. Oak ⅞″ x 1½″ tapered to 1″ at bow, 1¼″ at stern.

9. Cap. Oak, ½″ thick by 2″ wide to cover inwale and top edge of sheer plank. Sawn to shape, not bent. Extends from forward to after frame. Replaced from after frame to stern, and from forward frame to stem, with a narrower strip, beveled on its inner edge, which covers the edge of the sheer planks and laps on the inwale about ¼″.

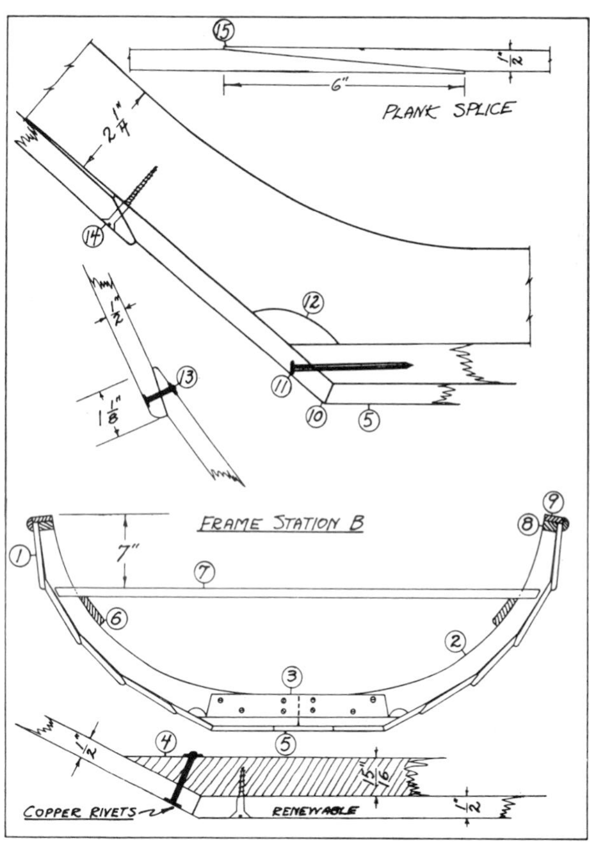

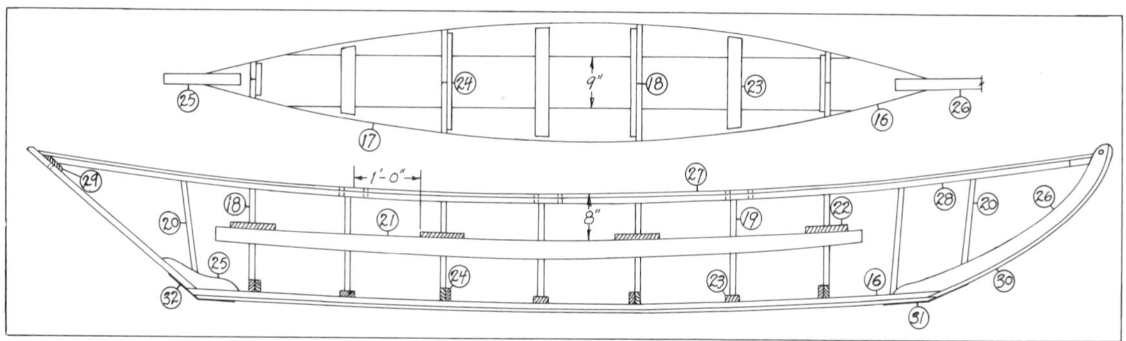

10. Note that the bottom edge of the garboard is not beveled off in line with the bottom, but is left square or approximately square for the false bottom to fit into.

11. At the ends of the boat where the bottom bevel is not suited to riveting, the lower edge of the garboard plank is fastened to the bottom with 10d nails, spaced 2½″ to 3″ apart. Nails can be galvanized iron common nails, bronze wire, or annular.

12. Limber to drain bottom of boat. When metal gussets are used to join frame futtocks, the joint in the frame is here.

13. The laps between the frames are fastened with copper rivets spaced 2½″ to 3″.

14. The laps are fastened into the sawn frames with 1¾″ No. 10 bronze wood screws.

15. Plank splices are made 12 times the thickness of the plank—½″ thick plank, 6″ splice. Scarphs are not planed to a sharp or feather edge, but are left ⅟₁₆″ thick on the ends. The splice clamps better this way, and the extra ⅟₁₆″ is planed off after the glue has thoroughly set. Scarphs are planed fair and true with a sharp block plane or smoother. Either epoxy or resorcinol glue can be used. Pressure is applied with a piece of oak on either side of the splice, held by four C-clamps. Wax the oak pressure blocks to prevent sticking.

16 & 17. Bottom boards.

18. Frame, same as No. 2.

19. Intermediate bent frames, oak 1″ x ½″. Steam bent and copper riveted through laps.

20. Cant frames in the ends of the dory. Same as No. 19.

21. Seat riser, same as No. 6.

22. Thwarts, same as No. 7.

23. Bottom cleats. Oak. ⅞″ x 2¼″.

24. Frame reinforcement, same as No. 3.

25. Transom knee. Oak, hackmatack, or fir. 1¾″ thick. 16″ overall length.

26. Stem. Oak, 2″ thick. Can be hackmatack or Douglas fir, laminated or solid.

27. Capping. Same as No. 9.

28. Inwale. Same as No. 8.

29. Transom cleat. Oak, ¾″ thick by 4½″ wide.

30. False stem. Oak, steam bent in place after planking is complete and plank ends faired.

31. Bronze strap to cover forward end of bottom and lower end of false stem.

32. Bronze strap, aft end of bottom and bottom of stern transom.

SAILING RIG

For those who would like to sail this Swampscott dory, as well as row her, I offer the following modifications. In adapting this dory for sail I have altered the interior arrangements of the rowing version in a few minor particulars. One of these was to raise the seat riser by one inch, which still leaves 6 inches between the surface of the rowing thwarts and the gunwales. One inch may seem a trivial amount, but it adds needed width to the centerboard without detracting from the rowing qualities of the boat. It is still comfortable to row. With the sail furled and the mast down and stowed in the boat, a single oarsman can row without interference from either thwart A or C, or both may be occupied at the same time with two men pulling. The thwart at station B can be left out entirely, and is not shown in the drawing. If desired, however, it could easily be installed in two pieces with the inboard ends supported by cleats screwed to the sides of the centerboard trunk.

As mentioned previously, the sailing balance of a small boat is affected by so many variables that it is difficult, and often impossible, to figure ahead of time just how the boat will behave in the water, and it is to be expected that adjustments will have to be made after launching and the first trial runs.

Charles G. Davis, who knew a great deal about small craft, both as a designer and as a sailor, was of the opinion that all too frequently in the design of a small sailboat the centerboard will be located too far forward. As it happens, this is especially true for some of the sailing dories, which in consequence have wicked weather helms.

Loading also has a lot to do with the sailing balance. Shifting weight forward or aft in a small boat can make a big difference under certain conditions, as is demonstrated by the behavior of the St. Lawrence River skiffs, which are sailed without rudders, steering being accomplished simply by moving back and forth in the boat to alter the trim.

In laying out the rig for this dory, I have done several things to enable adjustments in the sailing balance. For one thing, the centerboard has been made rather longer and larger than is usual for a boat of this size, and it is located well aft. By dropping it to different depths, or by raising it in the same manner, it will be possible to shift the boat's center of lateral resistance back and forth to some extent. To facilitate this, the oak board is given extra weight by adding a lead insert to give it positive drop, and it is raised by a rope pennant which makes fast to a cleat bolted to the oak capping of the centerboard trunk. In this manner the board is easily raised or lowered as desired.

In addition, there is a choice between two mast positions located 10 inches apart, which allows appreciable shift in the center of effort. By experimenting with mast position, centerboard depth, and weight placement in the boat, it should be possible to arrive at a combination giving satisfactory sailing balance, presumably with a slight weather helm, but not so much as to be tiring.

The indicated sail area is a moderate one with provision for reefing down in heavy weather. As there are no shrouds or stays, the entire rig as a unit is easily and quickly lifted out of the step for stowing in the boat. The spars are short enough to stow at one side, out of the way of the oarsman.

If desired, one might have one or more replacement rigs of smaller and/or larger size for different weather. This was a common practice early in this century at Marblehead, Beverly, and other towns on Boston's North Shore, where some dory fishermen had as many as three separate rigs—a large sail for summer racing, a medium working rig for the summer, and a small sail for winter fishing.

In the profile view on the next page showing a longitudinal section through the center of the boat, several features require additional com-

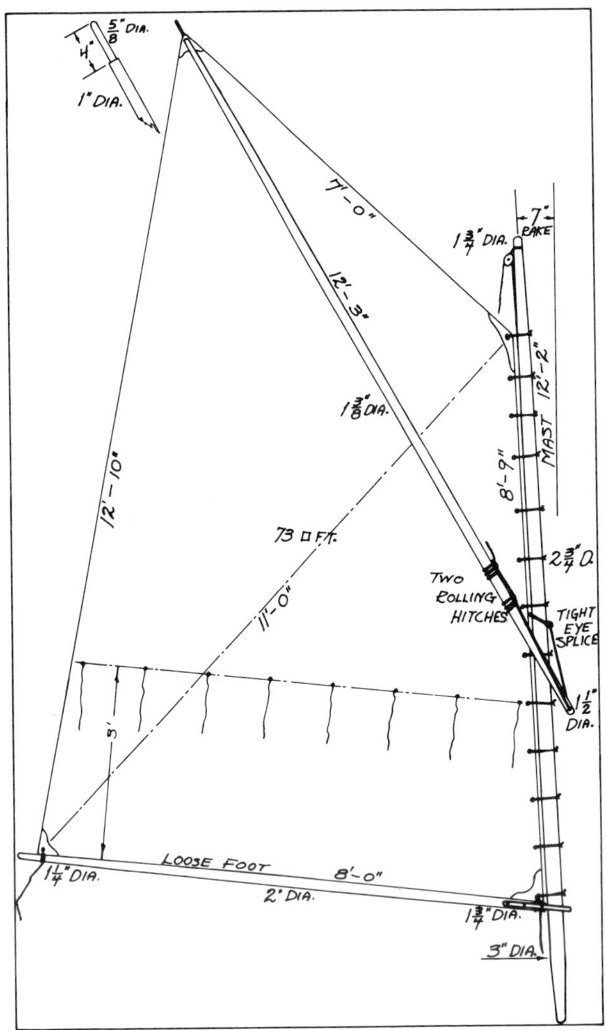

ment and explanation. The numbers in the explanation refer to the numbers in the drawing.

1. The forward thwart at station A is double width to permit two mast locations, and is braced and reinforced underneath with a fore-and-aft strip of oak 8 inches wide, and ⅞ inches thick. This should be well fastened from the top either with screws or rivets.

2. A pair of hanging knees is needed here for additional bracing. These should be oak, apple, or other hardwood, with a good run of grain—natural crooks, if available—and well fastened. As the riser is unsupported here for some 11 inches forward of the frame at station A, substantial knees at this location are a must.

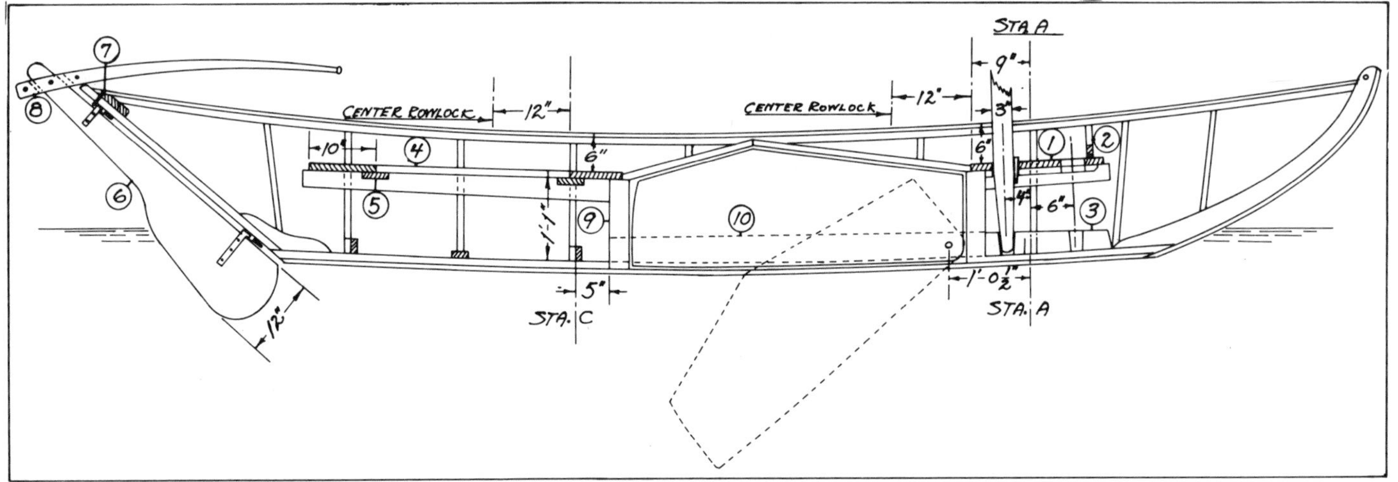

3. The mast step with its two tapered sockets for the end of the mast is in one piece molded 3 inches deep and notched over the bottom of the frame at station A. Four-and-one-half inches should give sufficient sided width. Pine or Douglas fir will do as well here as oak. The holes to receive the end of the mast should be accurately tapered for a snug fit to grip the end of the mast with enough friction to prevent it from jumping out easily. For further insurance against sudden lifting on the part of the unstayed mast, a soft pine wedge with a long taper fits in a slot about 1½" wide which is cut through the thwart on the forward side of the mast. If well fitted, a slight tap on top will secure the wedge against the mast, and it will be just as easily knocked out from the bottom in removing the mast.

4. Two fore-and-aft benches of the same stock as the cross thwarts and about 8 inches wide are fitted against the sides of the boat between the thwarts at stations C and D. These are for the convenience of the helmsman when the boat is sailing.

5. The oak blocks or cleats on the underside securing the ends of the fore-and-aft benches to the cross thwarts should be well fastened from the top with screws or rivets. The additional use here of epoxy glue would be desirable, as it would be elsewhere in the boat where members are fastened together in this way. Glue used in such places not only secures the joint, but if liberally applied, waterproofs it as well. Otherwise, when moisture collects between the mating surfaces of a joint, rot tends to start.

6. The rudder is made of oak ⅞ inches thick, with the blade tapered and thinned somewhat at the bottom and toward the outside. It can be got out of a single width of 12-inch board, or from two narrow boards pinned together with 5/16-inch drifts.

7. A removable pin ½ inch in diameter goes through the transom and the transom cleat, serving as a stopper to keep the rudder from slipping out. A push fit will suffice for easy removal, and it need not be otherwise secured.

8. Either oak or ash will do for a tiller, sided 2 inches at its after end to mortise for the rudder head, ⅞ inch thick. The mortise should be cut long enough to allow the tiller to swing up or down easily. The tiller pivots on a ½-inch diameter pin through the rudder head with a washer and cotter pin to hold it in. The after end of the tiller is reinforced with a through rivet on either side of the mortise. The tiller will, of course, be thinned and tapered both for appearance and to lighten it.

9. The end posts for the centerboard trunk are oak, molded 3 inches and sided 1¼ inches. This should give sufficient clearance for the ⅞ inch thick centerboard. The lower ends of these posts mortise through the bottom for caulking, but are covered by the false, or outer,

bottom. The ends of the bed logs are fastened to the end posts and each other with bolts passing through from side to side. Glue should be used here as well, to insure a strong watertight centerboard trunk.

10. Bed logs for the centerboard trunk, sided 2 inches and cut to fit the rocker of the bottom from pieces 4 inches wide, can very well be pine. Oak is not necessary for strength because of the substantial thickness of these members, made so as to give ample wood for bolting and to secure a lasting watertight fit with the bottom. In cutting through the bottom cleats in the way of the centerboard trunk, keep the cleats long enough for them to be notched into the sides of the bed logs, as shown in the drawing. They should be put in with glue. The bottom of the frame at station B is cut to fit snugly against the bed logs and is secured to them either with a knee or a metal angle piece. The assumption is that the trunk assembly will be installed as a completed unit, having been put together outside the boat.

If the hole for the centerboard pin is accurately bored for a moderate drive fit, it can be cut to come flush with the outside of the bed logs and will stay in place when driven. It is easily driven out should it become necessary to remove the board for painting or repair.

Instead of making the centerboard of two widths of oak board pinned together as shown, you can make it from a piece of plywood ¾ inch thick, or from two thicknesses of ⅜-inch plywood glued together. A plywood centerboard should be covered with fiberglass. Before this is done, it may be tapered slightly and the edges rounded.

Spars should be spruce, if possible. Sitka spruce is hard to get and very expensive. Instead, we suggest the use of the rough spruce now imported in large quantities from Canada for staging planks and boards. It is often possible to pick out pieces that are nearly clear. In cutting out the narrow strips required for gluing up these small spars, it is generally possible to avoid any bad knots. An occasional small pin knot does not matter.

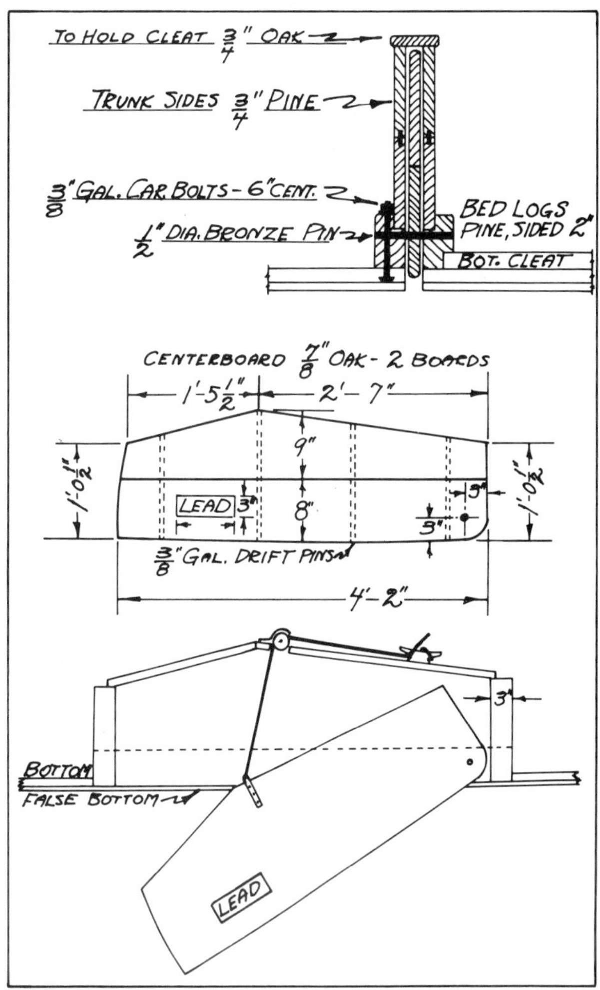

The sail could be laced to the mast, but the arrangement shown does just as well, and if it does not look quite as neat, it makes it much easier and quicker to bring down the sprit should it become necessary to reef. The two rolling hitches that secure the snotter to the sprit hold beautifully and are easy to tie and adjust.

12 A North Shore Surf Dory

Getting a boat on or off the beach in running surf requires a knack—also a special kind of boat. Back in the mid-1950s, when the Texas Petroleum Company was in need of a small surf boat on the west coast of Nicaragua, they sent up to New England. The boat they picked was a double-ended, round-sided surf dory of the sort developed in the North Shore fishing towns of Marblehead and Swampscott, Massachusetts. It was essentially a refinement of the fisherman's beach dory, with a trace of whaleboat, perhaps, and something from larger lifesaving craft as well as from the general heritage of scores of double-ended lapstrake work boat types once found on the North Atlantic coast.

The 19-foot surf dory was designed to carry at least four men and several hundred pounds of equipment and lines. In heavy surf there is normally a helmsman with a steering oar and three men pulling single oars. Under less severe conditions, however, two men, rowing in the ordinary manner with a pair of oars each, can handle the boat nicely and show a fair turn of speed. The boat is by no means so heavy or cumbersome that one capable oarsman cannot manage under most conditions, outside of surf.

The last builder to construct any number of surf dories of this sort was the late George L. Chaisson of Swampscott, Massachusetts. In the 1920s, Chaisson made them for local use and also shipped them to various parts of the country. They are listed in his catalog of that time as "Life and Surf Boats." What he had to say about them in this old catalog is interesting and informative:

> Small life-boats, suited for ocean-going yachts, or for surfboats to launch from the beach. Light, yet strongly built, and fitted with air tanks forward and aft. Cork sponsons on the outside. These boats have been adopted by the Metropolitan Park Commissioners as life-saving surf-boats along the New England Coast. Excellent sea boats and easily handled. Slightly flat on the bottom and will float in five inches of water. They have white oak frames, steam bent; cedar planking; oak bottom; gunwales and chafing strip, oak; cross seats, oak or spruce; copper fastened, and painted three coats of white, outside as in. Fitted with painter ring and hoisting bolts when required. Two pairs of ash oars and row-locks furnished with each boat. Built in lengths to suit the purchaser.

The Chaisson catalog also reproduced a letter from the Cummer Lumber Company of Jacksonville, Florida, dated October 10, 1923. After stating that a new surfboat, just received, had been placed in service, the letter went on to say: "Our beach is flat and naturally during high winds we have a very heavy broken surf to contend with. We succeeded in launching through a heavy northeaster two weeks ago, a feat which has never been accomplished on this beach before."

The surfboat built by Chaisson was certainly derived in large measure from the

(Left) Chamberlain's double-ended surf dory, built for the Metropolitan District Commission's Beach Patrol around 1900. (Right) The 19-foot surf dory designed and built for use as an oil company beach tender.

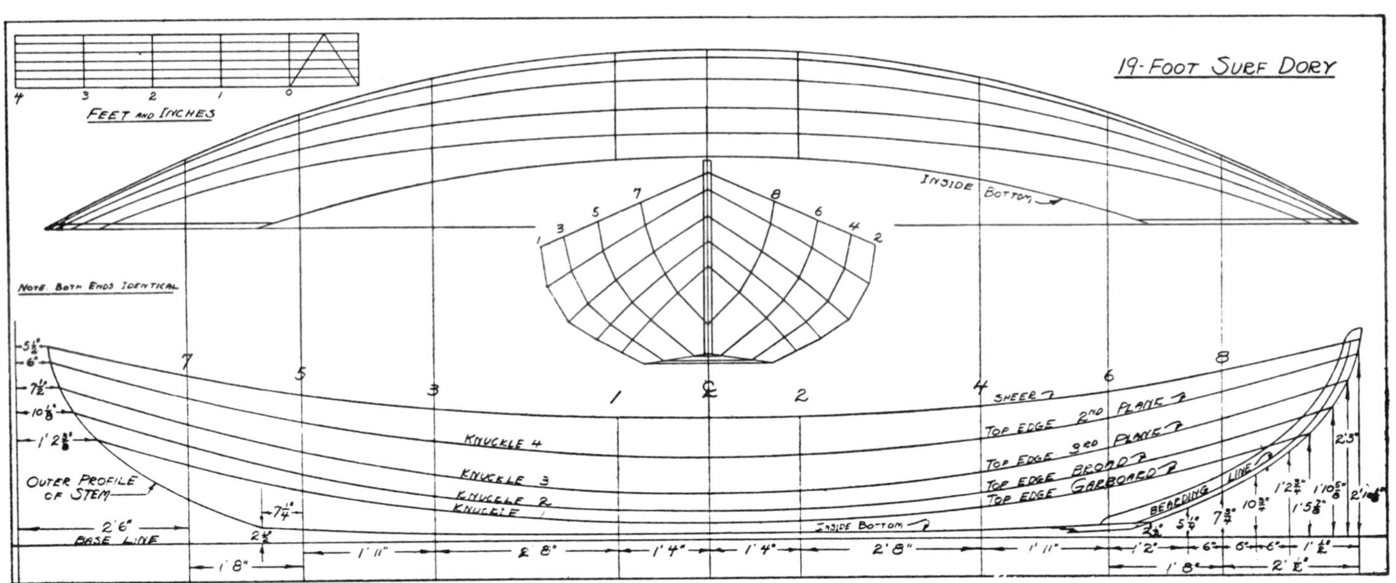

distinctive, round-sided work dories developed by the fishermen on the flat, sandy beaches of Swampscott and Lynn. But William Chamberlain built these surfboats or lifeboats in his Marblehead boatshop before Chaisson. And it appears to have been Chamberlain who designed the model or derived it, rather, from the common round-sided work dory. Possibly Chamberlain was indebted also to the design of the larger (30 feet) lifeboats of the Old Massachusetts Humane Society, which in Chamberlain's day maintained

19-Foot Surf Dory
Offsets — Feet, Inches, and Eighths

Stations		Stem	7 + 8	5 + 6	3 + 4	1 + 2
Heights	Sheer	2-10-1	2-4-6	2-1-2	1-10-7	1-9-2
	Knuckle 4	2-7-2	2-1-1	1-8-6	1-5-1	1-2-6
	" 3	2-3-0	1-8-4	1-3-5	0-11-4	0-8-4
	" 2	1-10-5	1-4-6	0-11-6	0 8-0	0-5-2
	" 1	1-5-7	1-1-8	0-8-6	0-5-3	0-3-2
	In. Bot.	0-2-4	Stem	0-2-2	0-1-4	0-1-2
Half-Breadths	Sheer	0-0-1	0-11-6	1-7-2	2-1-2	2-5-4
	Knuckle 4	"	0-11-1	1-6-3	2-0-1	2-4-2
	" 3	"	0-9-5	1-4-0	1-9-1	2-0-6
	" 2	"	0-7-5	1-1-2	1-5-1	1-7-6
	" 1	"	0-5-5	0-10-3	1-1-3	1-3-4
	In. Bot.	"	Stem	0-2-2	0-7-6	0-11-3

Offsets measured from baseline to inside plank, to inside bottom, to stem profile.

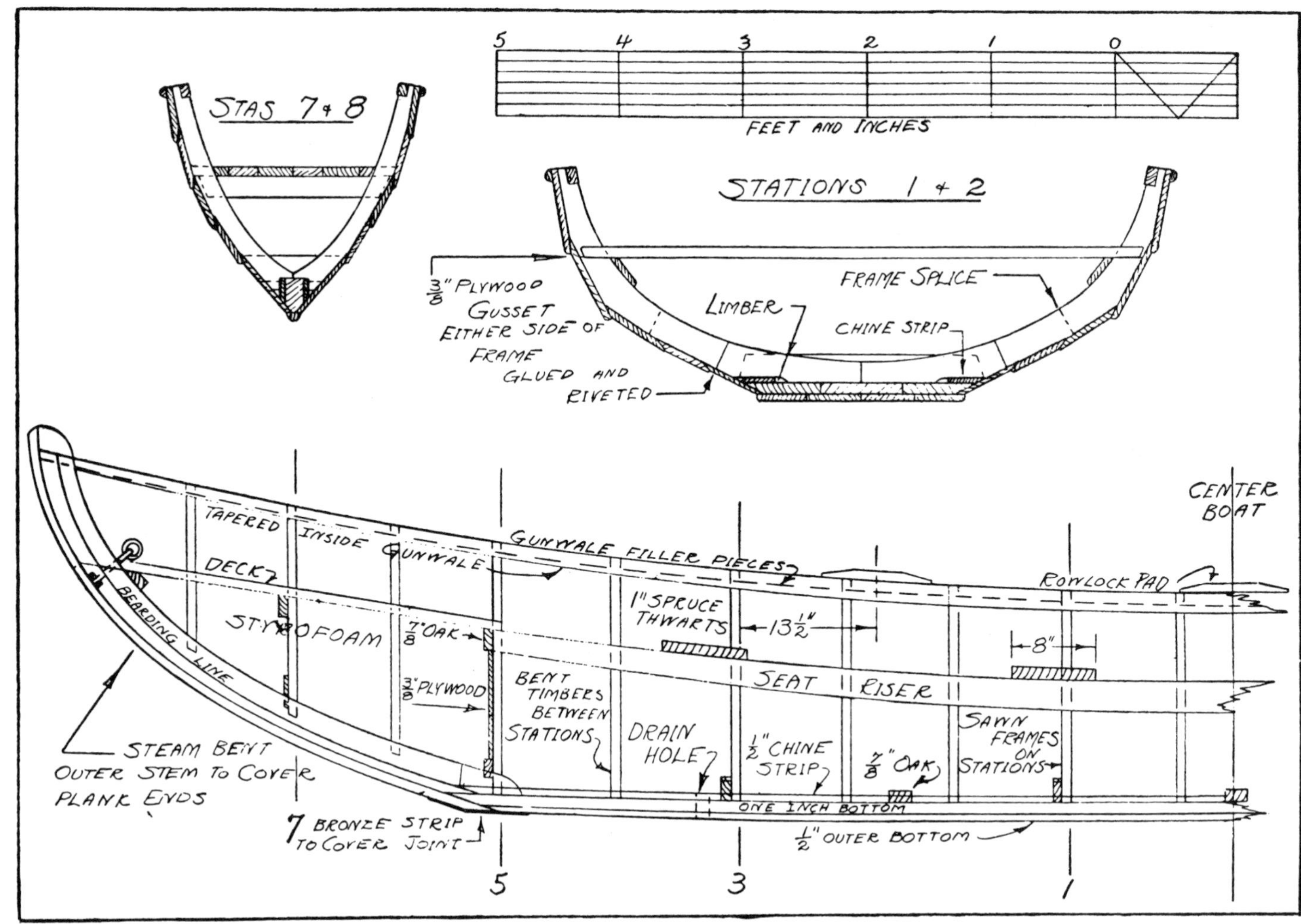

its Lifesaving Station No. 10 at Marblehead. The Humane Society's lifeboats, in turn, show a definite whaleboat influence.

The boat built for the Texas Petroleum Company, the lines and offsets for which are reproduced here, follows closely the old Chamberlain 19-footer, except that the new boat was given slightly more depth and beam to increase its carrying capacity as a working boat. In this respect, the new boat reverts somewhat to the proportions of its ancestor, the round-sided Swampscott work dory.

The leaner, slimmer, Chamberlain model would possibly row easier than the boat drawn here, but would carry less and likely would be less stable. Chamberlain built a 19-foot gunning dory similar to a surf dory, except that it had less sheer, was constructed lighter, and had four planks to a side instead of five as has the surf dory. (See Chapter 14). It was an exceptionally fast, easy-rowing boat even with only one man at the oars. But its exceptional lightness sometimes made it lively in rough water.

Several departures were made from Chamberlain's construction when the surf dory was built for the Texas Petroleum Company. Intermediate to the standard sawn dory frames, steam-bent white oak ribs were placed in the manner adopted by Chaisson, a structural feature of great importance in adding strength and stiffness to the hull. The garboards were made of 5-ply, ⅜-inch thick Douglas fir marine plywood, spliced in the middle. The garboards of this boat are so wide that suitable pine boards for them are nearly impossible to obtain today. (For more on plywood as a substitute for pine boards, see the Appendix.) Furthermore, plywood is stronger and does not split or rent, a common fault of old-style pine garboards. It was necessary, however, to take special measures to seal and to protect the edges of the plywood. A new method of locating the sawn frames up under the cross thwarts was employed to get a stronger frame and to avoid metal clips. An improved double bottom was adopted from one seen on a dory built by Fred Dion of Salem. For flotation, styrofoam was used instead of air tanks. Tanks can spring leaks. They are also difficult to make and expensive. Styrofoam is better in every way, and much cheaper. Instead of iron fastenings, bronze screws and copper rivets were used throughout. Modern waterproof glue as well as liquid rubber was employed. The inner bottom was made of mahogany, as mahogany gives a better hold for the garboard screws than pine, yet will not swell and shrink as much as an oak bottom would in the extreme conditions of the tropics.

Certain features of the hull should be noted. Both ends are identical to meet breakers either way, and the inside arrangement is such that the boat can be rowed in either direction. The ends are sharp to cut through the waves, yet full enough to have lots of lift. They are also carried high enough to keep above the crests. This means more than an ordinary amount of sheer when the ends are swept down to a moderate freeboard amidships to permit a good rowing angle for the oars and to keep down wind resistance. The bottom is straight and flat, which gives the boat a good seat on the beach and a very shoal draft, permitting the boat to go high up on the beach before grounding out. The bottom is also exceptionally solid to take pounding on a rough beach. The flotation is placed quite high in the ends to make the boat right easily in the water, should it ever capsize.

13 The Chamberlain Gunning Dory

This boat is a Marblehead gunning dory of up-to-date construction and the most modern materials built for James S. Rockefeller, Jr., of Camden, Maine, by Veli Holmstrom in his Vinalhaven, Maine, shop with the owner assisting. The lines of the boat, with minor changes, are the same that I showed in the February, 1960, issue of *Outdoor Maine*. These were taken off by me in 1942 from William Chamberlain's personal gunning dory, since broken up and destroyed, but owned in 1942 by Charles Briggs of Marblehead who used it for part-time lobster fishing during the early 1940s.

Using a gunning dory for lobstering is like hitching a spirited horse to a dump cart. But this superbly beautiful double-ender of ultra-light construction stood the gaff for several years in spite of advanced age and the roughest sort of treatment. Even under huge loads of lobster pots it rode the waves lightly, with infinite grace and with only slight urging on the oars. The gunning dory as perfected in Marblehead by William Chamberlain is the queen of all dories, and one of the handsomest double-enders ever built anywhere, not to mention its easy speed under oars and its unexcelled rough-water ability with capable hands at the oars.

The fame of the gunning dory reached the ears of James Rockefeller, an enthusiastic duck hunter who finds gunning among the islands and ledges in lower Penobscot Bay around Vinalhaven a fabulous and fascinating experience with a "certain mystique impossible to describe." He wanted to prolong the season into the first weeks of January, but that required a boat of unusual qualities, for as he observed, it can get quite nasty in a hurry on the offshore ledges in the winter time.

Rockefeller specified a boat large enough to hold two men with guns, decoys, and other gear, and to manage safely and comfortably in a bad chop. At the same time he wanted something that might double as a summer rowboat for his wife and two small children. And it must be light enough to drag up on the transom of his 36 foot lobsterboat with the aid of rollers.

In the beginning Rockefeller had not considered the possibility of sailing this boat, but when this was suggested he adopted the idea with alacrity. The original length of 19½ feet seemed excessive, particularly so, I suppose, in this decadent era of sawed-off, tubby outboard boats, but I held out for an overall length of nothing less than 18 feet and won my point.

The other changes in the lines were slight. I gave the modified version slightly more beam in proportion to length and widened the bottom a trifle aft. In lowering the deadrise angle just a bit, I attained a somewhat harder knuckle at the junction of the second and third planks with the object of giving stiffer bearing for sailing. In fact all changes in the lines, with the exception of

(Above) The 18-foot gunning dory under oars. The high bow, sharply raked ends, and low freeboard are key factors in the boat's exceptional rough water ability. (Left) The gunning dory under sail. The steering oar used can be replaced with the more efficient drop rudder described here.

shortening the length by about a foot under that of the original, were made with the object of making the boat stiffer under sail, yet without impairing her easy rowing qualities to any noticeable degree.

Originally the gunning dories carried a light, unstayed mast and a small sail for running before the wind. Naturally they required no centerboard. We had more ambitious plans for sailing, and borrowed the details for the centerboard and centerboard case from Chamberlain's famous 21-foot Beachcomber sailing dory (see Chapter 14). Otherwise we went about adapting this boat to sail cautiously and experimentally, starting out with a small sail area and an oar substituting for a rudder as originally used by the Swampscott and Marblehead lobstermen of 60 years ago when they sailed their working dories.

Even with meager canvas and the relatively clumsy steering oar, the new gunning dory sails surprisingly well. To some extent, this is certainly due to her exceptional lightness achieved without any sacrifice of strength by the use of a special seam batten construction utilizing laminated spruce framing, epoxy adhesive, and ¼-inch plywood planking reinforced with Dynel fabric set in epoxy resin. This is basically the same construction tested by me in the light pram described in Chapter 3. It combines lightness with great strength, insures perfect tightness, and obviates beveling for laps, which is generally a bugaboo for the inexperienced amateur builder.

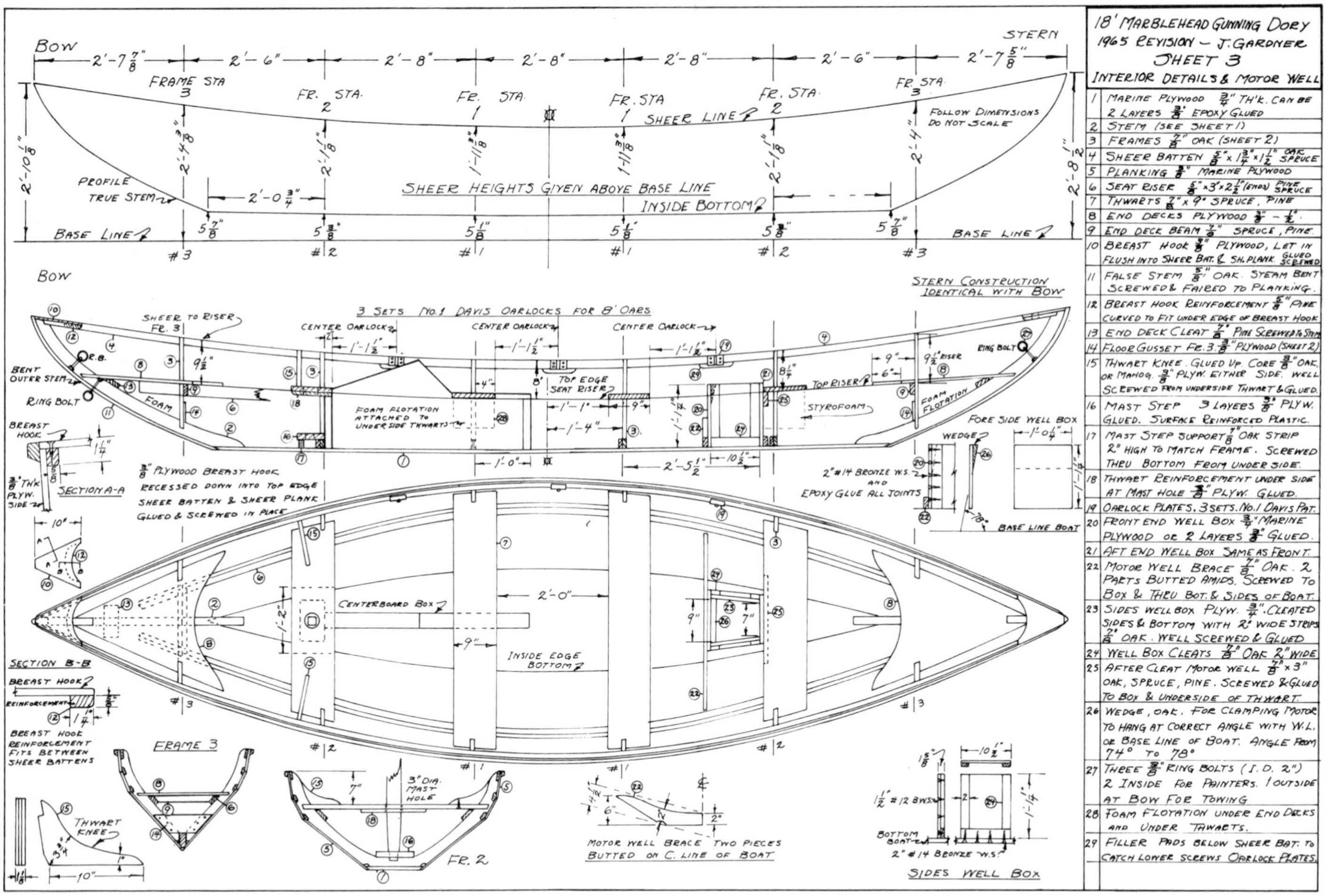

18' MARBLEHEAD GUNNING DORY
1965 REVISION – J. GARDNER
SHEET 3
INTERIOR DETAILS & MOTOR WELL

1	MARINE PLYWOOD 3/4" TH'K. CAN BE 2 LAYERS 3/8" EPOXY GLUED
2	STEM (SEE SHEET 1)
3	FRAMES 7/8" OAK (SHEET 2)
4	SHEER BATTEN 5/8" × 1 3/4" × 1 1/2" OAK SPRUCE
5	PLANKING 3/8" MARINE PLYWOOD
6	SEAT RISER 5/8" × 3" × 2 1/2" (ENDS) PINE SPRUCE
7	THWARTS 7/8" × 9" SPRUCE, PINE
8	END DECKS PLYWOOD 3/8" – 1/2".
9	END DECK BEAM 7/8" SPRUCE, PINE.
10	BREAST HOOK 3/8" PLYWOOD, LET IN FLUSH INTO SHEER BAT. & SH. PLANK. GLUED SCREWED
11	FALSE STEM 5/8" OAK. STEAM BENT SCREWED & FAIRED TO PLANKING.
12	BREAST HOOK REINFORCEMENT 5/8" PINE CURVED TO FIT UNDER EDGE OF BREAST HOOK
13	END DECK CLEAT 7/8" PINE SCREWED TO STEM
14	FLOOR GUSSET FR. 3. 3/8" PLYWOOD (SHEET 2)
15	THWART KNEE. GLUED UP. CORE 3/8" OAK, OR MAHOG. 3/8" PLYW. EITHER SIDE. WELL SCREWED FROM UNDERSIDE THWART & GLUED.
16	MAST STEP 3 LAYERS 3/8" PLYW. GLUED. SURFACE REINFORCED PLASTIC.
17	MAST STEP SUPPORT 7/8" OAK STRIP 2" HIGH TO MATCH FRAME. SCREWED THRU BOTTOM FROM UNDER SIDE.
18	THWART REINFORCEMENT UNDER SIDE AT MAST HOLE 3/8" PLYW. GLUED.
19	OARLOCK PLATES. 3 SETS. NO. 1 DAVIS PAT.
20	FRONT END WELL BOX 3/4" MARINE PLYWOOD OR 2 LAYERS 3/8" GLUED.
21	AFT END WELL BOX SAME AS FRONT.
22	MOTOR WELL BRACE 7/8" OAK. 2 PARTS BUTTED AMIDS. SCREWED TO BOX & THRU BOT. & SIDES OF BOAT.
23	SIDES WELL BOX PLYW. 3/4". CLEATED SIDES & BOTTOM WITH 2" WIDE STRIPS 7/8" OAK. WELL SCREWED & GLUED
24	WELL BOX CLEATS 7/8" OAK 2" WIDE
25	AFTER CLEAT MOTOR WELL 7/8" × 3" OAK, SPRUCE, PINE. SCREWED & GLUED TO BOX & UNDERSIDE OF THWART.
26	WEDGE, OAK. FOR CLAMPING MOTOR TO HANG AT CORRECT ANGLE WITH W.L. OR BASE LINE OF BOAT. ANGLE FROM 74° TO 78°
27	THREE 3/8" RING BOLTS (I. D. 2") 2 INSIDE FOR PAINTERS. 1 OUTSIDE AT BOW FOR TOWING
28	FOAM FLOTATION UNDER END DECKS AND UNDER THWARTS.
29	FILLER PADS BELOW SHEER BAT. TO CATCH LOWER SCREWS OARLOCK PLATES.

BOW — STERN

SHEER HEIGHTS GIVEN ABOVE BASE LINE

FOLLOW DIMENSIONS DO NOT SCALE

PROFILE TRUE STEM — SHEER LINE — INSIDE BOTTOM — BASE LINE

STERN CONSTRUCTION IDENTICAL WITH BOW

3 SETS NO. 1 DAVIS OARLOCKS FOR 8' OARS

3/8" PLYWOOD BREAST HOOK RECESSED DOWN INTO TOP EDGE SHEER BATTEN & SHEER PLANK GLUED & SCREWED IN PLACE

FOAM FLOTATION ATTACHED TO UNDER SIDE THWARTS

2" #14 BRONZE W.S. AND EPOXY GLUE ALL JOINTS

SECTION A-A — SECTION B-B — BREAST HOOK — REINFORCEMENT

BREAST HOOK REINFORCEMENT FITS BETWEEN SHEER BATTENS

FRAME 3 — FR. 2 — THWART KNEE — CENTERBOARD BOX — 3" DIA. MAST HOLE

MOTOR WELL BRACE TWO PIECES BUTTED ON C. LINE OF BOAT

FORE SIDE WELL BOX — SIDES WELL BOX — BASE LINE BOAT

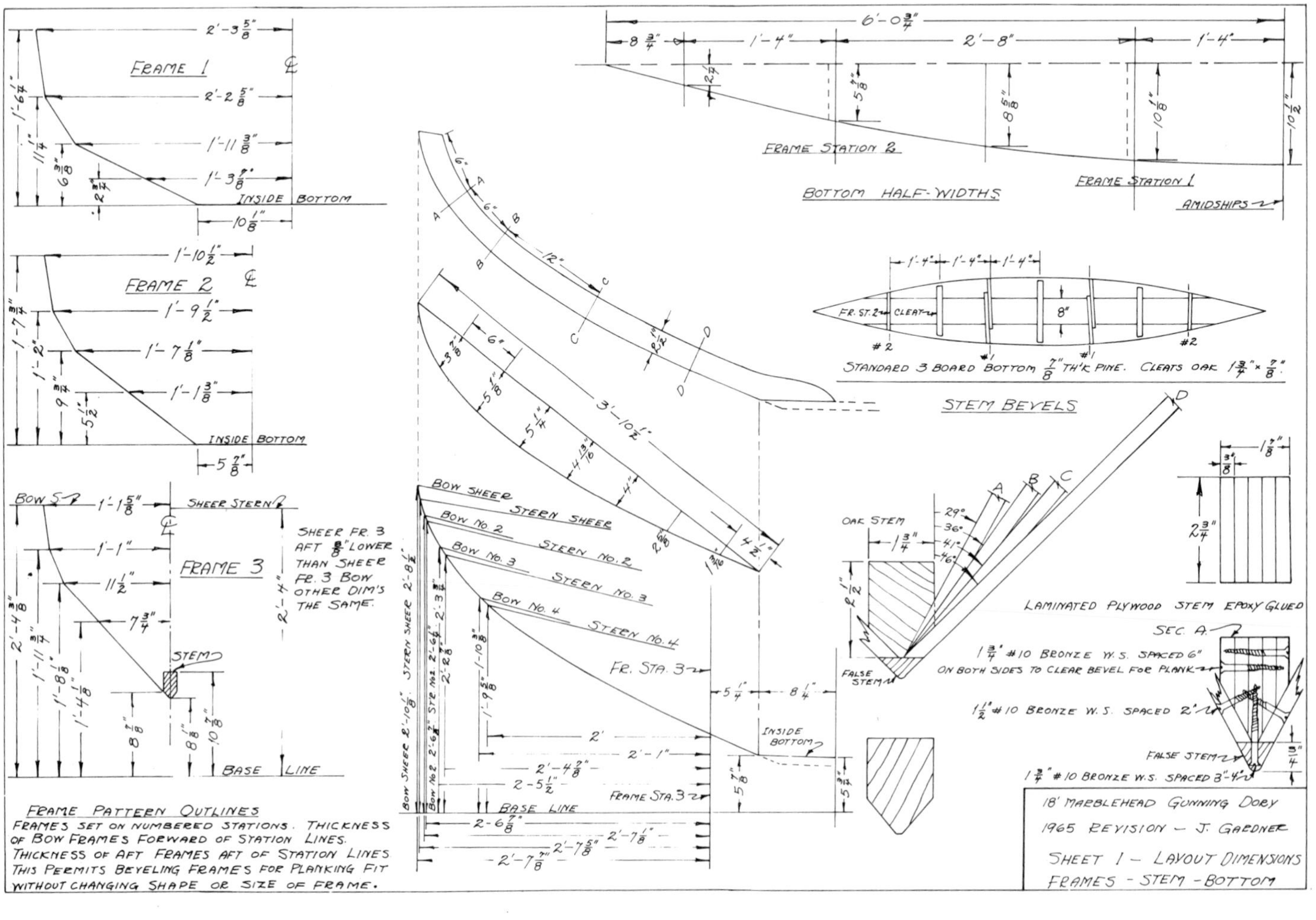

FRAME 1 — FRAME 2 — FRAME 3

SHEER FR. 3 AFT 5/8" LOWER THAN SHEER FR. 3 BOW OTHER DIM'S THE SAME.

FRAME PATTERN OUTLINES
FRAMES SET ON NUMBERED STATIONS. THICKNESS OF BOW FRAMES FORWARD OF STATION LINES. THICKNESS OF AFT FRAMES AFT OF STATION LINES. THIS PERMITS BEVELING FRAMES FOR PLANKING FIT WITHOUT CHANGING SHAPE OR SIZE OF FRAME.

BOTTOM HALF-WIDTHS — FRAME STATION 2 — FRAME STATION 1 — AMIDSHIPS

STANDARD 3 BOARD BOTTOM 7/8" TH'K PINE. CLEATS OAK 1 3/4" × 7/8".

STEM BEVELS — OAK STEM — FALSE STEM

LAMINATED PLYWOOD STEM EPOXY GLUED

SEC. A.

1 3/4" #10 BRONZE W.S. SPACED 6" ON BOTH SIDES TO CLEAR BEVEL FOR PLANK

1 1/2" #10 BRONZE W.S. SPACED 2"

1 3/4" #10 BRONZE W.S. SPACED 3"-4"

BOW SHEER — STERN SHEER — BOW NO. 2 — STERN NO. 2 — BOW NO. 3 — STERN NO. 3 — BOW NO. 4 — STERN NO. 4 — FR. STA. 3 — INSIDE BOTTOM — BASE LINE

18' MARBLEHEAD GUNNING DORY
1965 REVISION – J. GARDNER
SHEET 1 – LAYOUT DIMENSIONS
FRAMES – STEM – BOTTOM

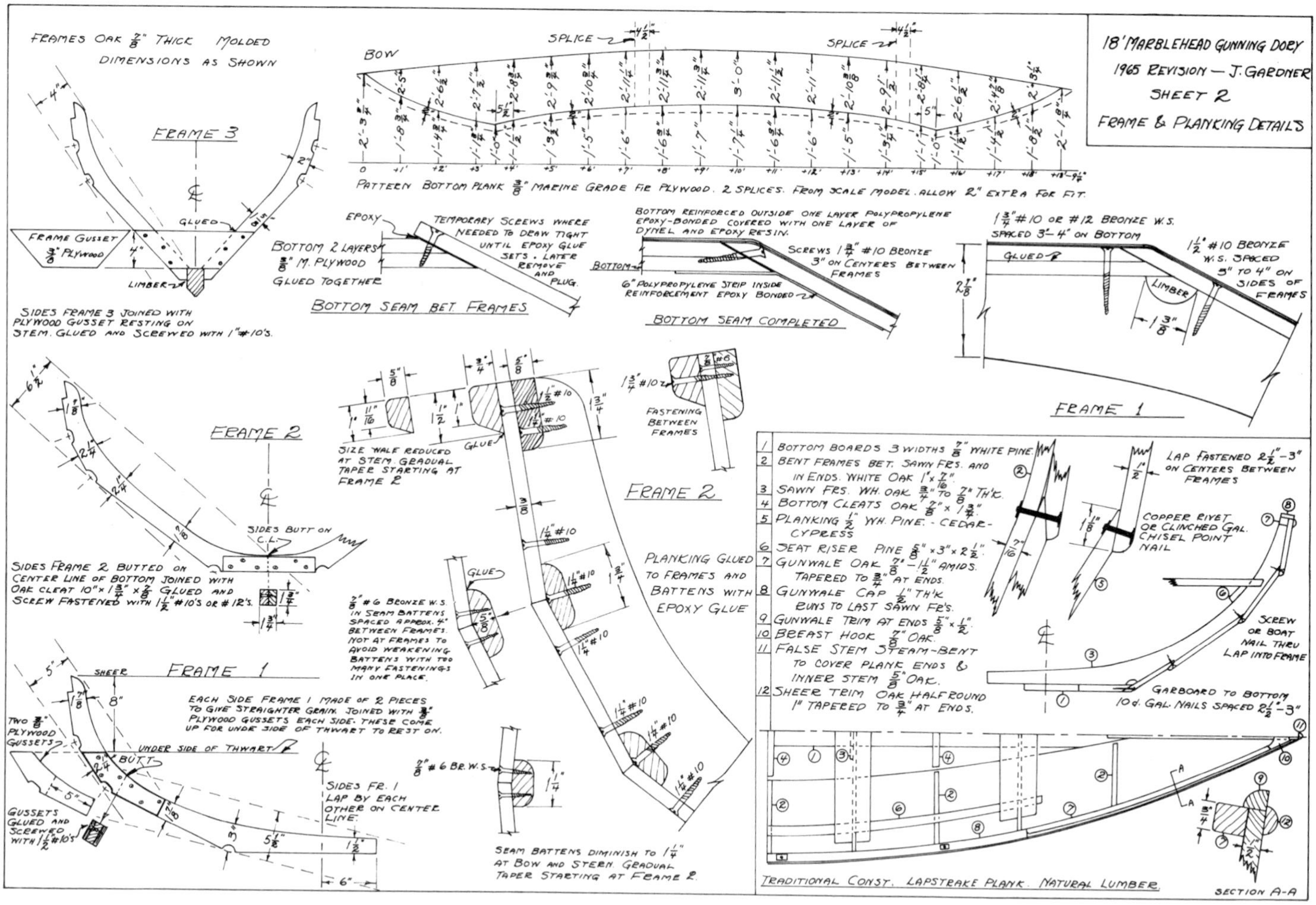

18' MARBLEHEAD GUNNING DORY
1965 REVISION — J. GARDNER
SHEET 2
FRAME & PLANKING DETAILS

18' MARBLEHEAD GUNNING DORY
1965 REVISION — J. GARDNER
SHEET 4
CENTERBOARD, SAIL & MISC.

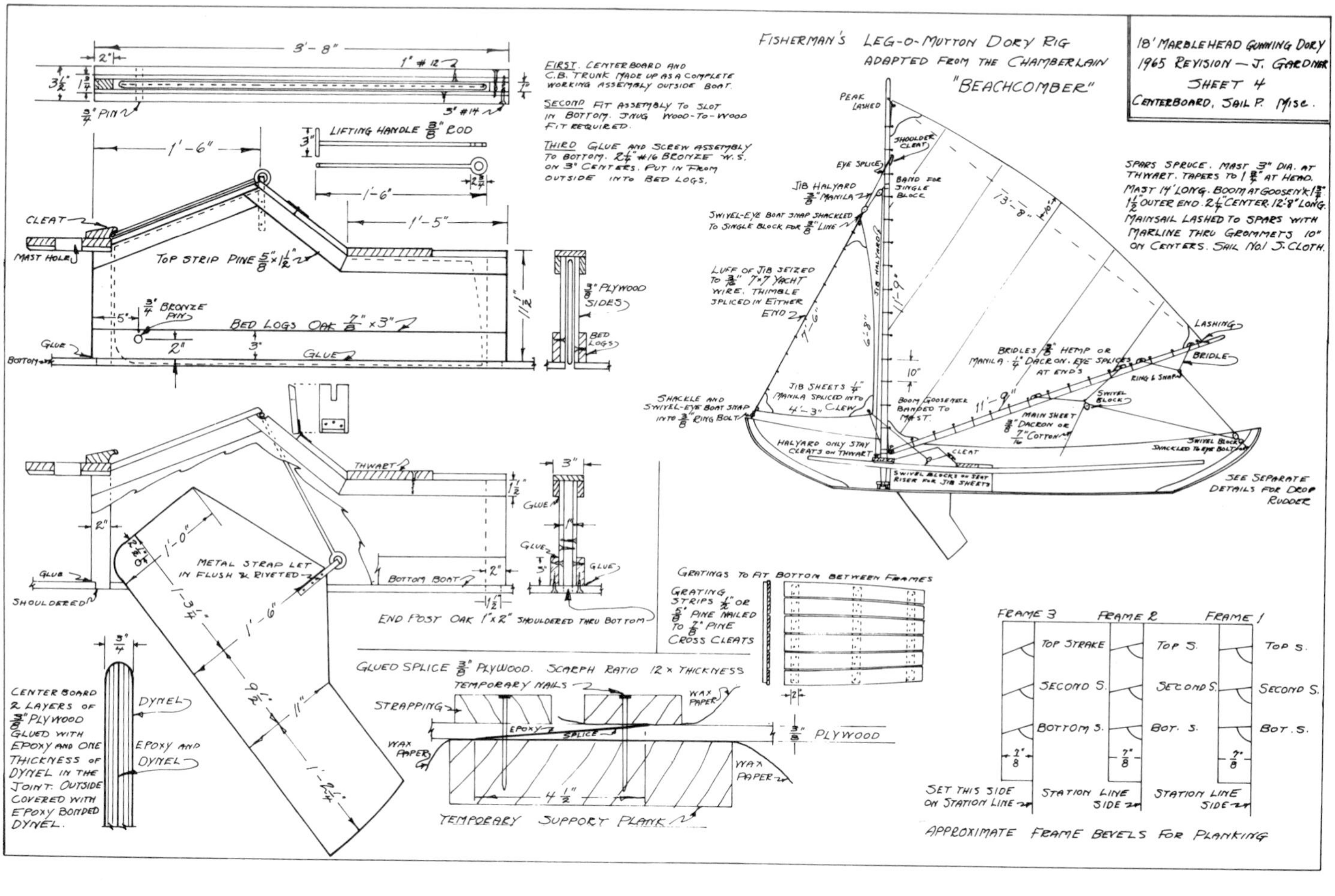

The gunning dory partly planked, showing laminated stem, plywood planking, and seam batten construction.

THE DROP RUDDER

The boat sails well, but would obviously sail much better with a suitable rudder. For one thing, a rudder would permit the helmsman to place his weight where it would do the most good, and a well adjusted rudder of suitable size would give much surer control. But fitting a rudder to this double-ended boat, considering the curve and rake of its stern post or rather its "stern stem," if the term may be permitted, involves a few problems. For one thing a rudder hung on an excessive rake tends to lift and lose its bite in the water when it is turned. Besides, the slant is awkward for the tiller or the tiller yoke. Certainly it was not possible to borrow the Beachcomber dory's rudder, as we had its centerboard, for the Beachcomber's "tombstone" is straight and not raked excessively.

In addition to the problem of mounting the rudder on a curved and overhanging stern there are other things to consider. It is desirable that the rudder be easily removed. The drop rudder shown comes off by loosening a single nut; the hinged blade also swings up by itself to clear any obstructions, and lifts and secures above the bottom so that the boat may be drawn out on the beach without disengaging the rudder.

The drop rudder is not new. Who invented it and when is uncertain, but 85 years ago drop rudders were in general use in this country for sailing canoes and other small craft used at that time for cruising and racing. The one shown here is adapted from W. P. Stephens's *Canoe And Boat Building*, Fourth Edition, 1889. Stephens, canoeing editor of *Forest and Stream*, was a pioneer authority on American small craft and the boatbuilding practices of his period then at a peak of perfection unapproached today. His building manual for amateurs is a treasure house of detail and a standard source book in small craft design. The rudder that I have worked out for our modernized version of the Chamberlain gunning dory is taken directly from the drop rudder formerly made by Charles Piepenbrink of Albany, N. Y. Stephens recommended it as "one of the best," and has detailed it carefully in his book.

This drop rudder is really not as complicated as might appear from a quick glance at the drawings. Unfamiliar drawings of detail frequently give such an impression until they have been studied awhile. Actually this rudder is quite a simple contrivance, made entirely from standard, easily obtained materials, and it is not difficult to construct.

The rudder stock and the rudder port are made out of standard brass pipe. The only lathe work is the solid plug closing the upper end of the rudder stock, which can be shouldered and threaded in 15 minutes. The two cheek pieces and the rib that joins and stiffens them can be

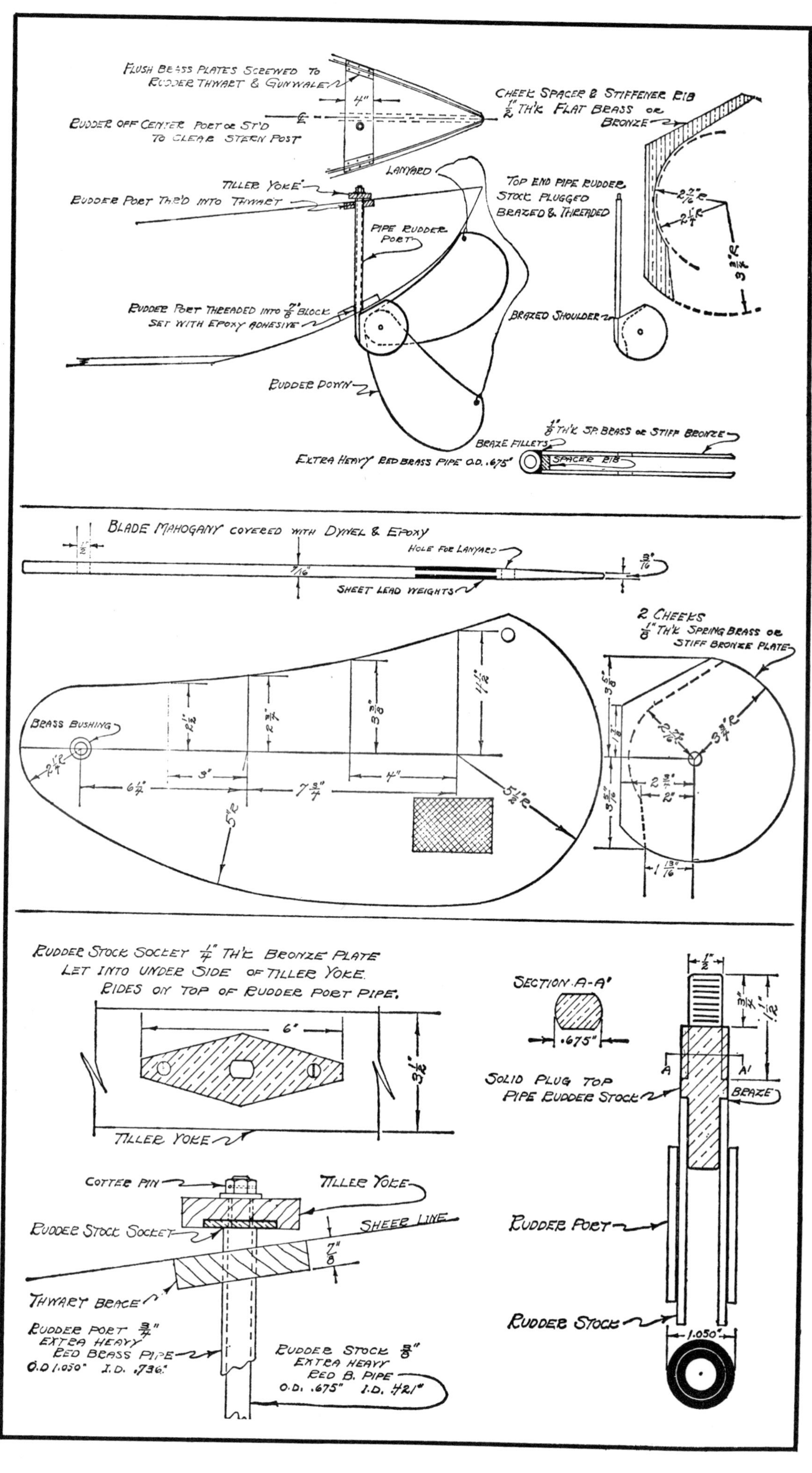

FLUSH BRASS PLATES SCREWED TO RUDDER THWART & GUNWALE
4"
RUDDER OFF CENTER PORT OR ST'D TO CLEAR STERN POST
CHEEK SPACER & STIFFENER RIB 1/2" TH'K FLAT BRASS OR BRONZE
LANYARD
TILLER YOKE
RUDDER PORT THR'D INTO THWART
TOP END PIPE RUDDER STOCK PLUGGED BRAZED & THREADED
PIPE RUDDER PORT
RUDDER PORT THREADED INTO 7/8" BLOCK SET WITH EPOXY ADHESIVE
BRAZED SHOULDER
RUDDER DOWN
1/8" TH'K SP. BRASS OR STIFF BRONZE
BRAZE FILLETS
SPACER RIB
EXTRA HEAVY RED BRASS PIPE O.D. .675"
BLADE MAHOGANY COVERED WITH DYNEL & EPOXY
HOLE FOR LANYARD
SHEET LEAD WEIGHTS
2 CHEEKS 1/8" TH'K SPRING BRASS OR STIFF BRONZE PLATE
BRASS BUSHING
RUDDER STOCK SOCKET 1/4" TH'K BRONZE PLATE LET INTO UNDER SIDE OF TILLER YOKE. RIDES ON TOP OF RUDDER PORT PIPE.
6"
3 1/2"
TILLER YOKE
SECTION A-A'
.675"
SOLID PLUG TOP PIPE RUDDER STOCK
BRAZE
COTTER PIN
TILLER YOKE
RUDDER STOCK SOCKET
SHEER LINE
7/8"
THWART BRACE
RUDDER PORT
RUDDER PORT 3/4" EXTRA HEAVY RED BRASS PIPE O.D 1.050" I.D. .736"
RUDDER STOCK 3/8" EXTRA HEAVY RED B. PIPE O.D. .675" I.D. .421"
RUDDER STOCK
1.050"

cut out just as quickly from ordinary flat brass or bronze on a metal-cutting bandsaw. A few holes are bored on the drill press and assembly is made by brazing. There is nothing beyond the skill of the capable amateur or the ordinary equipment of most boatshops.

There is enough clearance between the interior diameter of the ¾-inch extra heavy red brass pipe specified for the rudder port and the outside diameter of the ⅜-inch extra heavy red brass pipe used for the rudder stock to give a loose working fit, but not too loose. In locating the rudder port enough off center, either to port or starboard, sufficient to clear the stern post, no loss in rudder efficiency or any other undesirable effect may be expected.

The rudder port pipe is threaded on its lower end so as to screw tightly into the ⅞-inch thick wood block reinforcing the hull where the port goes through. If the pipe is threaded in tightly and glued with epoxy adhesive, the connection should be perfectly rigid and tight. The rudder port is also braced and held by the 4-inch thwart at the sheer line. The pipe port must be strongly secured, for it holds the entire weight of the rudder on its upper end. The underside of the tiller or tiller yoke, which is reinforced by a brass plate, turns on the upper end of this pipe.

The cheek plates brazed to the lower end of the rudder stock or shaft must be rigid enough to resist any side leverage exerted by the blade. The ½-inch thick rib which separates them and to which they are brazed adds greatly to their rigidity. To provide for strength and rigidity here I have specified spring brass or hard bronze for these cheek plates. If there is any doubt or difficulty in getting proper materials, it would be better if these cheeks were made 3/16 inch thick instead of ⅛ inch.

Clearance of 1/16 inch is allowed between the cheeks and the blade to prevent the latter from binding. A metal bushing in the blade for the pivot pin to go through will prevent wear and decrease friction. The lower portion of the cheek rib and spacer acts as a stop to prevent the blade from dropping too low or swinging under the boat. The after edge of the blade is tapered to streamline it somewhat. It should be completely covered with fiberglass or, better, Dynel, set in epoxy resin. The finished surface should be sanded as smooth as possible.

The lanyard passing through the hole in the upper, outer end of the blade should be a piece of light cord, preferably nylon, but strong enough to lift several times the weight of the rudder. It should be long enough so that when the upper end is tied inside the boat, the blade of the rudder can swing freely and with no hindrance. This cord or lanyard serves two purposes. By means of it the blade may be drawn up and tied to clear the bottom. Or, with the cord tied inside the boat, the rudder may be safely dropped in deep water and hauled aboard.

Whether an ordinary stick tiller is used or a tiller yoke and tiller lines is a matter still to be settled. Yoke and lines are seldom seen today, but Chamberlain favored them for dories and rigged his famous racing Beachcomber in this way. With lines for steering, the helmsman could sit amidships and could place his weight wherever he wished. It is necessary for a boat so equipped to carry a slight weather helm to keep a taut steering line. Besides some of the sailing dories, many of the old sailing canoes were steered with yoke and lines. Some of these almost forgotten craft carried light rigs to nearly ultimate refinement.

14 The Beachcomber-Alpha Dory

It looks as though this fine dory, once popular in Marblehead and Salem, Massachusetts, and a product of the Beachcomber and Alpha Dory Clubs, could be in for a revival of sorts now that the pertinent data is available. The Beachcomber-Alpha dory is a good boat to learn to sail in. It is a safe boat for youngsters in their early teens, but no toy. In fact, sailed hard and to its capacity, this craft can provide thrills and a vigorous workout for most adult sailors. It can be rowed as well as sailed and handles easily under oars, like the working dories of the Massachusetts Bay shore fishermen of the late nineteenth century from which it was derived. With a full rig, 50 pounds of lead ballast on either side the centerboard trunk, and a crew of three hiked out on the rail, this boat will draw smartly to windward and handle like a spirited colt.

The Beachcomber-Alpha is also an economy boat. The standard rig, contrived to be lifted out of the boat and carried home at night in a compact roll on the skipper's shoulder, is just about as simple and inexpensive as it is possible for a workable rig to be. It would be misleading to say that the hull is an easy one to build, yet it is not so difficult as to be out of the reach of amateur capability. It looks harder than it actually is.

For those who do not feel up to beveling and riveting lapstrake planking, an easier seam-batten planking construction can be substituted. This modified construction has been very successfully used on other dory hulls of Chamberlain design. Strakes of marine plywood are butted and glued on longitudinal seam battens, and, for reinforcement, the joint on the outside is bound with fiberglass tape set in epoxy glue. The result is absolutely and permanently tight as well as extremely strong. The difficulties of fitting laps are bypassed, and the problems of finding suitable lumber are virtually eliminated—plywood is easily obtainable.

EVOLUTION OF THE BEACHCOMBER-ALPHA

The Beachcomber-Alpha dories have had a long and interesting history. Central to their development was William Chamberlain, who was born in 1864 and who began building and racing dories sometime in the 1880s. Dory sailing was a coming sport in those days in Marblehead and neighboring North Shore towns, and boats like those that served the local fishermen on weekdays were raced on Sundays and holidays.

Chamberlain built superior dories, and won races and cups sailing them. Yet when the Beachcomber Dory Club was formed on the Marblehead waterfront sometime in the 1890s, Chamberlain may not have been sole builder of

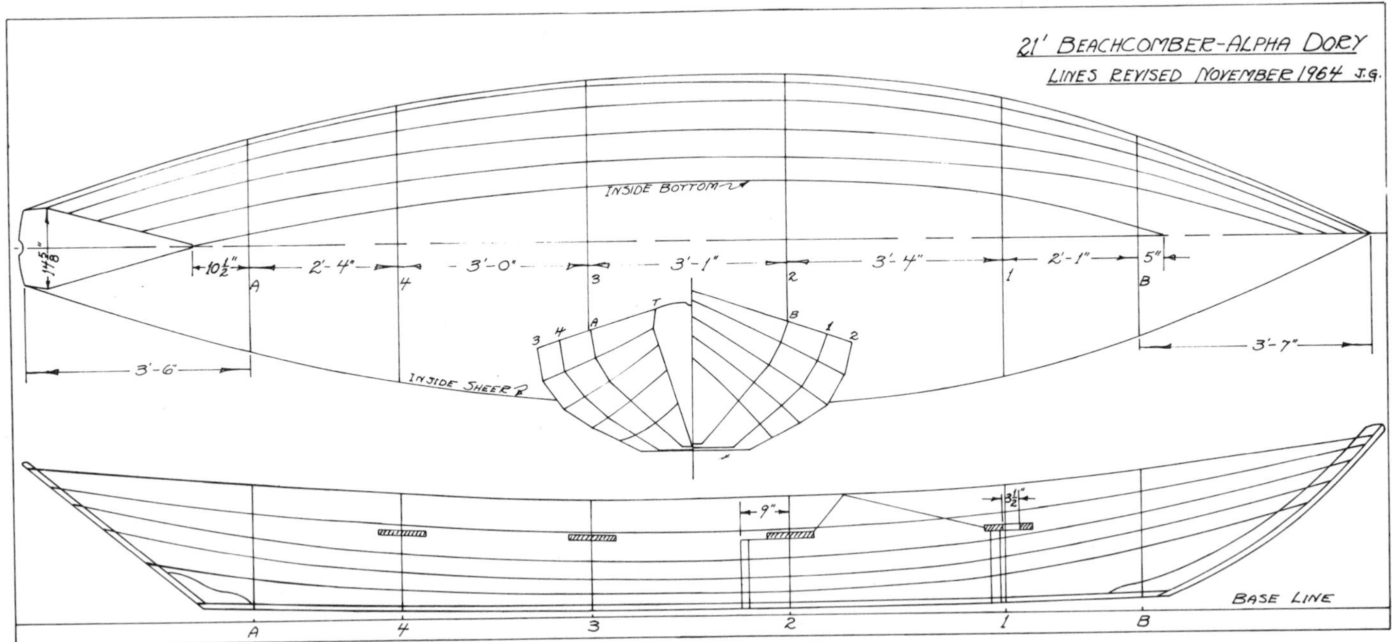

BEACHCOMBER-ALPHA OFFSETS, FEET, INCHES, EIGHTHS. INSIDE PLANKING AND BOTTOM. OUTSIDE STEM AND TRANSOM.									
	STATIONS	T	A	4	3	2	1	B	S
HEIGHTHS ABOVE BASE-LINE	SHEER	2-4-1	2-0-5	1-10-6	1-9-2	1-9-4	1-11-1	2-1-5	2-7-2
	1ST KNUCKLE	2-0-5	1-7-4	1-5-0	1-3-2	1-3-3	1-6-1	1-9-7	2-5-7
	2ND KNUCKLE	1-9-5	1-3-0	1-0-2	0-10-2	0-10-1	1-1-5	1-5-7	2-2-6
	3RD KNUCKLE	1-5-1	0-11-4	0-8-4	0-6-6	0-6-7	0-10-2	1-2-5	1-11-2
	4TH KNUCKLE	0-10-6	0-7-4	0-5-2	0-4-2	0-4-2	0-7-0	0-11-4	1-7-4
	BOTTOM	0-3-2	0-2-7	0-2-3	0-2-1	0-2-0	0-2-6	0-3-3	0-3-4
HALF-BREADTHS TO INSIDE PLANKING	SHEER	0-6-7	1-7-2	2-1-1	2-5-3	2-6-0	2-1-4	1-6-2	0-0-0+
	1ST KNUCKLE	0-7-3	1-6-3	2-0-0	2-4-2	2-4-4	1-11-5	1-4-7	0-0-0+
	2ND KNUCKLE	0-6-3	1-3-4	1-8-5	2-0-3	2-1-2	1-8-5	1-2-4	0-0-0+
	3RD KNUCKLE	0-4-6	0-11-6	1-4-1	1-7-3	1-8-1	1-4-6	1-11-7	0-0-0+
	4TH KNUCKLE	0-2-6	0-7-0	1-11-2	1-2-3	1-3-0	1-0-5	0-8-5	0-0-0+
		0-0-2	0-1-7	0-6-3	0-10-0	0-10-6	0-7-6	0-1-3	0-0-0+
T = TRANSOM. STATION A. 3'-6" FWD. SHEER AT TRANSOM. STATION B. 3'-7" AFT SHEER AT OUTBOARD STEM. S = STEM. TOLERANCE, PLUS OR MINUS 1/8". REVISED NOVEMBER 1964. J.G.									

club dories. There is evidence that, at first, members' boats and rigs were far from being uniform. But evidently Chamberlain's model soon became standard and had no competition until about 1912 when a young dory sailor by the name of Sam Brown, later to become a successful naval architect, designed the *Outlaw* for Ed Murphy.

The *Outlaw* was flatter on the sheer than Chamberlain's dory and faster around the harbor course. It constituted a further step in the evolutionary transition from the lobsterman's working dory to specialized racing class boats. As Ben Tutt of Marblehead once told me, the Outlaw "broke up the Beachcomber Club." Of course, the *Outlaw* actually didn't break up the Beachcomber Club or class there and then, for Beachcomber-Alpha dories were actively sailed and raced throughout the 1920s and even into the 1930s. But Tutt is right that the *Outlaw* started the evolution to larger, heavier, flatter, decked-over types with enlarged sail area and standing rigging that eventually replaced the lighter, slimmer, open dories directly copied from the workboats of the late nineteenth-century lobster fishermen.

After the *Outlaw*, it seems likely that Chamberlain may have modified the Beachcomber hull somewhat to increase its speed, but we do not know and have no way of knowing. It has been credibly reported that Chamberlain sometimes adjusted the shape of his dories slightly to suit the planking boards at hand. We know that he liked to experiment. It is reasonable to assume some progressive evolution as well as random variation in the succession of Beachcomber-Alpha hulls that came out of Chamberlain's Orne Street shop over a space of more than 30 years.

We do know about changes in the Beachcomber-Alpha rig, however, which were both extensive and distributed throughout the life of the class. The development of the rig will be discussed further later on in this chapter.

A 21-foot Beachcomber sailing dory built by Ernest Tarr of Gloucester, Massachusetts. (Photo courtesy of Mystic Seaport)

LINES AND OFFSETS

The lines and offsets for the Beachcomber-Alpha dory have been rechecked and revised since they first appeared in *Outdoor Maine* in 1961. The sheer has been lifted one inch higher on the stem, and the hood ends of the planks below the sheer have been lifted and relined accordingly, so as not to alter appreciably their widths at the stem. This might not seem to be much of a change, yet it improves the appearance noticeably, as I discovered when I constructed the scale model of the Beachcomber-Alpha now in the Peabody Museum of Salem.

The sheer, as it now stands, is probably closer to the sheer line of the fishing dories from which the Beachcomber-Alpha class originally derived. Later on, the boats were flattened out on top somewhat in what seems to have been an attempt to increase speed by cutting hull windage.

It is important not to overlook that the lines are drawn to the inside of the planking. This is noted on the lines and offsets, but some readers, unfamiliar with dories and small craft building practice, might overlook it. To work from the inside of the planking is easiest and most accurate, especially for clinker-planked boats with knuckled sides. It permits laying out

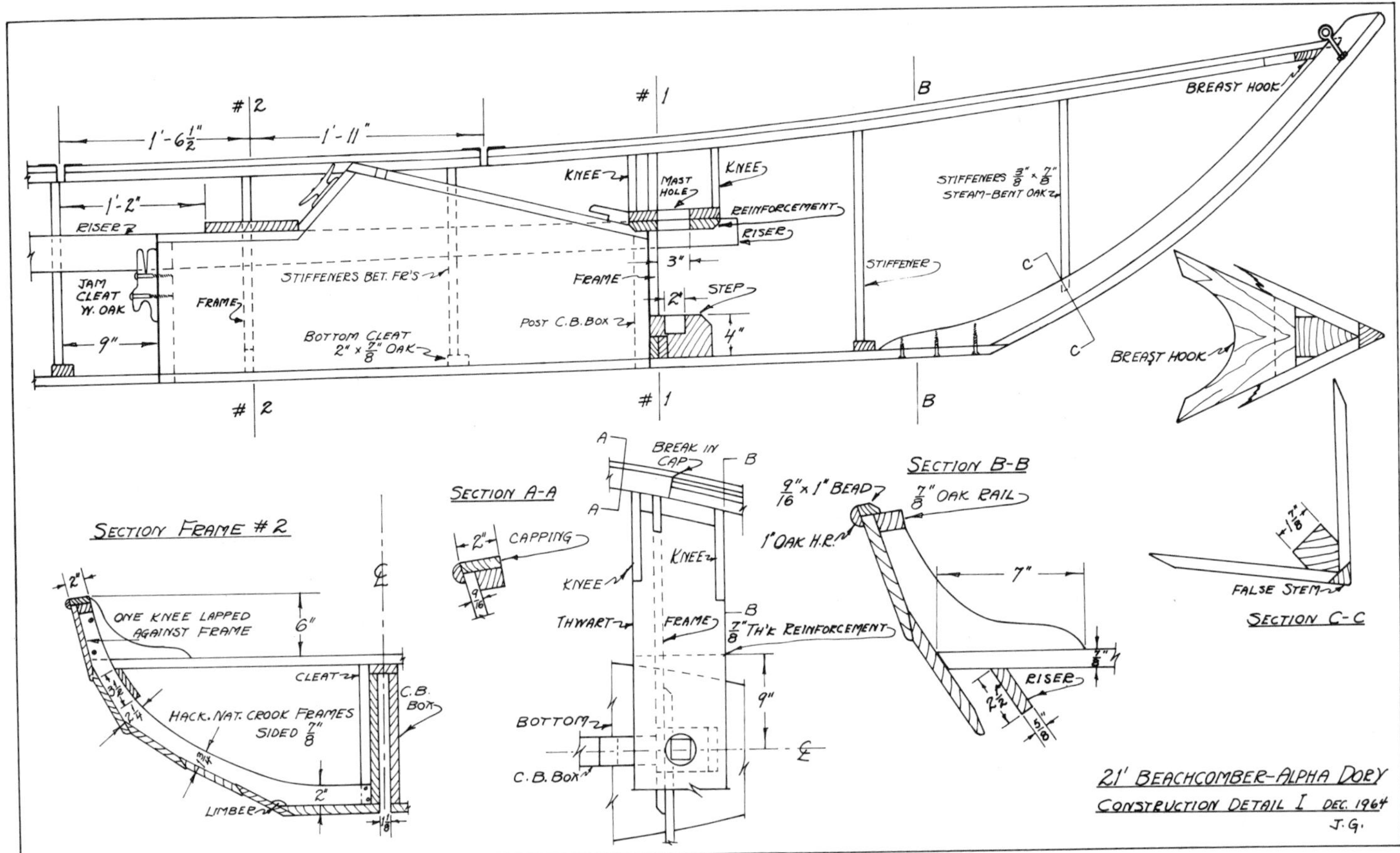

directly the shape of the frames which serve as building molds, without having to deduct plank thickness or to make an allowance for lap widths.

However, the planking lines as drawn do not represent the outside appearance of the hull after it has been planked. The finished plank lines will be lower by the width of the lap. This shows up especially in the width of the garboard, which will be reduced by the width of the lap, and in the sheer, which will be increased by the same amount.

The hood end of the sheer plank as it appears on the profile view of the lines might seem excessively narrow where it lands on the stem were it not understood that this is the inside view, less the lap, and that actually the end of the sheer plank will be wider by 1⅛ inches, which is the width of the lap. Even so, this makes the sheer plank quite narrow on the stem, but this is a characteristic of Chamberlain boats and one of the refinements by which he achieved a hull of outstanding grace and beauty. Also by keeping the hood ends of the upper planks quite narrow on the stem, and likewise on the transom, it is possible to peak up the ends of the garboard and so to straighten out the garboard's upper edge (when laid out flat), as well as to straighten out the run of the plank above. This ensures less work in planking, more efficient use of lumber, and stronger planking because of straighter grain.

A note on the table of offsets specifies a dimensional tolerance of plus or minus one-eighth inch. This is about as close as it is possible to scale offsets from a drawing laid out to a scale of one and one-half inches equals one foot. Even greater corrections or adjustments may be required in making a full-size lay-down of these lines for building. But this is to be expected, and as long as changes are kept as small as possible, and the general proportions of the lines adhered to while all is made fair and true, the result will be satisfactory.

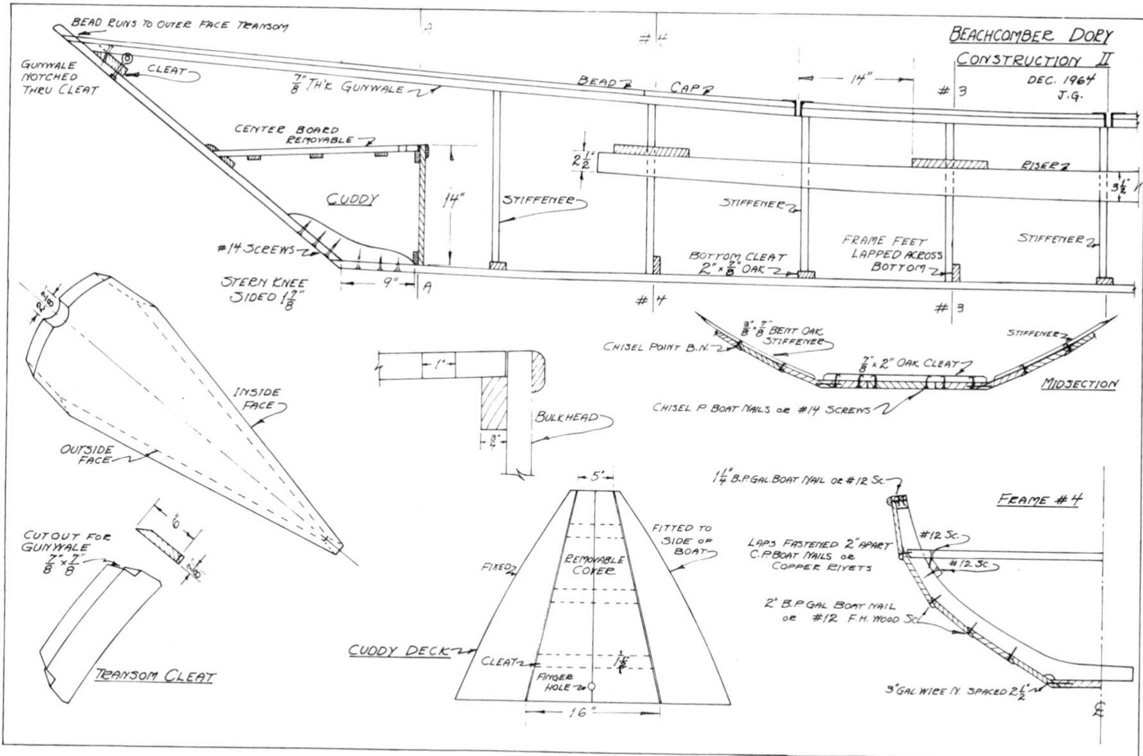

I believe that no two workmen, however skilled and careful, could ever achieve exactly the same lay-down, nor would there be any point in trying to. I am sure that Chamberlain never built any two Beachcombers exactly alike, although no hull ever left his shop that was not beautiful and true and that did not meet his very exacting specifications for the Beachcomber hull. Yet all Beachcombers were individuals, as alike as peas in a pod, and as different. This is the point where craft leaves off and art begins.

I would underline that lines and offsets alone are not enough for building this boat. They provide the raw materials for the fairing process, which, besides being a technical operation, is an artistic endeavor and a creative act.

MATERIALS

Originally the Beachcomber was built entirely of oak and pine lumber with the exception of hackmatack for its four sets of natural-crook sawn frames, and sometimes for thwart knees and breast hook. It was fastened throughout with galvanized boat nails, and the fittings and hardware were all of galvanized iron. All in all, scantlings and fastenings were on the light side to give as light a hull as possible for fast sailing, and it is a tribute to the inherent strength of dory construction, and the careful workmanship by which these dories were put together, that they lasted as long and stood up as well as they did.

In some of the older boats, weakened by years of hard sailing or by collision, a brace in the form of a ⅜-inch iron rod with a turnbuckle in the middle ran from gunwale to gunwale just forward of the mast. This was not standard equipment, however, and I have not drawn it in the plans.

Today a lighter and stronger boat could undoubtedly be built by the judicious substitution of modern materials, including screws, plywood, glue, and resin-bonded fabric reinforcements. Safety flotation can be supplied by plastic foams. Undoubtedly, if Chamberlain were alive today and building dories, he would take advantage of the newer materials. As it was, I believe that screws had to some extent replaced nails in the last of the Beachcombers.

A list of "General Specifications" for the Beachcomber has been found among Chamberlain's papers. It is not complete, although nearly all items of importance are included. We shall use it as an outline, considering each of the headings in turn and adding such supplementary data as is needed.

Bottom. White pine, ⅞ inch in thickness, which is about a minimum bottom thickness for nailing on a garboard. Normally, either two or three boards will be required to make up a maximum bottom width of 21½ inches. Standard nailing for garboards into the edge of the bottom is with 3-inch galvanized wire nails spaced about 2½ inches. A fine pilot hole for each nail is carefully sighted and drilled to prevent the nail from entering at the wrong angle, causing it to split through either one face or the other. As a substitute, bronze of monel Anchorfast nails will hold equally well or better and will last longer; they'll also cost considerably more.

A bottom of plywood, ½ inch or even ⅜ inch thick, would be adequate, except that an internal chine strip would be required for fastening the edges of the garboards. For additional reinforcement and complete watertightness, this bottom edge, when plywood is used, should be bound with glass fabric or Dynel set in epoxy resin.

Bottom cleats. The several boards making up the standard pine bottom are cleated athwartships between frame stations and at the ends with 2-inch strips of oak ⅞ inch thick and laid flat. These are made short enough to let water run around the ends. They were originally fastened on from the outside with 2-inch galvanized chisel-point boat nails with the points turned back and clinched into the wood, but now it is generally easier to secure them with No. 12 or No. 14 screws, 1½ inches or 1¾ inches long.

Stern transom. Oak, ⅞ inch thick. If one board is used, a width of 16½ inches is required, which is probably wider than is commonly obtainable. Two boards will do, provided one is quite wide and the two are solidly joined with No. 12 or No. 14 1½-inch screws into the stern cleat.

Stern knee. Oak, 1⅞ inches thick like the stem, fastened to the transom with No. 14 or No. 16 screws, 1½ inches to 3 inches long. Originally this would have been fastened with galvanized blunt-point boat nails of approximately the same lengths.

Stern cleat. Oak, ⅞ inch thick. The molded width of 6 inches is sufficient to allow for through-bolting of the ⅜-inch eyebolt for the main sheet block.

Stem. Oak, sided 1⅞ inches and molded 2¼ inches.

Outer or false stem. Oak, a strip about 2 inches wide by 1¼ inches thick, steam bent on the flat into place, nailed or screwed down tight, and finished to shape when cold.

Frames. Chamberlain lists: "4 sets hackmatack, sided ⅞ inch molded 2 inches between knuckles fastened to the bottom with galv. iron boat nails." Such natural-crook hack frames were crossed by each other across the bottom of the boat. More frequently, instead of such matched pairs of natural-crook frames, a three-part oak frame was substituted comprised of two side futtocks and a single piece across the bottom, the three joined together with riveted galvanized iron clips at the bottom knuckles. No. 12 or No. 14 screws 1¾ inches to 2 inches long fasten up through the bottom.

Stiffeners. Oak, ⅜ inch by ⅞ inch of tough, selected butt stock, steam-bent on the flat into place between the frame stations and in the ends to fit the shape of the boat, and fastened through the laps. Originally chisel-point boat nails were used with points turned back and clinched into the inside of the strip. Now that good chisel point nails are difficult to obtain, copper wire nails riveted over burrs make an excellent substitute.

Planking. Pine, 9/16 inch thick. Boards as wide as 16 inches are required for the garboards. Now that planks can be spliced with waterproof glues, great savings are possible by using pieced-out strakes glued up from shorter lengths of lumber. For the wide garboards (wide ends),

⅜-inch plywood may be substituted, scarphed and glue spliced from shorter pieces cut from 8-foot panels.

In fact, the boat may be planked entirely with plywood. Nor is it necessary to lap the plywood in the conventional way. The strakes may be butted and glued to internal longitudinal seam battens. In that case the joints may be bound with fabric tapes set in epoxy resin, or the whole surface of the hull may be covered with fabric set in epoxy.

In fastening conventional pine planking, No. 12 1¾-inch or 2-inch screws go through the laps into the frames, but only through the laps, for screws through the planks to the frames between laps are liable to split the planks. As previously mentioned, the lower edge of the garboards is nailed with 3-inch nails to the bottom.

The laps were fastened originally with clinched chisel-point nails spaced 2 inches to 2½ inches. Now, riveted copper wire nails would probably have to be substituted, but they are better and more lasting fastenings if properly put in. Incidentally, the 9/16-inch planking is beveled a width of 1⅛ inches.

Gunwales. Oak, ⅞ inch thick, and 1⅜ inches wide between frames, but tapering at the ends to ⅞ inch at the stem and stern. These are bent into place and fastened down into timberheads and through the sheer plank from the outside. Nails or screws may be used.

Capping. Oak, 9/16 inch thick and 2 inches wide, steamed, bent into place on the boat, and fastened down into the gunwales with nails or screws. The capping extends an inch or so past the frames at either end.

Beading. Oak, 9/16 inch thick by one inch wide, beveled on the inner edge, sprung to the shape of the boat at the ends, extending from where the capping stops to the stem and transom. It covers the top edge of the sheer plank and part of the gunwale, and can be fastened with screws or nails.

Breast hook. Natural crook hackmatack, apple, oak, ⅞ inch thick. It receives the ends of the gunwales, fastens to the stem, and takes fastenings through the sheer plank from outside.

Guard. Oak, half round, one inch wide. It should be planed so it tapers slightly at the ends for appearance. It can be nailed or screwed in place.

Thwarts. Pine, ⅞ inch thick by 9 inches wide. They are notched around the frames and screwed down to the seat risers with No. 12 2-inch screws.

Thwart knees. Hackmatack, apple, oak, ⅞ inch or ¾ inch thick. They are screwed where possible to the frames, thwarts, gunwale, and sheer plank, being fitted carefully against these.

Risers. Pine, ⅝ inch or ¾ inch thick and 3½ inches wide in the center, tapering to 2½ inches at the ends. They should be beveled on the top edge to receive the thwarts and screw fastened into the frames with 1½-inch No. 12 screws.

Centerboard trunk. Sides pine; lower half ⅞ inch thick, upper part can be 9/16 inch thick for lightness. The end posts, mortised through the bottom, are of oak, 1 1/16 inches thick by 1½ inches wide. The sides should be copper riveted through the posts.

Centerboard. Oak, finished ⅞ inch thick. It should be pinned with drifts of 5/16 inch rod and lead weighted.

Mast step. Oak block 4 inches by 4 inches by 6 inches notched over foot of No. 1 frame.

Mast hole reinforcement. Oak, ⅞ inch thick, by 9 inches wide.

Rudder. Oak, 1⅛ inches thick at the upper end of the stock, thinned to ¾ inch at the lower after edge. It should be pinned with 9/16-inch and ¼-inch rod.

Rudder yoke. Oak, ¾ inch thick.

Stern sheets cuddy. Pine, ¾ inch and 9/16 inch thick, fastened with No. 12 screws.

Gratings or racks. Pine, 9/16 inch thick, built to be removable.

Spars. Douglas fir, or spruce.

RUDDER AND CENTERBOARD

No surviving rudder or centerboard for the Beachcomber-Alpha is now to be found for copying, yet I have been able to get together enough reliable data from one source or another to reconstruct these essential accessories with

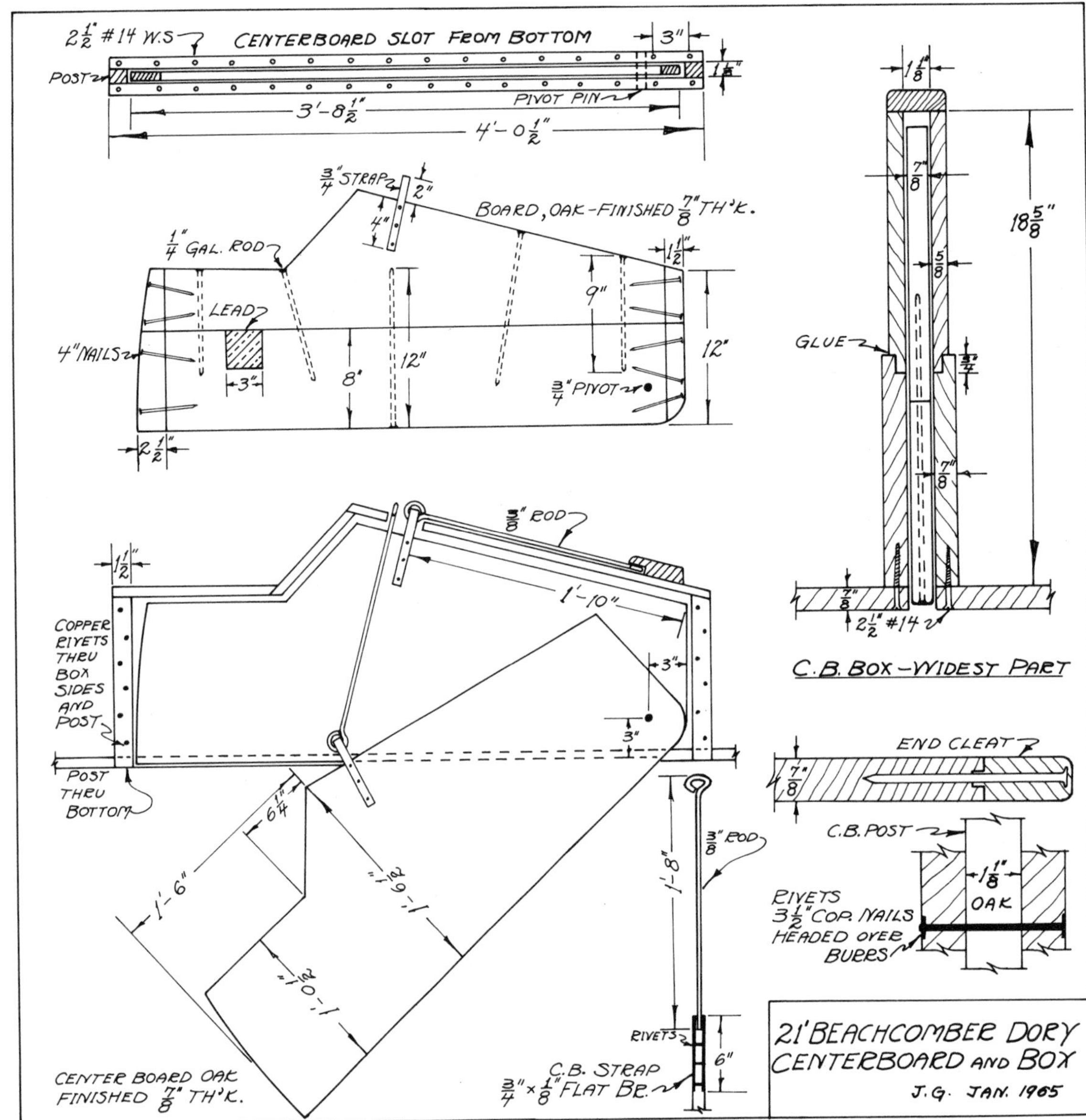

substantial accuracy. Both are typical of sailing dories of the period. Their design and construction are quite simple, yet even so, pains must be taken in putting them together, and there are several things that the amateur builder should be sure he understands before he sets to work.

Even if a single board wide enough to make the rudder in one piece were obtainable, it is better to make it of two boards, as I show, as a precaution against warping. And with two boards, the lumber should not be slash sawn, but as nearly rift sawn as possible, that is, with the grain of the annual rings running at right angles with the wide surface. Furthermore, when the two boards, or parts, are joined, they should be placed so that the grain in one runs opposite to the grain in the other. If warping takes place, the distortion in one part will tend to offset the distortion in the other, instead of adding to it, as happens when two or more boards are joined with their grain running in the same direction.

This precaution against warping is even more important in the construction of the

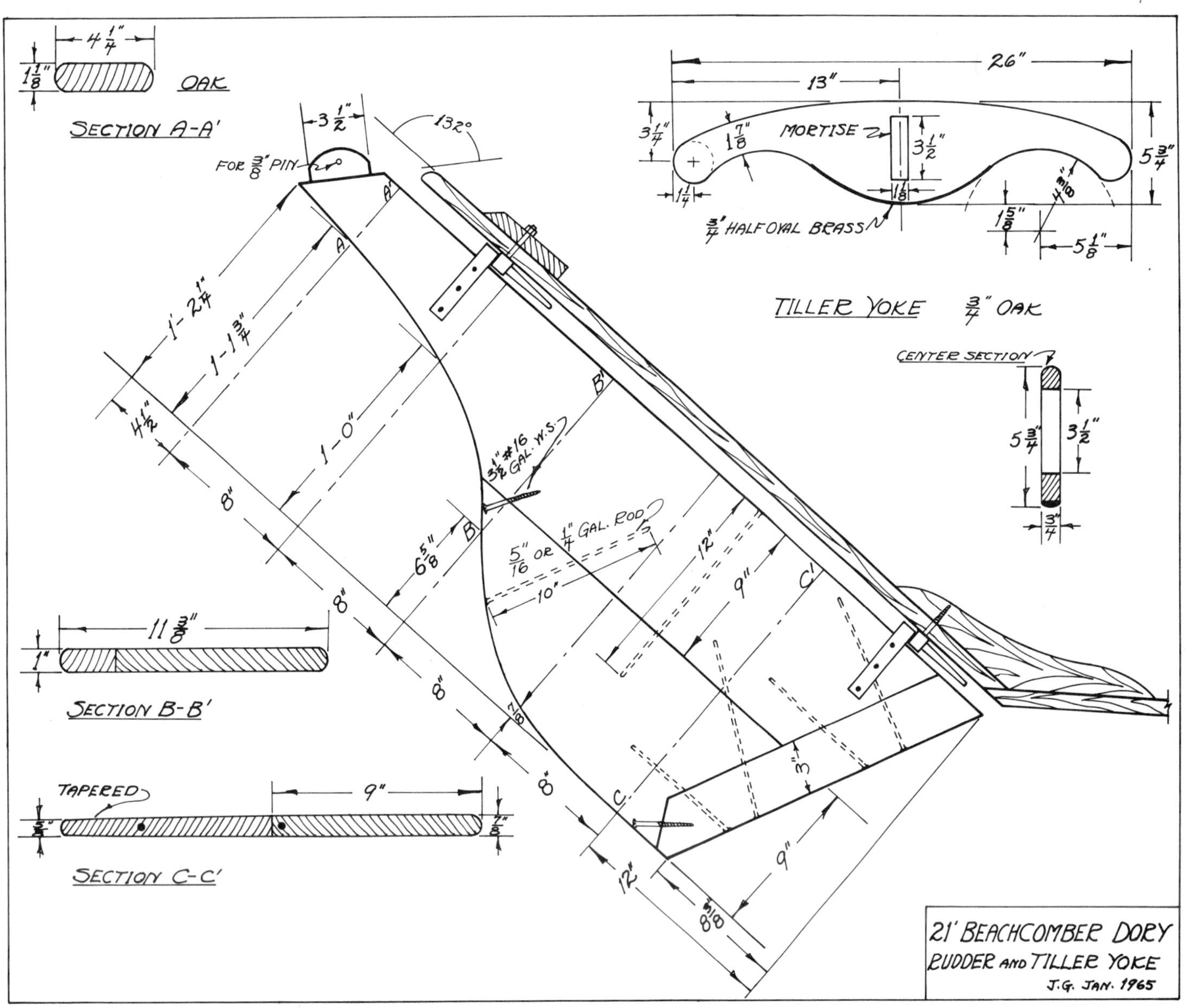

centerboard, for there, if even a small amount of warping or "dishing" takes place, the board will stick in its slot and will not be able to be put in or hauled out of its box. The cleats on the ends of the centerboard, like the cleat on the bottom of the rudder, are put there to stop warping or twisting, although they also help to hold the assemblies together.

For both rudder and centerboard, the lumber should be dry, well-seasoned oak. Green lumber—oak especially—is bound to twist and warp. Oak is specified because it is standard for New England dories, being what Chamberlain and other contemporary builders invariably used. A hard, solid grade of Philippine mahogany could be substituted. This wood keeps its shape and holds fastenings well, and costs less, or is no more expensive, now, than a good grade of seasoned oak.

Plywood could also be substituted for oak for both rudder and centerboard, but if this is done, it would be best to cover the plywood with a skin of Dynel fabric bedded in epoxy resin. This covering serves both to waterproof the plywood and to reinforce it. By making up these parts from plywood, the need for pinning and cleating would be bypassed, for each could be made in a single piece. This would save a lot of labor and might more than offset the cost and trouble of adding the Dynel fabric and epoxy resin. Should the rudder be made of fir plywood, it would be necessary to reinforce the tenon that passes through the rudder yoke. With waterproof mahogany or birch plywood, such reinforcement would not be required.

If oak is used, and pinned together as laid out in the drawings, the amateur should be briefed ahead of time as how best to go about this, for the operation is a fairly critical one that could easily be messed up for the want of the correct procedure. In boring for the pins, the uninstructed novice rarely gets his holes lined up accurately and too frequently puts his drill out through the side. Yet the operation is not essentially difficult. For detailed instructions on this, see the Appendix.

For the rudder, galvanized rod of 5/16 inch diameter is recommended for pinning, although 1/4-inch rod would do. Because the galvanizing adds slightly to the diameter, the drill should be the same size as the listed size of the rod. Even then it may be hard to drive without bending, especially the 1/4-inch rod. A heavy hammer is better for driving than a light one.

For the centerboard, 5/16-inch rod should be used. If the holes as laid out are drilled according to the method described in the Appendix, that is, from both sides of each piece separately, no bored depth would be greater than 4½ inches, so there should be little danger of running off.

After the rudder is pinned, it is planed smooth and tapered, and the positions of the pintles and gudgeons are located. The top gudgeon is easily bolted through the transom cleat for extra strength. The pintles specified open 7/8 inch between the straps. The straps of the top pintle will be let in slightly, for the rudder at that point is 1⅛ inches thick. The straps of the bottom pintle will slip on without cutting, since there the rudder is tapered to 7/8 inch. The pintle straps are fastened on with copper rivets.

The tenon on the rudder head must fit the mortise in the yoke snugly, so as not to wobble. A 3/8-inch removable pin further secures it. Only the weight of the rudder itself is required to keep the pintles from slipping out of the gudgeons under most conditions. If the rudder should come unshipped, the tiller lines would keep it from getting away.

The only feature of the yoke that needs mention is the reinforcement of ¾-inch half-oval brass that binds and reinforces the center part of the forward edge where there would be some danger, otherwise, of breaking because of the short grain. Normally, this brass would be secured by screws.

The centerboard box is rather light, but that is the way Chamberlain's specifications show it. I, myself, do not think that much weight is saved by reducing the thickness of the upper half of the box to 5/8 inch. In fact I would prefer that the sides of the box be 15/16 inch or even one inch throughout. The end posts should always extend through the bottom, as shown, both to stiffen the box and to permit caulking the ends from the outside. Copper rivets are the best fastenings for the ends of the box, but these must be well headed over and set up tightly so that they pull into the wood. I would like to see the box put together and bedded with waterproof adhesive, preferably epoxy, for additional strength as well as watertightness. The old builders like Chamberlain used white lead, which gave a tight seal but did not make the construction any stronger.

The centerboard pivot pin is sometimes made of white oak or locust, in which case, it ought to be 1 inch in diameter. I have shown it as ¾-inch diameter brass or bronze. It must fit tightly, yet be removable in case it is desired to drop the board.

Sometimes a large screw eye or even an eye bolt was fastened to the top of the board for attaching the rod used for raising and lowering the board. I show a simple strap arrangement of ¾-inch by ⅛-inch flat bronze, attached with copper rivets. The handle is easily formed of 3/8-inch rod with an eye to hook into the strap on the board and a T-shaped outer end. This T-end or cross-bar rests on the top of the box when the board is down, preventing it from going farther. When the board is up, the T-end slips under a special cleat on the front end of the box, locking the board in the up position. This is a simple but effective device that was generally used on centerboard dories of the Beachcomber period.

One thing that should be mentioned is that

the lumber thicknesses given are quite critical in some cases and should not be reduced even if retail lumberyards attempt to argue otherwise. For instance, ⅞-inch thick pine for the bottom or the sides of the centerboard box should under no circumstances be less than ⅞ inch thick. Most "one-inch" pine boards as sold today are actually only ¾ inch thick. So you may have to have your pine planed up special, and if you do, I, myself, would specify a "plump" ⅞ inch, which, if it ran to ¹⁵⁄₁₆ inch, would be all the better.

THE RIG

In describing the Beachcomber-Alpha rig, we shall start at the bow. The luff of the jib is laced or seized to a length of ³⁄₁₆-inch, 7 by 7 galvanized yacht wire with thimbles spliced in either end. The tack end attaches by a ³⁄₁₆-inch screw-pin shackle to a no. 1 galvanized swivel-eye boat snap, which hooks into a ⅜-inch galvanized eye bolt through the stem head. The upper eye of the jib luff wire takes another no. 1 swivel-eye boat snap, which is shackled to a single block for ⅜-inch line. Another single block of the same size shackles to a 4-inch or 5-inch galvanized eye plate, which screws to the mast at the height designated on the rigging plan. Two ³⁄₁₆-inch screw pin shackles are needed for a fast eye block; one for a swivel eye block.

The jib halyard of ⅜-inch manila carries an eyesplice in the upper end just large enough to slip over the masthead, supported about 3 feet 6 inches below on a wooden shoulder cleat. The lower end reeves through the block snapped into the thimble at the head of the jib, back through the block fixed to the mast and is hauled down taut, passing through a leader on the port top forward edge of the mast thwart, and securing to a 5-inch cleat on the after side of the thwart. This arrangement makes a separate headstay unnecessary.

The halyard arrangement is simplicity itself, but effective and generally substantial, although weak snaps have been known to break under the strain of pounding into a heavy chop. While ⁵⁄₁₆-inch manila might be sufficiently strong here, ⁵⁄₁₆-inch dacron would be more than ample. Dacron, except for its higher cost, is to be preferred here as in every other part of the rig, not only for its great strength and long wearing qualities but also because it handles easily and does not stretch.

The twin jib sheets of ¼-inch manila are permanently spliced into the clew of the jib, although some Beachcomber sailors preferred to have them on snaps. These sheets lead aft through swivel-eye single blocks shackled to ¼-inch galvanized eye bolts through the seat risers, either side, 15 inches forward of station 2, and secure to a 4-inch cleat on the after slope of the centerboard box, above and forward of the second thwart.

The mast and boom are solid sticks of Douglas fir, according to Chamberlain's specifications, but Sitka spruce or eastern red spruce would be just as good or better. The mast is 3½ inches in diameter where it passes through the thwart and tapers to 2 inches at the head. It rises 16 feet above the thwart and extends 1 foot below, requiring a length of 17 feet in all. The gooseneck for the boom attaches about 5 inches above the thwart. The gooseneck was generally of brass or bronze of a type that attached to the end of the boom with side straps fastened by through rivets. The boom, 15 feet 6 inches long, is 2½ inches in diameter centrally, tapering to 2 inches at the inner end and 1¾ inches at the outer.

The mainsail is lashed permanently to the boom and mast with Italian hemp marline or suitable Dacron cord by a continuous series of half hitches passing through small grommets set close to the edges of the sail and spaced on 10-inch centers. Grommets of the same size and spacing are likewise pierced through the luff of the jib for its lashings.

Larger, heavier grommets in the corners of the sails permit lashings at the ends of the spars. The head and the tack of the jib are held taut by lashings through respective eyes in the ends of the luff wire. The tack of the mainsail is lashed to the gooseneck. The head, in absence of a main halyard, is pulled up by lashings passing

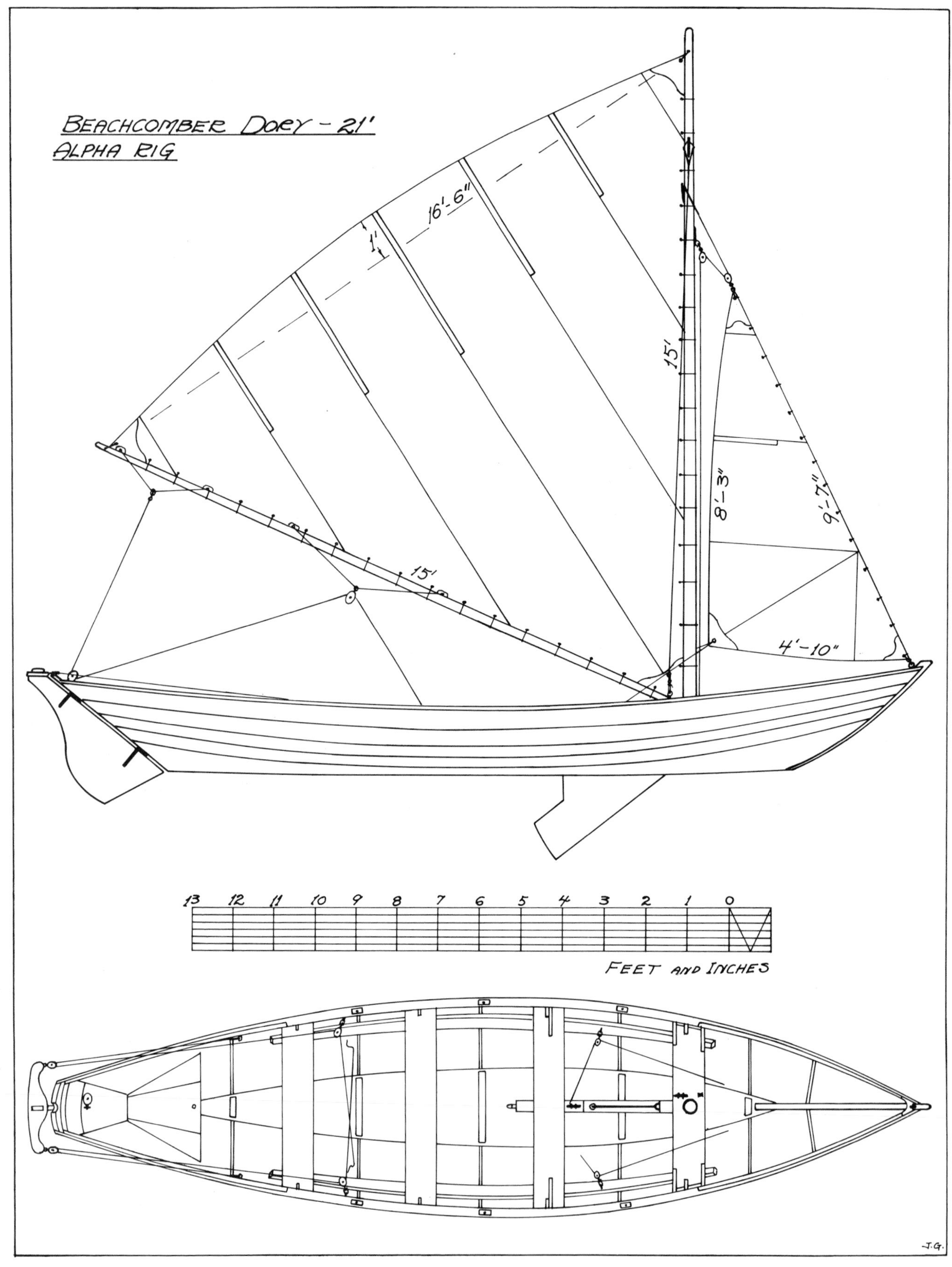
BEACHCOMBER DORY - 21'
ALPHA RIG
16'-6"
1'
15'
8'-3"
9'-7"
15'
4'-10"
13 12 11 10 9 8 7 6 5 4 3 2 1 0
FEET AND INCHES
J.G.

through a ⅜-inch hole bored through the top of the mast a couple of inches higher than the stretch of the sail. Likewise, a hole bored in the outer end of the boom allows a lashing from the clew that serves as an outhaul.

The two side stays or shrouds are 3/16-inch 7 by 7 galvanized yacht wire (stainless steel would be better) with eye splices served and varnished at the upper ends of a size to slip over the masthead and to lead neatly from ash shoulder cleats. Thimbles spliced into the lower ends allow lacing with light line to draw the stays taut. Turnbuckles are not used; instead, ⅜-inch galvanized iron eyebolts pass through the rail from 4 inches to 6 inches abaft the center of the mast. The eyes in the ends of the side stays hang about 6 inches above. A light line or lanyard threaded back and forth several times through these opposing eyes, secured with a couple of half hitches around the standing parts, puts sufficient tension in the stay. In an emergency two slashes with a knife will free the mast.

Formerly the main sheet was made of cotton line because it was softer on the hands than hemp or manila. Dacron would be best today, and for Dacron only ⅜-inch diameter line would be required, while cotton for this purpose should not be less than 7/16 inch.

The main sheet requires two bridles on the boom. Old photographs show considerable variation in the length and location of these bridles. It is suggested that the outer one at the end of the boom, with the ring at its mid-point to take the snap in the end of the main sheet, should be 1½ feet to 2 feet long with a drop of 6 inches, and that the inner or center bridle, which carries the main sheet block, should be 3½ feet to 4 feet long with a 12-inch drop. Further, there should be about 6 feet between the center points of the two.

These bridles have eye splices in their ends of a size to slip over the boom, and are held in position by small ash stops fastened with two screws each. It is important that these bridles should not stretch; no doubt hemp was originally used. Dacron resists stretching well, and the ⅜-inch dacron recommended for the sheet would do nicely for these straps as well.

As previously mentioned, the outer end of the main sheet snaps into a ring tied in the outer bridle. Thence it leads down through a single block, preferably swiveled, which is shackled to a ⅜-inch eyebolt passing through the center of the transom and vertically located slightly below the bottom of the sheer strake. From this block the sheet leads forward and up through another swiveled single block secured at the mid-point of the inner and larger bridle. Thence it leads downward and forward to be secured when desired on a jam cleat of ash or white oak bolted to the after vertical post of the centerboard box.

In the past, a few well-heeled skippers had brass snatch blocks attached to swivel deck plates which bolted to the bottom of the boat about a foot aft of the centerboard box.

Since 5/16-inch manila is ample for the two tiller lines, ¼-inch dacron will do nicely. One end of the tiller line snaps into a ¼-inch ring bolt or an equivalent screw eye set in the inner edge of the rail about 1 foot 5 inches aft of Station 3. The resulting two-part purchase is sufficient to work the rudder easily from almost any location in the middle of the boat. To secure the rudder, equivalent to lashing the tiller in other boats, the two lines are pulled tight thwartships and tied.

Rowlock sockets are set in the rail 12 inches aft of the after edges of the three forward thwarts so that the boat can be rowed from each of these thwarts if desired. When not in use, rowlocks are stored in the small after cuddy next to the transom. Here also could be stored the mooring line which was used without mooring chocks, being tied through the mast hole and lashed to the eye in the stemhead to hold it centrally.

A pair of 8-foot oars tied under the front thwart on either side, with the blades extending to the stem, were always carried in the old Beachcomber-Alphas. For rowing, some dories had a small hole through the upper part of the box through which a pin could be inserted to hold the board part way down to act as a keel for steadying the boat and holding it on course.

Now that we've seen how to rig the recreated Beachcomber-Alpha, let's look at the evolution of the rig.

HISTORICAL DEVELOPMENT OF THE RIG

The Beachcomber-Alpha sailing rig went through several evolutions over the years. We can trace the development of the rig from the recollections of those who owned and sailed these dories at various times. The features of the rig would be known and remembered by the dory sailor, while any precise apprehension of hull lines would not. Besides, numerous dated photographs of Beachcomber-Alpha dories have been preserved, showing comprehensive rigging details.

The committee representing the survivors of the Beachcomber and Alpha Dory Clubs, which recently presented to the Peabody Museum of Salem a scale model of a 21-foot Chamberlain Beachcomber-Alpha sailing dory constructed under their supervision and rigged to their specifications, diligently canvassed all former members of the two clubs that could be located concerning details of the rig as they recalled them. The secretary of the committee, Chesler L. Pattee, formerly of Salem, whose father helped organize the Salem club, and who, himself, had owned and skippered an Alpha dory from 1915 to 1924, headed up the rig research and furnished the sails for the museum model.

Pattee suggests that there were generally three eras of Beachcomber-Alpha evolution characterized by and, to some extent, caused by, marked departures in rig. He calls them:

1. The primeval period, extending from the class's inception in the 1890s through the first decade of this century.
2. The intermediate period, the second decade of the century with apogee circa 1915.
3. The sophisticated period, the third decade of the century and more precisely after 1925.

In the primeval period, side stays or shrouds had not appeared. The peak of the jib snapped into the eye of a short hemp pennant hung from the upper part of the mast. A piece of rope was spliced into the tack of the jib and was threaded through an eye in the stem head, pulled taut, and made fast. There was no jib halyard, so this arrangement was all there was to keep the mast from jumping out of its step.

An early modification and refinement of this first primitive arrangement is shown by photographs to have been the addition of a single sheave block to the end of the pennant that held the peak of the jib. This permitted the corresponding addition of a simple, single-purchase jib halyard. This was an important advance in the rig, for by changing the tension on the halyard, which served also as a headstay, the rake of the mast and the center of effort of the mainsail could be moved back and forth somewhat, better to suit the weather and to balance the rig.

The second or intermediate period was ushered in, Pattee is inclined to believe, not so much by the addition of side stays as by the adoption of a roached, "cross-cut" and battened mainsail, which rendered side stays necessary. Although no separate headstay appears at this time, the luff of the jib was beefed up with a length of rigging wire from the stemhead, and a second block was added to give extra purchase to the jib halyard, which doubled as forestay, permitting easy adjustment of tension for varying the rake of the mast.

The sophisticated, or final, stage brought permanent standing rigging, with metal turnbuckles replacing the simple lacings formerly used. Sails were enlarged and put on "runners," that is, track, necessitating another halyard. Heavier and more expensive fittings were added along with extras like mooring chocks. The rig was no longer capable of being lifted out at the end of a day's sailing to be carried home on the skipper's shoulder; now sails were furled and left on the boat. The boat was no longer rowed any more with the rig down, as was the lobsterman's dory from whence it evolved.

As the third decade closed, popular demand was for larger and more specialized racing types. In the ensuing competition with more powerful racing classes like the Massachusetts Bay Indian, also out of Chamberlain's shop, Sam Brown's Yankee Dory, the Marblehead Class, and the Alden O-Boat, the Beachcomber-Alpha rapidly lost ground, and after the death of Chamberlain in the early 1930s no more were built.

The ad hoc committee, set up in 1959 to

recover the Beachcomber-Alpha design and details to guide the construction of an authentic scale model, decided that the rig in general use circa 1915 was most representative. The committee researched this rig exhaustively. The immediate big difficulty that confronted the committee was that no specimen of the dories of the intermediate period had survived for measurement. Another vexing problem involved the dimensions of the sails.

A blueprint sail plan for the Beachcomber found among papers in possession of the Chamberlain family gave the dimensions as 15 feet equally on boom and hoist, 17 feet 11 inches on the leach, and a roach of 12 inches. But Chesler Pattee after inquiry and study, and from personal recollections, rejected the 17-foot 11-inch leach in favor of a 16-foot 6-inch leach dimension for the Alpha mainsail. His reasoning was as follows:

1. A mainsail for this dory with a leach longer than 16 feet 6 inches would drag excessively in the water when sailing on a broad reach in a stiff breeze.

2. The sail with the longer leach looks wrong when drawn to scale, and the lower boom angle does not correspond with contemporary photographs.

3. Recalling youthful experience, Pattee remembers it was quite a reach for a lad five feet tall to unsnap the main sheet from the bridle at the end of the boom when standing with one foot on the cuddy cover, which was about 12 inches above the bottom of the boat.

4. The helmsman on the third thwart would duck in coming about, more to dodge the main sheet pulley than to avoid being hit by the boom.

The late Samuel H. Brown, Jr., lifelong Marblehead doryman as well as a designer of successful sailing dories himself, in a letter to the committee in 1959, gave his recollections of the Alpha mainsail as 15 feet on boom and hoist, but failed to specify the distance across the leach. For the Beachcomber main, Brown recalled 16 feet 6 inches on the boom and hoist and 18 feet on the leach, which when laid out to scale gives approximately the same angle of rake for the boom as the 15-foot by 15-foot by 16½-foot sail, and this accords with the local tradition that the Beachcombers carried more canvas than the Alphas. Finally in a list of "General Specifications, Beachcomber (Swampscott) Dory" (no date), sails are described and dimensioned as "leg o' mutton style, of No. 1 sailcloth, 15 feet on boom, 15 feet on mast, 16½ feet on leach with 12 inch roach. Jib of proper size."

So 15 feet by 15 feet by 16 feet 6 inches then are the dimensions for the main as finally adopted for this design. Naturally that doesn't prevent anyone from experimenting with canvas of larger or smaller measurements, should he so desire. It is said that some Marblehead skippers had three separate sizes of spars and sails for their dories: an oversize rig for racing, a medium rig for ordinary sailing, and a cutdown rig for heavy weather.

It will bear emphasizing that the Beachcomber-Alpha class did not enforce rigid uniformity. Considerable variation in rigs obtained from boat to boat. While we can't be sure about possible alterations in lines, there were some differences in internal hull arrangements. Instead of cross thwarts, some boats had benches along the sides aft of the centerboard box. Others left out the bottom gratings. Some carried 50 pounds of lead ballast on either side the centerboard. A few were reinforced with a ⅜-inch galvanized iron rod and turnbuckles running from side to side through the sheer strake just forward of the mast.

It is not suggested that the rig described in detail previously is the best one or the only one worth considering. But it is the rig most used when the class was at the peak of its popularity. It will do to set a norm, but a norm that a present-day builder would probably want to depart from to some extent. It does constitute a tried and tested rig that is probably the least expensive and the least complicated of any that are workable and safe. But some of the newer things like Dacron yacht rope, stainless steel wire, and some of the newer fittings are more than worth the extra cost.

15 A Sharpie

The 18-foot sharpie *Shag*, formerly owned by Charles H. F. Storrow of Stonington, Connecticut, is ideal for the home builder who wants a family boat of proven qualities, and one that is simple and easy to build and not too expensive. Of course, with the price of lumber what it is today, no boat is going to be cheap to build at this time, but even so, the cost and availability of materials for *Shag* will stack up favorably with those for any comparable craft.

Charlie Storrow has generous words for *Shag*: "She is a wonderful boat. She sails well and is easy to handle, is surprisingly able in a hard breeze, and is ideal for picnics, landing on beaches and similar activities. On a broad reach in a good breeze she is really fast. She is, in my opinion, strikingly handsome. . . . As a day sailer for a family with young children, there could be no better boat. She would also be a great boat for the home builder because of her extreme simplicity." Yet—and there always is a yet of some kind—Storrow suggested two possible improvements. One: more canvas, for as she is rigged, she is a bit slow in light airs. Two: less weather helm. Both of these will be discussed at length later.

Shag served the Storrow family well for almost seven years, but eventually their need for a bigger boat capable of extended cruising impelled them to buy a large catboat. *Shag* was sold, but not until Charlie had carefully measured and recorded her lines and details. As Storrow is an architect by profession and an amateur builder of some experience (he completed the boatbuilding course at Mystic Seaport), the job was well done.

We would have reproduced his drawings as Storrow did them, except that they were too large, and some of the details were too small to permit the reproduction required to fit these pages. The drawings printed here follow Storrow's plans closely without any essential changes. I have added, however, a larger sail plan for a longer version of this sharpie, as will be discussed, and additional plans for the centerboard.

CONSTRUCTION

A few remarks about the construction: There is nothing difficult or unusual involved in building this boat, nothing that any one of a half-dozen current boatbuilding manuals cannot explain quite handily. Only common species of lumber are required—pine, cedar, Douglas fir, hard pine, and oak. For the most part, fastening can be done with galvanized nails. Decks should be ⅜-inch exterior fir plywood; spars, Douglas fir, if need be, spliced with epoxy glue.

Comments on the numbered references on the construction plan follow:

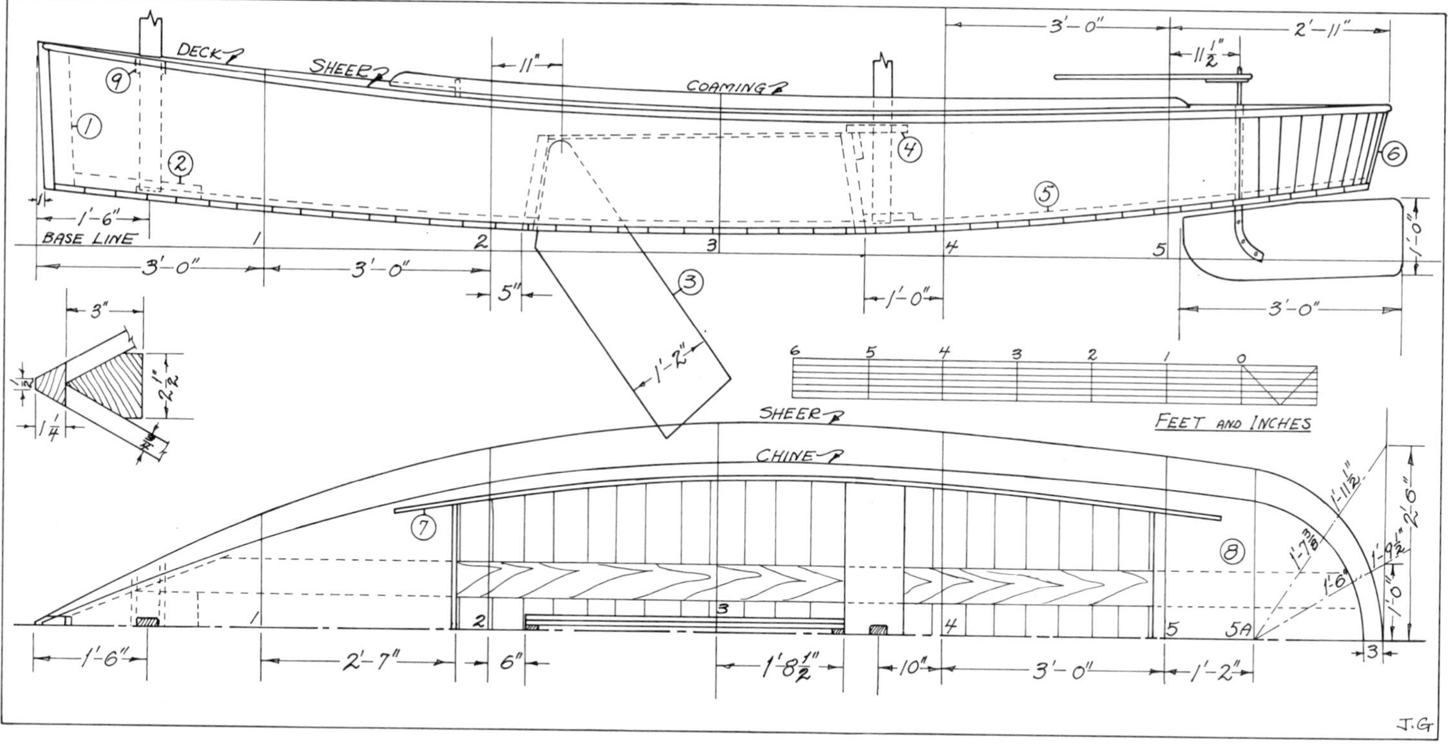

1. Inner stem—oak, hard pine, Douglas fir.

2. Mast step—oak, hard pine, Douglas fir, 1½ inches thick. Makes a solid reinforcement at the bow into which the short cross planks are well nailed with 8d galvanized wire nails.

3. Centerboard—¼-inch steel. Better made of wood. Heavy logs bolted to the bottom for the centerboard trunk. Without a cross brace, thwart or other, to stay the forward end of the trunk, there is need for extra heavy logs. Left open forward so that two people can sleep on the bottom, one on either side of the trunk. (More on the centerboard and trunk later.)

4. Combination thwart, centerboard trunk brace, bridge deck—oak, Douglas fir, ash. Full inch thick, if possible, reinforce on underside in way of mast.

5. Two keelsons—oak, Douglas fir, hard pine. Run inside the whole length of the bottom. Set in paint. Well nailed or screwed into each cross plank from the outside of the boat in.

6. Vertical staving—white pine or cedar—like the longitudinal side planking. Cypress very good if obtainable.

7. Coaming.

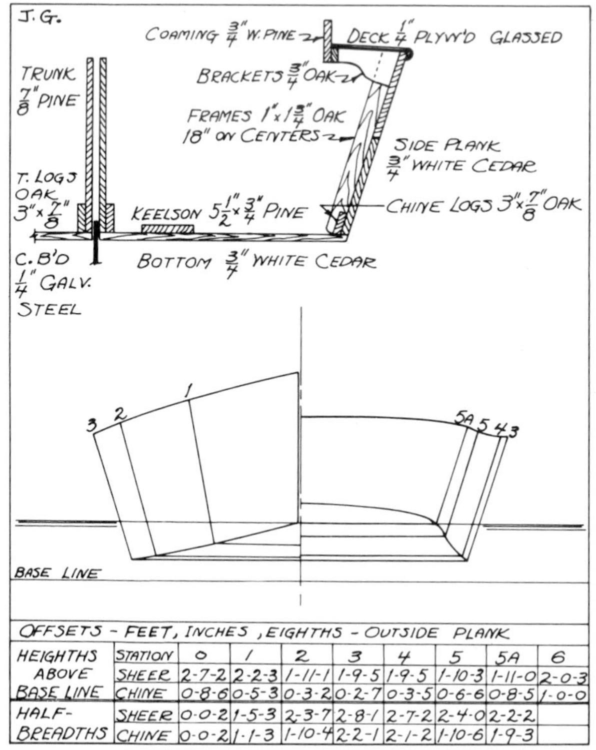

OFFSETS – FEET, INCHES, EIGHTHS – OUTSIDE PLANK

	STATION	0	1	2	3	4	5	5A	6
HEIGHTHS ABOVE BASE LINE	SHEER	2-7-2	2-2-3	1-11-1	1-9-5	1-9-5	1-10-3	1-11-0	2-0-3
	CHINE	0-8-6	0-5-3	0-3-2	0-2-7	0-3-5	0-6-6	0-8-5	1-0-0
HALF-BREADTHS	SHEER	0-0-2	1-5-3	2-3-7	2-8-1	2-7-2	2-4-0	2-2-2	
	CHINE	0-0-2	1-1-3	1-10-4	2-2-1	2-1-2	1-10-6	1-9-3	

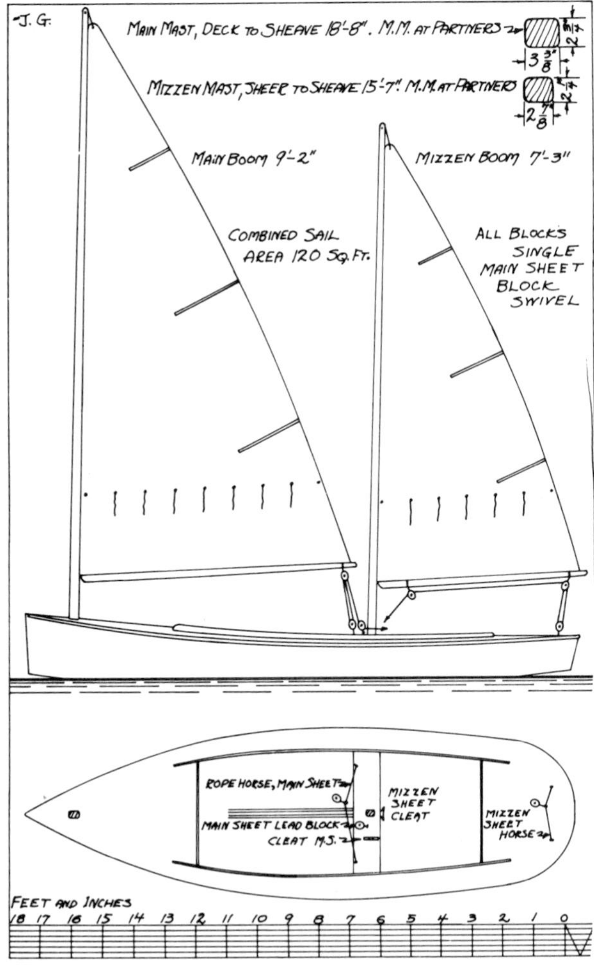

8. Deck, fore and aft—⅜-inch exterior fir plywood on slightly cambered deck beams, spruce, Douglas fir, oak.

9. Mast partners, also deck beams. Blocked under deck both sides.

The strength of this boat will be greatly increased by use of epoxy glue in all joints and on all contacting surfaces throughout.

THE SAILING RIG

Now let's go into the elements that could improve the boat. Charlie Storrow felt one of *Shag*'s weaknesses was light air performance. He experimented with a bowsprit and jib but the complication in rigging them did not seem worth the effort. But adding canvas will improve her performance. Together, we came up with a solution. In adding canvas, we felt that the essential character and proportions of the old rig should not be altered. As the main boom cannot be lengthened because of the location of the mizzen mast, the only way to increase the area of the mainsail would be to increase the height of the mast, but this was considered unwise, to the extent that would be required, for the obvious effect on stability.

There is a way to get more sail area without changing the character of the original rig. This is by lengthening the boat. *Shag*'s simple sharpie lines permit a 4-inch increase in station spacing—from 36 inches to 40 inches—without altering the basic shape, except for the increase in overall length of 2 feet. This allows longer booms as well as increasing stability somewhat to offset a greater area of sail, yet probably does not increase the wetted surface enough to slow the boat to any significant extent. I have included a sail plan for this longer hull. The same table of offsets can be used for both hulls—the 18-footer and the 20-footer—although it is recommended that, for the longer boat, these offsets represent the inside of the planking and the bottom, rather than the outside. This will simplify making the molds and frames, and will add a trifle to the beam and freeboard and, likewise, to stability.

As far as weather helm is concerned, Storrow felt *Shag* had an undue amount, which in his judgment slowed her down somewhat, even though she did not steer hard due to her balanced rudder. His suggestion was to move the centerboard aft, and possibly to increase its size. But how much to move it? As mentioned before in this book, there is no precise mathematical formula or reliable method for determining optimum balance for small craft rigs on the drawing board, before actual trials on the water. The calculations commonly resorted to are approximate and hit or miss. Often they don't even come close.

It will not be out of place here to review briefly the basic considerations underlying our problem. When a boat sails into the wind, the force of the wind on the sails tends to push the

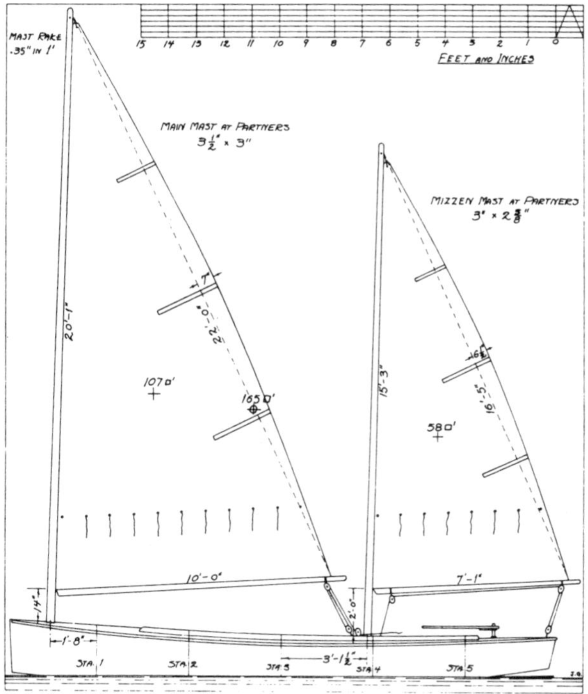

boat sideways in the water as well as to send her ahead. The effective force of the wind is concentrated at one point called the "center of effort." The resistance of the water against the side of the hull is likewise concentrated at one point, which is called the "center of lateral resistance." If the center of effort lies aft of the center of lateral resistance, the effect is to turn the bow into the wind. The rudder must counteract this turning force, and this is called weather helm. The greater the distance the center of effort is aft of the center of lateral resistance, the longer the lever arm turning the boat into the wind. The longer the lever arm, the more helm or rudder is required to keep the boat on course. But if the center of effort comes forward of the center of lateral resistance, the effect is the opposite. The bow seeks to turn away from the wind, and again the rudder must counteract. This is called lee helm. Lee helm is treacherous, and can lead to jibing and capsizing. A slight amount of weather helm, but not enough to drag, is desirable.

In rare instances, the force exerted by the wind and the counter force of the water against the hull will be so perfectly balanced that the boat all but steers herself. This does not happen often. With small boats, too many changing variables are involved: ballasting, heel, wind velocity, sail trim. Other factors include the area and location of the sails, the underwater shape of the hull, the shape and location of the centerboard, and the size and location of the rudder.

All of our traditional small sailing types are the result of long processes of trial and error in which the many diverse factors affecting performance have been brought more or less into workable and harmonious balance. Changes are not to be undertaken lightly, nor is it easy when changes are made to predict the results before trying them out.

THE CENTERBOARD AND TRUNK

In the present instance, it would seem logical to seek to lessen the amount of weather helm in the 18-foot boat by moving the centerboard aft to bring the center of lateral resistance closer to the center of effort, but it must not be moved back so far as to result in lee helm. Yet the centerboard trunk in the 18-foot boat is already as close to the mizzenmast as it will go, and to move the latter aft any distance would radically change the rig. One way to get around this would be to put the centerboard case slightly offcenter and alongside the mast. Locating the centerboard offcenter should not affect sailing performance noticeably, and is to be seen in the No Man's Land boat, the Barnegat sneakbox, and other types.

How far to move the board back is another matter, and is, in fact, anyone's guess. If I were to do this, I do not think I would go back more than a foot, and to do this I would merely extend the present trunk by a foot, leaving the forward end as it is and increasing the length of the board by a foot. At the same time, the width of the board might be increased by several inches, perhaps three or four. This would be a relatively safe gamble and easily hedged. If the board proved too long, some could easily be cut off. This is all simple, straightaway construction, requiring no diagrams.

For the 20-foot boat, we have worked out

quite a different arrangement. Here we have devised a centerboard that is easily moved forward or aft until the best of several positions has been determined by trial. In addition, because of the size and shape of the board, its effectiveness can be adjusted to some extent by raising or lowering with the tackle convenient to the helmsman's hand. This arrangement, it should be noted, was adapted from one worked out in 1912 or thereabouts by H. Willyams for a 16-foot sailing dinghy recently redrawn by William Garden.

Before the two pieces of ⅝-inch plywood which make up the centerboard are glued together, recesses are cut into the inside surfaces to hold the steel plate which forms the lever arm, and also the lead insert for weighting the board. These should fit tightly, but if not, any slack places can be filled with epoxy surfacer or putty. A stiff mix of the epoxy adhesive used and phenolic microballoons is excellent for this.

After the centerboard is glued together, the edges are rounded and sanded, and the sides are planed and smoothed to a streamlined taper in preparation for sheathing either with polypropylene or glass fabric set in epoxy. Do not use a polyester resin for this. But before the centerboard is sheathed, rivets are put in along the forward edge through the wood and the steel insert from side to side as shown in the drawing. These may be copper, as there is no danger of electrolytic action between the copper and the steel because the plastic sheathing will seal them from contact with water. Holes for the rivets are most easily bored on a drill press, but an ordinary electric hand drill will do. Actually, these rivets are probably not needed if the assembly is properly glued with epoxy adhesive, but they should be put in nevertheless to be on the safe side.

The lever arm is cut out of ordinary steel plate ⅜ inch thick. In changing the position of the board in the boat, a short length of rod is put through the one-inch diameter hole in the end of the lever arm to hold on to. In this way, it is quite easy to support the board until the pivot bolt has been shifted from one hole to another. All that is required for a pivot bolt is an ordinary ½-inch carriage bolt (6 inches or 6½ inches long). The holes through the board and the sides of the trunk for this bolt are 9/16 inch to provide clearance.

The case or trunk for the 20-foot boat is made heavier and is more securely braced than that for the 18-footer to take care of the larger board. Bed logs for the trunk are easily available from Douglas fir construction lumber 1½ inches thick, floor joist and the like. The ¾ inch thick sides of the trunk are not rabbeted into the bed logs as is usually done, but are glued to them and extend all the way down to the bottom of the boat. When the trunk is bolted on as shown, through the cross-planked bottom and the fore-and-aft stringer or keel piece on the outside, the result can hardly help being solid and leakproof.

The trunk end posts are morticed all the way through the bottom for caulking from the outside. A bedding compound that stays soft and tacky is desirable. Some have reported good results with ordinary asphalt roofing paste or compound. As an additional precaution against possible leaks, ⅜ inch pine stopwaters may be driven through each of the cross-plank bottom seams on either side of the centerboard slot. This will have to be done before the outer keel strip is put on.

The half-thwarts on either side of the forward end of the centerboard trunk are needed to brace the sidewise thrust of the big board. But they are made removable in case the boat is to be used for cruising with one or two persons sleeping on board. When these half-thwarts are removed, there is room for a sleeping bag on either side of the centerboard trunk. A tarp draped over the main boom, tied down securely, makes as snug a warm-weather shelter as anyone could want.

KEY TO CENTERBOARD DRAWING

1. Five 9/16″ holes 2″ apart through the centerboard trunk for hanging the centerboard and adjusting its location.
2. Tackle for raising and lowering the centerboard. Leads aft and is cleated within easy

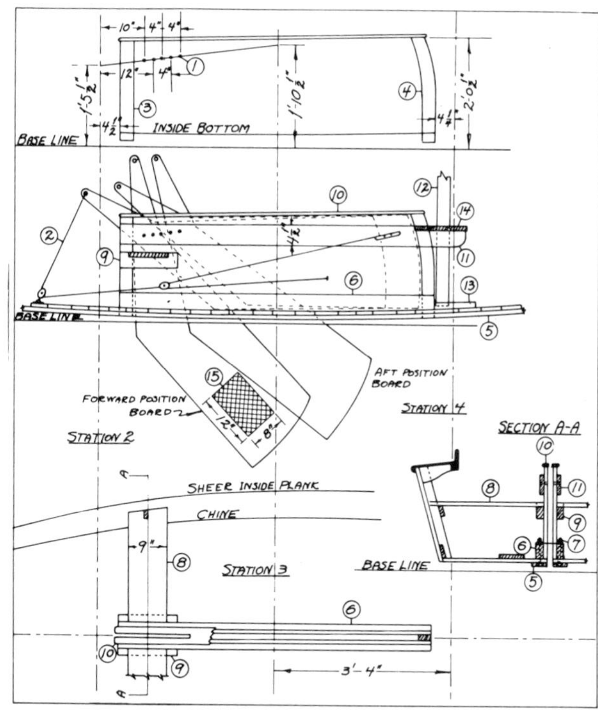

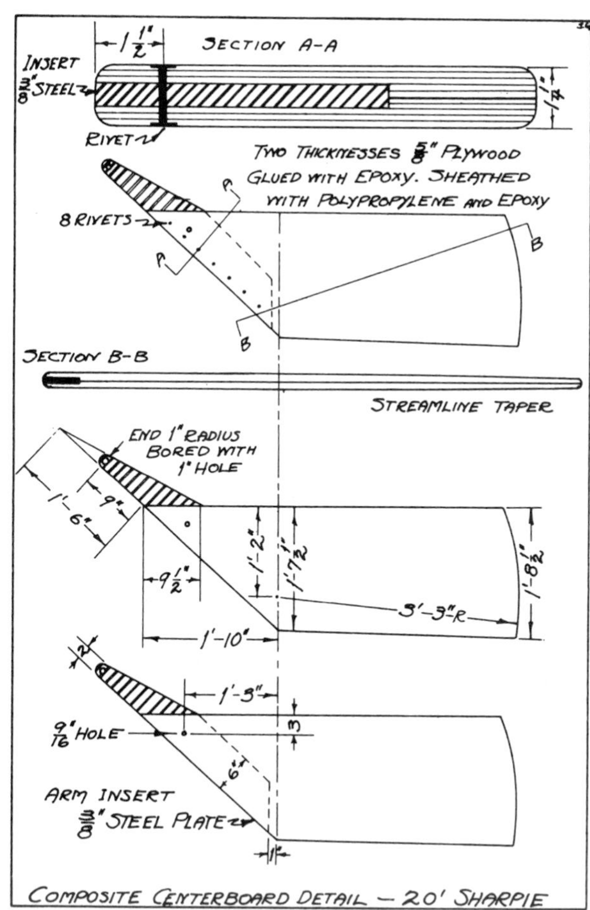

reach of the helmsman. Adapted from H. Willyams; redrawn by W. Garden.

3. Post, centerboard trunk—oak, Douglas fir, 3″ x 1½″. Mortised through the cross-planked bottom and fore-and-aft bottom stringer.

4. Aft post centerboard trunk—oak, Douglas fir construction lumber, 3″ x 1½″.

5. Fore-and-aft outside stringer or keel strip—oak, Douglas fir, 8″ x 1″. Tapers to 6″ wide at bow end.

6. Bed logs, centerboard trunk—Douglas fir, 3½″ x 1½″, glued to the sides of the centerboard trunk, which rests on the planked bottom. Bolted from side to side through the trunk end posts.

7. Bed logs bolted through the bottom and bottom stringer with 6½″ x ⅜″ galvanized carriage bolts spaced 6″ apart. Trunk scribed and fitted to the bottom curve, and set in non-drying bedding compound.

8. Removable thwarts—spruce or fir, 1″ x 9″ brace the centerboard trunk. Notch over side frame and fit into socketed cleat fastened to the side of the trunk.

9. Socketed cleat—fir, 1½″ thick.

10. Cap, centerboard trunk. Slotted forward end for centerboard lever arm.

11. Reinforcing strips—fir, 1″ x 4½″, extend the length of the trunk and under after thwart. Forward ends bored for centerboard pivot bolt. After ends support thwart and serve as partners for the mizzenmast.

12. Mizzenmast.

13. Mast step—fir or yellow pine, 1½″ thick.

14. Thwart—fir, 12″ x 1″.

15. Lead, approximately 20 pounds. Slab ½″ thick recessed into the interior of the centerboard before it is glued together.

THE RUDDER

It was well, I think, not to attempt any alteration in either the size or shape of the rudder for the 20-footer, at least not at first. If and when any problem should arise in this connection, there will be time enough to take care of it then.

The rudder shaft that came with the 18-foot boat was iron and seemingly hand-forged by a blacksmith, according to Storrow, with the lower end forked and curved to attach to the wooden blade of the rudder and at the same time to brace and reinforce it. It must have been quite old, and may have been salvaged from a former boat. Blacksmiths capable of such work are a rarity today. We had best consider some alternative.

The rudder, like the centerboard, can very well be made up of two thicknesses of ⅝-inch plywood glued together, streamlined somewhat by planing and sanding, and covered with fabric-reinforced plastic. For the rudder shaft, a short piece of brass or bronze rod approximately ⅞ inch in diameter will be just about right, if such can be had. Frequently, remnants or secondhand pieces of bronze propeller shafting long enough to serve can be found in boatyard scrap piles. With a hacksaw and a flat file, slot one end of this rod for a distance equal to about half the width of the rudder blade, and into this slot insert a rectangular piece of flat brass ¼-inch thick. This need not extend beyond the shaft more than 2 inches on either side. The two can be brazed together or through-riveted. Next, this assembly is recessed into the interior of the rudder blade before the two pieces of plywood which form it are glued together.

After the glue has cured, holes are bored through the wood and brass on either side of the shaft, for rivets, which are put in and drawn up tight. If the shaft is installed in this manner, it can never loosen as long as the blade of the rudder holds together.

The shaft turns in a length of pipe which is threaded tightly into a block of wood glued to the inside of the bottom. The upper end of the pipe is likewise threaded into a block glued to the underside of the deck. The rudder assembly hangs from two lock nuts and a washer. Should it be necessary to unship the rudder, the lock nuts are easily loosened. One of them could be bored for a cotter pin, if it were considered necessary. The wooden tiller is bolted to a short metal arm keyed to the head of the rudder shaft and held down with lock nuts and a washer.

In summary, this simple 20-foot boat has real possibilities for modest cruising for those who don't mind roughing it a bit. She is easily beached, and, with her shoal draft, it is possible to explore out-of-the-way places along the shore that the ordinary yacht never sees or dreams exist. For two teenagers who can sail and swim, but who have never before been strictly on their own, a boat like this can be a major part of growing up and a grand adventure.

16 The Peapod

Years ago as a boy down Quoddy way, I first heard a story about two lobstermen riding out a gale in a peapod, far from land. Nearby was a schooner, reefed down and pitching hard, which offered to take the men aboard. The men declined. They preferred to ride out the heavy seas in the safety of their pod. In other versions of this tale, the lobstermen became Indian porpoise hunters and their boat a canoe. No matter how the yarn went there must have been some truth in it, because the peapods, like the sea-going canoes they resemble, are wonderfully able boats.

Some say that peapods originated in the lower waters of the Penobscot Bay in the neighborhood of North Haven about 1870, but there were small double-ended boats on the Maine coast long before then. Chances are that some of them had a canoe shape, even if the peapod name didn't come until later.

Captain Ethan Allen Eliot of Calais had a small, cedar double-ender built in the 1840s when he stayed home several years from the West Indies trade to pilot on the St. Croix. His boat was very light, so if need be he could carry it over the mud flats on his back. When the tide favored he would put off down river to pick up incoming vessels—square-riggers to load with ton-timber for England. Outward-bound craft, once they got clear, would set him over the side in his little boat, and he would make his way back up river in all weather and at all hours. He carried a small sail to help.

Now and then he must have run across Passamaquoddy Indians in their sea-going canoes bound for Grand Manan or Pleasant Point. They, too, would be sailing sometimes, perhaps with a bunch of thick spruce brush high in the bow if they didn't have canvas.

Was the peapod copied from the canoe? Not deliberately, I would say. But everyone on the Coast was familiar with sea-going canoes. The first settlers borrowed the Indian canoe for use in their early fisheries. Long familiarity with the canoe and its good qualities had stamped the image in the minds of the fishermen so that later on when the special needs of the lobster fishery called for husky, easy-rowing boats, some of these would naturally turn out to resemble the canoe.

There were all manner of peapods. And it would be difficult to draw an exact line between pods and other small double-enders. Some deep, sailing pods were closer to double-enders like the Nomans Land boat than to the canoe. In others, resemblançes could be found to such early double-enders as the whale boat, the Merrimac River wherry, and the York boat. But the typical pod is closer to the canoe. Fifteen feet is the average length; both ends are exactly alike.

There are good reasons why the peapods had caught on in the Maine lobster fisheries before 1880. Lobsters were getting thinned out. Prices were low. Fishermen had to scratch to make a day's pay. In the lower Penobscot Bay where the pod was very popular, lobster fishing had begun in a serious way about 1848 or 1850.

At first lobsters were astonishingly abundant. In 1864, Captain S. S. Davis was running a lobster smack from the Muscle Ridges. He loaded 5,000 lobsters and averaged a trip every seven to nine days. Three men, tending from 40 to 50 pots each, caught all the count lobsters Davis could carry. But by 1879 the cream had been skimmed in that locality, and it took fifteen men instead of three to supply Captain Davis, and even then he was sometimes obliged to buy from still others to make up a load. As lobsters got scarcer, the fishermen had to tend more and more pots. For a few years in the late 1860s trawls were widely used, but after 1870 the use of trawls decreased as fishermen found they did better by scattering their pots over a wide area, which meant more and more rowing, and that is where the peapods came in.

Small sailing craft were also widely used—the Muscongus boat, Matinicus boats, and others. Unlike the large sailing pods, which usually carried spritsails, these boats were sloop rigged. But the wind has to be right for sailing, and it is not easy for one man to sail and tend pots at the same time, though some did it with the tiller rigged with a knife and comb arrangement that could be set to swing the boat in a wide circle while a pot was being hauled. Such maneuvers require plenty of room and call for gybing. Not a few men were lost from a clip on the head by a flying boom.

The peapods were not the only rowing workboats used by the Maine lobstermen before the gas engine gave oars the back seat. There were wherries, Whitehalls, Reach boats, dories, and others, named and nameless. But the favorite seems to have been the pod, and there must have been a lot of them in use, judging from the extent of the lobster fishery at that time.

Government figures for 1880 record close to 1,200 fishermen supplying 23 lobster canneries on the coast of Maine with 9,494,284 pounds of lobsters valued at $94,943 to the fishermen—one cent per pound. And this is only part of the story. There were 58 Maine-owned lobster smacks, 16 of which ran to Portland, where 1,900,000 pounds of lobsters were handled the same year. These figures represent a lot of rowing, in all kinds of weather. With one-cent lobsters, a man could not afford to lay up ashore much, even in those days.

Few peapods were identical, and some differed widely. There were lapstreak pods as well as those built smooth-seam or "set-works," an old-time New England boatbuilding term. Variation in the amount of deadrise and rocker was considerable. A few had a bottom plank instead of the usual keel projecting below the rabbet line. In some of the sailing pods that were kept in the water all the time, there were false keels as deep as six inches. Certain of the pods had a plumb stem like the Whitehall boats. Others had the forefoot cut well back, so the stem was quite raking. Some had slack bilges, and in others the bilges were very hard.

Pods were as different as the men who used them and built them. Maine fishermen, more often than not, are also competent boatbuilders. Many of the fishermen designed and built their own pods; in contrast, the dories of the Massachusetts lobstermen were standardized and mass produced by a few professional builders. Building their own boats, individual fishermen could experiment and adapt them to their own special preferences and requirements. In the long run this would mean improvement of the model.

COMPARING SOME PEAPODS

Comparison of some pods will give an idea of the range of the model and some of its possibilities. There isn't a better general example of the peapod type than the boat whose lines are reproduced from Howard I. Chapelle's book, *Boatbuilding* (W. W. Norton, 1941). This is the same pod Chapelle had as a tender for his pinky, *Glad Tidings*, and naturally he had ample opportunity to test its qualities. He has this to say about the boat: "It was a typical lobsterman's

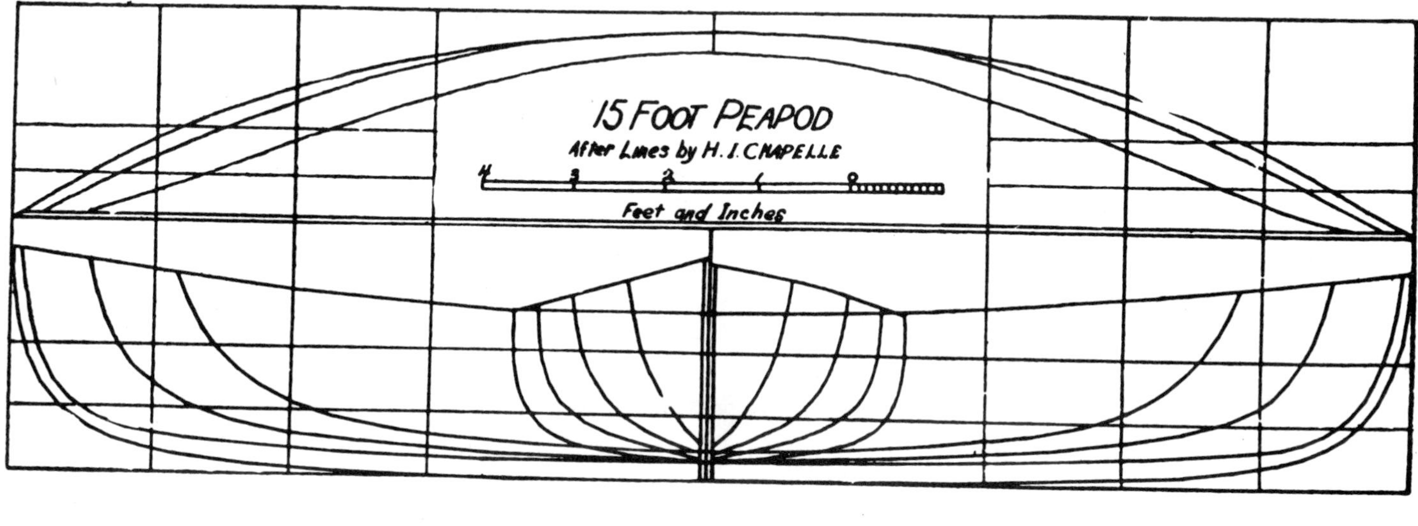

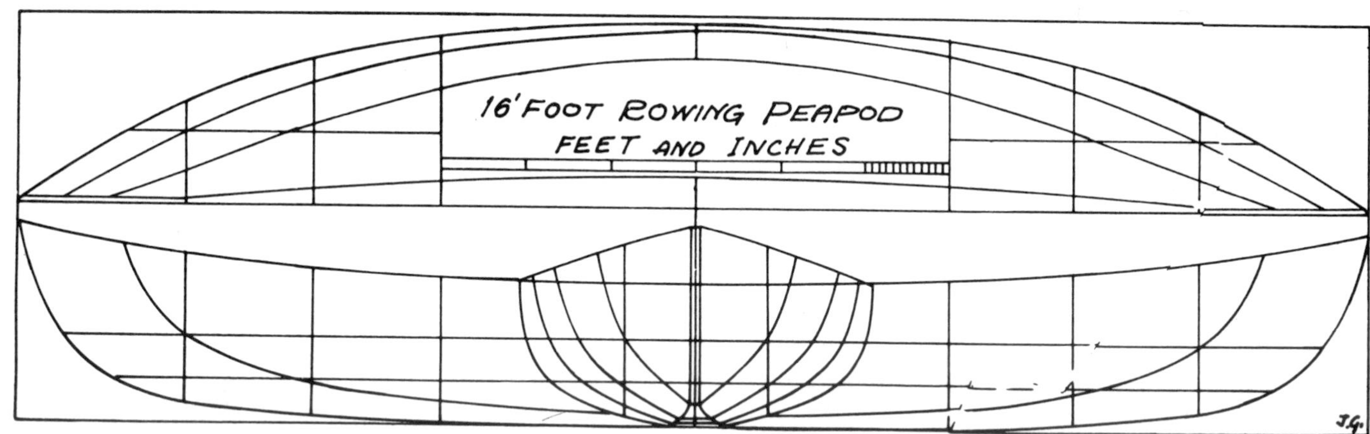

rowing pod and though very heavy she was wonderfully stiff and rowed very well into a wind and sea. For open-water work where the boat does not have to be lifted out, I would prefer a pod to any other small skiff I have ever seen." This is high praise, and coming from someone like Chapelle who really knew small boats as few others do, it means something. The construction details are on the heavy side, but that is the way the fishermen built them to stand the gaff of lobstering day in and day out.

The 16-foot rowing pod is my own idea for use on the St. Croix River. She is intended to be a much lighter boat, built lapstrake from three-eighths-inch cedar with a bottom plank, instead of the more usual keel, to make her easier to drag over the flats and also to facilitate the installation of a centerboard. To help her rowing

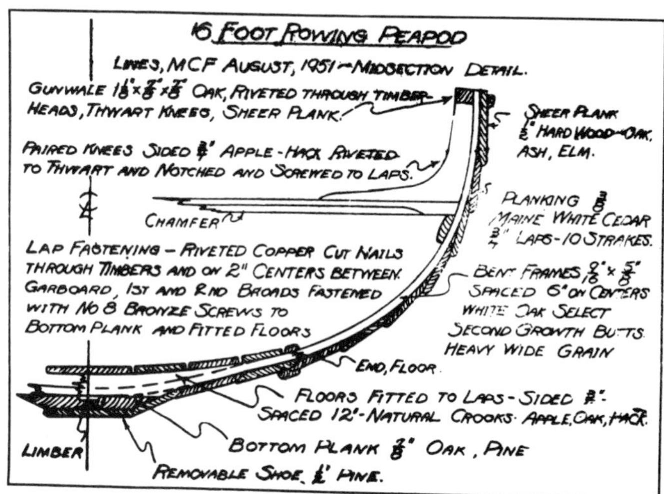

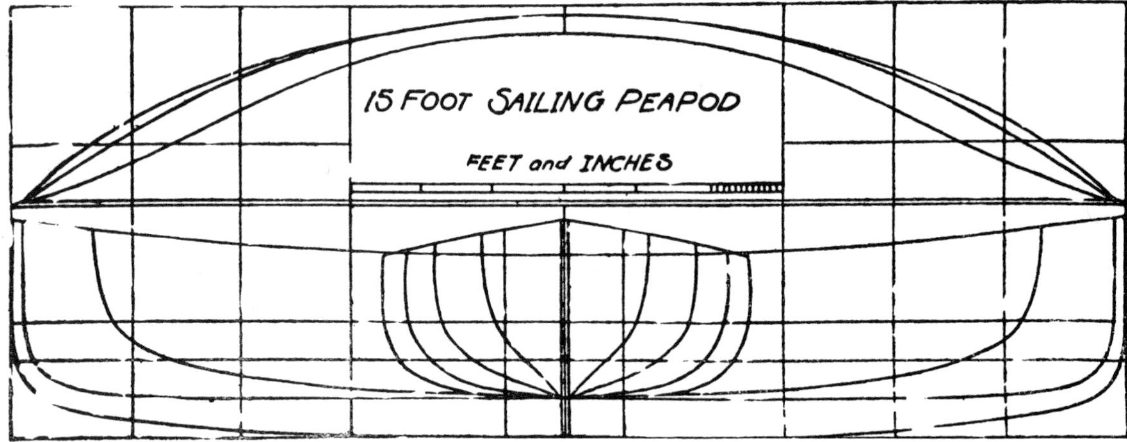

qualities, there is extra length, easy bilges, and considerable rocker. These features would make her an easy boat to plank. The forefoot is cut away for quick response in choppy water, as in some of the sea-going canoes of the Passamaquoddy Indians.

A very different pod is the fifteen-foot sailing model, whose rowing qualities have been reduced in favor of exceptional stiffness. Hard bilges and a five-foot beam would enable this boat to carry a lot of canvas for her length. Typically her rig would be a large spritsail furled by unstepping the mast. The sharp, deep forefoot and the deep, false keel would hold well against slippage to leeward. Such pods often had permanent rudders rigged with a yoke and tiller lines. Of the three, this boat would be the most difficult to build. Her planks would be crooked with lots of sny and bend.

A peapod of note is the one built in the winter of 1950 by Captain Charles F. Norton of Birch Harbor. The order called for a light but sturdy boat. Captain Norton furnished the following measurements and specifications for the design worked out by himself and his partner: 14 feet, 6 inches long; 4 feet, 4 inches beam; 18 inches depth amidships, with 8 inches sheer; very little deadrise—approximately 2 inches—and about the same amount of rocker. This pod was built on a bottom board instead of a keel, and planked smooth with eight strakes finished one-half inch thick. She has timbers one-half by one inch, seven inches on centers. She is built of Maine cedar on white oak.

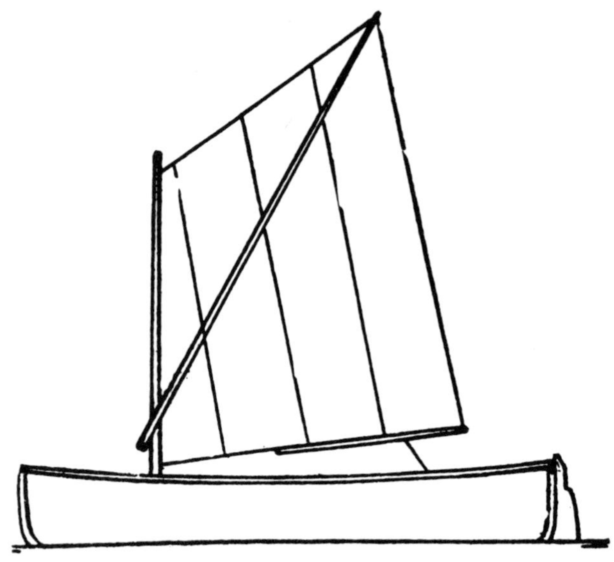

Captain Norton can qualify as an old-timer who knows a thing or two about pods. His model is pretty true to the type as described more than 75 years ago in the U. S. Fish Commission reports, when the pod was the leading workboat of Maine lobstermen. These old pods were commonly built with a bottom board, like Captain Norton's, but more were planked lapstrake than smooth. Average measurements were 15½ feet long, 4½ feet beam, and 1½ feet depth. Although the Fish Commission reports place the origin of the pod at North Haven, Captain Norton writes that to his knowledge the first were built at Milbridge, Maine, with Steuben and Addison taking up their building soon after.

The Chapelle pod, described previously,

came from Jonesport, and it is the same general model as the Norton boat, although it is built with a keel and is of much heavier construction: length, 15 feet; beam, 4 feet, 2 inches; depth, 19 inches.

A pod owned by John W. Twitchell of Barrington, Rhode Island, is of average beam, being 4 feet, 2 inches wide, but the length is only 13 feet and 2 inches. He states that the stem is nearly plumb, which would shorten the overall length somewhat. Her hard bilges are those of the sailing pods of the lower Penobscot Bay.

In 1941, Twitchell had two of these boats built by the late Nate S. Eaton of Mountainville, Deer Isle. He has the highest praise for them, saying that they are very fast both rowing and sailing. The pod has a centerboard, rudder, and a good-sized leg-of-mutton sail, unlike the older sailing pods which generally had deep, false keels and spritsails. The breasthooks and thwart knees, which Twitchell mentions with particular satisfaction, are characteristic of the better old-time construction, which utilized timber grown to shape for maximum strength and bracing.

The Van Ness pod, which was built by Bendix in Prospect Harbor 75 years ago, differs from the models so far considered. The bilge is slacker, and there is more deadrise and rocker. Indeed, there is an almost extreme amount of rocker rounding up into a forefoot that is cut away more than is usual. The waterlines show no reverse curve at the ends in contrast to the hollow entrance of most pods. Both Van Ness, who took off the lines, and Arnold Paine, who owned the boat at one time, agree that she was exceptionally able and easy to row and handle. She performed best with a load, they state, being somewhat tender when light. This is obvious from her slack bilges and exceptional

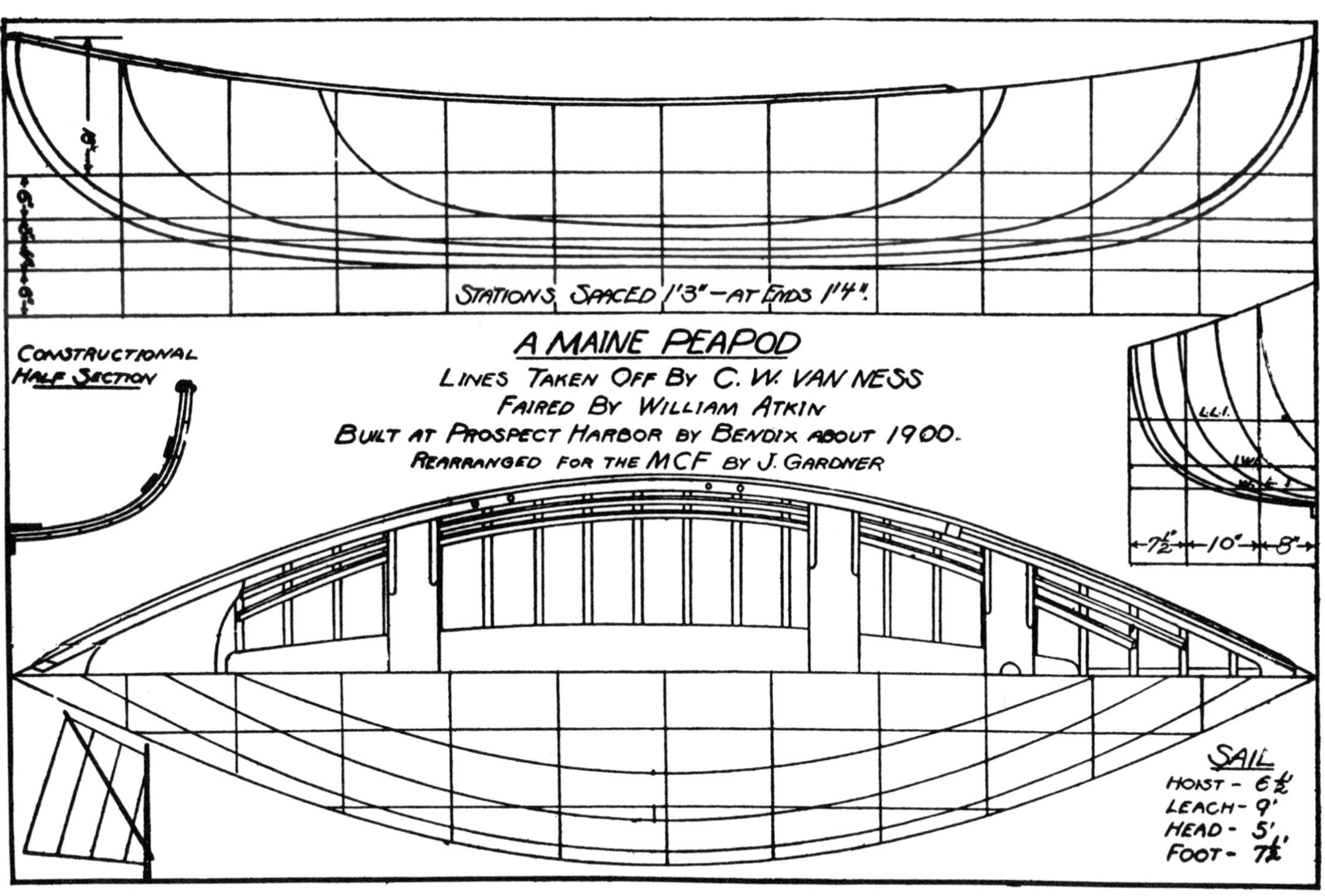

rocker, which would give her short bearing on the water without ballast to pull her down.

All the boats so far mentioned are smooth planked, but before 1900, lapstrake pods were in the majority, like the Jonesport model of 1883 in the National Watercraft Collection of the Smithsonian Institution. This boat is a keel pod that measures 15 feet, by 4½ feet, by 1½ feet. She has only seven strakes and her timbers are about two feet apart. This means heavy scantlings. The timbers would probably be sawn frames of hackmatack because of their large size and because that wood is plentiful in Washington County and good oak is not.

Only seven strakes on a boat of this depth and beam mean wide planks and thick ones—over half an inch. Such planks are stiff and must be put on as they bend naturally, without forcing. This will influence the shape of the hull, making for easy bilges, rising floors, no hollows or reverses in the waterlines, and no abrupt changes in line anywhere. Such construction is strong and rugged and not difficult to build, but makes a heavy boat—one too heavy to be pulled in and out of the water.

Alfred Brooks, writing in the *American Neptune* about the boats of Ash Point, Maine, of about 1900, describes several double-enders that I would consider peapods, although he does not use that name. These boats are exactly alike at both ends, a characteristic that sets pods off from some other double-enders, for example the small double-ended Reach boat built with a straight sternpost. What Brooks calls the best of these Ash Point boats shows lines much like those of my 16-foot rowing pod shown in this chapter. The similarity was accidental. What I did borrow from to some extent and used for checking and comparison was the fore half of the Herreshoff Columbia Lifeboat. There is also a similarity to the Van Ness pod.

My 16-foot peapod is planked lapstrake, for which this model is well adapted with its moderate bilge, ample rocker, and gradual waterlines. The indicated construction is light but strong—that of the standard yacht tender. Special emphasis is put on the use of natural crooks and woods that cannot be bought in ordinary lumberyards. Along the Maine coast, especially for those who own a farm or woodlot, it is possible to pick out choice logs and natural crooks of hackmatack, oak, elm, apple, and so forth, and have them sawed at a local mill, putting them away to season for future use. I recall sawing cut knees of apple and hackmatack by hand—it is surprising how much can be accomplished along this line with elbow grease and a sharp handsaw.

The stems for this boat would be made from single crooks without splicing, so that there is solid, unbroken grain running from breasthook to bottom board. Breasthooks from knees of suitable grain should be worked into both ends and securely riveted to the stem and gunwales. In combination with a hardwood top strake and well-fitted thwart knees, this will make a boat that will never sag or hog. As a primitive substitute for such bracing, the Indians would sometimes lash a strong log lengthwise in their canoes when obliged to cross a wide stretch of rough water.

The fitted floors are most essential. They give support to the garboard and the lower boards, which when unprotected rent and crack easily and are one of the weakest spots in an improperly constructed lapstrake boat. The floors also provide good fastening for the floor boards, which besides forming a surface to step on are also strengthening members. Many of the older pods had bent half-timbers across the keel besides their full-length frames. When this construction is used, the lower laps should be backed up by fitted wedges in the spaces between them and the frames to give solid bearing.

Great pains should be taken to get wide-grained white oak from the butts of fast-growing second-growth trees for the bent timbers. The heavier the wood the better, and it should be air-dried, and not too dry at that. Brittle, fine-grained, lightweight red oak is nearly worthless for bending stock. Elm would be a better choice, and if used the timbers should be a little larger. Copper cut nails are preferable to wire nails for rivet fastening. Bronze screws—an excellent fastening that they did not have in the old days—can be used to advantage in many places.

Brass screws are worthless. While galvanized fastenings are not suitable for light lapstrake construction, still, they can be used for heavier boats with larger members like the Jonesport model.

Today, carvel or smooth planking is generally preferred. Why, I don't know, because for my money lapstrake planking has the edge. I have built both kinds of boats, and I don't think that lapstrake is harder, as some claim; that is, once you get the tune in your head. Smooth planking requires more lumber—one-half inch being the minimum finished thickness for a smooth-seam peapod, and nine-sixteenths nearer the average. This means that planks must be backed out to fit the turn of the bilge, and this will require stock three-quarters of an inch thick and upwards. Lapstrake planks require no backing out, so that a one-inch board will give you a pair of three-eighths planks—one for each side of the boat, split apart after the board has been lined out and cut to shape.

In addition to backing out, smooth-seam plank require beveling, and a boat so planked must be planed smooth and fair after the plank are all on. Lapstrake plank have only to be beveled, and they can be smoothed and rough sanded on the bench. Of course there is some extra fastening with a lapstrake job, but no holes have to be bunged or puttied. Smooth-seam work is easier repaired, but replacing lapstrake planks is not too difficult. With a smooth-seam boat more depends upon the timbers, for that is all that holds it together. There is no question that a well-built lapstrake job will be lighter and stronger, and to my eyes it will look more like a boat.

Anyone thinking of building a pod will do well to give it a lot of thought and study. The flexibility of design holds great possibilities, and some pitfalls.

REFERENCES:

Chapelle, Howard I., *American Small Sailing Craft*, Norton, 1951, pages 217-222.

Chapelle, Howard I., *Boatbuilding*, Norton, 1941, page 402. Plans 15-foot pod.

Brooks, Alfred A., "The Boats of Ash Point, Maine," *The American Neptune*, October, 1942.

Van Ness, C. W., "A Maine Peapod," *Yachting*, February, 1932.

Mitman, Carl W., *Catalogue of the Watercraft Collection in the U. S. National Museum*, 1923, page 187. Description of Jonesport model.

Goode, George Brown, *The Fisheries and Fishery Industries of the United States*, Government Printing Office, 1887, Sec. V. Vol. 2, page 671. Description of Maine peapod.

BUILDING A 14-FOOT POD

To exemplify carvel construction in a course in recreational boatbuilding given at Mystic Seaport, we chose to build a peapod as our second boat. We picked the peapod as a distinctive New England workboat type—useful, aesthetically pleasing and attractive, not too large, too expensive to build, too fancy, or too difficult for construction by most learners, provided they have guidance.

We started from the beginning, going about it much the same as a fisherman would do, or used to do. That is, we looked over a number of pods, made some basic measurements—length, beam, rise of sheer, depth amidships, and the like—took a few rough templates, and proceeded to work out our own design. After sketching the basic shape on paper, we roughed out preliminary lines from which we made cardboard templates of the profile, sheer half breadth, and body sections. With these we began to shape a lift half-model of pine.

As this model took shape under plane and spokeshave, we could see exactly what alterations and refinements were required to give a fair hull with the characteristics we had previously decided upon. Shaping a three-dimensional half-model permits a much surer control over hull form than working in two dimensions on the drawing board. Besides this, the planking shapes, later on, can be lined out on the scaled half-model, a procedure which

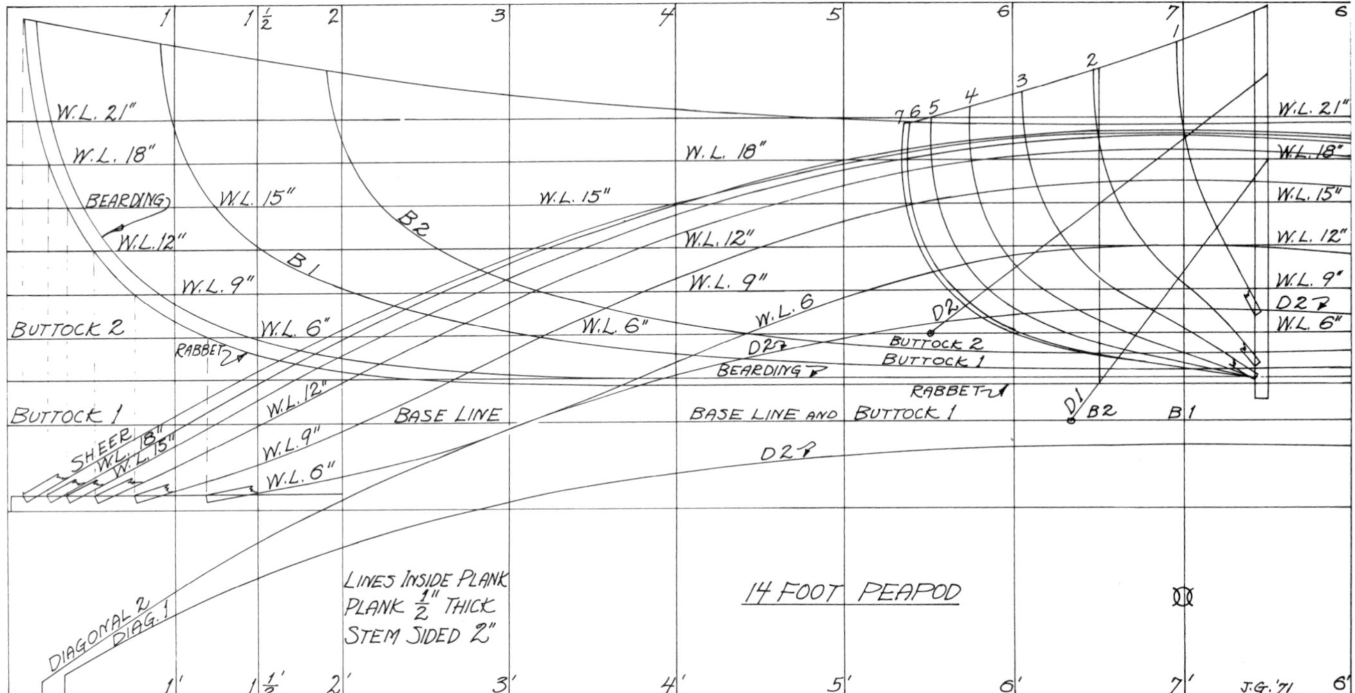

helps greatly when planking an unfamiliar hull for the first time.

Because this pod, like most pods, is a true double-ender, that is of identical shape on either side of the midsection, only one-half of a half-model was required—in actuality, a quarter-model. This permitted using a larger-than-usual scale, 3 inches to one foot, in fact, or one-quarter size, and this large scale in turn made possible more accurate measurement of lines and dimensions from the model.

As for the full-size laydown of this 14-foot boat, there is ample room for it on one standard 4 x 8 sheet of plywood, considering that only one-quarter of the hull need be drawn. This is an important consideration in setting up class instruction where a number of separate but identical laydowns are required in order to allow everyone in the group to participate in this basic boatbuilding operation—six separate laydowns in the present instance at Mystic Seaport in addition to the first, or master, laydown.

From the master laydown have been taken the lines, offsets, and stem dimensions reproduced here. The lines are laid out exactly as they would be drawn on a 4-foot by 8-foot sheet of

OFFSETS-14' PEAPOD MEASURED TO INSIDE PLANKING.

		STEM	STA. 1	STA. 1½	STA. 2	STA. 3	STA. 4	STA. 5	STA. 6	STA. 7
HEIGHTHS	SHEER	2-4-0	2-2-1+	2-1-1	2-0-1+	1-10-5	1-9-5	1-8-7+	1-8-5	1-8-4+
	BUTT. 1	—	1-8-2+	1-0-1+	0-9-3+	0-6-2	0-4-5	0-3-7	0-3-5	0-3-4+
	BUTT. 2	—	—	—	1-7-4	0-9-5+	0-6-7	0-5-3	0-4-6	0-4-5
	BEARDING	—	0-8-2+	0-5-6+	0-4-3+	0-3-2	0-3-0	0-3-0	0-3-0	0-3-0
	RABBET	—	0-7-0	0-4-5+	0-3-4	0-2-5	0-2-4	0-2-4	0-2-4	0-2-4
	KEEL	—	0-5-4	0-3-3+	0-2-3+	0-1-5	0-1-4	0-1-4	0-1-4	0-1-4
HALF-BREADTHS	SHEER	0-1-0	0-6-4-	0-9-4+	1-0-4-	1-5-3+	1-9-1+	1-11-6+	2-1-3+	2-1-7
	W.L. 18"	0-1-0	0-5-4	0-8-6	0-11-6	1-4-7+	1-9-0	1-11-7+	2-1-4+	2-2-0
	W.L. 15"	0-1-0	0-4-4-	0-7-4+	0-10-5-	1-3-7+	1-8-2	1-11-2+	2-1-1	2-1-5+
	W.L. 12"	0-1-0	0-2-7+	0-5-6-	0-8-6+	1-2-2	1-6-6+	1-10-2	2-0-1+	2-0-5+
	W.L. 9"	0-1-0	0-1-3-	0-3-1-	0-5-3+	0-10-6+	1-3-6+	1-7-6	1-10-1	1-10-4+
	W.L. 6"	0-1-0	—	0-1-0+	0-2-1+	0-5-4	0-10-0	1-2-4+	1-5-3+	1-6-0
	DIAGONAL 1	0-1-5	0-5-7-	—	0-10-3-	1-1-3-	1-3-4	1-4-5+	1-5-1	1-5-2-
	DIAGONAL 2	0-1-2	0-7-3	—	1-1-6-	1-6-4	1-10-1+	2-0-6+	2-2-4	2-2-6

DIAGONAL 1: OUT 1-2-0 ON BASELINE, UP 1-6-0 ABOVE BASE LINE.

DIAGONAL 2: OUT 2-0-0 ON W.L. 6, UP 2-0-0 ABOVE BASE LINE.

DIMENSIONS GIVEN IN FEET, INCHES, & EIGHTHS PLUS OR MINUS ONE-SIXTEENTH. J.G. '71

plywood. The overlap of lines so produced, while not usual on the drawing board, is common practice on the mold loft floor and is really not as confusing, given a little study, as might appear to some at first glance.

A brief word as to the characteristics of the pod laid out here. Its 14 feet overall of length is about average for working pods, and so is its ample maximum beam of 52 inches inside planking, 53 inches outside. An inside depth of

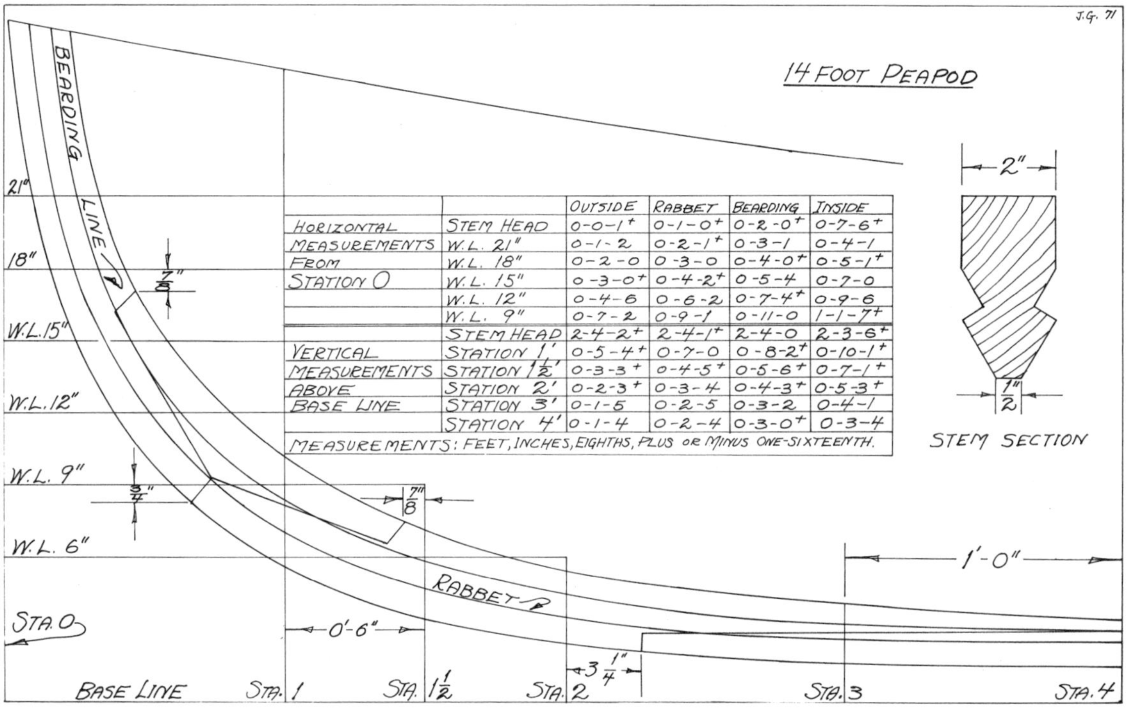

		OUTSIDE	RABBET	BEARDING	INSIDE
HORIZONTAL	STEM HEAD	0-0-1+	0-1-0+	0-2-0+	0-7-6+
MEASUREMENTS	W.L. 21"	0-1-2	0-2-1+	0-3-1	0-4-1
FROM	W.L. 18"	0-2-0	0-3-0	0-4-0+	0-5-1+
STATION 0	W.L. 15"	0-3-0+	0-4-2+	0-5-4	0-7-0
	W.L. 12"	0-4-6	0-6-2	0-7-4+	0-9-6
	W.L. 9"	0-7-2	0-9-1	0-11-0	1-1-7+
	STEM HEAD	2-4-2+	2-4-1+	2-4-0	2-3-6+
VERTICAL	STATION 1'	0-5-4+	0-7-0	0-8-2+	0-10-1+
MEASUREMENTS	STATION 1 1/2'	0-3-3+	0-4-5+	0-5-6+	0-7-1+
ABOVE	STATION 2'	0-2-3+	0-3-4	0-4-3+	0-5-3+
BASE LINE	STATION 3'	0-1-5	0-2-5	0-3-2	0-4-1
	STATION 4'	0-1-4	0-2-4	0-3-0+	0-3-4

MEASUREMENTS: FEET, INCHES, EIGHTHS, PLUS OR MINUS ONE-SIXTEENTH.

approximately 17½ inches amidships should give plenty of capacity and freeboard.

This boat shows rather more sheer than some, a rise of 8 inches from amidships to the extreme ends. She also has more deadrise than some of the flat-floored working pods; her underwater lines are hollow and gradual at the ends and fairly sharp for a boat as short yet as beamy as this one. These features in combination should make her fairly easy to row.

This hull, with its gradual bilges and rounded forefoot, should not prove difficult to plank with half-inch cedar. Unlike flat-floored pods, this boat has sufficient deadrise for an oak keel batten ½ inch by 3¾ inches, overlaying the keel sided 2 inches and molded 1½ inches. The keel batten provides a back rabbet for the garboards and for limbers alongside the keel.

Timbers are to be steam-bent white oak continuous from gunwale to gunwale where possible. Spaced 6 inches on centers, these timbers are to be ⅞ inch wide with a molded thickness of ⅝ inch. This permits fastening the half-inch planking with one-inch no. 8 silicon bronze screws, set slightly below the surface of the finished plank for puttying.

The building setup should be for right-side-up building, with the molds spaced 2 feet apart except at the ends, where extra molds are placed as needed to retain the designed shape. Ribbands are fastened to the molds with screws and washers, and spaced close enough to form and to support the timbers when they are bent in hot between the molds. By spacing the timbers on 6-inch centers and the molds 2 feet apart (one foot at the ends), all timbers can be bent in in one operation before the molds are removed.

The first plank to go on is the so-called "binder," that is the plank next below the sheer plank. The second is the garboard. Planking proceeds from the bottom up and from the topsides down with the last strake, or the "shutter," going in just above the turn of the bilge. Plank butts may be glue-spliced on the boat, so that butt blocks may be avoided if desired.

BUILDING A 14-FOOT LAPSTRAKE PEAPOD

In developing the design for this 14-foot rowing peapod, I kept the following objectives in mind:

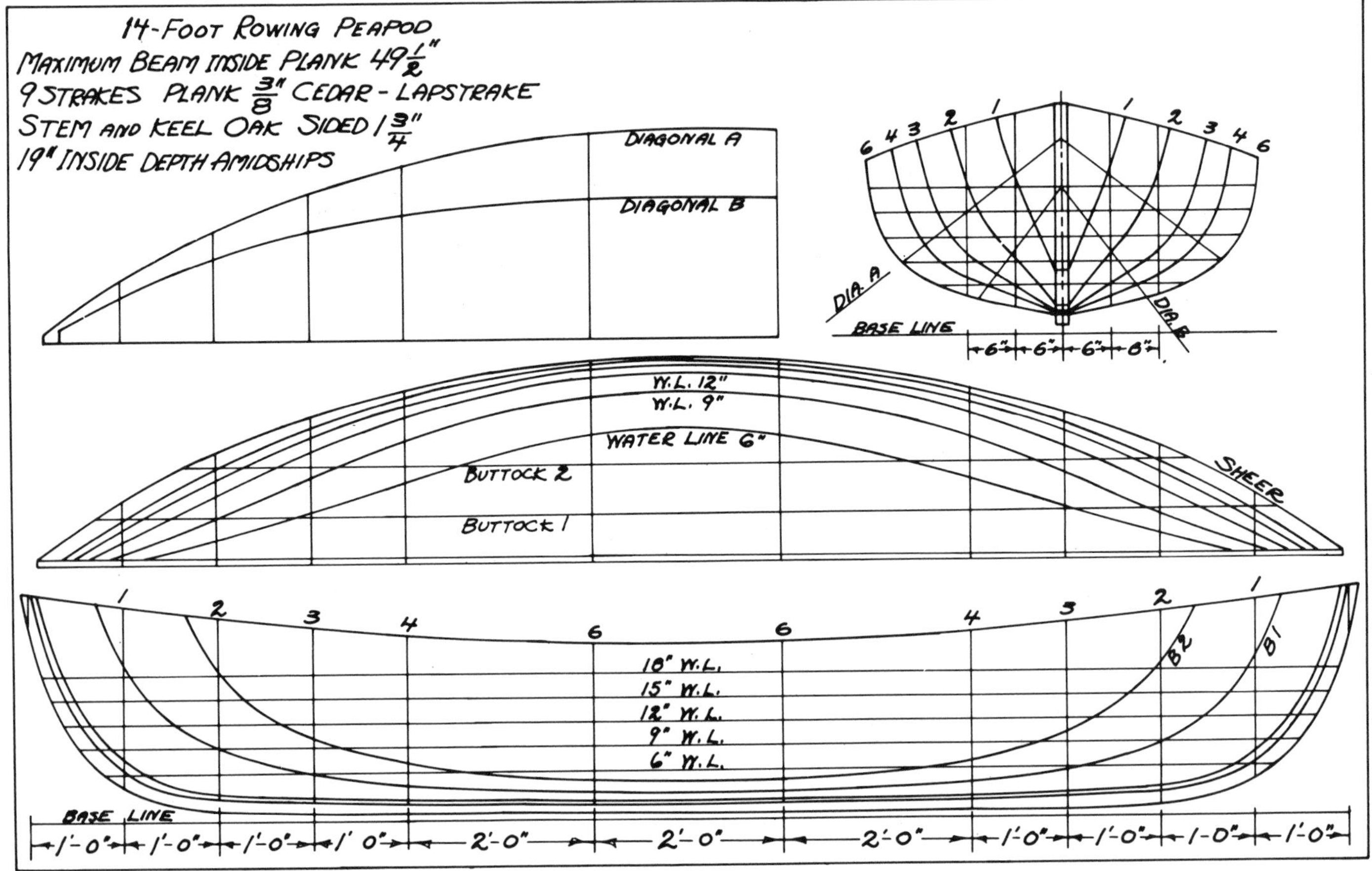

1. The boat should be as safe and seaworthy as it is reasonable to expect in an open 14-foot rowboat.

2. It should not be too much for one person to handle and should row easily. Although it is not intended for racing, it should be capable of a fair turn of speed.

3. It should not be too difficult to build in the ordinary home workshop by an amateur with modest woodworking skills, even though round-hull construction in general is not the easiest way to build a boat.

As mentioned previously in this book, in the past there were many variations of peapods depending upon where they were used, under what conditions they were used, and who used them. Some peapods were sailed, where long distances were covered, but more were rowed. Those that were sailed—for example, those developed for open-water sailing around Matinicus Island—were larger and more powerful than the ordinary rowing kind, and were fitted with plank-on-edge keels, which in some cases extended 5 inches or 6 inches below the bottom of the boat. Other sailing pods were fitted with centerboards, such as some that were built on Deer Isle.

OFFSETS 14-FOOT ROWING PEAPOD							
		STEM	STA. 1	STA. 2	STA. 3	STA. 4	STA. 6
HEIGHTS	SHEER	2-4-0	2-2-5	2-1-1	1-11-6	1-10-6	1-9-6
	BEARDING	—	0-7-6	0-3-3	0-2-7	0-2-5	0-2-4
	RABBET	—	0-6-1	0-2-7	0-2-3	0-2-2	0-2-1
	KEEL	—	0-4-2	0-1-2	0-0-7	0-0-6	0-0-4
	BUTTOCK 1	—	1-6 6	0-9-2	0-5-6	0-4-2	0-3-2
	BUTTOCK 2	—	—	1-6-3	0-10-1	0-6-7	0-4-6
HALF-BREADTHS	W.L. 6	0-0-7	—	0-2-7	0-6-2	0-9-7	1-3-6
	W.L. 9	0-0-7	0-1-3	0-5-5	0-10-5	1-3-2	1-8-2
	W.L. 12	0-0-7	0-2-7	0-8-4	1-1-6	1-6-0	1-10-6
	W.L. 15	0-0-7	0-4-2	0-10-3	1-3-5	1-7-3	1-11-7
	W.L. 18	0-0-7	0-5-4	0-11-6	1-4-6	1-8-3	2-0-3
	SHEER	0-0-7	0-7-7	1-1-6	1-6-3	1-9-4	2-1-0
DIAGONAL B		0-1-4	0-5-5	0-10-2	1-1-4	1-3-2	1-5-0
DIAGONAL A		0-1-2	0-7-6	1-1-4	1-6-2	1-9-5	2-1-3
DIAGONAL A 2' ABOVE BASE LINE OUT 1'-8" ON W.L. 9							
DIAGONAL B 1'-6" ABOVE B.L. OUT 1'-2" ON BASE LINE.							
OFFSETS MEASURED IN FEET, INCHES & EIGHTHS							
TO THE INSIDE OF THE PLANKING. J.G.							

For hauling lobster pots set among the rocks and ledges close to the shore, rowing pods were required. These were often quite flat in the floors, which in a round hull produced a wide, rather flat bottom with a sharp, quick turn at the bilge as it rounded up into the topsides. Such a hull had plenty of initial stability to support a heavy waterlogged lobster pot when it was hauled up and over the side. But boats like this were not the easiest kind to row, and, besides, that hard bilge with its quick, sharp turn was difficult to build, either carvel or clinker.

Examination of the mid-section shape at stations 4 and 6 in the accompanying lines of our new peapod will reveal how a hard, difficult bilge has been avoided by giving the bottom a moderate amount of deadrise (upward slope), and the topsides some outward rake or slant. The result is a relatively slow, easy turn at the bilge, which will help greatly in planking. A hull so shaped will heel quicker than one with a harder bilge such as is generally found in sailing models where stiffness, that is, resistance to heeling, is desirable.

But we are not offering a sailing model here, and the more moderate bilge curve as shown not only makes for easier planking, but for an easier rowing model as well. A harder bilge curve in these central body sections would necessarily produce more of a mid-section bulge in the waterline curves, resulting in increased resistance to hull movement through the water.

The buttock curves, as they appear in the profile view in the lines, show a relatively flat, easy run, which carries well into the ends of the boat. The entrance is relatively sharp as is shown by the hollow or reverse in the ends of the waterline curves. All these factors contribute to make this a low-resistance, easy-rowing hull.

The boat is a true double-ender with both ends exactly alike. This simplifies construction greatly, and there are no disadvantages for a rowing model. In a sailing model it is usually desirable to make the stern fuller to provide more bearing aft.

The stems are moderately raking and cut away at the forefoot. This obviates a tendency to yaw when towed, as generally occurs with boats with plumb stems when they are towed behind a larger vessel. This peapod could very well serve as a tender for a large yacht. Also, the shape to which the stems are laid out is an easy and economical one to build. As the detailed drawing shows, these stems can be made up of pieces got out of an ordinary oak plank. Steam bending is not required, nor is lumber with grown-in curves.

The keel can be cut to shape from a 12-foot oak plank 4½ inches wide and 1¾ inches thick.

The hull can be planked either carvel or lapstrake, but I recommend the latter, for a lapstrake hull is both lighter and stronger. Lapstrake planking can be got out and finished at the bench, including sanding, so that when the planks are fastened on the boat no additional surfacing and smoothing is required, as is necessary with carvel planking. Nor is any "backing," that is, hollowing the inside of the plank to fit the curve of the ribs, required either.

Beginners are frequently afraid of the beveling that has to be done in fitting the laps of clinker planking. It is far less difficult than it might appear to be, and planking for this hull has been laid out to make beveling as easy as possible.

Nineteen inches of depth amidships insures a generous amount of freeboard. The extra couple of inches of topside height will not increase windage appreciably, but it will add to the carrying capacity and the rough water capability of this boat. Three or even four adults can be carried easily; even more could be accommodated should the boat be used as a tender over short distances in relatively calm water.

The boat is designed to be built with nine strakes to the side of northern white cedar planking ⅜ inch thick. A few knots are no great matter. They can be replaced with tapered plugs (a little larger on the outside) of dry white pine or cedar. Better glue them in.

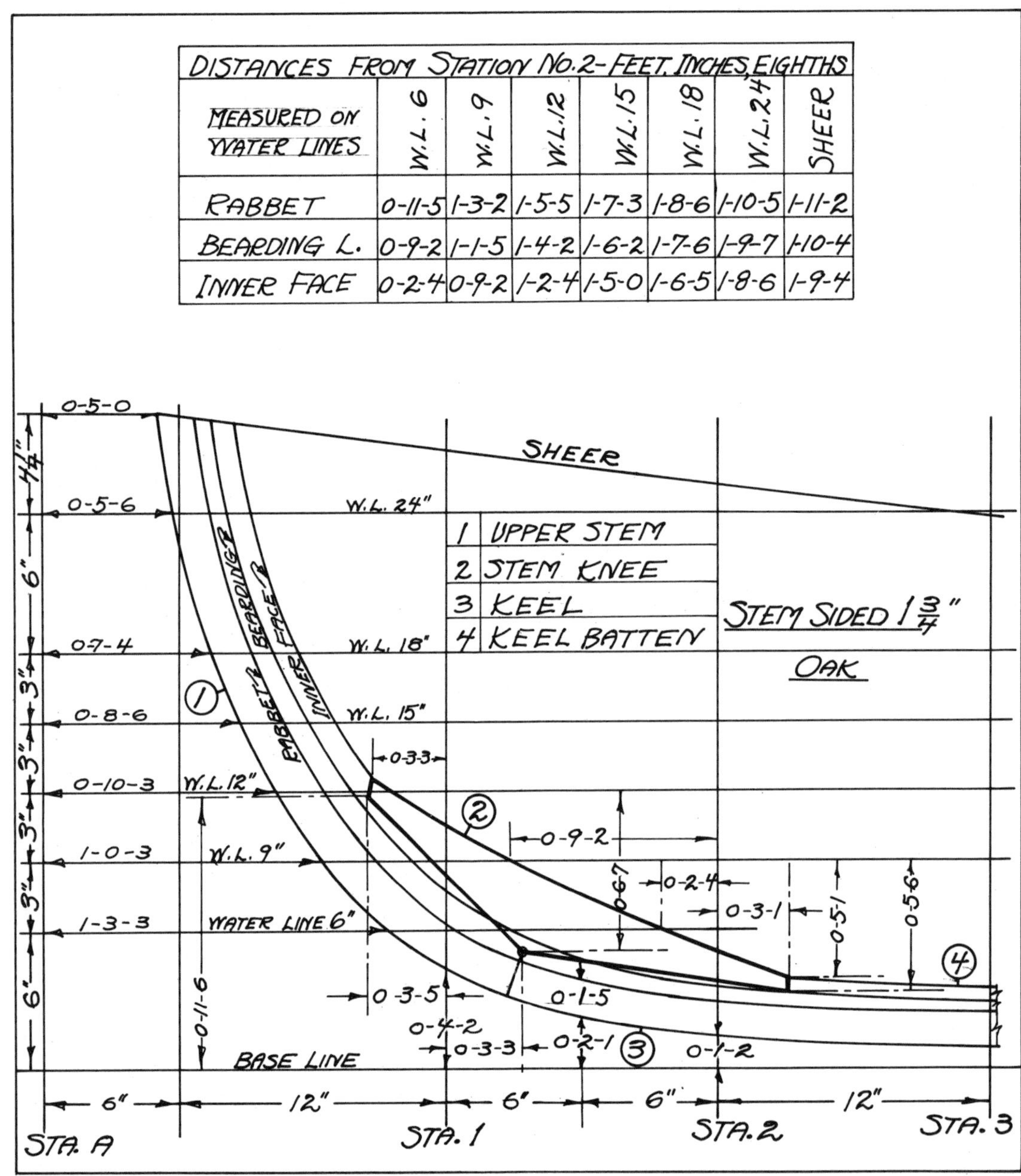

DISTANCES FROM STATION NO. 2 – FEET, INCHES, EIGHTHS							
MEASURED ON WATER LINES	W.L. 6	W.L. 9	W.L. 12	W.L. 15	W.L. 18	W.L. 24	SHEER
RABBET	0-11-5	1-3-2	1-5-5	1-7-3	1-8-6	1-10-5	1-11-2
BEARDING L.	0-9-2	1-1-5	1-4-2	1-6-2	1-7-6	1-9-7	1-10-4
INNER FACE	0-2-4	0-9-2	1-2-4	1-5-0	1-6-5	1-8-6	1-9-4

The stem and keel are oak, as is the keel batten. The keel requires a 12-foot piece at least 4½ inches wide and 1¾ inches thickness finished. A shorter piece the same thickness will make the stems and stem knees. If at all possible, this oak should be seasoned and dry, and the keel plank should be straight and true, without kinks or twists. A dense piece of red oak, yellow bark oak, or the equivalent, will do nicely and would probably be better here than a piece of white oak, which tends to twist and pull as the moisture content changes. With scantlings of this small size, there is little danger of red oak rotting if it is sound and solid to begin with.

Lay out the stem pieces, the stem knees, and the keel from the full-size laydown, presumably already made cut to the exact shape,

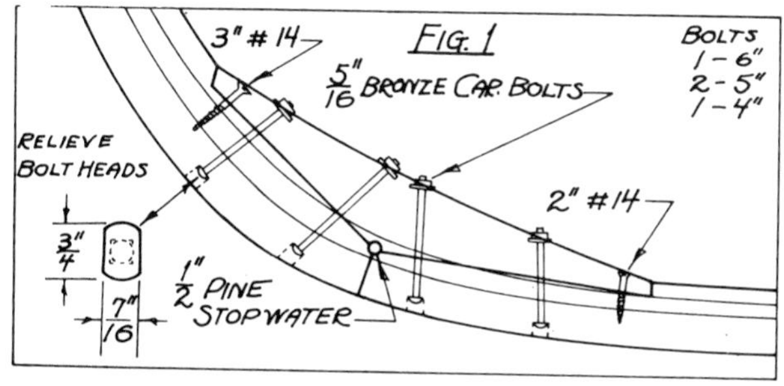

and fit together accurately. All the necessary dimensions are contained in the offsets and the drawing of the stem detail.

Figure 1 shows how the stem and keel assembly is bolted together. The direction in which the bolts run is important. They should be located as shown. This way they tend to pull the joint together when they are taken up tight. If they were slanted the other way, that is away from the middle joint, tightening them would act the other way, tending to open the joint.

Some builders would glue up this stem and keel assembly before bolting it, putting the screws in the ends of the stem knee to help hold it from slipping until the glue sets. Of course, the assembly must be well clamped and care must be taken to see that it does not slip out of true. After the glue has hardened, it is easier to bore for the bolts and put them in.

When the stem and keel are bolted together, but before the rabbet is cut, half-inch white pine stopwaters are put in as shown. These are tightly driven plugs or dowels of dry pine for tight swelling when the water strikes them. They are located in the joint just inside the rabbet line, and go through from side to side. Plank ends will cover them, and caulking will be driven in tightly against them later to stop any possible seepage of water through these joints at the base of the stem.

Before the boat can be set up for planking, molds must be made. Their shape will be taken from the body plan in the full-size laydown. When the set-up is made, the molds will be positioned 2 feet apart on stations 6, 4, and 2. As the ends of this pod are exactly alike, two molds for each of these three stations are all that are required. No. 2 common one-inch pine boards, actual thickness ¾ inch, will do nicely.

The mold shown in Figure 5 is for station 6, which comes at the widest part of the boat and is made up of four pieces cleated together. The No. 2 molds can be made of only two pieces each.

It will be seen that the mold shown in Figure 5 extends beyond the sheer to the ladder frame line. This is drawn in the full-size laydown 2 feet 4 inches above the baseline and parallel with it. All the molds are extended to this line. Thus, when they are set up on the ladder frame foundation, they will all stand at the right height in relation to one another. The centerline is clearly marked on the molds, which are notched to receive the keel batten, as shown in the full-size body plan.

This boat can be planked either right-side-up or bottom-up as shown in Figure 5. If he chooses to plank right-side-up, the builder can rivet the laps without assistance as he goes along, but everything else is harder: fairing the set-up, cutting the garboard rabbet, laying out the planks, fitting the laps, and so forth. Consequently, I recommend planking bottom-up on the ladder frame. A method has been worked out, as presently will be explained, for getting around the need to rivet the laps as the planks are put on.

For a thorough explanation of the ladder frame method of setting up a boat of this sort, see Chapter 2.

The stem rabbets are best cut with the stem and keel assembly lying flat before the keel batten is added and this assembly is laid over the molds in position on the ladder frame. Cutting a rabbet for the first time can be tricky. Figure 2 shows how it is done. The bearding line and the rabbet line are laid out from the offsets and the stem detail. Using the block as shown in Figure 2, points locating the *apex line* are obtained, and the apex line is drawn.

In cutting the rabbet, an apex line is carried straight down with the chisel, at the same time paring toward it with the chisel from either side, until the block fits, as shown.

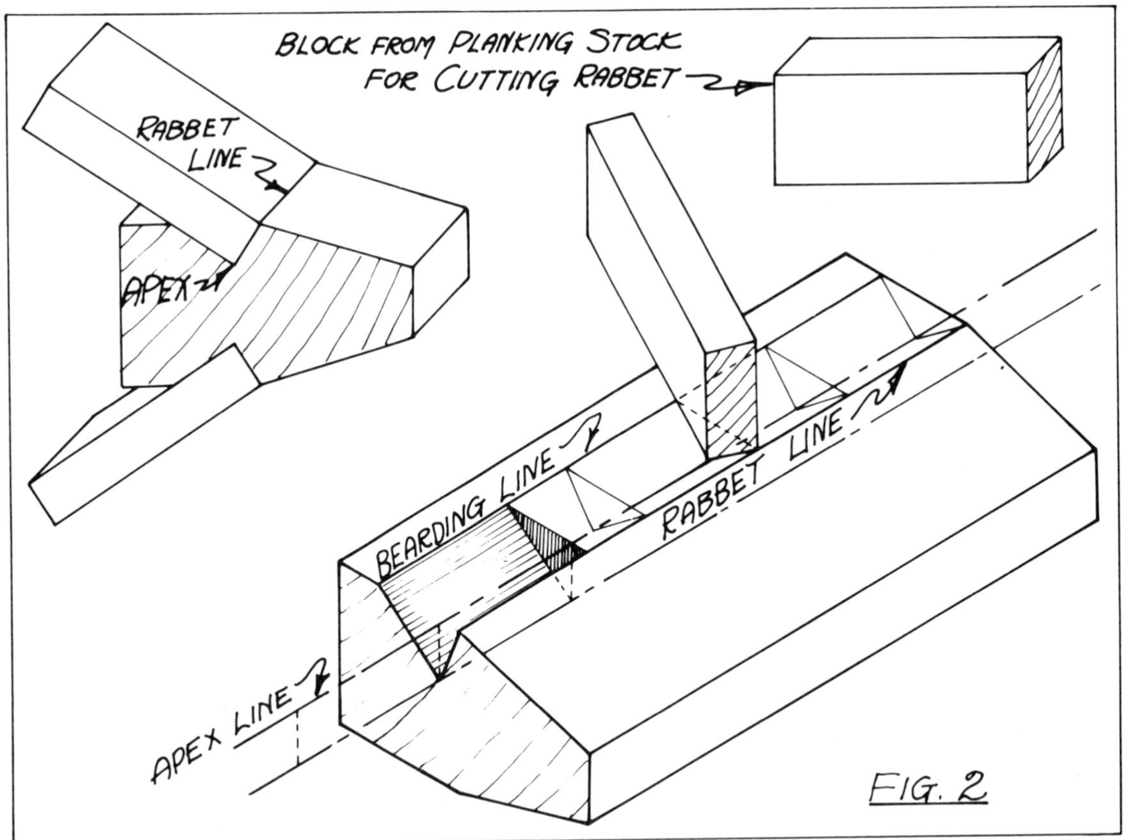

Without the apex line to go by, it is easy to go astray and to cut too much or in the wrong place. It is best to cut short sections of rabbet at intervals, and then clean out the intervening sections that remain.

The keel batten is oak, ⅝ inch thick and 3¼ inches wide, and it is screwed every 6 inches or thereabouts to the keel. Epoxy glue is also recommended. Beveling the keel batten to receive the garboards is best done on the set-up where the correct amount of bevel can be directly obtained from the station molds at 2-foot intervals.

Except at the ends of the boat, the keel batten bevel does not change much between stations, and what little there is can be easily worked fair with a rabbet plane. But toward the ends in the vicinity of Station 3 there is more bevel and it changes faster. Getting it right may not bother the experienced professional, but it can mean trouble for someone attempting this operation for the first time.

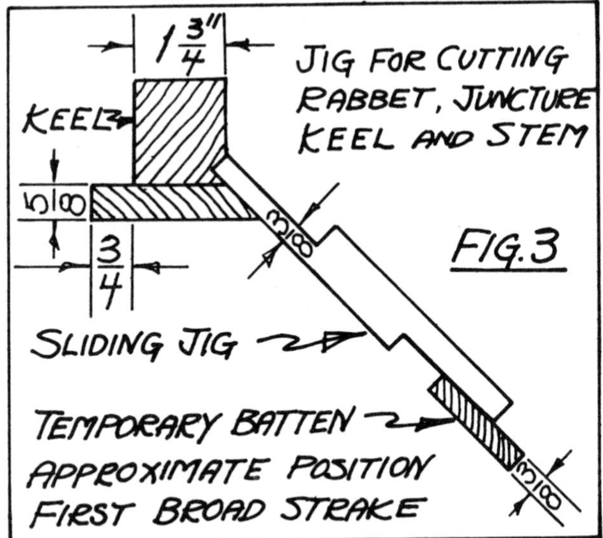

However, a sliding jig, as shown in Figure 3, takes out the guesswork. To set it up, a temporary batten the same thickness as the planking stock and 3 inches or 4 inches wide is bent around the forms in approximately the

PLANKING WIDTHS – APPROXIMATE CHECK WITH BATTENS TO LINE OUT LAPS					
STATIONS	6	4	3	2	1
GARBOARD	4 1/8	3 5/8	3 3/8	3 1/4	3/4
1	4 1/4	3 7/8	3 3/8	2 3/4	2 3/8
2	4 1/4	4	3 5/8	3	2 1/2
3	4 1/8	3 5/8	3 3/8	3	2 1/2
4	3 1/4	3 1/8	2 7/8	2 5/8	2 1/8
5	3 3/8	3	2 5/8	2 1/2	2 1/4
6	3 1/4	3	2 3/4	2 3/8	2 1/4
7	3 3/8	3	2 3/4	2 1/2	2 3/8
SHEER	4 1/2	4 1/4	4 1/8	3 7/8	3 3/8

same position that the plank above the garboard will later occupy, and is temporarily tacked in place with small nails. A sliding jig like the one shown in Figure 3 moved along this batten will give the correct bevel at any place that it is applied, and the cut can't help being right.

Much of the success of a clinker planking job depends on the number of plank, their widths, and how they line out. Nine strakes should be about right for this boat, and the widths given were carefully worked out on a scale half model. While they are not exact, they are close. Adjustment will need to be made, but in most cases this adjustment will not be more than 1/8 inch either way.

It is desirable to lay out all the plank on one side at the same time so that they can be viewed as a unit. Only in this way is it possible to harmonize all the adjustments, to equalize the widths, and to make sure that all is right, for boats are judged for appearance as completed units, and not separate plank by separate plank.

To lay out the plank, eight battens the length of the boat will be required, each 7/8 inch wide, the width of the planking laps, and 3/8 inch thick, the thickness of the plank. These will represent the planking laps and are temporarily tacked to the molds where the laps will later come, in accordance with the planking widths given.

After all of these battens are on, they are adjusted as necessary to give fair, pleasing, and uniform lines, their positions are marked on the molds and the stems, and these marks are carefully transferred to the other side of the boat.

Before attempting to plank this boat, the beginner is advised to read the sections that apply in the Appendix of this book.

The planking for this boat has been laid out as already noted for a 7/8-inch lap. In greater part, the upper edge of the planks, that is, the edge toward the sheer, will be thinned to 3/16 inch in planing the bevels. Exceptions, of which there are a very few, can be seen in the lay-out of the lap bevels shown in Figure 4. Number 1 shows that at Station 6 the upper edge of the sixth plank from the bottom has been thinned slightly less than 3/16 inch because the curvature of the side at that point requires this in order for the lap surfaces to close. This plank can be prepared and put on with the normal amount of lap bevel throughout, and the removal of a thin shaving or two with a small plane when the plank is in place on the boat will be all that is needed before the next plank goes on.

Number 3 of Figure 4 shows the top edge of the third plank from the bottom at Station 6 with less than the normal amount of bevel. This is because of the width of the plank above. If it were narrower, the angle with the mold, that is to say with the section curve, would change, permitting a normal amount of bevel. In this case the full amount of normal lap bevel is not planed off in preparing the plank at the bench. It will be observed that the more curvature there is in the sectional shape, the narrower the planks must be for the laps to close, but where the sectional shape

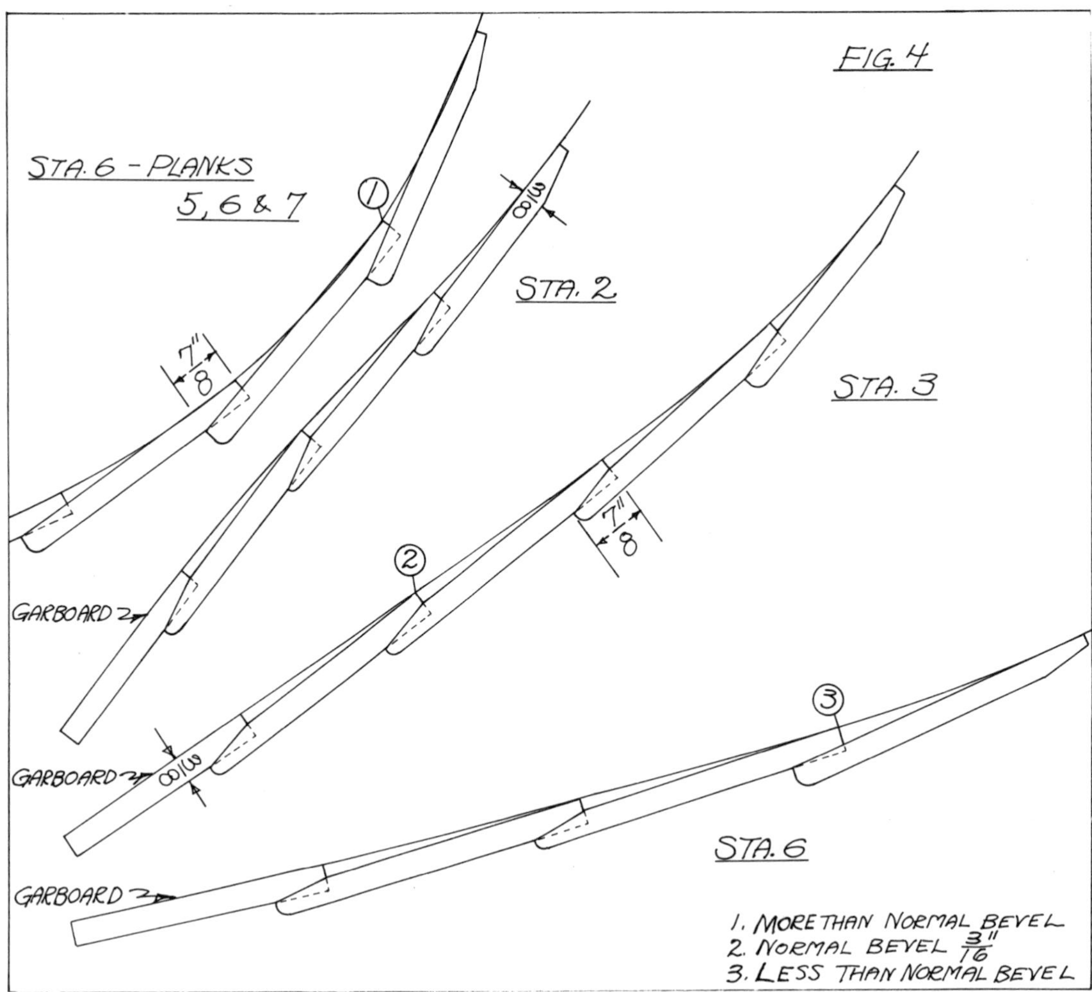

is straight or flat, width does not matter.

It is worth mentioning that an old fashioned spokeshave with a wood stock makes an excellent tool for roughing off the laps, to be finished with a small, sharp block plane.

For those unaccustomed to clinker planking, it will help to draw full-size sections of the planking at the various stations. To be useful, however, this must be done with precision and accuracy. When this is done, the builder can see ahead of time exactly what lap bevels will be required.

Actually this is not a hard boat to plank. For the most part the beveling is straightaway and uniform. I believe, nevertheless, that if I were laying out the planking for this boat a second time, I would make the garboard and the next two planks above slightly wider, which would allow the planks on the turn above to be slightly narrower. For one thing, this would normalize the lap bevel at Number 3, Figure 4, as already considered.

It is necessary to shape the ends of the planking, the hood ends so called, so that they will mate together and lie flat and level when fastened in the stem rabbet. The standard way to do this is detailed in Figure 6. An easy way of cutting the tapering recess into which the shouldered edge of the overlapping plank fits is to make a shallow kerf with a fine-tooth dovetail saw guided against a thin strip of straight batten tacked on the lap line. The necessary amount of wood can then be removed from the gain, so called, with a sharp chisel and finished with a small rabbet plane.

To hold the laps together and the planking

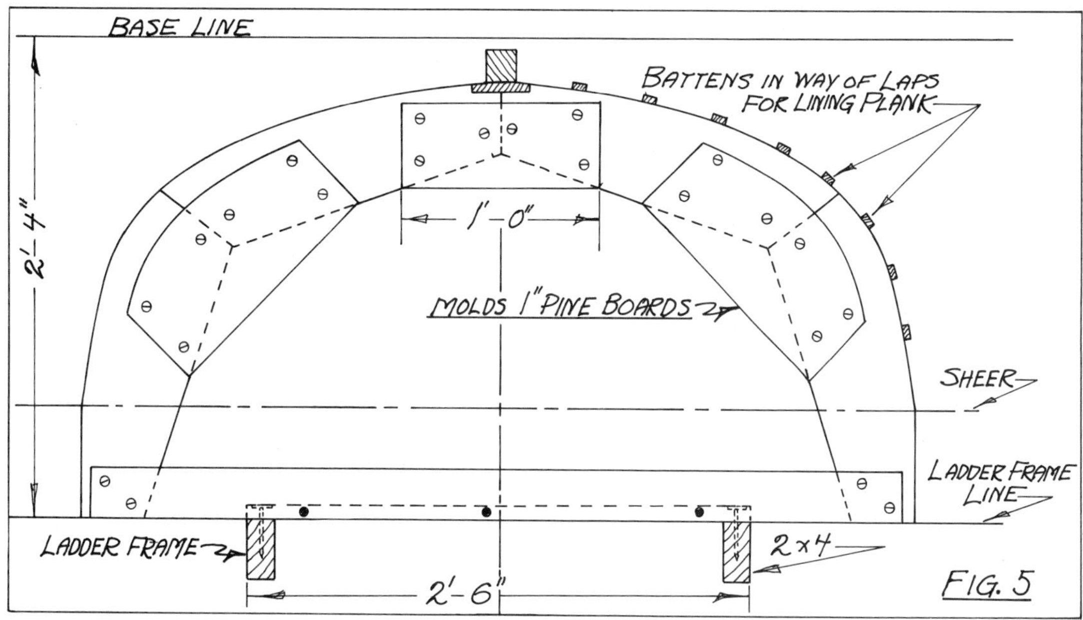

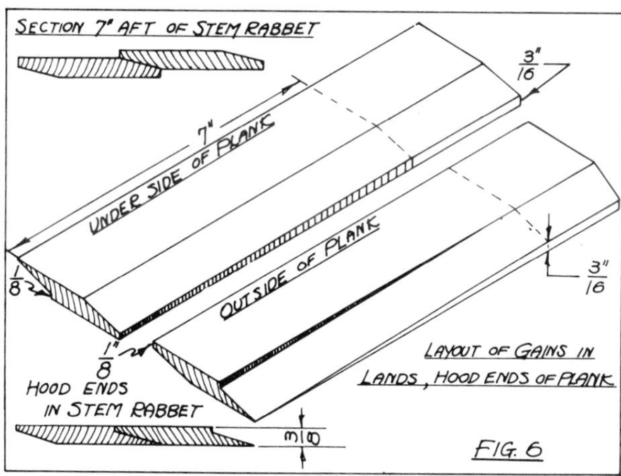

in place until the planking is finished and the boat can be turned over and riveted, the planks, as they are put on, are nailed through the laps into the molds. For this purpose, standard long, thin, coated nails are used with leather washers about ⅝ inch in diameter, dinked out of stiff, heavy leather with a hollow punch. These washers are then pierced with an ice pick to make a hole for the nail. This nail and washer arrangement holds well when driven through the lap, applying pressure to the lap, and is easily drawn out later with carpenter's tongs. When the time comes to timber out the boat after planking is completed, ribs will go in where the molds come out. Rivets through the laps and these ribs will occupy the same holes previously made by the nails.

Ribs or frames will be spaced 8 inches apart on centers, that is two ribs in each 2-foot space between stations, where there will also be the ribs that have replaced the molds. Thus, the rib spacing throughout the boat will be on 8-inch centers with rivets through the ribs, and with two rivets through the laps, equally spaced between each pair of ribs. Altogether, fastenings through the laps will be spaced approximately 2⅝ inches apart.

Ideally, ribs should be the best white oak from butts of young, fast-growing trees, steam bent and continuous from rail to rail. A thickness of 9/16 inch and a width of ⅞ inch would be sufficient. If it should be necessary to butt the ribs on the center of the keel batten, half ribs of the same size, continuous across the keel and extending from seat riser to seat riser, should double every other frame.

17 A Spurling Rowboat

As recently as 50 or 60 years ago—say before 1920—in most of the towns along Maine's more than a thousand miles of coastline, you could have found at least one man locally renowned as a boatbuilder. Not that boatbuilding had to be his sole, or chief, occupation. Often it wasn't and perhaps he didn't average a boat a year. But at a time when almost anyone could whack together something that would float, at least, this man was looked up to and respected as a master and his boats were sought after and imitated. Not infrequently his reputation and his boats lived long after he had passed away.

Boatbuilding in those days was more than a mechanical trade, it was esteemed as an art. Those who excelled set high standards for themselves and practiced building for pleasure as well as for profit, with the latter often the lesser consideration.

A glimpse of what it was like in those days is afforded by the account by Alfred Brooks, mentioned in the last chapter, of the boats of Ash Point, Maine. Today, Ash Point is only a few minutes' drive from Rockland, but back at the turn of the century the trip back and forth by horse and wagon, including shopping and other business, used up the better part of the day and was not too frequently made. People stayed home more in those days, and the people of the small fishing community of Ash Point were self-sufficient to an extent that is hard to realize now, producing much of what the simple needs of the time required. Of course, they built their own boats, of which four types, according to Brooks, were then in use: dories, wherries, double-enders, and small sloops.

Boatbuilding was a winter job. According to Brooks, many of the men built boats for their own use if they felt like it. However, Freeman Ratcliff and his son Paris built boats for others. "The ownership of a Ratcliff boat was like owning a Rolls-Royce car today," that is to say, in 1942, when Brooks wrote his article.

Another view of boatbuilding as it was practiced along the Maine coast several generations ago is to be found in the chapter on Isle au Haut fishermen in Wasson and Colcord's *Sailing Days on the Penobscot.* The construction of small boats, specifically peapods and wherries "flourished to an astonishing extent" in the Penobscot Bay area. Boatbuilding came naturally to these people, it seemed; nearly everyone had attempted a boat at one time or another.

Finished boats came out of the strangest places: attics, cellars, henhouses, and ramshackle waterfront sheds. Nearly everyone had a woodlot, and it was a general practice to cut logs for boat lumber in the wintertime along with the firewood. However, the roots of cedar and hackmatack for frames, stems, knees, and the like had to be dug when the ground was soft in the spring or fall.

A full bow and a fine run mark the Spurling skiff. This is the first boat Arthur Spurling built.

The would-be builder might have taken several years to accumulate the required lumber. How satisfying it must have been finally to complete a boat of lumber whose every piece had been selected, cut, and carefully stored away against the day of building. How different from the boat whose materials come from the store in a can! It may be that the latter sort of boat serves just as well for transportation, but a lot of the fun and satisfaction have been lost, notwithstanding.

Unlike furniture, small boats in the past were rarely stored under roofs. They were built to be replaced, and, when they wore out, they were abandoned to the weather and soon rotted away. So many fine examples of the boat-builder's art have perished utterly. So many superlative craftsmen have been all but forgotten in the short space of a couple of generations; their boats, shops, patterns, tools—everything—gone, reduced to names that only a few old-timers remember.

Nevertheless, more remains than often we might suppose. The question is for how long. It is my guess—may I say, educated guess—that if a thorough, coordinated search could be made from one end of the Maine coast to the other, and the Canadian Maritime provinces should be included as well, an immense amount of historic material, including actual boats, would still be found as surviving and recoverable. The institutional resources to undertake this job in a systematic fashion do not exist at this time, although marine museums and others are doing what they have the means for. Already, interested amateurs are beginning to make a significant contribution. One of the first things needing to be done is to search out and locate what still exists that is worth recording and preserving. Here the camera helps greatly. Photographs are only a part of the complete record, but an indispensable part.

The photographs taken in the summer of 1971 by Robert Sutter from White Plains, N. Y., of "set-works" (carvel) tenders built by Arthur M. Spurling of Islesford, Little Cranberry Isle, Maine, are a case in point. Spurling, now in his 90s, has not built a boat for more than 20 years, yet a number of his tenders are still in use and highly prized by their owners. In fact, the first one he ever built many years ago is still tight and seaworthy.

The photographs taken by Sutter tell a great deal, but need, of course, to be supplemented by detailed measurements and a list of specifications. The molds used by Spurling have disappeared, so that lines need to be taken off one or more of the boats. All Sutter was able to obtain in the way of patterns were several transom shapes laid out on building paper, yet even these by themselves are useful and more than worthy of preservation.

The photographs show a craft which was once much used along the coast of northern New England, both as a tender for larger boats and a general purpose rowboat. Twelve feet is

(Above) Detail photographs of the Spurling 12-foot tender. Note that the high stern knee prevents the use of an outboard motor. (Left) Arthur M. Spurling of Isleford, Maine, who was 94 when this photograph was taken in 1972.

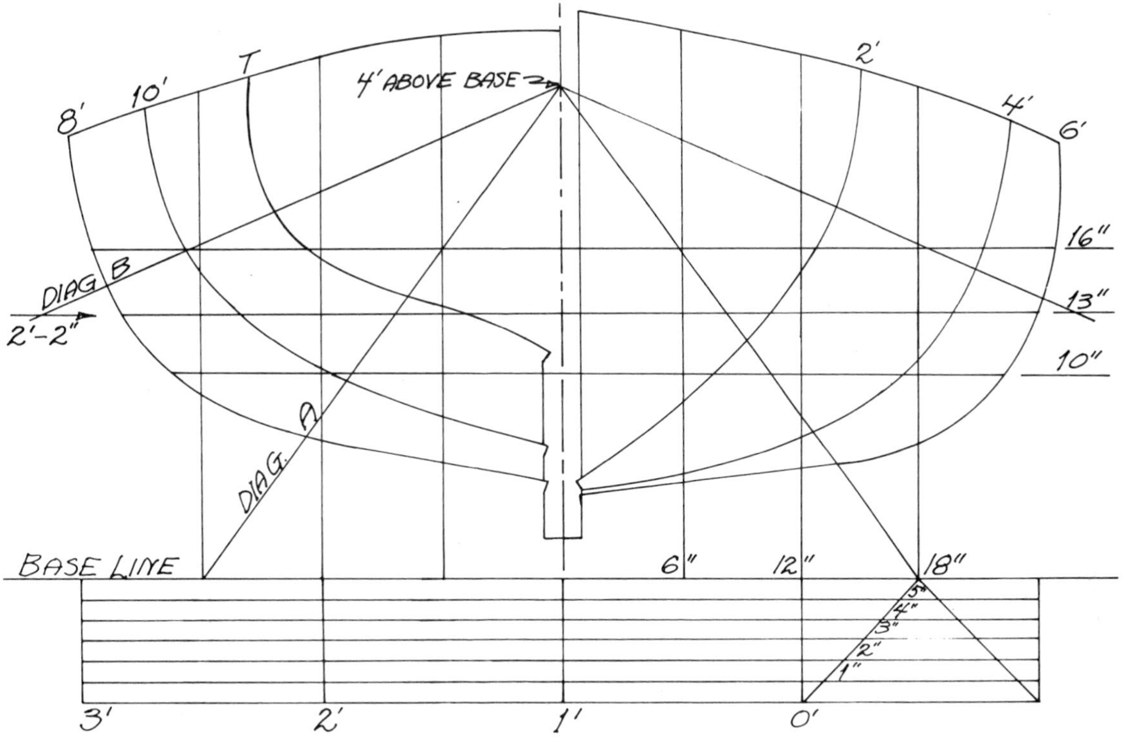

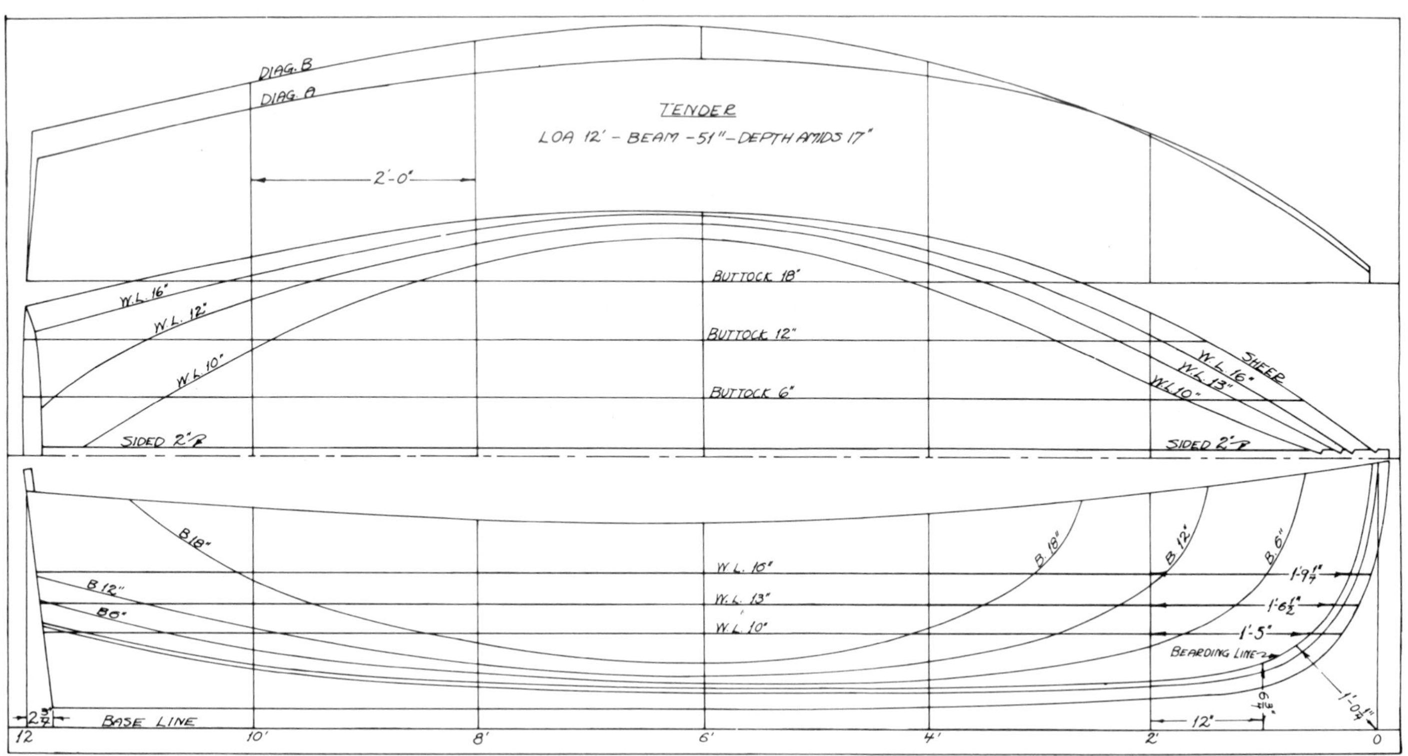

The lines above are for a 12-foot skiff similar to the Spurling model. The offsets for this boat are on the next page.

OFFSETS INSIDE OF PLANKING - FEET, INCHES, EIGHTHS.
12-FOOT SKIFF, NATIONAL FISHERMAN, SEPTEMBER 1972

	STATIONS	STEM	2'	4'	6'	8'	10'	TRAN.
HEIGHTHS ABOVE B.L.	SHEER	2-3-4	2-0-2	1-10-2	1-9-2	1-9-4	1-10-6	2-0-3
	KEEL BOTTOM	—	0-3-1	0-2-2	0-2-0	0-2-0	0-2-0	0-2-0
	PARTING LINE	—	0-4-6	0-4-1	0-4-1	0-4-6	0-6-5	0-10-7
	BUTTOCK 6"	—	0-8-5	0-5-1	0-4-5	0-5-5	0-8-1	1-1-2
	" 12"	—	1-3-0	0-6-7	0-5-3	0-6-6	0-10-2	1-3-5
	" 18"	—	—	0-10-4	0-6-5	0-8-7	1-3-2	—
HALF-BREADTHS	SHEER	—	1-3-2	1-10-6	2-1-1	2-0-5	1-8-6	1-3-4
	W.L. 16"	—	1-0-6	1-9-2	2-0-7	1-11-3	1-6-6	1-0-4
	W.L. 13"	—	0-10-4	1-7-6	2-0-0	1-9-7	1-4-0	0-4-6
	W.L. 10"	—	0-7-5	1-5-2	1-10-3	1-7-5	0-11-4	—
	KEEL	—	0-0-6	0-0-6	0-0-6	0-0-6	0-0-6	0-0-6
	DIAG. A.	—	1-3-4	1-9-0	1-11-0	1-9-2	1-5-7	1-0-6
	DIAG. B.	—	1-3-0	1-10-6	2-2-3	2-0-5	1-8-2	1-3-3

the most usual length, although some were built as small as 10 feet. Four feet or slightly more was the normal beam for a 12-foot boat. They were built both lapstrake and set works, but more often the latter. The set works boats were best planked of cedar, finished a plump ½-inch thick. Oak frames were often steam bent ahead of time on forms, beveled after cooling, and finally set in place to receive the planking. The frames would be joined across the keel and keel batten with a natural crook floor sawn out of apple, hackmatack, or more rarely an oak limb crook. Sometimes the frames were bent in continuous from gunwale to gunwale.

Such boats were for utility, not for show. Generally fastened with galvanized iron boat nails, and painted, the boats were heavier and more serviceable than the ultra-light, varnished yacht tenders which often resembled them in shape.

The lines reproduced herewith are not for the Spurling boat but are drawn from notes that I took some years ago from a boat closely like it. (The plans for her stem are reproduced in the Appendix, where cutting a stem rabbet is discussed.) The boat I measured also had a reputation for good capacity and easy rowing, and was a fine sea boat. I was told that the boat was built in Maine, in the Penobscot Bay region the owner thought, but he could not recall just where, or who the builder was.

One or more of the Spurling boats should be measured and recorded before they disappear. Aside from the historic record, this is a sturdy, useful type that would appeal to amateur builders if plans for it were available.

18 The Saint Lawrence River Skiff

Sailing without a rudder! A boat that handles smartly on all points of sailing with nothing resembling a rudder or substituting for it—no steering oar, no fin, no appendage of any sort extending overboard into the water. Most modern-day, salt water sailors are incredulous. Such a craft is outside their experience, and it is hard to imagine how it operates. On first consideration it seems impossible to sail without a rudder.

Yet it is possible, and is done, as it has been done for over a century, although it may develop that this sailing technique is older than now appears.

To maneuver without a rudder requires a particular type of boat, as shall be explained in detail later on. As far as we know the only craft so sailed is the St. Lawrence River skiff, a distinctive, lightly built, clinker double-ender, running up to 22 to 23 feet long for sailing models, a type which seems to have originated on the St. Lawrence River in the vicinity of the Thousand Islands, possibly at Clayton in Jefferson County, N. Y., in the late 1860s.

Directly in line between Clayton and the Canadian town of Gananoque in the Province of Ontario, midway in the St. Lawrence at a point where the river is several miles wide, lies Grindstone Island. Here, beginning in 1884, the American Canoe Association held its annual meets with hundreds of enthusiastic devotees of the canoeing sport, both with paddle and sail, in attendance. Here in 1886 an American canoeist won the international trophy cup in competition with visitors from England's Royal Canoe Club.

For a brief few years, the canoe, and particularly the sailing canoe, dominated the American sporting scene. Thus, in its Midsummer Holiday Number for August, 1885, *The Century Magazine*, the leading American magazine of that day, featured a long article by Henry Eckford titled "Camp Grindstone." While this was in the main an account of the exciting and fashionable goings-on of the ACA canoeing set at Grindstone Island, the author went out of his way to extol the admirable qualities of the St. Lawrence River skiff, as well as to describe the singular manner in which it was sailed. Apparently Eckford's was the first account of the skiff to appear in print.

Here is what he had to say about the skiff itself: "At the Thousand Islands there is an indigenous boat for fishing and rowing, remarkable for the methods by which it is managed under sail. Visitors call it a skiff, natives a skift. Holding five or six persons easily, it is of strong, yet light build, and in its lines probably the most beautiful rowboat afloat. Birchbark, Peterboro, Rob Roy, Shadow, Nautilus, Pearl, the hulls of all these must yield in gracefulness to the skiff."

This is high praise, indeed, for the names listed are those of the most popular and highly-

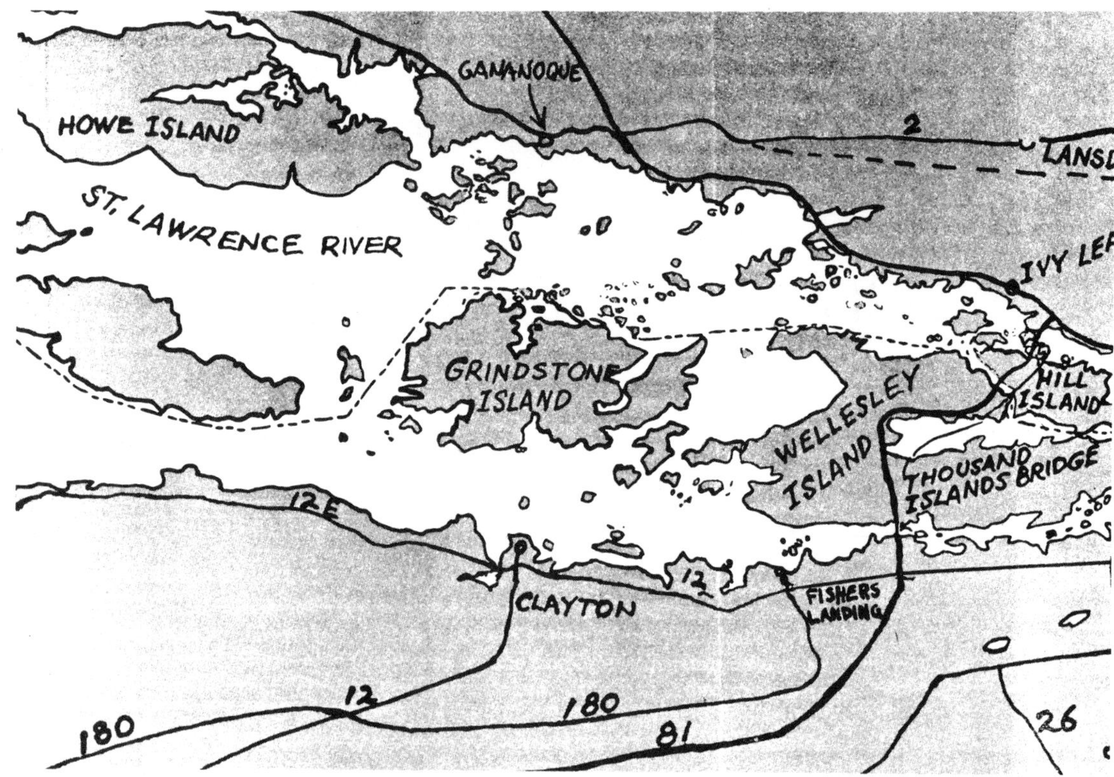

The Thousand Islands area around Clayton, New York, the center of St. Lawrence skiff development.

thought-of sporting canoes of that day.

Local tradition has it that the St. Lawrence River skiff was first built in all essentials the same as it has remained to this day in about 1868 by Xavier Colon in Clayton, N. Y. Whether research now in progress will confirm this, or whether some similar prior craft from which it may have developed will yet be revealed, remains to be seen.

However, it is clear that the skiff developed as a guide's workboat used primarily to take fishing parties to and from the fishing grounds in Thousand Islands waters. The Thousand Islands, so called, in reality number something like 1,800 islands and occupy a 50-mile stretch of river which is 12 miles wide at its upper end where it leaves Lake Ontario, and is still more than a mile wide at its lower end before the rapids begin. Here is some of the best, if not *the* best, muskellunge fishing in North America. Here also are to be found in abundance pike, pickerel, bass, perch, as well as numerous lesser species.

After the Civil War, the "summer visitor" came into increasing prominence in nineteenth century America. Farm boys, who had left the country in their youth to find fortune in the burgeoning cities of the Northeast, had in the decades following the Civil War accumulated the means permitting them to return with their families to vacation among the scenic beauties of unspoiled nature. They flocked to the seashore, to the mountains, and to inland rivers and lakes.

In New York the Adirondack woods and the Thousand Islands were greatly favored by vacationers. This was the era of vast, often palatial, summer hotels. While those of sedentary inclination relaxed on cool, spacious verandas, the more active took up canoeing or went fishing, especially the latter, for in those halcyon days the "big ones" had not all been caught, and pollution had not yet sullied the purity of aboriginal waters.

In the Thousand Islands region, because of the extent of fishing grounds and the distances

(Above) St. Lawrence skiffs in front of the Thousand Island House. The guides and sports are ready for a day of fishing. (Right) A fishing guide, one of many in a trade that provided motive power as well as fishing brains before the advent of the outboard motor.

needing to be traveled to reach them, a special sort of boat was required. This was before the day of motors. There were only two ways of moving a boat—by oars or by sail. Besides, it could get rough on the wide, open waters of the St. Lawrence, for example the windy stretch of water off Gananoque, called the Forty Acre Shoals, a favorite lurking place for muskellunge.

A boat for the Thousand Islands had to row as easily as possible when it was calm, yet be able to hoist canvas and sail when a breeze sprang up. Guiding fishermen was highly competitive. The guide who could get back and forth to the favorite fishing grounds in the least possible time with the least possible trouble naturally got the cream of the business.

An account in *Forest and Stream* in 1889 states that St. Lawrence River skiffs "are used everywhere about the Thousand Islands for fishing, rowing, and sailing, to the exclusion of all other small boats. They are handled by professional boatmen who show the greatest skill in their handling.... The chief peculiarity of the boat is the absence of a rudder, even in sailing, and steering being done by trimming the sheet and changing the balance of the boat. The boatsman brings her up into the wind by moving into the bow, and causes her to fall off by moving aft, handling her as perfectly as could be done by a rudder."

A longtime resident of Rochester, N. Y., a former summer visitor to the Thousand Islands whose experience with St. Lawrence River skiffs goes back to the 1890s, states in a letter written some 18 years ago that these skiffs were used by all fishing guides in the Thousand Islands region before the appearance of the small gas engine. Such skiffs, he explained, were very fast off the wind and were raced by the guides to and from the best fishing grounds. His father, who went on his honeymoon in such a skiff about 1880, had a St. Lawrence River skiff when he lived in

Stability test of a St. Lawrence skiff was shown in the Illustrated Catalogue of D.A. Bain, Clayton, New York, *about 1884. The guide rowed from the forward seat; the passengers relaxed in the comfortable after positions.*

Toronto, in which he used to sail to the Thousand Islands, camping on the shore at night, often in the company of friends also traveling in skiffs. When our informant and his brother were 10 years old, their father bought them skiffs.

"We used them on Lake Ontario," he related, "and almost every year sailed to the Thousand Islands in them, where we often brought them back by steamer because of prevailing westerly winds. Given fair weather and a southwesterly wind we could sail from Rochester to the Thousand Islands, a distance of about 150 miles, in about three days, camping on the shore at night."

Farther along in the letter, our correspondent goes on to say that "the St. Lawrence River guides in the Thousand Islands used to hold annual regattas. There was great rivalry between the guides of Gananoque, Ontario, and those belonging at Clayton, New York. The St. Lawrence skiffs were normally sailed without rudders by 'ballast.' To come about one moved his weight forward keeling the skiff to leeward. My father had rudders put on our boats for use on Lake Ontario where high waves frequently interfered with the ballast method of steering."

Rudders were also used on the so-called "batwing" boats, a special, over-rigged type of skiff developed prior to 1910 exclusively for racing. The name derives from the over-size sail which was heavily battened and of a shape somewhat similar to the wing of the nocturnal creature which it recalled.

Here is Henry Eckford's summary of how to sail a skiff from the August, 1885, issue of *The Century Magazine*:

> It sailed, with the aid of a small centerboard, by means of a large spritsail, the mast being stepped well forward when in use. The main peculiarity of the skiff under sail is that neither rudder nor oar nor paddle is needed to guide it. Some persons help themselves to come about on a fresh tack with the oars, but this is not at all necessary, and is held in great scorn by a good sailor. The latter walks unconcernedly up and down his boat, pays her off the wind, or brings her up close hauled as if by magic. The secret lies in distributing the weight of the sailor forward or backward. In order to bring the boat into the wind with the needed swiftness, he moves suddenly forward quite to the mast. This buries the bow of the boat, and the stern shaped like the bow, rises up and is swung around by the wind. As soon

A race among St. Lawrence skiffs.

as the sail shakes well in the wind, the skiff-man runs aft, thus raising the bow, which is helped about by the wind, and depressing at the same time the stern. All this without steering-oar or rudder, or the help of oars in the rowlocks.

It is curious to see how sensitive such a boat is to the weight of a man. Running free, he sits nearly aft. Should it be necessary to run directly before the wind, he gets as far astern as possible; while to come up into the wind the reverse movement is made. First lessons in this unique boat deal severely with the shins of the novice and with the paint inside the boat, but a little practice gives mastery. In the skiff it is considered dangerous to make the main-sheet fast to the gunwale, because the boat is so long, narrow, and shallow that it might be easily caught in one of the squalls that come with little warning down from the islands. Many will not use the running-block, caught to the gunwale with a snap-spring, which keeps the sail flat and holds it well. The simple rope is preferred and held in the hand ready to be loosed at once. The block and tackle might be hampered in an emergency and the boat turn over. Of course the skiff is not the best sailer to windward in the world, and a good regatta canoe under full sail can generally beat her, especially if the wind be light.

Another view of the sailing skiff is to be found in a short account of skiff sailing at Grindstone Island recently supplied by James C. White, M.D., of Boston. Dr. White, who has sailed skiffs for many years, is still an avid sailor. It is mighty fine sport as he describes it:

In the 1800's and '90's, before the days of motorboats, the Morgan and Leavitt families who summered at the head of Grindstone Island were entirely dependent on the combination rowing and sailing St. Lawrence skiffs, not only for their fishing, but for marketing as well. Indeed, our grandparents thought nothing of taking a guest with baggage the four miles from Clayton to the head of the island, or of sailing this distance to church and back on Sundays or to get a cake of ice to cool their drinks on other days of the week. Fishing, which in the old days was a frequent pastime, was done with the larger skiffs sailed or rowed by the boatmen.

After the advent of motorboats their offspring have used these superbly designed skiffs for many years. Races were usually held in a stiff southwesterly breeze over a figure-eight course which we called the "corkscrew." The first leg was around Papoose Island, then a reach with the wind abeam through the lee of Whiskey Island. After rounding it in the reverse direction by beating to windward the course was dead before the wind between Whiskey and Papoose where the puffs blew hardest.

The tricks to win were to get through the lees of the two islands with the minimal loss of headway, to tack the boat about smartly, and finally to jibe to cross the finish line at the Rum Point dock. In order to jibe you have to pull up the centerboard, sit on the extreme stern of the boat and haul in the sheet, hoping that you can pay it out smoothly enough not to capsize or get thrown overboard as the sail suddenly catches the wind on the other side and tilts the boat down to the gunwale. Some of the world's best yachtsmen, including Mike Vanderbilt, who skippered *America*'s Cup defenders, came to grief in this way.

A skiff race underway on the St. Lawrence in the old days.

To illustrate how maneuverable these little skiffs are when well handled, we used to play a game of tag within our small circle of islands. Each boat had a two-man crew, a tennis ball, and fish landing-net. The purpose was for the boat which was "it" to avoid being tagged by the tennis ball thrown by one of the crew of four or five pursuing boats. If the ball missed the dodging boat or its sail, it had to be retrieved with the fish-net. Collisions were rare and no skiffs were ever seriously injured.

The children of the oldtimers, who are now in their seventies, are too stiff and off balance to carry out the rapid, well-timed maneuvers required for this type of competition, but still enjoy sailing in quieter waters as much as ever. Unfortunately our boats are too old and valuable as antiques to let the grandchildren take over the old exciting games for which they were used for over a half a century.

As you can see, old-timers, and some not so old, who were reared on the upper reaches of the St. Lawrence, invariably praise the St. Lawrence River skiff in the highest of terms.

Admittedly the boat is good, but is it that good? This is a question that some are bound to ask, suspecting that local loyalties and long and fond associations might have colored such partisan views. But we do not have to rely on the word of the local advocate, nor trust his unsupported judgment, for there are others, both qualified to speak and unbiased by local ties, who are equally lavish in their praise.

One such fan of the skiff was the late Dwight S. Simpson of Boston, the eminent naval architect and international authority on wooden construction, who at the time of his death headed one of this country's leading firms specializing in the design of large commercial fishing vessels. Simpson did not mince words:

"The true St. Lawrence skiff," he said, "is about the best small boat ever developed for more or less open water."

This judgment is expressed in a piece Simpson once wrote for *Forest and Stream*, not to be confused with *Field & Stream*, currently published. *Forest and Stream*, going back to the second half of the nineteenth century, the first, and for a long period the leading, boating journal in this country, suspended publication some years ago, but complete files are to be found in some of the larger libraries, for example the New York Public Library, and specialized libraries like that of the Adirondack Museum at Blue Mountain Lake, New York. Simpson's article on the skiff is in Volume 93, beginning on page 248. It contains a set of lines, dimensioned details for the identical stems, and a table of offsets. Those desiring to build a skiff would do well to obtain a copy. However, they should insist on a photostat or even a photographic enlargement of the offsets, which were printed in reduced size.

Simpson's lines were based on extensive research. He consulted old catalogs, of which there were a considerable number, and visited and consulted builders of skiffs along the river.

"I was surprised to find in my research," he wrote, "that the skiffs of most (though not all) of the old builders, while sharp at both ends,

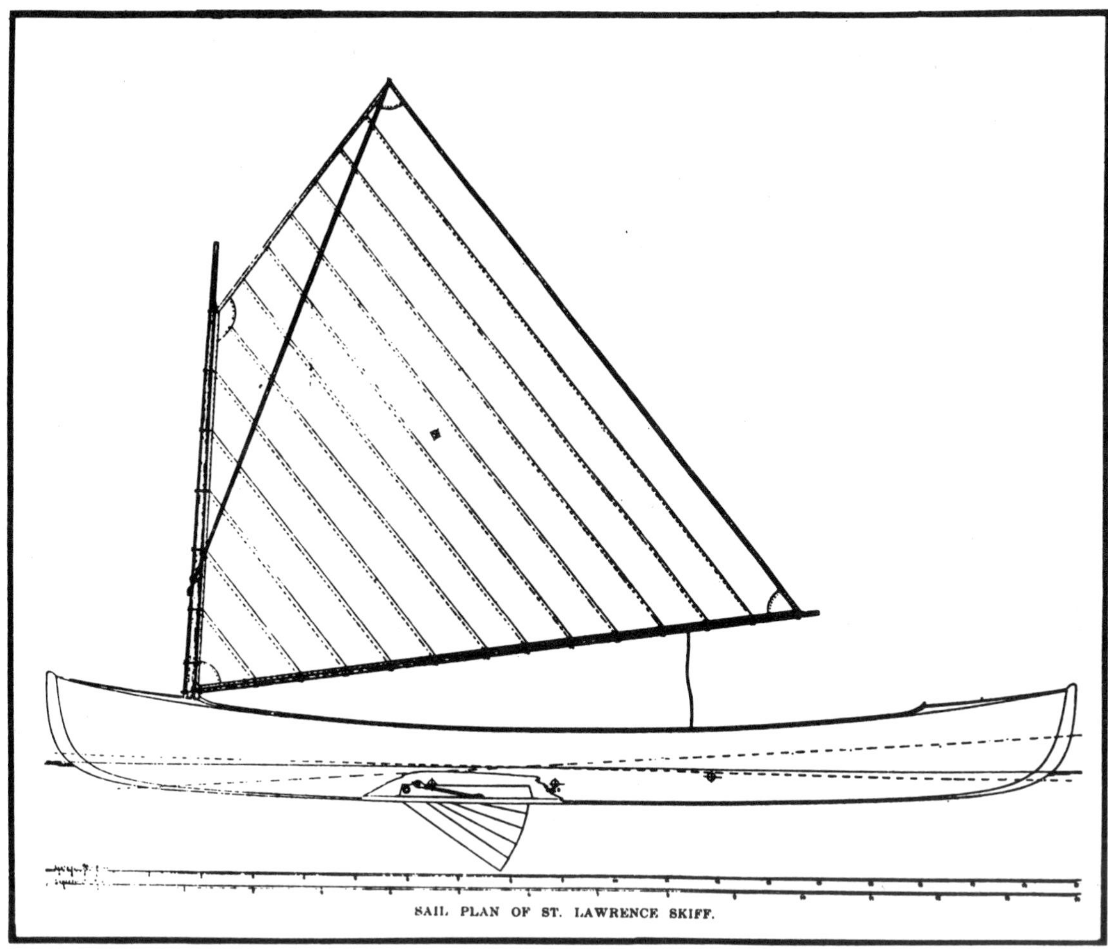
SAIL PLAN OF ST. LAWRENCE SKIFF.

were not really 'double enders,' the after body being decidedly finer than the fore body. The line of the sheer and keel and stem profile is the same for both ends, otherwise there is real difference in the modeling. . . . Owing to this difference the boat obtains the best possible trim—down slightly by the stern . . . without thought on the part of the casual user, whether loaded with one, two, three, or four passengers. This makes her row easily, and the high, full blow makes her dry and buoyant in a head sea."

Simpson treated the skiff solely as a pulling boat, not mentioning until his final paragraph, and more or less as an afterthought, it seems, that skiffs were sailed as well as rowed. "Skiffs were at first fitted with a single gaff-rigged sail, but later were rigged canoe fashion, and this boat will carry comfortably about 80 sq. ft. in the main and 25 in the mizzen. Usually sailed without a rudder, the steering being done by trim of the sails and shifting the weight of the crew forward or aft. A centerboard or other lateral plane should be fitted of about 2¼ sq. ft. in area."

The rigging observations, it must be said, are not entirely correct. Normally and originally these skiffs were sprit-rigged, not gaff-rigged. A few in time may have been canoe-ketch-rigged similar to the partly decked-over sailing canoes of the late nineteenth century, but these would have been exceptional and comparatively few. These canoe-ketch-rigged skiffs must have steered with rudders, as the mizzen would have interfered with the free movement of the crew essential for balance steering.

The standard sprit rig, which was early adopted and never improved upon for ordinary sailing, is shown in the sail plan published in *Forest and Stream* for April 25, 1889, and reproduced here. Offsets, scantling dimensions, and lines superbly drawn were also given in the 1889 issue of *Forest and Stream* and reproduced here. These details were furnished by Dr. A. Bain of Clayton, New York, who was the proprietor at that time of the St. Lawrence River Skiff, Canoe, and Steam Launch Company of the same town, having bought out Xavier Colon's original skiff-building business. Nevertheless, the skiff shown is Colon's model, which appears to have reached its final perfected form. I very much doubt if any basic improvement in skiff lines has since been made. Final proof of this waits, however, until lines of other and more recent builders have been drawn for comparison.

This 1889 Colon boat, like the skiffs Simpson observed much later, is not a true double-ender. While in profile the ends are alike, the after sections, as in the Simpson skiff, are molded leaner and sharper. Likewise, the Colon skiff, being fuller forward, will normally trim slightly down by the stern.

To sail these boats, agility, quick reflexes and a bit of daring are required. Yet they are safe enough for those who know how to manage them, and learning how is not so difficult, if one has instruction. The skiff is a remarkably stable craft for its size, and it is true that a 150-pound man can stand on the gunwale of a skiff of intermediate length in smooth water without putting it under. The 20 and 22-foot boats, more commonly used for sailing, are even more stable due to their greater length.

While it is possible for the tyro to capsize any small sailboat, an important part of sailing skill is knowing how to avoid a capsize, as well as what to do should it happen. On rare occasions in jibing the skiff in a strong wind, it might be necessary to go overboard momentarily to hold her upright, and then to clamber quickly back again over the end. That this is an advanced maneuver hardly needs saying; it is one that requires split-second timing, yet it is one which can be executed with safety, albeit with wet pants, by the experienced sailor.

Of course, the wise beginner does not attempt to jibe his skiff in a hard blow.

Experienced and avid skiff sailors claim

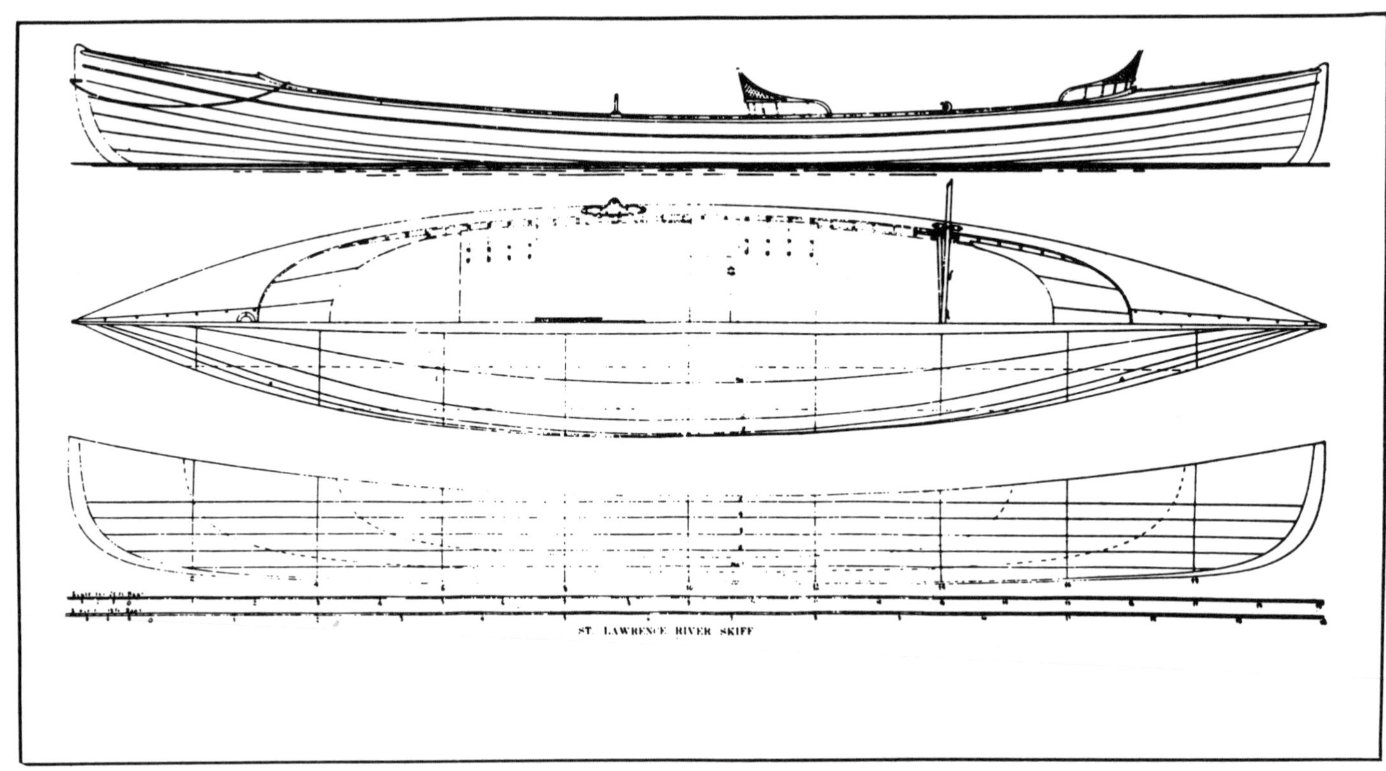

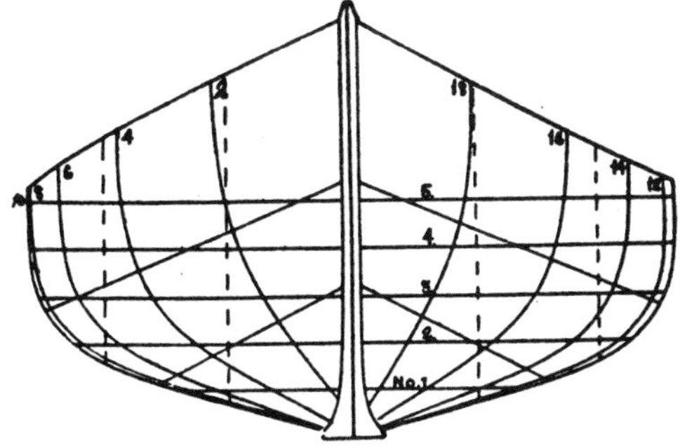

there is nothing quite like sailing the St. Lawrence River skiff. The exhilaration, the keen sense of movement and speed, and the lively action on the water add up to something that is close akin to flying, they say. Under the urging of a skillful sailor, his skiff comes alive—it responds almost like a part of his own body, becoming in a measure an extension of himself, and yielding sensations and experience not otherwise attainable.

Harold Herrick Jr., one of the most active promoters of the present skiff revival, has sailed skiffs from boyhood, and is still sailing skiffs with undiminished zest and enthusiasm. He learned to sail the hard way—by himself. Since then he has taught others, including his own children and the children of summer neighbors in the vicinity of Grindstone Island, and has found that the basic skills can be imparted by organized instruction in reasonable time and with a minimum of frustration, although only determined and continued practice makes perfect. From the beginning he has promoted the idea of an organized program of sailing instruction, finally initiated at Clayton. The following account sketching in part what is involved was written by Herrick at my request:

Lying four miles up river from the town of Clayton, New York, birthplace of the classic St. Lawrence River skiff, is the head of Grindstone Island commanding an unexcelled view of the river—18 miles west across open water to Kingston, Ontario, and extending north and south for a width of five miles from Gananoque, Ontario, to the American shore. Splitting this large body of water rise two majestic islands named Wolfe and Howe for British generals of historic renown.

It was here one summer as a youth that I first stepped into one of these unique double-ended boats with folding centerboard, 8-square sprit-rigged sail, and

	20ft. boat.	15ft. boat.
Length over all	20ft.	15ft.
L. W. L.	19ft. 1 in.	14ft. 3^{4}in.
Beam, extreme	3ft. 6 in.	2ft. 7^{4}in.
Draft	8 in.	6 in.
Least freeboard	8 in.	5^{6}in.
Sheer, Bow	10^{4}in.	8^{2}in.
Sheer, Stern	10^{4}in.	8^{2}in.
Fore side of stem to mast tube	2ft. 9 in.	2ft. 0^{6}in.
Coaming, Fore end	3ft. 11in.	2ft. 2^{6}in.
Coaming, After end	17ft.	12ft. 9 in.
Rowlocks	8ft. 9^{4}in.	6ft. 7^{4}in.
Slot, Fore end	6ft. 10in.	5ft. 1^{4}in.
Slot, After end	9ft. 5 in.	7ft. 0^{4}in.
Mast, deck to truck	8ft. 7 in.	6ft. 5 in.
Diameter, Deck	2^{6}in.	2 in.
Diameter, Truck	1 in.	0^{6}in.
Boom, length	12ft. 2 in.	9ft. 1^{4}in.
diameter	1^{2}in.	1 in.
Sprit, length	10ft. 6 in.	7ft. 11in.
diameter	1 in.	0^{7}in.
Sail, foot	11ft. 10in.	9ft. 10^{4}in.
luff	7ft. 1 in.	5ft. 4 in.
head	5ft. 6 in.	4ft. 1^{4}in.
leech	12ft. 9 in.	9ft. 7 in.
tack to peak	12ft.	9ft.
clew to throat	12ft. 8 in.	9ft. 6 in.
area	70sq. ft.	43sq. ft.

TABLE OF OFFSETS, 20FT. BOAT.

Stations.	Heights.		Half-Breadths.						
	Deck.	Rabbet.	Deck.	No. 5.	No. 4.	No. 3.	No. 2.	No. 1.	Rabbet.
0...	2 2^{4}	......	0^{1}	......	......	......	......	......	0^{4}
2...	1 10^{3}	2^{2}	8^{7}	8^{1}	7^{1}	1 5^{6}	3^{4}	1	0^{6}
4...	1 7^{3}	0^{3}	1 3^{3}	1 2^{7}	1 2^{3}	1 1	10	5	1^{3}
6...	1 5^{2}	0^{1}	1 7^{1}	1 6^{7}	1 6^{6}	1 5^{5}	1 2^{7}	8^{4}	1^{7}
8...	1 4	....	1 8^{7}	1 8^{6}	1 8^{4}	1 7^{7}	1 5^{4}	10^{5}	2
10...	1 3^{6}	....	1 9	1 8^{9}	1 8^{7}	1 8^{4}	1 6	11^{1}	2
12...	1 4	....	1 8^{3}	1 8^{3}	1 8^{2}	1 7^{4}	1 5^{1}	10^{4}	2
14...	1 5	0^{1}	1 6^{4}	1 6^{3}	1 6	1 4^{6}	1 2^{3}	8^{2}	1^{7}
16...	1 7^{1}	0^{6}	1 2^{3}	1 1^{7}	1 1^{2}	11^{6}	9^{1}	4^{7}	1^{3}
18...	1 10^{3}	2^{3}	8	7^{3}	6^{4}	5^{1}	3^{4}	1^{5}	0^{6}
20...	2 2^{4}	....	0^{1}	......	......	......	......	......	0^{4}

TABLE OF OFFSETS, 15FT. BOAT.

Stations.	Heights.		Half-Breadths.						
	Deck.	Rabbet.	Deck.	No. 5	No. 4.	No. 3.	No. 2.	No. 1.	Rabbet.
0...	1 8	....	0^{7}	......	......	......	......	......	0^{3}
2...	1 4^{6}	1^{6}	6^{5}	6^{1}	5^{2}	4^{1}	2^{6}	0^{6}	0^{4}
4...	1 9^{6}	0^{4}	11^{4}	11^{3}	10^{6}	9^{6}	7^{3}	8^{6}	1^{1}
6...	1 0^{6}	0^{1}	1 2^{3}	1 2^{3}	1 1^{6}	1 1^{2}	11^{2}	6^{8}	1^{3}
8...	11^{7}	....	1 3^{5}	1 3^{5}	1 8^{3}	1 2^{7}	1 1	7^{7}	1^{4}
10...	11^{3}	....	1 8^{6}	1 3^{6}	1 8^{5}	1 8^{2}	1 1^{4}	8^{3}	1^{4}
12...	11^{7}	....	1 8^{3}	1 3^{2}	1 8	1 2^{5}	1 0^{6}	7^{7}	1^{4}
14...	1 6^{6}	0^{1}	1 1^{6}	1 1^{3}	1 1^{3}	1 0^{4}	10^{6}	6^{2}	1^{3}
16...	1 2^{3}	0^{4}	10^{4}	10^{3}	9^{7}	8^{7}	6^{6}	3^{6}	
18...	1 4^{6}	1^{6}	6	5^{4}	4^{6}	3^{7}	2^{6}	1	
20...	1 8	....	0^{1}	......	......	......	......	......	0^{6}

Harold Herrick, Jr., self-taught yet now-expert skiff sailor, hauls the sail taut as he prepares to come about.

Start of tack shows sail drawing well. The sprit is too short; it's a substitute for the proper one, which was broken.

Body weight is brought forward to depress the bow and lift the stern, which is at the point of swinging about.

On the new tack, the boat slides easily through the water, leaving only a slight wake behind her sleek run.

Showing her power, a St. Lawrence skiff barrels across the finish line in a race.

unstayed mast. In a stiff breeze from the southwest I took off on a tack which was the beginning of many years of sailing pleasure on the river. Needless to say, I had to use oars at first to come about, and was forced to capsize the skiff to stop forward motion when coming in for a dock landing.

Through trial and error the technique of coming about without oars was mastered, and then began attempts to maneuver the jibe, resulting in a seemingly endless number of overturns. These are my early memories of wet pants and the challenge of the rudderless skiff.

Today this sailing craft still provides the same challenge and satisfaction and thrills of split-second timing. But with years of "hacking around" and racing, one's reflexes and habit patterns tend to become automatic like the trained field-trial retriever.

Anyone who can even in a small way acquire the knack of coordinating body movement with sail handling will have taken the first big step in attaining the alertness and sensitivity required for managing this rudderless sailing craft. Positioning body weight forward or aft as needed and to leeward with the sail is the basic secret of getting her going. This is something which must be learned by doing. Besides, I know of no reference books on skiff sailing.

In a heavy wind, one's movements are slow and deliberate, while in a light breeze the faster the better, especially in coming about. The sail is nipped in taut, centerboard jerked up, and with your rush to the bow the stern spins around. As the sail fills on the new tack, speed in moving aft and at the same time shoving down the centerboard is most critical for keeping full headway.

Many skiff races have been won or lost on the precision of this maneuver. In a heavy breeze, fast movement forward when coming about will result in taking water over the bow and leeward rail, and could end in "operation swamping."

In tacking one must also adjust weight position in the skiff with the sail. With practice the sailor gets the feel. How well is proven by his wake line. Here again, I have seen inexperienced racing sailors with their weight too far forward and the sail too closely hauled. Result: the skiff is only crawling along.

The skiff's leeward angle is also important. In a

heavy breeze it is not unusual to lash a spare sprit fore and aft across the thwarts to get toe purchase for hiking out, otherwise the sail cannot be hauled flat in order to obtain maximum speed without taking water to leeward.

Now we come to the most critical maneuver for a St. Lawrence skiff in a stiff breeze, the jibe. Body weight is concentrated in the extreme stern of the skiff as one sails down wind. The secret is to whip in the sail tight to swing the bow. If your weight concentration aft is not sufficient, you will not be able to jibe, as the bow will not swing around, being offset by the wind velocity on the sail. Should this be the case, one resorts to coming about.

However, when the bow has swung sufficiently to pick up the wind, shift your weight to windward and clear the sheet instantly as the boom swings around. The centerboard has been pulled up and the slightest mistake means "the drink." In a gale wind, with no downhaul, I have had the boom lift up in a jibe so that it swung completely around in front of the mast. Should this happen, drop the sheet, throw your body overboard to windward, and hold on! I have experienced this but once, a memorable occasion, in a 30-mile wind, and I should prefer not to have my reflexes tested again in this way.

Skill in the use of the four-bladed, folding metal centerboard, with a handle for working it up or down, can influence the performance of the skiff. A little centerboard is most necessary to substitute for a rudder in keeping a straight run down wind in the 19-foot Miller racing skiff.

And so finally to those seasoned sailors from both fresh and salt water who have never before taken on St. Lawrence River skiff sailing, I say: "Good luck, good swimming, and remember to take a long-handled pot for a bailer."

THE ST. LAWRENCE SKIFF COMPARED TO THE MAINE PEAPOD

Whether the St. Lawrence River skiff, developed for fresh water, is equally suited for use on the ocean is something to be considered. A few St. Lawrence River skiffs made their way to the ocean in times past, but what their performance was in comparison with saltwater craft appears not to be on record.

It is a well-known fact that waves build up very quickly, and to towering heights, on large freshwater lakes, and the Great Lakes in particular are notorious for rough water during storms. Yet at one time it was not uncommon for trips to be made in these skiffs, using both oars and sail, from one end of Lake Ontario to the other, with the voyagers camping out on the shore when night overtook them. Such trips occurred in summer, and presumably in good weather; yet even so, winds of moderate force must have been encountered, nor could the water always have been flat calm.

Nor was the water always calm in the vicinity of the Thousand Islands where the St. Lawrence leaves Lake Ontario. Between Clayton, New York, the birthplace of the skiff and Gananoque, Ontario, on the Canadian shore, lie several miles of open water. Bertha Fry Hall, daughter of Lucien Fry of Fry and Denny, famed builders of skiffs at Clayton in the late 1890s and early 1900s, recalling her girlhood, wrote me in a letter: "As you doubtless know, there is nothing more seaworthy than a good St. Lawrence skiff. I have rowed across the river in a gale when all the freighters were anchored or tied up."

Then she went on to make a most interesting and significant observation: "We were in Norway a number of years ago and visited the museums housing the Viking ships. They are mounted on supports; and as I stood at the bow looking aft, the lines were identical with those I had seen so often in my father's boat factory."

Apparently this refers in particular to the museum in Oslo where the large Gokstad burial ship is preserved together with the three smaller king's boats found in it, ranging from about 19 to 30 feet. These three double-enders are exhibited on inconspicuous supports at good height above the floor for viewing, and it is true that the lines of these king's boats are strikingly similar to those of the skiff. Also, these ancient Norse craft were superlative sea boats whose lines have not been improved upon in more than a thousand years.

This, then, provides support for the assumption that the skiff would also give a good account of itself at sea. It would make an interesting experiment to test the skiff on salt water in comparison with the performance of standard saltwater types.

The Maine peapod, in particular, comes to mind in this connection. In some of their features, the skiff and the pod, two nineteenth-century double-enders, are quite dissimilar. In other respects they have considerable features in common. The one makes a good foil for the other.

To begin with, the origins of both the skiff and the peapod, presumably dating from the early nineteenth century, are obscure. Both began as workboats, and while the peapod always remained such—a plain, functional craft without frills—some of the later skiffs attained the ultimate in finish, varnish inside and out, trimmings of walnut and mahogany, inlaid decks, and generally exquisite workmanship.

It has been theorized in the case of both craft that they developed from the Indian birch canoe. While it is clear that they both replaced aboriginal canoes, in a sense, and that they resemble canoes to the extent of being double-ended, there are nevertheless abundant double-ended craft of European origin that might have served as prototypes, including the Viking boats already mentioned.

The Indian birch was plying the St. Lawrence when the whites arrived and remained in use down to fairly recent times even after the bateau had superceded it to a large extent as a freight carrier. Certainly those who devised the forerunners of the perfected skiff were thoroughly familiar with the lines of the birch canoe.

An unsigned article on the skiff in *Forest and Stream* for April 25, 1889, states: "The exact origin of the boat is not quite clear: it is practically but a large canoe, and so it might be considered an enlargement of the ordinary open canoe so common on the St. Lawrence; but as the drawings show, it resembles much more closely the decked canoe of the States in model and construction."

The foregoing is not quite so. Let it be noted that while the lines of the skiff above the water do resemble the canoe, there is a marked and important difference below the water. The lines of the skiff show a rather considerable angle of straight deadrise, which the Indian birch does not have and cannot have on account of its manner of construction. And this amount of deadrise, which allows good bearing in combination with fairly deep displacement, is a critical factor in the skiff's superior performance, as it is in the Whitehall boat and other planked boats with similar underwater lines.

Indeed, the construction of the skiff is nothing like that of the canoe; the skiff could not possibly have borrowed anything essential from the canoe. "The decked canoe of the States" in its construction owed nothing to the Indian canoe, but was wholly in the wooden boatbuilding tradition of Europe.

The skiff built by Xavier Colon at Clayton, New York, in the early 1870s, or possibly a few years earlier, set the basic form. There was no subsequent evolution to speak of. Alterations or modifications by the numerous builders who followed Colon were never more than minor or superficial changes, limited mainly to finish. The pattern established by Colon was never improved upon.

Yet it is certain that Colon did not devise his perfected skiff all at once and all of a piece, without prototypes or precursors of some sort. The boats previously used on the river have not survived, and no plans, models, or detailed accounts of their construction can be found. But tradition has it that the early guides built their own boats in the wintertime, and even took part in skiff-building bees, helping each other.

For the fishing guide on the river before the day of motors, a good boat was all important. It was his livelihood, no less. The guides with the best boats got the cream of the business. To row 20 miles a day and often more, an easy pulling boat was desirable. That the boats were able is attested to by the lack of a single record of a guide's skiff ever having been involved in a fatal accident.

We do have one hint of what the earlier skiffs were like from an account of the Hon. Thomas G. Alvord's fishing experiences as published by Haddock in his *Souvenir of the St. Lawrence River.* Alvord, a Syracuse attorney and an inveterate fisherman, put out from Alexandria Bay one September morning in 1852 to wet a line for the first time in the famed waters of this river. As he explains in a letter written in 1895, "At that time Alexandria Bay was the Mecca of fishermen and Clayton the headquarters of square-timber cutting [shipbuilding], and no boatman or fisher-folk hailed from there until some years thereafter."

The fishing guide's boat at that time was not a canoe, yet apparently its only resemblance to the Colon skiff of 20 years later was its double-ended shape:

> The boats of that day were but the crude prototypes of the present exquisite ones, which have no superiors on the globe in form, finish or perfect adaptability, with their well-matched oars, centerboards, cushioned chairs, and other requisites, superior in all respects for the uses to which they are put. . . . I embarked on my first fishing excursion in a boat made of pine (not piano finished), sharp at each end, not more than 14 feet long, low-sided, with naked wooden boards, without back-rests, for seats. Loaded down almost invariably on the return from a day's fishing with their human cargo and catch of fish, the gunwales would be perilously near the level of the water of the river.

The early beginnings of the Maine peapods are even more obscure than those of the St. Lawrence skiff. The notion that they may have originated from birch canoes will not stand examination, either, although bark canoes were still used by Indians on the Maine coast until the late nineteenth century. It must be admitted that the large, low-ended bark canoes employed by the Passamaquoddy Tribe for shooting porpoise in the rough waters around Grand Manan Island were not unlike peapods in shape. In construction, however, there was nothing in common between the fisherman's pod and these sea-going canoes.

Fishermen commonly built their own pods, as guides appear to have built their own skiffs at one time. Occasionally, local boatshops and some builders became known for their excellent pods. But peapods were never produced in large commercial factories as skiffs were beginning in the 1880s, when the business established by Xavier Colon was taken over in 1887 by Dr. A. Bain of Clayton, who with the backing of New York City capital put up a factory measuring 50 feet by 100 feet and three stories high. Nor was there ever developed one standardized peapod model, as in the case of the Colon skiff. On the contrary, and within rather loose limits of size and form, a nearly infinite variety of pods was produced, nearly every one different according to the special requirements, or even whims, of individual fishermen and builders. Pods were built both clinker and carvel, with keels and with flat bottom boards, with abundant sheer and bottom rocker, as well as straight on the bottom and flat on the top.

In some, stems were plumb, in others, raking. Some showed slack bilges and a marked angle of deadrise, while others were broad of beam with very flat floors, the latter being favored by lobstermen willing to sacrifice rowing ease to gain initial stability for hauling their pots.

As far as I know, no mention of a peapod was ever included in a printed catalog, while at least a dozen different nineteenth century boatbuilding concerns issued catalogs in which St. Lawrence River skiffs are listed.

The first peapod lines to appear in print that I have seen accompanied a piece in *Yachting* for February, 1932, by C. W. Van Ness. (See Chapter 16.) Built by Bendix in Prospect Harbor, Maine, this pod used for lobstering had been put together in the local blacksmith shop and was framed with "natural bend hackmatack from the woods nearby." This pod showed an unusual amount of sheer and bottom rocker, which rounded up in raking stems very sloping and cut back in the forefoot. In a light condition a boat of this shape was bound to be lively and tender, but put a load in such a pod and she would settle down, yet continuing to pull easy. It is said that this pod was used in January for tending traps set nine miles offshore, and on more than one occasion got caught out in storms but always managed to make it home.

In 1969 Gordon Bennett of Clayton found a set of skiff molds in the old Colon house in that town. Presumably these were molds belonging to Xavier Colon, if not his original set. From outline tracings of these molds supplied me by Bennett, I worked up a set of skiff lines which turned out to be typical in all respects, and are shown herewith. The lines of the 16-foot rowing pod are also shown printed approximately to the same scale to facilitate comparison. The similarities between these two sets of lines are rather marked in several respects. Of course, as already stated, some pods would show entirely different lines.

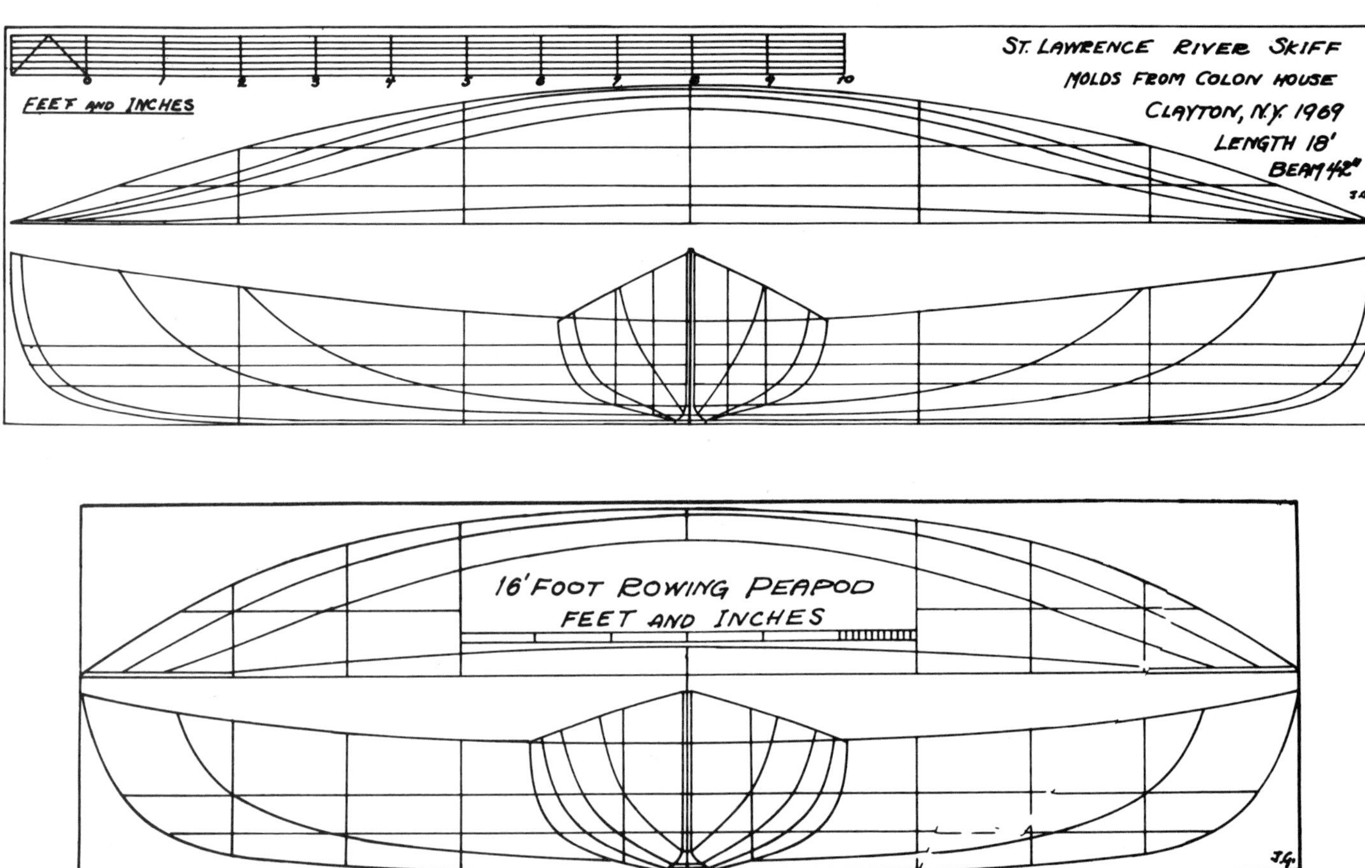

19 The Rangeley Boat

The Rangeley boat is a distinctive American sporting boat that has been in use on the Rangeley Lakes of Maine for something like 100 years and was well known to past generations of fishermen for its numerous excellent characteristics. It was not limited to the Rangeleys, for by 1900 it was in common use by fishermen on the Belgrade Lakes, on Sebago Lake, and on other large lakes in western and southern Maine.

Pictures of Rangeley boats have been published in abundance, but mostly in stories about fishing, where the attention was focused on the fishing and not on the boats. The boats were there as part of the Rangeley background—essential, but taken for granted. No one thought to pay the slightest attention as to how they were formed or constructed.

At one time there were at least three different boatshops at Rangeley actively engaged in building and repairing these boats. Now there are none. Local boatbuilders can make more money putting up camps and houses, and working on large government construction jobs. Mass-produced, factory-made boats have been brought in from the outside, decadent and inferior in design, yet capable of supporting an outboard motor.

There is still a limited demand for the old boats. There are still fishermen who like to row; as one expressed it in a letter to me: "Personally, I do not like to use a motor as I enjoy the response I get from a boat in rowing, and of course it is good exercise." Nor is the last such a minor consideration. There is no doubt that if there were more rowing and other similar regular wholesome exercise, there would be fewer heart attacks and other kinds of degenerative physical breakdown.

Unfortunately today's limited demand for Rangeley pulling boats is not enough to support professional builders. The old boats are fast falling into disrepair or wearing out completely, and there are no replacements.

On the other hand, there is amateur interest, and the model is a particularly good one for the amateur builder. By this, I do not mean the tyro without woodworking experience, but rather someone who has already built a boat or two, who has the feel of tools and materials, and who wants his next attempt to be at least a cut or two above a plywood boat or the ordinary kit boat.

The Rangeley boat's handsome shape and superior performance put it at least on a par with any boat in the same class and length range, yet its construction is fairly simple. This is because professional builders over the years simplified and standardized the construction in order to cut building costs. Besides, it was built for utility, not for show, and hence was painted, not varnished, and consequently does not require

A Rangeley boat at Belgrade Lakes, Maine, about 1900.

the fussy, time-consuming attention to finish that varnished construction exacts. If one has a good set of molds, in turn based upon a fair set of lines, and has practiced a little at fitting lapped, or clinker planking, the rest should be "duck soup," as the saying goes.

To appreciate fully the Rangeley boat, one needs to have experienced it in its native haunts. The Rangeley Lake region is unlike any other part of Maine—big lakes, wide expanses, mountains, sparkling, clear air, and deep woods close at hand. The fishing has always been superb. Our grandfathers and great-grandfathers sought refuge in such a place from the large city crowds—and once there, spent time in boats, boats very similar to the one whose lines are reproduced here, although not quite the same, for the one shown is a latter-day example, with a modified transom stern intended to support an outboard motor, but still not widened so much as to spoil the boat for rowing.

It appears that the first planked boats in the Rangeley Lakes region, following the Indian birch canoe, were built on a model brought from the New York lakes following the Civil War. And it further appears, although it is not definitely certain, that these early boats had small, high-tucked, transom sterns, as well as abundant sheer curves. Toward the end of the nineteenth century, however, the well-known double-ended model had established itself as the standard Rangeley type. The double ends persisted until some time after World War I, when increasing use of outboard motors forced a reversion to the transom stern.

Some double-enders were converted simply by sawing off one of the ends and nailing in a vertical bulkhead of heavy plank to support the motor. In the attempt to prevent such conversions from settling too much at the stern when underway, projecting flat, fin-like contrivances called "squat boards" were sometimes installed. Such improvised conversions of the double-ender were far from satisfactory. Instead, builders began experimentation with transom-stern models in which the after sections were widened and flattened to provide more support for the motor. Carried beyond a certain point,

Square-stern Rangeley boats at Quimby Pond, Rangeley, Maine, about 1900.

Fishing on the Belgrade Lakes about 1900. These two Rangeleys appear to be somewhat smaller in size than the standard model.

such modification in form can spoil the good rowing qualities of the model, and this is precisely what happened in too many cases.

As can be seen from the lines of the Ellis model, however, the boat remains essentially a double-ender below the waterline, although a transom for a motor was added and the after sections were filled out somewhat above the load line to prevent the stern from settling too far with the motor in place and running.

The transom is not large enough, however, to support large, high-powered motors, and for that reason this model is not to be considered a speedboat. It is axiomatic that speedboats are poor or useless as rowboats, and vice versa. This is a dual purpose craft—still a good rowboat, yet

This Rangeley is slightly smaller than the usual. She is 16 feet, 6 inches overall with a 45-inch beam. Her top two strakes are clinker, with carvel strakes below. This photo was taken at the Red Spot Fishing Club on Lake Umbagog, Upton, Maine, in 1967.

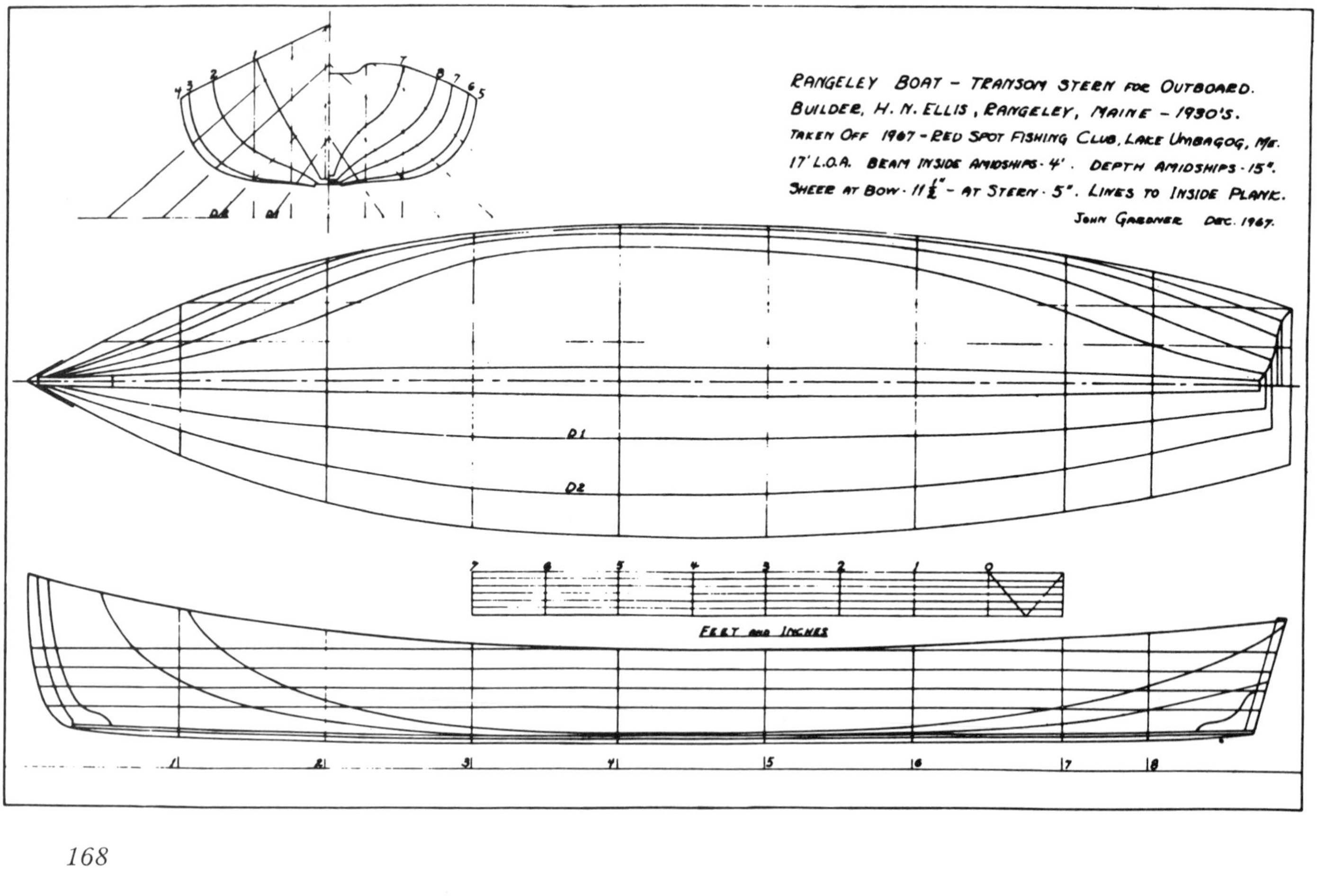

RANGELEY BOAT – TRANSOM STERN FOR OUTBOARD.
BUILDER, H. N. ELLIS, RANGELEY, MAINE – 1930'S.
TAKEN OFF 1967 – RED SPOT FISHING CLUB, LAKE UMBAGOG, ME.
17' L.O.A. BEAM INSIDE AMIDSHIPS · 4'. DEPTH AMIDSHIPS · 15".
SHEER AT BOW · 11½" – AT STERN · 5". LINES TO INSIDE PLANK.
JOHN GARDNER DEC. 1967.

D1
D2

FEET AND INCHES

one that can be driven efficiently at moderate speeds with light, low-horsepower outboard motors.

It might be mentioned in passing that the bow half of this Ellis boat is practically identical to that of the classic double-ender. Thus from these lines it would be easy to derive lines for a double-ender, simply by reversing the bow half and making it serve for the stern as well. In fact it would not be necessary even to redraw the lines. A double set of molds for the bow half would make the whole boat.

THE ELLIS RANGELEY BOAT

The boat from which our lines were taken was built some time in the 1930s for the Red Spot Fishing Camp on Lake Umbagog, the most southerly and westerly of the Rangeley chain. H. N. Ellis built the boat at his shop in Rangeley, Maine, and B. R. Burdsall, now president of the club, well remembers transporting the new boat from Rangeley to Upton on top of his Buick, although he is not sure of the precise year. This boat has been in service every summer since at the Red Spot Fishing Club and is tight and sound still. It was through the cooperation of the Red Spot Fishing Club that I was able to measure and record the details of this boat.

Lake Umbagog is quite shallow in places and lies open along its greatest length to prevailing winds, so that it can, and does, become extremely rough on short notice. It is known as a treacherous lake, and its summer storms are often sudden and violent. A boat that has given reliable service without any mishaps for a fishing camp on such a lake for over 30 years must be a

OFFSETS – 17 FOOT RANGELEY BOAT

	STATIONS	STEM	2'	4'	6'	8'	10'	12'	14'	15'-2"	TRAN.
HEIGHTS	SHEER	2-5-1	2-0-2	1-8-7	1-6-7	1-6-0	1-6-0	1-6-6	1-8-1	1-9-2	1-11-1
	KEEL	—	0-5-0	0-4-3	0-4-0	0-4-0	0-4-1	0-4-3	0-4-6	0-5-0	0-5-3
	3" BUTTOCK	—	0-8-3	0-5-5	0-4-3	0-4-3	0-4-4	0-4-7	0-5-6	0-7-0	0-10-7
	6" "	—	1-1-0	0-7-1	0-4-7	0-4-6	0-5-0	0-5-3	0-7-0	0-9-1	1-1-6
	9" "	—	1-6-2	0-8-4	0-5-3	0-5-0	0-5-1	0-5-6	0-8-0	0-10-7	1-4-1
	12" "	—	—	0-10-0	0-5-7	0-5-1	0-5-3	0-6-3	0-9-3	1-0-6	1-11-0
	15" "	—	—	1-0-3	0-7-0	0-5-6	0-6-0	0-7-4	0-11-1	1-3-3	—
	18" "	—	—	1-5-1	0-8-5	0-7-0	0-7-2	0-9-2	1-2-1	—	—
HALF-BREADTHS	SHEER	0-0-4	0-11-5	1-6-6	1-10-5	2-0-0	2-0-0	1-10-5	1-7-7	1-5-3	1-0-0
	KEEL	"	0-1-0	0-1-1	0-1-2	0-1-2	0-1-2	0-1-2	0-1-0	0-0-7	0-0-6
	9" WATER LINE	"	0-3-3	0-10-1	1-6-4	1-8-4	1-8-0	1-5-7	0-11-3	0-5-7	0-2-0
	12" " "	"	0-5-3	1-2-6	1-9-1	1-10-5	1-10-3	1-8-4	1-4-2	0-11-1	0-4-1
	15" " "	"	0-7-1	1-5-1	1-10-1	1-11-5	1-11-4	1-9-7	1-6-5	1-2-5	0-7-6
DIAG-ONALS	DIAGONAL A	—	0-4-6	0-6-5	0-9-0	0-9-1	0-8-7	0-8-4	0-7-2	0-5-7	0-3-4
	" B	—	0-7-5	1-0-6	1-4-6	1-5-4	1-5-3	1-4-1	1-1-2	0-10-6	0-6-6
	" C	—	0-10-5	1-6-5	1-11-3	2-0-7	2-0-4	1-11-0	1-7-4	1-4-3	0-11-5
	" D	—	1-0-5	1-9-6	2-4-4	2-4-0	2-3-6	2-2-1	1-11-1	1-8-1	1-2-1

MEASURED IN FEET, INCHES & EIGHTHS TO INSIDE OF PLANKING
LINES: NAT. FISHERMAN, JAN. 1968 & "BUILDING SMALL BOATS FOR OAR AND SAIL."

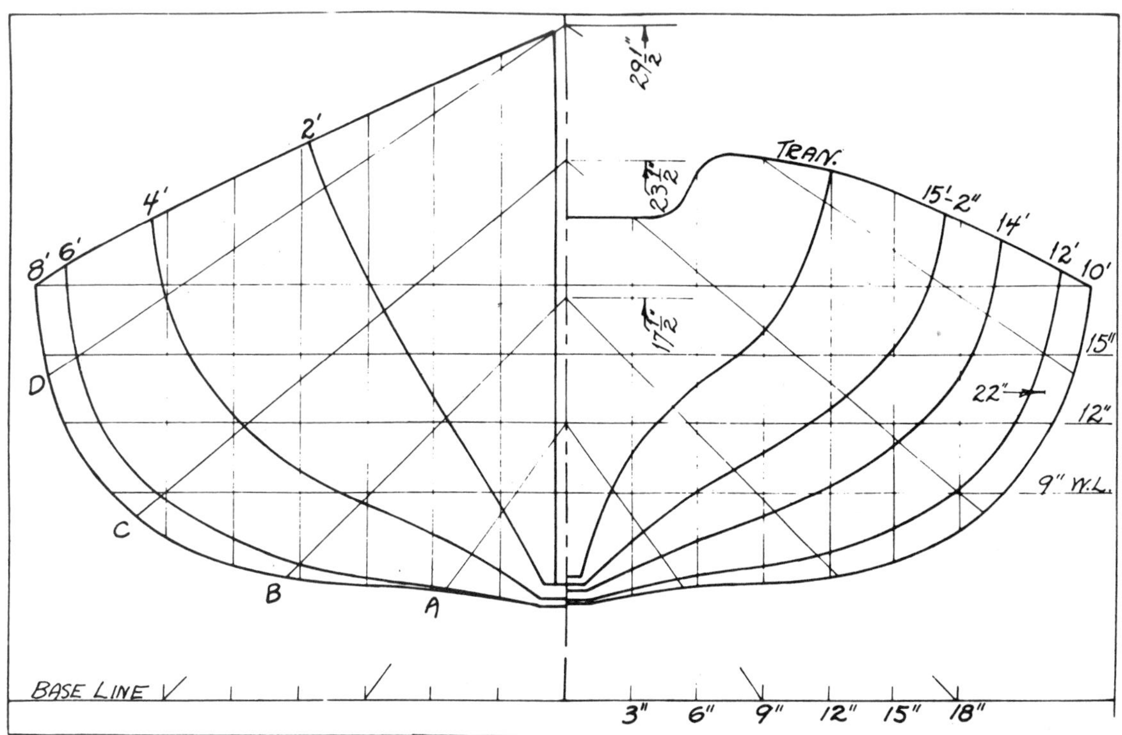

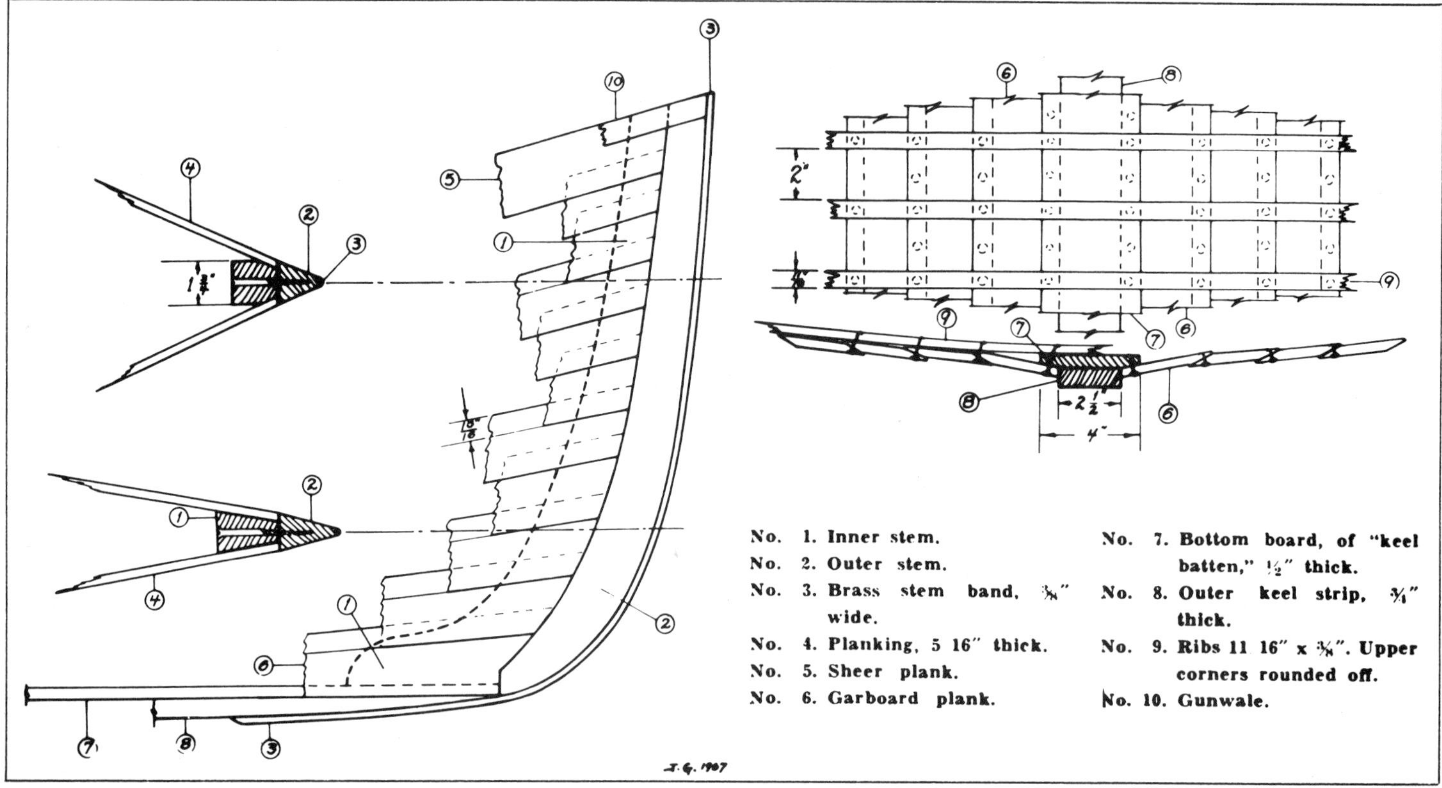

pretty good boat. Besides, the members of Red Spot Fishing Club are fishermen of the old school who row and like to row. They wouldn't have put up with a boat that long that didn't handle well.

The Red Spot Fishing Club was founded in 1908 by a small group of Boston and New York businessmen who liked to fish and who had previously summered in the Belgrades. The same families still hold and enjoy the club's 40 acres of unspoiled wilderness on the secluded shores of this beautiful mountain lake. One of the present members, first brought here as a small boy by his parents, has spent at least part of every summer here since the club opened in 1908.

As you must have guessed, "Red Spot" refers to the red spots found on the square-tailed trout (brook trout) that are caught in this lake. Such trout weighing as much as eight pounds have been caught here, as well as larger numbers of a somewhat smaller, but still respectable, size. Mounted specimens of the best hang on the walls of the dining hall in the main lodge to confound the doubting Thomases.

A few general words about the construction of the Ellis boat before we get specific:

No rabbeting is necessary although the effect achieved is that of rabbeted construction. The inner bottom board, or "keel batten," if you prefer, needs only slight beveling with a plane, and the outer keel strip covers the edges of the garboard exactly like a chiseled rabbet. In like manner, the inner stem piece is beveled with the plane as needed for the plank to lie fair, and after the planking is fastened on, its ends are covered by an outer stem piece, which is put on last.

The thin, narrow strakes of plank bend easily and conform without any difficulty or need for steaming to the rounded curves of this hull. Yet one thing that is somewhat tricky but not especially difficult is lining out the shape and widths of the plank. There are 11 of these on each side as the stem detail shows.

The laps originally were fastened with small

A party at the Red Spot Fishing Camp, about 1920. The guide is standing in a boat whose model is assumed to be the same as or similar to the first planked boats in the Rangeley lakes region. Note the small, high-tucked transom stern and the unusual amount of sheer curve. The boat at the left is a classic Rangeley double-ender.

nails or tacks of blued Swedish iron, which lasts sufficiently well in fresh water. They were merely bent over and clinched into the wood. Copper nails were not used, as experience proved they were softer than the iron nails and would not hold if merely clinched. To fasten with copper rivets would require a great deal more work, but rivets would be required if the boat were to be used in salt water, and are best in any case.

Ribs are not put in until planking is complete. The planking is done on several removable molds set up on the bottom board. These are removed as the ribs are bent in.

The reverse curve in the lower ends of the floors next to the keel assembly is not accidental. This brings the top, or inner surface of the bottom board in line with the top edges of the garboards and the planks above, so that there is no kink in the portion of the ribs extending across the bottom of the boat. The ribs are small; a kink here would tend to break them.

The ribs were fastened through the planking laps from the outside with nails that were clinched on the inside of the rib. Nails were left out of the laps where the ribs lie, until the ribs were bent in after planking was finished.

In building this boat the main things are good molds, a good planking job and careful fastening. If one is not familiar with clinker planking, some practicing should be done until one gets the hang of it. Basically, it is not difficult. The same holds for the fastening; practice at the bench a while before starting the actual job.

An Ellis-built transom-stern Rangeley at the Red Spot Fishing Club. This boat has a high, shapely bow that resembles that of the Adirondack guideboat.

SETTING UP

The offsets for this boat are measured to the inside of the plank, which is the proper way

Details of the Ellis square-stern Rangeley boat. (Above left) The midship thwart with a stool-top seat and tray for fishing gear. Note the stretcher across the walkway as a brace for the rower's feet. (Above right) The bow seat and inner stem. The walkway has been removed to show the bottom board or keel batten. (Right) The stern view shows the boat to be virtually a double-ender below the waterline. The transom has been outlined in white to make it stand out against the dark water.

for a small boat, allowing the molds to be made directly to the dimensions given without deductions. The planking thickness for this boat is $\frac{5}{16}$ inch. This is one boat whose lines, without fail, should be laid down full size and carefully faired before starting the building.

As mentioned previously, the Rangeley's two-piece stem is an ingenious simplification giving in effect a rabbeted stem without the difficulty of cutting the rabbet. The planking is fastened to the inner part and made leakproof. The outer part, which covers the ends of the planking, is not put on until after the planking operation has been completed. This permits the plank ends to be dressed off with a sharp block plane, an easy way of getting a good fit.

The outer stem, which is hardly more than a finishing piece and a cutwater, is fastened, as shown, by screws through the inner member. Thus it would be easy to renew, and can be tapered until it is nearly sharp at its outer edge, which is then covered by a very narrow half-round brass stem band.

The inner stem is probably best made of oak, although it could be spruce (treated with preservative), Douglas fir, or mahogany. It is got out of 1¾-inch stock to the dimensions and molded shape shown. When beveled, its outer edge will be a uniform one inch in width its whole length. Adding two thicknesses of 5/16-inch plank gives a total end width of 1⅝ inches for the outer stem to cover. Hence the outer stem cut to its molded shape is got out of stock of this thickness.

Instead of keeping the thickness of the stem uniform its entire length, it could be tapered somewhat from top to bottom, retaining the top siding of 1¾ inches but thinning it, let us say, to 1¼ inches at the bottom. There would still be enough landing or "back rabbet" for the planking, but to taper it thus would not lighten the boat by much, while adding considerably to the labor and difficulty of making the stem.

It should be noted that the makeup of the keel is similar to that of the stem; that is, there is an inner and an outer part, with the outer part serving to strengthen and to protect the bottom, but not needed to make the boat watertight. However, unlike the composite stem, the two members of the keel assembly are beveled and fastened together when the boat is first set up and before planking starts. The two should not be glued together, but merely dressed internally with a non-hardening bedding compound, so that if the outer keel piece should ever become badly worn on the rocks, it could be taken out and replaced by a new one.

As this is a lapstrake boat, it must be built right-side up. This is to give the planker easy access to both the outside and the inside of the laps, as the planking proceeds, which in lap-

KEEL SECTIONS
RANGELEY 17'
2'
12'
15'-2"

STEM DETAIL RANGELEY BOAT
OUTER STEM
INNER STEM

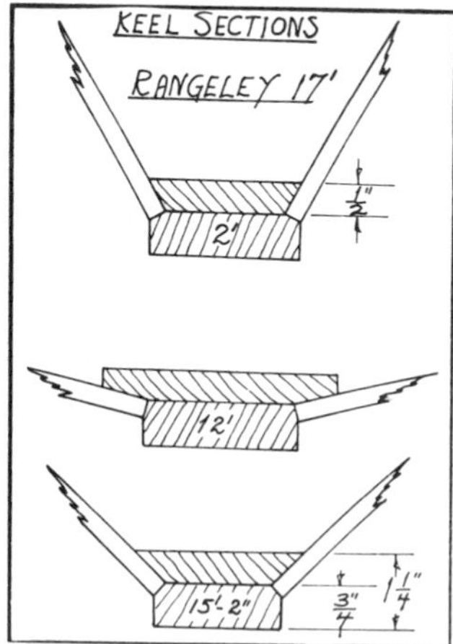

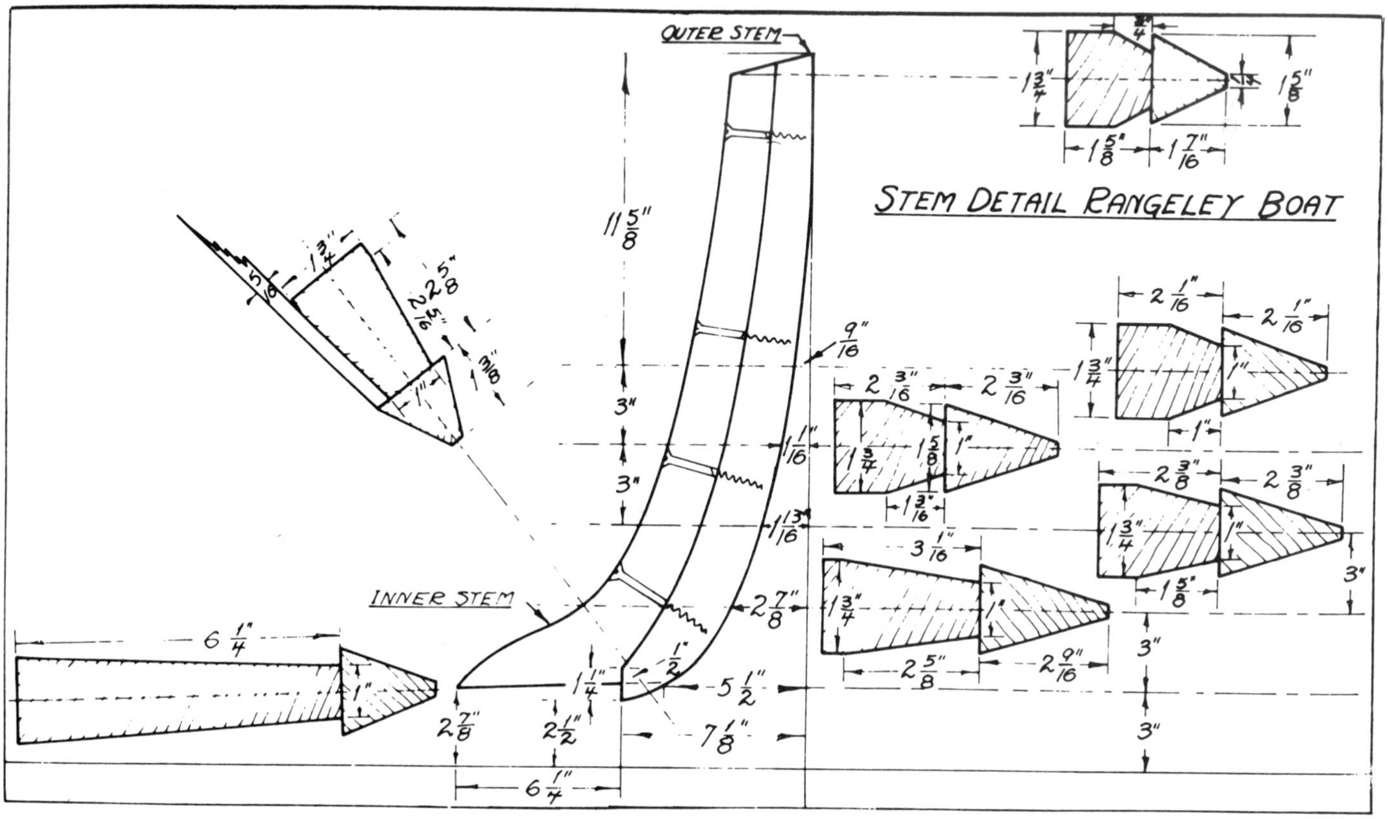

strake boats must start from the keel with the garboard and proceed upwards to the sheer, to allow each succeeding plank to lap over the one below it. When the boat is built upright in this way, the planker can reach over the top of each strake as it goes on to rivet or clinch the lap fastening from the inside, while with his left hand he can press the backing iron or "hold-on" against the head of the rivet or nail on the outside. In this manner one man by himself can manage the lap fastenings easily.

Should it be attempted to build the boat bottom-up, as works best with carvel planking, two men would be required to fasten the laps if rivets were used. One would have to crawl under the boat to rivet from the inside, while his partner held the backing iron on the outside. This requires double labor, and besides, riveting in the cramped quarters under the boat is awkward and inconvenient, at best.

To set up for building, the "backbone," consisting of the inner stem, the inner and outer keel strips, the stern transom, and the transom knee, are first assembled, fastened together, and set upright on posts, horses, or some other device. This set-up should be high enough to bring the boat up to a convenient height for working, but not so high as to make it difficult to rivet the topsides.

At 2-foot stations set up molds of pine (ordinary one-inch pine boards will serve nicely) made from the full-size laydown of the lines, which for a round hull of the Rangeley's shapeliness is absolutely essential. There are seven molds in all. Ordinarily there will be no mold at station 8, as this section was merely put in to aid in fairing the lines. These molds must be painstakingly plumbed, leveled, and squared with the centerline of the boat, so that they sit precisely on their individual section lines. Check each mold carefully athwartships with the level on the sheer line and the load waterline, both of which must be marked on the molds when they were assembled on the full-size laydown of lines on the floor. Once in position, the molds must be solidly secured with shores, braces, and temporary longitudinal battens, as needed; all will be removed as the planking proceeds.

The molds might have to be faired slightly if the temporary battens, or "ribbands," when bent on in more or less the same line that the plank will follow, do not lie exactly fair on all the molds, do not quite touch the molds in a few places, or in other places show "high" spots. The fairing process will require shimming up the low spots and planing off the high spots to bring everything perfectly into line. Unless this preliminary fairing is faithfully and accurately carried out ahead of time, it will be next to impossible to do a respectable job of planking.

There is another reason, as well, for getting the molds exactly where they belong on their respective section lines. This is so the exact location of the ribs can be measured from them and laid out as the planking is carried up the side. The ribs are bent in after planking is completed, and fastened through each lap. Obviously, the places where the rib fastenings will eventually go must be left vacant while planking is going on. Yet the lap fastenings between the ribs must be put in from the beginning to keep the planks in place and to hold the hull together until the ribs are fastened in.

The planks as they are bent on, or "hung," are temporarily fastened to the molds with screws, one at each station. These are later removed and plugged when the molds are taken out after planking is completed. It is a good plan to use small washers under the heads of these screws to keep them from hauling into the plank. Furthermore, such screws should be put in only at such points where the plank bears directly on the edge of the mold, for if there is not a wood-to-wood contact, pressure applied to the screw will almost invariably split the plank.

After the backbone is set up, before planking can start, the hull surface has to be divided up and lined out. (For a complete discussion of this process, see the Appendix.)

PLANKING

The Rangeley is planked lapstrake, or clinker as it is also called. Because beginners do not understand this method of planking, or know what is required, they tend to approach lapstrake planking as a fearsome bugaboo, when actually in such a type as the Rangeley, it is quite simple and easy, provided one knows how to go about it. Rather than presenting difficulties, this method of planking offers a number of advantages.

First, lapstrake plank do not need to be hollowed, or "backed out," on the inside surface to conform to the curve of the hull sections or ribs, which in the Rangeley show a marked amount of round. "Backing out" requires specially curved or rounded planes, and is a relatively skilled operation.

Furthermore, carvel planking, or "set-works" in old-time New England boatbuilding parlance, must be smoothed and made fair on the outside after it is on and fastened to the ribs, by planing, scraping, and sanding. This also is a skilled operation requiring experience and judgment to do properly. On large wooden vessels in the old days it was a trade by itself known as "outboard joinering," performed by a specialist who was called an "outboard joiner."

With lapstrake planking both backing out and outboard joinering are bypassed entirely. In fact lapstrake planking may be given its final smoothing on the bench before it is "hung" in place on the boat. For this, a modern power belt-sander gives excellent results and is a real time-saver.

Second, the lapstrake planking of the Rangeley bends easily into place without steaming, as would not be the case with some carvel plank that is thicker. This is partly because the Rangeley's clinker plank are narrow—there are 11 strakes to the side—and partly because they are quite thin—in fact only 5/16 inch thick. Lapstrake planking can be made thinner than carvel planking, and generally is, because doubling at the laps adds stiffness and strength, and because thickness for depth of seam is not needed to hold the caulking, which carvel plank requires to be made tight. Obviously, the Rangeley does not require caulking. Having so many strakes to a side means more work and more fastening, but the advantages more than make up for it.

There is much less danger of splitting or "renting" with narrow plank like these. As individual plank are quite narrow, cumulative changes in width from shrinking and swelling are reduced. Thus strain on fastenings is reduced, there is less tendency for the seams to open when the boat dries out, as well as less chance of the plank buckling when the boat remains in the water and becomes thoroughly soaked. Narrow plank are also easier bent, and when they are only 5/16 inch in thickness, like these, none of them will need to be steamed.

Third, the narrow clinker strakes of the Rangeley are easy to splice, which can be done on the boat as the planking operation proceeds, because the laps hold the splice scarphs. Scarphs are made with long matching bevels, in length eight to twelve times the thickness of the planking, and planed to a feather edge at each of the scarph ends. The mating surfaces of the scarph are lapped together with epoxy adhesive between, which, when set, makes a glue joint stronger than the original wood itself. (For a more detailed discussion of scarphing, see the Appendix.)

The ease with which plank can be spliced on this boat, together with the fact that the hull structure is not weakened in the least by numerous splices, and further that no heavy or clumsy butt blocks are required, adds up altogether to a very great advantage. It means that comparatively short lengths of planking stock can be used and that the grain can be kept straight for maximum strength. Knots and sapwood can be avoided, which provides both quality in planking lumber and its economical use.

The manner in which these planks are lapped gives maximum strength and tightness. First the lap bevels are of generous width, 13/16 inch on the average, but in actual practice probably ranging from 3/4 inch to 7/8 inch. This is more than twice the thickness of the plank. Yet the laps are not beveled excessively, so that ample wood remains for strength. In fact, as can be seen on the drawing, the four lower plank are hardly beveled at all—just enough wood is removed to bring the lap surfaces in contact. This means that the inner surfaces of these plank will

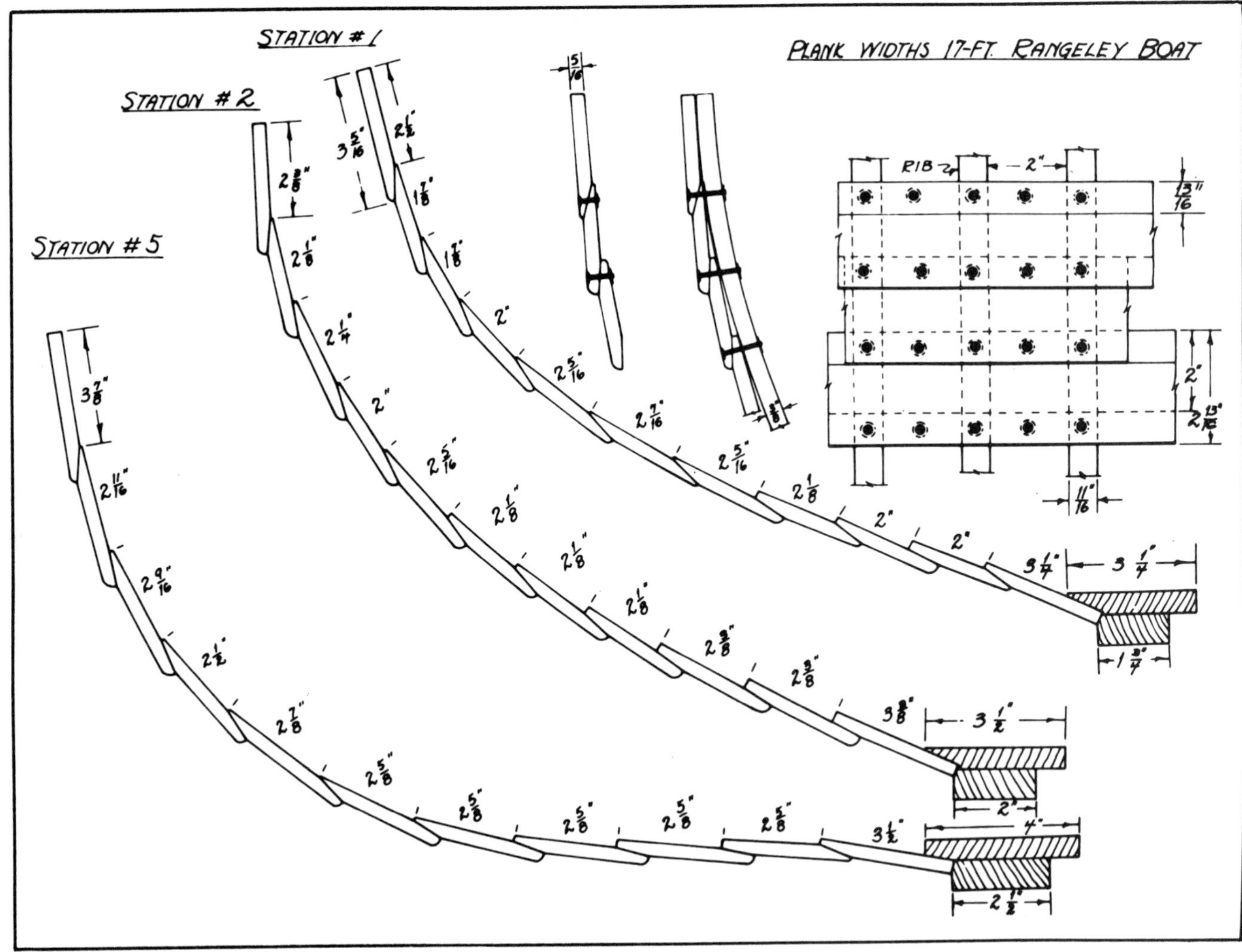

bear on the molds, and later on the ribs, only at one spot that is directly in back of the lap itself, which is all that is required, for that is where the fastening, or more precisely, the rivet goes through.

The rest of the plank coming above the four or five nearest to the keel are more or less uniformly beveled on their upper edges so that about ⅛-inch thickness at the edge remains. The inner lap of the plank next above, which comes down over and mates with the under bevel, is planed to fit.

As can be seen on the drawing, very little wood is removed to make a fit, due to the curved side of the hull. While the under bevel of these upper laps will be more or less uniform throughout, the outer bevel that matches or mates with it will change from station to station, and these changes in bevel will have to be picked up from the boat, and each plank fitted individually.

Changes in bevels are easily determined and measured with short sections of planking stock the same width as the plank being worked at the bench. Such pieces are held against the mold and lapped on the beveled edge of the plank already in place, exactly where the next plank is going, and by inspection are beveled to fit. This is done on separate short pieces at each mold station. These pieces are then taken to the bench where the bevels are transferred to the plank in preparation. The width of the lap bevel has already been scribed on with a pencil gauge of some sort. At each mold station as marked on the plank, the correct bevel is transferred from the block already fitted at that station. Thus, with a sharp block plane or spokeshave, the wood between these stations is carefully shaved down to get a fair, continuous beveled surface between each station.

Examination of the drawing of the planking laps will show that the inner bevels on the lower edges of the upper planks are extremely shallow. Only a shaving or two has to be removed to attain a snug fit against the beveled edge of the plank below. Thus a strong, heavy lap remains.

In fitting the laps of this boat, one general principle applies: lay out the lap bevels so as to take off just as little wood as possible.

Beveling the laps is an operation which often panics the beginner. If he will keep his cool, go slowly, practice a little at the bench, be content even if he spoils a plank or two at the beginning, he will make out all right and will find before he reaches the end of the job that he can often tell by "eye" how much bevel is required, and will be at a loss to understand what it was about this operation that scared him so much at the outset.

An experienced planker will make perfectly fitted laps so that once they are drawn up by rivets they need nothing between them and are perfectly tight as they are. For laps that do not fit that snugly, some kind of flexible sealer between is not a bad idea. Sometimes all that is needed is to turn the boat upside down so that paint will run into the laps. But if the right sort of adhesive sealer is put on the inside surfaces of the laps during planking, not only will water-tightness be insured, but also the adhesion will strengthen the hull over and beyond the regular metal lap fastenings. Whatever is used should be flexible enough to allow the laps to give in order to work with the boat, both when the planks swell or shrink and when the boat moves in a seaway.

As the finished planking on this boat is only 5/16 inch thick, it is often possible to get out planks for both sides at once from one-inch thick planking stock, to be split in two with a thin circular saw or bandsaw after being sawed and planed to shape. Often this method can be used to save both time and lumber, as well as to insure identical plank on both sides of the boat.

TIMBERING AND FASTENING

As originally built at Rangeley, these boats were fastened with a small clinch nail of pure Swedish iron, which, without any galvanizing, lasted well enough in fresh water. Copper nails had been tried, but they were not strong enough and consequently loosened. Copper rivets had not been used because of the additional work which they required.

Today, the old type of iron nails are not available, so far as I know, and if there were any chance that the boat would be used in salt water, they would not be suitable. I do not hesitate to recommend copper rivets—they are somewhat more work, perhaps, but well worth it. (See the Appendix for riveting instructions.)

Usually when timbers are bent into a boat after it has been planked, the laps are pre-bored for the nails and the nails inserted in the holes ready for driving through the timber once it is bent down into place. Nails put in in this way pull the timber tightly against the planking all the way around for a snug fit. But the timber must be hot so as not to split, and the timbers for this boat are so small that they would be bound to cool quickly, so quickly that it might not be safe to try to nail through them without boring.

For rivets for this boat, I suggest copper nails about 1½ inches long. Cut copper nails are preferred, but wire copper nails will do quite well. Over 2,000 will be needed. That's a lot of riveting, it's true, but not too excessive, once the builder has the hang of it. And it will make a wonderfully tight, strong job.

After the boat is planked and riveted, a light sponging with hot water will swell out the dents made by the riveting hammer, and after a light finish-sanding the boat is ready for paint.

FINISHING OFF

The interior arrangement of the Rangeley is simplicity itself, yet the location of the two rowing thwarts is critical for rowing trim and balance. As for the stern sheets, the builder can

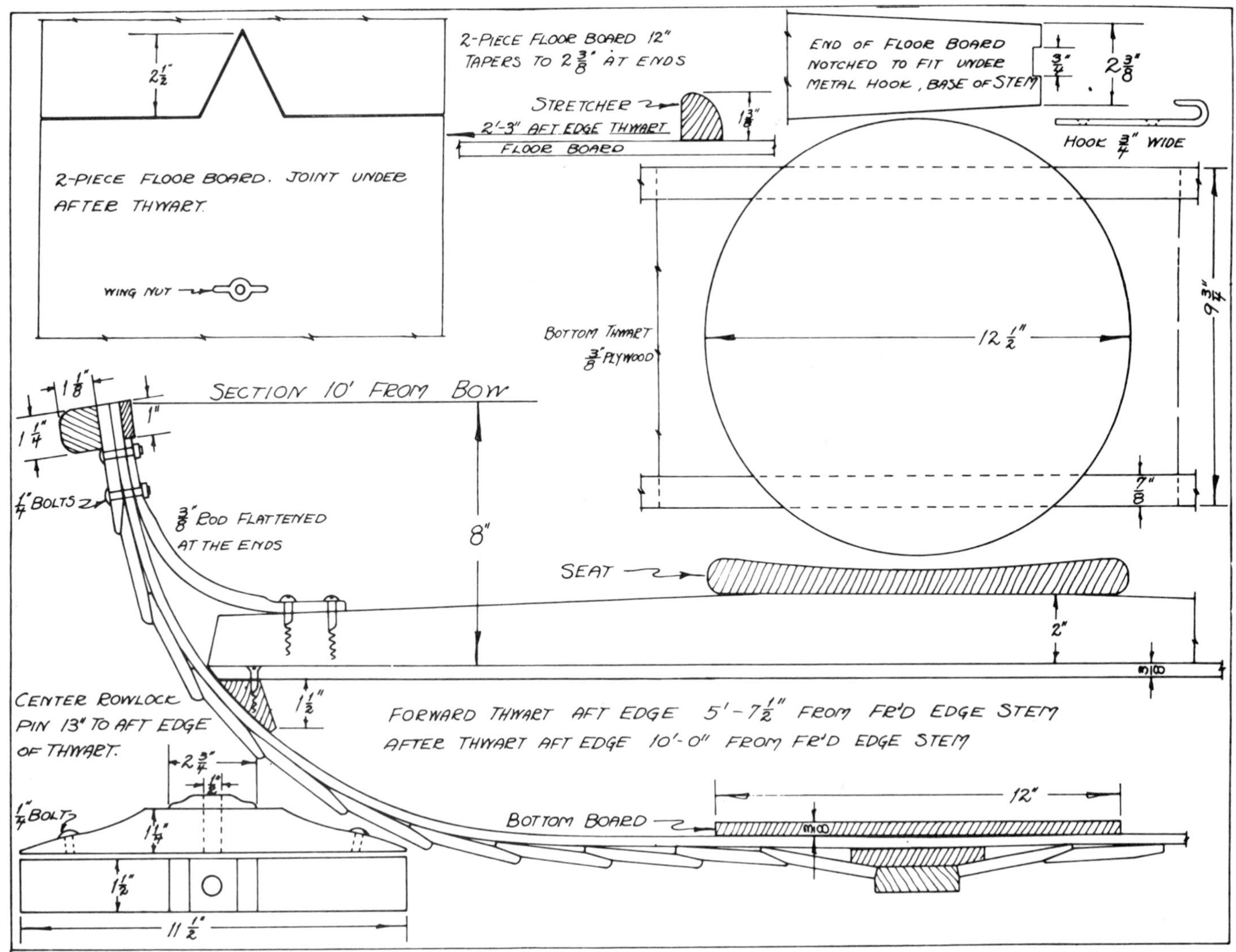

put them in to suit himself, or leave them out entirely. A small stowage compartment or locker could be built underneath if one wanted to. This is purely a matter of personal preference, as any normal construction here would not affect the performance of the boat.

The rowing thwarts are unusual, if not unique. The raised round seat in the center, like the top of a stool, is comfortable to sit on, in part because it is hollowed out somewhat. It can be fitted with a thin cushion for the fisherman who spends long hours out on the lake.

On either side is a handy shelf with sides on it so that things put into this recess cannot fall out into the bottom of the boat—a most convenient feature for the fisherman. The bottom of these thwarts is made of 3/8-inch plywood, which is glued and screwed to the stiffening supports on either side. These stiffeners should be of spruce or Douglas fir, preferably, although almost anything, even pine, will do.

The thwarts are braced on either side with metal angle braces made of 3/8-inch rod with the ends flattened, as shown on the drawing, and bored with 1/4-inch holes for bolts and round head screws. Ordinary iron rod is generally used for boats kept in fresh water. In working bronze rod, care must be taken not to heat the metal too hot, as it will crumble. Brass should not be used as it is worthless for this purpose.

The removable floorboard is made in two pieces that fit together endwise under the middle thwart. One bolt projecting from the bottom with a wing nut is sufficient to hold these in place. The ends are secured by metal hooks, as shown in the drawing.

The rowlocks now commonly used in these boats are of the ring type, sometimes called "round socket rowlocks." They remain on the oar permanently and have a pin which slips into a socket in the gunwale. Such oarlocks permit the oars to trail in the water when playing a fish, providing, of course, that the oars have leathers with shoulders which prevent the oars from sliding out of the oarlocks.

Stretchers to brace the feet against when rowing are shown screwed to the bottom board. Modern rowboats do not always have stretchers, but it is difficult to row properly without good bracing for the feet, and these should not be overlooked or omitted.

20 The Wherry

The old working wherries once extensively employed by New England fishermen have all but disappeared. Except for the meager sketches by Alfred A. Brooks illustrating his account of "The Boats of Ash Point, Maine" in the *American Neptune* for October, 1942, and the lines of the boats reprinted herein from the pages of the *National Fisherman*, no representation of lines for the New England wherry can be found in print.

The so-called "wherries" formerly built for the U. S. Navy seem to have been quite a different kind of boat, and it would be interesting to learn how they happened to get their name. Sheet 2 of the U. S. Navy Standard Plan No. 226, being lines and offsets for a 14-foot wherry, dated July 24, 1912, has been reproduced in much reduced size by Bill Durham in his privately printed *Standard Boats of the United States Navy, 1900-1915.* This boat, very much the same as standard dinghies of Whitehall derivation, does not have a bottom board, but has rather the conventional rabbeted keel of uniform siding throughout, in a word what H. I. Chapelle called a "scantling" keel.

If there is one single characteristic above all others which is distinctive of the old working wherry, it is its plank keel, which provides its flat bottom. The wherry's bottom is not as wide as the bottom of the Banks dory, but rather like that of the Swampscott dory; it is quite wide enough for the boat to ground out firmly in an upright position, and to serve as a shoe for dragging the boat up and down the beach. Indeed, there is a close resemblance between the New England wherry and the Swampscott dory, and because the former appears to have been the older boat, the latter may well have been derived from it.

Before dories were built at Swampscott, Massachusetts, the fishermen of that town imported their boats from Salisbury Point on the Merrimack River above Newburyport where the Lowell family had been building boats since pre-Revolutionary times. These boats, according to investigations by Andrew L. Harris, reported in John Albree's historical sketch, "The Swampscott Beaches" published in 1905 in the *Register* of the Lynn, Massachusetts, Historical Society, were called "wherries" and were hauled over the road on wagons for delivery at Swampscott. This would have been prior to 1840, for this is the approximate date when boatbuilding as a business was started on the Lynn and Swampscott beaches.

Perhaps the "wherries" observed by Rev. William Bentley, Salem diarist, at Halibut Point off the extreme tip of Cape Ann in May of 1799, had also been built by the Lowells at Salisbury Point. As Bentley recounts: "We then put out into the bay among the wherries, which are small flatbottom boats and are as numerous

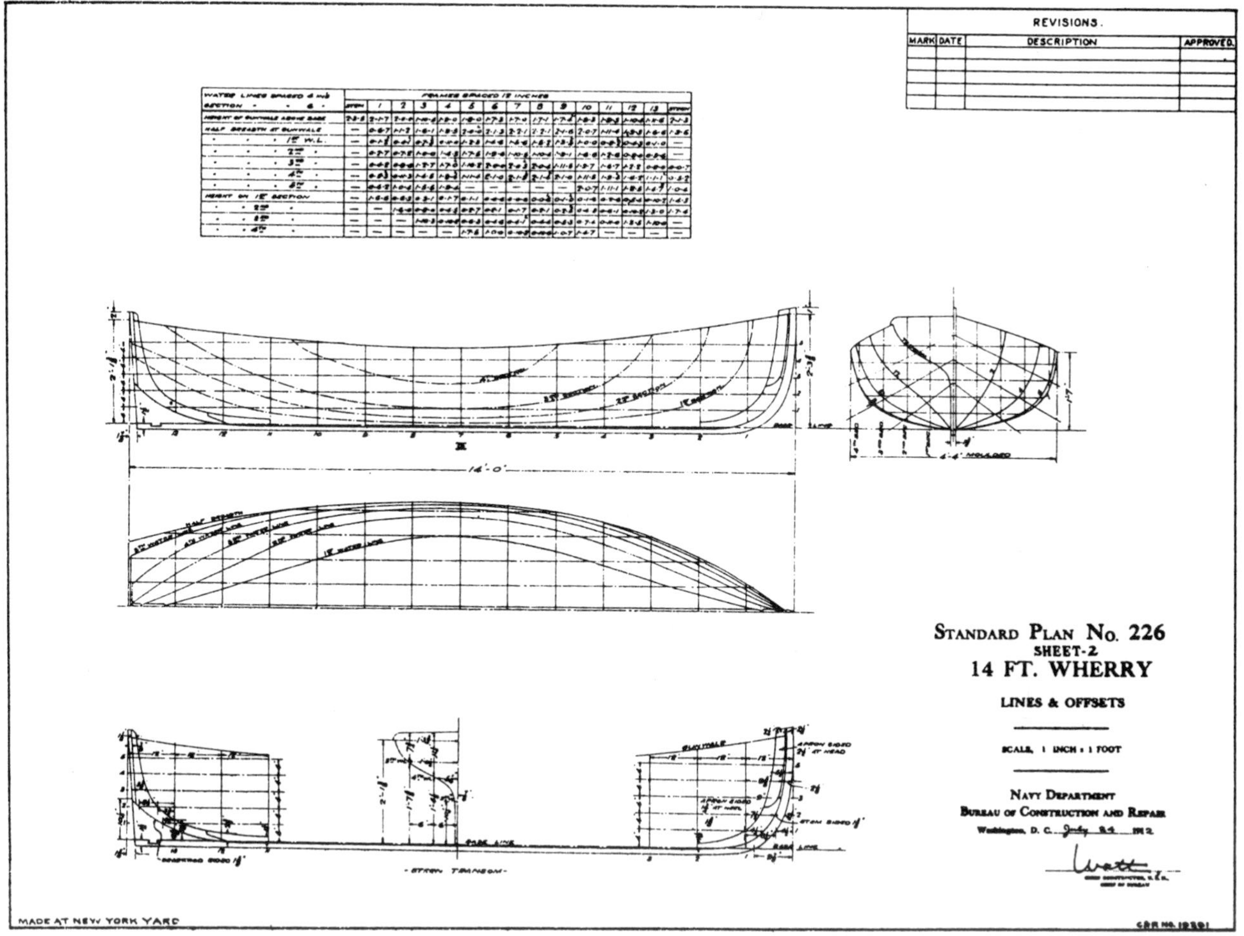

U.S. Navy wherry from Standard Boats of the United States Navy, 1900-1915, *by Bill Durham.*

as Jebacco Boats and which in good weather make two fares a day & sometimes take as many as five hundred Cod & Haddock. They are rowed cross handed by one man & even by boys of 10 & 12 years."

In another entry in his diary made from Gloucester 18 years later, Bentley noted "40 wherries within the piers near Straightsmouth."

Nor was the resemblance of the Swampscott dory to the wherry overlooked by Brooks in his *American Neptune* article already cited, although his opinion of this dory is not high, stating he "never could see any justification for the round-sided or Swampscott dory, they are as hard to build as a wherry and neither as fast or as seaworthy under sail or oars."

Colonial wherries were built without benefit of designers' lines, and mostly by amateurs. By "amateurs" I mean those not regularly working at boatbuilding as their main occupation. The working tradesman regularly employed the year round for wages in the commercial boatshop does not appear on the American scene until quite late, for the most part. In fact there were almost no commercial boatshops in early times that limited their production to small craft.

On the other hand, the shipyard for the construction of large vessels was an ancient establishment that required numerous specialized tradesmen regularly employed for wages. Building vessels of any size was an enterprise of magnitude for which were needed large amounts of capital and equipment and many trained "hands"—shipwrights, caulkers, riggers, shipsmiths, and others.

This view of Newburyport, Massachusetts, in the nineteenth century shows a variety of ships and small craft, including what appears to be a wherry, center, also seen in the enlarged detail at the right.

There were men in eighteenth-century shipyards who swung the broad-axe all their lives and did nothing else, and others who bored holes for treenails until old age overtook them. Only with a specialized labor force regularly employed was it possible to build large wooden vessels with any dispatch in a day when everything had to be done by hand. The ship carpenter could not very well be self-employed. To find work at his trade he had to hire out at some shipyard.

Building a small boat was quite a different proposition. The nails and lumber for a skiff or a wherry were easily come by, and farmers and fishermen could, and did, build themselves boats in their barns and dooryards at odd times when they didn't have anything else to do.

Although the larger shipyards had skilled

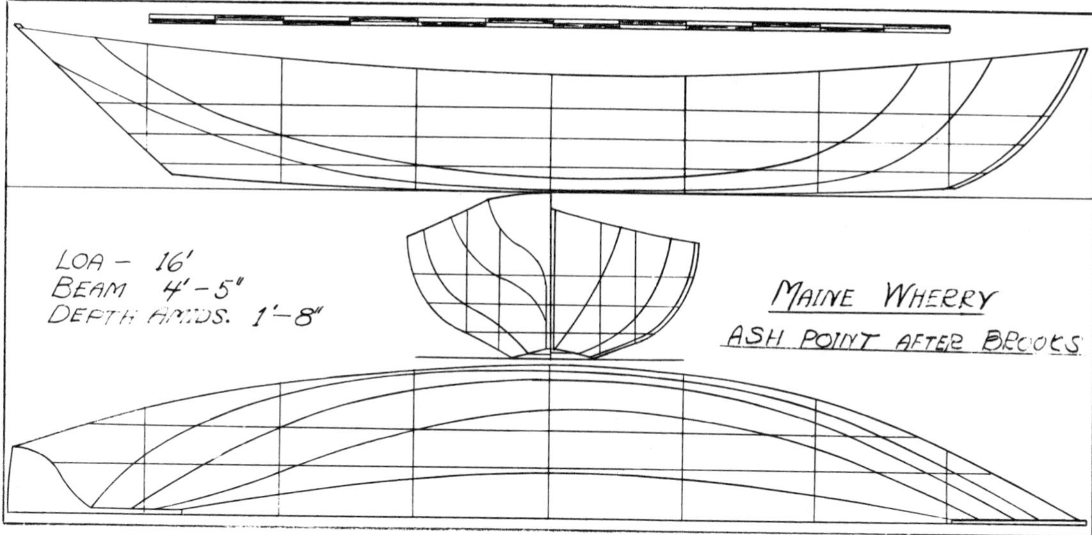

specialists who turned out yawl boats, gigs, and other small craft with which to equip their new vessels, such comprised only a minor fraction of the small boats in use in colonial New England, when nearly everyone lived within sight of the water, when travel was generally easier by water than by land, and when the small boat occupied much the same place in the economic and social life of that time as the auto does today.

Life could not have gone on in pre-Revolutionary New England without its multitude of small boats, yet these were so common and so taken for granted that they scarcely ever got into the historical record except as an occasional bare name. Those who wrote, wrote about politics and religion but not about such lowly subjects as small boats or household furniture. Much of the latter has come down to us intact in the interiors of old buildings. Eighteenth century tables, chairs, and chests have survived mainly because the wood of which they were constructed was protected from the weather. But the small boats of that period, subjected to hard use and exposed to the elements, sooner or later wore out and rotted away.

These small boats were not entirely lost, for some small pockets of eighteenth-century culture continued to exist in isolated areas on the coast of Maine well into the nineteenth century, retaining folkways and artifacts that elsewhere had long since disappeared. Some of the peapods and wherries built in Penobscot Bay until quite recently were definitely colonial survivors.

There are two sorts of Maine peapods. The more recent is a typical late-nineteenth-century boat, carvel or smooth planked, with a keel and steam-bent oak ribs. In addition it is a true double-ender, being identical at the bow and the stern. The old type was quite different. It was a heavier boat, clinker planked with a bottom board and natural-crook sawn frames. While sharp at either end, the older pods were often fuller and higher at the bow.

In construction the older pods and the Maine wherries were identical or nearly so. In hull form the chief difference was the wherry's small, high-tucked transom stern. However, at the load waterline the wherry was virtually a double-ender which launched as well stern-first into the surf as any peapod.

In short, the older pods and the wherries were much the same kind of boat as appears from descriptions by George Wasson, in *Sailing Days on the Penobscot*, and Alfred Brooks, in "*The Boats of Ash Point, Maine*," both of whom were well acquainted with the boats about which they wrote. Wasson had much to say about pods, but strangely he did not mention wherries, although he must have seen them. Brooks had much to say about both wherries and "double-enders," although he never referred to the latter as "peapods." Of the Ash Point double-enders and wherries, Brooks stated that they both had a flat bottom board 6 inches to 12 inches wide, and both had much the same shaped hull in its lower part.

In *Sailing Days On The Penobscot*, George Wasson, born in 1855, wrote in delightful detail of Isle au Haut as it once was. Even as late as the period of Wasson's own personal recollection, life on this isolated Penobscot Bay island still moved in much the same way as it had a century earlier. For instance he noted the absence of horses and wheeled carts and told how supplies were hauled across the island on sleds by oxen.

As previously mentioned in this book, on this island, as well as throughout the bay region, small-boat building burgeoned. Every sailor and fisherman, it seemed, was an occasional boatbuilder as well. Nearly everyone had built, was building, or planned to build a boat. From out of barns, sheds, cellars, one-time henhouses, and dooryards the new boats kept coming. Boatbuilding was in the blood and the breed. It was something to do in between times, something to dream about, something to plan for, something to talk about around the stove at the store. It was economic gain, recreation, and an art form all in one.

The favorite type, according to Wasson, was the peapod, clinker-built with planks got out of "live-edge" cedar boards, and ribbed with natural-crook hackmatack frames. A "wide, heavy bottom board" allowed the boat to be run aground and to be dragged over rough beaches with impunity. The flat bottom board both in the wherry and the old-time pod is extremely convenient for beach work, especially where tides run strong on rocky shores. Some of the wherries were built so that the bottom board, when worn, could be easily removed and replaced. Some were made with the bottom board in two layers so that the outer one, or "false bottom," as it was called, could be renewed with a minimum of difficulty.

Besides allowing the boat to sit upright on the beach, run easily on rollers, and withstand dragging, the flat bottom board on its inner side afforded a convenient and solid landing for the feet of the natural-crook side frames. A heavy bottom board of hardwood, as they were often made in both the wherries and the older pods, is not a disadvantage as some might suppose. Some weight in the lower part of a pulling craft used in rough water helps to keep it moving ahead steadily between strokes of the oars once headway has been attained, especially when the boat is laboring in a seaway.

THE BUILDING PROCEDURE

Brooks observed that the Ash Point wherries and double-enders were not built with benefit of drawn lines or lofting. The same was true for Isle au Haut peapods and Lincolnville salmon wherries. The building procedure for all of these old clinker types must have been essentially the same. First off, the bottom board, stem, and transom were got out, sometimes from patterns, borrowed, inherited, or saved from earlier ventures, and sometimes by "eye." These were then assembled and set upright on horses or stocks of some sort at a convenient height for working. Bevels and rabbets as necessary were cut. The bottom board was shored down to the required camber or "rocker." A center mold or "shadow," as it was called, was inserted amidship. After a final check with level and plumb, and when everything had been securely shored and braced, preparations for planking were complete.

Planking proceeded by "eye" from the bottom up, starting at the garboard and getting out the plank in identical pairs, so that both sides could be carried up together. As the planks went on, the laps were riveted.

Today's first-time builders may require additional molds. The old builders of lapstrake boats seemed generally to have managed well enough with the single center mold or "shadow." They did not try to force the strakes, permitting the natural bend of the lumber to influence the shape of the boat. Lapstrake planks, especially the thicker sort, cannot be forced, bent, and twisted to anywhere near the extent that steamed carvel planks can.

The old way was not to fit the ribs or frames until the planking was complete. Brooks stated that in his day the Ash Point builders used strips of white oak soaked in water but not steamed. Wasson related that, on Isle au Haut, peapods were ribbed with natural crooks of hackmatack carefully notched to fit the jogs of the laps. This is the method still employed in England, and possibly was commonly used in this country in colonial times, although rarely seen now.

The frames of the salmon wherry examined by Smithsonian experts in 1959 were cut from natural crooks obtained from white cedar stumps or roots. They were not notched to fit the laps. Furthermore, they are fairly light, so as to be almost frail in appearance, yet, having endured more than 60 years of hard use without serious breaks, they cannot be considered inadequate. Obviously, these frames were fitted and installed after the planking was done, especially the first set of frames in the fore end of the boat. These are true cant frames set out of square with the centerline of the hull. This permits them to lie flat against the curve of the planking without beveling. This also gives them a forward slant as they run up the side of the boat.

Cant frames such as these were formerly employed to frame full-ended vessels in order to avoid excessive beveling of the frames. Such frames are not difficult to scribe into place after the planking is on, but they are extremely difficult to lay out accurately ahead of time on the mold loft floor.

The planking of the Robie Ames salmon wherry whose lines are shown here is native

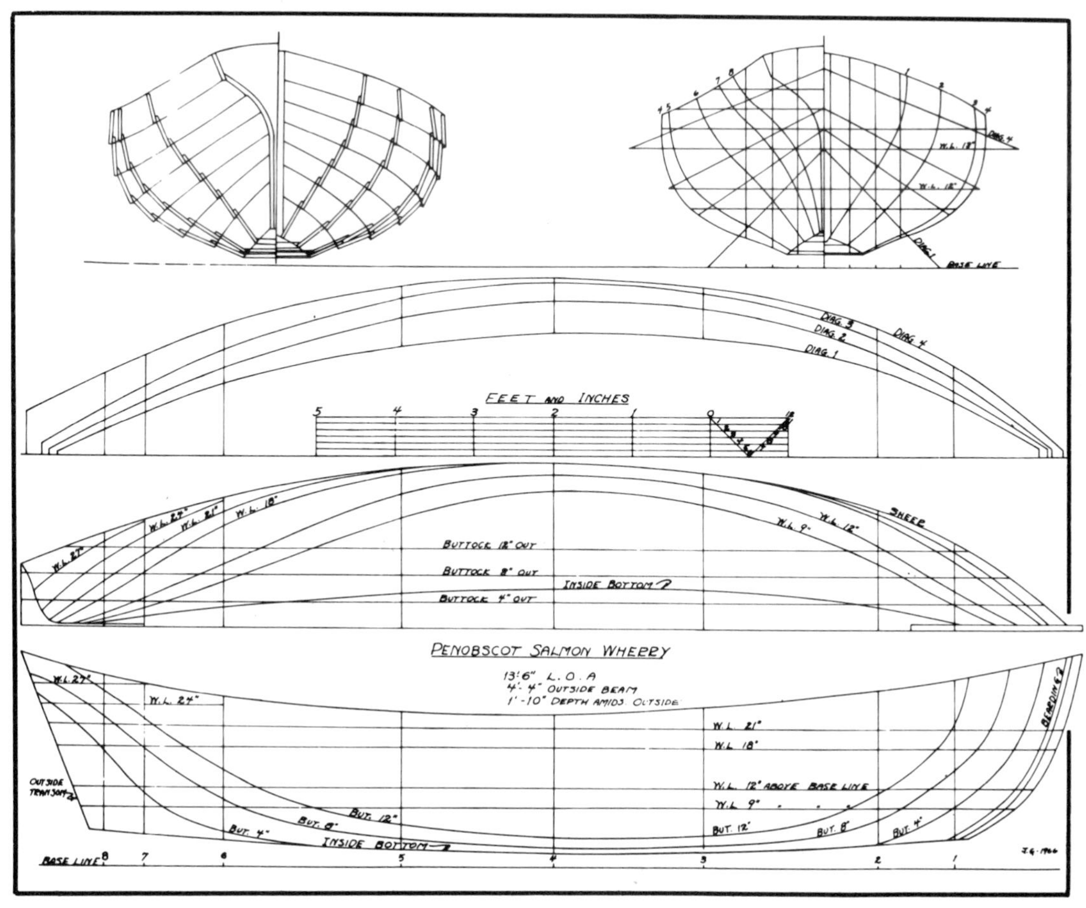

Maine white cedar ½ inch thick and lapped 1⅛ inches. There is very little beveling of the laps. Half-inch planking for a clinker boat of this size is fairly heavy, and this with the stout laps gives the hull extra strength. Besides, Maine white cedar, with sound knots and twisted grain, while harder to work, is tougher and more resistant to splitting than the clear straight-grained species such as most Virginia white cedar.

The lapped planking and the native cedar in combination produced an exceptionally strong, flexible, lasting hull; otherwise it would never have stood up so well under continuous severe use for longer than a man's ordinary working lifetime. The principle strength of this remarkable boat resides in its clinker plank.

In summing up the foregoing, two points may be made. The first is that the rugged strength and endurance of this archaic type of lapstrake hull came from its Maine white cedar and copper-riveted laps. The second is that this kind of lapstrake construction was widely used, very successfully, by farmers and fishermen who were not professional boatbuilders, although they had a good eye for boats. Only the simplest hand tools were available to them, they had never studied drafting or design, and not one in a hundred had the slightest notion of lofting a set of lines.

I do not say that some clunkers were not built. There are vast individual differences among men in mechanical aptitude, as well as in patience and in perseverance. Still, on the whole, craft that did meet the test of use and endurance—and sometimes even beauty—were produced by those who were essentially home builders and amateurs. Craft at least as good can still be built of the old materials according to the old designs and methods with hand tools by amateurs of ordinary ability and skill, provided they are willing to take the time and care required.

THE MERRIMACK RIVER WHERRY

One wherry that was an exceptionally good boat, according to Ephraim C. S. Clark, who drew its lines as he recollected them in 1961, was the Merrimack River wherry *Axa*. This boat was Clark's first boat when he was a boy growing up on the Newburyport waterfront. The *Axa* was the tender for a sailing scow of the same name, belonging to his grandfather, Otis Dwinells, who used it 60 years ago and earlier to freight coal up the Merrimack to Groveland. Ordinarily, when not in use, the tender hung athwartships against the transom of the scow, above the water, parbuckled close, sheer in and bottom out.

The wherry *Axa*, as Clark remembers, had six frames sawn from hackmatack knees, and six strakes of lapped cedar planking. The ends of the garboards were wider than the other strakes, like those of a dory, running up on the stem and stern post to straighten the top edge of the plank and the planking lines above.

Axa's stem construction was the same as in a dory; that is, instead of a single rabbeted stem, the stem was made in two pieces, the principal inner part beveled sharp to receive the planking, and the outer part, or "false stem," as it is sometimes called, bent in place to cover the plank ends and fastened by nailing through into the inner member. This method avoids the difficulty and labor of cutting rabbets, yet the result in small craft of this sort is just as strong, tight, and lasting. The line in the drawing representing the stem shows the location and profile shape of the inner part before the outer, or "false," stem is bent in place.

The stern of the *Axa*, although typically wherry in shape, was made in an unusual way. Clark recalls that the entire stern, comprising a 12-inch transom, curved stern post, and stern knee joining the bottom board, had been hewed out in a single piece from a cedar stump. A large stump would have been required and much patient and skillful axe work must have gone into the job. At the Adirondack Museum there is a primitive guideboat with its transom stern sculptured from a spruce stump in the same manner. This is an old method. It harks back to the ancient dugout. The specialized boatshop, making its appearance on the American scene in the nineteenth century, could not afford such

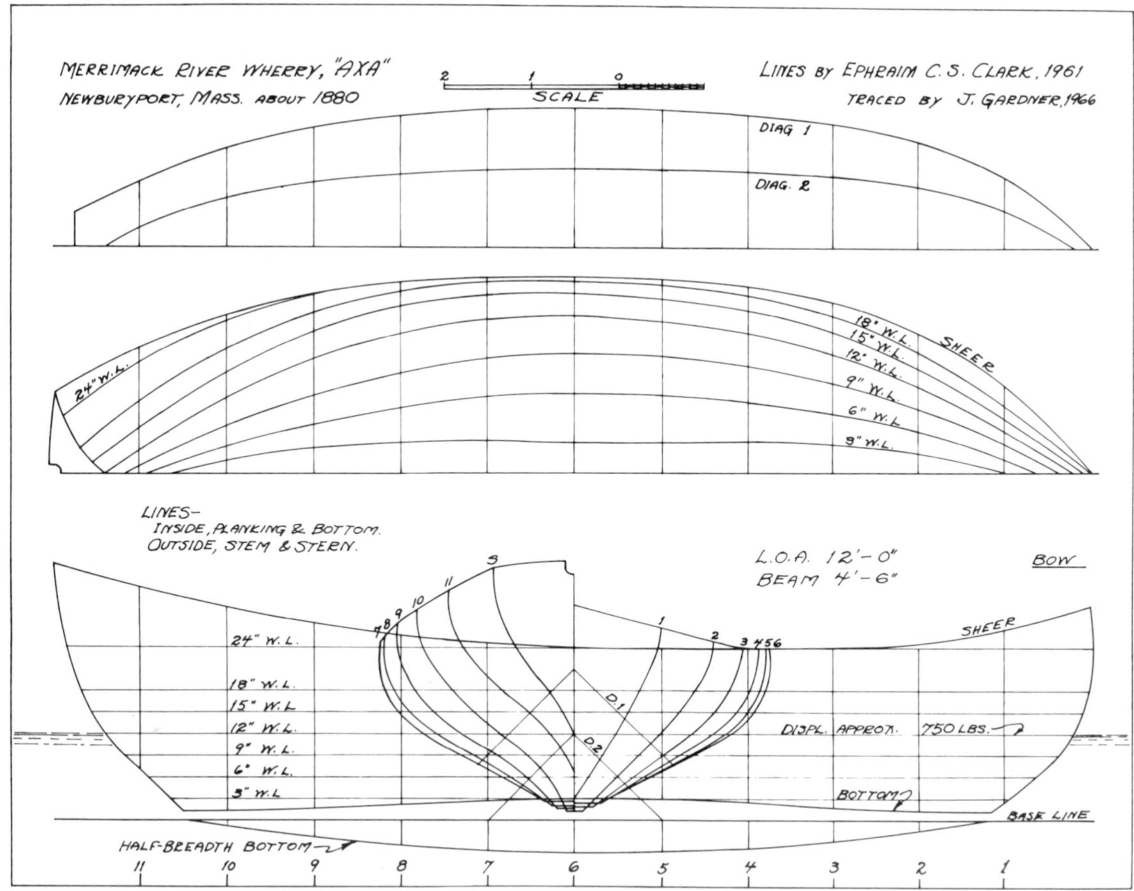

work. It did not suit mass production or "hurry-up" methods. This is the sort of thing a man would do for himself when time was not too pressing.

As in older construction, natural grown crooks or knees figured extensively in the *Axa*'s build. The two thwarts were kneed in, as was the transom at the sheer on either side. Another natural crook formed the breast hook.

The *Axa* was rowed with oar straps instead of thole pins. A hole for a small mast went through the forward thwart.

All in all there was nothing too unusual about *Axa*'s build, except it might have been slightly old-fashioned even in 1880. What is unusual about the *Axa* is her shape, particularly her snubbed ends and the reverse rocker of her bottom. Clark called attention to these two unique features, and I would add another—her unusual amount of deadrise, which gives her almost a V bottom, even though her bottom board amidships is 9 inches wide.

Clark thinks the wherry might have had snubbed ends so they wouldn't project past the transom of the scow. As for the "reverse rocker" in the bottom board, which makes it appear hogged, this was supposed to have some connection with the boat's excellent qualities in sea and surf, but just how is not too clear. Perhaps the boat was accidentally hogged without any adverse effect on her original good performance, or perhaps the hog was purposely put in by the builder in accordance with some theory of his own. I am sure such "reverse rocker" in the bottom was never typical or common in wherries, and indeed the *Axa* is the only one with this peculiarity I have come across so far.

The angle of *Axa*'s deadrise is quite extreme and it is possible that Clark's recollection has exaggerated it slightly. In a light condition this boat would balance delicately and would heel so sharply that it could pitch the unwary occupant overboard, although she could only roll down so far. With a load, however, the *Axa* must have been exceptionally steady and stable, for in that condition her unusual hull form would have combined both broad bearing and deep draft. For 12 feet of length, the *Axa* is exceptionally burdensome. She is deep and has body, unlike some craft which seem to be all ends with no middle.

Loaded to her 12-inch waterline (12 inches above the baseline) the *Axa*, as represented by Clark's lines, would displace approximately 750 pounds, ample for at least three ordinary occupants plus the weight of the boat. Freeboard amidships would then be 12 inches, while draft would be approximately the same (depth to inside of bottom, 10½ inches). The amidships bearing on the water at the 12-inch loadline is 43 inches, as much as the total beam for many ordinary 12-foot rowboats. However, the sides of the *Axa* from this level upward round out rapidly, permitting several hundred pounds of additional weight to be added without diminishing the freeboard to any hazardous or uncomfortable extent, while increasing steadiness and stability.

The *Axa* is not a racing shell but a working tender, burdensome and stable (when loaded) and good both in sea and surf. Her lines deserve to be known and might be well worth study and experimentation where ordinary types do not fill the bill or leave something to be desired.

THE LINCOLNVILLE SALMON WHERRY

Let's look at a downeast wherry. Reproduced here are the lines and details of a salmon wherry surviving from the now defunct salmon fishery formerly carried on off the beach at Lincolnville, Maine. Through the kindness of the owner, Osborne Wade of Lincolnville, we had the boat on loan at Mystic Seaport a few years ago, where we were able to photograph it and measure it accurately. As far as I have been able to determine, only three of the salmon wherries once used in the fishery at Lincolnville yet remain, this one and another belonging to Wade, and the

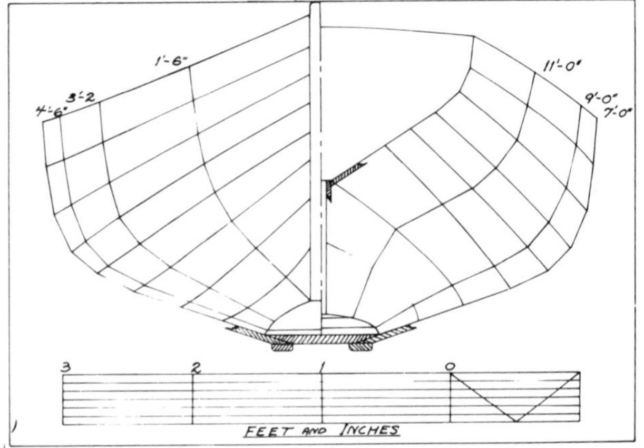

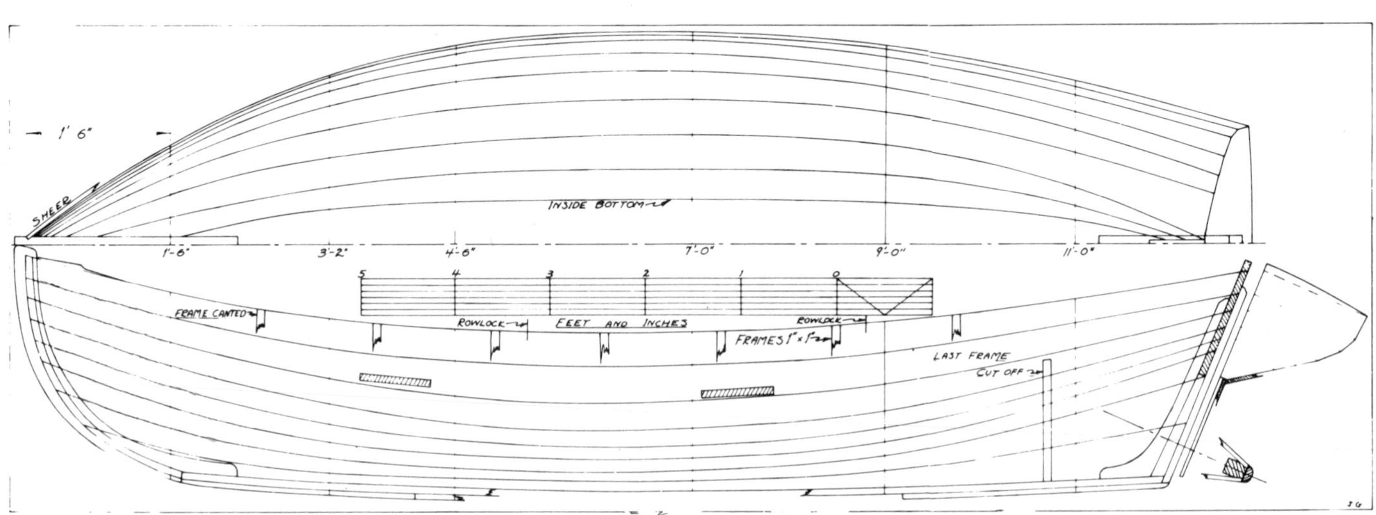

Robie Ames wherry formerly at the Adirondack Museum and now in the small craft collection at Mystic Seaport.

The New England wherry, it seems, came about as close to extinction and oblivion as is possible without disappearing completely. The Ash Point wherries have long since gone. The Cape Roseway wherry (could this have been the Cape Rosier wherry?) was described briefly by George Brown Goode in his *Fisheries and Fishery Industries of the United States*, 1887, Sec. V, Vol. II, p. 672.

According to Chapelle, this type may be considered extinct as no model has been found. Described by Goode, "The Cape Roseway wherry employed in the lobster and inshore fisheries of Penobscot Bay, Maine, especially in the vicinity of Castine, is a lap-streak boat with a sharp bow, round bilge, narrow, flat bottom, and very narrow, heart-shaped stern. It ranges from 12 to 18 feet, is entirely open, and seldom provided with sails."

The sharp bow of the Cape Roseway model differs from the round bow of the specialized salmon wherry, and besides, wherries were commonly sailed as well as rowed both at Lincolnville and Ash Point. Otherwise the Goode description applies quite accurately to these other Penobscot Bay wherries.

If such boats were once found quite widely distributed in Penobscot Bay and possibly to the eastward of it, might there not still be survivors hidden away which have gone unnoticed to date? The prospect is an intriguing one. Some painstaking detective work might yet pay off.

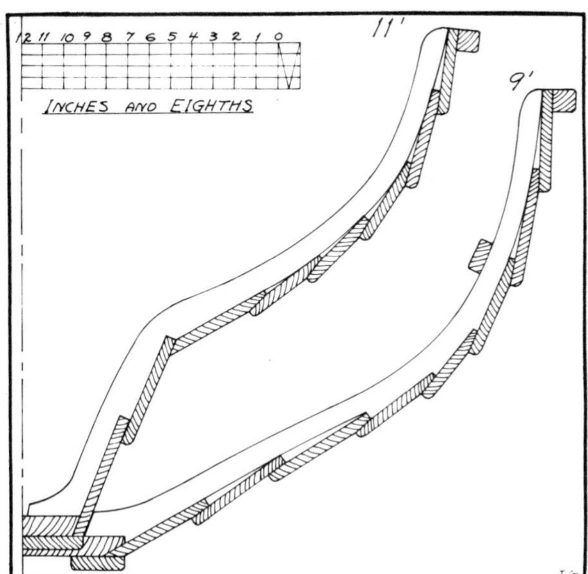

Although the Wade wherry was built for the Lincolnville fishery, and was so used for many years, it differs somewhat in two respects from most of the other salmon wherries. The bow of the Wade wherry, while fairly full, is not as round as most of the other boats, and its stern with its wider transom is not quite as high as was generally the case.

The salmon fisherman knelt in the bow of his boat directly abaft the stem to overhaul his nets and bring the fish aboard. Some of these salmon were big and scrappy, and, if the fisherman was a heavy man, as well, more than ordinary fullness and displacement was required at the bow. The photograph of a wherry with centerboard and spritsail taken at Lincolnville Beach about 30 years ago by John Leavitt shows a full-bowed, lean-sterned boat more typical of the general run of the salmon wherries than the Wade boat.

The lean, high-tucked stern with its small transom was functional, for it facilitated launching stern-first into the surf, as was frequently required in getting these boats off the beach. In the Robie Ames wherry, the stern stands higher than the bow, a feature found in some fishing dories, and for the same reason.

Although the stern of the Wade wherry is not as high as some of the other salmon wherries, it is still relatively high, making the boat a virtual double-ender on its waterline even when loaded. Its additional bearing aft carried through to the relatively wide transom adds greatly to steadiness aft.

It is worth noting that the shape of the stern, deep and sharp below, yet flattening out directly above the tuck, is not unlike that of the Staten Island oyster skiff or the New Jersey beach skiff. All three are flat-bottom, clinker-built craft with sufficient likenesses to suggest derivation from a common ancestral type, possibly a prototype Colonial wherry now completely forgotten.

Osborne Wade and the wherry he loaned to Mystic Seaport at the left, foreground. The smaller wherry at the right has an inwale and what appears to be slightly more delicate lines. (Photo by John Kochiss)

The Wade salmon wherry in profile shows her full lines. (Photo by Lester D. Olin)

Less highly specialized than the usual run of salmon wherries, that is, neither so full in the bow nor so lean at the stern, the Wade wherry is undoubtedly better suited for general use, and indeed it is an excellent small sea boat either for oars or for sail with the addition of a centerboard. This boat will handle easily, show fair speed under either oars or sail, carry a load, stand some weather, and take a lot of punishment. The build is quite rugged.

The false bottom can be seen here. The removable pieces served to absorb punishment on rocky beaches and could be replaced when worn out. (Photo by Lester D. Olin)

Interior view of the Wade wherry shows the broad bottom plank, the mark of the type. (Photo by Lester D. Olin)

The Wade wherry's double flat bottom with replaceable outer layer is made to take the wear of rough beaches and enables the boat to sit firmly upright when hauled out. One man can pull it on or off the beach and take it in or out through moderate surf.

There is nothing fancy about this boat, nor is it actually too hard or too fussy for the handy amateur to build. In fact, the construction is fairly simple, and, for a tough, reliable little ship to knock about the shore in, no other boat of its size comes to mind that would serve any better.

Planking is Maine cedar a half-inch thick. Any northern white cedar is first choice for planking, but Virginia cedar is not recommended, as this southern cedar is too brittle and splits too easily. Small knots won't do any harm, if they are sound. The planks are really tougher and stronger because of them, and if a few are loose, these are easily plugged. As the boat is painted, knots will not show when the job is finished. The shape of the Wade wherry is such that I believe it could be planked without steam provided the cedar is not too dry. However, steam for some of the planks would make things easier. For planking the replica of the Robie Ames salmon wherry built at Mystic Seaport a few years ago, steam was required because of the full, round bow.

With the seat removed, one can see how the garboard and second planks are faired into the sternpost, making the wherry a virtual double-ender.

Width of lap is normally 1⅛ inches, although where the side curve is greatest, the lap width may have to be slightly reduced to obtain wood-to-wood closure of the laps. In fitting the laps, just as little wood is removed as is possible to get a snug fit. For some of the laps no wood at all has to be planed off. This gives a strong hull which depends on its lap fastenings to hold

(Left) This salmon wherry fitted for sailing with a spritsail and centerboard was photographed in Lincolnville, Maine, in the early 1940s by John Leavitt. (Right) Salmon wherry on display at the Adirondack Museum. The low platform that should cover the base of the stem is hanging from the framing in the stern. It was used by the kneeling net tender. Because of the camera angle, the bow does not appear as full as it actually is. (Photo courtesy of the Adirondack Museum)

it together and tight, at least as much as internal framing.

The lines are drawn to the inside of the planking, and the points that determine these lines lie in the upper inside edges of the inner bottom and the eight strakes of plank. By working from these points located at the intersection of the sections with the inner lines of the planking, the laps may be laid out as I have done for the two sections in the accompanying drawing. In this way, if laid out full size, the precise amount of beveling required for each plank is easily determined.

Lap fastenings are copper nails spaced approximately 2½ inches apart and riveted over burrs. The inner bottom, ⅞ inch thick, was usually made in Lincolnville wherries of old-growth yellow birch. Oak would do as well, or even good quality mahogany could serve as a substitute.

The ribs or frames in the Lincolnville wherries are most unusual, being got out of white cedar roots selected and dug to give the shape required. The siding and molding is approximately one inch, but rather more than this than less, particularly the molding toward the foot, and at the stern where the frames take a reverse curve, and are scribed to fit the jogs of the lower planks.

Note that there is no inwale, and that the gunwale on the outside is in section about one inch square, tapered to ¾ inch at the ends. The breasthook and likewise the stern quarter knees are exceptionally large, and got out of natural-crook cedar roots like the frames.

The rabbeted stem, sided 2 inches and molded approximately 3 inches, is likewise cut from a cedar knee, as is the inner stern knee or stern post. These members do not have to be cedar crooks, which in the past were easily obtainable at Lincolnville, but could just as well be hackmatack or any other suitable boatbuilding timber. Nor is it necessary to use natural crooks. The frames could be laminations glued to shape on a form.

It is not necessary to follow these lines exactly, although it would be wise not to depart too far from them and only for well considered reasons. No two wherries, I believe, were ever built exactly alike. The wherries sketched by Brooks in the *American Neptune* show some marked variations both in size and hull shape, yet all are easily recognizable as wherries. A wherry intended mainly for sailing would conceivably differ considerably from one built for rowing. One of the great attractions of a type like the New England wherry for the amateur designer and builder is the scope it gives for variation and individuality.

21 The Origin of the Whitehall

All sail set, a ship rounds Race Point off the tip of Cape Cod bound for Boston. Racing out to meet her, oars flashing, their leg-o-mutton sails drawing, are several small, open boats. Each is provided with a long, slender pole with a hook at the end to which is lashed a length of nine-thread line. Someone in the foremost boat dexterously hooks the rapidly moving vessel at her fore lee chains, pays out to a safe distance, then warps alongside, and one of the occupants springs nimbly aboard. He is a runner from some "deepwater boarding house," or from one of the competing outfitting establishments located on Boston's Hanover and North streets in the 1870s and the 1880s. He is out to line up trade before Jack Tar makes port, and a sly half-pint discreetly slipped here and there to the crew when the officers are looking the other way can work wonders in getting prospective customers into a receptive frame of mind.

The slim, tidy craft that brought the successful runner all the way out across Massachusetts Bay was a Whitehall boat, in length not more than 20 feet, perhaps only 18 feet, and not a great deal over 4 feet in beam. Thwarts, stern bench, and the top strake would probably have been finished bright, as would have been the varnished backrest with the boat's name in gold leaf.

The authority for this description is the late Captain Charleton L. Smith of Marblehead, Massachusetts, from whose recollections of Boston Whitehalls in *The Rudder* for August, 1943, the above brief account is paraphrased. Captain Smith, who was born in 1869, grew up on the Boston waterfront.

The port of Boston in those days teemed with enterprise. The harbor was white with incoming and outgoing sail. A flood-tide of commerce surged across the wharves. Vessels large and small from far and near discharged and took on cargo in a kaleidoscope of activity, color, sounds, and smells, and Smith as a lad was there and took it all in and never forgot. Once, as he recalled, he counted 18 Whitehalls in the "Cow Pen," as the enclosure at the forked end of Lewis's wharf was then called. When Whitehalls were at their peak in Boston, it has been estimated that there were 75 in service in the harbor.

For all their fancy trimmings, these runners' Whitehalls were workboats as hardy and as business-like as the men who owned them. One of these owners, according to Captain Smith, was a saltwater boarding house owner by the name of Sorensen, Captain Alfred Sorensen, who had a case full of rowing prizes and life-saving medals for sailors he had pulled out of the briny deep. As one story goes, Sorensen once far outran the Whitehall fleet. It was in the winter-time and, broad off the tip of Cape Cod, the wind freshened to a "howling gale." Did Alfred panic? Not a bit. Stowing mast and sail, he payed out his warp for a sea anchor and lay head

These two Whitehalls of classic design were built recently to meet their owners' wish for fine pulling boats aboard their sailing vessels. The elaborately finished yawl boat above was built for the replica schooner America *by R.D. Culler and the Concordia Boat Company of South Dartmouth, Massachusetts. Below is one of the sleek ship's boats built by Dick Shew of South Bristol, Maine, for the topsail schooner* Shenandoah.

into the storm for some 36 hours, until he picked up an inbound ship and came home.

The beginnings of the Boston Whitehall are vague, just as the beginnings of the Whitehall type in general, in spite of its popularity and renown, are also vague and shadowy. Some even question that it originated on this side of the Atlantic, holding that the boat was introduced from England and that its name was taken from Whitehall in London.

However, there is also a Whitehall Street in New York City where Howard I. Chapelle and others have written these boats were first built. Chapelle cites the opinion of W. P. Stephens, who thought that the type came into existence sometime in the 1820s in New York City, having first been built by former Navy Yard apprentices who had derived their model to some extent from the old naval gig.

Of course the Whitehall had antecedents, if only we knew how to unravel that tangled skein of history, as all distinctive boat types have antecedents and are a combination of old and new elements, with much more of the former than the latter. The pronounced conservatism of sailors and seafaring men, often noted, and their predilection for sticking with the tried and the tested, have always worked to insure a high degree of continuity in the development of hull design, both for small craft and for larger vessels.

If the Whitehall did first appear as a distinct and recognizable type in New York City in the 1820s, it was quickly and widely adopted in use. Chapelle thought that Whitehalls were in mass production in New York boatshops by 1840. The water taxi service carried on by "Battery boatmen" recalled the celebrated ferrying service of the Thames watermen, part of the pageant of London since the sixteenth century.

The Whitehall was not a ship's boat but a vehicle of harbor and coastwise transportation. Intended primarily to be rowed, but capable of a good showing under sail as well, it was fast, seaworthy, and trim. Whitehalls were in great demand in the days of sail on the waterfront of a busy commercial port such as was New York City in the early nineteenth century. Not only were these boats the choice of crimps and boarding house runners, but of nearly everyone else as well who required reliable and expeditious transportation about the waterfront or from one part of the harbor to another—ship chandlers, brokers, newspaper reporters, insurance agents, doctors, pilots, ships officers, port officials, and many others.

Gentlemen of that day, seeking a pleasure boat, frequently adopted modifications of the Whitehall workboat. Naturally, Whitehalls were raced. Perhaps it was the influence of the Whitehall as much as anything else that made rowing the principal American competitive sport on the Eastern seaboard at the midpoint of the nineteenth century. The rise and decline of rowing as a major competitive sport in this country, from the eighteenth century to nearly the end of the nineteenth, will some day make a fascinating book. At least one section of that book will be devoted to the Whitehall.

Once the Whitehall was established in both Boston and New York, inter-city competition began. Captain Smith, from Boston, relates that an early challenge from New York resulted in a match race for $1,000 (a large sum in those days) rowed between a New York Whitehall and a Boston Whitehall on neutral water at Springfield, Massachusetts. The Boston Whitehall, the *Gookin Brothers*, a fast runner's boat built by Partelow, won in a morning race. To satisfy the disgruntled challengers, a second race for a wager of $500 was rowed on the afternoon of the same day with the same result, clearly establishing the superiority of the Boston boat and its crew.

When and how the Whitehall first arrived in Boston is not clear, but if it was brought from New York, it must have been quite soon after its inception. No evidence for an independent derivation for the Boston Whitehall has yet appeared, although the Boston Whitehall has some distinct differences in construction from the New York Whitehall, at least as far as we can tell, considering that no authentic specimens of early New York Whitehalls, with one possible exception, are to be found. Two examples of the Boston Whitehall, however, exhibiting its distinctive construction, have survived and are now to be seen in the small craft collection at Mystic Seaport.

Captain Smith was of the opinion that the first Boston Whitehalls were produced about 1870 by Charles M. Partelow in his shop on Commercial Street. It is true that C. M. Partelow was an early builder of the Boston Whitehall, but it is doubtful if he was the first, or if he originated its distinctive features of construction. There were several Whitehall builders contemporary with Partelow, two of the best known being Dick Sullivan and Cragin & Sheldon. However, as we shall see, the boatbuilding firm later organized and managed by C. M. Partelow's second oldest son, H. V. Partelow, did eventually initiate a new method of framing and planking which cheapened Whitehall construction and changed it radically.

The most distinctive feature of the classic Boston Whitehall as built approximately 100 years ago was the special manner in which it was framed and planked. There seem also to have been less readily discernible characteristics of the shape or hull form which in combined effect produced a unique boat in contrast with the New York Whitehall. Yet this is difficult to determine or analyze concretely, for as far as I know, no contemporary New York Whitehalls have survived for direct comparison. H. I. Chapelle, on page 197 of his *American Small Sailing Craft*, gives the lines and some construction details for a boat built at the Brooklyn Navy Yard in 1890, and claimed to be representative of the standard New York Whitehall of the period between 1860 and 1895. While similar to the Boston boats, its proportions are not quite the same. For one thing it is a slightly beamier boat with shallower deadrise. Also, it is built with a flat plank keel 6½ inches wide amidships.

Neither of the two Boston Whitehalls which survive at Mystic Seaport are standard runner's workboats of the 1870s. According to Captain Smith, such boats in order to be eligible for rowing competition had to conform to certain restrictions laid down by the Boston boat clubs of the time to prevent the appearance of racing freaks. The rules read that boats must be between 17 and 20 feet in length, not less than 4 feet in beam or 19 inches in depth amidships, and must be rowed on the gunwales.

The standard runner's boat brought to near perfection in racing competition set the norm for the type. Two such, mentioned by Captain Smith as "very fast boats on the Charles at that time," and both built by Partelow, were the *P. F. Gilmore* and the *Joseph Edwards.* But if such runner's boats established the norm, there were numerous variations within the norm—Whitehalls built in different lengths and sizes, for different purposes, yet all recognizable as Whitehalls. The smallest seem to have been the 12-foot rowboats once to be seen on the pond in the Public Gardens. In boats any shorter than this the superior characteristics of the type would mostly disappear, though the construction would not differ from full-size boats. Few, if any, were ever built longer than the 21-foot runner's boat in which, according to Captain Smith, August Motto won all the cups and first-place money in the final days of the sport, before the motorboat put an end to it.

In their annual catalog for 1891, H. V. Partelow & Co. listed six grades of "fancy Whitehall row and pleasure boats" ranging in price from $6 per foot for Grade A, down to $3.75 per foot for the cheapest galvanized fastened grade, the length of the boat to be specified by the customer to suit his individual requirements.

A 17-FOOT WHITEHALL

The longer of the two Boston Whitehalls at Mystic Seaport is a fancy pleasure Whitehall apparently built at Boston, Massachusetts, in 1879: length 16 feet 9 inches, beam to outside of planking, 3 feet 7 inches, inside depth amidships to top of keel, 15½ inches. This boat was intended to be sailed as well as rowed, for it is fitted with a box for a metal daggerboard, 9 inches wide by ¼ inch thick. There are two separate sockets for a 2½-inch diameter mast, one considerably aft of the other, apparently so that the position of the mast could be changed to suit different rigs. A sliding seat for the oarsman on runners extending over the top of the daggerboard case is a refinement not to be found in the runner's workboat. Yet in essentials the boat conforms to standard Boston Whitehall construction, although its scantlings are reduced to an absolute minimum, and its hull lines are drawn extra lean and fine.

Edwin M. Bailey of Amesbury, Massachusetts, the donor of this boat, has this to say about it:

> The boat belonged to my father, E. Wm. Bailey, who was born in 1863 in East Pittston, Maine. He went to high school in Charlestown, Mass., graduating in 1881. He had the boat when he was in high school, and I am fairly sure that he bought it second hand. So I would guess it was built in the late 1870's.
>
> In 1882 he moved to Amesbury, and sailed the boat around Cape Ann to the Merrimack River and up the river six miles to Amesbury. I do not think it was built in Amesbury, in fact, I am sure it was not.
>
> The boat lay upside down in my grandfather's cellar for over 40 years. Before my father died in 1940, he told me to take the boat out of the cellar, and if it was in good condition, to use her, if not, to burn her. After he

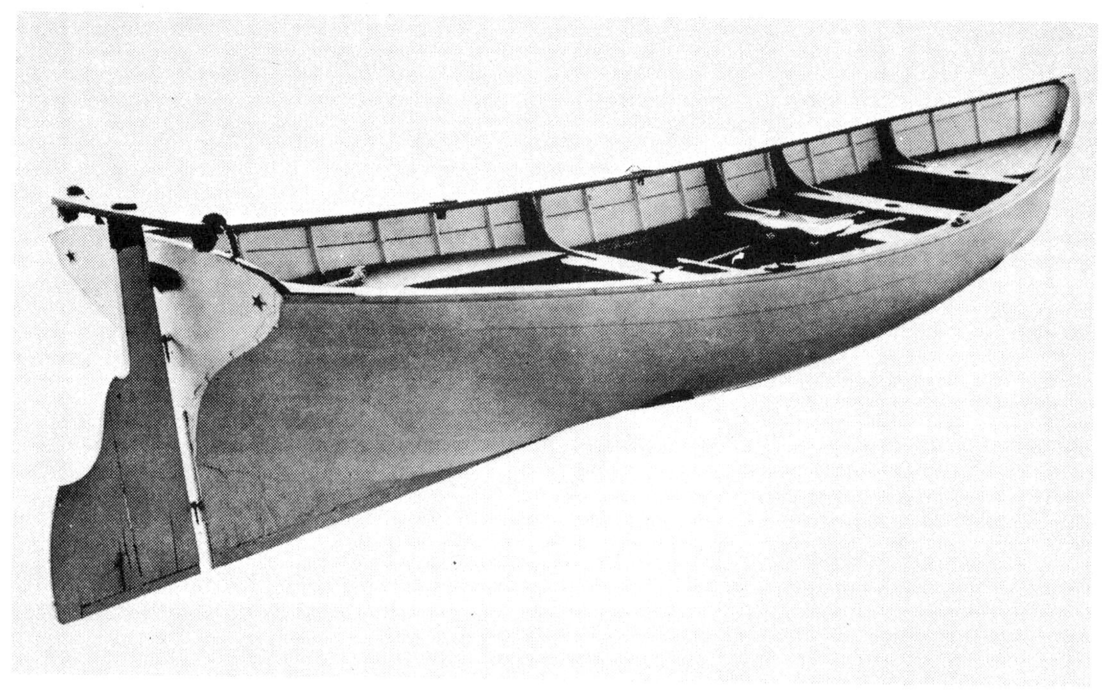

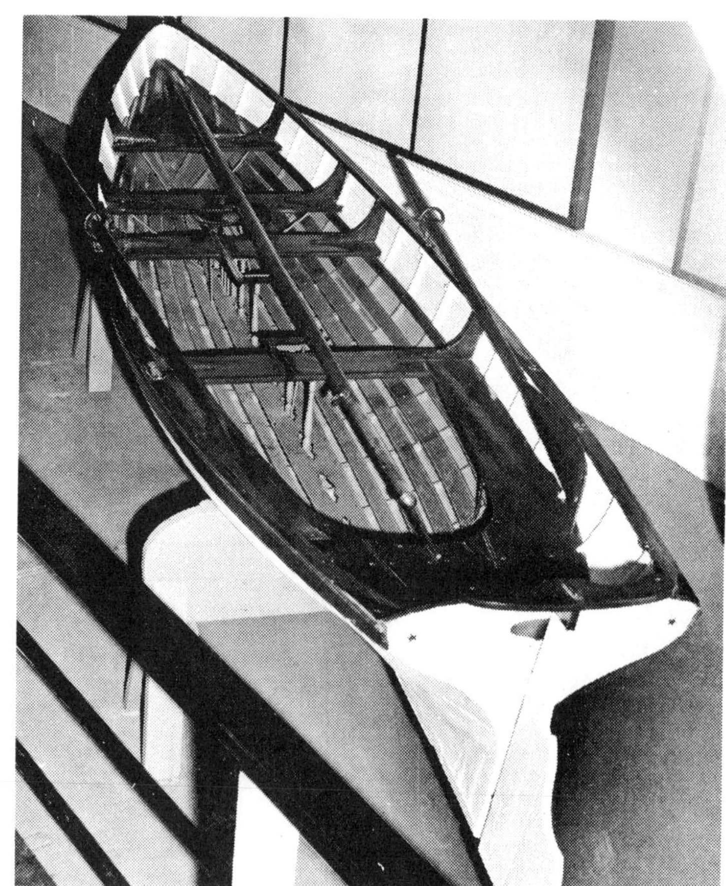

(Above, right, and opposite page) A fancy 17-foot Whitehall on display in the North Boat Shed of Mystic Seaport. She is obviously a pleasure boat, not a working boat, yet the construction is practically identical, though lighter with smaller scantlings. Note the sliding seat, the spoon oars, and the very unusual circular oarlocks with a moving inner ring attached to the oar, producing the effect of a universal joint. The boat is fitted for sail with two mast steps and a metal daggerboard. (Photos by Russel A. Fowler)

died, my brother and I pulled her out of the cellar and found her to be in good condition. We found the spoon oars, the machined, fitted oarlocks, the boom and gaff, the hand-sewn sail and jib, and the rudder. We never found the backrest for the stern sheets. I made a dagger board out of sheet steel, and sailed her in the Merrimack River for two seasons. Then a leak developed around the dagger board box and I did not launch her again. . . .

It was a very easy rowing boat, as you no doubt know, and I could sail her sometimes for half an hour without touching the tiller ropes, by moving my weight backwards and forward. This was with the wind two points forward of the beam to two points abaft the beam. Closehauled or running free, she required the rudder.

The peerless workmanship found in this boat, its exquisite lines, and delicate yet sturdy construction which has lasted so well after so many years, bespeak the hand of a master craftsman. Although we do not know the name of the builder, there is good reason to conclude that this boat came out of one of the leading Boston boatshops of the era, when the boatbuilding craft was practiced on a level which we do not begin to approach in this country today.

One characteristic of this Boston Whitehall mentioned by the former owner deserves comment. On certain points of sailing she steered without touching the rudder merely by shifting weight forward or aft, that is by slight changes in the fore-and-aft balance of the boat. This is precisely the way St. Lawrence River skiffs are sailed, as explained in a previous chapter. Both these types are long and lean of hull and lightly built, with rigs basically much the same.

A 13-FOOT WHITEHALL

The shorter of the two Whitehalls at Mystic Seaport donated to the museum's small craft collection by William F. Peach of Marblehead is 13½ feet in length, 4 feet amidships inside the planking, and 19 inches deep inside from the sheerline amidships to the top of the keel. Its precise origin and date of construction are uncertain. Apparently the boat was built in Maine in the 1920s, yet we have it on the authority of a master boatbuilder who as a

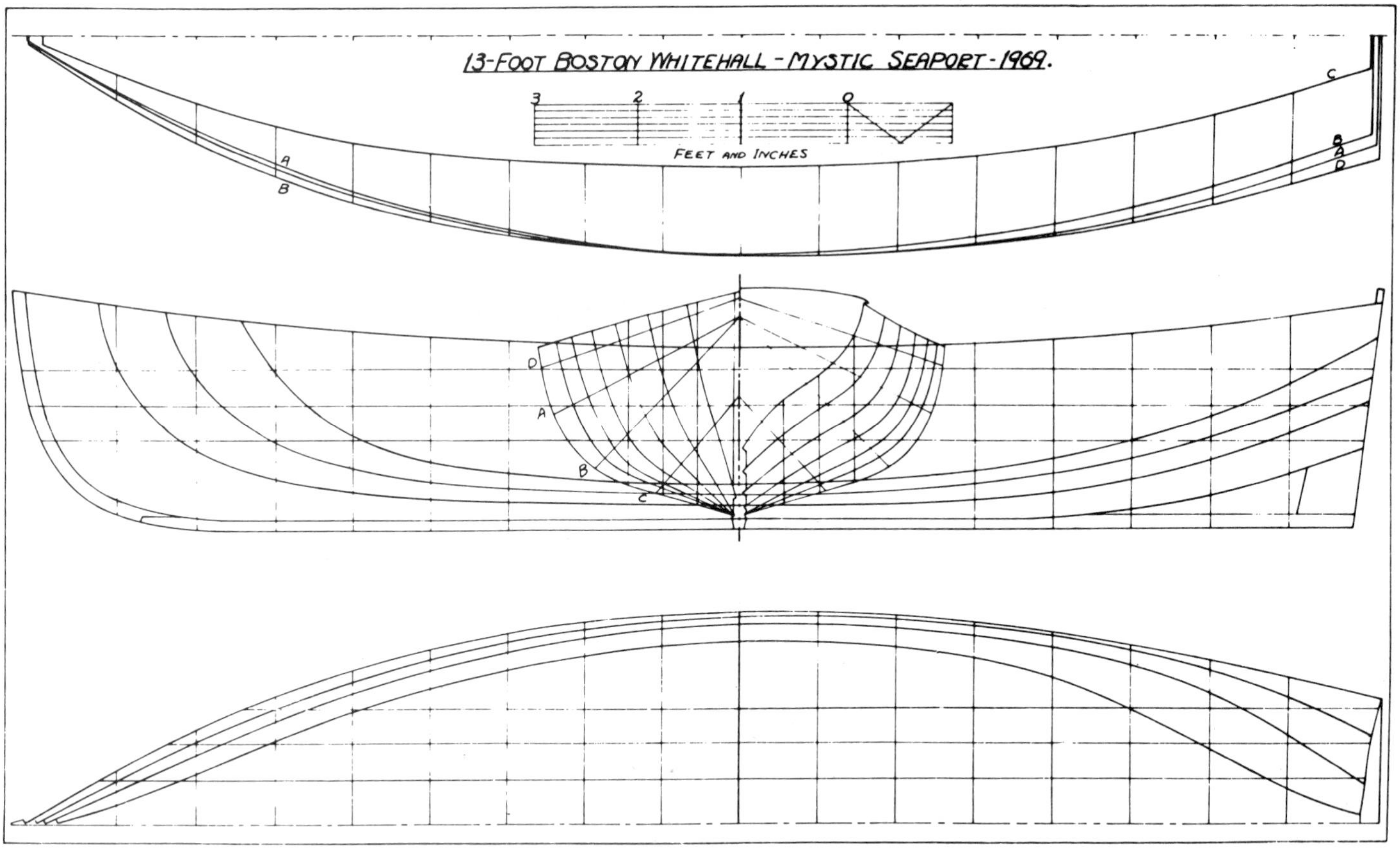

13-FOOT BOSTON WHITEHALL - MYSTIC SEAPORT - 1969.

FEET AND INCHES

The 13-foot Whitehall as she appeared when donated to Mystic Seaport by William F. Peach.

young man worked for the Partelow firm in Boston building Whitehalls and other small craft, and who subsequently built Whitehalls elsewhere, that this particular boat is an authentic Boston Whitehall in its general details, and that in the main it can be considered representative of the nineteenth-century Boston boats. Admittedly it is only galvanized-nailed instead of being copper-fastened and burred, and it does not have the fine hardwoods, the finish, or the varnish and gold leaf of the fancier boats, yet in its proportions and basic construction it is essentially true to the type.

The man who made this identification was Charles A. Lawton, a native of St. John, New Brunswick, born in 1858, who came to Boston as a young man, going to work as a boatbuilder for H. V. Partelow & Co. at their Auburndale plant on the Charles River in 1882. H. V. Partelow's chief claim to our remembrance today is that he was the one who built the famous

Boston swan boats still plying the pond in the Public Gardens.

Charles M. Partelow had four sons. The second oldest, H. V. Partelow, had in Charlie Lawton's words, "a head for business." He took over the management of his father's boatshop, and, by the early 1880s, expanded it to include a canoe factory at Auburndale, a thriving boat livery at Riverside Station on the Charles across from the shop and livery of J. R. Robertson, a rival builder, a large showroom occupying two storefronts on Atlantic Avenue in Boston, and a marine railway, a yacht yard, and a boat and steam launch factory at Marblehead. In the 1891 issue of their annual catalog of boats, canoes, engines, marine hardware, and miscellaneous fittings and equipment, running to 59 pages, H. V. Partelow & Co., after claiming 50 years of experience in the boat manufacturing business, stated that they were confident that they produced the finest and largest variety of boats and canoes in the United States.

According to Lawton, the Partelow concern revolutionized the construction of Whitehall boats about this time when they started planking them over molds, and bending in steamed ribs after planking was completed. This new method of construction, subsequently adopted almost universally for the production of yacht tenders and similar craft, did not produce a superior Whitehall, but it did substantially reduce building time and cost. For a time thereafter, as Lawton recalled, the Partelows did a "whale" of a business.

Yet, not so long after revolutionizing Whitehall construction, the firm failed, started up again, and then within a few years, failed again, both times for large amounts, and, after a third abortive attempt at continuing in business in Charlestown, finally closed down for good. It seems to have been the canvas canoe, as much as anything else, that finished the company off.

Quite suddenly about the turn of the century, hundreds, if not thousands, of canvas canoes appeared on the Charles River, displacing the more expensive Adirondacks, St. Lawrence River skiffs, pleasure Whitehalls, and varnished, all-wood canoes which had been the mainstay of the Partelow business. Boatbuilding within Boston's city limits went into permanent decline, which no doubt was the reason Lawton left around 1900 to go to work for E. Gerry Emmons in Swampscott. In 1908 Lawton removed to Marblehead to work for James E. Graves, where, well along in his 80s, he was still building fine yacht tenders when I made his acquaintance in the early 1940s.

Charles Lawton was a superb craftsman. His pre-eminence as a boatbuilder was unquestioned in Marblehead. His reputation was prodigious. His last boat, completed in his 90th year, was a fine, varnished 12-foot yacht tender which showed the Whitehall influence, although it was not a Whitehall. Few builders in the prime of life and professional career could have equaled it.

My acquaintance with Charlie Lawton soon ripened into friendship. Naturally, I admired his skill as a boatbuilder, and was much impressed with reports of his past achievements, for even then Charlie Lawton was well on the way to becoming a legend in Marblehead. Whenever the opportunity presented itself, I encouraged him to talk of his early experiences. He thought highly of Whitehall boats, and often spoke of them, recalling the early years in Boston when he was building Whitehalls for the Partelows. That concern was frequently hard put to meet its payroll, it seems, and the crew was never quite sure, according to Charlie, whether or not they would get paid at the end of the week.

There were other noted builders of Whitehalls, Dick Sullivan, for one, whose Commercial Street shop had for a sign a three-foot replica of a Whitehall hanging over its entrance. Sullivan also had come to Boston from St. John, where he had once worked for a time for Charlie's father and uncle. Charlie's great-grandfather, John Lawton, a Philadelphia boatbuilder born in 1758, and a Loyalist at the time of the American Revolution, had emigrated in the 1780s to St. John.

Somehow in talking with Charlie, I became enamored of the Whitehall. Charlie explained classic Whitehall construction to me in detail,

The simple construction of the after end of the 13-foot Whitehall is revealed here. Note the hogging piece over the keel and the boxed frame ends. (Mystic Seaport photo by Louis S. Martel)

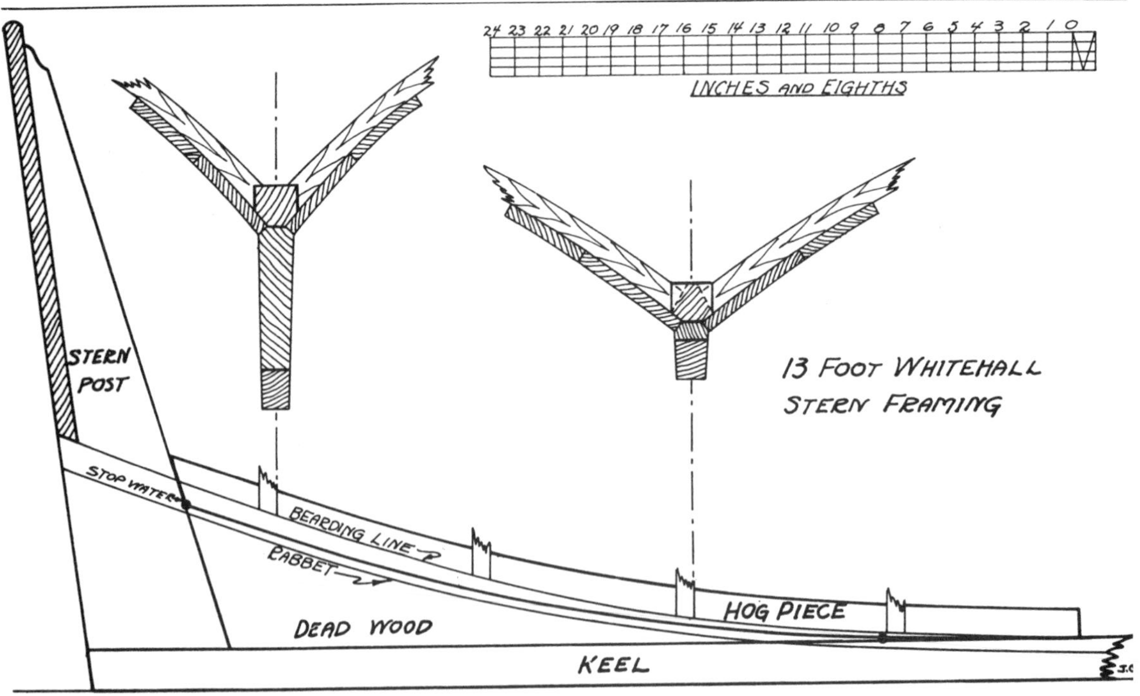

and let me copy a draft of Whitehall lines he had made, as well as trace the outlines of molds for Whitehall stem and stern transom assemblies retained from his Boston days, molds which he later gave to me and which I still have. It was he who called my attention to the smaller of the two Whitehalls now at Mystic Seaport. At that time, in the early 1940s, this boat was in use in Marblehead during the summer as a yacht tender, and was stored in the winter at Graves's Front Street yard.

After Charlie recommended this boat as a good example of Whitehall construction, I studied it closely from all angles, took measurements, and went back occasionally for another look, and thus got its details stamped indelibly into memory. Then I left Marblehead, and with the passing years lost trace of the boat completely. A couple of times I made inquiries as to its whereabouts, but with no success. Finally I reluctantly assumed that it had disappeared without leaving a trace.

Then one summer, Captain Jerry Smith, son of Captain Charleton Smith, notified me that his neighbor Bill Peach on Stony Brook Road, Marblehead, had a boat in his backyard that I might want to take the lines from. The first look told me that it was the same Boston Whitehall that I had given up for lost, although in the intervening years its color had changed from white to black, long storage away from the water had opened gaping seams, and along the way it had acquired an ugly rope bumper around its sheer after the manner of a yacht tender. Otherwise it was in fine condition, little changed from the way I remembered it nearly 25 years earlier.

In the acquisition of this boat, Mystic Seaport made a significant addition to its small craft collection. As H. I. Chapelle observed, the Whitehall is "perhaps the most noted of American rowing workboats." The Boston Whitehall was a principal sub-type of the basic Whitehall. This boat is the only reliably documented example of this sub-type so far found and available for study. It complements beautifully Mystic's other Whitehall, the 16-foot 9-inch boat presumably built at Boston in the 1870's, also a very rare survival, and substantiates much of the detail found in Captain Charleton Smith's account of the Boston Whitehall published in *The Rudder* in August, 1943.

AN UNUSUAL ONE-PIECE STEM

When the 13-foot Boston Whitehall was prepared for exhibit at Mystic Seaport, it was found necessary to remove the floorboards and bow and stern sheets in order to strip and repaint the inside of the boat. This allowed an unobstructed view of the interior and the framing, so that details of construction ordinarily hidden could be seen. These details are of particular interest to prospective builders, and, because they are permanently out of sight when the boat is in use, which is the condition in which it was to be exhibited, we had the photographs taken of the stripped interior, which are reproduced here. These will repay close study. While it has often been said that a picture is worth a thousand words, there are many things in boatbuilding that must be seen, touched, or otherwise directly experienced through the five senses, that no amount of explanatory verbiage can convey.

The construction of the stem was puzzling at first, and it would have been impossible to determine how it was made without the removal of the bow sheets and the cleat on the inner face of the stem which supported it. Getting this out of the way not only allowed the inner to be viewed and photographed, but, more important, permitted the making of a template of the inside of the stem.

By relating this template to a corresponding template taken from the curve of the stem rabbet on the outside of the boat, it was possible to determine the molded width of the stem, which could not have been done otherwise except by removing the planking or drilling holes through the stem.

The result was surprising. When these two templates, one for the inner curve of the stem, and the other for the outer, were correctly positioned with relation to each other, we found

Exterior view of the bow shows how the keel is scarphed to the stem. With the paint removed, the irregular grain of the stem is revealed. The stem actually runs aft all the way to the left of the photo. (Mystic Seaport photo by Louis S. Martel)

that the greatest molded width, occurring at the turn of the forefoot, was no less than 4¾". This is more than had appeared and more than we had expected.

True, it was obvious from the first that this stem was out of the ordinary. The usual construction method is to build up the stem from a three-piece assembly: first, the stem, proper, which can be got out of an ordinary plank, if need be, although some curve in the grain of the lower end is desirable; second, a knee of curved natural-crook grain, if possible, which fits against, and reinforces, the inner side of the forefoot extending a short distance along the top of the straight keel where it meets the stem, tying the two together; and, third, an apron piece of greater width of siding than the outer and principal stem piece, fitting against its inner side and running from the upper end of the forefoot knee to the stemhead. The apron provides backing (back rabbet) and fastening for the hood ends of the planking.

As it was clear from the first glance that the stem of this boat was not fabricated in this manner, the possibility was considered that it might have been steam-bent, and that perhaps it was made up of two or more steam-bent pieces joined together. For instance, if of two parts, the inner and outer parts could have been joined lengthwise, with the joint hidden by the rabbet. However, examination of the stemhead revealed no such separation or joint. Nor were there any breaks or joints to be found either on the inside or the outside of the stem, except where the straight keel was scarphed in at the end of the stem. It then became clear that the stem was one piece throughout.

Could the stem have been steam-bent as a single piece? This seemed unlikely when we determined the amount of molded width. While it is possible, of course, to steam-bend oak of this width to curves as sharp as this, it is not easy, and special equipment not found in the ordinary boatshop would be required. Besides, inspection of the grain of the wood in this stem showed it to be irregular rather than straight,

(Above and below) Interior views show the framing and the one-piece stem, which ends at a natural-crook floor timber. Note the lapped sheer strake and the bead on the wide plank below it. (Mystic Seaport photos by Louis S. Martel)

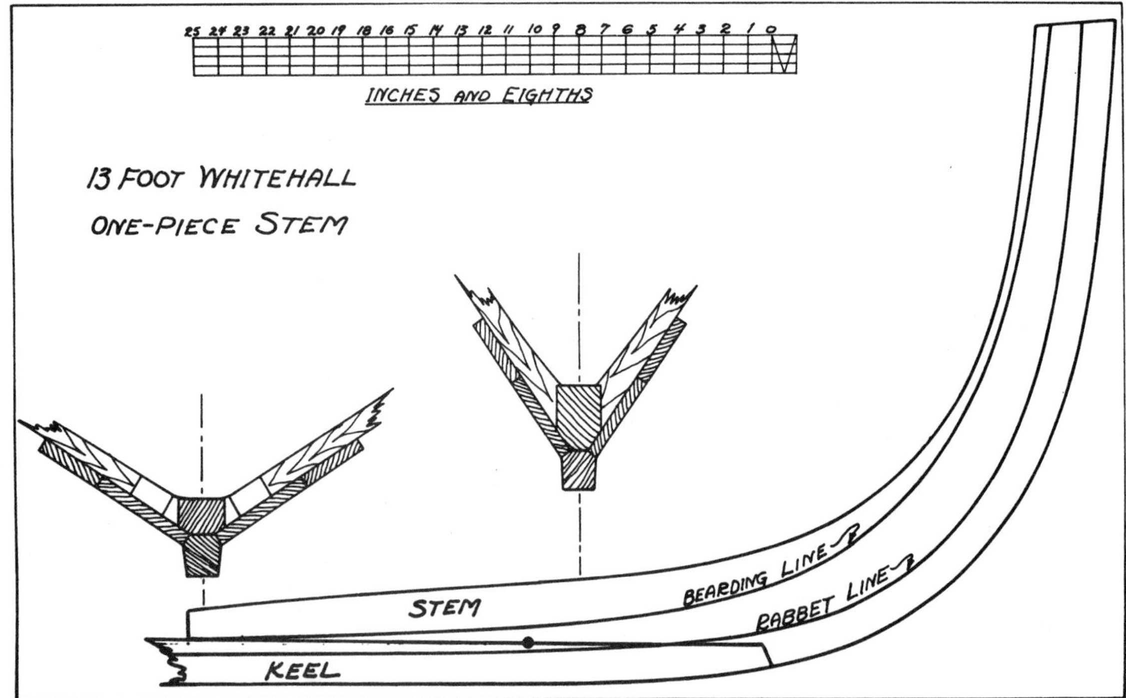

and running slashwise in places rather than parallel to the lengthwise run of the stick. In selecting lumber for a bend as difficult as this, it would be strange not to choose wood with a straight, regular grain.

Taking all these things into consideration, we can only conclude that this stem was gotten out of a natural-grown crook of some sort. Although limb crooks of oak of the required curvature are sometimes found, stump crooks or knees of the requisite shape occur more commonly. In either case, natural crooks make the best possible stems, and, while oak was used for this boat throughout, hackmatack also makes a perfectly adequate stem for boats of this size.

Using natural crooks means problems for most amateur builders. Unless the builder can go into the woods and dig a suitable knee, or find a limb crook of the right curve, he will have to settle for something else. It hardly needs saying that timber of this sort is not to be found in lumberyards.

However, there are two perfectly acceptable alternatives; one, the ordinary three-piece stem assembly already mentioned, and the other, a glued, laminated stem. Epoxy glue for this latter purpose has now been thoroughly proved, and the technique is simplicity itself: A rough form is used to give the shape, and a few clamps are used to pull the strips together and hold them until the resin has hardened.

There are two methods of lamination to choose from. One uses strips thin enough to bend without steaming, and gluing takes place immediately. The other calls for fewer but heavier and thicker strips, which must be steamed to bend. These are then allowed to dry out before gluing and reclamping. Those who still can't bring themselves to trust glue completely and who would feel better using some reinforcement can add a number of long, thin, bronze screws put in from the inside, but they are really not needed.

There is one thing about the one-piece stem which should be mentioned, for it might escape notice even though it is shown in the drawing. The siding of the stem on its after side inside the planking is 1⅝ inches, while at the rabbet line it is only 1⅜ inches. This means that the outer portion or edge of the stem must be thinned by ¼ inch (⅛ inch on each side) before the rabbet is recessed. There is special reason for this. It is done so that the stem will not appear to be too thick and clumsy from the outside of the boat, while at the same time providing sufficient wood inside to afford good backing for the hood ends of the planking. As already pointed out, with the standard three-piece stem assembly, the apron, which is molded heavier than the main stem piece, provides this required extra width of backing, or "back rabbet," for the plank ends.

Rabbeting the one-piece stem is undoubtedly the fussiest and most difficult operation in building a Whitehall, and the beginner is advised to go slowly and to be sure he understands what he is doing, otherwise he may find himself in trouble. The standard composite stem is considerably easier to rabbet.

As to how close the tolerances are in rabbeting the single-piece stem, note that in the diagram of the rabbeted stemhead of this 13-foot Whitehall, the ends of the planking are not shown square, but are cut back about ⅛ inch on the inside. This leaves a little additional thickness of undisturbed wood between the two rabbet cut-outs. There is nothing extra to spare than this.

The internal structure at the stern is simplicity itself. The strip that is fastened on top of the deadwood to afford back rabbet for the garboards where they rise toward the stern is oak sided 1¾ inches, which is ⅛ inch more than the siding of the inside after edge of the stem, and ⅜ inch thicker than the sternpost, keel, and deadwood. This member, added to the top of the deadwood and after end of the keel, is neither a knee nor a keel batten, but possibly might be called a "hogging" piece by the British. It can be sawn out of an ordinary oak plank, as it has no curve to mention, and is fastened down with screws. The lower ends of the after frames are boxed into it, which is a neat way of securing them, besides adding to the structural strength of the after bottom.

Hidden from sight in the photographs, but critically essential nonetheless, are the two stopwaters, one in the rabbet at either end of the deadwood to close the joints and prevent leakage at these two points into the bottom of the boat.

THE IMPORTANCE OF A FLOOR KNEE

Among the W. P. Stephens papers in the manuscript collection of the G. W. Blunt White Library at the Mystic Seaport is an outline tracing bearing the following penciled notation printed across its length: "Floor Knee From Meredith's Shop, Presumably Deadrise Of Whitehall Boat. W. P. S."

This is more important for the history of the Whitehall boat, I am inclined to believe, than might first appear. To my satisfaction at least, this simple outline furnishes the needed clue to a number of perplexing questions concerning the form and construction of the Whitehall and bearing upon the origin and use of the original New York working boats. In a real sense this floor knee outline constitutes a "missing link." To my knowledge, about the only tangible bit remaining of the New York working boats, at least that we can put our hands on, is this outline of a floor knee.

If this one molded shape can be accepted as authentic, as I believe it can, and as I shall presently attempt to show, we shall have more to work from than might at first be supposed. Quite a lot can be told from it, both as to what the Whitehall was and what it was not. Besides, this molded shape does constitute a link to some Boston Whitehalls which have survived, for instance the two that are now preserved in the small craft collection at Mystic Seaport.

Just as the paleontologist from an ancient, fragmentary, fossilized bone can often determine to a considerable extent the characteristics of the prehistoric animal of which it once formed a part, so the small craft historian from the shape of this floor knee should be able to reconstruct and establish some significant features of the working Whitehall boats of New York. By great good fortune it happens that preserved in the simple molded shape of this floor knee is one of the principal determining elements of the boat's shape. If we had had a choice, we could hardly have picked for examination a more significant single member of the craft's structure.

First, however, it is necessary to establish

the authenticity of the molded shape of this floor knee, and to place it within the historical context in which it acquires significance. To do this we must consider the source from whence it comes. How did it happen to be found among W. P. Stephens's papers?

No man could have been better qualified by experience, interest, and specialized knowledge to rescue the Whitehall from oblivion than W. P. Stephens. Yet time was against him, and the job was never finished. Born in 1854 in a day when rowing was the foremost American competitive sport, Stephens took up sculling early and came into intimate contact with some of the best oarsmen of the time, both American and British. After graduation as a civil engineer from Rutgers, he began building boats, and in 1880, at the age of 26, he was operating his own boatshop in Rahway, N. J. That same year he participated in founding the American Canoe Association, becoming one of its 23 charter members. At the first meet held at Lake George, N. Y., in August of 1880, Stephens won the first race in one of his own "Jersey Blue" sailing and paddling canoes.

The following year Stephens moved operations to West New Brighton, Staten Island, renting a boatshop formerly occupied by a builder of working Whitehalls, William Meredith by name, but known about the waterfront as "Billy English." Billy English, was supposed to have built a fast boat to satisfy the requirements of his clientele, reputed to have been mainly harbor thieves and junkmen.

Stephens was a frequent and popular contributor, under the pen name of "Jersey Blue," to *Forest and Stream*, the foremost boating publication of the period. He was not long in becoming its canoeing editor at the time the sailing canoe, derived from the British Rob Roy, was at the height of its popularity in the Northeast. In 1884, *Forest and Stream* brought out the first edition of Stephens's *Canoe and Boat Building for Amateurs* with 24 plates. Within the next 25 years this book was to pass through more than a dozen editions with an increase in the number of plates of drawings to 30 and finally to 50. This book was probably the most widely read and influential work on small craft construction ever published.

With the decline of the sailing canoe and its permanent eclipse before the end of the century, Stephens turned to yachting. There seems to have been a period when writing and editorial work did not suffice for a living, for in a letter to Captain Charleton L. Smith, written when Stephens was 82, Stephens mentioned that he was sailing his little ketch, *Snikersnee*, probably for the last season, attempting to make up for the years of duty on tugboats and steam yachts when he missed all personal sailing. Incidentally, it proved not to be the last season for *Snikersnee*, for in May, three years later, he explained to a correspondent that he was about to go down to the yacht club to beach and pump out his little yacht, which was leaking badly.

Duty at sea did not seem to have interfered either with Stephens's writing or yacht designing. His ability as a designer was demonstrated in one notable instance by his 15-foot waterline *Ethelwynn*, first winner of the Seawanhaka Cup, defeating the challenger, the English half-rater, *Spruce IV*, in 1895, as well as boats by Herreshoff and other eminent American designers. As a writer he continued to publish, in time winning distinction as the foremost reporter of international yacht racing.

With the inception of *Lloyds Register of American Yachts*, Stephens became its editor, a position he continued to hold until he was past 80. In addition to Stephens's early *Canoe and Boat Building for Amateurs* were *American Yachting*, 1904; *Traditions And Memories of American Yachting*, 1942, reprinted from *Motor Boating*; and *The Seawanhaka Corinthian Yacht Club, Origins And Early History, 1871-1896*, published posthumously in 1963. This last book and related investigations into yachting history took much of his time and effort toward the end of his life, preventing the completion of his investigation of the Whitehall. Stephens died in 1946 at the age of 92.

What a pity Stephens could not have carried his Whitehall research to its conclusion! His qualifications for the job were perfect: his skill as a working boatbuilder, his background in competitive rowing and sailing both as a sailor and a designer, his knowledge of yachting and his experience as a yachtsman, his achievements as writer, reporter, and historian, and in addition his personal recollection of the New York harbor scene when working Whitehalls were still in use—these taken altogether are pre-eminent qualifications. And for these same reasons, what he did do deserves our particular consideration, even though some of his work is incomplete.

At the outset of the 1930s a stir of interest in the Whitehall boat and early days on the New York waterfront found expression in letters published in the local newspapers. Stephens took a leading part in this exchange. The "race boats" of the early nineteenth century came in for particular attention. The New York *Sun* on March 9, 1934, published a letter by Eugene L. Baptiste of Montclair, N. J., claiming that the race boat, *Knickerbocker*, built by his ancestor, John Baptiste, in 1811, was the first Whitehall rowboat. After winning a notable race by a quarter of a mile against an "English" challenger (apparently a New York boat, but produced by a builder of English extraction), the letter continued, the *Knickerbocker*, painted white with a green gunwale and a gold stripe, was hung for public view in Scudder's Museum from which it was later transferred to the American Museum at Broadway and Ann Street. Also known as Barnum's Museum, the building with all its contents was destroyed by fire in 1865. Incidentally, Stephens as a small boy had visited this museum, but failed to recall seeing this boat.

Other winning race boats by John Baptiste (sometimes Baptis) were the *New York* in 1818 and the *General Lafayette* in 1824, which beat a rival race boat, the *Mapes*, in an historic race.

John Baptiste was succeeded by his son Edward who later sold the business and boatshop at 660 Water Street to a famous builder of metal lifeboats by the name of Raymond. According to claims put forward by the descendants of John Baptiste, his race boats were never beaten in an important race, yet ironically it was the race boat *American Star*, built by Baptiste's arch rival and oft-defeated competitor, the "Englishman" Chambers, that the Whitehallers of New York presented to General Lafayette in 1825 during his visit to America; and that Lafayette took back with him to France on his return.

Because the professional boatmen who early in the nineteenth century frequented Whitehall slip at the foot of Whitehall Street and were known as Whitehallers took a prominent part in race boat competition, some have concluded that the working Whitehall used in harbor service was derived from the race boat. Stephens believed that this was not the case. As to which came first, service boats or race boats, Stephens felt certain it was the former, a point on which he proceeded to correct his admirer and collaborator, Captain Charleton L. Smith of Marblehead, who had assumed priority for the race boats in an early piece on Whitehalls published in a Boston newspaper.

To support his view that the service boats came first, Stephens cites evidence for a more or less continuous ferry service between lower Manhattan and the New Jersey shore from at least 1661, and most probably carried on to a large extent, especially in the beginning, in rowboats. While none of the actual boats so used come into clear view earlier than the beginning of the nineteenth century, Stephens assumed that there must have been a gradual evolution from heavy ships' boats. As the city grew, need arose for larger craft capable of transporting horses and horsedrawn vehicles, and for this purpose periaugers came to be used, described by Stephens as large flat boats fitted with two masts and sails.

The first Commodore Vanderbilt, Stephens observed, began life as a skipper of a periauger plying between Staten Island and the Battery. The *Boston Weekly News Letter* of March 18, 1756, has it that one of the Staten Island ferryboats, presumably a periauger, with 13 passengers and three horses, sank between Bedlows and Oyster Island with 11 drowned.

Apparently not all of the early periaugers or pettiaugers were large flat craft fitted with sails. Derived from log dugouts or pirogues, some of these pettiaugers must have been sharp craft and fast, or relatively so, under oars. From the *Boston Weekly News Letter* of May 6, 1756, we learn that a Cape Cod whaleboat with a crew of six on the way to Albany stopped off at Manhattan to race one of the local pettiaugers for a wager of $20, winning with "greatest ease."

These early boats, pettiaugers and the like, have receded into the depths of time, leaving hardly more than their names. Only with the race boats after 1811 or thereabouts and the working harbor-service craft of the Whitehallers and the Battery boatmen from about the same time or a little later do actual boats appear. Certainly by the time we are able to distinguish the race boats and the working boats, they are distinctly different types. The former were clinker planked, the latter carvel. The race boat was nearly flat of sheer, lean, long and narrow in proportion to its over-all length. Thus the *Mapes*, beaten by John Baptiste's *General Lafayette*, was 25 feet over-all, while the *American Star* was slightly less than 27½ feet. The race boat was crewed by a coxswain and four men, each pulling a single oar.

The largest of the working Whitehalls of 19 feet were pulled ordinarily by two pair of 9-foot sculls, although the smaller 17-foot boats used for running lines to the piers were operated at times with only one pair. There were other differences as well.

These two types were not the only pulling boats to be found in New York harbor prior to the Civil War. In a large painting depicting the arrival of the *Great Western* in New York in 1839, Stephens distinguished, besides race boats and working Whitehalls, a pleasure barge with ladies in the stern sheets. In commenting on the annual spring race of the working Whitehalls around Robbins Reef Buoy, the only race in which these boats engaged, Stephens explained that most of the racing about New York at that time was done in shells, gigs, barges, and the "New York working boat," which was between a shell and "a half-outrigged gig."

In a letter written in 1934 to a correspondent who suggested the Whitehall might have originally been a lake boat from Whitehall, N. Y., Stephens is quite definite in rejecting this hypothesis. He explained: "I have seen a great many light rowing boats built on South Street years ago, but those which might be called pleasure boats were distinctly different from the Whitehalls. While the pleasure boats were all lapstrake, the working boats were carvel built; but there was a still greater difference in model. I would attribute the origin of the Whitehall boat to ships boats and similar small craft in use about New York City and not to a model from an inland lake."

Again in 1936 he wrote: "We had in New York fifty years ago many fine light rowing boats similar to the Whitehall boat, but lighter in build and more elaborate in finish—a distinct type."

Elsewhere he explained: "Great numbers of these were sent throughout the country from the New York boatshops, the Whitehall name accompanying them."

Today, almost any small pulling boat with a nearly plumb stem, rounded bilge, and "wine glass" stern is called a "Whitehall," and this is not likely to change. Yet while form is part of it, and an essential part, the main thing is the unique way in which the true Whitehall was framed and put together. No true Whitehall can have the following: clinker planking, an open gunwale, or strip ribs bent in hot after planking is complete. In these respects the working Whitehalls of both New York and Boston seem to have been nearly identical.

The exchange in the newspapers concerning race boats and Whitehalls set Stephens in motion, and he undertook to see if he could locate any of the old boats or anyone who had rowed, or who had built them.

On May 7, 1934, Stephens talked with Ernie Akers, then foreman of the Nevins yard at City Island, who told him that in 1888, when he was 18 years old, he had worked for Tom Blackwell, a boatbuilder in Astoria, building Whitehall boats for junkmen. Some of the boats were sold to Staten Island.

These boats, Akers recalled, were about 19 feet in length, carvel planked of ½" white cedar on frames approximately ¾ inch by ⅞ inch, spaced 9 inches. A top strake of white oak was beveled on its lower edge to lap over a matching beveled edge on the plank below, and was ornamented with a small bead which came just above the lap fastenings. The inside was finished with a foresheets, two rowing thwarts, and a horseshoe bench aft. Flat thole pins about 2½ inches by ⅝ inch were mortised through the gunwale to socket in a steadying cleat below.

Just a year later on May 8, 1935, Stephens spoke with Captain Bill Quigley, last of the Battery boatmen, whom he found on the Battery Wall. Quigley, 73 and retired from the water, had been born at No. 6 State Street and had rowed in the harbor for 55 years. According to his recollection, the large service boats, the same for the Battery boatmen and the Whitehallers, were 19 feet long, confirming Akers. In beam they were 4½ feet and in depth 20 inches. After the large boats went out, the 17-foot boats continued to be used to run lines to the piers. In his recollection of interior detail, including the flat thole pins, Quigley did not differ materially from Akers. Quigley was able to furnish a lead to a surviving boat, but upon investigation this boat was found to be heavily and crudely constructed and hence unrepresentative. The following year Stephens talked with Quigley again, but it seems without learning anything further of any importance.

Toward the end of 1935, after H. I. Chapelle had apparently informed Stephens that Captain Charleton L. Smith of Marblehead was an authority on Whitehalls, Stephens wrote him. Smith lost no time in replying. He greatly admired and respected Stephens and the subject of Whitehalls was dear to him. Besides, he and Stephens had much in common, for Smith was also a fine boatbuilder, a deepwater sailor and a yachtsman, and an author as well: he had published two books of juvenile fiction about adventures at sea and was a frequent contributor on nautical subjects to Boston newspapers. An exchange of letters and information followed, extending over a period of nine months, during which there was some slight give and take, yet remarkable agreement on essentials throughout. It seems clear that working, rowed-on-the-gunwales Whitehalls both at Boston and New York during the 1870s, the 1880s, and the 1890s were practically identical.

Captain Smith accepted Stephens's correction on the origin of the service Whitehall, that is to say that the working boat had not developed from an eariler race boat, and in consequence Smith left this out of his final article on the Whitehall, the previously mentioned one published in *Rudder* in August, 1943, shortly before his death.

Stephens for his part stated that Smith's account of the method and procedure of Whitehall construction had refreshed his recollection, and he gracefully accepted Smith's correction of timber dimensions previously obtained from Akers.

The method of timbering a Whitehall is worth going into in some detail, for it is unique to the Whitehall, as far as I know, and is one of its most distinctive features. Timbers are set up square with the centerline of the boat in matched pairs, one futtock to a side, before planking starts, so that the carvel strakes can be fitted and fastened to the timbers ahead of time over the same mold or "timber block" shaped to a somewhat greater curvature than that of the sides of the boat. In preparing a pair of timbers to go into the boat, they are straightened out as much as necessary to fit against the ribbands at the station they are to occupy, and they must also be beveled at the bench to fit the fore-and-aft curvature of the sides, for, as previously mentioned, they are always set square with the centerline of the boat. Timbers are also tapered lengthwise. The molded depth of the timber at the head where it jogs into the underside of the gunwale is considerably less than the molded depth at the bottom end or the heel.

Captain Smith, in correcting the uniform ⅞-inch molding dimension which Stephens obtained from Akers, stated that a correctly proportioned timber of standard ¾-inch siding would be molded ¾ inch at the head, but at the heel it would be molded 1⅜ inches. This last dimension I consider to be excessive, except, perhaps, for a very heavily built 20-foot boat.

In the 13-foot Whitehall now at Mystic Seaport, the timbers, which are sided ¾ inch, are

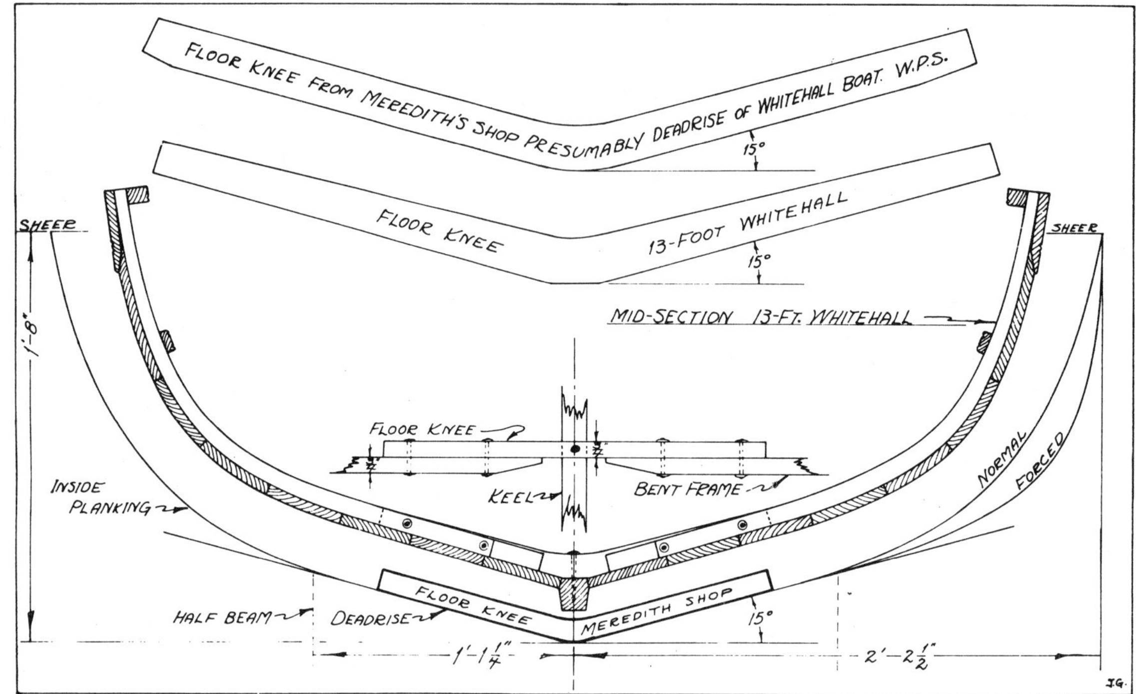

molded ⅞ inch at the heel, tapering to a molding of ½ inch under the gunwale, and this is not a lightly built boat by any means, in spite of the fact that it is only 13 feet long.

As Captain Smith explained in his letter of January 3, 1936, to Stephens: "Yes, it was the custom to bend a great many timbers at one steaming, and force them under window sills, work benches or other convenient places, where they wouldn't straighten out. When ready to timber a boat, they shaped one pair of these frames to suit the eye and placed them amidships. Next they straightened out a pair by eye to go half way from the bow. Then the same thing was done half way to the transom. A few ribbands were bent around these few frames, and they shaped the timbers to the ribbands until the boat was all timbered out. Invariably they had a beveled frame with taper from heel to head."

What is not mentioned is that each pair of timbers was riveted through the heels to a natural-crook floor knee, which passed across the top of the keel and was fastened to it. This made an exceptionally strong and neat arrangement. This floor knee, cut out to the deadrise angle of the boat, extended out 10 or 12 inches on either side of the keel in the midsection of the boat. Thus, in a boat of 4 to 4½ feet in beam, the floor knee extended across half the width of the boat, the center half. This conforms closely to the old standard rule for deadrise in small boats, a rule handed down from the eighteenth century or possibly earlier, namely that the deadrise of the bottom (rise from the dead flat) should be half the beam of the boat.

The very term "deadrise" means a straight rise of bottom or floor extended out from the side of the keel at whatever angle of rise a particular design calls for. In a slack-bilged boat like the working Whitehall, the angle of deadrise is relatively steep. Thus, in the 13-foot Whitehall at Mystic Seaport, the angle of deadrise amidships is 15 degrees, which turns out to be identical with the angle of deadrise for the floor-knee pattern found among Stephens's papers. Captain Smith in one of his letters, in commenting on a Whitehall model which seemed to him to have a rather flat sheer, observed, "I never considered a Whitehall very flat; rather they were easy shaped in every way, with a sharp floor, next to no bilge, and a very S-like stern." This is indeed the Whitehall shape, and given the width of beam, the depth amidships, and a floor pattern with the angle of deadrise, the shape of the midsection is predetermined within rather close limits. The curvature from bilge to sheer cannot vary much one way or the other. The boatbuilder's experienced eye can find the happy medium without recourse to thwartship molds.

When Stephens took over the Meredith shop in West New Brighton in 1881, he found, according to his letter to C. G. Davis, March 8, "a timber block for bending the frames, molds for the stem, forward rabbet, transom and after deadwood, and odd parts," but no thwartship, or section, molds. Assuming that there had been thwartship molds originally, he concluded that Meredith's son-in-law must have taken them. But why only these without the rest of the molds?

All through the intervening years Stephens had retained the Billy English molds, as he explained in writing to Captain Smith on August 9, 1936. "I have . . . the stem mould, rabbet mould, after deadwood and timber block for the 19 foot boat; also a complete stem ready for the apron, and other moulds for the 17 foot boat. I have no thwartship moulds. If there were any, there were probably three. What I lack to plot from these are three or four breadths at the gunwale and the rise of the dead flat; of course the timber block shows over bending."

The foregoing is from his last letter to Smith, at least the last that we have. Three years later in replying to an inquiry from the West Coast asking about progress in his investigation of the Whitehall, he explained that there is much in this connection that he would like to do, but that so far he had been unable to go farther. His study of yachting history was taking most of his time. Stephens was then 85.

My surmise is that Stephens never quite gave up the idea of sometime completing his work of Whitehall restoration. I would guess that subsequently in going over the Meredith molds, and in particular the "odd pieces" mentioned in his letter to Davis, he discovered the floor knee, or at least came fully to realize its significance, as he had not previously.

With the angle of deadrise obtained from this knee, together with the approximate beam, which he had, and the depth amidships, a thwartships mold was hardly necessary. Being aware of the importance of this piece for a future reconstruction of the working Whitehall, Stephens traced its shape, marked it for identification, and placed the pattern among his papers.

BOATS SIMILAR TO THE WHITEHALL

There are so many small boats, similar in some respects and different in others, which have been called Whitehalls, that in discussing them complete confusion reigns unless there is some established and recognized norm to which they can be related and compared. While it is common and convenient to use the term, Whitehall, when describing a boat, it is often inaccurate and misleading to do so, for many variations of the type have appeared at different times and in different places.

Since boats bearing the Whitehall name first came into view, there has been considerable evolutionary change. This development presents us with the problem of determining or deciding what constitutes the true Whitehall, the Whitehall norm, so to speak.

Shall it be the early Whitehall as built in New York, or the later model developed in Boston, or a composite of the two, with possibly the inclusion of features from other sources as well? And if we should decide on working out a composite norm, by what standard or procedure should we attempt to do this? We know definitely, and precisely, and in detail what the Boston Whitehall was like, since two authentic models are available for study at Mystic Seaport. For me the Whitehall type attained the summit of its development in the classic Boston boat, which justifies taking it as the "norm" for comparing and classifying other boats with Whitehall characteristics to a greater or lesser degree.

In my judgment the ultimate Whitehall is exemplified by the fancy 16-foot 9-inch Boston

This large, heavily built boat, photographed in Falmouth Foreside, Maine, in 1952, shows a Whitehall influence. Neither the cast bronze thwart knees nor the small half-round finishing off the bottom edge of the top strake are typical of the classic Whitehall.

An excellent pulling boat similar to a Whitehall. Unlike the classic Whitehall, she has a clinker build, flat, closely spaced bent ribs, and a transom without a wine-glass reverse curve. This boat is also beamier than the true Whitehall and is flatter in her floors.

Star of Noank, *which is a replica of* Favorite, *a 11′9″ strip-built boat of Whitehall lines built somewhere east of Boston about 1900.* Favorite *is now in the small craft collection at Mystic Seaport.*

Whitehall formerly belonging to E. Wm. Bailey of Amesbury, and now at Mystic Seaport. It is to be understood, then, that henceforth when I use the term "Whitehall," it is the Boston Whitehall which I have in mind, and to which I make reference.

One small pulling boat often taken to be a Whitehall is the *Favorite*, which first came to Mystic Seaport on loan more than a quarter of a century ago. In 1951 when her owner, Captain Elwell B. Thomas of Stonington, Connecticut, finally donated her to the Museum, he stated he believed she had been built somewhere east of Boston "about 50 years ago," bringing her within the period of Whitehall dominance. Quite small for a Whitehall, in fact only 11 feet 9 inches overall, *Favorite*'s lines are basically Whitehall; her construction is different, however, for she is strip-built. This is most unusual, both in consideration of her lines and from the standpoint of her size.

In 1966, Robert Bruce Small, crew coach at South Kent School, South Kent, Connecticut, secured lines and construction details from Mystic Seaport and had a replica of this boat built for his personal use, except that the new boat was strip-built entirely of mahogany, which finished bright inside gives an unusually handsome appearance. *Star of Noank*, as she was named, has proved to be a most satisfactory and "pleasurable" craft, according to her owner.

Let him explain in his own words:

> She handles quite well. In flat water she will carry at one stroke per minute, and she will cruise a mile in twenty minutes (with moderate effort). For a boat of her size, she has good cruising range, a maximum of five miles in Fishers Island Sound from Groton Long Point. She has some shortcomings (but what boat doesn't?). Mainly she is quite quick in her motion as one moves about aboard her. I suspect that this quickness of motion could be smoothed out by the addition of 50 to 75 pounds of ballast. Surprisingly enough, she tows quite well at moderate speeds and is a pretty good boat in a sea. . . . Although *Favorite* is not a true Whitehall, I think she would provide a good basis for a 14′ pulling boat. I would retain her tumble home aft—it is a handsome line—and I would retain her unique keel/skeg arrangement with slight modification. However, I think she would be improved by having slightly less deadrise amidships, a slightly sharper entry, and more flare forward to increase her stability. Finally, I think I would want a slightly deeper forefoot to keep her on course in

A 15½-footer belonging to Bob Rose of Lake Linden, Michigan. She is not a true Whitehall but resembles one in certain respects, such as her narrow beam of 44 inches. It appears that the boat does not have the solid deadwood aft of a true Whitehall; rather it is planked down to the bottom of the keel, producing "hollow garboards," an excellent method of building but not Whitehall construction. The boat may have been built around 1900.

This pretty 12-foot yacht tender, though not a Whitehall, shows a definite Whitehall influence. She was built by by Charles Lawton in his 90th year (1948) and is an example of the fine craftmanship of the old-time builders.

quartering head wind. I know these ideas would complicate building problems and increase costs; but, I believe, the end result would be worth it.

For individual enjoyment of rowing and the beneficial effects of this wholesome exercise (at least the equal of jogging) several of the traditional workboat pulling types are particularly well suited, namely dories, wherries, peapods, guideboats, Rangeley boats, a wide selection of skiffs, and, of course, the Whitehall. It is this latter type of rowing involving adaptations of our traditional small pulling workboats which especially needs to be encouraged, but first off suitable boats must be more easily available than they now are. So on to the construction of a 17-foot Whitehall.

22 A Whitehall Pulling Boat

Whitehalls were built from 12 to 20 feet long. Some of the larger ones intended for sailing were quite beamy and were fitted with centerboards. But the best of the Whitehalls and the most typical were 17 to 18 feet long. If built shorter than this, they tended to lose their good qualities, so that the very short ones of 12 and 13 feet were somewhat degenerate. It is often forgotten, now, what an important factor length is for the best performance of small craft to be driven at moderate speeds. The longer boat moves easier through the water and is more seaworthy than the shorter one.

Most yacht tenders are too short to row really well or to take much weather. Francis Herreshoff has stated that prior to 1890 his father modeled his yacht tenders on the Whitehall, as was the common practice in that period. This boat, he recalls, rowed easily when loaded, but towed poorly and rated only fair as a sea boat. Later N. G. Herreshoff discarded this Whitehall-derived model for improved tender models he worked out himself. The Lawley tender, it should be noted, though of superb construction, remained close to its Whitehall ancestry, and is generally acknowledged by those who have used both kinds to have been inferior in performance to the later Herreshoff models.

Now this might seem a poor recommendation for the Whitehall boat, but the point is that the model suffers greatly when shortened to yacht-tender length, and should not be judged in this abbreviated length. But 70 or 80 years ago, the reputation of the larger Whitehalls was so pre-eminent and good boatbuilders were so thoroughly steeped in the habits of Whitehall construction, that when they built yacht tenders, these naturally took shape as miniature Whitehalls. And, as has been noted, even the 12-foot and 13-foot Whitehalls did pull very easily, far easier than most of the scurvy tubs that pass for rowboats today. This was due in large measure to the fine entrance and clean delivery of these boats, and because the length of the load waterline was stretched to the absolute limit by making the stem plumb and the forefoot deep and sharp. The plumb stem is the main reason why they did not tow well. The deep forefoot would bite into the seas, causing the boat to yaw.

As for the larger Whitehall, the true exemplars of the type, these are by no means obsolete, and their suitability for modern use will bear investigation. For those who want a boat of dual utility, that will give superior performance for both rowing and sailing, the Whitehall is as good as there is. For lake fishing, the 17- or 18-foot Whitehall powered with a small air-cooled inboard engine should prove a natural. The model drives easily and quietly. Moving at a good turn of speed or throttled

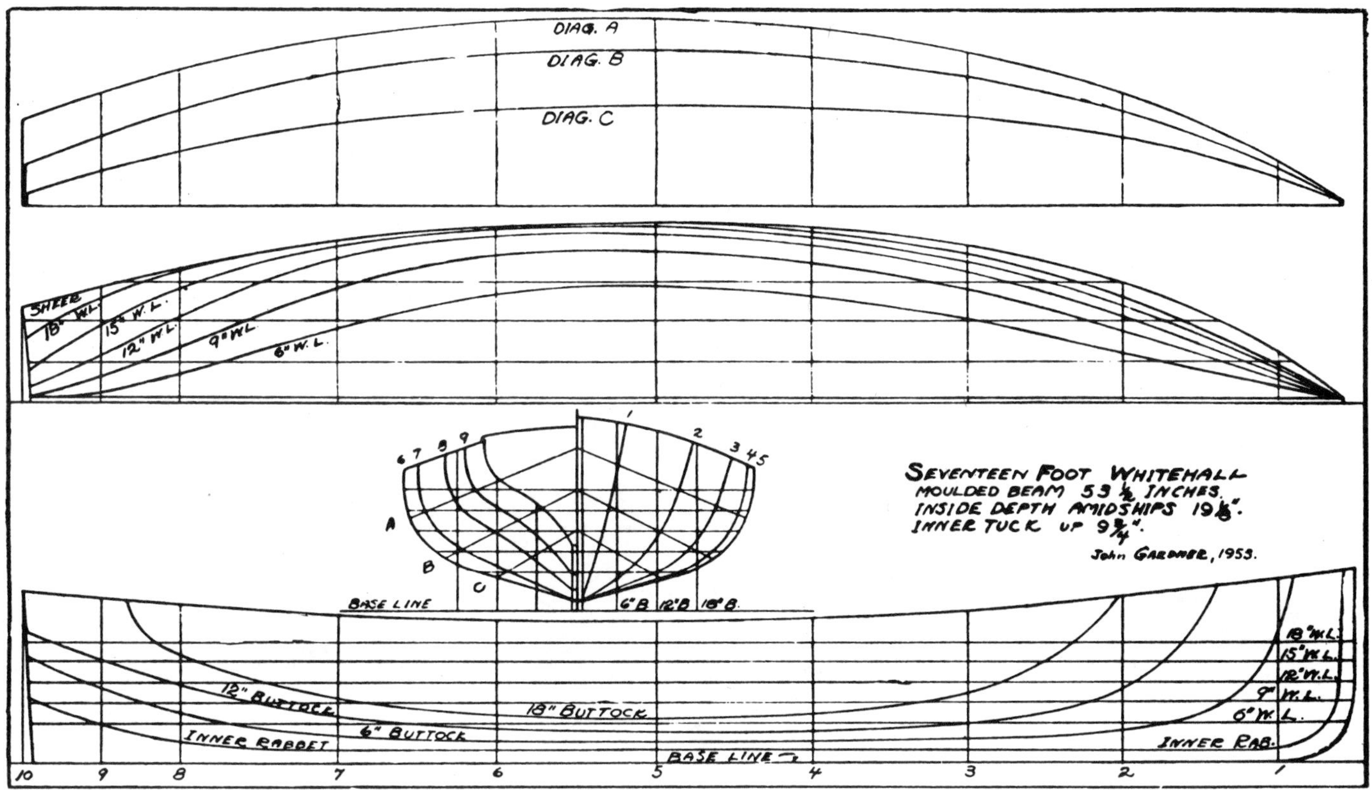

down to a crawl, this hull should be comfortable, stable, and completely seaworthy.

Every good boat is a compromise—or more accurately, many compromises. Desired qualities often clash. A tender broad as a sawed-off molasses puncheon would be very buoyant and steady to step in and out of, but try to row it. On the other hand, the slack-bilged splinter that slips along without a ripple may need its oars in the water to keep it right-side up. Length in a small boat is always a prime virtue, and it is a great harmonizer of conflicting elements. In the 17-foot or 18-foot Whitehall there is an excellent reconciliation of the diverse qualities needed to make a good boat. Its long waterlines combine a fine, sharp entrance and a clean, tapering delivery. There is no drag aft, even when the boat is deeply loaded. The upper works forward have sufficient fullness and flare to keep her head above the seas and to turn these outboard.

A moderate amount of deadrise eases the bilge but does not permit the boat to drop so deep as to preclude passage and landing in shallow water. Without bunching, the after quarters are buoyant enough to give steady bearing and a firm seat on the water. The small, high, heart-shaped transom affords ample room in the stern sheets, while allowing a stern shape nearly equal in weatherly qualities to the double-ended boat of comparable capacity, and permitting a saving, over the double-ended boat, of at least a couple of feet in overall length.

THE LINES

The lines of the 17-foot model shown here embody a lot of research and comparison of data from several sources. I think that the resulting lines are fairly typical of the larger Whitehalls, somewhat an average of the type as built in Boston and the vicinity. Of course with any boat built as extensively as the Whitehalls, there was bound to be a lot of variation. No doubt if we had the data, the step-by-step evolution of

SEVENTEEN FOOT WHITEHALL BOAT

	STATIONS	BOW	1	2	3	4	5	6	7	8	9	TRAN.
HEIGHTS ABOVE BASE	SHEER	2-4-4	2-3-3	2-0-5	1-10-4	1-9-3	1-8-7	1-9-1	1-9-7	1-11-2	2-0-1	2-1-3
	BUT. 18"	~	~	~	0-10-1	0-7-1	0-6-4	0-7-0	0-9-5	1-3-5	~	~
	BUT. 12"	~	~	0-10-6	0-5-6	0-4-6	0-4-4	0-4-7	0-6-6	0-11-4	1-3-2	1-7-3
	BUT. 6"	~	1-8-3	0-4-5	0-3-3	0-3-0	0-3-0	0-3-1	0-4-1	0-7-3	0-11-0	1-3-6
	INNER RAB.	~	0-2-0	0-1-6	0-1-6	0-1-6	0-1-6	0-1-6	0-1-6	0-3-0	0-5-5	0-9-6
HALF BREADTHS	SHEER	0-0-7	0-7-4	1-5-7	1-11-4	2-2-0	2-2-6	2-2-1	2-0-0	1-7-7	1-5-1	1-2-0
	W.L. 18" UP	0-0-7	0-5-5	1-3-4	1-10-2	2-1-3	2-2-5	2-2-1	1-11-7	1-7-3	1-3-5	0-9-5
	W.L. 15" UP	0-0-7	0-4-7	1-2-3	1-9-1	2-0-5	2-2-1	2-1-5	1-11-1	1-5-3	0-11-5	0-4-7
	W.L. 12" UP	0-0-7	0-4-1	1-0-7	1-7-4	1-11-2	2-0-7	2-0-4	1-9-3	1-0-7	0-7-1	0-2-0
	W.L. 9" UP	0-0-7	0-3-2	0-10-5	1-4-7	1-8-5	1-10-3	1-9-7	1-5-0	0-8-2	0-3-7	0-0-7
	W.L. 6" UP	0-0-7	0-2-3	0-7-4	1-0-4	1-3-6	1-4-7	1-3-6	0-10-3	0-4-2	0-1-2	0-0-7
	INNER RAB.	0-0-7	0-0-7	0-0-7	0-0-7	0-0-7	0-0-7	0-0-7	0-0-7	0-0-7	0-0-7	0-0-7
DIAGS.	DIAG. A	~	0-6-6	1-4-5	1-10-6	2-2-4	2-3-5	2-3-2	2-0-6	1-8-1	1-4-5	1-0-4
	DIAG. B	~	0-5-5	1-2-1	1-7-3	1-10-0	1-11-1	1-10-4	1-7-4	1-2-0	0-10-2	0-6-0
	DIAG. C	~	0-4-0	0-10-2	1-1-2	1-2-4	1-2-6	1-2-1	1-0-0	0-7-7	0-5-0	0-1-5

STATION 1 TO INNER RAB. STEM	6" W.L.	9" W.L.	12" W.L.	15" W.L.	18" W.L.	SHEER
	0-7-3	0-8-6	0-9-1	0-9-3	0-9-5	0-10-0

STERN RAKE 0-1-5 MEASURED ON BASE LINE FR'D OF STA. 10. STATIONS 1 TO 8 SPACED 2'. STATIONS 8 TO 10 SPACED 1 FT. WATER LINES SPACED 3". BUTTOCKS SPACED 6". BASE LINE BOTTOM OF KEEL. LINES TO INSIDE OF PLANK. DIAGONAL "A" UP 2', OUT 2'6" ON 12" W.L. DIAGONAL "B" UP 18", OUT 18" ON 9" W.L. DIAGONAL "C" UP 12", OUT 1'9" ON BASE LINE. OFFSETS IN FEET, INCHES & EIGHTHS.

the type could be traced. There would be superior Whitehalls, and some not so good, but in the long run the model would strike a general average—a run-of-the-mill Whitehall that some scores of ordinarily competent journeymen boatbuilders by long practice could build with their eyes closed, if need be.

The design for this 17-foot Whitehall is based on the data and molds, previously mentioned, given me by Charles Lawton before he died. The molds included a mold for his Whitehall transom and the rabbet mold for the deadwood and tuck. He also gave me a sketch of the lines that he drew about 1940 for a 13-foot "fancy Whitehall." This sketch was never faired thoroughly and shows the influence of his many years of building yacht tenders.

For the 17-foot Whitehall I have taken the transom shape and size, also the height of the tuck and sweep of the after rabbet, almost exactly from Lawton's molds. Checking, I have found that this transom is very close, in fact surprisingly so, to the transom shown by Chapelle in his drawing of the lines of a 16-foot Boston Whitehall as taken off by Albert Green in 1876. The rise of the after rabbet to the tuck, following Lawton's mold, is flatter and more gradual than the curve shown in Greens' lines, which in my judgment is rather too quick to plank easily.

For over-all depth and beam, I have worked within the limits established by the old Boston Boat Clubs for racing Whitehall workboats. These were given by the late Captain Charleton L. Smith in his article on the Whitehall boat in *Rudder* for August, 1943—overall length between 17 and 20 feet, beam not less than 4 feet, depth not less than 19 inches, rowed on the gunwale, and weighing not less than 265 pounds. I have followed the midsection shape shown by Captain Smith in his specimen lines, which seems a good average for the Whitehall type.

While it is true that Lawton's lines for his fancy Whitehall do not show the deadrise as being straight, still he often told me that the old rule for the Whitehall was a straight deadrise amidships for half the width of the boat, and that is the way I have made it in my lines.

Another feature mentioned as characteristic by Lawton was considerable flare of the topsides forward, sometimes giving a slight reverse curve to the shape of the first set of frames. But most Whitehall lines I have examined get ample flare forward without such reverse. I have avoided this reverse as it tends to put a difficult twist in the top planks.

Whitehall construction, now nearly unknown and lost to this generation of boatbuilders, combined strength and lightness with numerous shortcuts that developed during the years that the Whitehall was mass-produced by the hundreds if not the thousands. The amateur builder will do well to adopt, at times, certain of the Whitehall methods, especially that of shaping and beveling the timbers in pairs after they have previously been steam-bent and have cooled, using these timbers as secondary molds, and planking on them directly.

THE FOUNDATION

Whitehall construction was a method worked out by scores of smart builders over many years under exacting competition. It was simplified and highly standardized. There was very little that was not thought of or tried out. All legitimate shortcuts were adopted but without sacrifice of quality. Framed with white oak, planked with northern white cedar, and copper fastened throughout, the Whitehall was tops.

Although occasional laydowns must have been made, the practiced builder did not generally bother with offsets. He had the tune in his head, so to speak. In ordering a new boat, it was sufficient to specify a few key dimensions—the LOA, beam, depth amidship, height of tuck, and possibly width of transom and amount of sheer. (The tuck is the point where the garboard, transom, and sternpost come together.)

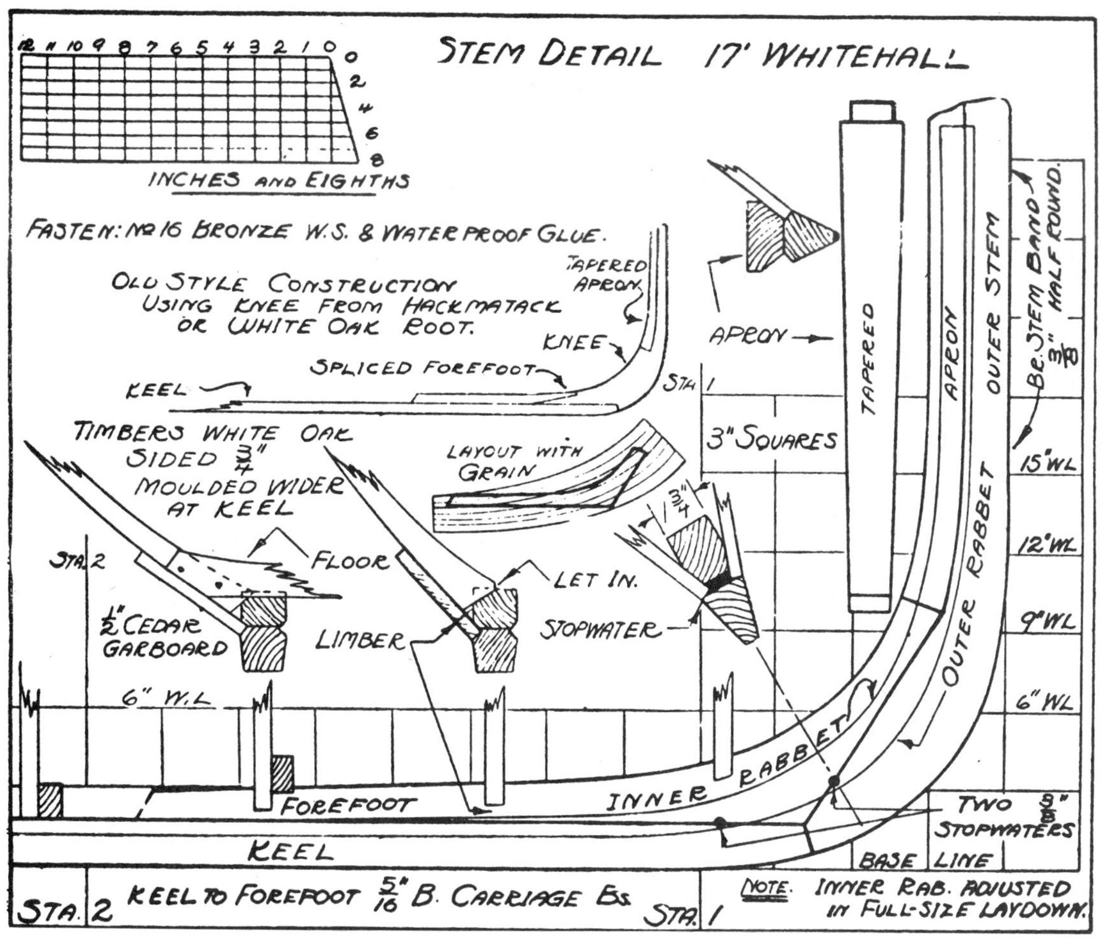

From standard molds of thin pine, the stem, transom, deadwood, and other curved members would be marked out and cut to shape. For example, a single transom mold, cut to the contour of one of the symmetrical halves of a standard transom would suffice to lay out a Whitehall transom of any desired size, the mold being adjusted on the rough stock according to the required depth and width. The stem rabbet and also the curve of the rabbet aft along the deadwood were marked out from standard rabbet molds that were moved a little this way or that to suit the builder's eye and the dimensions of the particular boat under construction. It should be noted in this connection that even a considerable difference in length did not change the sectional dimensions much, so that a couple of additional feet in length overall might not mean more than an extra inch of depth and two or three extra inches of beam.

The backbone of the boat, sometimes called the "foundation" was all of the best white or "yankee" oak. The members that comprise it—including the apron and forefoot, the keel, deadwood, stern post, and transom—were fastened together and secured right-side up on a stout horse made of a wide, straight, two-inch plank set on edge. The keel of the Whitehall is perfectly straight and was laid level about two feet off the floor to bring the boat to a convenient height for working. The stem and sternpost were plumbed and the transom was horned to a perfect right angle with the longitudinal centerline. Staylathes tacked to the walls of the shop and to the rafters secured these members in position.

The Boston Whitehalls had a "scantling" keel, that is, a straight strip uniform in section varying from 1½ inches to 1¾ inches square. Aft, the sternpost and deadwood stood on top of it, and forward, the keel met the stem and was reinforced by an extension of the forefoot which ran back on top of the keel for 2 feet and sometimes more.

Between the forefoot and deadwood there was no keel batten or anything to form a back rabbet for the garboards, so that the cross floors connecting the butts of the ribs rested directly on top of the keel and were fastened to it. In this midsection the top corners of the keel were beveled so the square edge of the garboard would fit perfectly snug with only a slight caulking seam on the outside.

Of course the stem, forefoot, and deadwood were rabbeted in the conventional way. Most of this was cut out at the bench, except that some wood was frequently left in the stem rabbet to enable adjustment there after the frames were raised and faired as insurance for getting a perfect fit for the garboards and hood ends. Rabbets were simple as pie for the practiced professional. But the amateur and occasional builder will do well to go slowly and carefully here, and take the greatest pains, even laying out in pencil numerous full-sized sections of the rabbet to cut from.

The old builders commonly used only one section mold, called a "shadow." This was made to the inside shape of the midsection. The shadow method, by the way, is still employed occasionally by older builders, as I observed in 1952 in the Whalen Brothers shop in Calais, Maine. It requires special skill, however, and is not recommended for beginners, who should make separate molds for each section in their laydown.

The shadow was set in place and carefully plumbed and horned, and then secured. Around it were sprung fairing battens, the same thickness as the plank (½-inch pine). These battens were put on symmetrically in pairs, running from the stem rabbet to the transom. Their lay determined the shape of the boat, and judgement and a sure eye were required to spring them properly. It was a quick method, but the amateur need not despair. With multiple molds made from a carefully faired lay-down, he can achieve the same results, but with a much greater expenditure of time.

After the battens are on comes timbering. The ribs are put in cold in fitted pairs, shaped and beveled identically so that both sides of the boat will be the same. Timbers are of white oak, preferably selected from the butts of young, fast-growing trees that yield heavy wood and wide grain. The timber blanks are steam-bent to

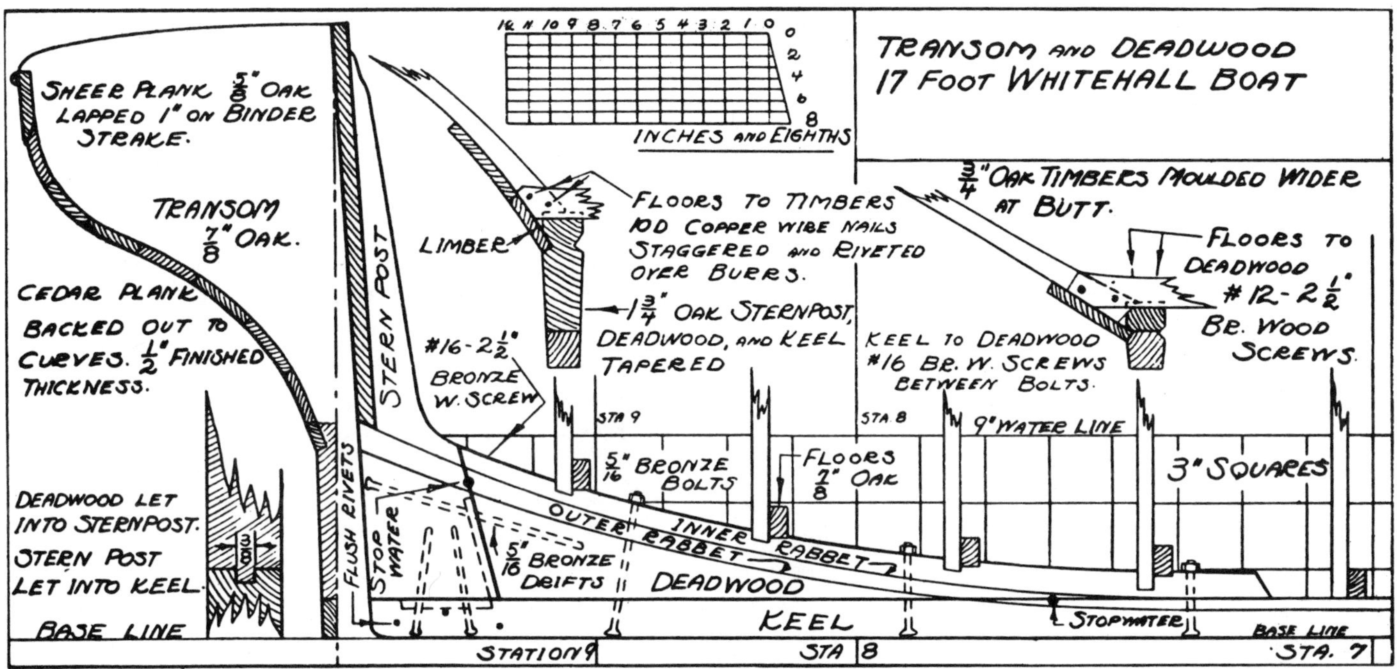

shape around forms and allowed to dry out for several days or weeks. They are given a little more bend than is required, for they can always be straightened out a trifle, if necessary, while it is impossible to give them more bend once they are cool and set. The shape from station to station does not change radically, making it possible to get along with only a few different bending forms for the entire boat. One of the tricks is to leave the timber blanks quite a bit longer at either end than will be needed. When cool and set, the bends can be adjusted lengthwise to get just the right curve.

The blanks should be about 1¾ inches wide, so a pair of timbers of ¾-inch siding can be split out of them on the circular saw, after the bend is in. Also, allowance in thickness should be made for a heavier butt, which is sometimes molded 1⅛ inches where it is riveted to the floor. Extra wood must also be allowed for bevels, which are put on at the bench with plane and spokeshave as the frame is tried in place against the ribbands, from time to time, until it lies flat and true.

The inside of the timbers should be beveled parallel to the outside, giving a diamond-shaped cross-section for the frames toward the ends of the boat. Each pair of timbers is joined together at the butts by an oak floor, which is screwed to the keel. The ribs are riveted to the floor with ten-penny copper nails. Amidships, the floors will extend on either side of the keel 10 to 12 inches, conforming to the pitch of the deadrise, which is straight in the Whitehall for about half the width of the boat. Thus, these floors will have something of a flattened vee shape, so that it is best for strength to get them out of crooked live-edge boards with a run of grain conforming somewhat to this shape.

In some of the shorter, lighter Whitehalls, the floors were omitted on top of the forefoot and deadwood, and the frames that ended here were notched rather deeply into these members and nailed securely. While this is a neat, easy method, cross floors are stronger, and I have indicated these for the 17-foot model except for the two forward sets of frames.

The floors, which are sided ⅞ inch, are to be fastened to the keel with two screws far enough apart to allow a ⅜-inch limber to be cut between them out of the bottom of the floor. Fore and aft where the lower ends of the ribs come against the siding of the forefoot and the deadwood, respectively, their tips are snipped off to provide limbers. Limbers are most important so that the boat can drain the entire length of its bottom.

When the ribs and floors are all beveled and in and fastened securely, the boat is ready for planking. But before going on to that stage, it is necessary to revert to some details that need more explanation.

When possible, a knee from hackmatack or white oak should be used for the stem; such natural knees were much used in the best of the old boats. Lacking a knee, there is an excellent substitute construction in which parts of a pieced stem are cut out of oak plank. Of course, a curved plank with a swirling grain should be selected, especially for the end of the forefoot that fastens on to the bottom of the fore part of the stem. This method of framing a stem, as shown in the detail drawing, was widely used in Boston shops in the late nineteenth century for plumb-stemmed small craft, including St. Lawrence River skiffs and the double-ended Adirondack, popular for rowing on the Charles in the 1890s and sometimes mistaken, today, for a variety of peapod. The extra siding of the tapered apron is to give more bearing in the rabbet for the hood ends, as the topsides get fuller at the bow. The apron is let in as far as the apex line of the rabbet for convenience in cutting the rabbet. The forefoot is made to run back on top of the keel for reinforcement and to provide a back-rabbet for the forward ends of the garboards.

In the past, the stem assembly was fastened with bolts or riveted drifts. It can just as well be fastened with heavy bronze screws—No. 16s or No. 18s—and with several advantages. Properly put in, screws pull up very tightly. They do not stick out like bolts and do not require boring through and plugging the outer edge of the stem, which is thinned down to ⅜ inch. Waterproof glue can also be used to advantage on the stem joints, but it must genuinely waterproof and not merely "water resistant." It may be advantageous to bolt the keel to the forefoot. Five-sixteenths inch diameter bronze carriage bolts are suitable.

Wherever the rabbet crosses a joint, as between the keel and forefoot, or deadwood and sternpost, a stopwater must be put in to prevent leakage. These round, pine plugs that run at right angles through the joint from side to side, must fit tightly, and the holes for them should be bored just inside the outer line of the rabbet so that the caulking in the garboard seam bears firmly on them. The most common mistake is to bore the hole too far inside the rabbet, where the caulking cannot reach the stopwater, allowing the water to seep in between. Four ⅜-inch stopwaters are called for, as indicated.

Five-sixteenth-inch diameter bronze bolts are proposed for the deadwood, and bronze drifts of the same diameter should be used to secure the lower end of the stern post. It is important that the members that join the sternpost be let in to one another as shown in the detail. Waterproof glue is also desirable here. True, the old builders had neither waterproof glue nor bronze screws, but as good mechanics who in their day prided themselves on being up-and-coming and up-to-date, they would certainly have adopted both screws and glue had they been available.

It might seem that there is not enough fastening in the stern assembly, so it may be pointed out that the after end will become amply strong and rigid when the boat is complete, that is, when the plank are screwed to the transom, the gunwales and their connecting knees riveted to the transom, and the stern bench is in place and secured to the sternpost and to the after frames. The stern bench is not merely a place to sit. It is also a bracing member that ties the entire stern together, imparting great rigidity to the end of the boat when properly fastened in.

There is a chance that the after end of the keel could split where it is bored for the drifts that pass up into the sternpost. For reinforcement, three flush rivets are shown. A better, but more expensive device would be a bronze casting let in flush to cover the end of the keel and to run partway up the sternpost. In case a rudder were to be shipped, a socket might be provided in this casting for the bottom pintle.

To secure the floors to the keel, I settled on

No. 12 bronze screws, but not without some misgivings. Bronze screws, even Everdur, do not last too well in damp oak. Nor is a large screw desirable, as boring for it could unduly weaken the narrow floors. Copper nails would loosen. Through rivets would be very long, indeed. Perhaps 2½ or 2¾-inch hot-dipped galvanized blunt-point boat nails would be the strongest and most lasting fastenings here—two to a floor and toed in to pull against each other.

Comparing the scantlings of this 17-footer with that of an original 13-foot Whitehall, differences will be found that might seem to anyone other than a boatbuilder too slight to notice. Yet I have had to argue with myself to justify each of these increases, and it may be that this boat is slightly on the heavy side. This is not such a bad fault in a 17-foot boat that can stand a little extra weight; it is not intended to be tossed around like a light tender.

Compared to a 13-footer, the siding of the stem, keel, deadwood, and sternpost has been increased from 1½ to 1¾ inches. The keel is molded ¼ inch deeper. The transom thickness has been increased from ¾ inch to ⅞ inch. The timbers are spaced on 9-inch centers instead of 9½-inch, and, while their siding of ¾ inch has not been changed, they are molded heavier at the butt and ⅛ inch heavier at the gunwale. The floors have been increased from ¾ inch by 1 inch to ⅞ inch by 1¼ inches. The cedar planking is ½ inch finished, and the oak sheer strake 9/16 inch. The gunwales will be about ⅛ wider and thicker all around, with corresponding increases in the breasthook and interior knees. While ship carpenters might not have needed divisions less than 8ths marked on their rules, as old Tom Hines used to say, your builder of small boats was a different breed of cat who was very fussy over 16th and even 32nds.

PLANKING

Whitehall planking shows a few special features, otherwise standard planking methods are used. It might prove helpful to run through the main planking operations as used by professionals for the Whitehall. These operations, which apply to smooth-seam boats, even upwards of 40 feet, are as follows:

1. *Lining*, which is dividing up the hull surface and lining out fair, uniform plank shapes of desirable width and taper.
2. *Spiling*, which is picking up the plank shapes from the curved surface of the hull and laying them out flat on the planking stock.
3. *Getting Out*, which is sawing out the plank to shape, planing the edges true and to the line, and beveling them, and backing out, that is, planing the back of the plank hollow to fit the curve of the ribs.
4. *Hanging*, which is bending, setting down, and fastening the plank in place.

After these four steps, the planked hull is planed smooth, caulked, scraped, and sanded.

And now, a few special features of Whitehall planking:

When the ribbands are spaced and bent on prior to timbering, the position of the binding plank is determined and a space is left for it so it can be put on without disturbing any ribbands. The binding plank, or "binder," which is the plank below the sheer plank, is the first to go on. This is required because the sheer plank laps over it exactly as if the boat were clinker built. The sheer plank in this boat is 9/16-inch oak, lapped 1¼ inches and chamfered to ¼ inch on the lap edge, which is finished in all true Boston Whitehalls with a shallow ¼-inch bead for appearance. Riveted up solid, this heavy, lapped sheer plank is the staunchest of construction.

Next, after the binder and the sheer planks are on, the two planks directly below them are hung and fastened. At this point in Whitehall construction, planking is interrupted, and the builder proceeds to install gunwales, breast hook, risers, thwarts, bench, knees, and all interior work. The boat, being right-side-up, is in a convenient position for this work—chips and shavings can fall through the unplanked bottom—and the boat is made rigid by this interior work, so that when it is turned over to get at the bottom, it does not go out of shape.

This interior work completed, the boat is removed from its "landing," that is, the heavy

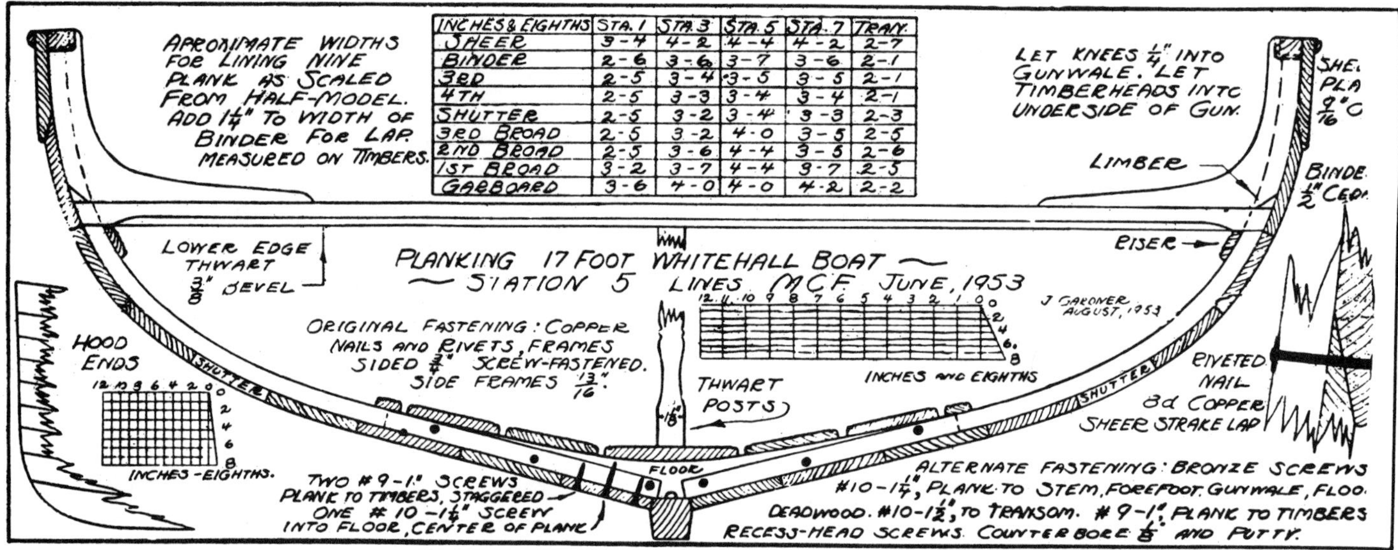

INCHES & EIGHTHS	STA. 1	STA. 3	STA. 5	STA. 7	TRAN.
SHEER	3-4	4-2	4-4	4-2	2-7
BINDER	2-6	3-6	3-7	3-6	2-1
3RD	2-5	3-4	3-5	3-5	2-1
4TH	2-5	3-3	3-4	3-4	2-1
SHUTTER	2-5	3-2	3-4	3-3	2-3
3RD BROAD	2-5	3-2	4-0	3-5	2-5
2ND BROAD	2-5	3-6	4-4	3-5	2-6
1ST BROAD	3-2	3-7	4-4	3-7	2-5
GARBOARD	3-6	4-0	4-0	4-2	2-2

plank set edgewise under the keel, and is turned bottom up on two horses of convenient height. Planking is resumed, starting with the garboards. In this particular boat, three broads will follow them, and finally the shutter at the turn of the bilge will finish the job. Of course plank is always hung and fastened in symmetrical strakes, so that one side is never more than one plank ahead of the other.

Originally, copper nails and rivets were used in plank fastening, but I believe that bronze screws properly selected for size and correctly put in would be just as strong and lasting, would pull tighter, and are certainly easier and quicker to use. In this type of construction it is essential to calculate the size of the fastenings very precisely, for the best of woodwork is to no avail when a boat gets "nailsick." In case screws are used, it might be on the safe side to make the timbers slightly heavier, say 13/16 inch instead of 3/4 inch.

Even if screws are to be used, it is perhaps best to rivet the sheer strake lap with 8-penny nails, heads set flush as I have shown. This is strong and looks neat with the top strake bright, as is proper for the Whitehall. Opinion may differ as to the size of screws, but for plank to timbers I would choose No. 9, 1 inch long. These would be set below the finished surface 1/8 inch and puttied, which means they would extend 5/8 inch into the white oak timbers.

The holes should be bored exactly the right size, as experimentally determined, to give the threads maximum grip, but not to strain the screw when driving or split the timbers. Lubricate the screws with soap. I prefer putty instead of bungs, because bungs would have to be 3/8 inch in diameter, which requires going too deeply into 1/2-inch plank to make the bung secure. As the boat is to be painted, the appearance of putty or wood bungs is all the same.

For planking to stem, forefoot, gunwales, thwart knees, floors, deadwood, and all other places where there is plenty of wood in the backing member, a slightly larger screw is desirable, that is a No. 10 in lengths of 1 1/8 inches and 1 1/4 inches. For the plank ends on the transom, a No. 10, 1 1/2 inches should be used, because the screw will be going into end-grain wood. Bronze is the only acceptable kind of screw. Brass is too weak, and galvanized screws do not hold well in small sizes because of their inferior threads. The recessed-head screw is far superior to any other kind, both for driving and for appearance.

Nine plank to a side are best for this boat. Eight plank would do, but with 10 plank the hood ends would be too narrow. Plank should be lined in fair, sweeping curves, as straight as possible. For this a lining batten is required. This is a straight, uniform strip of wood, longer than the boat, that will take a fair curve when bent edgewise. White pine is the best wood for such a batten, which for this boat would be ⅜ inch thick by about 1¾ inches wide.

For lining, consider the hull shape of a boat like the Whitehall in two sections—the first section is the topsides down to a fair sweep running along the turn of the bilge, which is obtained by tacking the lining batten on the timbers in an easy, natural position, and the second section is the bottom. Divide up the topsides so the plank will line out to be as straight and uniform as possible, except that the sheer plank is made somewhat wider both for strength and appearance. For the bottom, the planks can be wider than those in the topside, as the term "broads" indicates.

Try to manage the lining of the broads so as to avoid excessive curves; being out of sight, the shape does not matter so much as in the topsides. In this boat run both ends of the garboard up as high as possible without "fishtailing" the plank—a fishtailed plank is one wider at the ends than in the center. Keeping up the ends of the garboard will tend to straighten out the broads. Besides, upsweeping plank ends, so long as they are not overdone, are desirable for appearance. When the hood ends sag, especially in a full-ended boat, an ugly, drooping condition results. This is known as "moose shoulders" down Nova Scotia way. (For more details on battens and spiling, see the Appendix.)

Now on to getting out the plank: After the planks are roughed out to shape by saw, their edges are jointed with the plane exactly to the lines. Some put on the edge bevels next, and back out last to fit the curve of the ribs. For plank as thin as ½ inch, and for a boat of the size and curvature of this 17-foot Whitehall, the old builders often backed out the plank before beveling, hollowing them exactly to templates of thin wood marked against the ribs. For hollowing, a couple of backing-out planes are needed, that is, wooden smoothing planes with slightly convex soles and irons ground to suit. Too much curve in the bottoms of the planes makes it difficult to do an exact job.

After the planks were backed out, the edges are beveled. To get the correct bevel, which increases, a small planker's square with a tongue about 1 inch long (see drawing) is used. This is held against the inside of the hollow, the angle of the blade of the square indicating the amount to be planed off the side edge of the plank. In this way the bevel is divided between the two abutting planks, which is neater construction and better for caulking than leaving one plank edge square and putting all the bevel on the other.

On a boat like this, the planks should form a perfectly tight seam on the inside, and should open just enough on the outside to permit a very thin thread of wicking to be rolled in. Some open the seam slightly after the boat is planked by plowing it with a thin, sharp, flat fid of lignum vitae. Another way is to burnish or compress the outer edges of the plank, before the plank is hung, by rubbing them firmly lengthwise with the hammer handle. After the wicking has been rolled into such seams and primed with thin paint, they may be sponged with hot water, and they will close tightly around the cotton.

This boat is a slack-bilged model that will take plank easily. It may be necessary to soften a couple of feet on the fore ends of the garboard and broads to get them to twist into place, but steaming is not necessary. To make the hood ends pliable, a teakettle of boiling water is sufficient. Wrap the end of the plank in some old woolen rags to hold the heat and soak with hot water, letting the rag-wrapped plank set a while to soften.

Start hanging the plank by clamping the hood end securely into the stem rabbet. Wrap the plank around the timbers firmly and carefully. Don't jump it. Use plenty of clamps, sets, wedges, and whatever else is necessary to get the plank down snugly and tightly throughout. A way positively guaranteed to split a plank is to try to pull it into place with its fastenings. In thin planks like these, planks and timbers must be wood-to-wood before any fastening is attempted. If a seam does not close up properly, by all means take the plank off and fix it. As has

Though classic Whitehalls were carvel planked, lapstrake versions have been built. The photographs above and right show Golden Wings, *built to the lines of the 17-foot Whitehall by Bob Coe of Waldron Island, Washington. The hull is finished bright.*

been explained, great pains should be taken with the fastening, especially in light construction like this where there is no margin for error. Drills need to be exactly the right size. Counterboring should be neither too deep nor too shallow.

If the shutter is spiled with care, it should give no trouble. A snug fit is desirable, but not so snug that hard pounding is required to force the shutter down into place. Half-inch cedar is too soft to hammer much. Don't be afraid to take the plank out several times to plane off a fine shaving where required.

After the boat is planked, very little outboard planing should be necessary. In fact, the backed-out plank should be gauged ½ inch at the bench and the outside rounded off nearly to thickness on a convex curve corresponding to the hollow of the inside. If this is done accurately, only a few shavings will need to be planed off after planking, and the wicking may be rolled directly into the seams after the plank are on. Planing should be done first in a fore-and-aft direction, then all over lightly at an angle of 45 degrees. This last is called "traversing," and is required for a smooth job. In scraping and sanding, the hull should also be traversed as well as gone over in a fore-and-aft direction.

Of course the hood ends of the plank in the stem rabbet, and the garboard seam next to the keel and deadwood, will need to be caulked with a thin iron and the mallet. In these parts the cotton must be driven firmly, but not so hard as to strain the plank or fastenings, or to go through where there is no back-rabbet. The boat is puttied and painted in the conventional way, except that usually the top-strake, transom, gunwale, thwarts, bench, and interior knees were finished bright in the original Whitehalls.

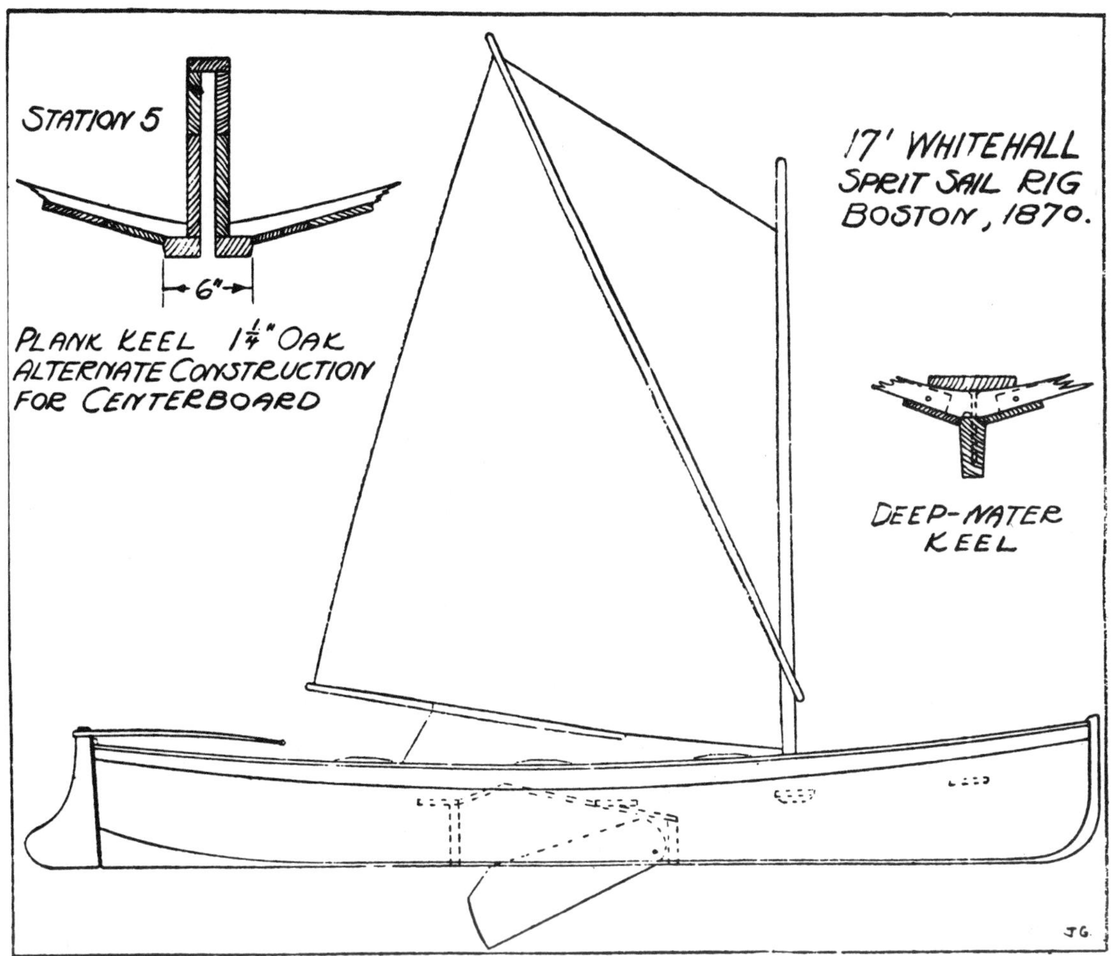

THE SAILING RIG

Whitehalls were tuned for an ash breeze, but like most small boats in the pre-gasoline era, they were generally rigged for canvas, too. When special provision for sailing was desired, builders increased the beam and often installed a centerboard.

The 17-foot model described here for building is of generous beam for a Whitehall, without being too wide to row. If a centerboard is wanted, it must be located so that the rig can be balanced. Also it should not take up any more space than is absolutely necessary or obstruct rowing. Furthermore it must be tight, and constructed so as not to weaken the boat. It is best, if a centerboard is to be installed, to use a plank keel about 6 inches wide amidships where the board goes through, tapering to the siding of the stem and sternpost at the ends. If there is any question about scantling, err on the heavy side, for a box that works or leaks is good for nothing.

The suggested rig is modest. Certainly the hull would carry more sail, but this is safe and practical to start with. Anyone who intended to sail this boat a lot would undoubtedly want to work out his own rig by experiment, to suit his own needs and preferences. The spritsail was typical and very widely used by contemporary small sailing craft, although the leg-of-mutton sail was also seen. Sometimes a small jib was used.

As shown, the sail can be furled in an instant by wrapping it around the mast, which is light spruce and unstayed. The mast can then be

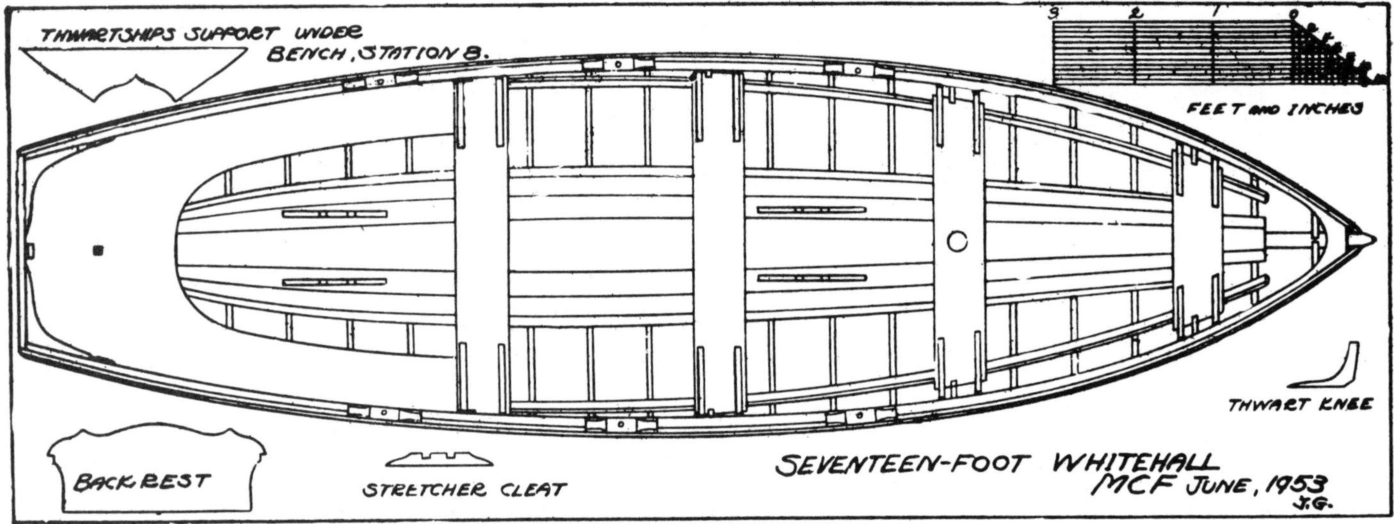

quickly unstepped, lifted through the thwart, and stowed along the thwarts when the boat is under oars, or while waiting for a breeze. The sail is shown with a club. Sometimes spritsails had full-length booms, but more frequently they were loose-footed.

FINISHING OUT

The interior construction of the Whitehall is simple, light, and strong. Essentially it is the same construction more recently used for fine yacht tenders such as those that Lawley built at Neponset, Massachusetts, except that these later boats had the modern open gunwale bent in on the inside of the timbers instead of forming a tight cap over the timberheads.

As was previously explained, the Whitehall interior, with the exception of the floorboards, was put in before the bottom was planked while the boat was still upright on its landing. The gunwales are ⅞-inch oak 1⅛ inches wide on the flat and tapering at the extreme ends to ⅞ inch. They are installed in one continuous piece running from the transom to a snug fit against the apron, and are beveled slightly so they pitch outboard to conform, for appearance, to a moderate thwartships camber.

The gunwale rests on top of the timberheads, which are let into its under side about ⅛ inch, enough to lock them securely. The bow is tied together with a breasthook, preferably made from a natural crook of apple or white oak. This is rivet-fastened with 10-penny copper wire nails through the gunwales and top strakes. The stem, apron and breasthook are drawn together by a through-length of ¼-inch copper rod riveted up tightly. At the stern the knees are also riveted to the sheer and transom.

The seat risers are screwed to the timbers eight to 8½ inches below the top of the gunwales. These risers should be ½ inch by 2 inches, tapering to 1¾ inches at the ends. This will bring the upper surface of the thwarts 7 to 7½ inches below the top of the gunwales, which is the standard distance.

The thwarts are 8 inches wide, ⅞ inch thick, run to the skin, and are notched snugly around the frames. Originally the best workmanship called for two knees on either end of the thwarts. Ralph Davidson of New Castle, New Hampshire, used this construction 50 years ago. I have seen such boats on the St. Croix built at that time or earlier with double sets of knees all around. As a boy I knew a retired boatbuilder from Portsmouth, New Hampshire, who told me he went into his father's shop in that city some years before the Civil War as a young lad of 13. His first job, he recalled, was pushing a hand saw 10 hours a day roughing out applewood knees. Lots of them were used in those days.

While suitable crooks for thwart knees are not to be found in modern lumberyards—even hackmatack knees are almost unheard of today—there are still plenty of apple trees, and, if a person has in mind to build a boat, he can keep a lookout for suitable timber and store it away against the day of building.

There is a good substitute for natural-grown knees—laminated knees. These are glued up from ⅛-inch strips of ash or mahogany. Oak is harder to glue properly because of an acid in that wood.

The strips for laminated knees should be got out about 2 inches wide on the circular saw. A lamination this wide can be split into a pair of matched knees. The prepared strips should be bent around a form of suitable shape and drawn up with plenty of clamps until the glue has set. If the strips are got out on a sharp, well-filed saw, they will be smooth enough as they come from the saw to glue.

The thwarts and thwart-knees join the gunwales and upper planks, and, with their supporting posts, form important bracing members—they are trusses as well as seats. The thwarts need to be strong. Ash or mahogany are good timber for them, but oak is too heavy. In spacing them in a boat of this size, seating capacity has to be taken into account, but above all it is necessary to provide for good rowing trim, either for one or two oarsmen. Where the mast hole goes through the second thwart, a heavy oak cleat for reinforcement is required on the underside.

The bench that occupies the stern sheets braces and stiffens the entire after end of the boat. Of course the bench is laid out especially for sailing. When the boat is being rowed, one or two may sit in the stern, and for their comfort a backrest is indicated, as was customary in such boats. The backrest fits into shallow notches in the gunwales and a ⅜-inch pin in the bottom of the rest slips into a hole in a small plate set flush into the surface of the bench. The bench is made of the same stuff as the thwarts and is notched to fit tightly around the sternpost and timbers. It is screwed down to cleats on the transom and to the seat risers. At station No. 8, the bench rests on a bridging cross-member, the ends of which halve on to the pair of timbers closest to that station, forming a partial bulkhead. The forward ends of the bench are joined to the after thwart and are securely cleated underneath.

The longitudinal floorboards are sometimes fitted snugly and are sometimes spaced slightly apart. They will be ½ inch thick, except the center one, which is thicker so that it can be shaped on the underside to fit the top of the cross floors. Under the last thwart, which is the low point of the boat, the center strip has a 4-inch hole for sponging out the bottom. For proper drainage it is well to have a light brass chain threaded through the limbers, for these are small and easily plugged with loose dirt. Also, they are out of reach, for the floor strips form a partial ceiling and are screwed down tightly to the cross-floors, not the frames. This ties the bottom together and strengthens and stiffens it a great deal. Pulling the chain back and forth clears the limbers.

Chocks are indicated for stretchers for the oarsmen to brace against. Obviously these should be as low as possible, with corners well rounded off. Three sets of rowlocks are shown. The standard location is to center them 11 inches aft of the aft edge of the rowing thwart. The rowlock socket is set into an oak pad ⅝ inch by 1¾ inches by 11 inches, and beveled as shown. This is a reinforcing piece that fastens into the sheer strake and gunwale.

For ornamentation, the old Whitehalls had a shallow ¼-inch bead run on the following members: lower edge of the gunwale, both edges of the seat risers, both edges of the floor ceiling and both upper edges of the thwarts. The under edges of the thwarts were chamfered ⅜ inch to give them a slimmer appearance.

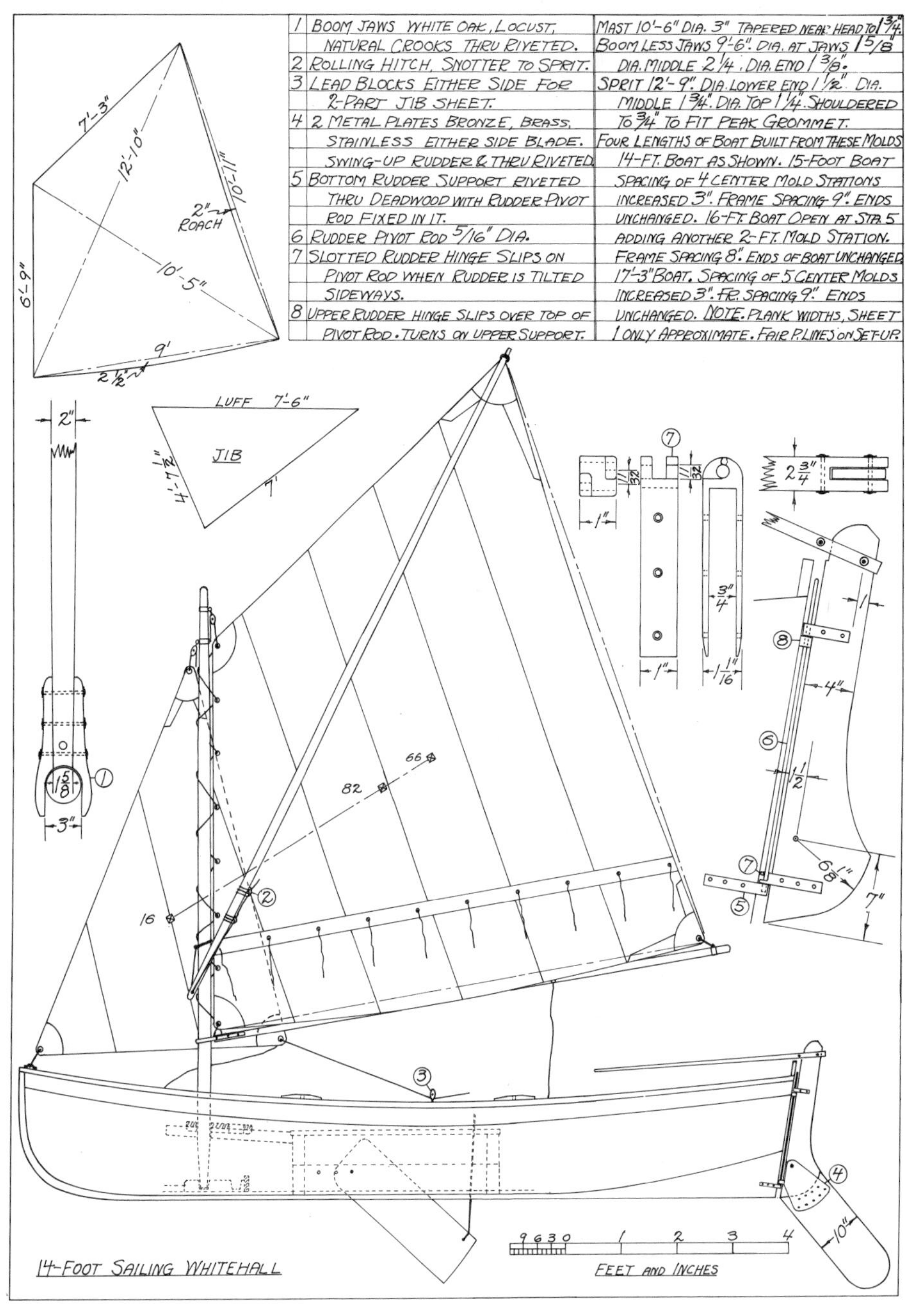

Plans for a 14-foot sailing Whitehall. The sail plan above and the plans on the next two pages provide sufficient detail for the amateur to build a good multi-purpose Whitehall. The planking widths, the first ever shown for a Whitehall, were taken off a 2"=1' scale model of the boat. A description of the building process for this boat appeared in the February and March, 1977, issues of the National Fisherman.

14 Foot Whitehall

OFFSETS INSIDE OF PLANKING — FEET, INCHES, EIGHTHS		STEM	1	2	3	4	5	6	7	8	TRAN.
HALF-BREADTHS	SHEER	0-0-6	0-9-0	1-2-0	1-6-2	2-0-1	2-1-2	2-0-3	1-9-1	1-6-1	1-2-4
	20" WATER LINE	0-0-6	0-8-3	1-1-2	1-5-6	2-0-0	2-1-2	2-0-2	1-8-4	1-5-1	1-0-6
	16" W.L.	0-0-6	0-7-2	1-0-1	1-4-4	1-11-0	2-0-4	1-11-2	1-7-2	1-3-1	0-8-6
	12" W.L.	0-0-6	0-5-6	0-10-1	1-2-5	1-9-3	1-11-0	1-9-5	1-4-5	0-9-3	0-2-4
	8" W.L.	0-0-6	0-3-6	0-7-2	0-11-4	1-6-5	1-8-0	1-5-5	0-10-1	0-1-7	—
HEIGHTS ABOVE B.L.	SHEER	2-3-4	2-1-2	1-11-4	1-10-2	1-8-4	1-8-2	1-9-0	1-10-6	2-0-2	2-2-1
	BEARDING LINE	0-1-4	0-2-6	0-1-6	0-1-4	0-1-4	0-1-4	0-1-4	0-4-0	0-7-2	0-10-4
	BUTTOCK 6"	—	1-0-4	0-6-6	0-4-4	0-2-7	0-2-7	0-3-3	0-6-2	0-10-2	1-2-5
	BUTT. 12"	—	—	1-4-0	0-8-5	0-4-4	0-4-3	0-5-4	0-9-0	1-1-4	1-7-0
	BUTT. 17"	—	—	—	1-6-0	0-6-6	0-6-0	0-7-6	1-0-4	1-7-7	—
	DIAGONAL A	0-0-7	0-8-5	1-1-2	1-5-2	1-11-0	2-0-1	—	—	—	—
	DIAG. B	0-1-0	0-7-2	0-10-6	1-1-5	1-5-0	1-5-1	—	—	—	—
	DIAG. C	—	—	—	—	—	2-0-4	1-11-4	1-8-6	1-4-7	1-1-1
	DIAG D	—	—	—	—	—	2-3-0	2-1-7	1-9-7	1-6-0	1-1-7

DIAG. A 1-9-0 ABOVE B.L. OUT 1-9-0 ON 8" W.L. DIAG. B 1-4-0 ABOVE B.L. OUT 1-5-4 ON B.L. DIAG C, 2-2-0 ABOVE B.L. OUT 1-0-0 ON B.L. DIAG D 2-2-0 ABOVE B.L. OUT 2-0-0.

STEM OAK $1\frac{1}{2}$" TH'K

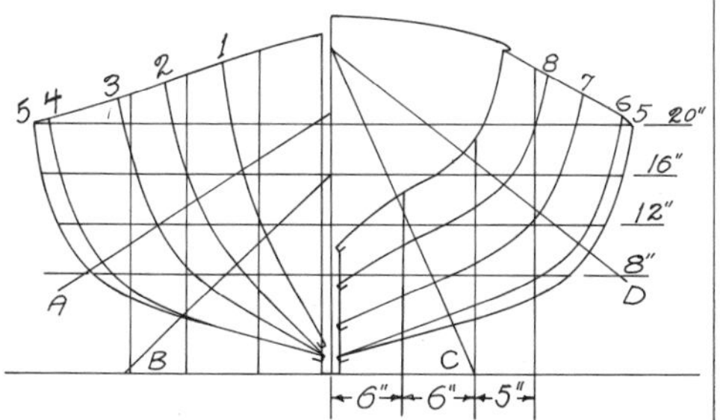

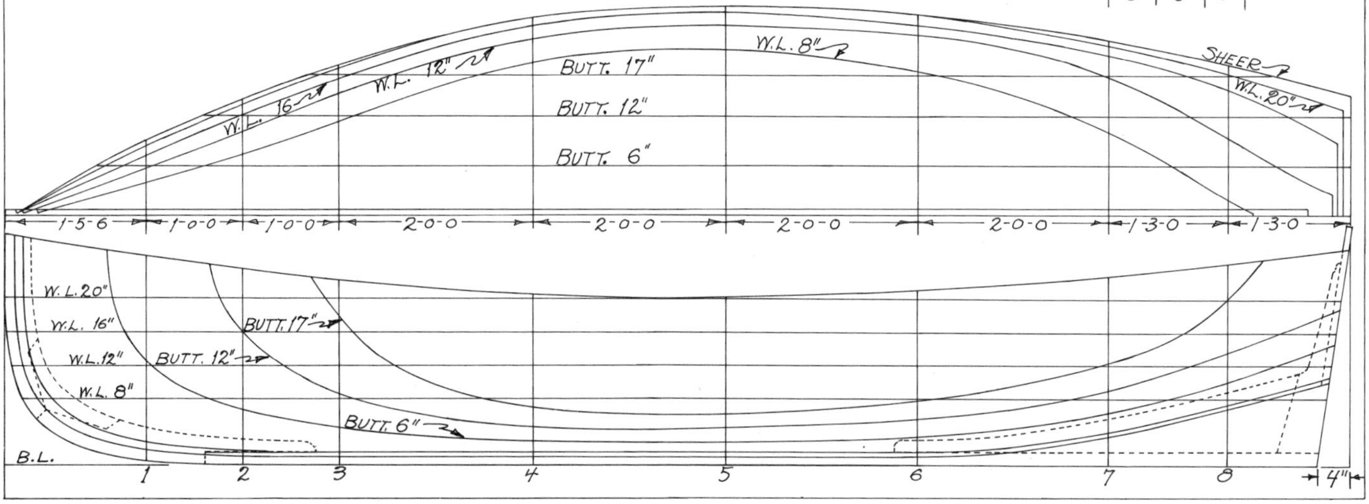

HORIZONTAL MEASUREMENTS FROM STA. 1	SHEER	W.L. 20	W.L. 16	W.L. 12	W.L. 8
OUTSIDE	1-5-6	1-5-6	1-5-4	1-4-7	1-3-4
RABBET	1-4-4	1-4-3	1-4-2	1-3-4	1-1-5
BEARDING	1-3-3	1-3-2	1-3-0	1-2-0	0-11-4
INSIDE	1-2-2	1-2-1	1-1-6	1-0-3	0-9-0

VERTICAL MEASUREMENTS DOWN FROM W.L. 8"	INSIDE	BEARDING	RABBET	OUTSIDE
STA. 3	—	0-6-3	0-7-0	0-8-0
STA. 2	0-4-6	0-6-2	0-7-0	0-8-0
STA. 1	0-3-4	0-5-1	0-6-1	0-7-4
STA. A	0-0-0	0-2-1	0-3-6	0-5-4

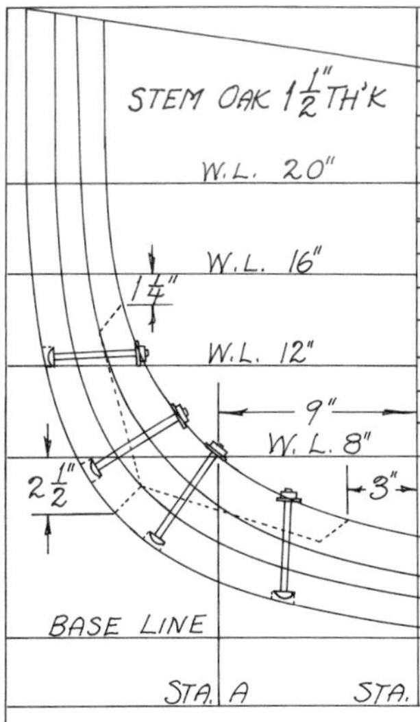

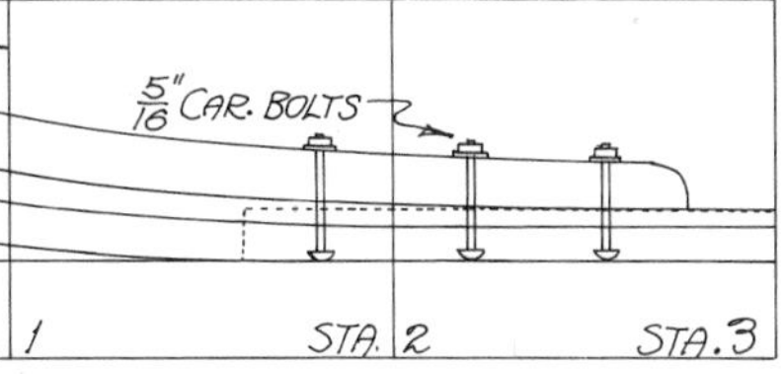

PLANKS	GAR'D	2	3	4	5	6	7	SHEER
STEM	—	2-5	2-5	2-5	2-5	2-5	4-0	4-0
STA. 1	3-3	2-5	3-0	2-6	2-7	2-7	4-1	4-4
STA. 2	3-4	3-0	3-0	3-0	3-0	3-0	4-4	4-4
STA. 3	3-6	3-3	3-4	3-3	3-3	3-1	4-6	4-5
STA. 4	4-2	4-1	4-3	4-0	3-6	3-6	5-1	5-0
STA. 5	4-5	4-3	4-4	4-1	3-5	3-6	5-3	5-0
STA. 6	4-6	4-2	4-2	4-0	3-6	3-6	5-1	5-0
STA. 7	4-5	3-6	3-4	3-4	3-2	3-2	4-7	4-4
STA. 8	3-1	3-2	3-0	3-1	2-7	2-7	4-3	3-7
TRANSOM	2-4	3-0	2-4	2-4	2-4	2-4	4-0	3-6

PLANK WIDTHS INCHES & EIGHTHS — INSIDE PLANK. SHEER PLANK OVERLAPS NO. 7 $1\frac{1}{8}$ INCHES. WIDTHS STEM & STERN MEASURED SQUARE WITH RUN OF PLANK. FAIR WIDTHS ON BOAT WITH BATTEN.

$\frac{5}{16}$" CAR. BOLTS

Station 6

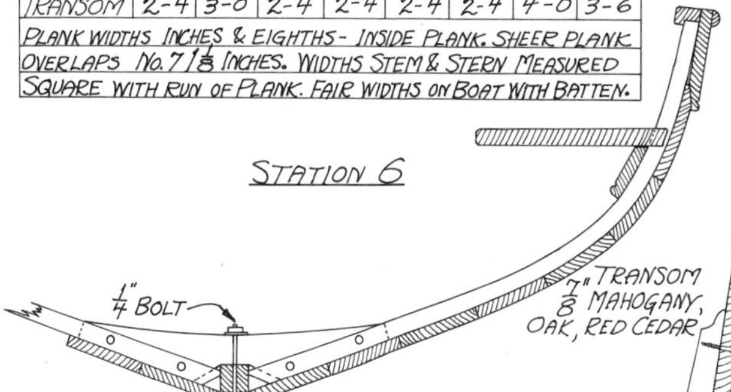

$\frac{1}{4}$" BOLT

$\frac{7}{8}$" TRANSOM MAHOGANY, OAK, RED CEDAR

Station 8

STERN SHEETS

RIVET

SHEER PLANK $\frac{5}{8}$" OAK

$\frac{1}{4}$" PIN

FEET AND INCHES

PLANKING CEDAR $\frac{9}{16}$" WT. PINE FINISH

BEARDING

STOP WATER

RABBET LINE

$\frac{3}{8}$" TENNON

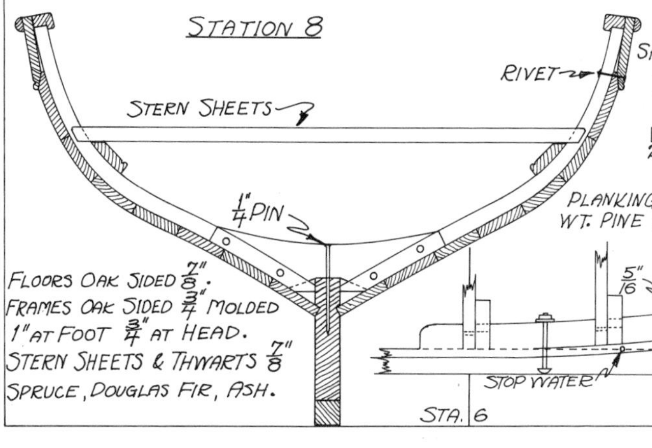

FLOORS OAK SIDED $\frac{7}{8}$". FRAMES OAK SIDED $\frac{3}{4}$" MOLDED 1" AT FOOT $\frac{3}{4}$" AT HEAD. STERN SHEETS & THWARTS $\frac{7}{8}$" SPRUCE, DOUGLAS FIR, ASH.

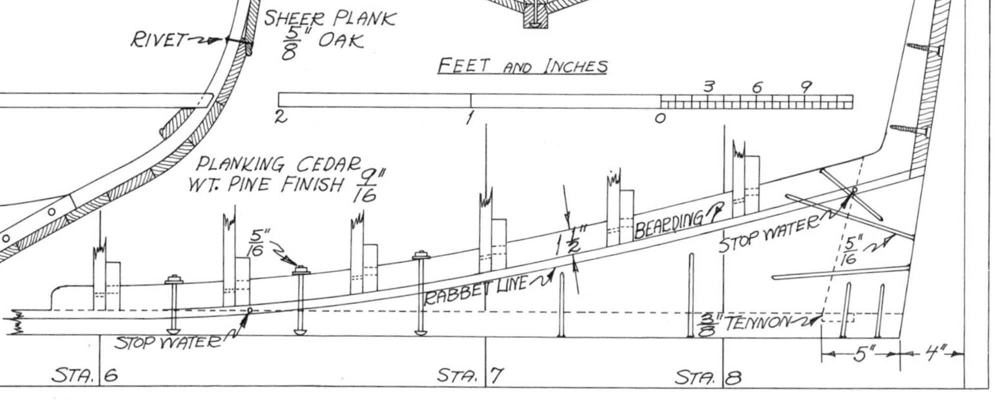

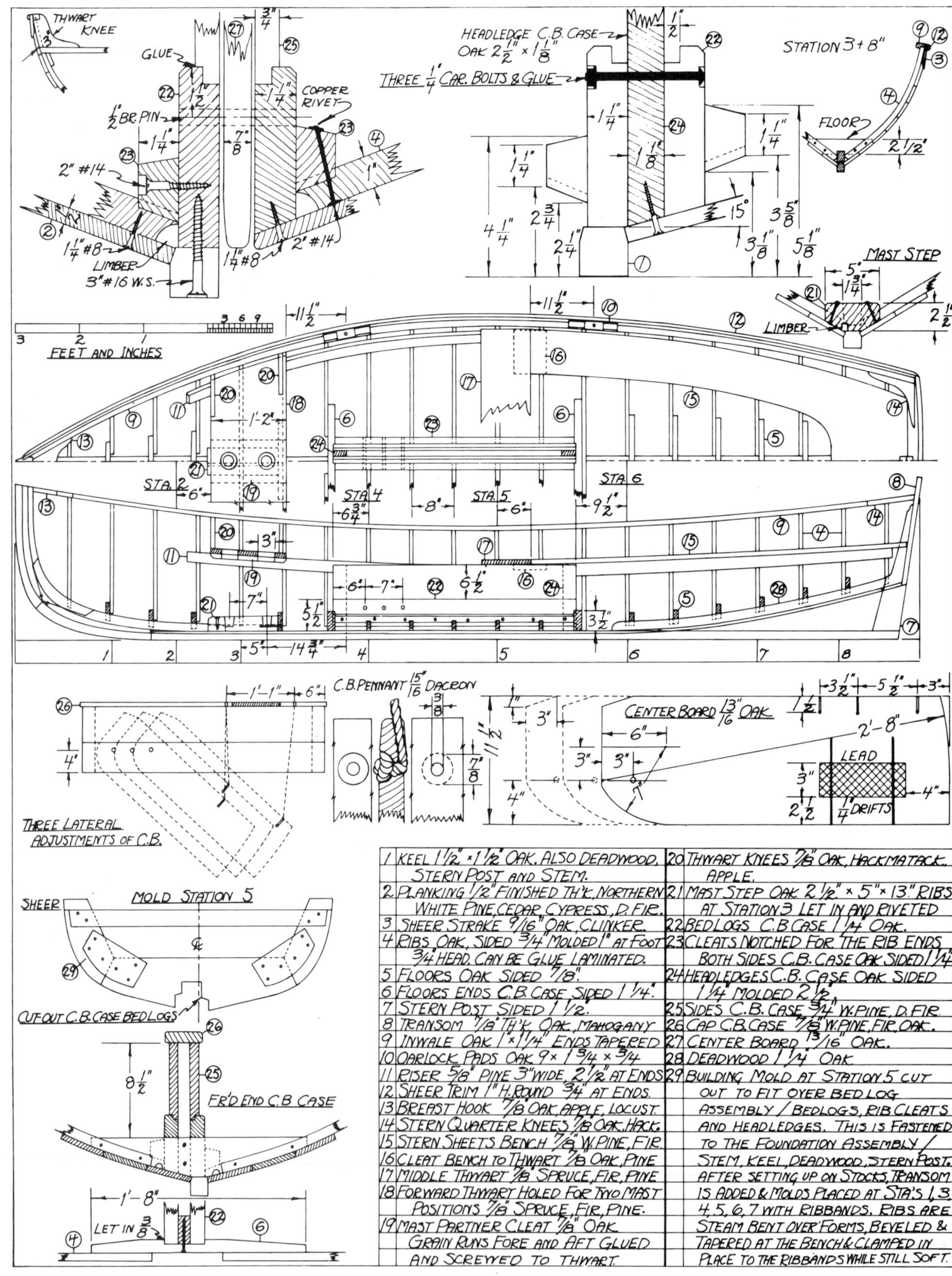

1	KEEL 1 1/2" × 1 1/2" OAK. ALSO DEADWOOD, STERN POST AND STEM.
2	PLANKING 1/2" FINISHED TH'K, NORTHERN WHITE PINE, CEDAR, CYPRESS, D. FIR.
3	SHEER STRAKE 9/16" OAK, CLINKER.
4	RIBS, OAK, SIDED 3/4" MOLDED 1" AT FOOT 3/4" HEAD. CAN BE GLUE LAMINATED.
5	FLOORS OAK SIDED 7/8".
6	FLOORS ENDS C.B. CASE SIDED 1 1/4".
7	STERN POST SIDED 1 1/2.
8	TRANSOM 7/8" TH'K, OAK, MAHOGANY
9	INWALE OAK 1" × 1 1/4" ENDS TAPERED
10	OARLOCK PADS OAK 9 × 1 3/4 × 3/4
11	RISER 5/8" PINE 3" WIDE, 2 1/2" AT ENDS
12	SHEER TRIM 1" H. ROUND 3/4" AT ENDS.
13	BREAST HOOK 7/8 OAK, APPLE, LOCUST.
14	STERN QUARTER KNEES 7/8 OAK, HACK.
15	STERN SHEETS BENCH 7/8" W. PINE, FIR.
16	CLEAT BENCH TO THWART 7/8 OAK, PINE
17	MIDDLE THWART 7/8 SPRUCE, FIR, PINE
18	FORWARD THWART HOLED FOR TWO MAST POSITIONS 7/8" SPRUCE, FIR, PINE.
19	MAST PARTNER CLEAT 7/8" OAK GRAIN RUNS FORE AND AFT GLUED AND SCREWED TO THWART.
20	THWART KNEES 7/8" OAK, HACKMATACK, APPLE.
21	MAST STEP OAK 2 1/2" × 5" × 13." RIBS AT STATION 3 LET IN AND RIVETED
22	BEDLOGS C.B CASE 1 1/4" OAK.
23	CLEATS NOTCHED FOR THE RIB ENDS BOTH SIDES C.B. CASE OAK SIDED 1 1/4"
24	HEADLEDGES C.B. CASE OAK SIDED 1 1/4" MOLDED 2 1/2".
25	SIDES C.B. CASE 3/4" W. PINE, D. FIR.
26	CAP C.B. CASE 7/8" W. PINE, FIR, OAK.
27	CENTER BOARD 13/16" OAK.
28	DEADWOOD 1 1/4" OAK
29	BUILDING MOLD AT STATION 5 CUT OUT TO FIT OVER BED LOG ASSEMBLY / BEDLOGS, RIB CLEATS AND HEADLEDGES. THIS IS FASTENED TO THE FOUNDATION ASSEMBLY / STEM, KEEL, DEADWOOD, STERN POST. AFTER SETTING UP ON STOCKS, TRANSOM IS ADDED & MOLDS PLACED AT STA'S 1, 3, 4, 5, 6, 7 WITH RIBBANDS. RIBS ARE STEAM BENT OVER FORMS, BEVELED & TAPERED AT THE BENCH & CLAMPED IN PLACE TO THE RIBBANDS WHILE STILL SOFT.

(Above) A 15-foot Whitehall built at Mystic Seaport. (Below) The Whitehall Donoughue, *restored by Bob Baker. (Courtesy of Mystic Seaport)*

23 The Sea Bright Skiff

Before the gasoline engine, the shore fisheries in various locations along our northeast coast developed several closely related small boats for getting off and on the beach, often through moderate surf. These were of clinker build, virtually double-enders on their load lines and below, with relatively narrow, flat bottoms and round bilges. Of particular note are the wherries of colonial New England, of which a few surviving examples are still to be found on the Maine coast, the round-sided Swampscott dory, and the Sea Bright skiff of the New Jersey beaches. While their flat bottoms allowed these boats to sit upright on the beach, their sharp, high sterns permitted launching stern-first into the surf, as well as riding back on the surf bow-first when coming in to land on the beach.

The renown of the sea skiff of the New Jersey beaches, or the Sea Bright skiff, its more distinctive name, as a sea boat—able in surf, seakindly and safe in capable hands beyond most small craft of its size—has spread far beyond the exposed beaches of northern New Jersey. That the Sea Bright skiff originated as a special and possibly a unique development of those beaches alone, as is sometimes claimed, is a highly doubtful hypothesis, for there are several other American small craft types as old, if not older, which so closely resemble it and each other in all important respects that it is most unlikely they originated independently of each other.

The Maine salmon wherry of the Penobscot Bay region, the Saint John River salmon boat, the Staten Island skiff (also known as the "Yankee skiff" in the Chesapeake where it was once extensively used in the oyster fishery), and to some lesser extent the round-sided Swampscott fishing dory—all of these have so much in common with the early New Jersey sea or beach skiffs, before their gradual transformation brought about by their adaptation for the gasoline engine, that there is good reason for surmising all these craft to be the offspring of a common ancestor—the military bateaus of the French and Indian Wars of the mid-eighteenth century.

Peter Guthorn in his important book, *The Sea Bright Skiff and Other Jersey Shore Boats* (Rutgers University Press, Brunswick, N. J.), makes no attempt to go back to the eighteenth century, but starts with the boat adopted by fishermen operating off the beaches of northern Monmouth County near what is now Sea Bright, beginning about 1845. At that time a rising influx into New York City of large numbers of immigrants accustomed to fish in their diet made a profitable venture of fishing off the beaches south of Sandy Hook, which were close enough to market for the catch to arrive there in a fresh condition. According to Guthorn, in 1850 in the Long Beach area, fishing engaged 63 proprietors, each with two to four employees, as well as boats, seines, and other equipment.

No boat, accurate drawing, picture, or half-model has survived from this earliest period. Nevertheless, Guthorn's research has produced a considerable body of information as to what these early boats were like. This information is by no means complete, in fact it contains serious gaps, yet there is enough to enable us to make a start in the rescue from oblivion of this worthy craft. By bringing together, comparing, and collating bits and pieces of data from many diverse sources, by extrapolating from similar but later craft to supply missing details, by calling upon a boatbuilder's judgment and intuition, by utilizing acquaintance with trade practices and the characteristics of the building materials used, we may be able to recover and organize sufficient detail to enable present-day builders to construct reproductions of the early beach skiff worthy of its prototype and not inferior to it in performance.

At the beginning of his book, Guthorn lists some of the dimensions and other characteristics of the earliest beach skiffs. They were about 15 feet long, he tells us, with 5 feet of beam, increasing in length after 1880 to 17 feet. The flat, slightly rockered bottom was tapered toward the ends from a maximum width amidships of approximately one-third the beam; this varied somewhat with different builders. At the stern, a transom, which he describes as U-shaped, raked about 30 degrees from the vertical. The bilge was round or rounded. Planking was lapstrake of white cedar. Single garboards twisted or rolled as they extended aft from amidships to fasten vertically on the sternpost, producing a planked-up skeg and a reverse chine at the after end where the garboard and the plank above (the "tuck" plank) came together.

This is scarcely enough information to draw a set of lines from, but enough to set some definite boundaries within which to work. Although the Jersey beach skiff reaches back to the 1840s and even somewhat earlier, it seems safe to assume that it did not change much for several decades, that is, comparatively little before 1880 when Guthorn states that the length of the fishing skiffs was generally increased to 17 feet. Thus we can accept with some confidence as typical of the early skiffs the three tintype photographs of the *Lizzie*, a beach skiff built by Isaac or William Seaman before 1872, presumably about 15 or 16 feet in length. The Seamans of Jersey were early and leading builders of sea skiffs who figured prominently in the development of this craft. In fact the term "sea skiff" first appears in print in an advertisement by William Seaman in 1885. The importance of these early photos of the *Lizzie*. then, as primary sources of information, can hardly be over-stressed.

From the photo giving a clear view of the stern from almost directly aft, the relative length of the skeg in comparison with the vertical length of the transom is readily determined. The *Lizzie*'s transom is not U-shaped, but quite definitely forms a broad V, five planks high with the top strake standing plumb or approximately so. Not until a later period, after the sea skiff had become a much larger and chunkier power

Two boat types with a planked-up skeg and reverse chine construction similar to the Sea Bright skiff. On the left is a St. John River Salmon boat from New Brunswick (Photo by Russell A. Fowler) and below is a Lincolnville Salmon wherry from Maine (Photo by Lester D. Olin)

(Above) Beach skiff Lizzie *being launched into the surf in 1892. (Left)* Lizzie *under oars with mast and sail stowed aft. (Below) Half-model of a typical rowing-sailing beach skiff of about 1900 as built in 15- and 17-foot lengths by Neill Campbell of Belmar, N.J. The model shows a skeg modified to take a stern bearing for a gas engine. (Photos from* The Sea Bright Skiff and Other Jersey Shore Boats *by Peter J. Guthorn; Rutgers University Press)*

craft, did the transom assume a U-shape. From this photograph the general shape and proportions of the transom and skeg are easily sketched, although we shall not be able until later to assign precise dimensions to them as parts of the craft we are undertaking to reconstruct.

An enlargement of the second photo of the *Lizzie*, a broadside view of the boat under oars, provides an outline of the boat in profile, allowing an estimate of the amount of stern rake, which appears to be 36 degrees rather than 30. Taken together, these three photos of the *Lizzie* reveal a great deal to the boatbuilder's eye, a great deal more in fact than is easily set down in print. They are of prime assistance in laying out the boat for one thing, in lining out the plank, of which there are six strakes, not to mention giving the location of the mast, the shape and approximate size of the sails, and the position of the rowing thwarts.

What is principally lacking up to this point is a profile outline from which, assuming the length to be 16 feet, we can pick off with proportional dividers the least depth amidships and the heights of the bow and stern, from which in turn the amount and curve of the sheer, as well as the bottom rocker, can be drawn. We also lack enough of a halfbreadth view, assuming a width amidships of 5 feet, to give the width of the stern as well as proportional dimensions for laying out the halfbreadth shape. Also, we lack a midsection outline for comparison, and as a check. All three of these desiderata—profile, halfbreadth, and midsection—are to be found in Guthorn's book. An adequate profile view for scaling with the proportional dividers is obtained from enlargements of two broadside views of the same Campbell half-model, which the author states is typical of the 15- to 17-foot rowing and sailing beach skiffs of about 1900. The general proportions of this half-model correspond rather closely with what can be observed in the three tintype photos of the *Lizzie.*

However, it should not be overlooked that on the model the lower part of the planked-up skeg projects somewhat and stands vertical, an innovation found in conversions to power of the rowing and sailing skiff to provide a seat for bolting on an outside stern bearing and stuffing box. This is clearly to be seen in a photo of skiffs on the beach at Sea Bright about 1907. Otherwise the 1907 skiffs are definitely of the rowing and sailing model with abundant sheer, a well-raked V transom, and six planks to a side.

The use of the profile view of the Campbell half-model requires judgment and some discretion. The stern rake seems excessive and is found to be something like 40 degrees. At the bow the stem also appears to rake more than is shown by photos of the older boats. Such differences may be discrepancies due to camera distortion, which must be taken into account in scaling all photographs of boats, or they may be special Campbell characteristics, for according to the author, each of the builders had his own characteristic model, which differed in certain respects from those built by the others.

A number of halfbreadth views of the beach skiffs are included in Guthorn's book, but they are all for larger and newer boats, yet neither so large or so new as to be significantly altered in their basic proportions. Witness to a long established halfbreadth shape is obtained by comparing the beam to the transom width in a number of representative skiffs dating from about 1870 to 1940.

A 25-foot surf boat on skiff lines drawn some time between 1870 and 1880 by William A. Seaman of Branchport for the U. S. Life Saving Service has a transom width that is 65 percent of its greatest beam, as scaled with proportional dividers. A comparison of section widths of pound boats built by Seaman and L. B. Newman, as recorded in a boatbuilder's notebook and reproduced by Guthorn, yields transom-to-beam ratios of 65 and 68 percent. For a typical 21-foot Seaman skiff built in 1919, the transom width is 66 percent of the beam. A 21-foot regulation sea skiff advertised by Seaman about 1935 shows a transom width that is 67 percent of the beam. A 26-foot open-type sea skiff advertised by the Keyport Boat Works in 1925 has a transom width that is 69 percent of the beam. For the Seaman pound boat model as built from 1918 to 1940, the transom width was 66 percent of the beam.

Thus in all these boats examined, the greatest difference in transom-to-beam ratios amounts only to four percent—from 65 to 69 percent. Taking these ratios into consideration, we settled on a transom width for our reconstructed model of 68 percent of the given beam of 5 feet, amounting to a transom width at the sheer line of 3 feet 4¾ inches.

By working from the profile proportions developed from the Campbell half-model, we established a height for the transom. By scaling the enlarged photo of the stern of the *Lizzie*, we not only derived the vertical measurement of the transom scaled along the rake of the stern, but also a measurement for the planked-up skeg, and, in addition, transom widths at measured intervals. We could not accept the 40 degrees of transom rake as taken from the Campbell model of 1895, particularly as another photo of what appears to be the same model seems to show a rake of 38 degrees, strongly suggesting the possibility of camera distortion. Neither could we accept a rake of only 30 degrees, feeling this was not enough, and was closer to the later power skiffs, rather than to the earlier boats for oars and sail.

In checking, we found the Seaman surf boat of 1870-80 to have a stern rake of 33 degrees.

The stern rake of the *Lizzie*, as far as can be determined from the broadside photo, is 36 degrees. The typical 21-foot Seaman power skiff of 1919 shows a stern rake of only 16 degrees, for, as the development of the power skiff proceeded, the angle of stern rake became progressively less. Judging 40 degrees to be too much and 30 degrees too little, we kept close to the angle measured for the *Lizzie* by adopting an angle of stern rake of 35 degrees.

For purposes of comparison we were able to scale off with proportional dividers the midsection shape of the Seaman surf boat of 1870-80 from her lines published in Guthorn's book. As we have the beam, height, and bottom for the midsection of our reconstruction, it is principally for a comparison of deadrise and bilge curves that the midsection shape of the surf boat was obtained. The surf boat shows more topside flare than we have estimated to be representative of the early beach boats, and we have been guided here to a large extent by the photos of the *Lizzie*, the 17-foot by 6-foot Joralemon utility skiff of 1905, and the fishing skiffs on the beach at Sea Bright in 1907 and 1908, all appearing in Guthorn's book.

After deriving lines, drawn to a scale of 1½ inches equals 1 foot, principally from the sources reviewed, these were translated into wood, that is to say a working half-model, which was made as fair as possible and yet as close to the shape of the *Lizzie* as could be determined from her photos. Likewise, six strakes of plank, the same as the *Lizzie*'s, were carefully laid out on the half-model, using thin pine battens and dressmakers' pins, lining the strakes as nearly as we could to conform to those on the *Lizzie*.

The lines were then taken off the half-model and laid out on the drawing board as they are reproduced here. They are drawn to the inside of the planking, and are laid out much the same as dory lines, as these beach skiffs, also called beach dories, are closely similar to dories both in shape and construction. The principal construction differences for the beach skiff are a rabbeted stem, a thick bottom board rabbeted

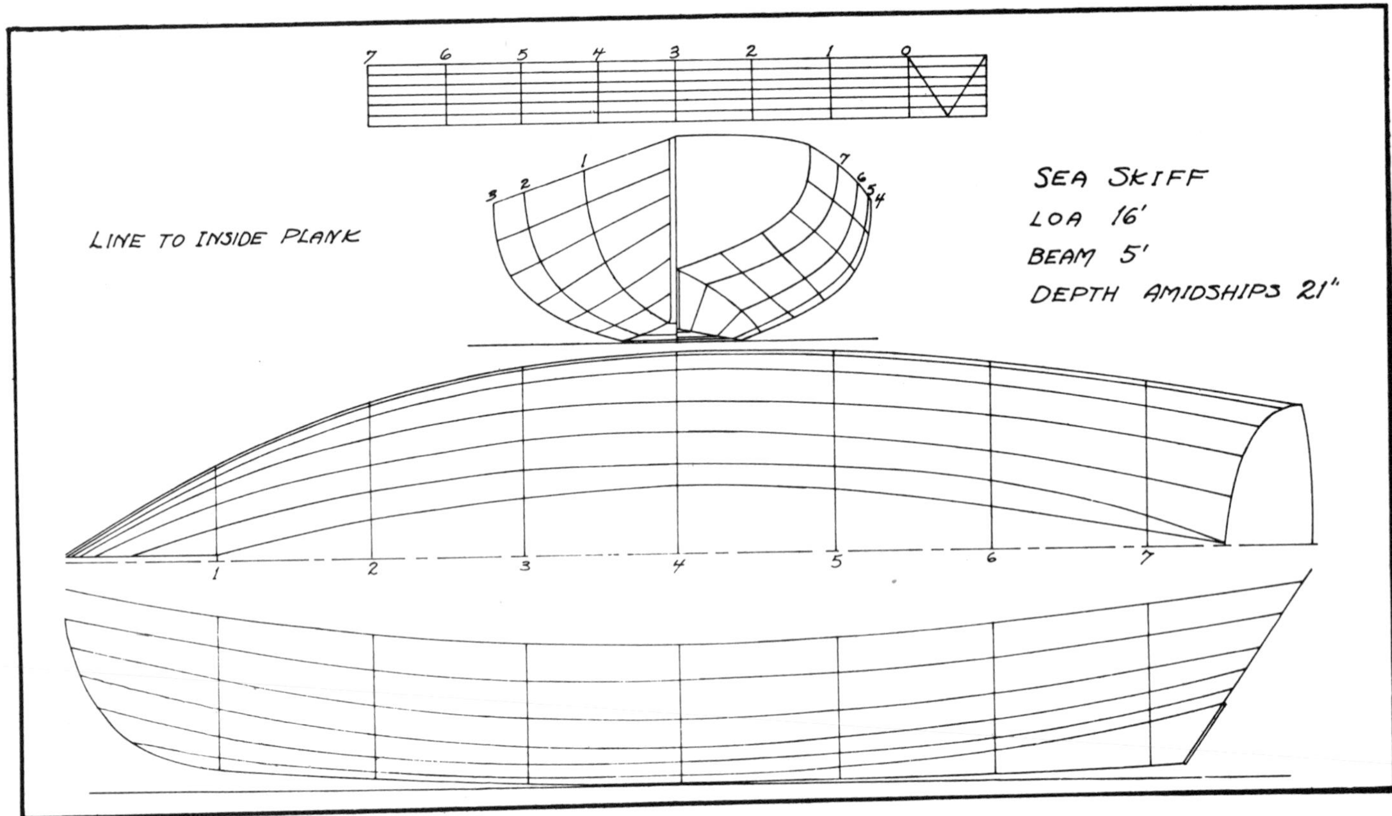

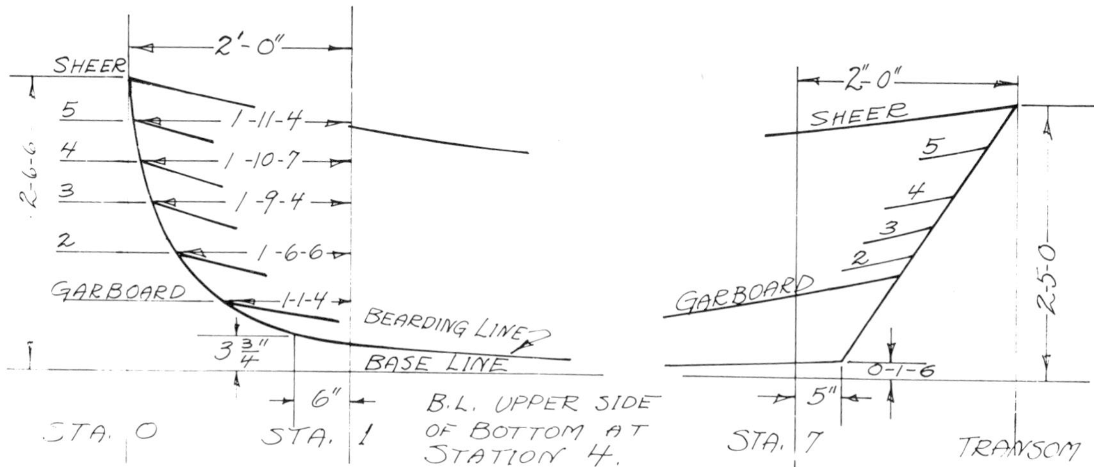

for the garboard, and the combination of planked-up skeg and reverse chine. The reverse chine—not a very good term, but the best we have for this particular feature of construction—is also found in the Maine salmon wherry, the Saint John River salmon boat, and the Staten Island skiff. It is their most distinctive feature, and is indicative of a common origin.

SIXTEEN FOOT SEA SKIFF

		STEM	1	2	3	4	5	6	7	TRAN.
HEIGHTS	SHEER	2-6-6	2-1-5	1-10-5	1-8-7	1-8-3	1-9-2	1-11-2	2-1-7	2-5-0
	5	2-2-1	1-8-7	1-5-4	1-3-7	1-3-2	1-4-1	1-5-7	1-8-7	2-0-2
	4	1-10-0	1-4-0	1-0-1	0-10-3	0-9-5	0-10-7	1-0-6	1-4-0	1-7-2
	3	1-5-6	1-0-0	0-8-0	0-6-1	0-5-4	0-6-6	0-9-1	1-0-5	1-4-0
	2	1-0-6	0-8-3	0-5-2	0-3-0	0-3-0	0-4-0	0-6-3	0-10-2	1-1-1
	GARBOARD	0-7-0	0-5-3	0-3-0	0-1-5	0-1-1	0-2-0	0-4-5	0-8-6	0-10-7
	BOTTOM	—	0-2-6	0-1-3	0-0-2	0-0-0	0-0-1	0-0-7	0-1-5	0-1-6
HALF-BREADTHS	SHEER	0-1-0	1-2-1	1-10-7	2-4-0	2-5-7	2-5-4	2-3-5	2-0-6	1-8-7
	5	0-1-0	1-1-6	1-10-3	2-3-5	2-5-4	2-5-2	2-2-6	1-11-5	1-8-1
	4	0-1-0	1-0-1	1-8-4	2-1-4	2-3-2	2-2-5	2-0-3	1-8-5	1-5-5
	3	0-1-0	0-10-0	1-4-7	1-9-4	1-10-5	1-10-0	1-7-5	1-3-7	1-1-1
	2	0-1-0	0-7-3	1-1-1	1-5-2	1-6-1	1-5-2	1-2-2	0-9-6	0-7-1
	GARBOARD	0-1-0	0-4-2	0-9-2	1-0-5	1-1-3	1-0-5	0-9-6	0-4-2	0-0-4
	BOTTOM	—	0-1-0	0-5-4	0-8-4	0-10-1	0-9-2	0-6-2	0-1-2	—

OFFSETS IN FEET, INCHES, AND EIGHTHS. TAKEN TO INSIDE OF PLANKING, INSIDE OF BOTTOM, TO BEARDING LINE ON RABBETED STEM, AND OUTSIDE OF TRANSOM. STATIONS SPACED 2 FEET APART.

SETTING UP

The lines represent the upper inside edges of the six strakes of this clinker hull. The upper inside edge of the flat bottom board is also shown. Because we are working from the inside of the planking, measurements for the bearding line on the stem, rather than for the rabbet line, are given in the offsets. How the latter is derived is shown in one of the drawings and will be explained in detail later.

While this skiff is planked much the same as a Swampscott dory, it has a rabbeted stem and bottom board, and, in this particular case, a rabbeted stern post, which the dory does not have. These features increase the difficulty of construction considerably, and there is some question whether they are worth the extra effort. A well-built Swampscott dory will last as long and take as much abuse and pounding on beaches and in the surf as a Jersey sea skiff, as the double-ended surf dories built by William Chamberlain of Marblehead for lifesaving boats for the Boston Metropolitan Commission have amply demonstrated. Likewise these same 19-foot surf dories later built in Swampscott by George Chaisson proved themselves in service along the whole length of our eastern seaboard.

The necessity for cutting a stem rabbet is avoided by the dory's two-piece stem construction. The inner stem is beveled to take the hood ends of the plank, which extend to the stem's outer edge. These are fastened and planed off square to conform to the curve of the stem profile. The outer, or "false," stem is then bent on to cover the plank ends and is securely fastened into the inner stem. The result is for all practical purposes the same as a rabbeted stem but is much simpler and more easily attained.

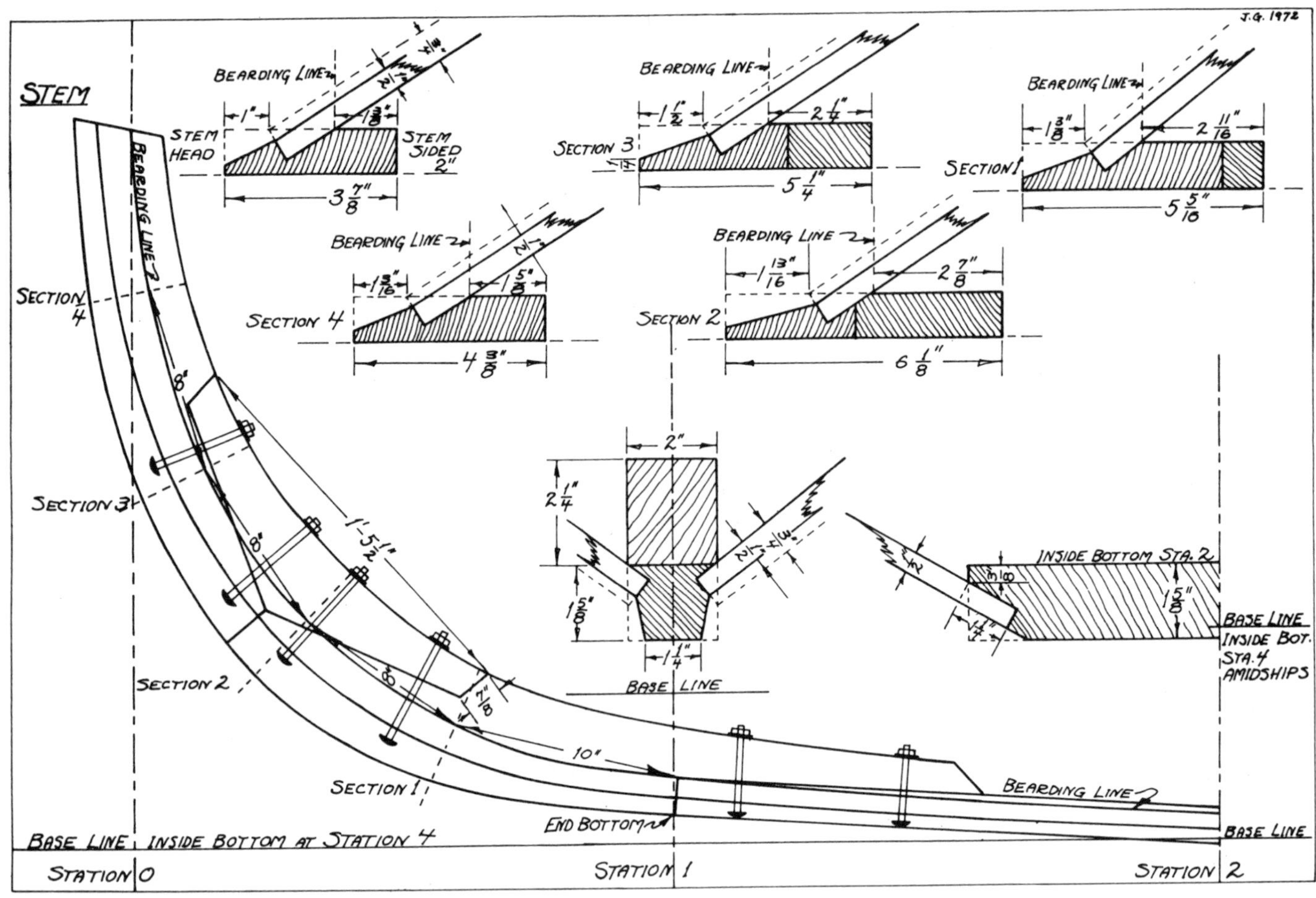

It would be quite easy to substitute a dory-type stem for the rabbeted stem shown here for the Sea Bright skiff. In that case, the inner stem could be laminated to the shape of the stem profile, and the outer stem could be a piece of steam-bent oak. This assembly adequately through-fastened would make a good, strong job. Alternately, the inner stem could be steam bent, although this would be a somewhat more difficult bending job than required for the lighter outer stem.

Guthorn, in his book, lists scantling dimensions for a typical 16-foot general service skiff. The stem as given there is steam-bent white oak, sided 1⅞ inches with a 4-inch molded dimension. Bending 4-inch oak requires special equipment, easy enough for the commercial boatshop but beyond the reach of most amateur, one-time builders. For that reason I show a pieced-stem easily put together from ordinary straight-grained 2-inch thick oak plank. Of course, if one could get a natural crook of oak or hackmatack of the right shape for the stem, that would be my first choice and, in my estimation, the best stem of all, but such timber is so unusual and difficult to obtain today that it hardly need be considered.

As previously mentioned, in laying out the stem rabbet for this skiff we work from the bearding line, the measurements for which are given in the offsets. Although this skiff is clinker planked with strakes finished ½ inch thick, I have laid out the stem rabbet for ¾-inch thick planking. After the rabbet is cut, it is easy to mark the rabbet for half-inch plank using a small section of ½-inch thick block for a gauge, which is slipped around in the rabbet to mark against. On the forward face or edge of the stem a ½-

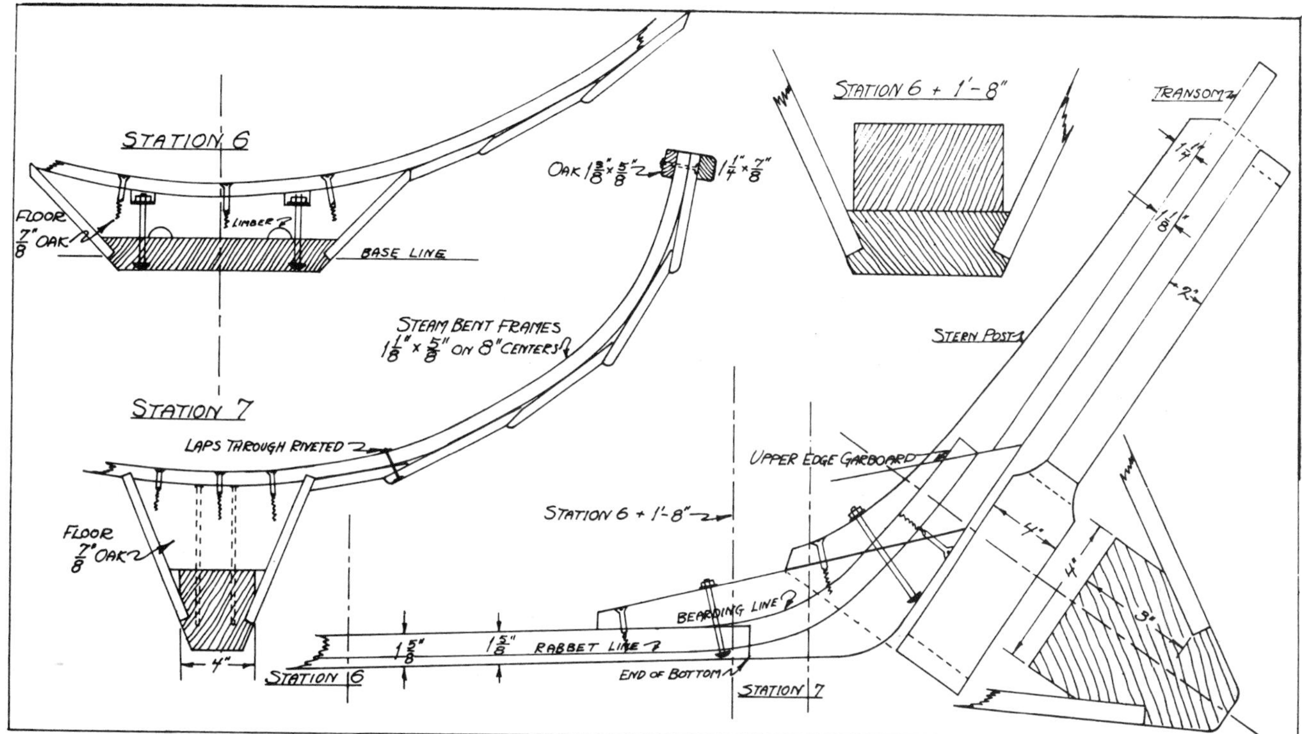

inch-wide strip is marked in the center for the stem band, either half-round or half-oval brass. The excess wood is next cut away between the line marked inside the rabbet and the line marking the outside edge of the stem band. By this method, instead of merely laying out and cutting a ½-inch rabbet to begin with, two advantages are secured. More back rabbet surface is obtained for landing the hood ends of the planking on and for fastening them, while the outer part of the stem, forward of the planking, is made thinner both for improved looks and for a sharper, easier entrance.

Even though I have increased the stem siding of 1⅞ inches given by Guthorn to 2 inches, there will be less wood in the finished stem because of the amount cut away in trimming down the ¾-inch rabbet, yet the greater stem siding gives more back rabbet surface for landing the plank.

The flat bottom, or plank keel, as this is sometimes called, is pine, 1⅝ inches thick. A dory bottom in a boat this size might be one inch thick, more likely ⅞ inch, but the dory would have an outer bottom of ½ inch or ⅝ inch, or at least part of an outer bottom along the outside covering the bottom edges of the garboard strakes. This double-bottom construction is like the two-piece stem, in that it is easier to construct than the single, thick, rabbeted bottom. Also, the outer part is easily renewed, should it become battered or worn on the beach.

I have shown a rabbeted bottom for this boat because this construction was usual for beach skiffs, although it seems that the double bottom was occasionally used for beach skiffs and favored by a few builders. I think I would probably use a double bottom myself. While the Maine salmon wherry has what amounts to a double bottom, this is only at the ends and along the sides, with the inner, middle portion uncovered. It is important that the side pieces should be straight on the inside edges and parallel to the centerline of the boat. If the side strips are curved more or less to conform to the sides of the boat, their inner edges will drag.

The stern construction as shown for this boat may appear to some to be heavier than needed. Yet the after end of the bottom takes a lot of pounding on landing and in getting off the beach. If the after end of the bottom board is brought to a shim point and is not covered or protected in some way, trouble can result.

In this skiff both the end of the bottom board and the ends of the garboard are recessed into a solid sternpost with plenty of bearing, with good fastening, and well forward of possible impact damage. A rabbeted sternpost such as this is more work but worth it, I think. The 4-inch siding of the post in the heel makes it possible to bore a shaft hole in case it is desired to install a small inboard engine. In that case the fastenings holding the two-part sternpost assembly together could be placed on either side of the center to permit a small shaft hole to be bored on the centerline between them. Enough wood should be left on the bottom of the sternpost aft of the rabbet to allow bolting on the outside stuffing box and bearing. In case this boat should be considered for power, it would be quite easy to make it 18 feet long instead of 16 feet by adding 2 feet in the middle, with almost no other changes.

The two-piece sternpost shown is readily got out of ordinary 4-inch stock. No wide widths are required. Oak is not necessary, but good quality hard, or longleaf, pine will do nicely. In fact the whole stern, including the transom, can very well be made of hard pine. Guthorn's specifications call for 1¼-inch white cedar for the transom. I would rather have hard pine, but not over 1⅛ inches thick.

As I previously indicated in connection with the stem, a natural grown knee of the right shape for the sternpost would be ideal. In that case the siding could be 3 inches or even narrower, this depending in part on whether or not it is to be bored for a shaft. A capable builder can shape such a natural knee so that its siding tapers from, say 4 inches where the end of the bottom jogs into it, to less than an inch at its extreme after edge.

In the Maine salmon wherry, the natural crook sternpost got out of a large white cedar root is tapered to a sharp edge under the transom and the after ends of the garboard, and one or two of the strakes above are run back and sawn off square and flush with this after edge after they are in place and fastened. These plank ends are covered with a beveled strip of oak similar to the dory's false stem and through-fastened into the sternpost on the inside. This strip extends partway up the width of the transom and is fastened into it and through into the upper part of the sternpost, which reinforces the inside of the transom. This is a solid way of finishing off the stern, although a bit clumsy in appearance. The bottom end, which otherwise would be exposed, is covered by the wherry's false bottom.

This same construction could be used for the sea skiff. In fact it would be both possible and easy to build this skiff with a two-part dory stem, a double bottom without rabbeting, and a wherry stern, also without rabbeting. In such a boat no rabbeting in any part would be required, with a considerable saving in labor, especially for the inexperienced builder.

FRAMING AND PLANKING

Guthorn's specifications call for planking of ½-inch or ⅝-inch thick white cedar, but ⅝ inch seems pretty heavy for a 16-foot boat and for that reason I have drawn up this boat for ½-inch planking. For myself, I'd rather have good quality northern white pine than cedar for planking, or Maine, rather than Virginia, cedar. With small, sound knots, the Maine cedar is ever so much tougher than some of the wide, clear southern cedar that looks beautiful in the board but splits so easily.

White oak frames ⅝ inch by 1⅛ inches, spaced 8 inches on centers, are called for. The oak should be the best obtainable, from butt logs, if possible, newly cut, and sawn to follow the grain. There is a great difference in oak, and some of the light, open-grain red oak is quite worthless.

The planking laps, 1⅛ inches in width, should be copper riveted, between the frames as well as through them. At stations 6 and 7, I have shown floors in the hollow trough between the garboards with their upper edges curved and the frames bent in on top of them and running continuously from gunwale to gunwale. Aft of station 6 such floors will not be in the way and they add greatly to the strength of the boat where it is especially needed.

This boat could be framed with natural crook timbers, which was the old way and the method of framing still to be seen in survivals of the Maine salmon wherries and the St. John River salmon boats. Also laminated frames, epoxy/Versamid-glued, could be made up to simulate natural crooks, if one wished to do so. It is only fair to say that more work is required for laminations than most realize who haven't done this previously.

According to Guthorn, skiff bottoms were made of spruce or cedar. I like neither for this purpose. Spruce rots too easily and cedar is quite soft. For my part I would choose pine, either northern white or southern yellow, or good quality Douglas fir.

FINISHING OFF

Brass screws are mentioned on an equal footing with bronze, but I want no part of the former. Brass screws are too weak and do not last especially well either. I would want bronze bolts also. The price difference between poor and superior fastenings for a boat of this size amounts to so little that it is hardly worth considering.

Inwales and gunwales, I believe these are what Guthorn calls clamps and rub strakes, are best made of oak. Dimensions for clamps are given as ⅝ inch by 1⅜ inches and rub strakes as ⅞ inch by 1¼ inches. Clamps or inwales are to be fastened through the timberheads and sheer strake with 8d copper nails riveted over burrs, while the gunwales or rub rails can be screwed on.

Thwart knees, breasthook, and quarter knees are best made out of natural crooks, limb or root, of apple, hackmatack, oak, or other, if you can get them. In a pinch, laminated substitutes can be glued up. Thwarts can be made of spruce, for the wood is stiff, strong, and light, and there is little chance of rot developing here.

THE SAILING RIG

Primary propulsion for the original beach-launched working craft of the northeast coast was supplied by ever-reliable oars, but many of the early boats were also rigged to sail. Small spritsails predominated, except for the Swampscott's leg-o-mutton sail and small jib. Eventually many of these boats rigged to sail were equipped with centerboards, but just when centerboards were first put into such craft is uncertain.

In Swampscott, Massachusetts, in the old days, the summer dory fishermen in good weather used to leave the beach under oars at dawn, usually in a dead calm. By late afternoon, when it was time to start home, a brisk on-shore breeze would have sprung up, so sails were raised and the loaded boats would come riding in before it. No centerboard was required and an oar sufficed to steer. As time went on, sailing rigs were enlarged and improved, and modified sailing versions of such craft were developed with centerboards and rudders.

Alfred A. Brooks, in his account of the boats of Ash Point, Maine, in the early decades of this century, as published in the October, 1942, issue of the *American Neptune*, shows the lines and rig for two large sailing wherries; one, a capacious 16-footer built by Luther Hurd about 1870, and the other, Elmer Witham's 18-foot *Siroc*. Of something like 1,500 pounds displacement, *Siroc* was partly decked and carvel planked, although built on wherry lines. Neither of these Ash Point sailing wherries was equipped with a centerboard, and consequently, while fast and seaworthy off the wind, they did not do so well to windward. Both carried a sprit main and a small jib, a rig very similar in fact to that of the Jersey beach skiff *Lizzie*, which we have attempted to reconstruct here.

Of these various beach craft which we have been considering, the Swampscott dory was carried farthest in its development as a sailboat. From about 1900 to 1920 and even somewhat later, dories were the most numerous and popular small sailing craft in this country. Still remembered are such dories as the Beachcomber

The Lizzie, *set up on the beach in 1892 to have her picture taken. (From* The Sea Bright Skiff and Other Jersey Shore Boats *by Peter J. Guthorn; Rutgers University Press)*

and Alpha, the Clipper dory, the X-dory, the Riverside dory, followed by larger and more powerful craft like the Yankee dory, the Massachusetts Bay Indian, and the Marblehead Town Class, which has recently taken a new lease on life in fiberglass.

The Jersey sea skiff, to the contrary, developed in the direction of power rather than sail. Peter Guthorn's book does not include details of a single example of these boats rigged to sail within the past 100 years. However, the photograph he shows of fishing skiffs on the beach at Sea Bright in 1908 gives evidence that some of these boats still carried small sails at that time. In at least three boats out of more than the score shown on the beach, spars lying flat with the sails rolled up on them can be seen, and one of the boats has mast and sail raised. Another photo of working skiffs at Sea Bright the previous year does not have a single spar or sail showing. This was taken at the very beginning of the transition to power, as is indicated by a boat in the photograph with its primitive installation of a small inboard engine.

It appears that the Sea Bright skiff was never popular as a small sailboat either for racing or for other pleasure sailing. The reason is not at all clear, considering the great popularity achieved by the sailing dories. There is no intrinsic reason why the sea skiff could not have been developed as an outstanding small sailboat. Only it wasn't. Nevertheless, for those today who want a boat that can be both rowed and sailed, one that is a fine sea boat, that handles easily on and off the beach, the early Jersey beach skiff, exemplified by the *Lizzie*, is certainly to be considered.

When it comes to picking a sail plan, there are a number of different rigs which would be suitable. But we have chosen to follow, as closely as careful scaling with dividers allows, the old tintype photo of the *Lizzie* under sail, which Guthorn reproduces in his book. Basing our scale on the assumption that the *Lizzie*'s length was 16 feet, although it just as likely was a foot shorter, we get a sail area of 70 square feet for the main, and 15 square feet for the jib, or 85 square feet combined sail area, which is not excessive for a boat of this size. The boat could probably carry more, but general utility and ease of handling is the object here rather than ultimate speed.

The rig could hardly be simpler, with the sprit main lashed to the short, unstayed mast

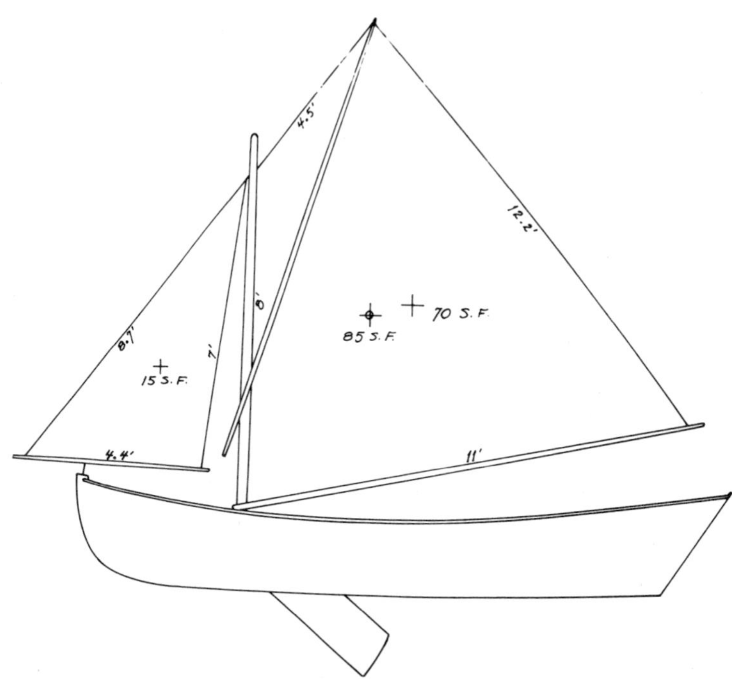

(Above) Suggested sail plan for the Sea Bright skiff. (Left) Robert Crockett's 16-foot Sea Bright skiff has a similar sail plan, though the jib club is not balanced. This boat was built by the Rose Bay Boat Shop in Lunenburg, Nova Scotia.

but not to the boom. In the photograph the end of the boom seems to extend by the mast somewhat like a sprit, but this is not clear, and it might have had crude boom jaws, although there was definitely no gooseneck fitting. To douse the rig one merely has to unsnap the jib club from the stemhead, lift the boom, wrap the sprit and sails around the mast, and lift the whole rig out of the step and mast thwart. The spars are short enough so that the resulting compact bundle is easily stowed within the boat.

The mast should be spruce, 3 inches in diameter at the bury through the thwart, tapering to 2 inches at the head. The main boom tapering toward either end should not be over 2 inches at its thickest part, the sprit and jib club likewise not over 1½ inches. Sitka spruce for the spars is excellent, of course, but expensive and often difficult to obtain. Many lumberyards today carry rough Canadian spruce ledger boards, which come 16 feet long. Selected boards stripped up on the circular saw to avoid knots, and glued up with epoxy, can be shaped into spars of the finest kind. Or if one lives Down East, it is possible in some areas to find suitable spars growing on the stump in spruce thickets. After cutting, these should be protected from weather and worms until they have seasoned before being worked down to size with drawknife and plane.

In the photographs of the *Lizzie* the thwart that serves for mast partners seems to be at gunwale height. This is not necessary, and as putting this thwart at gunwale height tends to fill up the boat, I have drawn it in the reconstructed plan at the same height as the rowing thwarts. This is the way it was generally found in dories and wherries. In the latter, there were sometimes two mast positions for different rigs and sail areas.

It is extremely difficult to achieve a well-balanced rig by calculating sail areas and mast positions ahead of time on the drawing board. There are so many variables, and the values for these are so easily changed in a small boat by changing conditions of trim, heel, and loading, that generally one must try a new rig, experiment with it, and make various changes and adjustments before it is satisfactory. In the case of different rigs and different sail areas for different weather conditions, having more than one mast position is desirable if not essential. Likewise the design and positioning of the centerboard is an important element in achieving a balanced rig.

None of the photographs that we have of the *Lizzie* shows a centerboard or centerboard trunk. In assuming that there was a centerboard, and in including one in my reconstruction, I have consequently had a free hand. The heavy, wide pine bottom of this skiff is ideal for the installation of a centerboard trunk and is strengthened rather than weakened by the addition of such centerboard construction as is shown here. In addition to centering it approximately under the combined centers of effort of the two sails, which brings the forward end up close to the mast as in sailing dories, I have made

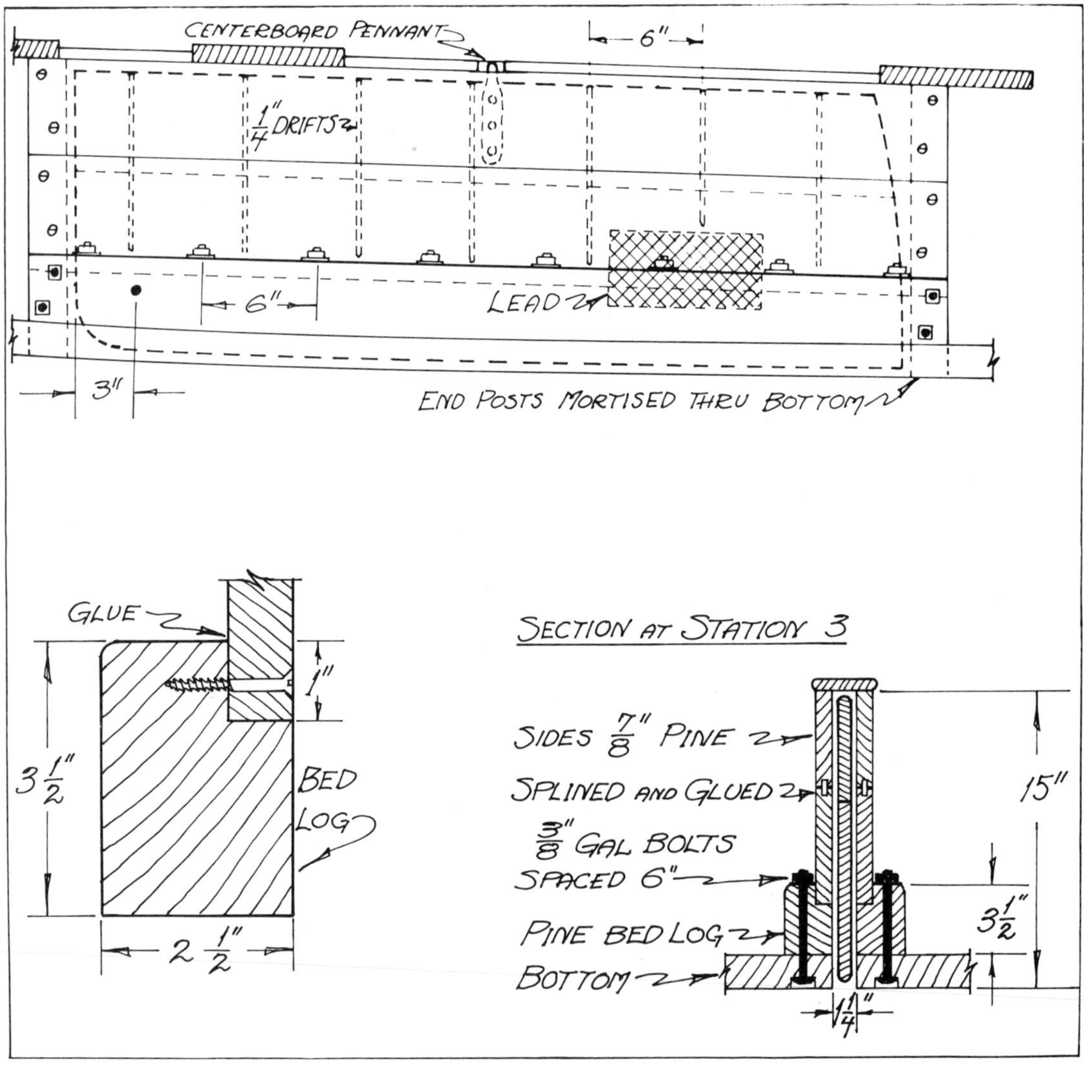

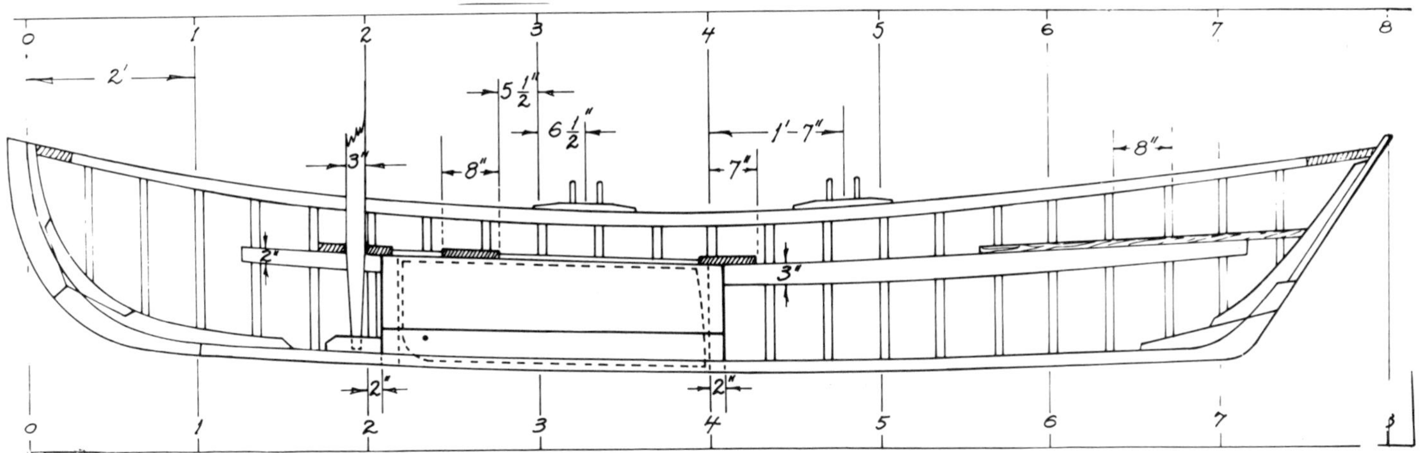

the board quite long, yet narrow enough to fit under the rowing thwarts. The extra length makes up in area what the board lacks in width, although 14 inches is not excessively narrow. When a long board is raised and lowered, the center of lateral resistance shifts considerably in the fore-and-aft direction. This affords flexibility in achieving balance of rig. Besides, keeping the board below the thwarts does not interfere in any way with the use of the boat for rowing, and at the same time the thwarts brace and secure the centerboard trunk.

The bed logs for the trunk are not oak, but pine, a full 2½ inches thick and bolted through the 1⅝-inch thick pine bottom with ⅜-inch galvanized iron carriage bolts on 6-inch centers. This generous fastening with the wide bearing surface of pine bed logs coated with a non-hardening bedding compound should give a solid, perfectly tight box. End posts are oak 2 inches wide and extending through the bottom slot for caulking from the outside.

The bolts through the bottom should be set so that their heads come just under the surface, to be covered with bottom compound rather than bunged. It may be desirable to tighten the nuts slightly several times at intervals after the installation of the trunk, and each time this is done, the heads will tend to draw up a little deeper into the bottom, so it is wise not to set them too deep to begin with.

The board, made of two pieces of oak finished ⅞ inch thick, is pinned together with 5/16-inch diameter drifts spaced 6 inches on centers as shown and precisely marked and bored. The upper section 5 inches in width is bored halfway through from either edge. The holes can be bored to meet exactly in the center if the drill is sighted both ways (by the operator of the drill and an assistant) as drilling proceeds and the drill is made to follow exactly the line of the hole as marked across the surface of the board.

A piece of lead is set into the board as shown to add weight to it in addition to the weight of the oak and the drift pins. The lead can either be run in hot, or a block of lead of the right thickness and shape can be set in cold and swelled around the edges with a hammer and punch so that it grips the wood solidly and cannot move or fall out.

A short rope pennant spliced into the strap eye on the upper side of the board serves to raise or lower the weighted board to the desired height and is made fast to a cleat on the outside of the box. For a pivot a piece of ½-inch brass rod will do nicely and needs only to be driven through tightly fitting holes bored through the trunk logs and cut to come flush on either side.

No rudder is shown, although one might easily be added. The main reason for this is that it seems that the *Lizzie*, like early Swampscott dories, did not have a rudder, but was steered with an oar.

24 The Barnegat Sneakbox

One of the old small-boat favorites is the famous Barnegat sneakbox. Tradition has it that the first sneakbox was built on Barnegat Bay in 1836. Its flat, spoon-shaped hull draws little water and is easily dragged over mud or sand. Sitting very low in the water, the sneakbox is easily disguised as a shooting blind. Originally, this type of hunting skiff was built of a size small enough to be easily handled by a single hunter, that is, about 12 feet by 4 feet, and was rigged with a small spritsail.

According to W. P. Stephens, most of the early Barnegat boats were fitted with a daggerboard inserted through a small trunk from which it could be removed entirely. H. I. Chapelle explained that at first these daggerboards were "scimitar-shaped" and were hung to one side well off-center. This was to permit the hunter to stretch out full length beside the board in a 12-foot boat. Later when the type was developed and enlarged for recreational sailing and for cruising, the location of the board was shifted to a more "normal" position on the centerline of the hull, and the removable daggerboard was replaced by a pivoting centerboard, sometimes of galvanized iron boiler plate.

Soon after the inception of the sneakbox, someone, no doubt shocked by its novelty, dubbed it a "devil's coffin." Its low, flat, "melon-seed" hull might have looked precarious and unsafe, but actually it is not so at all. Used as intended and not overloaded with canvas, the sneakbox is to be trusted fully. She is not an oceangoing packet, it is true, but when used in sheltered and semi-sheltered waters, she is a comfortable, secure, and surprisingly able little craft.

Indeed, the good qualities of the sneakbox and its inherent potential beyond a limited specialization as a shooting boat were soon recognized by boating enthusiasts. Following the Civil War came a flowering of recreational boating in this country. The widespread and intense activity involving small craft, and sailing canoes in particular, during the 1870s and 1880s is often lost sight of today. One has only to dig back in the files of *Forest & Stream* for these decades to discover how highly the sneakbox was then regarded among sportsmen and small craft amateurs and sailors.

Some of this material on sneakboxes is to be found in *Canoe and Boat Building—A Complete Manual For Amateurs*, by W. P. Stephens. The drawings of the Barnegat Cruiser that are reproduced with this article are adapted from Plate No. 39, which accompanied the Stephens book. Plate No. 38 shows a large 16-foot shooting box.

I might add that Stephens's plates were printed separately on individual sheets and folded in a packet which went with the book. Over the years many of these separate plates have been mislaid or destroyed, so that few complete sets remain, with popular items like the sneakbox particularly hard to find. Persons interested in the sneakbox should not fail to get Stephens's book from the library to read the relevant sections in the text, which provides dimensions, a sail plan, and much miscellaneous data of importance.

A much easier source to obtain, and one fully as important in its way as Stephens, is Chapelle's *American Small Sailing Craft*, published by W. W. Norton in 1951. Both of the sneakbox drawings included by Chapelle, a hunter's box built in 1880 and a more modern "arc-bottom" modification, were made from take-offs of the actual boats by the author. They are complete to the minutest detail, and include offsets and sail plans. In contrast, Stephens's drawings omit some minor details, such that any knowledgeable boatbuilder, either amateur or professional, might be expected to supply himself without difficulty. Neither Stephens nor Chapelle provides complete step-by-step building directions, although Stephens gives more of such information than Chapelle, whose book is a technical and historical treatise and not a building manual.

The modified sneakbox or Barnegat Cruiser shown by Stephens is the culmination of a great deal of special study and experimentation with sailing and cruising sneakboxes by N. H. Bishop of Toms River, N. J. At the time Stephens was writing his book, Bishop had under his supervision a number of such Barnegat Cruisers building at Toms River for members of the American Single-handed Cruising Club. The lines were taken from Seneca's boat previously described in *Forest & Stream.* "Seneca" was the pen name of a popular contributor to *Forest & Stream* who wrote extensively on sneakboxes. As Bishop was the man who took a sneakbox from Pittsburgh to the Gulf of Mexico down the Ohio and the Mississippi, later recounting his experiences in a book, *Four Months In a Sneak Box*, the Barnegat Cruiser comes to us with the highest of recommendations.

Stephens's paragraph of introduction to the Barnegat Cruiser is worth reproducing:

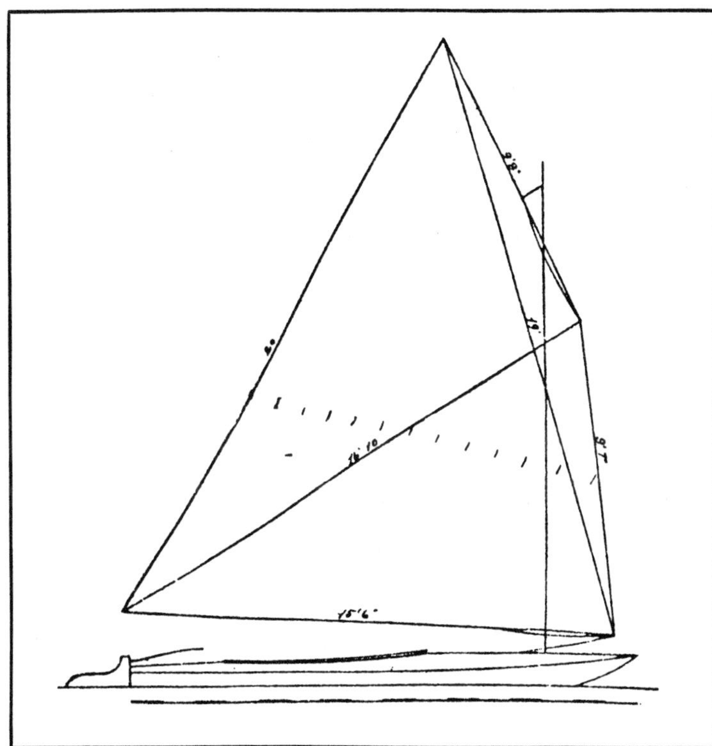

The sail plan for W.P. Stephens's sneakbox featured a balanced lug rig.

> The prominence given to cruising of late years by the increased growth and importance of canoeing has brought many into the ranks who do not care for so small a boat as the canoe, but who wish a strong, roomy and serviceable boat, either for cruising or for general sailing, alone or with one or two friends. The canoe is really a boat for one person, and must be capable of being paddled, sailed, and handled on shore by one; but where these conditions do not prevail a different type of boat may often be used to advantage. In places where the boat must lie afloat and a fine canoe would be damaged; in open waters where there is no occasion to haul up the boat, and where transit by rail is not an object; in shooting trips and other cruises where several persons, and perhaps a dog, must be carried, the boat shown in Plate XXXIX will answer admirably.

Dimensions furnished by Stephens for the Barnegat Cruiser are as follows: Length 14 feet 0 inches. Beam 4 feet 6 inches. Depth at gunwale 1 foot 1 inch. Sheer, bow 8½ inches. Sheer, stern 4 inches. Draft, loaded 6 inches. Freeboard 7 inches. Crown of deck 8 inches. Fore side of stem to mast tube 2 feet 9½ inches; to trunk, fore end 3 feet 1 inch; to trunk, aft end 6 feet 3 inches; to well, fore end 11 feet; to rowlocks 9 feet 1 inch; to bulkhead 12 feet. Diameter of

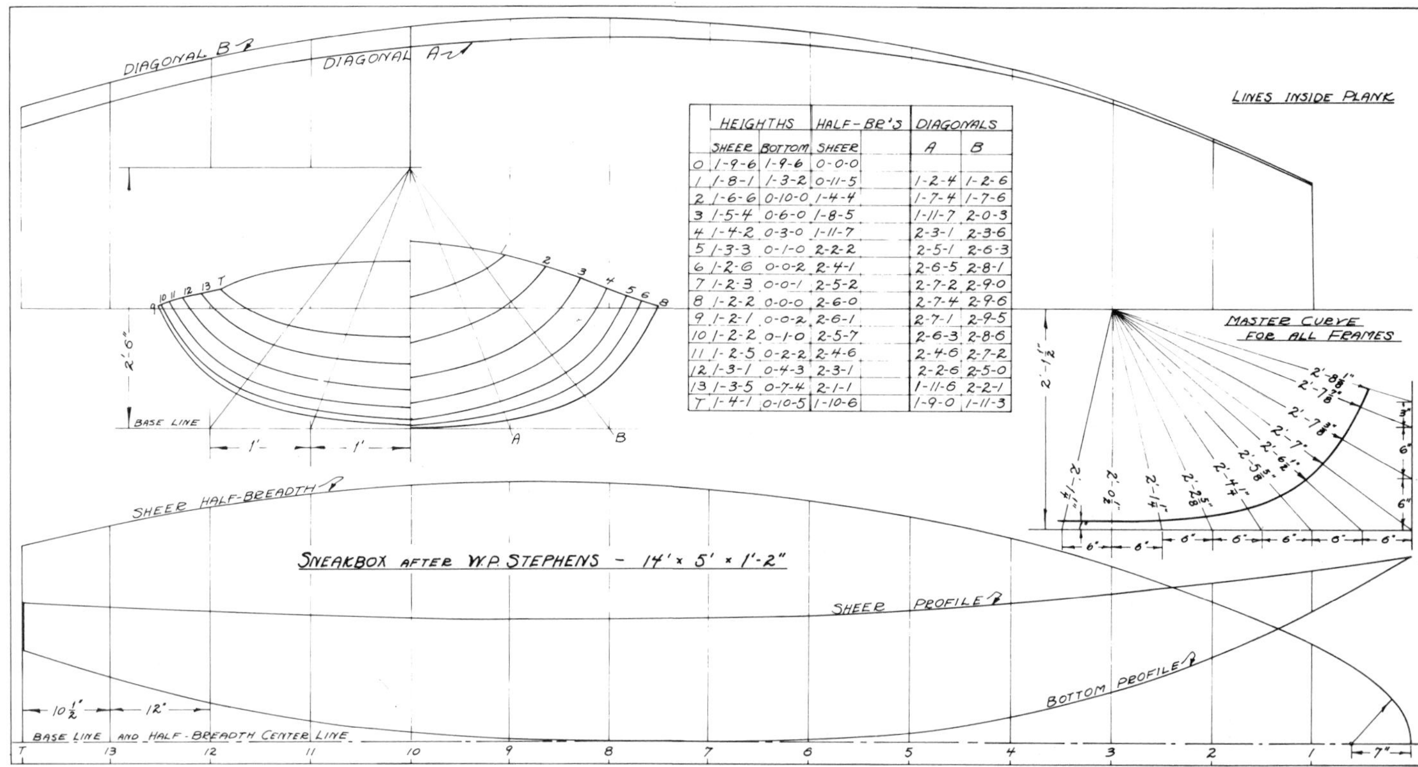

	HEIGHTHS		HALF-BR'S		DIAGONALS	
	SHEER	BOTTOM	SHEER		A	B
0	1-9-6	1-9-6	0-0-0			
1	1-8-1	1-3-2	0-11-5		1-2-4	1-2-6
2	1-6-6	0-10-0	1-4-4		1-7-4	1-7-6
3	1-5-4	0-6-0	1-8-5		1-11-7	2-0-3
4	1-4-2	0-3-0	1-11-7		2-3-1	2-3-6
5	1-3-3	0-1-0	2-2-2		2-5-1	2-6-3
6	1-2-6	0-0-2	2-4-1		2-6-5	2-8-1
7	1-2-3	0-0-1	2-5-2		2-7-2	2-9-0
8	1-2-2	0-0-0	2-6-0		2-7-4	2-9-6
9	1-2-1	0-0-2	2-6-1		2-7-1	2-9-5
10	1-2-2	0-1-0	2-5-7		2-6-3	2-8-6
11	1-2-5	0-2-2	2-4-6		2-4-6	2-7-2
12	1-3-1	0-4-3	2-3-1		2-2-6	2-5-0
13	1-3-5	0-7-4	2-1-1		1-11-6	2-2-1
T	1-4-1	0-10-5	1-10-6		1-9-0	1-11-3

mast tube 3 inches. The rig is a balance lug of 118 square feet in area.

ORIGINAL CONSTRUCTION

The directions for the construction of the hull furnished by Stephens, which follow verbatim below, are worth close study, for the same general order of building procedure applies in composite construction:

> In shape the new cruiser resembles the old sneakboxes, but is deeper than most of the latter. The board is of steel plate ¼" thick, pivoted at the fore end in place of the daggerboards once common in these craft. The construction is quite peculiar. Both keel and planking are of white cedar ⅝" thick. The keel is flat, in one piece. . . . There is no stem piece, but the keel is bent up, forming the stem. The garboards . . . end along the gunwale, instead of in a rabbet in the stem, as in most boats.
>
> In building, after the keel is fastened to the stocks, with the proper curve, the stern and moulds are put in place. Then two [harping] pieces are sawn out of 1" the shape being taken from the deck line on the floor. These pieces are screwed in place, at the height of the lower side of the deck, and remain permanently in the boat. The ribs are now bent and fitted in place, nailed to the keel, and the upper ends of the forward ones are nailed to [the harping] pieces. The correct breadths of each plank may be taken from the body plan on every frame. The frames are of sawn cedar 1⅛"–1⅙" and spaced 10". The trunk is of pine, deck and ceiling ½" cedar. . . .

MODERNIZED CONSTRUCTION

For a number of reasons, as will appear, the sneakbox hull is particularly suited to a construction utilizing glued splices and laminations, plywood and synthetic reinforced thermoplastic (SRP) covering. While such construction is neither particularly simple nor easy, the amateur may find it easier than older methods, especially the planking with ⅝-inch cedar, which would certainly require steaming, as well as careful lining, backing out and rounding, beveling, fitting, and caulking.

One should not get the idea that the new materials are particularly cheap; to the contrary they are relatively expensive. The expense is worth it, however. A covering of SRP greatly strengthens a hull without adding much weight, renders it completely and permanently watertight, and prevents water soaking, something that invariably happens to cedar planking when left for long periods in the water.

Composite wood-plastic construction requiring gluing procedures and the applications of plastic reinforcement tends to be time consuming and often goes very slowly in building new and unfamiliar designs. This may be a serious disadvantage for the commercial boatshop, which must figure its labor costs today closely. The amateur should not mind spending extra time if it produces superior results. Any amateur considering boat construction should think twice before undertaking a project, if he must be niggardly with his time. It is no good to rush, particularly with adhesives and plastic.

In adapting Stephens's Barnegat Cruiser for building with modern materials, I have made some changes to improve the sneakbox for present-day use and home construction. The principal change is an increase of 6 inches in the beam, so that this 14-foot boat is now 5 feet at its widest point. This amount of beam would be excessive for most craft of the same length, but not for this shallow, spoon-shaped hull with its rounded, overhanging sides. The additional beam adds appreciably to sailing stability without undesirable effects, such as a significant increase in weight, and it also provides a greater displacement without an increase in draft. With two occupants and a considerable amount of equipment and camping gear, this widened version can still slide across water too shallow for any other craft except the lightest canoes.

The most remarkable thing about these lines is that all hull cross-sections in the body plan are, in outline, parts of the same master curve. The practical import of this is that, as the boat is built with laminated frames, only one gluing form is required for all the frames in the boat. This means a considerable saving in labor.

FRAMING

The frames, spaced on one-foot centers, are laminated spruce glued with epoxy adhesive. For both frames and deck beams, laminations of spruce glued with epoxy adhesive are recommended. An inexpensive source of excellent lumber for laminated frames is widely available in rough, air-dried spruce ledger boards of good quality, selected and stripped up with the circular saw to avoid large and unsound knots. A few small, sound knots well distributed throughout the lamination does not detract from its strength. Strips ⅛ inch to 3/16 inch thick and roughly 2 inches wide are got out on the circular saw, which gives a slightly rough surface ideal for epoxy gluing. Enough of these strips are bent around the form to give 1¼ inches of molded width when the rib is finished. Two half ribs of ⅞-inch finished siding can be got out of each glued assembly of 2-inch wide strips. As a glance at the drawings will discover, each complete frame is made up of two half ribs. The construction sections show the half-ribs butted on the bottom centerline and joined by an oak floor molded 2 inches and sided ⅞ inch, and fastened with ¼-inch through bolts. Another way would be to let the ends of the half-ribs extend by one another across the bottom.

Forms for gluing both frame and deck beam laminations are easily made from a flat piece of heavy plywood to which are bolted pieces of 2 by 4 sawn to conform to a desired curve as previously marked out on the plywood. A light brushing of hot paraffin is all that is needed as a release to prevent the glue from sticking to the form. Curved mating blocks and plenty of C-clamps pull the strips firmly into position against the form until the glue sets.

While laminated frames and deck beams may be made up in advance of their use, assembly starts with the formation of the laminated curved keel or keel batten, the forward extremity of which also serves for the stem. The strips or layers of ¼-inch marine plywood, which comprise the inner keel, are bent to shape and glued on stocks cut to the required profile curve of the bottom. The skeg of tapered 1¼-inch oak forms the after portion of the stocks, and the keel batten is fastened to it permanently. Forward, a plank on edge sawn to the profile curve is set up, plumbed, and secured, and the keel strips coated with glue internally are bent into its hollow and temporarily fastened.

Next, the frames are put in place and are beveled and secured for planking. The frames themselves act as molds, but a few battens serving as ribbands will facilitate setting the frames, especially the forward ones, which require considerable beveling. Also a couple of battens temporarily fastened on either side will help to hold the faired shape secure until planking has started, for which the boat must be turned over.

Forward where the keel sharpens slightly in a widened V-section, frame ends and floor will rest on top of the inside of the keel strip or batten. Aft, where the bottom is nearly flat, it will be necessary to recess the floor and frame feet slightly so as to drop them enough to give a flat bearing for the garboards. This is shown in the accompanying construction sketch. Note also the provision for limbers, for it is of critical importance for the bottom to drain completely to its lowest point about amidships.

As part of the framing-out operation, the sheer harpings at the bow are cut out to the half-breadth shape of the deck, are notched to receive the timberheads of the first three frames, and are fitted in place and fastened to the head of the inner keel or keel batten where it rounds up in place of a stem. Aft of the harpings, two ⅜-inch by 1½-inch battens with glue between are fastened to the inside of the timberheads along the deck or sheer line. This is more easily done with two battens because of the twist. Outward of this laminated clamp, the spaces between the timber heads are filled in solid with pieces the width of the laminated clamp and glued to it. This makes a solid landing at the deck line the whole length of the boat for fastening the plank ends, which, because of the spoon shape of the hull, round up and terminate along the sheer.

Of course, the outer surfaces of the sheer harping at the bow, as well as the filler blocks between the timberheads, must be carefully beveled to conform to the rake of the side flare, but this is done, or finished, after the framed-out hull is turned over for planking. The keel batten is also beveled and faired at this juncture.

Considerable beveling of the inner keel is required toward the bow where some sharpness or V-section develops. Hardly any beveling is required aft. Because of this the inner keel is made three layers thick at the bow and back nearly to station 7, while aft of this it drops off to two layers, so continuing to the stern.

PLANKING

The distinctive and unusual shape of this hull—more specifically its relatively great beam, its shallowness, together with the open round of its extreme side flare—constitutes a special planking problem. Instead of the bow ends of the planking (the "hood" ends in older terminology) landing in a stem rabbet in the usual way, they run up to the sheer on the curved bow to meet the deck and fasten into the solid harping piece ingeniously provided for just this purpose. Who first devised this manner of securing the plank ends is not known, but Stephens showed it in the 1880s, and presumably this planking practice originated long before Stephens reported it. It is possibly unique to the sneakbox.

Offhand, I cannot recall just this same method of lining plank and handling plank ends as used for any other hull. The nearest thing to it is the Scandinavian pram with the hood ends of its planks landing on a small, steeply raked bow transom. Actually there is some resemblance between the two types, except that the sneakbox is relatively much wider and shallower and more flaring than the pram.

For his 16 feet by 4 feet 11 inches by 1 foot sailing sneakbox, W. P. Stephens specifies carvel plank finished 9/16 inch thick. Although the lining of the plank is not shown, Stephens, in the construction section for his Barnegat Cruiser, does indicate representative planking widths ranging from 4 inches to 6 inches. This would mean that some hollowing or "backing out" of the inner sides of the planks would be required, even though the wide and gradually

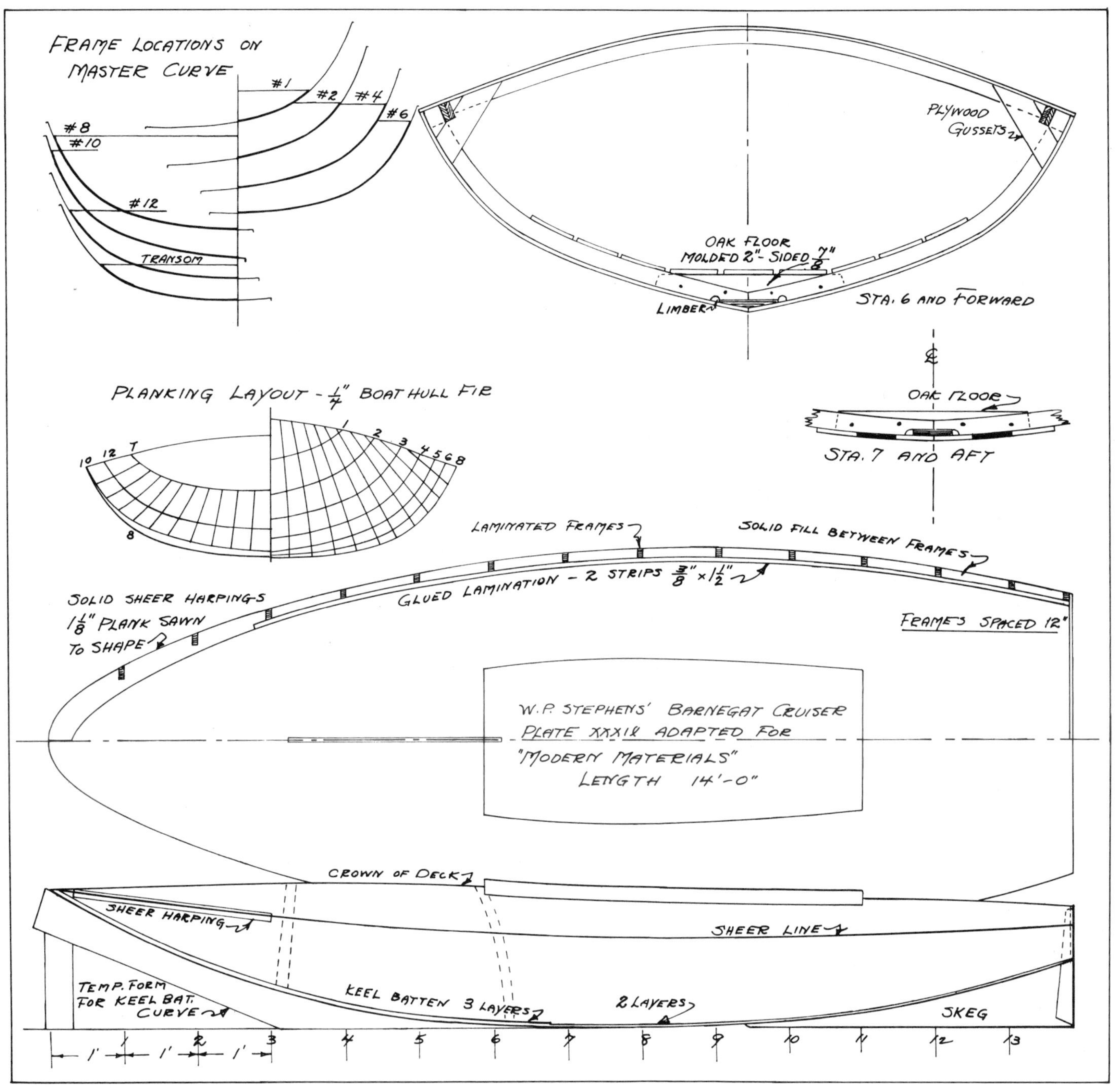

flaring sides of the sneakbox do not show any abrupt curves or sharp turns. Because of this, that is, because the side curves of the sneakbox hull are so flat and gradual, even though it is a round-sided boat, it is possible to plank it with perfectly flat strips, provided these are kept fairly narrow. This makes it possible to plank with strips of thin plywood without hollowing or backing out, and yet to achieve a satisfactorily round hull surface with only light sanding.

For the 14-foot by 5-foot by 1-foot 2-inch composite hull for which the lines and offsets are given here, 11 to 12 strakes of ¼-inch marine fir plywood on either side are recommended. Where the hull curves are practically flat, the planking can be as wide as 4 inches. Where there is more curve and at the ends, planks will narrow to 2 inches and even less.

Planks will be put on in continuous strips, in one piece from bow to stern, spliced before installation from standard 8-foot by 4-foot panels. The length of the scarph tapers should be 12 times the thickness of the planking stock, or 3-inches for ¼-inch plywood. The scarphs should be epoxy glued and sanded smooth on both sides after the glue has set. Well-made scarphs after sanding should be nearly invisible and are just as strong as the rest of the plywood. Plank splices must be systematically staggered on the boat.

Narrow plywood strakes pulled tightly against the frames with No. 6 1-inch bronze screws or No. 8 1-inch brass screws (the increase in size is to make up for the weaker metal) should give a hull surface very close to round when completed. Any slight tendency to show knuckled seams can be removed by sanding before the outer covering of SRP is applied. As bronze screws are extremely expensive, some economy may be achieved by using 1¼-inch Anchorfast nails in the less critical areas of the hull surface.

FINISHING OUT

After the boat is planked it is turned back on its bottom so that access may be gained to the interior, and narrow fiberglass or polypropylene tapes set in a stiff epoxy mix are laid over all inside planking seams, carefully cutting for length to fit between the frames. After the tape reinforcements have set up hard, the boat is turned back again bottom up.

In most cases a single layer of 4-ounce Vectra or Versatex polypropylene fabric set in epoxy resin will suffice, plus an overlay of Dynel (for its greater resistance to abrasion) to cover the bottom. As the sneakbox is a shallow-water craft that will be frequently grounded on sand and gravel, this overlay of Dynel, also epoxy-bonded, should not be omitted.

Inside the hull, the plywood before painting should be thoroughly soaked with a good oil-based wood preservative like Wood-Life or Cuprinol. In addition, an application of heated linseed oil diluted to help penetration would be all to the good. This should not be applied until after all epoxy adhesives and surfacing resin on the outside have hardened.

Next the deck beams and deck are installed. Each frame is topped by a deck beam of laminated spruce. The deck beams and frames are joined at the ends with plywood gussets glued and screwed in place and notched slightly to fit against the underside of the sheer clamp, previously put in. Some of the deck beams could have been put in previously, serving in place of cross spalls to hold the shape of the hull during planking, but not so many as to prevent convenient access to the interior before the tape reinforcements are put on the planking seams. Of course, the centerboard trunk must be installed before the deck is in place. Some builders might prefer to attend to the trunk before the boat is planked. This is a boatbuilder's option and depends in part upon the style of trunk and board selected.

The deck should be of ¼-inch marine fir plywood covered with SRP. This makes a deck both stronger and tighter than the ½-inch pine originally specified by Stephens.

We cannot give here completed details and directions for constructing a sneakbox throughout. For such further details, and for building directions to some extent, you should refer to previously published sources, especially W. P. Stephens and H. I. Chapelle. All we have attempted to do here is to show how the traditional sneakbox hull may be adapted to composite wood-plastic construction. By such construction it is possible to get, I believe, a hull of superior strength and lightness, to be made from materials more easily and widely obtainable today than is suitable natural sawn cedar for planking, for instance, as well as a hull easier for home builders to frame and plank than if they used the older methods.

Appendix: Notes on Boatbuilding Methods

ASSEMBLING AND RABBETING STEMS

Assembling and rabbeting a stem seems to be a difficult operation, though it is not. Because procedures for putting together, shaping and rabbeting stem assemblies are often treated perfunctorily in boatbuilding manuals, it will be worthwhile, I think, to examine these operations in detail. As an example, I include on pages 256 and 257 the details of the stem for the 12-foot round-bottom skiff shown in Chapter 18.

The term stem derives from the older word, stam, which the English Oxford Dictionary defines as a "stem or stalk, a trunk or stump of a tree," citing a seventeenth-century agricultural work, which mentions stamwood as "the roots of trees grubbed up." The original material for boat stems was stamwood, whence the name, and there is nothing better to this day for a boat stem than stamwood, providing you can get it.

In the past, builders of fine varnished yacht tenders got their stems, as a rule, out of hackmatack knees. Hackmatack, also known as tamarack, is a species of eastern larch whose principal roots grow out approximately at right angles from the stumps, and close to, or on, the surface of the ground. Root wood is the toughest part of the tree, and usually it was possible to select knees whose curved grain conformed closely, if not exactly, to the designed shape of the stem. Thus it was possible to get out the stem in one piece without cutting across the grain, achieving maximum strength without excessive bulk of timber. Hackmatack made a handsome stem in which toughness was combined with light weight.

Still lighter stems for the Adirondack guideboats were cut from red spruce root crooks obtained from stumps left by the lumbermen. White oak knees are the finest kind, but were used to a lesser extent for boat stems, possibly due to the difficulty of digging them. Even root crooks of northern white cedar served for the stems of Maine salmon wherries.

Of course, you won't find stump knees or root crooks for sale in today's lumberyards. There are plenty still growing in the woods, but unless the modern boatbuilder undertakes to dig his own, he will have to be content with substitutes. There are a number of ways of piecing together several short, relatively straight, sections of lumber to get the desired curvature. Also, it is possible to steam-bend straight pieces to the designed shape, and, in addition, the same result can be attained by laminating a number of strips thin enough to bend easily. (See the next section of this Appendix.)

A composite three-piece stem is recommended for the boat under consideration. In this case the continuous curved section will be on the outside, backed up by an apron piece, so called, at the top, joined below by another inner

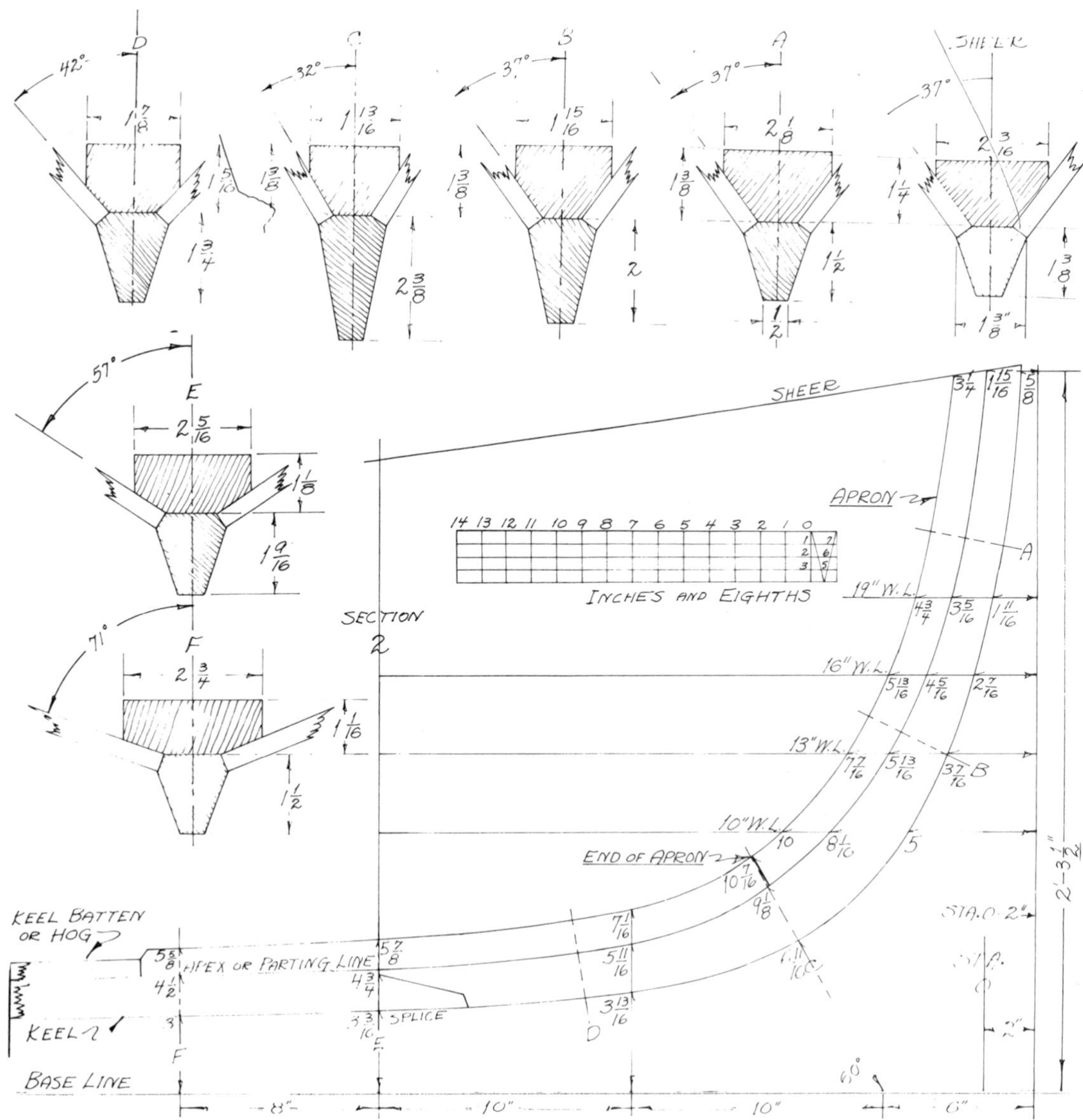

backing piece, which extends aft on top of the keel some 8 inches and is securely fastened to it. We do not have any specific name for this lower backing piece that I know of, although, according to Eric McKee, it would be called a "dead wood" piece in the south of England.

The curved outer piece, continuous from stemhead to where it splices into the keel, could either be glue-laminated from oak strips or a single piece steam bent. I recommend the former for a number of reasons. For one, good bending stock, and the means for steaming a piece of the required size are not always readily available, while lamination offers no special problems—except the clamps needed, possibly, but with some ingenuity effective substitutes can be improvised.

I want especially to direct attention to the way in which a stem assembly like this should be put together, and why it is made up as it is. Essentially it is made up of two layers: an outside layer of laminated or steam-bent wood in one continuous length and an inner layer in two sections placed end to end. These two layers are laid out so that they come together on the apex line of the planking rabbet, which I also refer to as the parting line precisely because the stem assembly is intended to separate along this line

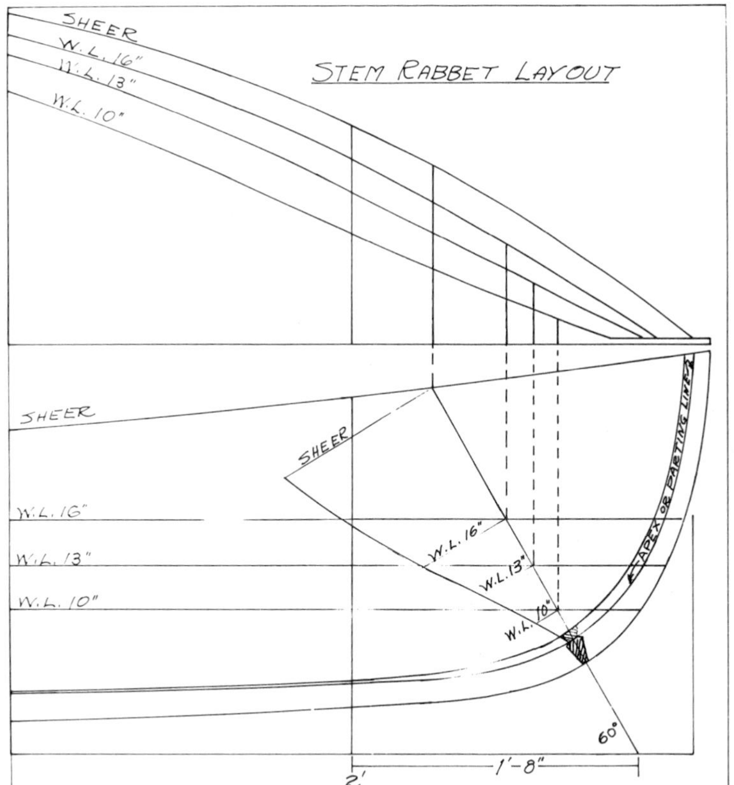

in order to facilitate cutting the planking rabbet.

Otherwise, the different "sidings" (thwartship thicknesses) of the inner and outer stem-pieces would have made the planking rabbet extremely difficult to lay out accurately. The different sidings or thicknesses of the parts that make up this composite stem range from 1⅜ inches to 2¾ inches, which greatly complicates lofting and layout if the stem assembly is treated as a unit rather than as separate pieces to be joined together after the planking rabbet has been cut, the method we have adopted here.

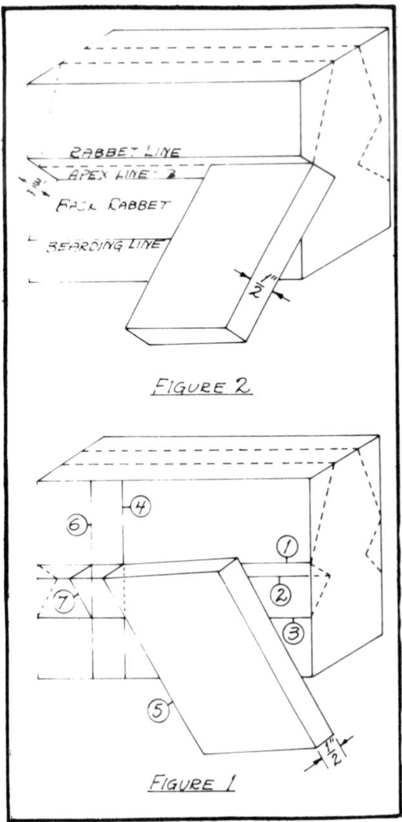

FIGURE 2

FIGURE 1

The simplest sort of stem is the one-piece stem with the same siding throughout, which is another way of saying that its port and starboard side surfaces are flat and parallel to each other. Lofting of the planking rabbet lines is quite simple and their transfer to the stem piece equally easy.

The procedure for cutting the planking rabbet under these circumstances is illustrated in the accompanying diagrams labeled Figure 1 and Figure 2. Figure 1 shows a short section of a stem of uniform siding with the planking rabbet marked out on one side but not cut. Number 1 is the rabbet line; number 2, the apex line; number 3, the bearding line. Numbers 1 and 3 are given in the original lines and are marked on the stem pattern when that is lifted from the full-size laydown.

After numbers 1 and 3 have been transferred to the stem piece, number 2, or the apex line, is derived as follows: A series of construction lines, numbers 4 and 6, as well as others like them, are drawn. These cross lines are laid out square with the rabbet and bearding lines when these are straight, and where they are curved the cross lines are drawn "normal" to the curve, which is to say they take the shortest distance across.

Number 5 is a small rectangular block of the planking stock to be used, which has been accurately squared at either end. This is applied edgewise. One corner is placed directly over the intersection of the cross line with the rabbet line, and the line of the opposite surface or face is made to pass through the intersection of the cross line with the bearding line. If the two edges lying over the space between the rabbet line and the bearding line are marked, the outline will appear as a right triangle when the block is removed, as is seen at number 7. The hypotenuse of this triangle extends between the rabbet and the bearding lines and its two legs intersect in the apex line. After a series of these points have been established along the length of the stem piece, a batten is run through them and the apex line marked, preliminary to cutting the planking rabbet.

It should be noted that if any one of these triangles so marked could be made to rotate on its hypotenuse as an axis, the path it would describe in passing through the wood of the stem would correspond exactly to the shape of the planking recess or rabbet when it is correctly cut.

It should be added that in cutting a stem rabbet of this kind, a perpendicular cut with a sharp chisel is made along the apex line first. Then the wood is carefully pared away with a sharp chisel, working toward the apex line from both the rabbet line and the bearding line, until the sample block of planking stock fits perfectly.

In Figure 2, the plank rabbet was first laid out for planking ¾ inch thick. This was done on the lines laydown. The stem pattern was marked accordingly, and the stem was so laid out. When the planking rabbet was cut, a block ¾ inch thick was used. Figure 2 shows a ½-inch thick block being used to mark the excess wood to be removed when ½-inch thick planking is used for this boat. The reason for doing this is to provide additional back rabbet surface for supporting and fastening the hood ends of the planking.

Compare the difference in the width of the back rabbet surface in Figure 1 and Figure 2. As the angle at which the hood ends of the planking meet the stem grows larger and becomes more obtuse, the width of back rabbet surface decreases. In some full-ended boats, an ordinary parallel-sided stem with uniform siding throughout would not provide enough back rabbet surface to afford secure fastening for the hood ends of the top-side planking. The method generally used to correct this is to back up the upper part of the stem on the inside with a thicker piece called an apron. A convenient way of doing this is to fit the apron to the outer stem at the apex line. This is what we show here for both the upper and lower backing members of this composite stem.

The outer section of this stem is of a uniform 1⅜-inch siding throughout. This is quite sufficient for the exposed portion of the stem for this boat, affording a sharp entrance and a neat, trim appearance. However, if this narrow siding were extended to the whole stem, there wouldn't be sufficient width of back rabbet to land the ends of the upper planks securely, or the forward end of the garboard. For this reason the inner portions of the stem were given an increased siding ranging up to 2¾ inches.

The three parts of the stem assembly are first got out to their molded shape and accurately fitted together and temporarily fastened with large screws from the inside. These screws are next removed, and the pieces taken apart and beveled. The back rabbet bevels are cut on the inner pieces, as are the bevels to receive the ends of the planking on the outer portion of the stem. This is done according to full-size sectional outlines laid out at regular intervals along the stem as shown in the drawing at an approximate 8-inch spacing.

A separate diagram shows one method for laying out these sections from the lines plan. Actually all that is needed for laying out a section is the angle at which the planking meets the center plane of the boat, except that this angle must be taken normal to the curve of the stem, or "square" with it, in boatbuilders' parlance, at the point where the section is laid out.

The angles used to lay out the stem sections are easily taken from a half model should one prefer to work directly from a model rather than lines, and, even if lines are used, a half model can be a great help and is well worth making. Such a half model should be shaped to the inside of the planking, and its stem profile should represent the apex line of the hull rather than the rabbet line.

After the stem pieces have been beveled according to the sectional diagrams laid out as explained, they are reassembled using an application of epoxy glue and drawing up tightly on the screws. When the glue has set, this composite stem should be as strong, or stronger, than if it had been got out of a single piece.

THE TWO-PIECE DORY STEM

As can be seen in the various plans for boats in this book, stems can be rabbetted or made up of two parts—an inner main stem and an outer false stem. For the latter type of construction, let's take a look at the stems for a Lawton dory skiff and the Chamberlain skiff shown in Chapter 5. The dimensioned layouts of both boats' stems are shown here.

Note that these layouts are for the shape of the inner or main stem. The outer false stem, which covers the plank ends, is, in standard dory construction, a strip of oak, put on last, steamed, bent into place, and fastened while it is still hot. After it has cooled, it is planed to shape. It should be faired off nicely in conformance with the lines of the bow, to give as easy an entrance as possible.

The main stem can be made solid or laminated. Here we will consider a laminated one.

The best way to make a gluing form for a laminated main stem is first to lay out the shape on a piece of plywood, ½ inch thick or thicker. Generally a scrap, or secondhand, piece can be obtained for this, to save the expense of new wood. Next, solid backing blocks for clamping against are fitted to the line of the stem and screwed on through the plywood from underneath. As the stem will finish to a 1½-inch siding

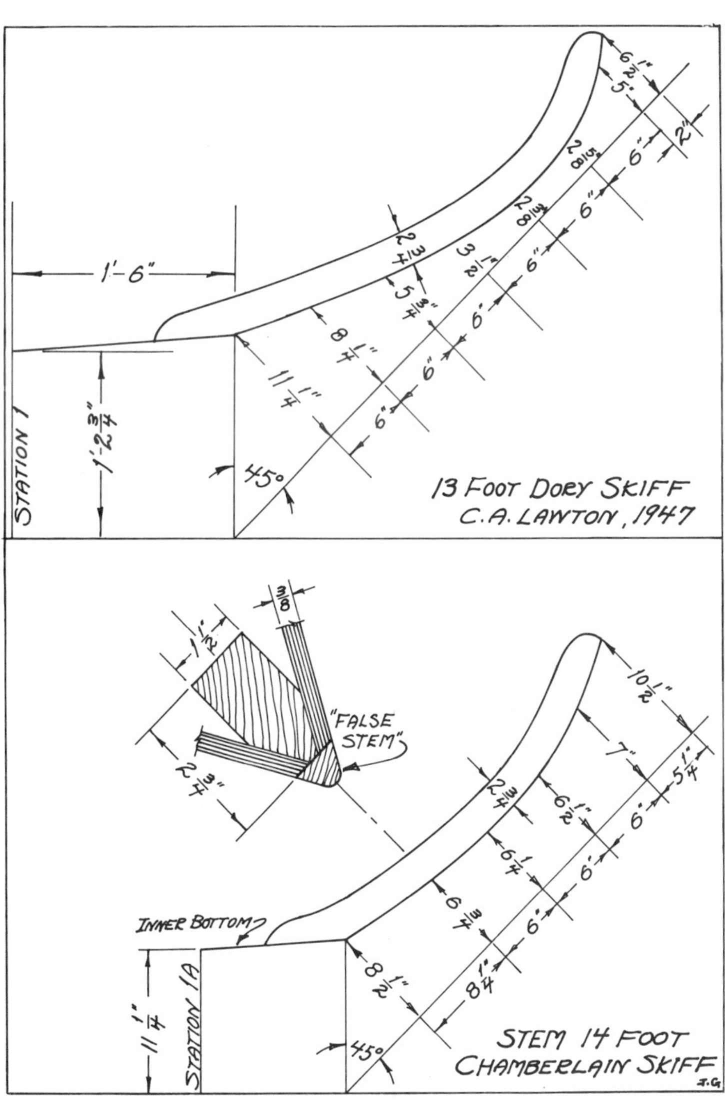

and will be glued up from strips slightly wider to compensate for any slight irregularities that might result from slippage during gluing, the backing blocks can be bandsawed out of short pieces of 2 x 4s. The blocks should be fastened on with plenty of 2-inch No. 12 or No. 14 screws; to glue them on as well would be an excellent idea, for this form must be absolutely rigid and adequately strong to withstand powerful clamping pressures, especially if a resorcinol resin glue is used.

I prefer to place my clamping blocks on the concave side of the stem curve, so that the clamps pull the laminations into a cavity, so to speak. Whether this is the better way, I cannot say for sure, but it seems to work better for me.

The form should be well waxed with several coats of Simonize or an equivalent wax to prevent the glue from sticking to it. The surfaces of the laminating strips should be rough, just as are usually left by the ordinary circular saw, for this helps to hold a film of glue in the joint, which is essential for a strong bond when gluing with epoxy. The laminations, after preliminary clamping, are tapped down with a block and hammer to rest snugly against the plywood base throughout. This evens them up edgewise and at the same time seals the bottom of the stem lamination so that the epoxy adhesive does not settle by its own weight and leak out before it has hardened. The epoxy adhesive should be applied liberally. It is far better to have too much glue rather than too little, as the excess is easily planed off after it has hardened.

Once laminated, the stem could be beveled at the bench to receive the planking before it is attached to the bottom. The bevels are quite easily obtained from the laydown. However, this is unnecessary, and I do not especially recommend it. For the amateur, it is probably easier to bevel the stem after the frames have been set up and are being faired for planking. A long strip of plywood serving as a fairing batten and extended across the frames in a fore-and-aft direction to overlap the stem will show exactly how much must be planed off in order to receive the ends of the planking. A centerline is marked on the outside surface of the stem, and the bevel is cut to about ⅛ inch of this line on either side of it.

Those who laminate the main stem may decide to laminate the false stem also. This can be done on the same form used for gluing the inner stem, with some slight adaptations, or it can be done directly on the boat itself, provided the epoxy glue used is thick enough not to run out of the joints before it hardens. It can be thickened by the addition of Cab-O-Sil, a thixotropic agent, which is a very fluffy, finely divided, powdered silica manufactured by the Cabot Company of Boston, and obtainable from most plastic supply firms.

The recommended technique for laminating the false stem directly on the boat is to tack each layer as it is applied with just enough fine brads to hold it in place. After the required number have been bent on, several temporary pressure blocks are screwed in place to hold the laminations in firm contact until the glue has hardened. These temporary pressure blocks can be sawn out of any convenient scrap stock, and are cut to fit the curve of the stem. They are fastened with long, slim screws, which go through the laminations into the main stem beneath.

Screw holes must be bored to prevent splitting the thin layers, especially if these are oak. After the glue has set, the pressure blocks, which need not be especially thick, by the way, are removed and discarded, and the screws which held them, if slim enough and not too long, may be set in and bunged, to remain as the permanent fastening of the outer stem.

It might be mentioned also that the strips forming the laminations of the outer stem are put on somewhat wider than this member will be when finished, and are later planed off and faired after the glue has hardened.

If a resorcinol glue should be used by someone sensitive to epoxy, the laminated outer stem should be glued on a form so that the requisite pressure can be secured by the use of clamps. Resorcinol resin glue requires ample pressure for satisfactory joints, which in this case means at least six or eight strong C-clamps as well as solid, fitted pressure blocks to transmit the clamping pressure evenly throughout the gluing surfaces. I should caution you, however, that some of the resorcinol resin glues are not always reliable with certain species of oak, in particular some of the white oaks.

PLANKING

Most of the boats in this book—the Rangeley for instance—are relatively easy to plank, although some who do not know might think otherwise. To say that a boat is easy to plank does not mean that it will plank up quickly. The contrary is more apt to be true. But to the amateur builder, the amount of time required is not too important, for his labor comes for free. Aside from the cost of materials, the amateur's main concern is whether the job falls within the range of his capability. He will be well advised not to venture into undertakings too exacting and advanced for his limited experience and skill.

Planking is not too difficult for the amateur, provided he is not in a hurry, can follow directions, and is able to use hand woodworking tools with fair proficiency. It must be set down at the outset, although it might seem too elementary to need saying, that no one should even think of building a planked boat unless he can measure accurately with rule and square, sharpen and set a plane, saw to a line, and otherwise employ carpenters' tools with moderate facility. There was a time when American boys in growing up acquired such basic woodworking skills as a matter of course. No more. In this button-pushing age, one can no longer take such fundamentals for granted.

This said, we may further explain that the Rangeley and other classic craft described here are better adapted to amateur construction than some other models, because over the years the professionals who built these boats to sell simplified and rationalized their construction. They did this to save labor and to keep the cost down so they might compete favorably in the market with other small-craft types, yet still retain the boats' superior characteristics and fine performance.

While all operations in building small craft are important and require care and competence, still the planking of a boat must be accounted the principal operation, and it is a good planking job above all else that makes a superior, or even an acceptable, boat. Planking is the boatbuilding skill par excellence. A good finish house carpenter can step into a boatshop and lay deck or cabin sole, scribe in bulkheads, build lockers and berths, or do a number of similar things first off as well, or nearly as well, as the experienced boatbuilder, but put him at planking without preliminary instruction or practice, and he is sure to botch it. This is because planking is a highly specialized operation, with methods, procedures, "tricks of the trade," if you will, that are not needed or used elsewhere.

In all the books on boatbuilding written in the last hundred years or so since books on boatbuilding (not shipbuilding) began to be written, there is no adequate treatment of planking that I know of, and the aggregate of planking information in all of them put together does not get into the subject in depth. This is mainly because those who so far have written the books are not the actual builders of boats with tools in hand, but rather persons somewhat removed from the building operation, that is to say architects, designers, engineers, and draftsmen. These people know all there is to know about hull lines, mathematical computations, and theory in general, but none, as far as I know, has as yet paid much attention to the practical problems involved in covering the hull surface with suitably proportioned strakes of wooden planking. To this day this essential operation has been left to the working boatbuilder. He has not written it down for various reasons, but mainly because he is usually not a writer, and thus much of traditional planking methods and procedures have remained virtual "trade secrets" in a day when there are not many trade secrets left.

For the foregoing reasons, the planking operation is prone to give the amateur trouble, and because he cannot find the instruction he needs in books, he goes haltingly and tends to exaggerate the difficulties that confront him.

LINING PLANK

In lining out plank, the builder tries to get shapes that will run as straight as possible when laid out in the flat on the planking stock. Excessively curved or crooked planks not only waste lumber, but are weaker than straight planks, because their curved sweeps cut across the natural grain of the board. The builder also tries to get shapes that look well on the boat, and this is especially important in clinker boats like the Rangeley where the lap lines stand out prominently. Not infrequently these two desiderata conflict, requiring artful compromise. Nevertheless, with certain hull shapes some crooked strakes are unavoidable.

With some such crooked strakes it would be difficult, if not impossible, to find boards wide enough to get them out full-length in one piece. Crooked strakes are usually made up of two or more shorter lengths, to save lumber and to give a straighter grain in the component pieces. One common example of the use of the spliced strake to permit the use of narrower boards, and to give a straighter, stronger grain, is the sheer plank of the knuckle-sided Swampscott dory, which is commonly made in two parts joined somewhat aft of the center of the boat. The strakes of the Adirondack guideboat were made up of two and three pieces each, primarily to get as straight a grain as possible for maximum strength. The narrow, clinker strakes of the Rangeley are also easily spliced. One thing that must be remembered is that splices in planks must be well separated from plank to plank. A judicious use of scarphed splices well distributed throughout the planking fabric makes planking easier and saves lumber, but under no condition should such splices be bunched up or allowed too close together in adjoining strakes.

The hull surfaces of different small craft types vary greatly in shape and proportion, each presenting its own special problems to the planker. Those experienced with one type often have trouble when they attempt to line out the planking for another type with which they are not familiar. In this connection, let me repeat a suggestion that has proved helpful in the past. Anyone planning to plank an unfamiliar hull shape should first make a scale half-model, and on this practice laying out the planking with light strips of pine for battens held in place with thumbtacks or large pins. By trial and error in this manner, he can work out pleasing and uniformly proportioned planking lines, the spacings between which are then scaled off and transferred full size to the molds of the actual boat.

It may be helpful to the non-professional to cite a few common problems met with in spacing off and lining out plank. First, consider the dory garboard, the top edge of which is lined out on the boat (that is to say, on the frames serving as molds and the stem and stern transom) to show a pronounced curve or sweep with the ends running up quite high on the stem, and usually almost as high at the stern. Judging from the lining batten as it is thus tacked in place on the side of the boat, it appears that this plank has a great amount of hollow curve in its upper edge. However, when the shape of the plank is spiled off and laid out on the planking stock in the flat, it will be found that the top edge of this plank is actually nearly straight. Had it been lined out to look flatter or straighter on the boat, the top edge of this plank, when laid out flat, would have taken a convex curve, necessitating a corresponding concavity or hollow curve in the bottom edge of the plank next above, causing this next plank to be quite crooked. By running the ends of the dory garboard up high on the stem and at the stern, the lower planks of the dory are made nearly straight, which saves planking material and produces stronger planks because of their straighter grain.

Because of the dory's high sheer, enough uncovered stem surface still remains above the upswept garboard to provide ample landing width for the hood ends of the remaining plank. This would not be the case if the dory had a straight sheer like the standard round-sided yacht tender, made to lie as flat and low as possible when turned bottom up on deck. Such a tender will be relatively big-bellied to carry a load, yet the stem will be short because of the flat sheer. Nine or ten strakes will be required to fill out the girth amidships. Yet, should the garboard be carried up high on the stem as in a dory, sufficient length of stem rabbet would not remain to allow sufficient width for the hood ends of the eight or nine plank remaining. To get them all on, these ends would have to be made too narrow and pointed to look good or to fasten properly.

I have seen many poorly lined planking jobs and they were most unsightly as well as structurally inferior. Some years ago a boatshop in Amesbury, Massachusetts, which had formerly built dories exclusively, added a round-hull stock sailboat to its line. Built like dories by dory builders, obviously, these boats the first year showed extremely ugly plank shapes, a wide, high-swept garboard, and wedge-shaped upper plank with narrow pointed hood ends. Later this was rectified after the plankers learned how to line this round hull.

When properly lined, the upper edge of the garboard of the standard round yacht tender will look, when the boat is viewed in profile and square off from the side, straight or nearly so. But lay this plank out in the flat and you will see that the fore end is narrow and that it hooks down somewhat. This is due to the twist, and the pinched-in shape of the entrance below the load waterline, as well as the necessity of keeping the end of the garboard low. This ugly hook in the end of the plank disappears when the plank is bent and twisted into place on the hull. Sometimes, due to a bad job of lining, such a hook can still be seen in the fore ends of planks after they are in place on the boat. Such drooping ends, aptly called "moose shoulders," offend the eye and are avoided by the professional planker.

The Rangeley is not a hard boat to line for plank; this is particularly true for the 17-foot H. N. Ellis boat described in Chapter 20. While its 4-foot beam gives considerable center girth, the stem is high enough, because of the ample sheer, to provide ample landing room for 10 planks above the garboard. The ends of these can be kept wide enough to look and fasten well.

But let's get specific: lining the shape of the plank does not take place until after the boat has been set up and faired for planking. This means that the backbone—stem, keel, and transom—is set in place with section molds at indicated stations. For example, in the Rangeley boat (Chapter 20), the molds are spaced 2 feet apart, making seven molds in all. Ordinarily there would be no mold at the No. 8 station shown on the drawing as this section was put in merely to aid in fairing the lines.

In the case of a new boat being built for the first time from scratch, it is necessary to decide on the number of planks and their approximate widths, and to space them off on the stem, transom, and at the center of the boat. In very few boat plans are the number and the widths of the planks given.

In dividing up the sides of the hull into equal plank spacings at various selected locations, a simple but convenient device called a "diminishing batten" is easily prepared and used (see next page). Of course, the same results can be obtained with a rule and arithmetic, but the diminishing batten is quicker and avoids figuring. It is not needed as much on small craft as on larger vessels where planing widths have frequently to be adjusted and where there are many more stations to measure. It is important to realize that a separate diminishing batten must be marked out for each different number of plank.

After the line representing the upper edge of a strake of plank has been tentatively and approximately located and marked at the bow, stern, and midsection, and possibly at other locations in between, a fair lining batten is run through these spots and temporarily tacked in place with small nails only partly driven in so that they may be easily pulled with the claw hammer. Usually it is best to start nailing at the center of the boat and work either way to the ends. Directions for making up a lining batten follow this section.

After the batten is in place, it is sighted carefully from various heights, stances, and angles. In this way, unfair places, if any, are discovered, and are corrected by raising the batten slightly here or depressing it slightly there. When

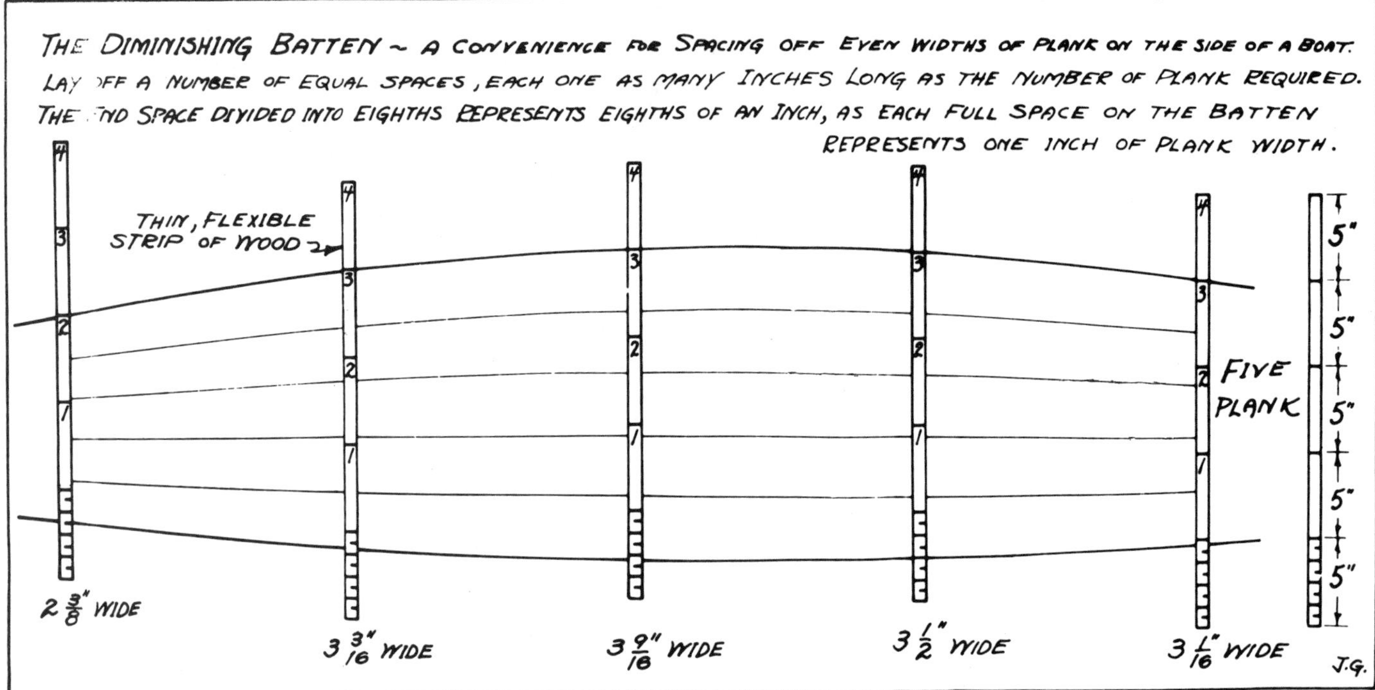

the plank line is finally true and fair throughout, it is clearly marked on the molds at each station.

The inherent tendency of a properly made lining batten is naturally to assume a fair curve or sweep when bent without being forced at any point. Often when a place shows unfairness, it is necessary only to pull a single nail for the batten to spring into place and thus to correct its line more or less automatically. Thus, in lining plank, a good batten supplements the boatbuilder's eye, and one serves as a check on the other. The boatbuilder's eye is educated by sighting the batten, and by the judicious and painstaking use of the batten, the novice can usually do an acceptable job of lining, which otherwise would be impossible for him. The lining batten is an indispensable planking tool that must be kept in good condition, so that it does not become twisted, warped, split, or scarred along its edges.

Some builders line all the planks at the start. Others work piecemeal. Often as planking proceeds, and in clinker planking especially, slight cumulative errors creep in after a few strakes are on, requiring adjustment in lines laid out previously if the planking is to come out right. Thus, as the planking goes up the side of the boat, it may be necessary to reline some of the upper strakes. Here the diminishing batten may be used to advantage to check plank widths and spacings. However, it is always the lining batten that has the last word as to what the widths and shape of the strakes will be.

To keep the planking on both sides of the boat running the same is not quite as easy as it sounds. Frequently, inexperienced plankers fail to keep port and starboard hood ends on the stem of equal height and width. The two ends on either side of the stem rabbet should match exactly. Slight discrepancies from side to side in the mid-part of the hull, where the eye cannot easily detect them, are not particularly serious, that is, as long as they remain small, but a close watch should be kept for them nevertheless, and immediate adjustments made to minimize them as quickly as possible when found.

THE LINING BATTEN

As already discussed, lining out a boat hull for planking requires a lining batten, which the builder must make for himself. Such a batten is a uniform strip of wood with parallel sides, a flat, rectangular cross section, and a length somewhat greater than the boat to be planked. For example, the Rangeley boat (Chapter 20), requires a suitable lining batten that would be something like 1¾ inches to 2 inches in width, 5⁄16 inch to ⅜ inch in thickness, and 19 feet to 20 feet long. Clear, soft, straight-grained northern white pine is probably the best material for a batten, since it is a wood that is close grained, springy and uniform in bend, and soft enough to take nails without splitting.

The edges of a lining batten must be perfectly regular and true, so that in whatever way it is bent, a fair curve or sweep is produced. "Fair" is a trade term meaning a continuous, uniform sweep without lumps, holes, or irregularities of line of any sort. The ultimate test of fairness is what boatbuilders call a "good eye," which a few seem to come by naturally, but which most must acquire through practice and experience. As the old boatbuilder would say, "If it looks right, it is right." But it depends, of course, on who is looking. Fortunately for the novice, there is an aid to the unpracticed eye. The fair line is inherent in straight-grain wood itself, that is to say the long uniform cell fibers of straight-grain wood naturally assume fair curves or sweeps when they are bent.

In picking out pine for a lining batten, considerable pains should be taken in selecting the wood, for the quality of individual planks or boards can vary considerably. Try to get a section of plank that is straight, free from knots, and quite soft. Occasionally pine planks will be found that are harder than is normal for the species and some will be found with a pronounced grain that is not characteristic of pine. "Brashy" is the old Maine word for such lumber, which is strictly to be avoided. Brashy lumber comes from deformed, misgrown trees that are sometimes found on rocky, exposed hillsides. The wood has ingrown stresses and is prone to warp and split. Far better for our purpose is the softer wood from lush pines that grew fast, straight, and tall in rich bottom land.

Soft, straight-grained spruce can be used for lining battens but is more likely to warp than northern white pine. Port Orford cedar is quite good, and less apt to warp than our native northern white cedar. A select grade of soft Philippine mahogany will serve, as will cypress possibly, although it splits easily. By and large, a soft wood with as little grain as possible is to be preferred.

The hardwood species are of no use whatsoever for lining battens. A warped or twisted batten is useless, and any that get into this condition should be discarded. Obviously, battens when not in use should be stored in such a manner as to minimize the possibility of warping and twisting. Preferably they should lie flat and straight on a long rack where the air can reach all sides equally.

Long boats require long battens. For instance, as previously mentioned, the Rangeley boat will require a lining batten some 19 to 20 feet long for best results. Pine lumber of suitable quality in such lengths is not easily come by today. Fortunately, however, long battens can be spliced up from shorter lengths of stock, and, if this is properly done, the result is just as good as the unspliced batten from full-length lumber. It may even be possible to produce a better batten in this way, for the same quality of wood may be had throughout from the same high-grade section of plank.

If the finished width of the batten is to be 2 inches wide, the strips from which it is to be spliced up should be at least 3 inches wide to start with in order to provide ample extra wood for edging and sizing. The number of scarphs will depend on the length of the stock available. Three or four in a 20-foot batten are not too many. The length of the scarph bevel should be at least 12 times the thickness of the stock, and this should be left thicker when spliced than the finished thickness of the batten to permit straightening and sizing.

The scarph bevels must be accurately planed to a feather edge at the ends in order to secure perfectly fitting joints. Strong glue and careful procedure are required to obtain a perfect glue joint. As the batten will be kept dry and under cover, a completely waterproof glue is not required. If epoxy adhesive is used, the meeting surfaces of the scarph should be slightly and evenly roughened with a fine wood rasp or coarse sandpaper, for it is necessary that a thin film of resin be retained in the joint.

For a simple but excellent gluing jig or press, two pieces of smooth board slightly wider and longer than the scarph are required. One side of each is thoroughly waxed. On the waxed surface of one block the scarph to which glue has been applied is assembled and tacked in place with several fine brads to prevent slippage. The other block is laid on top, with the waxed surface over the scarph, and firm pressure is applied with two or three C-clamps. The wax prevents the glue, which is squeezed from the scarph, from sticking to the pressure blocks. When the glue has thoroughly hardened, the clamps and blocks are removed and the brads pulled out.

After the batten is glued, it is laid on the bench, or on a long plank serving as a bench. One side is planed smooth and true with a sharp jack plane. Next it is turned on edge, and the upper edge is planed as true as possible with the longest plane available, a long joiner if possible.

The batten is now ready for the circular saw, which should be sharp and smooth cutting; a planer-tooth blade is best. The edge already planed is run against the fence, which is set wide enough so that the saw blade barely brushes the other edge of the batten when it is run through. The fence is then set in an eighth of an inch or so, and the batten, turned over to reverse the edges, is run through again. This process is repeated several times, trimming one edge and then the other, until the width has been cut down to the desired 2 inches. By then, the two edges should be perfectly even and true, and parallel throughout. The fence is then set ⅜ inch from the blade, or according to whatever thickness is desired for the batten, which is run by the saw on edge with the previously planed surface against the fence. The batten is now trued and sized and ready for use.

Any extra care or labor expended in making a good lining batten will be repaid many times over before the boat is finished. To the experienced boatbuilder, all this may seem so obvious and simple as not to be worthwhile considering in detail. For the novice, however, it should serve to smooth over some otherwise rough going.

CLINKER OR LAPSTRAKE PLANKING

Clinker or lapstrake planking deserves to be more widely used. It has a number of advantages over carvel planking, and for some hull forms is the easier method. But inexperienced builders tend to shy away from it. This is because they do not understand how it is done, and because it has never been explained to them.

To the best of my knowledge no fully adequate explanation of clinker planking techniques has yet found its way into print. Some of the books hardly mention it. Others go only part of the way, skipping over, or leaving out entirely, essential steps and procedures.

Books at best, with their drawings and printed explanations, are only partly effective and a poor substitute for actual planking experience under the tutelage of a skilled craftsman. Still it is possible to convey enough with words and sketches to put the beginner on the right track, and to give him some directions to go by, enough to insure a reasonable chance of success, provided he keeps his wits about him. There are in fact a number of books that take up lapstrake planking which are worth looking into, and they are quite good as far as they go, but none is complete in all details, and all of them, at least all that I have seen, leave out things here and there that I consider important or even essential.

High on the list of books to be considered is H. I. Chapelle's *Boatbuilding* (W. W. Norton, N.Y.), for 35 years a standard work in its field. A much less extensive treatment of clinker planking is to be found in Robert M. Steward's more recent *Boatbuilding Manual* (International Marine Publishing Company, Camden, Maine), but one that will bear looking over, nonetheless.

Quite recently there have been two books

by British authors devoted entirely to this method of boatbuilding. Eric McKee's *Clenched Lap or Clinker* (National Maritime Museum, Greenwich, England), although only 30 pages long, contains considerable which is new to print, and John Leather's *Clinker Boatbuilding* (International Marine Publishing Company, Camden, Maine), a full-length book, includes much supplementary information. Both McKee and Leather treat the subject according to British methods, which frequently differ from American building practices. But the contrast between British ways and American ways can be instructive.

It is important to understand some of the advantages as well as the disadvantages of lapstrake construction. Although it is not suitable for some hull types and should not be considered for them, for others it is the natural and proper method and superior to any other that might be used.

While I have done my part to bring modern materials to the attention of amateur builders, and do not regret having done so, I must say I am sometimes disturbed when I find someone using glued-strip construction for a classic type that is better and easier built clinker. Generally this happens because the builder does not understand the advantages of clinker construction, or is afraid to try it, having never done it, but having heard somewhere that clinker is too difficult except for highly skilled professionals. Actually this is not so at all.

What are the advantages? Clinker boats tend to be light and strong, but flexible, making them faster and easier in a seaway, a characteristic of lapstrake craft since the time of the Viking longships. Clinker planks can be finished and sanded smooth at the bench before they are bent in place on the boat. This means substantial saving in labor over carvel planking, for the latter method requires that planks be hollowed on the inside, that is "backed out," to fit the curve of the frames, and after the hull is planked, the outside must be planed fair and sanded smooth. In addition the planking seams on a carvel hull must be caulked, while clinker hulls do not require caulking.

In order to hold caulking, carvel planking is rarely made thinner than ½ inch finished thickness, and to allow for the backing required for round-sided hulls the planking stock to start with will need to be from ⅛ inch to ¼ inch thicker than this, requiring a total thickness of ⅝ inch to ¾ inch or more. For clinker-planked boats of approximately the same size, the planking ordinarily will not be more than ⅜ inch thick and possibly only 5/16 inch. This means that for some of the classic clinker types such as the Rangeley boats, St. Lawrence skiffs, light yacht tenders, dinghies, and similar craft, the strakes for both sides can be laid out in single thickness on one-inch rough lumber to be split in two edgewise with a fine rip saw or band saw after being cut to shape. This can result in a substantial saving in lumber, not to be taken lightly considering current prices of planking stock.

One disadvantage of clinker boats is that it is not easy to replace damaged planks. However, with the epoxy glues and related materials now available, split planks can often be repaired on the boat without removing them.

Not every hull shape is suitable for clinker planking. Carvel planking is more versatile in this respect. By hollowing, bending, and twisting, carvel plank can be forced into all sorts of difficult shapes, as clinker plank cannot. The novice will be well advised to stick with classic clinker types, at least to start with, and be content to copy proven craft, adhering closely to them in such things as lap width, plank thickness, number and widths of planks, and especially to the way the hull surface is laid out or "lined" for planking.

What seems most to worry many beginners is fitting the laps, for of course a tight wood-to-wood fit of the lap surfaces must be secured throughout if the boat is not to leak. It is possible to secure a tight, leak-proof boat by using a flexible polysulphide compound in the laps, even in badly fitting ones, although applying this material is likely to be a messy procedure.

Laps should never be glued, as this prevents the normal slight movement back and forth of the lap surfaces occasioned by swelling and shrinking as the boat absorbs moisture or dries out. Splits in the plank or the laps will almost inevitably occur if the laps are rigidly glued.

Swelling and shrinking of the plank can be minimized and the wood stabilized to a great extent by soaking the planking with hot linseed oil (heated in a double boiler and diluted about 20 per cent with paint thinner or turps). Several applications until the wood is saturated, applied before painting, are required for best results. Clinker plank so treated will remain permanently tight under most conditions, provided they are well fitted to start with. In painting, after the oil has dried, the paint should be thoroughly worked into the laps.

But to return to fitting the laps. Where the sides of the boat are straight or only slightly curved, there is no problem. All that is required here is careful planing to get a tight fit. But where the frames show more curve, and particularly amidships on the turn of the bilge on hard-bilged boats, it may not be so easy to close the laps, unless the operation is carefully laid out in advance.

Four factors need to be taken into consideration: (1) the curvature of the hull, (2) the width of the plank, (3) the thickness of the plank, and (4) the width of the lap.

If the curvature of the hull is too abrupt, or the width of the plank too great, or the plank too thin, or the lap too wide, it will be difficult, and perhaps impossible, to close the lap. Of the four, plank width is most readily adjusted. Once a model is selected, the curvature of the sides can hardly be altered without basic alteration of the design. The plank thickness is generally established at the outset, and likewise is not open to adjustment as construction proceeds.

While lap width may not be reduced below the minimum required for secure fastening, there is still some slight margin for adjustment. But plank widths can generally be made as wide or as narrow as required, without adverse effect on the structure or appearance of the boat, if the planks are lined out properly. How to go about this will be explained shortly.

On Sheet 1 are shown planking layouts for the midsections of four clinker workboats ranging in length from 14 feet to 15 feet 5 inches. In all four the sheer planks and the bottom planks are wider than those on the round of the bilge. The first boat, left to right, is a wide, heavy working skiff 14 feet 5 inches long with 5 feet of beam. This is closely like a working skiff built in Rhode Island a hundred years ago, and in active use there until quite recently. The half-inch-thick planking is unusually heavy for a clinker boat of this size and the 1⅛ inches laps are extra wide. This hull shows a good amount of deadrise and some flare at the sheer, hence the turn at the bilge is moderate.

By making the sheer plank, the garboard, and the broad quite wide, it is possible to plank this boat with only seven strakes. However, the planks on the turn are only about half the width of the garboard and the sheer planks, yet even so, the laps for planks 5 and 6 do not quite close at the bottom. This does no harm, and is done to give ample wood for the lap fastenings. Besides this slight gap will fill with paint, and will not show when the boat is in use. The same thing occurs with the lap of the fifth plank of the wherry.

In all four boats the plank widths are laid out so that those planks on the turn of the bilge, where the greatest curvature is, are considerably narrower than the bottom and sheer planks where the side, or sectional, shape is straighter. As these narrower planks—that is, narrower amidships—carry forward to the stem and aft to the stern, they will hold their widths to a greater extent than will the top and bottom planks, that is, they will not "diminish" as much, to use the trade term. Or to put it another way, these middle planks will line out more nearly parallel sided. In most cases it is desirable for the ends of all the plank landing on the middle and upper stem,

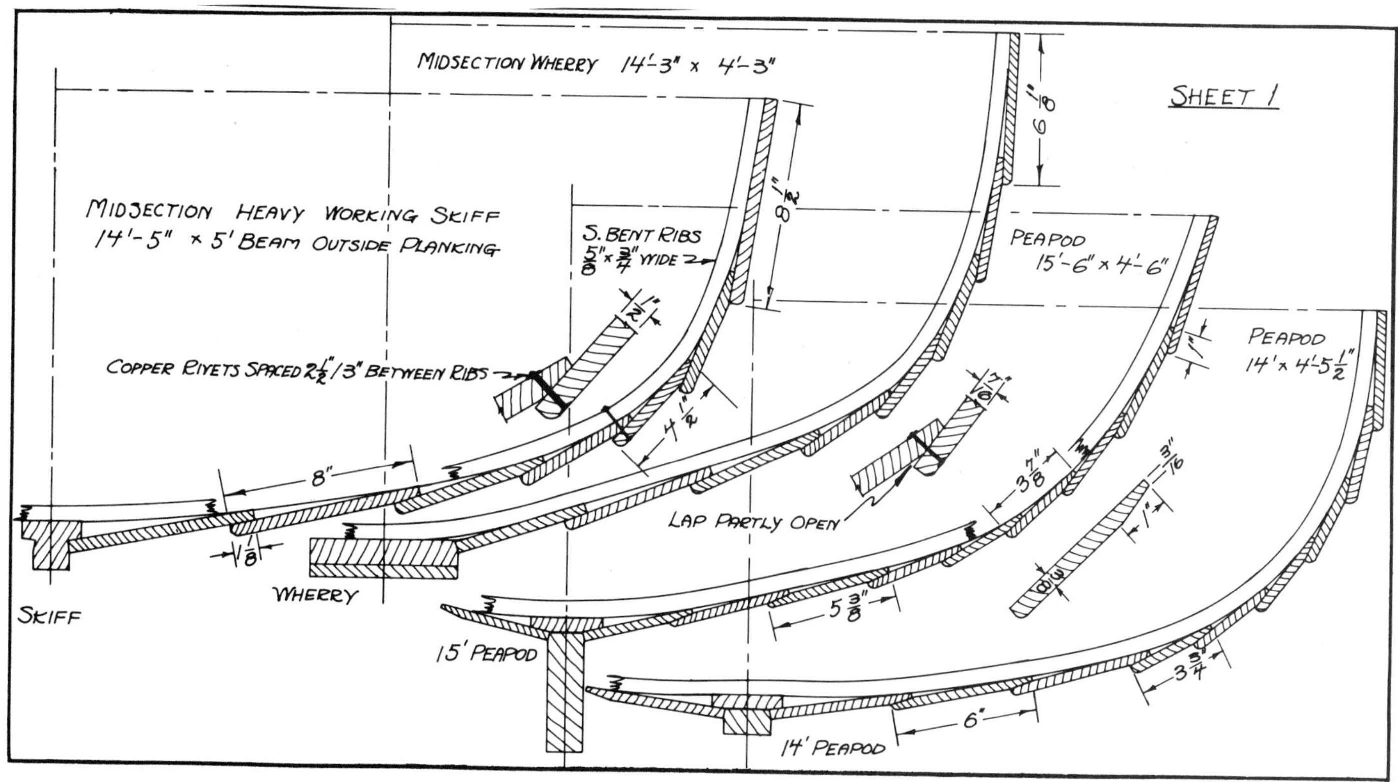

with the exception of the sheer, to show approximately the same width. Generally the sheer plank should be wider.

The lining or layout operation that established the planking lines, that is the planking widths, shapes, and relative locations on the hull, is a highly critical part of clinker construction, much more so than for carvel planking. Not only is this important, as we have seen, to get laps that will close easily, or even close at all, but the planking lines stand out so distinctly on a clinker hull that, unless they are right, the appearance is spoiled.

In building a first boat, it is highly desirable to have access to one already built to go by. With such a model it will be easy to copy the planking layout, number of planks, their widths, lining, lap widths and bevels, and so forth. With a little care, even the most inexperienced builder should be able to avoid serious mistakes.

If one undertakes to build from a drawing without having an example of the craft at hand to consult, chances are that some details will be missing. In fact most building plans now available for small craft do not go into planking at all, leaving this up to the builder. If it is his first boat, or even his first clinker boat, it will not be strange if he makes a mess of it, unless he has something more to go on.

How to proceed under such circumstances? As soon as the lines have been laid down, the body section with the greatest amount of curvature (usually the midsection) should be reproduced full size on the drawing board so that a layout of the plank sections can be worked out for it. This will consist mainly of adjusting the widths of the given number of strakes to get good closure of the laps without making some of the strakes excessively wide and others too narrow. Extremes should be avoided. Plank thickness, lap width, and number of planks are usually given or established at the outset, but conceivably any one, or all, of these might have to be adjusted to get a satisfactory planking arrangement. In some cases, additional sectional layouts of the planking at other hull locations might be desirable for comparison.

The results obtained from the sectional layout provide the basis for the lining operation; that is, the lengthwise layout from stern to stem of planking width and shapes. I cannot recommend too strongly that the inexperienced builder start by making an accurate scale half-model of the hull of convenient size, say, on the order of 1½ inches equals 1 foot for a 16-foot boat. A trial layout of the planking is made on this half model, lining out the planks with miniature white pine battens representing the planking laps (made to scale, of course) and held in place with dressmaking pins. This procedure allows the builder to see the planking layout as a unit, and permits such adjustments as are required to correct any unfairness and to insure a pleasing and harmonious planking arrangement throughout. The corrected batten or lap locations are marked on the half model before the battens are removed.

Some experienced builders may feel that they can skip the half model, but I recommend that they use battens to lay out the lap locations on the building molds as soon as they are set up and secured in position. These lap-width battens should be stiff enough to bend fair between the molds, and battens for all of the planking laps should be put on the molds at the same time so that the planking arrangement can be viewed as a unit.

Plank locations previously worked out on the half-model are transferred to the full-size setup. Adjustments, and more than a few, will nearly always have to be made, until all of the battens run fair and the whole arrangement looks pleasing and right as a unit. This will take sighting and resighting from every angle, and this fairing process should not be hurried. In fact it is best to go away and come back several times before the fairing operation is completed.

Finally, the adjusted lap locations are marked top and bottom on the molds, and transferred to the other side of the boat so that both sides are identical, and the planking as it proceeds should be held strictly to these lap locations. In this way it is easy to maintain fair planking lines and to come out right at the end, something not easy for the inexperienced builder to do otherwise.

Beveling the laps can be a real bugaboo for the inexperienced. It takes care, and it takes knowing how, and what complicates things is there are several different ways of going about it, each applying to some particular boat or type with its own special requirements.

Some of the St. Lawrence skiffs, for example, have their laps brought to a feather edge and are planed so they are quite smooth outside, almost like a carvel hull. Some boats like the heavy working skiff on Sheet 1 have a minimum amount of wood removed in fitting the laps, so that some of the lap joints are not planed at all, in this case the lap between the garboard and the next plank above. British boats are more apt to be built this way with only the least possible amount of wood removed in fitting the laps, what the British call "hemming," according to Eric McKee. Leaving as much wood as possible in fitting the laps makes for a strong lap joint, but it tends to produce a heavy, not to say clumsy, look which can be avoided by thinning the lap somewhat, but not to the extent of weakening it unduly.

Where the model permits it, and this is governed by the amount of curve in the sectional shapes, a uniform amount of bevel can be planed off the underside of the lower edge of the overlapping plank, and the lap bevel on the underside of the plank below can be planed to fit.

An example of this is shown by Lap Diagram No. 1 on Sheet 2, where a uniform bevel of ⅛ inch by ¾ inch is planed off the lower inside edge of the planks when they are prepared at the bench. Lap Diagram No. 2 shows how a thicker, heavier lap joint would result if the overlapping edge were not beveled.

The method that I am suggesting here, and it is not the only method by any means, for fitting and "hemming" the laps consists of planing whatever is required for a fit off the bevel on the top edge of the under plank and doing this on the boat. This amount is not uniform or constant, but varies from thicker to thinner as the curvature of the side varies.

Generally, the professional will first cut the correct lap bevel at each mold station using a gauge of some sort representing a cross section of the upper, or overlapping, plank at that station in order to get the correct amount of bevel. When this is done for all the stations, he will next proceed to bevel the sections between the stations, depending more or less on his eye and acquired skill to get the lap sections true and fair from station to station. This is not easy for beginners who are apt to take off too much or too little wood, producing a lumpy lap surface which will not close tight.

However, if the beginner will adapt the method detailed on Sheet 2, he can, by taking care, plane a perfect lap. A small, sharp plane set fine is needed. One small enough to fit in the palm of the hand is best for this.

A batten as long as or longer than the boat, and stiff enough to bend true and fair, is temporarily tacked to the section molds so that its lower edge (it is understood, of course, that the boat is being built right-side-up) coincides with the marks on the molds representing the extreme upper edge of the plank in the process of being hung. A gauge for testing the lap bevel, such as is shown on Sheet 2, can then be applied at any place along the side of the boat to indicate the exact amount of lap bevel required on the under plank. There is absolutely no guesswork. With ordinary care a perfect fit can be achieved throughout.

There are various ways of reducing the thickness of the laps at the ends so that the

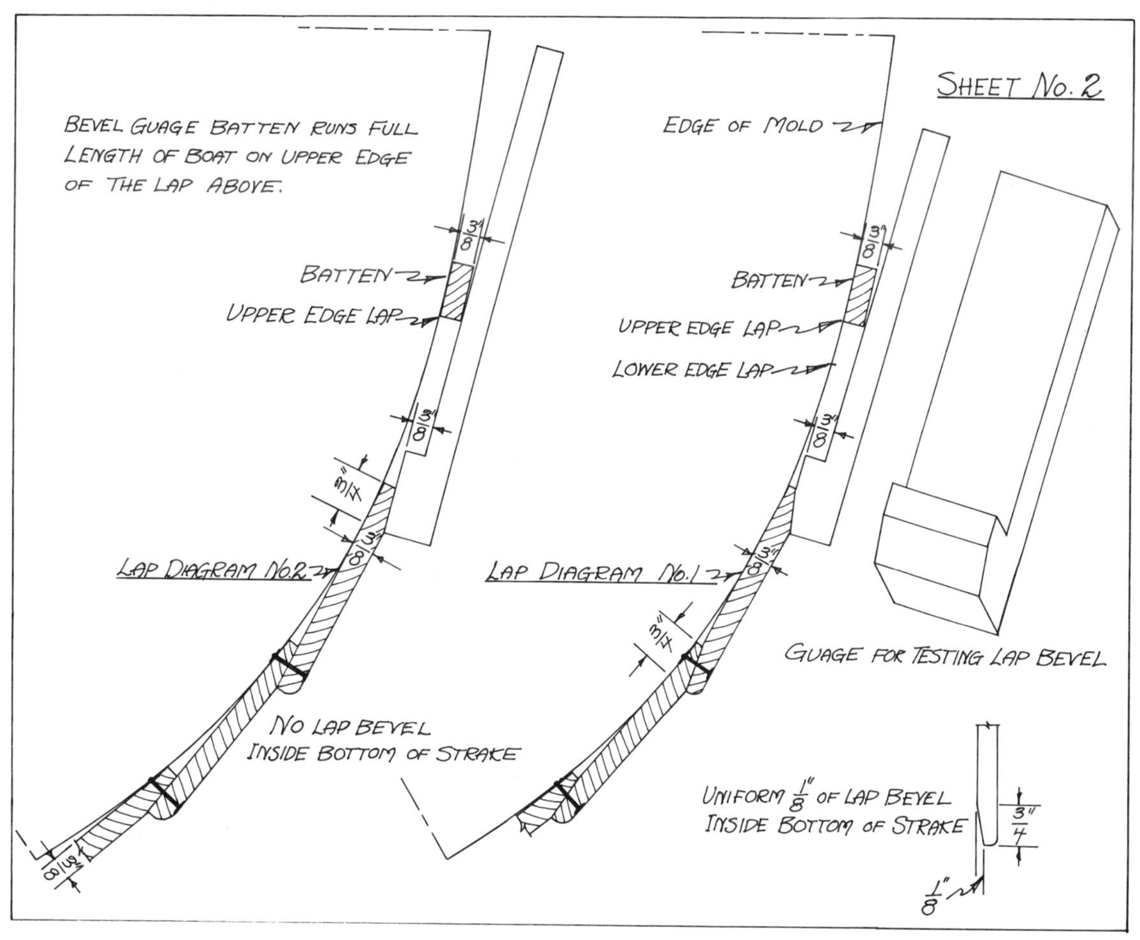

ends of the planks will fit together to lie flush in the stem rabbet and on the transom, what McKee calls "chasing." These methods have been pretty well explained already in the books previously mentioned.

There is one more thing I should mention about lapstrake planking. For a one-off job, and especially for a first boat, I would recommend building it right-side-up, but set up high enough to work under comfortably. If this should require a plank a foot or so off the floor to stand on while working on the top side, that would be quite all right. Building right-side-up permits the builder to rivet the laps as he goes along without the assistance of a helper. In the production shop, boats are often built upside-down on a special form with all the riveting being done at one time after the planking is completed and the boat has been removed from the form and turned right-side-up. But I do not recommend this for the beginner and his first lapstrake boat.

SPILING

Spiling is the technique that enables a boatbuilder to take off the shape and dimensions of any structural part of the hull, and to transfer that shape to a flat plank, timber, sheet of plywood, or whatever, so that when it is cut to the line, and bent, twisted, or otherwise forced into place on the boat, it will fit perfectly.

A boat is all curves and bevels. Because many of its component parts assume different shapes when they are incorporated into the hull fabric than what they had laid out flat (planking in particular), the methods of the house builder, utilizing mainly the square and the plumb line, do not suffice for the boatbuilder.

The shapes that boatbuilders have to deal with are so complex that without a special technique with which to determine them, and to duplicate them, boatbuilding would be a slow, tedious process, and one extremely wasteful of materials. Boats probably could be built by hit-or-miss methods of cutting and trying, and cutting and trying again until a fit was achieved with methods that miss far more often than they hit, methods sometimes resorted to by the inexperienced and the unskilled, although there is a better and an easier one at hand.

There is nothing difficult or mysterious about spiling, although it might seem so at times. Quite the contrary, spiling procedures are simple and straightforward, yet few of the numerous boatbuilding books and manuals now in print treat this subject competently and adequately. More often their directions are defective and misleading.

One recent, widely touted work, purportedly on "simplified boatbuilding" for amateurs and home boatbuilders, fails to include spiling in the index, although it allots a full half-page of text and three sketchy diagrams to its consideration. All three of the diagrams are defective, with one seriously in error. This last is a diagram of the "reference line" method of spiling, in which reference lines fail to appear on the spiling batten shown transferred to the planking stock, which is where reference lines are required, and the only reason for having them. In redrawing this diagram, the author apparently saw fit to dispense with reference lines in the precise place where they are indispensible.

This may seem an extreme example, but another comes to mind almost as horrible. About 30 years ago, a Massachusetts man got into the public eye by building a vessel in his backyard intended for a voyage around the world. In the process he became a boatbuilding expert, and one spin-off was an article in a national yachting magazine presenting a spiling gadget of his own devising, which, in addition to everything else, mounted a spirit level. Nothing could have been more unnecessary, useless, or ludicrous to a professional boatbuilder.

While the principles underlying spiling procedures are quite simple, their application, depending on the circumstances, can take many different forms and variations. Much of this is difficult to put into words. In boatbuilding as a whole, as well as in the other manual trades, much is involved that words—and especially printed words—do not cover very well. Yet, in spite of this, it is possible to set down some useful notes and directions for spiling.

As previously pointed out, spiling is a method developed by boatbuilders for transferring shapes. In order to transfer shapes, they must first be recorded in some way. In spiling, this is most commonly done by marking thin strips of wood, called "spiling battens," as are used in the planking operations. Spilings are also marked on templates of approximate shape, as in fitting plywood bulkheads in the interior of a vessel.

If the correct procedure is followed, and the required steps of the spiling operation are accurately performed, the shape of any part of the hull can be marked for duplication—quickly, easily, and accurately enough for any practical need. Considering the geometry of some of the complex curves involved in planking a round-sided boat, it will be seen that a great deal of intricate mathematics is bypassed by this simple manual procedure.

In marking spiling battens or templates, three different methods are most commonly used, and these we shall consider here without going into others of more limited applications, such as the use of a chalk line to take the shape of the planking of large wooden vessels, such as nineteenth century Gloucester fishing schooners.

The three different methods for marking spiling to be considered here are shown in the diagrams on page 275: (1) reference lines, (2) intersecting arcs, and (3) the spiling block. Some boatbuilders prefer one, some another, but generally make use of all three at one time or another, for each works best in certain situations or places, as usually becomes evident in actual practice.

Spiling is commonly thought of in connection with planking, although, as we have seen, it can be employed for taking the shape of any part of the vessel. Spiling battens used in planking are wooden strips of varying lengths, or widths, roughly approximately the same as the planking, and of pine, fir, cedar, or other soft wood that planes and nails easily. Battens are used over and over again, with the pencil marking planed off each time, so that they tend to become quite thin. To begin with, they are usually under a half-inch thick.

Thin battens in long lengths tend to be flimsy, and in long lengths they are apt to sag edgewise when they are being temporarily tacked in place on the side of the boat unless precautions are taken. In tacking a batten on the side of a boat, be it long or short, it is best to start at the center of the batten and work out toward the ends. In the case of a long batten, if there is an assistant handy to hold up the ends until the nails are in, so much the better.

Edge-set—edgewise springing or sagging of the batten—must be prevented when using a spiling batten. Should it get into the batten when it is put on the boat, or afterwards when it is tacked on the planking stock, the identical amount of distortion will be automatically transferred to the plank, which will then have to be sprung (edge-set) back into place to make it fit when it is hung on the boat. This can present serious difficulties, especially with clinker planking.

For holding spiling battens on the side of the boat, for cleating them together (unless small screws are used), and for tacking them to the planking material so they won't slip out of position while the marks are being transferred, small common nails 1 inch to 1¼ inches in length are used. These are not driven all the way in—enough of each nail is left out for the claw hammer to catch. These tacking nails hold better in cleating together two short lengths of spiling batten if they are driven in at an angle, first in one direction then in another. It is better to put in a few extra, rather than too few, for if the cleat should slip, the spiling operation must be done over.

When a spiling is to be taken for a long, curved plank, it is best to use two or three short pieces tacked on the boat end to end to make up the required length. The spiling is marked, and then the ends of the short battens are well cleated together before disturbing them, so that they can be removed from the boat in one continuous length and placed on the planking stock (board) without any change in their relative positions one to the others. When the spiling batten is put on the boat, it could be cleated together before it is marked, but then some of the marks would come on the cleats, with more chance for inaccuracy.

After the batten is placed on the wood, the marks are checked to see if they all come on the wood, and that defects like sap and bad knots are avoided. When the optimum position for the batten is found, each of the component pieces of the batten are temporarily tacked in place with two or more small nails so that they cannot accidentally slip or be moved, after which the cleats holding them together are removed so that the spiling marks beneath them can be reached for transfer.

Although edge-set should be avoided as a rule, there are times when it cannot be helped or is even deliberately put in. Some planking species, including white cedar, retain grown-in stresses, especially in flitch-sawn, or live-edge, boards, so that when planks are sawn out of such boards, their shape as marked tends to change. If the change is slight, the plank can generally be sprung into place, otherwise it may have to be discarded.

Now and again, it will be found that the board intended for a plank is not quite wide enough to get the plank out as spiled. However, it may be possible to get wood enough for the batten by springing (edge-setting) it slightly in and tacking it on. If this is done gradually, with care to get a uniform change of curve throughout, the board can often be saved. The resulting plank, although slightly straightened, will have the requisite width and a fair edge so that it can usually be sprung into place to give a tight fit

The longer a plank is and the thicker it is in relation to its width, the easier it is to bend edgewise; consequently, with large vessels, edge-setting planks was frequently resorted to by design to save lumber and to expedite the planking process. On small craft, however, it is not recommended, as a rule, and especially not in the case of clinker planking.

Clinker planking is usually both thinner and wider than carvel planking for the same size craft. The laps of clinker plank that are edge-set tend to gape open and are hard to get tight. In addition, the frames in lapstrake boats are usually not put in until after the boat is planked, consequently there are no frames to fasten into as planking proceeds to hold the plank in place, as in a carvel-built boat. Thus, edge-setting the planks of a clinker boat is very apt to lift the planks off the molds, altering the intended shape of the hull.

In spiling for clinker plank, special precautions are advised for the best results. If the plank is at all long and/or crooked, the spiling batten should be made up, as previously described, of two or three short pieces cleated together, and in light construction small screws, say No. 4s or No. 5s, are to be preferred over nails for fastening the cleats.

The width of the spiling batten should be about the same as the plank, and it is best put on like a plank so that it overlaps the edge of the plank from which the spiling is taken, and it would be advantageous to under-bevel the overlapping edge of the batten somewhat, very much as if it actually were a plank.

All this may seem over fussy and tedious to some, but believe me, it is worth doing and will pay off, especially for the novice and the occasional builder. There is an old saying that applies here: "The long way around is the shortest way home."

Each of the three methods for marking the spiling batten and the plank in turn, which have already been mentioned and are illustrated in the accompanying diagrams, require some additional explanation.

1. *Reference lines*: This may be the oldest method, and it seems to be the most commonly used in Great Britain. After the batten is tacked in place on the side of the boat, lines—at intervals ranging from a few inches apart to a foot or more—are drawn across the

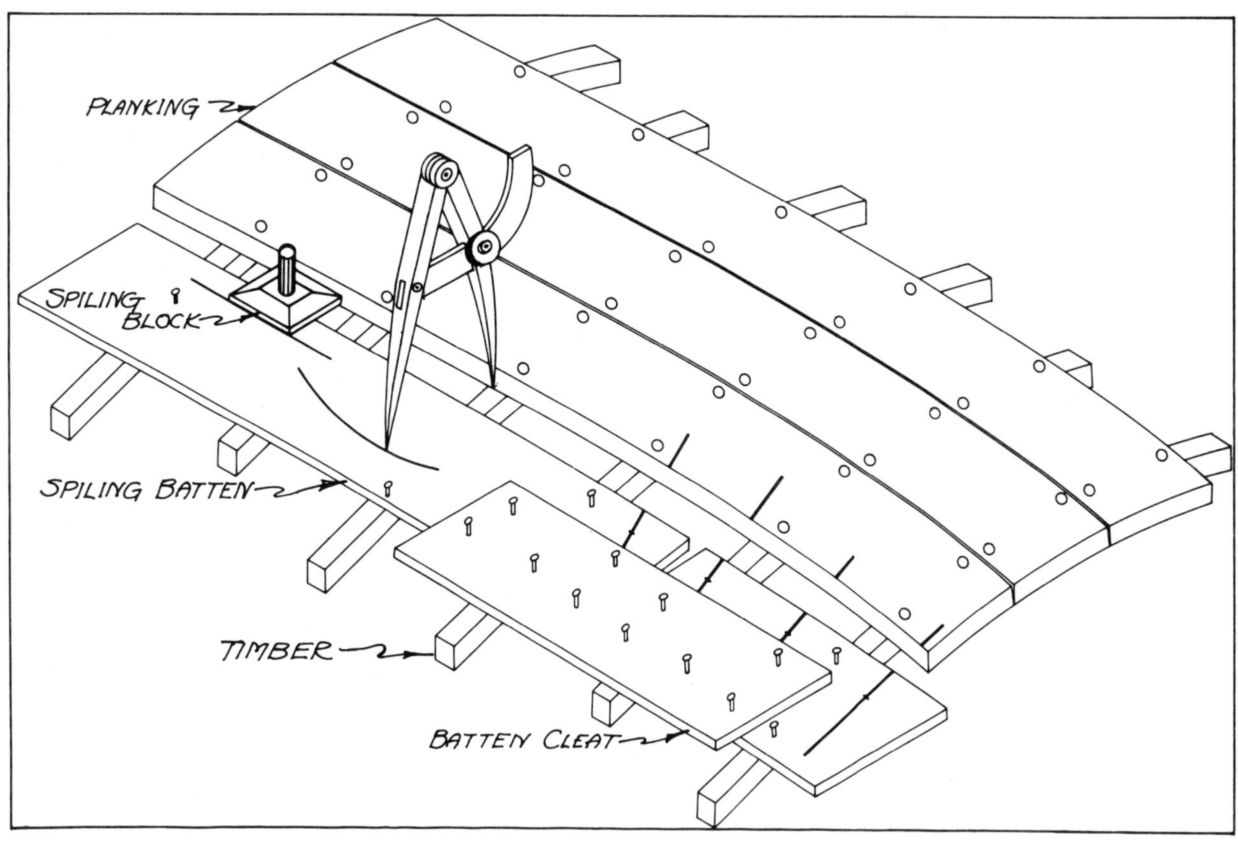
PLANKING
SPILING BLOCK
SPILING BATTEN
TIMBER
BATTEN CLEAT

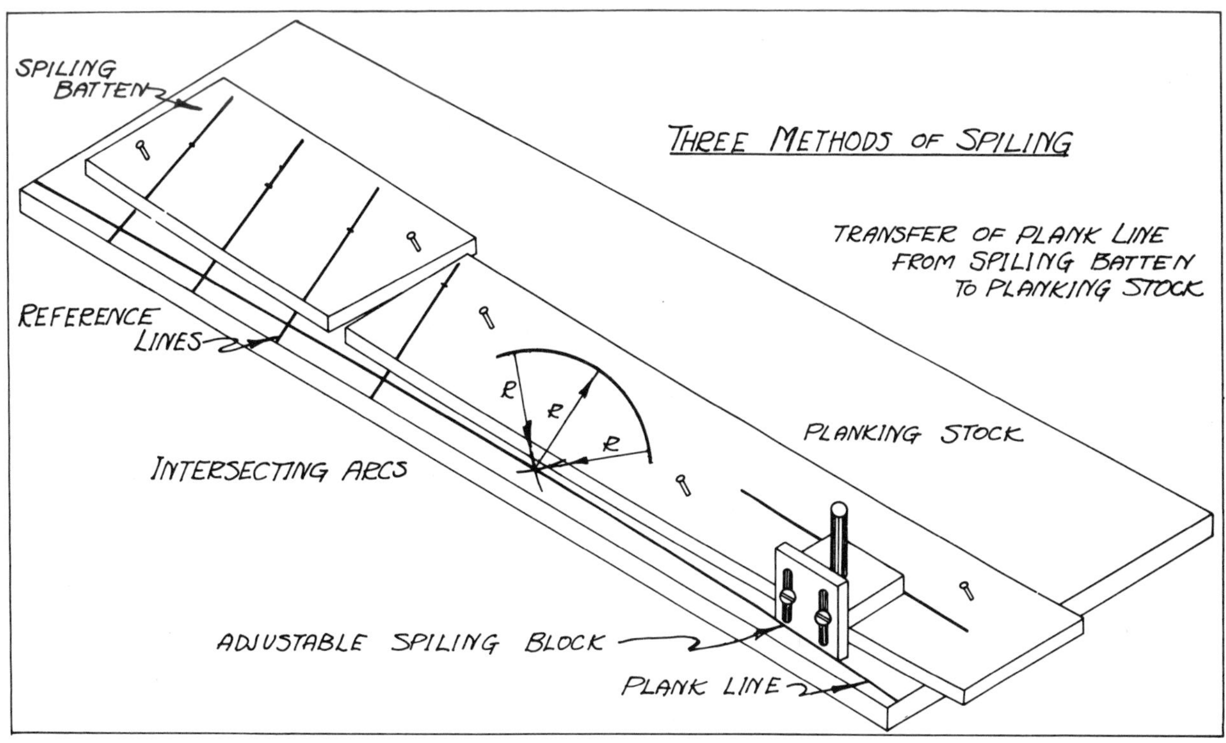
SPILING BATTEN
THREE METHODS OF SPILING
TRANSFER OF PLANK LINE FROM SPILING BATTEN TO PLANKING STOCK
REFERENCE LINES
R
R
R
PLANKING STOCK
INTERSECTING ARCS
ADJUSTABLE SPILING BLOCK
PLANK LINE

batten and carried on to the edge of the plank, from which the spiling is to be taken. These lines run more or less square with the edge of the plank, or normal with its curve, and are commonly drawn by the professional using a pencil marking along the edge of his folded two-foot pocket rule.

Next, dividers are set to a convenient distance that will reach from the edge of the plank on to the batten all along its length. When this setting has been referenced on the batten so that it could be recovered if it were accidentally lost, it is stepped off from the edge of the plank along each line, and plainly marked on the reference lines on the batten. After the batten has been lifted from the boat and located and tacked in place on the planking stock, the reference lines are extended on to the board using the straight edge of the rule and the pencil.

Next, the original setting of the dividers is checked on the batten to make sure it has not changed, is stepped off along each reference line from the point on the batten to give a point on the extension of the line on the board, being the original spiling procedure exactly in reverse. This gives a row of points on the board through which a fair batten is run or "lined," which, when marked, produces a line exactly the same as the line of the edge of the plank on the boat—that is, if the spiling has been accurately done.

Basically, it is all a matter of measuring along the reference lines. How best to lay out these lines—the fine points, that is—will vary somewhat from job to job, and calls for experience and judgment, yet the method is very nearly foolproof if care is taken and the procedure is carried out accurately. It is best to make a reference mark, or "sir mark," so-called, at whichever end of the plank goes on the boat first, usually the bow end, so that the plank can be hung exactly where it belongs on the first try by matching the mark on the plank with the mark on the boat. This is especially necessary for garboards. Also, for the bow end of garboards, where they turn up sharply in an abrupt curve, best results are often obtained by making an exact template for a short distance and cleating it to the end of the spiling batten when the latter is tacked in place and before the spiling is taken. The dividers should be applied uniformly with all measurements taken from the top of the plank or from its bottom edge, as may be decided for a particular job, but never haphazardly from both top and bottom.

2. *Intersecting arcs*: This is probably the method most used in this country in recent years. Spiling by intersecting arcs is quick and accurate, and generally applicable to any situation in boatbuilding. Pencil dividers are opened to a convenient setting, which is marked on the batten for reference in case the dividers are dropped or some other mishap occurs to alter the setting. With the pointed end of the pivot leg placed exactly on the edge of the plank being spiled, an arc is swung marking the spiling batten. If the position of the legs of the dividers is now reversed so that the point of the pivot leg is placed anywhere on the arc marking the batten, an arc now swung will pass through the original point on the edge of the plank and the intersection of any two secondary arcs swung from points separately located anywhere on the original arc will establish the location of the original point. In this manner, points for the plank line on the planking stock are established from arcs on the spiling batten. This may sound involved, but it isn't. A glance at the diagram on page 275 should make it all perfectly clear.

Accuracy will be increased if the points for the intersecting secondary arcs are taken a good distance apart on the original arc rather than close together, and for that reason, the arcs on the spiling batten should be as long, within reason, as is convenient to make them. Here again, experience and judgment enter in, and sometimes arcs must be quite short due to special circumstances.

Aside from the manner in which points are established, as just explained, the method of spiling with intersecting arcs is governed by the same considerations as already explained for reference lines.

3. *The spiling block*: In using the spiling block, the batten is handled exactly the same as for the other two methods. When the spiling block is used, it is of particular importance for the batten cleat to be put on after the batten is marked, for obvious reasons.

The block is placed on the batten with one edge coinciding with the line to be transferred, and a pencil is drawn along the opposite edge of the block marking the batten. In some cases, a continuous line is drawn on the batten; that is, the line is transferred in its entirety, but more often it is not. A series of short lines suffice, which, when they are transferred to the planking stock, are connected with the lining batten exactly as if they were a row of points.

The diagrams on page 275 show two types of blocks—one that is flat, and another which is adjustable. It is plain that when the flat block is used to transfer lines from the batten to the planking stock, the edge of the block will be raised above the planking stock the thickness of the batten, and unless the pencil point is held exactly plumb and directly under the edge of the block, the mark will not be accurate. To insure against error from this source, an adjustable block is sometimes used, but through practice the professional generally learns to get accurate results with the flat block, not bothering with the adjustable one.

Flat blocks so used are generally rectangular in shape, 1½ inches by 2¼ inches. Both the long way and the short way can be used, depending on the width of the gap to be spanned in order to get a mark on the template, but when the long way of the block is used, the line on the batten so obtained should be clearly and immediately marked for identification as such, otherwise confusion and errors are bound to occur.

Best results for taking complicated templates for interior bulkheads of plywood and the like are obtained by using the spiling block. It is best adapted for short lines and intricate shapes. With care and some practice, the most intricate shapes can be fitted perfectly using templates and the spiling block.

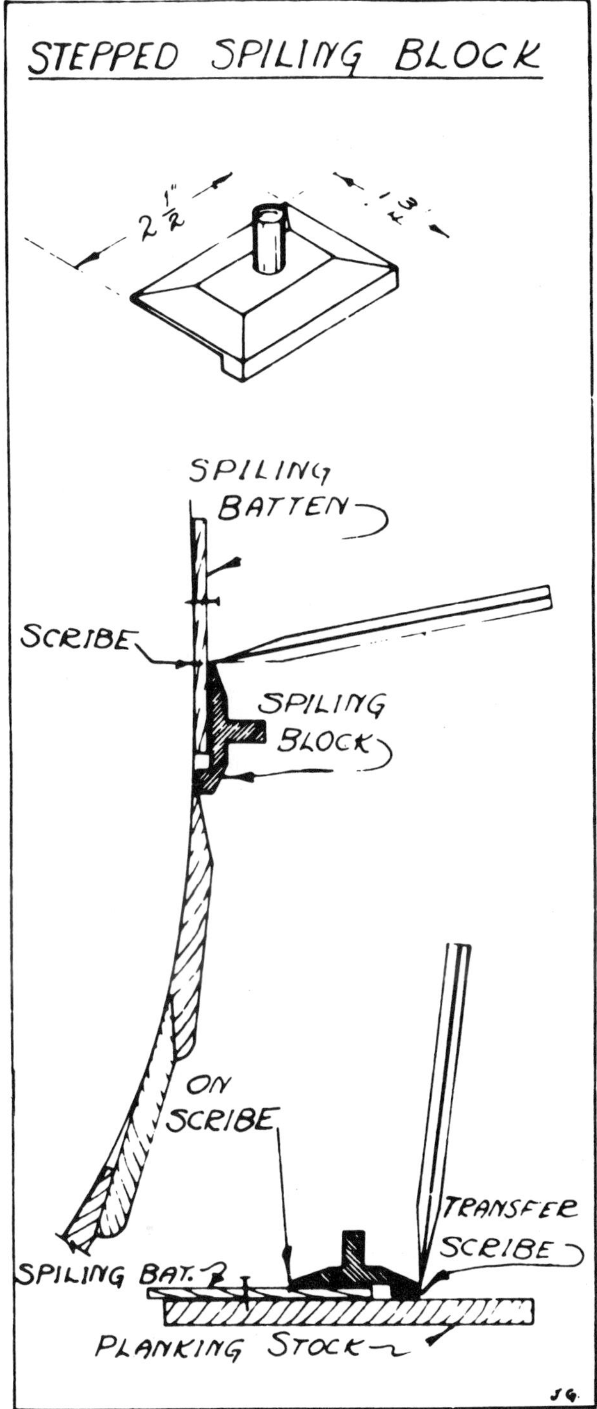

Of course, with all spiling methods allowance must be made for bevels. In addition there are numerous other fine points that will become apparent as you proceed. As with everything else, facility and accuracy come with experience and practice.

SCARPHING

Since so many of the boats described for building in this book call for scarphed planking, some general directions for making epoxy-glued splices, both of plywood and ordinary boards of sawn lumber, will be useful. First of all, scarphs to be joined should be neatly made, of course, so they fit well when brought together. Yet the meeting surfaces should be slightly roughened with a rasp or sandpaper, for epoxy is strongest when a slight film of glue (a few thousandths of an inch thick) remains on the joint.

Epoxy does not require high clamping pressures (like the resorcinol glues for example). Often when clamps are not available, or in places where ordinary clamps won't reach or fit, glue joints can be drawn together by nailing. Sometimes the nails can be left in; other times they are removed after the glue has set. In the latter case, they are generally driven through pads or strips of plywood or other material, so they will exert pressure, yet permitting access to their heads so they may be easily removed later on.

Using epoxy glue, it is possible—and not difficult—to splice plywood of any width. The width of a scarph should be not less than eight times the thickness of the plywood, but 12 times the thickness is better. The scarph bevels of the joining ends are cut on a fair uniform taper and are brought nearly to a feather edge, but not quite. The excess is sanded off after the glue has set. When this has been done, a well-made splice can hardly be found.

If much plywood splicing is to be done, a simple but adequate jig can be set up for use with a power router. For a boat that requires only a few splices, a sharp, low-angle block plane is all that is required. The plane's blade or iron should be set at an angle of 10 to 12 degrees. Low-angle planes are made for smoothing end grain, and plywood is approximately half end grain.

One other important tip in planing scarphs for splicing plywood: the thin end should be supported during the planing. Usually the end of the bench will do nicely for this. If the bench is uneven, another piece of plywood or a wide board can be placed underneath the end and just even with it to give the necessary support when scarphing.

Before gluing a plywood scarph, it is prudent to check the alignment of the splice by clamping the pieces in place on the boat. Also, it is best not to cut the panels to exact size and shape until after the splices have been glued. Some extra wood left on the edges of the panels will permit a final adjustment before the piece is fastened, should this be required.

One simple method of gluing up a splice in plywood as wide as the sides of a boat is to apply glue to both surfaces, fit them together, and rest them on a large, heavy plank. A couple of small nails into the plank will keep the surfaces from slipping out of alignment. Then a strip of board is laid across the top, roughly the width of the scarph and directly over it. A line of 10d nails driven through the scarph into the plank beneath at intervals of 3 to 4 inches will apply enough pressure to pull the joining surfaces together. Of course, the surfaces of the plank and the board must be either waxed or covered with paper to keep glue squeezed out of the splice from sticking to them.

For pulling together glue joints and holding them until the glue has set, double-headed, or "staging" nails, so called, are useful. They can be driven in tightly enough to exert considerable pressure, yet the protruding outer head makes them easy to draw later with a claw hammer or bar. In gluing softwood planks with epoxy glue, staging nails can be used in place of clamps to a considerable extent.

After the glue is set, the nails can be pulled, their holes plugged, and the splice sanded on both sides. Properly done, the splice will hardly show, not at all if painted, and the result will be as strong as the rest of the panel.

Besides plywood, ordinary boards of sawn lumber can be spliced. For instance, I suggested that scarphing the clinker planking of the Rangeley (Chapter 20) offers two distinct advantages: (1) butt blocks, as are required for joining lengths of carvel plank, are avoided, and (2) short lengths of planking lumber can be used. This means substantial saving in the cost of planking material, for some of the strakes for the Rangeley in full length take pronounced curves, which to get out in one piece would require premium-priced wide boards, difficult to obtain nowadays, at best. Even lumber with some knots may be used, for in getting out shorter lengths of plank, it is often possible to lay out the cuts in such a way as to avoid the knots.

Furthermore, in full-length strakes of marked curvature, some cross-grained wood cannot be avoided, resulting in a loss of strength. But with spliced strakes of several shorter lengths, the grain can be kept straight throughout, so that spliced strakes make a stronger boat, provided the scarphs are well distributed or "staggered," as boatbuilders say, in addition to being properly made and glued.

Splices in sawn boards should be bevel scarphed to a feather edge on each side; the length of the bevel should be eight to twelve times the thickness of the plank. The scarph surfaces should be glued with epoxy adhesive on or off the boat. If the scarph is glued on the boat, it should be clamped with the simple clamping jig shown in the accompanying sketch. This jig is merely two blocks of wood (hardwood is best) well waxed on the inner surface to prevent sticking, and drawn tight with one 1¾-inch No. 12 wood screw, which passes through the splice and hauls it tightly between the two blocks. When the glue has set up hard, the jig is removed by loosening the screw, and the hole is plugged. This jig fits between the laps, so as not to interfere with planking, and thus planking can proceed from strake to strake without waiting for splices to harden, or the removal of the clamping jigs.

If you prefer, splices can be glued off the boat. One way is identical to the plywood scarph method already described: Assemble the splice on a plank with a short piece of board on top covering the splice, and drive a few nails through this "sandwich" to hold the surfaces of the splice in place and in contact until the glue is set. Afterwards, the nails can be pulled and plugged. The bottom plank and covering board may either be waxed or covered with paper to prevent the excess glue from sticking.

Scarph laps in sawn boards are easily planed with a sharp block plane, although in commercial boatshops, such as those operated at Rangeley, a planing jig was used. The plank end to be scarphed was inserted in the jig, a handle was pushed back and forth a few times, and the sharp cutter attached to it and set on an angle produced a perfect scarph bevel more or less automatically. Such a device is a great time-saver and more or less a necessity in a commercial shop. It is not difficult to contrive, and, even though planking scarphs are easily made with a block plane, some amateur builders might want to devise a scarphing jig. This could easily be done today with a high-speed router, which many amateur woodworkers have and are familiar with. With the plank end clamped in position in the jig, and with a few passes of the router, the scarph bevel would be perfectly cut in the proverbial "jig time."

RIVETING AND TIMBERING

The planking laps of classic lapstrake boats can be fastened with rivets or clinched fastenings. Copper rivets are used to fasten the planking laps of many of the boats discussed in this book, both through the timbers and between them, instead of clinched fastenings. Although rivets may mean a little more work, I believe they pull up tighter and are not as apt to work loose as clinched fastenings, when properly put in. J. Henry Rushton of Canton, New York, the famous nineteenth century builder of light boats and canoes, thought otherwise and used clinched fastenings. In one of his catalogs he explained why: "When we try to rivet-fasten the ribs of a cedar boat, the result is seldom satisfactory . . . with the clinch fastening the slender end of the nail will curve back into the wood before the shank will upset. The annealed copper is not weakened by such a clinch, and it is our experience that such a fastening will last as long in the wood."

Rushton's implication here is that, unless properly done, rivet fastening is inferior. When riveting is incorrectly done, that is, when too big a hammer is used and the blows struck are too heavy, when the rivets are not clipped short enough, when the burrs used are sloppy and don't hold firmly when forced down with the burr set—especially when all of these conditions obtain together—the rivets will buckle and cripple within the wood, without drawing tight, even to the point of sometimes splitting the lap. When this happens it is not the fault of the rivet, but rather the fault of the riveter.

By the same token, if nails are not properly clinched so that the points turn neatly back into the wood, they will not draw tight and will also sometimes split the lap. Furthermore, for a proper clinch job, nails must be exactly the right length, neither too long nor too short, and they must be a particular type of cut, clinch nail. Wire nails won't do at all for clinching, but they can be used for riveting, although they are not as good for driving through hot timbers as cut nails.

I believe it takes more skill to clinch lap fastenings, and to do it right, than to put in rivet fastenings, although the former is certainly the faster method of the two for the skilled professional who has acquired the knack through long practice. W. P. Stephens, Rushton's contemporary and competition, held for rivets.

Riveted laps were standard for clinker yacht tenders and other fine small craft built along the coast, and indeed, before small screws were available, rivet fastening was used for the best carvel construction as well, which almost invariably was built with soft cedar planking.

The Rangeley boat was clinch fastened, but the nails used were of imported pure Swedish iron, which lasts quite well in fresh water, as ordinary steel nails do not. However, I was informed that copper nails had been tried previously for clinch fastening Rangeley boats but had been given up because the clinched copper nails were too soft and thus "worked" in use, thus allowing the laps to loosen in time. Whether Rushton's soft copper nails ever loosened, I do not know. Perhaps bronze nails would work if those of suitable shape for clinching could be had, with metal hard enough to hold firmly. Yet bronze nails might be too stiff, with a tendency to split delicate laps when clinched.

All things considered, perhaps it is best to confine ourselves to rivets and learn to do riveting correctly. First, the right kind of a nail is needed. Copper wire nails can be used, but copper cut nails are far superior. The copper cut nail is desirable because its square (really rectangular) point can be driven through hot timbers with less chance of splitting them than a round wire nail. Furthermore, the right size is important. A nail that is too large or too heavy will strain or split delicate laps, as large nails require too much hammering to head up. Bronze nails or other "hard" nails should not be used because they are too hard to head over. Only soft copper nails head over easily.

Second, the burr, or rove, as this is sometimes called, must not be sloppy, that is, too large. Rather, its hole should be tight enough so that, when the burr is driven over the point of the nail and forced down firmly against the wood on the inside of the lap, it will hang tightly until the rivet has been headed over.

Third, the excess length of rivet protruding beyond the burr must be clipped off just right—enough for a good head and not a bit more, for any extra length left on for heading will tend to make the shank of the rivet buckle or "cripple" in the wood. This is extremely important. Exactly the right amount of length must be left for heading, no more or no less.

Fourth, a proper riveting hammer must be used. For small-boat work the hammer should be under half a pound in weight, including the handle. The latter should be of hickory, shaved down close to the head to the diameter of a lead pencil, to give the handle flexibility. For some reason, not wholly clear, a hammer with a long, narrow head works better and balances better than one that is short headed (assuming, of course, that the two hammers are of equal weight).

More than likely, a suitable riveting hammer will not be found for purchase, although some light upholsterer's hammers could possibly be adapted and give good results. However, a perfectly serviceable hammer can be made from

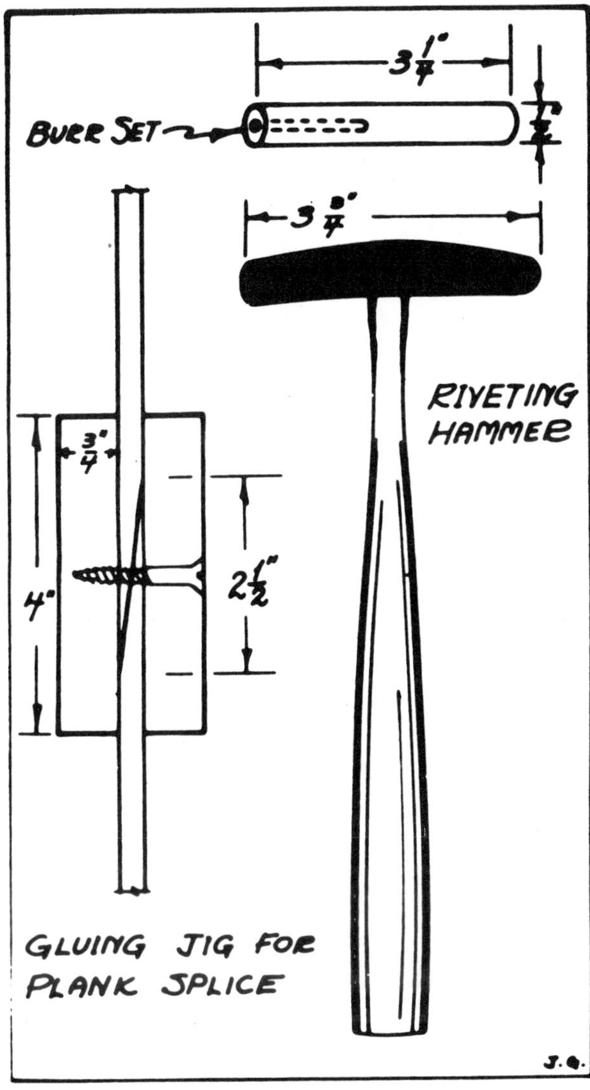

a piece of steel drill rod ⅝ inch in diameter and 3¾ inches long. One end is squared off and given a very slight convex round, the other should be rounded like the ball end of a ball peen hammer. The middle of this head is drilled at right angles to take a hickory handle. No hardening is needed, as the copper to be pounded is much softer than the steel. The hole for the handle should be elongated so as to give enough room for the handle without weakening the head unduly. This is an easy way to make a good hammer, which, I doubt, you could find to buy today.

For a burr set, a piece of the same ⅝-inch drill rod 4 inches long will do. Drill a 3/16 inch hole lengthwise into one end about 1½ inches.

In addition to the hammer and the burr set, you will also have to have a "hold-on." Here, weight (as much as you can conveniently hold in one hand) is an advantage. It should fit the left hand (if you are right-handed) comfortably, with the surface that is applied against the wood smooth and slightly convex. There should be no sharp edges or corners to dig into the plank inadvertently.

When riveting, that is, when forming a head over the burr on the inside of the lap, with many light, quick blows of the hammer, the hold-on must be pressed tightly and firmly against the head of the nail on the outside of the lap, else a bent or crippled rivet or even a split lap will result.

Nails should not be driven through the laps without drilling for them first; the holes should be slightly smaller than the shank of the nail to insure a tight fit. Those who are new to riveting should practice at the bench on laps identical to those on the boat until they get the hang of it. Not until they can head over rivets perfectly should they attempt it on the boat. Those who leave their practicing for the boat will surely regret it. Riveting small copper fastenings is best done with very light but rapid blows. These upset a head without bending or crushing the rivet itself. With a heavy hammer and a few heavy blows, the rivet is likely to bend and split the wood, and it never draws tight. With many rapid tapping blows, a nice head forms, the burr draws up tightly, and the rivet itself is not mashed, deformed, or crippled into the wood.

For a specific example of riveting and timbering, let's take the pram in Chapter 2. When all the locations of the fastenings are marked, the molds are removed from the planked-up shell, and holes are bored through the laps where the timber rivets are to come. Next, nails are driven in from the outside so that their points are just flush with the inside of the skin. In this condition the hull resembles a huge pincushion. In the meantime the timbers have been prepared and are steaming. After an hour of hot, wet steam, timbers of this size, if of good quality white oak and not fully seasoned to begin with, will be soft and limber enough to "tie into knots."

The hot timber is quickly forced down into the interior of the boat along the lines previously marked for it. Clamped to the sheer at either side, the timberheads projecting above the sheer may be tapped with a nail hammer to drive the hot timber down against the laps. Generally it is tacked into the keel batten with a small nail to keep it from slipping out of place.

Quickly, then, the boatbuilder, starting on the outside from the bottom or garboard with his nailing hammer, drives the nails already entered in the laps, driving each in turn as he goes up the side to the sheer, while he backs up on the inside with a heavy hold-on, applied against the timber as close as he can get to the nail he is driving without preventing its going through. The inertia of the heavy hold-on forces the hot timber tightly against the inside surface of the lap, and twists the timber, as may be required, making it lie flat against the inside of the planking. Once the timber is down in place, the nails will hold it until the timber cools, which quickly occurs, and then nothing will move until the riveting can be done. This is usually done later and in one operation.

When laid out and organized in this manner, timbering is quickly and simply accomplished. Otherwise, all sorts of difficulties might be met with. Unless the position and location of the timbers are marked in advance, they could never be got in evenly. Unless the holes are bored through the laps and the nails inserted ahead of time, timbers could neither be fastened before they cooled, nor drawn tightly to the inside of the boat while still hot and flexible. The nails used should be blunt-ended cut nails. Sharp-pointed nails are likely to split the timbers. To be on the safe side, the nails should be bored for.

FRAMING WOOD

As far as I am concerned, the only wood to use for steam-bent timbers for the boats in this book is the best genuine white oak that can be obtained. It should not be over dry. Long seasoning tends to make wood brittle, oak especially. In fact, wood for steam-bent timbers can come directly off the stump, for steaming drives out the sap and seasons the wood, so that small timbers, although growing the day before they go into the boat, will be as hard as a piece of horn after they have been steamed and then dried out for a couple of weeks.

The best wood for white oak timbers comes from the butts of young, healthy trees that have grown fast. The wider the grain and the heavier the wood the better. Wood from the upper parts of the tree is always softer and weaker. Some of the red oaks are worthless for timbers, especially the weak, brittle, fine-grained wood from old, large, slow-growing trees of the species appropriately known in the boatshops as "piss" oak.

Rushton specified red elm for timbers, but I have never used it and do not know enough about it to recommend it for this purpose. Many of the Rangeley boats also used elm timbers. White ash bends beautifully, and some selected white ash from the butts of young trees is nearly as hard and strong as good oak. But unfortunately ash rots easily when exposed to weather. Perhaps it could be treated with preservative of some sort, but I don't recommend risking it until some experimentation has been done.

LAMINATING FRAMES

An alternative to steam-bent frames is glued, laminated frames, bent in and fastened while the glue is still soft. This becomes especially feasible with an epoxy/Thiokol adhesive, which will not run out of the joints, especially those which are vertical, before it sets up. Epoxy resin is a fairly heavy material, and some adhesive formulations, especially the slow-setting ones, like some of the Versamid mixes, have a bad tendency of leaking or creeping out of joints when there is any chance for the still-liquid glue to run downhill. The "buttery" consistency of the epoxy/Thiokol obviates this.

For a laminated frame of ⅝ inch thickness or molding, five strips of ⅛ inch thickness will be required. Such strips are got out carefully to their exact size on the circular saw and are made long enough to bend in from gunwale to gunwale, with a little extra to extend above the gunwale on either side, for ease of handling. (The example given here is for continuous frames; the method is applicable to single frames as well.)

In putting in a frame, five strips are first selected, adhesive is applied to their meeting surfaces, and the strips are stacked one on top of the other as they are to go on the boat. The bundle is then tightly wrapped at intervals with several turns of masking tape to hold the lifts together, although they can still slip against one another in a lengthwise direction. The bundle is then bent into place in the boat in accordance with the line of the frame already marked. Forced down approximately into position, the two ends of the frame are clamped to the sheer on either side so that they can be tapped down to make contact with each side plank and the bottom, by pounding the ends with a hammer.

The frame is now ready to fasten in place. The fastenings, either screws or rivets, if properly put in, will draw the frame layers tightly together and hold them in position until the glue hardens. The turns of masking tape should hold the laminae pretty nearly where they belong as the frame is fastened, but to insure perfect alignment, several small hand screws will be useful and convenient. Such hand screws have wooden jaws and threaded steel spindles. A small size is best for these hand screws—those with a 4-inch jaw and a 2-inch opening. A couple will suffice. In fact, one is all that is absolutely necessary, to be used wherever a fastening is about to be put in to force the laminae into perfect sidewise alignment, and to hold them there until the fastening takes over. The hand screw is then shifted to the location for the next fastening and so on. However, several hand screws at various places along the frame are a great convenience.

If this procedure is followed, ordinary care taken, and the excess glue is wiped off with a cloth after the fastening of the frame is completed, it will be hard to tell after the job is done whether the frame is laminated or solid—at least to the cursory glance.

PLYWOOD FOR DORY CONSTRUCTION

Dory construction was perfected before plywood or waterproof glues were developed. Your oldtime dory builder managed quite adequately without these materials, yet that is no reason for our not using them. In fact, plywood and glue can be employed to advantage for dories, as well as for the construction of many of the other older types of small boats. Thus the design of the 19-foot surf-dory (Chapter 13) and many other boats in this book call for both.

The theory has been advanced that the dory developed from an abundance of wide pine boards. Given the wide lumber from the primeval pine forests of New England, and the need for strong and inexpensive boats for the fisheries, the various dories naturally took shape as the most economical way of putting together wide boards into boats of the desired characteristics. But the big pines are gone, and it is far from easy today to get white pine boards sixteen to eighteen inches wide as are required for the garboards of a surf-dory. If plywood can be made to do, here is a plentiful supply of wide lumber the use of which will permit the retention of the advantages of wide-board design. However, in using plywood for garboards, the right sort of plywood must be selected, and several minor departures from standard dory construction will have to be made in applying it to the boat.

For the 19-foot surf-dory in Chapter 13, the plywood selected was marine grade, ⅜ inch thick, 5-ply Douglas fir. This was for the garboards, for gussets for splicing the frame futtocks and the two-piece stems, and for the bulkheads of the two end-compartments enclosing the styrofoam flotation. As the garboards of the surf-dory are approximately 19 feet long, they are spliced in the center, which is their narrowest part, and as the boat is identical at both ends, one pattern can be used for marking out the four pieces needed for making up the two garboards. Thus it is possible, by taking care, to lay out the garboard pieces on a 4-foot by 10-foot sheet and to have enough left over to make the frame and stem gussets, as well as the end bulkheads. This procedure requires laying out a garboard pattern before the frames are assembled and the boat is set up. Such a pattern may be obtained with sufficient accuracy from a scale half-model of the boat, most conveniently made 1½ inches to the foot.

Douglas fir plywood was chosen for the good and sufficient reason that that was the only kind of marine grade available at that time. Apparently for such reasons as the abundance and the large size of Douglas fir timber, the good gluing qualities of that wood, and its high strength-weight ratio, Douglas fir dominates the plywood field. Other woods or combinations of woods, however, can now be found in marine plywood.

Superior grades of exterior (waterproof) plywood are manufactured especially for boat-building purposes. Different manufacturers designate this special grade with various names, for instance "Armorbond," "Marine," and "Boathull." No matter the designation used, the inner plies of marine plywood with respect to core gaps, solid veneer, and the like are better than those of industrial exterior-type plywood. However, there is no difference in glue, as all exterior grades have the same waterproof glueline.

Anyone who intends to use plywood for small boat construction will do well to inform himself thoroughly about plywood specifications, select his wood with care, and demand a product that conforms to standards. (A good place to get such information is the Douglas Fir Plywood Association, 1119 A Street, Tacoma, Washington.) The requirements for small boat construction are fairly critical, especially as dimensions must be kept down to save weight, but without sacrifice of strength.

There is an important reason why 5-ply plywood is to be preferred over that of 3 plies for planking and other boat parts subject to immersion and soaking. That is because in the 5-ply product there is less wood in the thinner veneers to swell and shrink as the moisture content varies, hence less strain on the glueline. In 5-ply plywood, a greater proportion of the wood is glue impregnated, reducing swelling and shrinking stresses still more. Plywood is made with the grain of its composite veneers crossing at right angles, and recurrent stresses are set up by the expansion and contraction of these veneers. Thus the wood as it gets wet, and dries out, is always pulling at the glueline. Modern waterproof glues have tremendous holding power, but good boatbuilding practice calls for all possible measures to mitigate the strains to which the glueline of plywood will be subjected. One of these is to coat the surface of the wood with paint and special sealers to prevent it from soaking up water too fast or drying out too quickly. It is the powerful stress set up by abrupt change in moisture content that does the worst damage.

As the edges of the plywood, by their exposure of end-grain wood, take up or give off moisture most rapidly, they are the most vulnerable part of the plywood and need special protection. On the edges, the veneers first separate or are split apart by accidental blows, abrasion, or other mechanical injury. In the surf-dory the lower edges of the garboards are not only coated with applications of sealer and paint, but also the ½ inch outer bottom of oak is extended to cover the garboard edges, with a liberal coating of bedding compound placed between. The upper edges of the garboards, beveled 1⅛ inches to lap under the broad strake, are coated with three applications of No. 900 rubber sealer before the lap is riveted together. At both ends of the boat the garboards are sealed and bedded before being covered by the steam-bent false or outer stem. Thus all edges of the garboards are protected by sealing and covering with other members of solid wood. It may be positively stated that good building practice requires that plywood edges always be covered, and when plywood is adapted to traditional boat types, design and construction should be modified to permit such covering.

In the past the garboards of a standard 19-foot dory would have been of pine ⅝ inch thick; for light construction, 9⁄16 inch thick. Chamberlain built his gunning dories with planking of ½-inch cedar. In substituting plywood for the garboards, that of ⅜ inch thickness is the best choice. Plywood ¼ inch thick, available only in 3-ply construction, is not solid enough for a boat of this size, nor is it stiff enough to bend fairly in the garboard width around frame-molds spaced 32 inches apart. On the other hand ½-inch plywood would be unnecessarily heavy and stiff. Possibly 5/16-inch 5-ply Mexican or African mahogany plywood would be the best choice of all for garboards for a 19-foot dory, if such a plywood could be found.

In the dry condition, ⅜-inch plywood garboards will be a little lighter in weight than garboards of ⅝-inch pine, in spite of the added weight of the glue in the plywood. In a water-soaked condition, the thicker pine planking would certainly be considerably heavier, especially as a portion of the plywood is made impervious to water by its four layers of glue.

BORING FOR CENTERBOARDS AND RUDDERS

When assembling large, flat pieces, such as centerboards and rudders, some amateur boatbuilders have difficulty boring for the fastenings. Care must be taken to bore a hole that is straight and true. The following instructions should help simplify the job:

For both rudders and centerboards, cut out the component pieces and fit them, temporarily assembling them on a flat surface like a level bench top. These pieces will all be of the same thickness of stock, for any tapering and thinning is left until the assembly is solidly pinned together.

Clamp this preliminary assembly so it can't move, and exactly mark on the exposed upper surface the location of each pin with a firm straight line the length of the pin. This line represents the center of the pin. Separate the parts and square the pin lines down across the edges of the piece. Next, with a combination square or some other gauge, set to half the thickness of the boards, mark through the lines already squared across the edges, gauging always from the upper, marked side of the boards.

Now the exact locations for boring the holes for the pins have been found and are marked on all edges by the intersection of the squared-down pin line with the gauge line. At these intersections holes of the right size for the pins may be precisely centered and started with a sharp-spurred bit in a hand brace.

If a pin is to pass entirely through a board, the hole is started on both edges and is bored halfway through from either side to halve possible error. If the two holes do not meet precisely, they usually come close enough so that the drill bit will lead through from side to side, so that, after reaming, a pin can be driven through. The important thing is that by this method the correct location of the holes on the edges of joining pieces is maintained. An attempt, starting at one edge, to bore a long hole edgewise through two or more thin boards will generally result in having the drill break out through one side or the other before the hole is complete.

A better way, when several thin pieces or boards are to be pinned together edgewise, is to bore each piece separately. If preassembled and properly marked to begin with, and provided the marks are followed, the holes will line up perfectly when the parts are reassembled, and the pins can be driven without trouble.

A spurred bit is not suitable for boring long holes, for such bits have a tendency to "run off." Either a "bare-foot" ship's auger or a long twist drill is better. (A short twist drill may be lengthened by brazing on an extension of drill rod.) It is assumed that an electric machine will be used.

When drilling the builder will need assistance for sighting. The piece to be drilled is clamped flat on the bench. A straight, narrow strip of board is laid with one edge exactly on the marked line of the hole to be drilled, and it should extend somewhat beyond the piece toward the drill. By sighting along the edge of this stick, the man with the drill can line his hole one way. The hole is lined the other way, that is up and down, by an assistant standing off some distance at right angles. He calls out to the drill operator to move up or down to keep the shank of the drill parallel to the run or line of the sighting stick.

By using this method and exercising care, holes 8 inches or 10 inches, or longer, of nearly perfect alignment, can be bored edgewise through thin, flat stock.

ASHCROFT CONSTRUCTION

Many classic craft are adaptable to the Ashcroft method of construction, which uses planking made up of two layers of narrow, thin strips, laid diagonally with the boat's centerline and glued together. To describe this method, let's look at the Rangeley boat, which has an ideal form for the task.

Construction by the Ashcroft method lies well within the capability of the amateur with modest woodworking skill, and it will not be overly expensive, as prices run today. In fact, one of my guiding considerations in including this material was to help keep down costs. Low-cost, easily obtainable lumber is specified, and the use of expensive metal fastenings has been kept to a minimum. The amount and kind of adhesives required should not run the price up excessively. The number of tools required is small—in addition to a few standard hand tools, a staple gun will be needed, as well as the use of a circular saw to rip out the planking strips.

This method of planking was first devised and successfully used in the early years of this century by an Englishman, Herbert J. Ashcroft. Ashcroft planking, as it came to be called, achieved considerable popularity for a time, especially in Australia, and Ashcroft's book, *Boatbuilding Simplified*, was published in several editions—the third revised edition, and the last, as far as I know, appearing in London about 1920.

What Ashcroft lacked was waterproof glue, which did not become available to the boatbuilding trade until the 1940s, during World War II. Although Ashcroft built successful boats without modern adhesives, special care had to be taken to get a leak-proof hull without them. Given a reliable waterproof glue, the effectiveness of Ashcroft construction is immensely enhanced. The revival of up-dated Ashcroft building methods, using modern glues, is overdue, offering special inducements to the unskilled builder.

As its originator claimed, Ashcroft is a simplified method, avoiding the principal difficulties of both clinker and carvel planking—there is no need to line out and diminish planks, spile their shapes, back them out to fit the round of the ribs, or bevel clinker laps. Mainly what is required in the way of planking is a quantity of thin, narrow strips got out to uniform width and thickness on a circular saw, and ordinary care in applying them to the building form.

For planking strips, almost any wood will do that is not too hard, that takes glue well, and that bends fairly easily. Naturally, woods which rot easily should be avoided. For the boat we are considering, I suggest spruce, northern white pine (but not Ponderosa), and Douglas fir. These can be had in comparatively inexpensive construction grades and are commonly carried by local retail lumber dealers. There are several kinds of cedar, both eastern and western, and particularly northern white cedar, which would be excellent, but cedar is apt to be more expensive and is not as widely stocked as the other types.

Because the strips required for this boat are less than 3 feet long and not more than 2 inches wide, they may be got out of the cheaper grades with knots and other defects by cutting up the material so as to avoid the blemished parts. Thus, rough spruce staging boards, No. 2 common white pine, or Douglas fir framing lumber can be made to serve quite adequately. Considerable wastage occurs in stripping up this material on the saw, which makes a thin, sharp blade desirable. The strips need not be smoothed or planed. In fact, they glue better with epoxy just as they come from the saw.

Bob Sheffields, of Binghamton, N. Y., who built a 16-foot Adirondack guideboat using the Ashcroft method, found that ⅛ inch thick spruce was quite adequate. Because white pine is neither as stiff nor as strong as spruce, probably

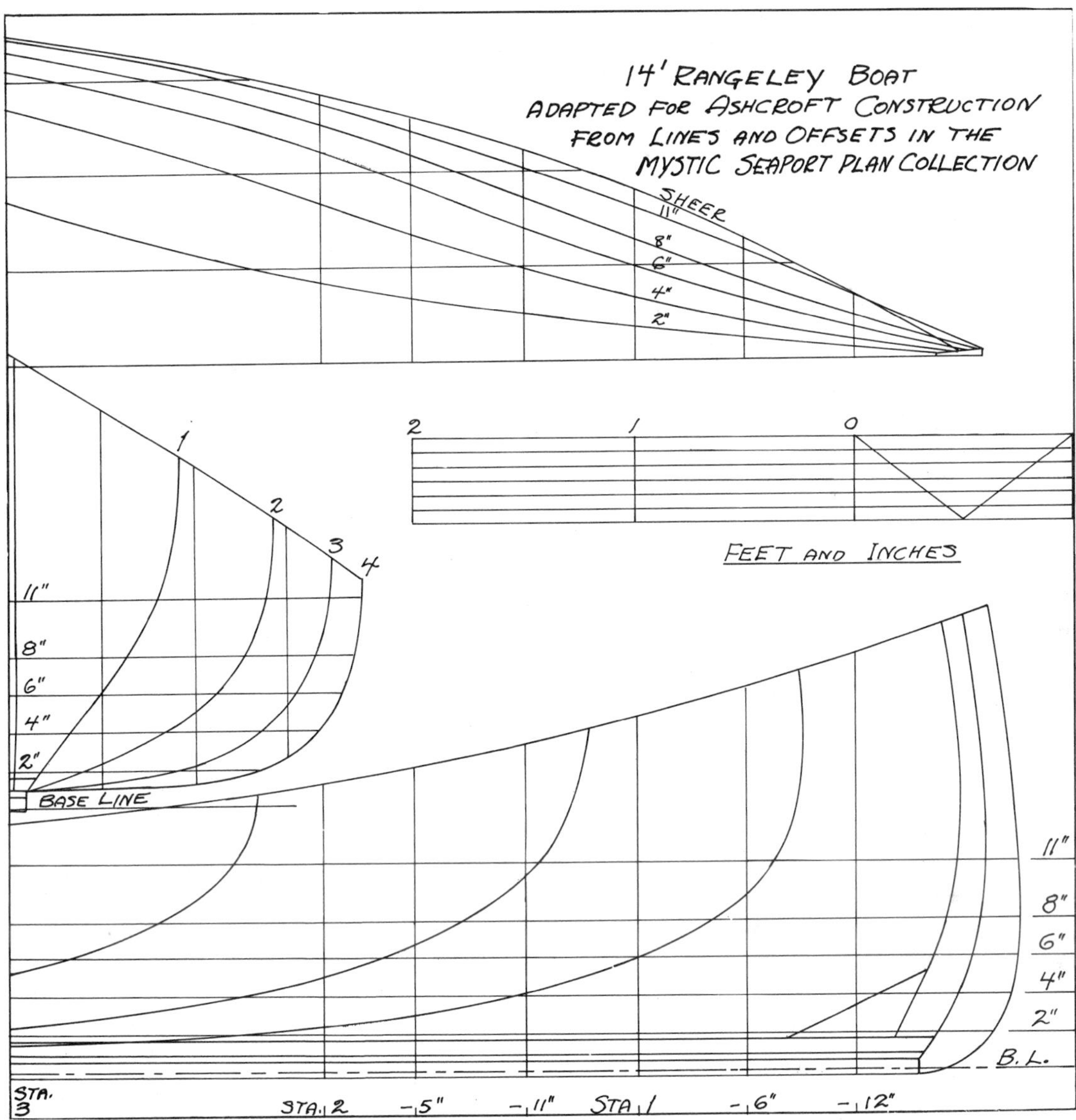

a thickness of 3/16 inch would be better if pine is used, which I am suggesting for this boat. For Douglas fir, 1/8-inch or 5/32-inch strips will suffice.

Even though the strips are thin enough to be relatively flexible, best results will be obtained if they are softened by steaming before they are bent on the form. Boiling them will serve just as well, and in some cases, boiling will be easier to accomplish. Various devices can be improvised for doing this. One is easily made from a section of large-diameter copper tubing slightly longer than the strips to be boiled. Secured in an upright position, with its lower end capped or plugged, the tube is filled with water and the flame from an ordinary small soldering torch is applied to the side of the tube. The water will soon boil. A few minutes in the tube will render strips pliable enough to bend easily, and as heated strips are removed to go on the boat, fresh ones are inserted to keep the planking operation proceeding continuously.

If a suitable length of large tubing is not to be had, a narrow, tight wooden box can be substituted. Through its closed lower end there should protrude a foot or so of smaller-diameter copper tubing, its bottom end capped or plugged. A torch applied here will soon bring the water in the box to a boil. This box can be

The Ashcroft method. (Top) Setting up the first form. (Center) The ribbands and stringers in place. (Bottom) The beginning of planking. In the original method, both layers of strips were put on together. (From Ashcroft's Boatbuilding Simplified)

nailed up almost anywhere and, with care, is quite safe. Such a box is easily made out of four pine boards well nailed together, with the seams caulked with a strand of cotton wicking set in heavy paint or mastic of some sort.

Before the strips are bent in place on the boat, a proper form must be constructed to receive them. Such a form set bottom up can be seen in the accompanying illustration reproduced from the third edition of Ashcroft's book. Molds are made in the usual way from the faired lines of the body sections, from which the thickness of the longitudinal ribbands or stringers has been deducted.

Building is done bottom-up, and the best way of setting up the building form is by the ladder-frame method, which is fully explained for the light 10-foot Herreshoff pram described in Chapter 2. Incidentally, this pram has an ideal shape for Ashcroft construction.

As the final shape of the boat can be no fairer than the form on which it is planked, no pains should be spared in getting it right. If the boat is to have fair lines, the ribbands or stringers must run fair and true, and there must be enough of them to support the planking strips in fair curves when these are bent into place. If the supporting stringers are placed too far apart, unsightly knuckles could develop in the skin of the finished hull. At the turn of the bilge, where the curve is quickest, the stringers will need to be closer together than on the flat of the bottom or high on the topsides. As shown in one of the illustrations in Ashcroft's book, the stringers appear to be rather far apart.

In the original Ashcroft method, planking strips were nailed to the longitudinal stringers, which remained in the finished hull as an integral part of the structure. But because of the added strength derived by gluing together the two layers of planking strips, we should not need to retain all of our form ribbands as permanent hull stringers. Perhaps four on each side so retained would be sufficient, with the hull lighter and its interior less cluttered as a consequence.

For permanent stringers for the boat under consideration, I suggest one at the turn of the bilge, one on the flat of the bottom about midway between the turn and the keel batten, another above the turn to serve as a seat-riser, and the fourth along the sheer line to become the inwale. Additional ribbands would be necessary to get a fair shape, but these would be fastened to the molds and would remain with the form when the finished hull is lifted off. The stringers that are to become part of the completed hull may be tied to the molds with thin but strong cord to hold them in place preliminary to planking. If they were nailed or screwed to the molds, there would be no way of removing these fastenings after the hull was planked. Fine, strong wire twisted to draw tight could also be used to hold the permanent stringers in place, to be clipped and pulled out of the finished hull afterwards.

Stringers for this boat might well be made ¾ inch thick by 1 inch wide. Those which are to remain in the hull should be smoothed and sanded with the inside corners nicely rounded. Spruce or Douglas fir would be suitable material, or some other wood which holds nails at least moderately well. White pine and white cedar are too soft.

The Rangeley boat is perfectly straight along the bottom, which makes it easy to set up. The inner keel or keel batten, either oak or selected Douglas fir, is a strip ¾ inch thick, 4 inches wide and tapered at the ends. This taper and the amount of beveling required is shown in the accompanying drawings. Likewise are shown the filler pieces at each end and how they are shaped and beveled also.

As this boat is exactly alike at either end, two identical inner stem pieces are worked out of 2-inch thick stock, either oak or Douglas fir, according to the shape and dimensions given. In fastening these to either end of the keel batten, two triangular knees of the same 2-inch thick stem stock are required, thinned and tapered to the thickness of the inner stem and the end of the keel batten.

The inner stem pieces, stem knees, and keel batten are nailed and glued together before being placed on the molds already set up and secured on the ladder frame. After the keel batten assembly is in place, its bottom is beveled, and the bottom filler strips are glued and fitted at either end.

The ends of the longitudinal ribbands or

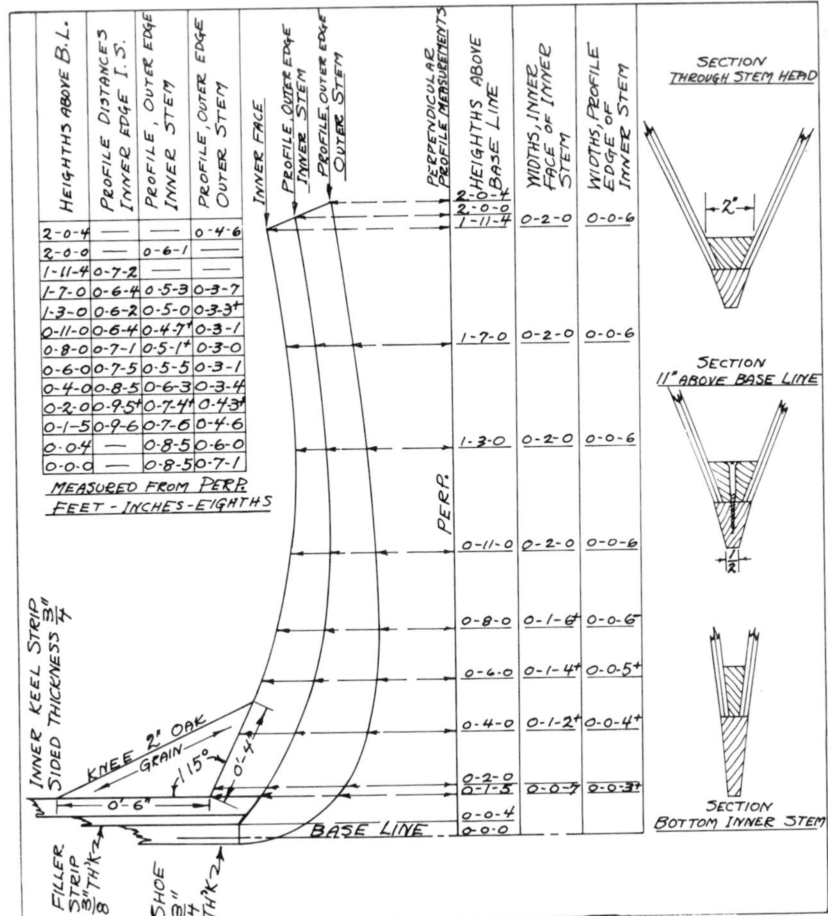

HEIGHTHS ABOVE B.L.	PROFILE DISTANCES INNER EDGE I.S.	PROFILE, OUTER EDGE INNER STEM	PROFILE, OUTER EDGE OUTER STEM
2-0-4	—	—	0-4-6
2-0-0	—	0-6-1	—
1-11-4	0-7-2	—	—
1-7-0	0-6-4	0-5-3	0-3-7
1-3-0	0-6-2	0-5-0	0-3-3+
0-11-0	0-6-4	0-4-7+	0-3-1
0-8-0	0-7-1	0-5-1+	0-3-0
0-6-0	0-7-5	0-5-5	0-3-1
0-4-0	0-8-5	0-6-3	0-3-4
0-2-0	0-9-5+	0-7-4+	0-4-3+
0-1-5	0-9-6	0-7-6	0-4-6
0-0-4	—	0-8-5	0-6-0
0-0-0	—	0-8-5	0-7-1

MEASURED FROM PERP.
FEET - INCHES - EIGHTHS

HEIGHTHS ABOVE BASE LINE	WIDTHS, INNER FACE OF INNER STEM	WIDTHS, PROFILE EDGE OF INNER STEM
2-0-4		
2-0-0		
1-11-4	0-2-0	0-0-6
1-7-0	0-2-0	0-0-6
1-3-0	0-2-0	0-0-6
0-11-0	0-2-0	0-0-6
0-8-0	0-1-6+	0-0-6−
0-6-0	0-1-4+	0-0-5+
0-4-0	0-1-2+	0-0-4+
0-2-0		
0-1-5	0-0-7	0-0-3+
0-0-4		
0-0-0		

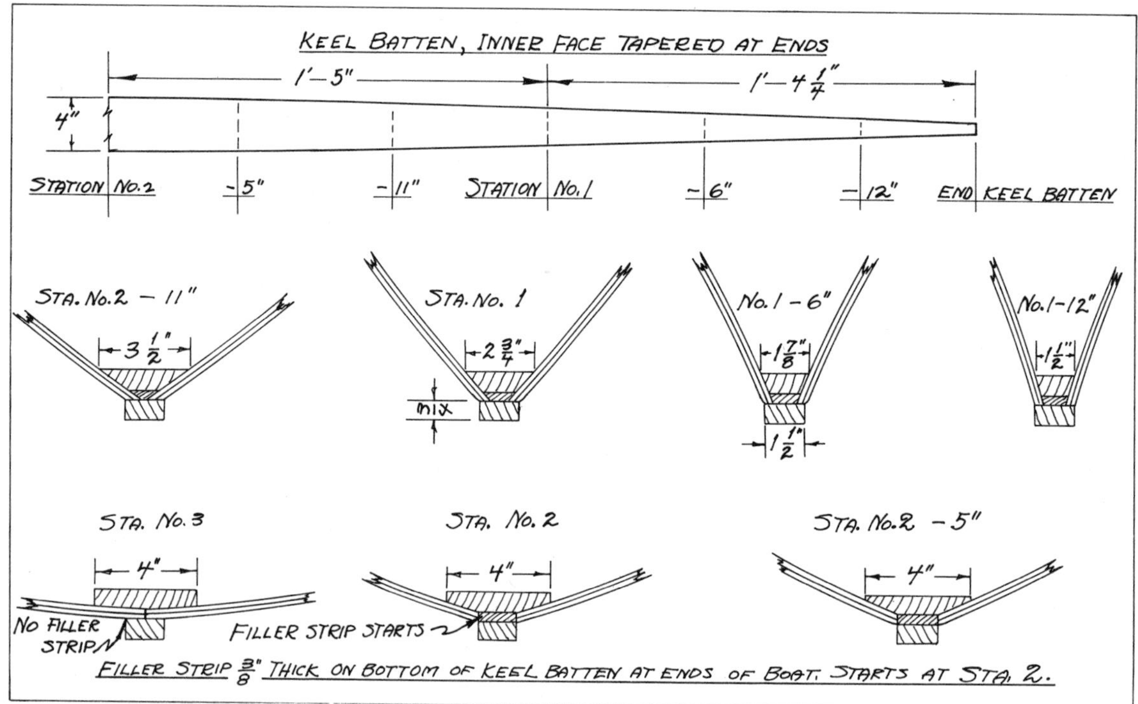

stringers must land precisely against the back of the inner stem pieces, and also must line up exactly with the fayed or beveled surfaces of these inner stems. Perhaps some planing will be required here to achieve a fair backing surface for the planking strips. Stringers that are to remain in the hull must be fitted neatly where they come together and fasten behind the inner stem.

When all underlying surfaces are fair and smooth, the planking strips are put on. According to the original Ashcroft method, both layers were put on together, the under layer one strip in advance of the upper, with the seams in the top layer falling midway on the strips in the under layer. Of course, both layers had to run at the same angle and in the same direction. In this way there were no openings to leak, that is if the two layers were pulled snugly together, with paint or flexible bedding of some sort between. The strips were nailed through and clinched, both to the permanent stringers and to themselves as the planking proceeded. Steaming the strips to make them soft for easy bending did not interfere with this process, as it would have if glue had been used between the two layers. It is doubtful if reliable results could be obtained by applying glue directly to steamed or boiled wood before it has cooled or dried.

When glue is used, an alternate method may be adopted. The strips softened by steaming or boiling are bent on at an angle of approximately 45 degrees from the centerline, starting at the middle of the boat and working toward the ends. They are laid as close together as possible, and are held down in place with staples put in wherever needed. The entire hull surface is covered in one operation and left to dry. When sufficiently dry, the strips, starting at the middle of the boat, are removed one at a time, edge-trimmed with a sharp block plane to lie snugly against the adjoining strip, and fastened permanently in place, both with glue and nails to the keel batten and the permanent stringers. Small annular nails of bronze or Monel, ¾ inch long, are best for tacking down this inner layer.

The first layer of strips should fit together as tightly as possible, so that when the outer layer is glued on, the adhesive does not leak through. It is well, in any case, to wax the ribbands that remain on the mold, so that if glue does work through, it will not stick to them. In any case, for best results, a thick epoxy paste should be used between the two layers, either a proprietary formulation or ordinary liquid epoxy well thickened by the addition of Cabot's Cab-O-Sil.

After the first layer is permanently nailed in place and the glue has set, the surface can be rough sanded to prepare for the application of the second layer, which is done like the first. Before the bending operation starts, however, the position of the underlying ribbands and the permanent stringers should be clearly lined out and marked on the surface of the under layer to guide nailing. Instead of laying the second layer in the same direction as the first, as Ashcroft did, a stronger hull will result if we put on the top layer at right angles to the one underneath. With glue between the two layers, there is no chance of leaks where the strips cross.

The procedure for the outer layer is the same as for the under layer. The softened strips are bent on and temporarily stapled in place. After they have dried, the staples are removed, and the strips are fitted and put back permanently with glue and nails. For the latter, annular nails 1 inch long can be used. The heads are set slightly below the surface, and the indentations filled with hard facing compound, which also is used to fill any slight openings between the strips. When this has hardened, the outer surface is sanded true and painted.

The completed hull is next removed from the mold, and its inner surface is treated in the same manner as the outer. It is then ready for the addition of seats, floorboards, flotation, gunwales, rowlock pads and sockets, and the two outer stem pieces. The latter are carefully fitted to the outer surface of the inner stems. A thick coating of epoxy paste is applied, and the outer stem piece is drawn up tightly with large screws through the inner stem from the inside.

The last piece to go on is the outer keel strip, for which screws and glue are also used. Finally, if desired, half-inch-wide, half-oval brass stembands, extending down over the ends of the outer keel strip, may be added, both for reinforcement and to dress up the appearance of the boat.

BOATBUILDING GLUES

Glues are now used so extensively in wooden boatbuilding as to be practically indispensable. With quality boat lumber in diminishing supply and constantly rising in price, boatbuilders are being forced to consider glued construction. The regular use of glues in the boatshop is a fairly recent development; it began about thirty years ago or so during World War II when adhesives embodying various synthetic thermoplastic resins first began to be used by boatbuilders. Prior to this, casein glue was used since early in the century for gluing hollow spars. Casein glue is an organic compound, the basis of which is milk. Water resistant but not waterproof, it still proved satisfactory for gluing spars provided the joints were protected by varnish. In the 1930's, phenol-formaldehyde resins requiring heat and high pressure during the curing cycle were developed by the plywood industry to obtain a waterproof, chemically inert, high-strength bond, but these resins were too critical and exacting in their application for ordinary boatshop use.

In the 1940's, wartime demands upon the boating industry stimulated the introduction of new methods and new materials, including thermoplastic adhesives. First to appear were urea-formaldehyde, or plastic resin, glues, then resorcinal resin glues, followed closely by the epoxies. Since then a number of other plastic adhesives have been introduced, but because of their limited and specialized application, we shall not consider them here.

Urea-formaldehyde glues. There are two distinctly different types of urea-formaldehyde glues. The best known and the most widely used is the one-part type exemplified by Weldwood plastic resin glue distributed as a dry brown powder that is dissolved in water before applying. The other is a two-part system developed by the CIBA Co., Ltd., sold as Aerolite 306. It consists of a white powdered resin made liquid by adding water before it is applied to one surface of the joint. The other joint surface is moistened with a separate liquid hardener, and the two surfaces are brought into contact to effect the cure.

Weldwood plastic resin is relatively cheap and easily obtained because of its wide retail distribution. In accurately made, closely fitted joints, it cures stronger than the wood, but loses strength rapidly where there is a build-up of thickness in the glue line of an ill-fitting joint. Directions for its use specify a temperature of 70° F or higher for a proper cure, and enough clamping pressure is required to force the glue out of the joint.

CIBA's dual-system urea-formaldehyde glue, namely Aerolite, was developed in Britain during World War II for the manufacture of Mosquito bombers. Joints made with it are stronger than the wood, completely waterproof, mold-proof, insect-proof, and do not deteriorate with age or from exposure to the elements. It is gap filling without loss of strength up to a glue-line thickness of 1/16 inch. Only enough clamping pressure on joints to bring the meeting surfaces into firm contact is required. Although it will be retarded, cure will take place at temperatures as low as 50° F. Cost is moderate. It is easy and clean to use, and economical because there is no wastage in applying it. It does not stain, and the glue line in well-made joints is nearly invisible. For splicing planking and plywood, for gluing up spars, for laminating deck beams and curved ribs, and for other similar uses, Aerolite is not likely to be excelled.

Resorcinol Glue. As a boatbuilding glue, resorcinol has served well, and some boatbuilders still swear by it. Yet there can be little doubt that everything that resorcinol can do, epoxy can do better. Close, accurately fitted joints glued with resorcinol are waterproof, lasting, and stronger than the wood, but resorcinol is not gap filling at full strength, and for best results, according to the U.S. Plywood Corp., the glue line should not be thicker than 0.005 inch. High pressure clamping is required. The curing temperature should not fall below 70° F, and resorcinol should not be used when the moisture content of the wood is above 15 per cent. Furthermore, resorcinol stains wood badly, and for that reason is not desirable for gluing wood that is to be varnished. On the plus side, it is reasonably priced and readily available in retail quantities almost everywhere.

Epoxies. Epoxy's versatility and superior adhesive qualities may be judged from the literally hundreds of different epoxy formulations now in use throughout industry for gluing wood, metal, and plastic. In short, it is used for practically every gluing need. Most of the large manufacturers of chemicals, such as Shell, Dow, Union Carbide, and General Mills, produce extensive lines of epoxy resins as well as their own lines of hardening agents and copolymers. By selection and combination, chemists can formulate tailor-made epoxy adhesives with almost any desired combination of characteristics—slow cure, rapid cure, resilient or rigid bond, resistance to chemicals, adhesion to damp wood, and so forth. Because wooden boatbuilding on a commercial scale has come close to dying out in recent years, there has not been the same incentive as elsewhere in industry to develop epoxy formulations especially adapted to boatbuilding needs. Nevertheless, epoxy is available to boatbuilders in a number of formulations with characteristics no other adhesive products can match.

If the boatbuilder has some elementary knowledge of chemistry and the inclination to experiment with various standard epoxy resins, copolymers, hardeners, activators, and the like (obtainable from dealers in thermoplastic supplies), he may be able to formulate his own adhesive combinations that will work well for him. When epoxy adhesives for boat work were something of a novelty and had not been as widely adopted as they are today (1990), that was definitely a way to go, and one that I considered in detail in the first edition of this book.

Since that time, however, in response to greatly increased demand, numerous proprietary formulations of adhesive epoxy have come on the market and are now widely distributed, and when not obtainable over the counter they may by ordered by mail. The best of these have been thoroughly tested and proven in use. For occasional use and for the one-off boatbuilder, such superior proprietary formulations remove any reason to attempt to mix one's own, saving time and expense and insuring successful gluing results.

Three brands that I have used with first-rate results are Chem-Tech, Inc., 4669 Lander Road, Chagrin Falls, OH 44022; Fibre-Glass Evercoat Co., 6600 Cornell Rd., Cincinnati, OH 45242; and System Three Resins, Inc. 5965 Fourth Ave. S., Seattle, WA 98108. The epoxy adhesives put out under these three brand names have a number of desirable if not essential characteristics. In all likelihood there are others that share these same characteristics and are equally good, but I have used the three named and can vouch for them from experience. Their superior qualities are as follows:

1. Under ordinary conditions and when used with reasonable precautions, they are nonsensitizing and nonhazardous for all but a very few individuals who are naturally allergic to epoxy and should not attempt its use under any circumstances.

2. They are comparatively slow-setting, which is desirable for the nonprofessional builder, who often finds that a gluing operation takes longer than planned. Ample time for unforeseen adjustments can make the difference between a proper job and a botched one.

3. They are easy to mix in either one-part or two-part proportions that are not highly critical as to exact amounts. This makes for convenient and economical use of materials.

4. It is highly desirable for the glue mix to stay where it is put—not to run freely and not to leak out of critical joints. This is the case with Fibre-Glass Evercoat. Small amounts of a thickening agent like Cab-o-Sil, for one, added to Chem-Tech or System Three will bring them to the optimum consistency. A liquid, runny mix is difficult to handle, messes up the work, and is all but impossible to keep off hands and clothing, increasing the chance of becoming sensitized.

5. They have some resilience after hardening, and joints glued with them are capable of absorbing a moderate impact without shattering, which is not the case with some glue mixes that cure glass-hard.

Both Chem-Tech and System Three issue brochures with directions for using their products as well as epoxy adhesives in general. And of course there is much additional material in print that would be helpful to the inexperienced.

Index